The Cambridge Economic History of Modern Britain
Volume III: Structural Change and Growth, 1939–2000

The Cambridge Economic History of Modern Britain provides a readable and comprehensive survey of the economic history of Britain since industrialisation, based on the most up-to-date research into the subject. Roderick Floud and Paul Johnson have assembled a team of fifty leading scholars from around the world to produce a set of volumes which is both a lucid textbook for undergraduate and postgraduate students and an authoritative guide to the subject. The text pays particular attention to the explanation of quantitative and theory-based enquiry, but all forms of historical research are used to provide a comprehensive account of the development of the British economy. Volume I covers the period 1700–1860 when Britain led the world in the process of industrialisation. Volume II examines the period 1860–1939 when British economic power was at its height. The focus of volume III is 1939–2000, when Britain adjusted to a decline in manufacturing, an expansion of the service economy, and a repositioning of external economic activity towards Europe. The books provide an invaluable guide for undergraduate and postgraduate students in history, economics and other social sciences.

RODERICK FLOUD is Vice-Chancellor of London Metropolitan University, a Fellow of the British Academy, an Academician of the Social Sciences and a Fellow of the City and Guilds of London Institute. His publications include *An Introduction to Quantitative Methods for Historians* and (with D. McCloskey) *The Economic History of Britain since 1700*.

PAUL JOHNSON is Professor of Economic History at the London School of Economics and an Academician of the Social Sciences. He has authored or edited seven books and over fifty articles and chapters on various aspects of the economic, social and legal history of modern Britain, and on the economics of ageing and pensions. Publications include *Saving and Spending: The Working-Class Economy in Britain 1870–1939*, *Ageing and Economic Welfare* and *Old Age: From Antiquity to Post-Modernity*.

The Cambridge Economic History of Modern Britain
Volume III: Structural Change and Growth, 1939–2000

Edited by Roderick Floud

London Metropolitan University

and Paul Johnson

London School of Economics

CAMBRIDGE
UNIVERSITY PRESS

PUBLISHED BY THE PRESS SYNDICATE OF THE UNIVERSITY OF CAMBRIDGE
The Pitt Building, Trumpington Street, Cambridge, United Kingdom

CAMBRIDGE UNIVERSITY PRESS
The Edinburgh Building, Cambridge CB2 2RU, UK
40 West 20th Street, New York, NY 10011–4211, USA
477 Williamstown Road, Port Melbourne, VIC 3207, Australia
Ruiz de Alarcón 13, 28014 Madrid, Spain
Dock House, The Waterfront, Cape Town 8001, South Africa

http://www.cambridge.org

First published 2004

Printed in the United Kingdom at the University Press, Cambridge

Typeface Swift 9.5/12.5 pt. and Formata   *System* LaTeX 2_ε [TB]

A catalogue record for this book is available from the British Library

ISBN 0 521 82038 3
ISBN 0 521 52738 4

To Louisa and Oriana

Contents

Figures

Tables

Contributors

STEPHEN BROADBERRY is Professor of Economic History at the University of Warwick

WILLIAM BROWN is Master of Darwin College and Professor of Industrial Relations at the University of Cambridge

TOM CLARK was formerly Senior Research Economist at the Institute for Fiscal Studies, London

ANDREW DILNOT is Principal of St Hugh's College Oxford, and was formerly Director of the Institute for Fiscal Studies, London

RODERICK FLOUD is Vice-Chancellor of London Metropolitan University

LESLIE HANNAH is Professor of Economics at the University of Tokyo

PETER HOWLETT is Senior Lecturer in Economic History at the London School of Economics

SUSAN HOWSON is Professor of Economics at the University of Toronto

PAUL JOHNSON is Professor of Economic History at the London School of Economics

MICHAEL KITSON is University Lecturer in Macro-economics at the Judge Institute of Management, University of Cambridge

ROBERT MILLWARD is Professor of Economic History at the University of Manchester

LARRY NEAL is Professor of Economics at the University of Illinois at Urbana-Champaign

MARY O'MAHONY is Senior Research Fellow at the National Institute of Economic and Social Research, London

PETER SCOTT is Lecturer in Management at the University of Reading

JIM TOMLINSON is Professor of Economic History at Brunel University

NICK VON TUNZELMANN is Professor in the Economics of Science and Technology at SPRU, University of Sussex

KATHERINE WATSON is Lecturer in Modern History at the University of Birmingham

Preface

In their gloomier moments, academics are prone to predict the demise of their subject. As the tastes of students change, as the economy waxes and wanes, as the number of academic jobs fluctuates and the average age of academics increases, so it is easy to discern a long-term decline in the attractiveness of any subject.

Economic historians, above all, ought to be wary of such speculation. After all, if there is one single thing which is taught by study of the subject of economic history, it is that change is continuous and usually slow. As economists put it, 'change is at the margin'; it proceeds by tiny increments or decrements and the end, or even the direction, is rarely to be seen by those who are living through the changes. But change is always with us, a lesson which needs to be learned by each generation. It should be learned particularly by those eminent economic commentators who, at each stage of the business cycle, confidently predict that that stage, whether of boom or bust, will go on forever. But it must be learned also by those who predict that an academic subject is in terminal decline.

On the evidence of the three volumes of *The Cambridge Economic History of Modern Britain*, reports of the death of economic history are clearly premature and probably mistaken. The volumes demonstrate a vibrant subject, reaching out into new areas of research and using new techniques to explore new and old problems. Economic history, as revealed in these pages, is a true interdisciplinary subject, a point emphasised also by the contributors to *Living Economic and Social History* (Hudson 2001) which was published to celebrate the 75th anniversary of the Economic History Society, the guardian of the subject in the United Kingdom.

As Pat Hudson emphasises, the subject has certainly changed. The rotund phrases of Ephraim Lipson, the beautifully crafted analyses of John Clapham, have given way to equations, to the quantitative analysis of bizarre sources such as human skeletal remains and to the increasing emphasis on the study of national economic histories within their global environment. Yet the essence of the subject remains: in the words which used each Sunday to advertise *the News of the World*, 'all human life is here'. Economic history is about the behaviour of human beings in an uncertain world, as they struggle to earn a living, as they decide when to have a child, as they band together in a common cause or, all too often, fall out and resort to conflict or war.

The economic history of modern Britain, the subject of these volumes, has seen all these and billions more human acts, collective and individual. In most cases, economic history is about collective behaviour. There are few 'great men' (and even fewer 'great women') in British economic history, mainly because economic change can very rarely be attributed to a single person. Even if, on occasion, economic historians identify one person as an inventor who has changed the world, other historians will usually jump in to claim the credit for another, or at the extreme will claim that, counter-factually, the invention really did not make much difference. This alone is enough to keep the subject changing. But also, because we cannot directly observe collective behaviour or describe myriad individual acts, the subject has to theorise as well as describe. Only through theory can we hope to make sense of the economic past.

Some academic subjects, in such circumstances, turn in on themselves and allow theory to predominate. Often, they become the preserve of the favoured few, writing and publishing for each other, theorising in increasingly arcane language. New technologies of academe, the email and the working paper, abet these tendencies as the results of research are circulated within an inner circle and only emerge, months or years later, to inform a wider audience.

The Cambridge Economic History of Modern Britain, by contrast, belongs to a tradition which believes that research and scholarship have no purpose if they are not used, if they are not disseminated as soon as possible to as wide an audience as possible. In other words, its editors and authors have a mission to explain. This certainly does not obviate the use of the most ingenious and complex techniques to tease out the mysteries of the past; it does demand, however, that the techniques and the results that stem from them are explained clearly, concisely and in language which anyone interested in the topic can understand. This was the aspiration which lay, for example, behind *The Economic History of Britain since 1700* (Floud and McCloskey 1981, 1994) and it still animates these volumes. They belong to an academic tradition exemplified by Lord Rutherford, the great Cambridge scientist, who believed (in somewhat antiquated parlance) that 'The good scientist should be able to explain his results to the charlady in his lab.'

These volumes, therefore, are textbooks, in the best sense of books which explain their subject. They are written by leading researchers, drawn from many countries around the world, who have themselves recently contributed to our understanding of British economic history; usually with pleasure, they accept the obligation to tell students and others with an interest in their subjects about the results of academic enquiry by themselves and others in the field. It is not always possible, of course, to be sure of the background knowledge which each reader will possess; most of the techniques and technical terms have been explained as they are used in the chapters which follow, but some readers – if they are puzzled – may need to consult a dictionary or a dictionary of economics.

All authors need critics. A phrase which seems limpidly clear to one person may baffle another and only an informed critic can help the author to express complex notions in a comprehensible way. For this reason, all the drafts of the chapters which follow were discussed, not only by the editors, but by all the other authors within each volume and by a number of invited commentators who gathered together at a conference held in London Guildhall University. The editors are grateful to those commentators: Martin Daunton, Tim Leunig, Richard Smith, Emmett Sullivan, Barry Supple, Rick Trainor and Peter Wardley. Our grateful thanks go also to the Economic and Social Research Council, the British Academy, the Gatsby Foundation and Cambridge University Press for their support for the conference and the production of these volumes. Richard Fisher, Elizabeth Howard and Helen Barton at Cambridge University Press have encouraged us throughout the process of publication and we have also had the invaluable support of an exemplary research assistant, Claudia Edwards.

Roderick Floud and Paul Johnson

1

The war-time economy, 1939–1945

PETER HOWLETT

Contents

INTRODUCTION

During the Second World War Britain was transformed from a predominantly free-market economy into a centrally managed economy as it moved from a peacetime footing to one of full-scale war mobilisation. The transformation is shown in Table 1.1: expenditure on war-related activities increased from around 7 per cent of net national expenditure in 1938 to 53 per cent by 1941 and peaked at 55 per cent in 1943, at which time it totalled £4,512 million. This increase was achieved through substantial negative non-war capital formation and by severely curtailing the growth in the consumption of non-war goods and services. In 1938 the latter had stood at £4,090 million but, despite the rapid war-time growth of the economy, it had reached only £4,526 million by 1943 and its share of net national expenditure had fallen by 32 percentage points. The greater involvement of the state in the economy is also clearly demonstrated by Table 1.1: government expenditure rose dramatically and as early as 1940

Table 1.1   The distribution of net national expenditure: 1938–1944 (%)

Year	Consumption	War	Non-war investment	Government
1938	87.2	7.4	5.4	17.4
1939	82.6	15.3	2.1	25.1
1940	71.1	43.8	−14.9	51.0
1941	62.4	52.7	−15.1	60.6
1942	59.0	51.9	−10.8	60.2
1943	55.5	55.3	−10.8	63.5
1944	56.5	53.4	−9.9	62.1

Note: Net national expenditure is the sum of expenditure on consumption, war and net non-war capital formation. 'Government' expenditure is the sum of government expenditure on non-war current services (part of 'Consumption') and government war expenditure (part of 'War').

Source: Combined Committee on Non-Food Consumption (1945: 144).

accounted for more than half of the net national expenditure; this transformation was almost entirely due to its increased expenditure on war.

This chapter will examine several issues related to the war economy. Why did the role of the state increase? How did the war affect GDP, productivity and the broad industrial structure of the economy? How did Britain perform relative to other combatant nations? What were the constraints that the war-time economy operated under and how did it deal with them? Did the war have any long-term impact on the British economy?

WAR AND THE MARKET ECONOMY

Why was the war-time transformation from a predominantly free-market economy to a centrally managed economy necessary? To answer this question one must consider the nature of the free-market economy. The abstract neoclassical free-market economy can be characterised by perfectly mobile factors of production, fully informed and rational economic agents, and market clearing. Its essence is that pure competition between self-interested economic agents will, through the operation of the price mechanism, not only lead to the full employment of all resources but also ensure that those resources are employed efficiently. If for any reason the economy is in a state of disequilibrium then the unfettered forces of the free market will cause a return to the desired full employment equilibrium. Of course, the British economy in 1939 was not a pure free-market economy: labour and capital did not move freely; tariffs, employer cartels and trade unions all hindered the operation of the price mechanism; and markets did not clear, as the mass unemployment of the period testifies. However, the interwar economy did, in essence, resemble a free-market economy more closely than a planned economy. The war was to change this. There were many reasons for the abandonment of the free-market economy but the three most important were: the fear of inflation, the adjustment time (that is, the length of time it takes for an economy to adjust to a new set of economic conditions), and the system of rewards and penalties. The problems these posed could only jointly be solved by government intervention.

War and inflation are common bedfellows and the reasons for this can be explained in simple terms. The advent of war will lead to an increase in the demand for munitions and at the same time raw materials may become scarce due to the loss of external supplies, such as imported iron ore, or simply because of the pressures of internal war-time mobilisation, which may reveal, for example, shortages of skilled labour. Thus prices will rise. Furthermore the civilian sector of the economy is likely to contract, in order to release resources for the war effort, reducing the amount of consumption goods available just as money incomes increase due to the increased demand for labour. This adds to the inflationary burden. Although inflation may provide the government with a short-term windfall, by providing a stimulus to output and increasing revenue via the 'inflation tax',[1] it also increases the cost to it of buying goods and services and could also cause it political and social problems which might possibly result in open dissent. Thus, in order to ease the financial burden of the war and to appease the populace the government is forced to take action to control inflation.

The second reason why a neoclassical free-market economy model is inappropriate is the weakness of the model in its time specification (Eatwell and Robinson 1973: 161–5). In the context of a war economy, in particular, the adjustment time, the time it takes for the economy to adjust from a peacetime economy to a war-time economy, is crucial. It is not possible to wait for the unspecified length of time – a month? a year? ten years? longer? – that it would take for a free-market system to adjust properly to the new demands. To take an extreme case, it could be envisaged that if Britain had failed to produce a sufficient quantity of fighter aircraft in the space of a few months in mid-1940 it might have lost the war. The neoclassical free-market model cannot explain the vast and rapid movements of resources and labour that occur in the war economy; nor would it have achieved such a readjustment within the time horizon called for had it been allowed to try. Such a readjustment can only occur through the central direction of the economy (Robinson 1951: 34).

Another reason why the state is likely to become more directly involved in the economy in war-time is related to the reliance of the price mechanism on rewards and penalties. In war-time, producers want higher rewards than in peacetime because of both the low current consumable output, a result of the increasing proportion devoted to war, and the uncertainty surrounding future, post-war, output. Higher rewards for the producers inevitably mean higher prices, and thus, *ceteris paribus*, lower living standards for the consumers. As producers are few and consumers are many, this is potentially a recipe for revolution; at best it could demoralise the workforce and adversely affect production. In order to prevent such a situation developing, and to gain the support of the many which

---

[1] An inflationary increase in the price level will tend to raise indirect taxes proportionately, and an increase in personal and corporate incomes will tend to bring more individuals and companies into higher-rate tax bands. Thus inflation will increase government tax revenue.

is an implicit necessity for victory, the government must be seen to support and enforce a reasonable degree of equality. Hence, for example, the measures adopted by the British government in both World Wars to control profits and to ration goods.

Problems concerning inflation, adjustment time and the rewards and penalties system therefore make it inevitable that the role of the government in the war-time economy will grow. Why does this invalidate the neoclassical free-market economy model? In an economy where the government is dominant, such as that of Britain in the Second World War, the causal mechanism operates from society as a whole, as represented by the state, to the firm and from the firm to the individual. This is the exact opposite to the situation in the free-market system. Efficiency in the latter is ensured because the allocation is first sorted out at the individual, or microeconomic, level and then aggregated to derive the state, or macroeconomic, level. The system works because no individual, or group of individuals, is able to dominate any other individual, or group of individuals: all economic units are 'price-takers'. In a war economy, however, the state is not interested in the needs of the individual but in the needs of the state. Indeed, in war-time the state may interfere with even the choice of individuals about whether to work or not, where to work and what sort of work they will perform. The state would argue that in the long run the two needs were identical but in the short run they could conflict. The needs of the state are largely decided, in war, by exogenous factors, i.e. strategic conditions, which create demands that must be met if the state is to survive, even if this means creating disequilibrium in the economy – indeed, this is often unavoidable. However, although the imperatives of total war called for a temporary displacement of the market economy it has been argued that the success of the war-time British economy was based on its market economy inheritance (Broadberry and Howlett, forthcoming).

THE PERFORMANCE OF THE WAR ECONOMY: A NATIONAL PERSPECTIVE

Output and productivity

Table 1.2 charts the war-time performance of the British real gross domestic product (RGDP) and offers two measures of productivity. The productivity measures are measures of labour productivity only since capital data for the war period is extremely sketchy; for example, the gross domestic capital formation figures given in the relevant National Income statistics were not based on any actual returns but were in fact merely a residual and since this was the first time such statistics had been produced there is considerable doubt about their reliability (Mars 1952). The lack of capital data and the widespread use of rationing and fixed-price contracts makes the use of standard productivity measures, such as total factor productivity, inappropriate. The labour productivity measures must also be treated with caution as they cannot capture such effects as changes in product quality or labour intensity. Nor is it possible to quantify the impact of warfare itself, through air raids, blackouts and the forced dispersal of industry, and it is therefore highly probable that such a measure will understate the actual changes in war-time productivity (Elliot 1976: 53, 67).

RGDP grew rapidly, peaking in 1943 at a level 27 per cent higher than in 1938, an average annual rate of growth of 4.9 per cent. Given the burden of paying for the war the growth in real output was a crucial ingredient in the war effort, supplying more than half of the necessary domestic finance for war expenditure (Harrison 1988: 185). The RGDP

Table 1.2　Real GDP at 1938 factor cost and related measures, selected years *(1938 = 100)*

Year	RGDP	RGDP per head	RGDP per person employed
1925	94.9	82.1	89.8
1929	96.2	87.9	92.9
1935	98.7	92.5	97.6
1939	101.0	100.5	97.0
1940	111.1	110.0	103.0
1941	121.2	120.0	108.2
1942	124.2	122.5	107.3
1943	127.0	124.2	108.8
1944	121.9	118.7	105.7
1945	116.6	113.2	103.2
1946	111.5	108.1	103.8
1951	106.5	117.4	113.5
1957	108.8	132.3	126.0

Note: The RGDP measure is Feinstein's compromise estimate. Total employed labour force includes the armed forces but excludes ex-members of the Armed Forces on release but not yet in employment. The years 1925, 1929, 1935, 1951 and 1957 are included to place the war performance in a longer historical perspective. The years were chosen as they represented peak years in the Feinstein RGDP series, except for 1935 which was the year prior to the beginning of the pre-war rearmament drive. Also, 1951 is, in effect, another war year as this was the period of the Korean War.

Source: Calculated from Feinstein (1972: tabs. 6, 55 and 57).

per head of population, like production, peaked in 1943. Its movements also reflect the general trend of war-time production. The cautious build-up of the 'Phoney War' period, in which civilian and military demands still competed against each other in the market for resources, was followed by the rapid expansion of 1940–1 and the transition to a truly managed economy. Finally there was the 1943 peak and subsequent decline, reflecting the D-Day demands, the increased American supplies and the reaching of limits to labour mobilisation.

RGDP per head is not, however, a good indicator of industrial labour productivity because it says nothing of the proportion of the population involved in actual production. The employed labour force grew faster than the actual population because of the decrease in unemployment and the greater absorption of female workers. The mobilisation of women was impressive: the female participation rate rose from 30 per cent in mid-1939 to a peak of 45.3 per cent in September 1943. This mobilisation was necessary because of the vast numbers of men absorbed by the Armed Forces, some of whom came from the ranks of the unemployed but the majority of whom were drawn from industry and who had to be replaced. As early as mid-1941 95 per cent of men of working age had been mobilised for the war effort (Ince 1946: 33). In Table 1.2 the more usual measure of overall productivity, RGDP per head of the employed labour force, had more or less reached its peak by 1941. This is consistent with the claim by Postan (1952: 45) that in 'the history of war production the eighteen months between the summer of 1940 and the end of 1941 – the period when Britain stood alone – were the period of great achievement'. It also possibly reflects the fact that after 1941 increases in the labour force were achieved by absorbing untrained labour, although it also undoubtedly reflects the fall in the capital–labour ratio.

Ideally we would want to adjust the raw RGDP per employee figures for the changes in the average amount of hours worked but unfortunately available data is too crude to give meaningful results. Nevertheless what evidence we do have suggests that the average hours worked in industry increased during the war: from 47.7 hours in 1938 to a peak of 52.9 hours in 1943 for male manual workers and from 43.5 hours to 45.9 hours for female manual workers over the same period (Department of Employment and Productivity 1971: 104). These official figures probably underestimate the increase in the average amount of hours worked because, at the end of 1941, the government advised the Select Committee on National Expenditure that the average working week for men should not exceed 60 hours and for women, 55 hours. This implies that the actual hours worked were greater than these guidelines which were themselves higher than the officially recorded figures for both 1938 and 1943. The official concern for limiting the hours worked followed reports that indicated that absenteeism increased with the number of hours worked (Parker 1957: 445). This suggests that if the RGDP per employee figures were calculated on the basis of hours worked, they would be reduced, possibly by a substantial margin.

The figures also hide some important factors bearing on productivity. For example, there was a dilution of labour throughout the war and, although Postan (1952: 152) has claimed it could have been carried out more effectively, it probably helped to improve productivity levels in those cases where the skill barrier was an artificial one which merely hid restrictive practices (Matthews *et al.* 1982: 114). However, there was a shortage of skilled labour and this must have acted as a brake on productivity, a situation not helped by the slow utilisation of training facilities (Postan 1952: 96–8; Ministry of Labour and National Service 1947: 348–9). The official labour statistics also ignored the input of many groups of workers, such as Irish labour and prisoners-of-war. For example, by the end of the war, 240,000 prisoners-of-war were economically active, working mainly in agriculture and general labouring. Voluntary workers, mainly female, numbered 1 million at their peak whilst men over the age of 64 and women over the age of 59 accounted for over 1 million workers at their peak. Part-time female workers, whose numbers rose from 380,000 in June 1942 to 900,000 a year later, almost certainly contributed more to the war effort than the half-worker the official statistics equated them to.

Finally, many full-time workers, such as bank workers, also did part-time work in the munitions industries outside their normal working hours (Ministry of Labour and National Service 1947: 54–68). If it was possible to take this under-recorded labour supply properly into account this would again significantly diminish the labour productivity figures.

Industry and agriculture

The most obvious feature of war-time industrial policy was the deliberate decision to contract the production of consumer goods in order to release raw materials, labour and capital for the munitions industries. This was achieved by controlling both demand and supply: demand was controlled through various means such as rationing (see below) whilst supply was controlled through import restrictions and the Limitation of Supply Orders which set a quantity ceiling, which was progressively reduced, on what wholesalers could sell. Once quantity ceilings were imposed the state was then able to concentrate the production of particular industries in selected firms, known as nucleus firms. The idea was that the designated nucleus firm would absorb other firms in the industry in some manner, by, for example, buying all of their raw material ration, taking on their machinery or even buying the whole firm outright (Allen 1951). These measures and other war-time pressures resulted in a severe contraction in several consumer industries. For example, between 1939 and 1943 paper production fell by 51 per cent, cotton yarn production by 35 per cent and the gross value of activity in the building and civil engineering industry fell, in real terms, by 45 per cent (Central Statistical Office with Howlett 1995: 138, 141; Kohan 1952: 426, 488). Over the same period employment in industries such as cotton spinning and weaving, woollen and worsted and silk and rayon declined by a third whilst the declines were even sharper in industries such as hosiery, lace, furniture and upholstery (Hargreaves and Gowing 1952: 641).

The contraction of the civilian sector was matched by a massive expansion in the war sector. For example, between 1939 and 1943 the annual production of light anti-aircraft guns increased from 30 to 5,570, mortars from 2,822 to 17,121, rifles from 34,416 to almost 1 million, tanks from 969 to 7,476, heavy bombers from zero to 4,615, light bombers and fighters from 2,403 to 11,103, and the tonnage of naval ships produced increased more than sixfold (Central Statistical Office with Howlett 1995: 151–70). An index of the total munitions output of the UK suggests that it increased fourfold between the outbreak of the war and the last quarter of 1941 and more than doubled again when it reached its peak in the first quarter of 1944 (Harrison 1990). This expansion looks even more impressive when it is realised that it was carried out against a background of almost constant modification of existing armaments which continually disrupted the production process: Milward (1977: 192) cites the example of the Spitfire whose design underwent over 1,000 technical modifications during the war. There were also other war-related problems, such as air raids and the forced relocation of industry to less vulnerable areas, which prevented munitions production from scaling even greater heights.

The agricultural sector was also very important to Britain's war-time success: it increased the supply and variety of domestically produced food; this reduced food imports, which had accounted for 70 per cent of pre-war food requirements, and thus released valuable shipping space for other vital imports (Murray 1955: 242). The net calorie output of British agriculture increased by over 90 per cent between 1938/9 and 1943/4, and the calorific reliance on imports was cut by 75 per cent (Milward 1977: 245–55; Hammond 1951: 394). An important reason for this increase was the war-time structural change in UK agriculture that saw arable farming expand at the expense of livestock farming. Between 1939 and its 1944 peak the acreage devoted to arable land increased from 12.9 million to 19.3 million whilst that devoted to permanent grassland fell from 18.8 million to 11.7 million. Thus, war-time domestic meat production fell by more than a third whilst wheat production increased by 81 per cent (Central Statistical Office with Howlett 1995: 67–9, 78).

Martin (2000) has argued that the increase in war-time agricultural production was due to increased inputs, particularly land, rather than increased technical efficiency: taking into account the rise in land devoted to temporary grassland, the total area of cultivated land in the UK increased by almost 7 million acres between 1939 and 1944. However, there were pronounced productivity gains. Broadberry and Howlett (1998: 62–3) have shown that labour productivity, measured in terms of calorific output per employee rather than its monetary value, rose by 77 per cent between 1939/40 and 1943/4. This process was aided by increased mechanisation and by the increased use of fertilisers.

Another important factor was the role of the state. Although pre-war agricultural preparations have been subject to some criticism they have generally been judged to have been successful and to have laid a solid foundation for the war-time experience in terms of both policy and organisation (Murray 1955: 62–4; Wilt 2001). The state, through legislative and other means and through an extensive national organisation, was able to plan and direct war-time agricultural production (Wilt 2001: 182–222). For example, it provided farmers with price incentives that resulted in them increasing their income greatly, indeed they benefited far more than any other group from the war. The increased price of food products was not, however, passed on to the consumers, who were protected by government subsidies. The subsidisation of agriculture by the government, a process that obviously interferes with the efficient operation of the free market, was an important change that extended into the post-war world. It was not abolished until Britain joined the EEC and the national subsidisation was replaced by supra-national subsidisation (Milward 1977: 285–6).

Despite its seemingly impressive performance, Barnett (1986) has attacked the industrial record of the war economy. He argues that the British grossly exaggerated their war-time achievements, ignoring, for example, the invaluable assistance of American 'lend-lease', and thus created the welfare state on a weak foundation, on an economy whose industrial performance was poor in several key areas. The first thing to note about this thesis is that it is not really about the performance of the economy during the war at all, but about what Barnett sees as the long-term structural problems of the British economy. Thus, we are not told how the British economy in this period compared with previous periods nor are we told if the relative disadvantage that Barnett identifies between the British and the German and American economies increased or decreased during the war years. An interesting contrast is to compare Barnett's (1986: 143–58) very pessimistic assessment of the war-time performance of the British aircraft industry with the much more positive picture presented by Overy (1980: 168–71) in his truly comparative study.

Further, Barnett is primarily interested in showing the poor productivity performance of the British economy during the war relative to other nations, particularly Germany and the USA; and he argues that the war offers an excellent opportunity to assess the productivity performance because, during this period, the economy was pushed to its limits. This, however, ignores a fundamental problem: the most important concern of the government during the war was not productivity; its foremost concern was with simply increasing the output of those goods deemed necessary by the strategic demands facing the country within, again strategically determined, time horizons. In terms of labour productivity this meant that as long as the numerator increased (to meet the production target) there was little concern, at least initially, over what was happening to the denominator. This is not to argue that Barnett is wrong, there were industrial problems in many war-time industries, notably coal and shipbuilding – indeed he provides much interesting information on the war-time performance of certain key industries – but merely to warn the unwary that his agenda and that of the war-time government were not the same and that work on war-time industrial productivity, both at a national and an international level, is still in its infancy.

THE PERFORMANCE OF THE WAR ECONOMY: A COMPARATIVE PERSPECTIVE

Having discussed the war-time performance of the UK economy, we will now compare it to that of other combatant nations. However, it is far from clear that this is an entirely objective exercise. The assessment of comparative economic performances over long periods of time does have a strong theoretical justification in that the achievement of most

Table 1.3   Real GDP of the main combatants, 1938–1945 (1938 = 100)

Year	UK	USA	USSR	Germany	Italy	Japan
1939	101	109	102	109	107	109
1940	111	118	116	110	104	114
1941	121	137	100	117	102	116
1942	124	154	76	119	103	117
1943	127	175	85	121	97	115
1944	122	187	101	125	83	112
1945	117	184	96	88	65	85

Source: Harrison (1998: 10; forthcoming, tab. 1).

socio-economic goals relies on having the resources to meet them and, in the long run, that means achieving sustainable economic growth. However, such comparisons made over short periods of time have a less sound foundation: any economy could, in theory, achieve rapid growth over a short period of time by simply mobilising all its available resources. This does not mean that such growth is sustainable over a longer period. The desire for such a mobilisation will normally come from the political leaders but the ability to achieve it will depend on its acceptance by the population, and possibly also by the suppliers of external capital, and the existing economic infrastructure. The fact that an economy is at war does not change these constraints or choices, it simply means that the social utility function may change so that, for example, the population is more willing to endure a postponement of present consumption. Thus in the Second World War the growth of each individual economy was governed by political, strategic and social considerations which may have, at least initially, called for different responses.

Table 1.3 considers the performance of the major belligerent economies during the war (see the national contributions in Harrison (1998) for a detailed discussion of each economy). The UK performance was only exceeded by the powerhouse of the US economy, which expanded by more than 70 per cent between 1938 and 1945. For the USSR the dominant factor was its initial loss of territory, and hence resources, to German military advance in 1941 and the subsequent regaining of territory after 1942 (Ranki 1988: 314–31). The USSR was a relatively poor economy and such economies typically collapse when subjected to massive attack, as was the case with Italy. However, Harrison (1998: 18, 24) has argued that the USSR proved an exception to this rule because it was able to maintain its economic integration despite the intense stress it faced. Initially, Germany and Japan witnessed similar rates of war-time economic growth, although we should note that Japan had been at war with China since 1937, but whereas Germany experienced a marked spurt in 1943, matched by a spurt in armaments production, the Japanese economy declined, as the Allied advance cut off supplies of imported raw materials that Japan was dependent upon.

Harrison (1988) provides an interesting comparison of the degree of resource mobilisation within the war-time economies of the UK, the USA, the USSR and Germany. He defines two measures of war-time mobilisation. The first, which he calls *national utilisation*, is an attempt to measure national priorities and encompasses all resources supplied to the war effort of a country irrespective of their origin. The second, which he calls *domestic mobilisation*, measures the domestic finance of resources supplied to the war effort of a country irrespective of utilisation. For example, American war-time aid to the UK, which was substantial (see below), would be included in the UK figure of *national utilisation* but not in the UK figure for *domestic mobilisation*. His conclusion is that whilst in *national utilisation* terms the UK allocated more resources to the war effort than the USA, the situation was reversed in terms of *domestic mobilisation*.

THE CONSTRAINTS OF THE WAR ECONOMY

Robinson (1951) identified five major constraints facing the British war economy: gold and foreign currency reserves, materials, manpower, shipping and capacity. War-time planners had to be aware of where and when potential bottlenecks in the system would occur and what the limits of mobilisation were. These constraints were discussed explicitly within government and dealing with them was a central part of economic policy. Many academic economists were drafted into the government as advisors and they imposed their technical language and knowledge on the ensuing debates (Booth and Coats 1980). Initially the government was concerned about financial constraints, both internal and external, but this was soon replaced with worries about the physical constraints facing the economy. Thus, the running of the war moved from relying on financial controls to physical controls.

Budgetary policy

The government was faced with two related problems in terms of its budgetary policy: how to pay for the war and how to dampen the inflationary pressures in the economy. It was important to tackle the latter for social and political reasons as well as economic reasons: in the First World War both Britain and Germany had experienced serious social disruption as a result of the distorting effects of war-time inflation, which had changed both income distribution and the rewards system (Milward 1977: 106). Keynes (1940) argued that the traditional method of assessing potential government revenue used by the Treasury, which worked on the principle of 'what the taxpayer could bear', started at the wrong end. He felt that the Treasury should first calculate National Income, including its main components, in order to judge the war potential of the economy as a whole. Then it could calculate the level of taxation and forced savings that would bring about that level of transfer of National Income from taxpayers to the government that was necessary to stop inflation. To explain the problem of inflation Keynes referred to the notion of an 'inflationary gap', that is, a gap between aggregate demand and aggregate supply.

The inflationary gap was inevitable given the war-time pressures which would ensure that aggregate demand would rise just as the amount of consumer goods available would fall, as the consumer goods industries were deliberately contracted in order to release resources for war production. If the government did not intervene the potential gap between demand and supply would be closed automatically by an inflationary rise. In order to prevent such inflation the government, according to Keynes, should mop up the potential excess demand, through taxation and forced savings, thereby closing the potential inflationary gap (Sayers 1983: 112).

Initially these proposals faced opposition from two sources. The Treasury opposed Keynes because it believed that there was some 'natural flow' of voluntary savings and it felt that if the level of forced savings called for by Keynes, as a supplement to taxation, exceeded the natural level it would cause inflation rather than prevent it. Nor was the Treasury impressed by the figures quoted by Keynes. The Labour Party also opposed what it saw as the increased taxation of the working classes. Even the attempt by Keynes to try and soften the blow by arguing that war-time taxation should be treated as deferred pay that would be repaid after the war did not convince them (Booth 1989: 63; Peden 1985: 132–3). However, the paralysis of the Treasury in the face of war-time inflation, coupled with the shock of military defeat in the spring of 1940 and the subsequent change in government, paved the way for the adoption of Keynes' main proposals. Indeed, Keynes himself was co-opted to the Treasury in June 1940.

The turning point was the budget presented on 7 April 1941 by the chancellor of the exchequer, Kingsley Wood. Before the war, budgetary policy was largely conducted in terms of financing government expenditure and attempting to achieve a balanced budget. However, the 1941 budget transformed the annual budget speech into 'a comprehensive survey of the national economy' and made price and income stabilisation explicit concerns (Sayers 1983: 108). It introduced two innovations: the economic theory that informed it, the explicit introduction of Keynesianism, and the underlying national income accounting framework it used (Feinstein 1983: 12–13). The budget also tried to strike a balance between being seen to promote social justice and ensuring that there remained adequate economic incentives (Sayers 1983: 110).

A crucial and innovative aspect of the 1941 budget was that it was conceived in National Income terms and was accompanied by a White Paper setting out the official estimates of National Income and Expenditure (HMSO 1941). This was the result of the work of two young economists, James Meade and Richard Stone. Meade produced the initial double-entry framework for the national income accounts and Stone played the major role in filling in the numbers (Meade and Stone 1941; Stone 1951). Their estimates of national income were still rudimentary, with many of the items calculated as residuals, but has been described as 'a revolutionary departure in British official statistics' (Booth 1989: 66–7) and it would have an impact beyond the British economy and beyond 1945. Despite the importance of the national income accounts, however, they were not used in the actual planning of the war effort; this was done almost entirely in terms of physical resources (Robinson 1951: 40).

The 1941 budget proposed a two-pronged attack on inflation: taxation and forced savings were to be used to tackle the problem of demand-pull inflation and cost of living subsidies were to be used against cost-push inflation. It was hoped that stabilising the cost of living index would lead to moderation in wage settlements because of the widespread indexation. The two-pronged attack was necessary since rapid wage inflation would defeat the attempt to mop up excess demand through taxation and if the inflationary gap was not closed by the government it would be difficult to prevent wage inflation: the two were really the different sides of the same economic coin (Sayers 1983: 107, 113).

It was hoped to close £200–300 million of the estimated potential £500 million inflationary gap by promoting a policy of forced savings. This was to be achieved by a series of measures: suspending various investment opportunities; putting pressure on the clearing banks to turn all their available resources, their idle balances, over to the government; restricting bank advances intended for use for capital construction; and making attractive offers to savers through Government bonds. The decreased availability of consumption goods also helped this process as it restricted even the opportunity to consume above a certain level. The remaining part of the inflationary gap was to be closed through taxation: the standard rate of income tax went up from eight and a half shillings (42.5 per cent) to ten shillings (50 per cent) in the pound; personal allowances were reduced; purchase tax was increased on a broad front; the excess profits tax, a tax intended to stop war-time profiteering by, at least theoretically, taxing profits that were in excess of peacetime levels, was increased from 60 per cent to 100 per cent. These anti-inflationary measures would also help to pay for the war by raising government revenue (Sayers 1983: 112–13). The approach outlined in the 1941 budget was refined throughout the war – for example: in September 1943 the Pay As You Earn (PAYE) scheme was introduced which made tax collection easier and more efficient; purchase tax was developed as a weapon to restrict and influence consumption; and the number of households liable to pay income tax increased dramatically, from 3.8 million in 1938 to more than 12 million in 1945 (Pollard 1983: 213; Chapter 14 below).

The success of the strategy of increasing taxation and forced savings is shown in Table 1.4. Direct taxation more than doubled between 1939 and 1941 and almost doubled again between 1941 and 1945, by tripling income tax receipts and by introducing the excess profits tax. At its peak the latter brought in £482 million, a quarter of total direct taxation.

Table 1.4 Taxation and public borrowing, 1939–1945 (in £m)							
	1939	1940	1941	1942	1943	1944	1945
Indirect taxation	465	676	1,000	1,137	1,233	1,239	1,211
Direct taxation	515	706	1,143	1,426	1,819	2,023	2,054
of which –							
income tax and surtax	410	551	741	921	1,184	1,353	1,426
excess profits tax	0	44	211	318	453	482	440
Public borrowing at home	352	1,550	2,553	2,576	2,972	2,792	2,442
of which –							
small savings	62	466	602	600	719	702	668
other public issues (net)	10	567	1,031	1,047	1,059	896	1,176

Source: Sayers (1956: 493–4).

Receipts from indirect taxation also surged, although most of the increase had already occurred by 1942. Forced savings are measured in the table by public borrowing. This saw a massive expansion in the first year of the war, increasing almost fourfold, before almost doubling again between 1940 and 1943. Within public borrowing small savings and net other public issues became more important: in 1939 they had accounted for only 20 per cent of public borrowing but by 1945 that figure had leapt to 76 per cent.

The subsidisation of key items in the cost of living index also appeared to be successful in its aim of restraining wages as labour mobilisation reached its limits. The cost of living index had increased sharply between 1939 and 1941 but thereafter it remained fairly steady and this led to a deceleration in the rate of increase of the average weekly wage, from 10 per cent in 1940 to only 4 per cent in 1943 (Central Statistical Office with Howlett 1995: 237). A major feature of this success was the massive growth of food subsidies. In 1939–40 the net cost of food subsidies borne by the Ministry of Food was £13 million but by the end of the war that figure had leapt to £162 million, a more than twelvefold increase (Hammond 1951: 398; Nash 1951). In evaluating the success of the policy two things should be borne in mind: first, the manipulation of the official cost of living index did not eliminate inflation but merely disguised it (Peden 1985: 130–1); secondly, factors such as the increased availability of overtime and the dilution of jobs that had been deemed skilled and semi-skilled meant that average earnings increased faster than wages (Department of Employment and Productivity 1971: 99).

Taxation, forced savings and stabilisation of the cost of living index, however, were not considered enough to close the inflationary gap. In particular it was felt that if taxation was too heavy it could, even in war-time, adversely affect incentives and that it might also fail to curb consumption if people responded by drawing on their savings (Reddaway 1951: 182). Even if aggregate consumption was reduced there was no guarantee that the consumption of specific key goods, such as petrol and sugar, would be cut. Thus, rationing, which had been introduced as early as 1940, was gradually extended and by the end of the war it covered about one-third of all consumer goods and services. Its importance as an anti-inflationary tool has been highlighted by Capie and Wood (2002), who have argued that rationing was the crucial element in war-time efforts to control price inflation.

Two different types of rationing schemes were operated. The coupon scheme covered most basic foodstuffs and gave every consumer a minimum fixed weekly quantity of the foods covered. The points scheme was more flexible in that coupon points could be 'spent' at the preference of the consumer on a limited number of goods (Booth 1985). Of the exceptions to rationing the most important were bread, potatoes, fish and fresh vegetables, whose prices were strictly controlled, and tobacco and alcohol, whose exemption helped to boost morale and provided the Treasury with a lucrative source of revenue. Despite the existence of a significant black market and extensive circumvention of rationing legislation (Zweiniger-Bargielowska 2000), the British system of rationing operated far more effectively than schemes tried in other combatant nations. This was mainly due to the panoply of controls, backed up by both financial and legal resources, which ensured that there was relatively strict supervision of both production and distribution. It also reflected the fact that the control of materials and foodstuffs is simplified in an island economy that imports a high percentage of such goods (Mills and Rockoff 1987).

External policy and 'lend-lease'

The Treasury initially believed that the war could be financed through the sale of gold and foreign exchange and higher exports. Hence the war began with what in retrospect seems to be a rash export drive which only served to add a further strain on the resources of the fledgeling war economy. As the cost of the war exploded and reality dawned on ministers and officials about the folly of the export policy, its high economic priority was dropped (Sayers 1956: 267). This accelerated the decline in exports that had already occurred. In volume terms exports fell by 71 per cent between 1938 and 1943 and export earnings were cut in half; at the same time the cost of imports rose by a third, even though the volume of imports fell (Central Statistical Office with Howlett 1995: 207). In terms of the external account the result of these changes was dramatic: external liabilities more than doubled between December 1939 and December 1941, by mid-1940 assets in North America were being sold off cheaply in a desperate attempt to pay for American goods, and by the beginning of 1941 hard currency reserves had been exhausted (Sayers 1956: 438–64). The situation was rescued when, in March 1941, the American government passed the Lend-Lease Act which effectively gave Britain, and the

USSR, free access to the amazing powerhouse of the US war economy. The 'lend-lease' agreement removed all existing restrictions on purchases in the USA and, crucially, deferred the payment for American goods and services until after the war.

The total net value of US 'lend-lease' aid to all countries during the war was $43.6 billion of which the UK, excluding the Empire, received $27 billion (62 per cent) and the USSR $11 billion (25 per cent) (Allen 1946: 250, 258). The UK also received aid from the Empire, notably Canada who supplied $1.2 billion of Mutual Aid during the war and more or less wrote this off after the war (Milward 1977: 351). The UK did provide reciprocal aid to the USA that amounted to $5.7 billion, leaving the net US contribution at $21 billion, but even so the contribution of the American economy to the UK war effort should not be underestimated. In Britain 'lend-lease' took an enormous burden off the productive shoulders of the country with US supplies being equivalent to, for example, 104 per cent of the UK's war-time production of tanks, 24 per cent of combat aircraft, 60 per cent of landing craft and ships, 67 per cent of small arms ammunition, and so on (Postan 1952: 247). In total US 'lend-lease' aid supplied 17 per cent of all British Empire munitions during the war (Allen 1946: 268). This helped to ease many of the constraints on the British economy, particularly that of labour.

The evaluation of 'lend-lease' has, however, been a fertile ground for disagreement. Churchill (1949: 503), for example, said that 'lend-lease' was 'the most unsordid act in the history of any nation'. But others have seen it as a hard-nosed business deal by the Americans, which would reflate the American economy and denude their greatest potential rival of any real economic power in the post-war world. The latter view was expounded by no less a figure than Keynes. He was very much involved in 'lend-lease' discussions with the Americans and was under no illusion about the supposed generosity of the 'lend-lease' programme. He claimed that the US government 'was very careful to take every possible precaution to see that the British were as near as possible bankrupt before any assistance was given' and that they operated the programme with the aim of 'leaving the British at the end of the war . . . hopelessly insolvent' (quoted in Salant 1980: 1059). This cynical view of how the USA perceived 'lend-lease' even finds support among contemporary American historians (see, for example, Vatter 1985: 30–1). The almost indecent swiftness with which the USA ended the 'lend-lease' arrangement – it was promptly terminated one minute into the first day of official peace – offers some support to this view since it left Britain with an immediate bill for $650 million just at the time it was facing a dollar crisis (Cairncross 1985: 4–10). A more favourable stance could be that the Americans were simply being too inflexible in how they viewed 'lend-lease'. Allen, for example, has argued that the Allies engaged in a form of international division of labour during the war with a greater mobilisation of troops by Britain, the USSR, Australia and India compensated by a greater provision of munitions by the USA and Canada (Allen 1946: 247–9). Therefore 'it could surely be argued, for example, that in those cases where British tank crews had used American tanks it would make at least as much sense to charge the US for the crew as the UK for the tank. But this was not the view taken in the US' (Milward 1977: 351). Furthermore it was largely orders from the UK and France that enabled the USA to expand its pre-war capacity and thus created the strong base from which it was to launch its war effort. Allen (1946: 246) has claimed that the post-war settlement of 'lend-lease' took all such factors into account because the Americans effectively wrote off about $20 billion of the outstanding debt. The counter argument, though, would be that it was not the sum of the 'lend-lease' credit itself that was important but the conditions attached to it and the strength it gave to the US bargaining position in the post-war world.

Table 1.5   The financing of the UK external debt, 1940–1945

| Year | External debit (£m) (1) | As a percentage of (1) | | | |
		Credits (2)	Net US grants (3)	Liability accumulation (4)	Other (5)
1940	1.5	47	0	13	40
1941	1.9	42	16	32	11
1942	2.6	35	38	19	8
1943	3.6	42	56	19	−17
1944	4.2	40	57	17	−14
1945	2.8	43	36	25	−4
Total	16.6	41	40	20	−1

Note: The external debit is the sum of imports plus shipping plus government overseas expenditure (minus munitions). The current account credits include exports, reciprocal aid, other governments' expenditure in the UK, shipping and errors and omissions. 'Other' includes other net grants, sale of investments, requisitioning of balances of gold and dollars and net drawings on gold and reserves.

Source: Sayers (1956: 499).

Whatever the long-term impact of 'lend-lease', there is no doubting its short-term benefits for the UK economy, as Table 1.5 demonstrates. Over the period of the war as a whole only 41 per cent of the external debits were financed by credits which left a large gap to be filled. Sayers (1956: 499) believes that the total debit noted in Table 1.5 may be an overestimate, because 'to some extent the pricing of lend-lease goods was too high for purposes of comparing economic efforts', possibly by as much as £1.6 million. The shortfall was made up in many ways, including capital disinvestment and drawing on the gold and dollar reserves, but the two most important means were increasing overseas liabilities and the US 'lend-lease' scheme. The importance of 'lend-lease', which was the dominant component of net US grants, can be seen by comparing 1941 and 1942. In 1941 the accumulation of overseas liabilities helped to finance almost one-third of the external debits and was threatening to get out of hand. However, as 'lend-lease' came on stream it started to take up most of the burden and by 1943 more than half of the debit was being effectively paid for by 'lend-lease' aid. Thus, 'lend-lease' eased the pressure on the UK to accelerate its rate of overseas liability accumulation; although by the end of the war such liabilities had still increased massively – from £0.5 billion in June 1939 to £3.4 billion by June 1945 (Sayers 1956: 497).

Labour as a constraint

Those at the centre of policy making in Britain in the Second World War believed that manpower was the ultimate constraint on the performance of the war-time economy. Indeed, from the end of 1942 onwards, when it seemed that the limits of labour mobilisation were being reached, the most important planning tool was the manpower budget (Robinson 1951: 48–55). The first manpower budget of the war, produced at the end of 1940, was a comprehensive survey but it did not tackle the central problem of the allocation of manpower to the production programmes of different government departments. This is not surprising as the bottle-necks in the economy at the time were raw materials, machine tools and skilled labour, and not the general supply of labour (Gowing 1972: 149–59). It would not be until December 1942, by when the voracious appetite of the Armed Forces for manpower meant that the scarcity of labour was threatening to spread from the specific to the general, that the manpower budget would seriously tackle the issue of allocation.

The dramatic expansion of the Armed Forces is the most significant trend shown in Table 1.6. From a total of 480,000 men before the outbreak of war their numbers rose rapidly and by 1944 had reached 4,500,000, at which time there were also 467,000 women in the Auxiliary and Nursing Services. The expansion was made possible by drawing on two main sources: decreasing unemployment, which was well over 1 million at the beginning of the war, and withdrawing labour from civil employment. However, the troops needed to be supplied with weapons, clothed and fed and so the withdrawals from civil employment had to be, at least partly, replaced. This was done by expanding the size of the working population: it rose by 13 per cent, from 19,473,000 in 1939 to a peak of 22,285,000 in 1943. About one fifth of the increase was due to natural population in-crease (Milward 1977: 218). However, by far the most important factor was the increase in the number of women absorbed into the labour force: four out of every five new workers was a woman (for a general discussion of the employment of women in war-time Britain see Summerfield (1984)). The increased participation of women in employment during the war was a phenomenon replicated in other combatant nations although the actual scale and timing of the expansion differed across countries (Rupp 1978: 185–6; Saunders 1946: 18). In Britain, unemployment among women had actually risen in the first year of the war, by 12,000, possibly because the dislocation of the economy as it moved to a war footing meant that there was a mismatch between women coming on to the labour market and the actual jobs available. By mid-1941, however, over 1 million women not previously in the labour market had been mobilised; this despite the fact that compulsory registration for women did not begin until April of that year (Ince 1946: 36–7). By 1943 women accounted for 34 per cent of the total insured workforce in engineering (compared to only 10 per cent

Table 1.6 The distribution of the working population (WP) of Great Britain *(at June each year)*							
	1939	1940	1941	1942	1943	1944	1945
WP (in 000)							
Total	19,473	20,766	21,332	22,056	22,285	22,008	21,649
Male	14,476	15,104	15,222	15,141	15,032	14,901	14,881
Female	4,997	5,572	6,110	6,915	7,253	7,107	6,768
WP (as % of total)							
Female	26	27	29	31	33	32	31
Unemployed	6	3	1	...	...	...	1
Armed Forces	2	11	16	19	21	23	24
Civil Defence	...	2	2	2	1	1	1
Civil employment	92	84	81	79	77	76	75
of which:							
Group I	16	17	20	23	23	23	20
Group II	27	25	26	25	25	25	26
Group III	49	41	36	32	28	28	29

Note: For the definition of Groups I, II and III see text.
... negligible (less than 0.5%).

Source: Central Statistical Office with Howlett (1995: 38).

in 1939), 52 per cent in the chemical industry (27 per cent, 1939) and 46 per cent in miscellaneous metals industries (34 per cent) (Summerfield 1984: 199).

The net result of these changes in terms of the distribution of civil employment is shown in Table 1.6. War-time planners categorised civil employment into three groups. Group I industries, those concerned with munitions production such as metals, engineering, aircraft production, shipbuilding and chemicals, expanded rapidly and by mid-1943 were employing more than 5 million workers. Employment in Group II industries, 'other essential industries' such as agriculture, mining, transportation and the utilities, remained fairly stable at approximately 5.5 million. Finally, Group III industries, those deemed 'less essential' such as textiles, building and services contracted severely, falling from over 9 million workers at the beginning of the war to 6 million by mid-1944. The signs that the economy was reaching the limits of possible labour mobilisation had been clear since 1942, as the absorption of women into the working population slowed and the well of unemployment ran dry. Furthermore, the contraction of the Group III industries was so severe that by 1944 it was felt that it had reached its limit and Table 1.6 implies that the expansion of the Armed Forces after that date was solely at the expense of the munitions industries.

The enormous expansion and redistribution of the working population was achieved through a system of legislative measures and administrative controls (Ince 1946: 18–27). In particular, the Schedule of Reserved

Occupations and the Essential Work Orders were used to control the supply and movement of labour and at a local level the Employment Exchanges played a crucial role in matching demand and supply. However, although the state gave itself wide powers of labour compulsion they used these powers with great care and avoided recourse to them whenever and wherever possible (Robinson 1951: 51). This reluctance to be heavy handed, and to rely as much as possible on voluntarism and co-operation, partly reflected the desires of the Minister of Labour Ernest Bevin who, prior to his appointment in the coalition government, had been the outstanding trade union leader in the country (Bullock 1967). It also, though, reflected the general awareness within government of the need to avoid industrial unrest, which might adversely affect production programmes. Trade union leaders and workers in general were not blinded by patriotism to the need to protect and improve their job, its environment and their wages. Indeed, the war saw an expansion in trade union membership, from 6 million in 1938 to 7.9 million in 1945. Furthermore, strikes, despite their war-time illegality, were more numerous between 1940 and 1945 than in the whole of the 1930s, although the average days lost per strike during the war was about a quarter of those lost during the 1930s (Department of Employment and Productivity 1971: 395–6). In order to appease the labour force, and to compensate it for the pressures of war-time work, the government actively encouraged improvements in the working environment and in the social care of workers (Milward 1977: 241). It also tackled the potential menace of inflationary wage demands by providing significant cost of living subsidies (see above).

Capital as a constraint

Although there is no study that shows clearly how, in quantitative terms, the manpower constraint affected potential war-time production, it is widely accepted that it was the most important limitation placed on the war economy. A similar consensus exists that capital, on the whole, was not a constraint (Milward 1977: 229). In fact, as was seen in Table 1.1, current production of war goods and services was expanded partly by capital disinvestment: in effect, some future consumption, that is, investment, was foregone in order to increase current consumption. However, there is some debate about how to classify war expenditure. Kuznets (1945: viii) argued that since the ultimate aim of war production is to 'sustain or augment the capacity of the nation's economy to produce goods in the future' it should be classified as investment (see, also, Higgs 1992; Rockoff 1998: 84–5).

Capital investment in war-time is perceived as extremely risky. At one level there is the very real risk that your newly acquired plant or machinery may be destroyed by the enemy, and in terms of financial planning it is virtually impossible to determine if the investment will show a positive return. Thus, what new investment did occur during the war was mostly financed by the state, which tended to base its decisions not on monetary considerations but on the availability of other resources, particularly manpower (Robinson 1951: 53–5). Given the role of the state in war-time capital investment it is not surprising to find that such investment was geared towards meeting the military priorities, which primarily meant expanding the capacity to produce finished armaments.

These trends are borne out by the figures for gross domestic fixed capital formation, which fell in both absolute and relative terms during the war. Between 1939 and 1943 gross domestic fixed capital formation dropped from £530 million to £170 million at 1938 prices, or by approximately two-thirds. In current prices its share of GNP at factor cost shrank from 11.4 per cent in 1938 to 3.3 per cent in 1944. The fall in capital formation combined with both the massive labour mobilisation and the surge in output led to decreases in the capital–labour ratio and the capital–output ratio, by respectively 13.1 per cent and 20 per cent (Feinstein 1972: tabs. 2, 20 and 40).

Another significant feature of war-time capital formation was the shift in its composition and, in particular, the reversal in the position of buildings relative to plant and machinery. In 1939 buildings had accounted for more than half the gross domestic fixed capital formation whilst plant and machinery accounted for about one-third; in the following year it was plant and machinery that accounted for more than half and buildings which accounted for only a third (Feinstein 1972: tab. 39). This partly reflected the need to expand the output of specialist machine tools and other items vital to the war effort; for example, alloy steel capacity had to be increased. Indeed, in the first year of the war one of the major bottlenecks in production was the supply of drop forgings. The squeezing of civilian house building was one obvious way to re-allocate investment resources in favour of war production and it was a method the German war economy also adopted (Overy 1988: 622).

LONG-TERM IMPACT

This section will consider some of the long-term consequences of the war. In Britain the successful prosecution of the war was seen to vindicate an expanded and more interventionist state whereas in the USA it was mainly attributed to big business, either directly in terms of the role of the major firms in expanding war-time production or indirectly in the prominent role taken by leading businessmen in the war-time state. Chapters 3, 8 and 14 below all touch on both of these popular Anglo-Saxon mythologies and demonstrate their resonance in post-war Britain.

The conduit for spreading the American 'big business' influence to the post-war British economy was the Anglo-American Council on

Productivity (AACP) and its sponsored visits of British managers and trade unionists to study American industry in the late 1940s and early 1950s (see chapter 3 below). The war had demonstrated the much higher productivity of many American industries and the AACP was an attempt by the post-war Labour government to find out if American technology and methods could be transferred to British industry in order to raise its productivity levels. Broadberry argues that the attempt to introduce American mass production techniques, based on 'Simplification, Standardisation and Specialisation', to British industry between the 1950s and 1970s were problematic. In too many cases it caused industrial relations to deteriorate, as unions tried to protect craft skills and their control of the shopfloor (see also chapter 15 below) and management struggled to come to terms with the demands of the new production methods. The nature, extent and success of this exercise in the Americanisation of British industry is not without controversy (see Tiratsoo and Tomlinson 1997; Booth 2001: 116–19) and nor is the role of the war in the process. British manufacturing productivity had been roughly half that of the USA since the mid nineteenth century (Broadberry 1997c). Thus, it could be argued that even without the war it was likely that British manufacturing would have attempted to learn from the more successful American industry. However, two facts suggest that the war was an important catalyst for the 'Americanisation' process: first the war saw a significant increase in the American productivity lead (Broadberry 1997c: 36); secondly, the Anglo-Saxon war effort was a joint effort which meant that the two economies shared knowledge and experience which must have made the American productivity lead more obvious to the British and thus probably made it more likely that something like the AACP would appear in the post-war period.

The 'big state' influence on post-war Britain appears clearer in that the size and scope of the state were both unambiguously greater after the Second World War than before. Clark and Dilnot (chapter 14 below), echoing the work of Peacock and Wiseman (1961), point out that the war produced a 'displacement effect': although state expenditure and state revenue both declined in the post-war years they still remained significantly higher than they had been previous to the war. They argue that this was because war eased the peacetime electoral constraint on politicians raising taxes and therefore also increased their scope for non-military spending after the war. Tomlinson (chapter 8 below) goes further and argues that the war meant that the state had to become more actively involved in providing economic security and social improvements for its citizens. This, coupled with the greater fiscal and planning role of the war-time state, helped to establish what he calls the national economic management (NEM) of the post-war era.

One important aspect of the new interventionism was the creation of the Welfare State. It is generally agreed that one of the most influential reports to appear during the war was the Beveridge Report, published in 1942, which mapped out the future Welfare State. Its aim was to take all the existing ad hoc social insurance schemes and gather them into one overall scheme that would provide cover for every crisis in life, from maternity grants to funeral grants, from the cradle to the grave. It also aimed to provide a national minimum income in the form of National Assistance (Beveridge 1942). Perhaps even more important than the scheme itself were the three assumptions that the Beveridge Report rested on: family allowances would be paid for all children; a National Health Service would be set up; full employment would be guaranteed by the state. The Report was later followed by a series of White Papers that laid down the foundations of the Welfare State: in February 1944 the National Health Service was the focus of a White Paper; in May, full employment; in September, National Insurance; in March 1945, housing. The other important building block of the new post-war state was the Education Act of 1944 (see chapter 5 below). Johnson (chapter 9 below) considers these developments in more depth but he does not see the creation of the Welfare State as a process that was initiated, or indeed ended, by the war. He argues that the war-time developments were the result of a process whose origins preceded the war and that the process they initiated was refined for many years after the war.

Another significant area of debate among historians has been the impact of the war on female employment. We have seen that the war led to a dramatic upsurge in the participation rate of women. For example, by September 1943 46 per cent of women aged between 14 and 59 were in civil employment or the Auxiliary Services, as were 90 per cent of able-bodied single women and 80 per cent of married women with no children aged between 18 and 40 (Smith 1984: 934). Thus it is not surprising that there has been much recent literature on the impact the war had on the attitude of women to, among other things, the labour market both during and after the war (Summerfield 1998; Lewis 1992). Historians initially argued that the war had led to a positive revolution in the position of women in work (Marwick 1974) but since the 1970s a new orthodoxy has emerged that has emphasised that war-time changes in the participation and position of women in the labour market were either transitory or had much less significant long-term impact (Wilson 1980; Thane 1991). Smith (1984), for example, has argued that the abolition of the marriage bar in teaching and the civil service in the immediate post-war years reflected the tightness of the labour market in those years rather than a significant change in attitude by the state, trade unions or employers to the position of women. One apparent long-term change induced by the war was the higher participation of married women in the British labour market: this increased from 10.0 per cent in 1931, to 21.7 per cent in 1951, to 29.7 per cent in 1961, to 43.4 per cent in 1973 (Matthews *et al.* 1982: 564). However, Smith (1984: 944) again argues that in the immediate post-war period this change was not an outcome of the war but reflected labour market tightness and demographic factors, for example that due mainly to falling birth rates there were 1 million fewer women aged 14 to 24 in 1951 than there were in 1931. Furthermore, female labour force participation during the war had been overwhelmingly full-time whereas much of the post-war expansion in female participation rates was due to the expansion of part-time work: thus, in 1943 only 7 per cent of women workers were part-time whereas by 1951 that figure was 12 per cent, 29 per cent by 1964 and 35 per cent by 1973 (Matthews *et al.* 1982: 627).

The most obvious cost of the Second World War was the massive loss of human life. For many countries the number of deaths attributable to the war is still controversial although throughout the world it probably accounted for more than 40 million deaths. The best recent estimates suggest that these included 24 million Russians, 6 million Germans, 6 million Poles, more than 2.5 million Chinese and 2.4 million Japanese (Harrison 1998: 291; Milward 1977: 211). Britain and the USA suffered far fewer casualties. American deaths attributable to the war numbered 324,000, whereas the UK suffered war losses of 358,950, including 63,635 civilians, and the Commonwealth suffered another 612,000 casualties (Milward 1977: 211; Central Statistical Office with Howlett 1995: 15, 18). Given that the UK had a high pre-war level of national income per head, however, its aggregate human capital loss, at least in monetary terms, was higher, although still far less than the loss suffered by Germany or Russia (Broadberry 1988: 30–1).

The war-time destruction of physical capital in the form of land, structures, inventories and shipping (including cargoes) amounted to £1,240 million at 1938 prices. Taking into account also internal and external disinvestment, Broadberry and Howlett (1998) have estimated that the net loss of national wealth due to the war was £4,595 million at 1938 prices, equivalent to 18.6 per cent of pre-war wealth. They also offer a more tentative estimate that if human capital is included, the war-time loss was equivalent to 12.3 per cent of pre-war wealth.

Did these losses of human and physical capital have an effect on the long-term growth of the economy? Perhaps surprisingly Crafts and Mills (1996), using sophisticated statistical analysis, argue that there was no negative war-time shock to British growth and that the trend rate of growth was more rapid after 1950 than before 1940. However, others have argued that the war did have a significant impact on long-term economic growth. For example, in terms of the destruction of physical capital the loss suffered by the defeated powers was greater than that suffered by Britain. Despite this it is Germany and Japan that were to be the miracles of the post-war world, not Britain. This has led some to claim that their success was built on the fact that the destruction of their physical capital was so great that it meant that they had to build their economies from scratch in the post-war period and thus invested in the latest technology. This gave them a capital stock that was to be younger and more productive than that of Britain. Broadberry (1988) has dismissed this folk view of the post-war success of Germany and Japan. He cites the studies of Rostas and the AACP which implied that it was not the age of machinery but its utilisation and the utilisation of 'best-practice techniques' that explained the productivity gap between the UK and the USA, and the study of post-war economic growth by Denison which did not find the decrease in the age of capital to be a significant factor.

There is also a perverse logic that says that war is good for economic growth because it encourages inventions and innovations that have positive long-term 'spin-off' effects. On this simple criterion the Second World War was indeed a boon for mankind. The war-time work done on the long-range bomber and the jet engine laid the basis for the post-war development of long-distance passenger aircraft. The loss of vital raw material supplies due to war-time disruption led to the development of synthetic oil and rubber. There were numerous advances in the fields of medicine and chemicals during the war, including penicillin, synthetic quinine and DDT. Radar, nuclear fission and many new metal fabrication methods also saw their first applications during the war (Milward 1977: 169–207; Vatter 1985: 146). However, the crucial question is whether such developments would have occurred without the impetus of war. Milward (1977: 175, 180) concludes that the pro-war case is far from proven. He even argues against the idea that at the very least the war acted as a catalyst for such inventions and innovations by pointing out that non-war-related activities were denied funds thus preventing other potential developments. Evidence about British R&D expenditure during the war suggests that, although it increased, this reflected a shift into more expensive war-related activities, such as aeronautical research, and that the increase was entirely due to an expansion in state expenditure – private expenditure, if anything, declined (Edgerton and Horrocks 1994).

Another argument about the long-term impact of the war concerns the Olson (1982) thesis. This states that over time certain groups emerge, such as unions or employer cartels, that gain some form of monopoly power in the economy and therefore, in pursuing their own vested interests, contribute to a long-run deceleration of economic growth – over time the economy becomes sclerotic. The argument is usually applied to the national economy and war can be seen in a positive light if it helps to sweep away the institutional structures that are contributing to the economic sclerosis. This, it is argued, is what the Second World War did in Japan and Germany but not in the UK or the USA. Perhaps the most important effect of the war, in terms of institutional sclerosis, was not, however, on the nation state but on the international arena. The post-war international settlement aimed to replace the chaotic and protectionist stage of the 1930s with a more ordered and freer environment via such new structures as the Bretton Woods system, the International Monetary Fund, the World Bank and the General Agreement on Tariffs and Trade (Vatter 1985: 157–69). Within Europe the European Common Market, and all its attendant bodies, would rise from the ashes of destruction and lay the foundations for rapid recovery from the war and create a new and powerful economic bloc (Milward 1984: 59–75, 1977: 329–65). Eichengreen (1996) has persuasively argued that these new post-war institutions helped to solve commitment and co-ordination problems and so contributed to a prolonged post-war boom known as the 'golden age', which lasted for approximately twenty-five years. Thus, it was in the encouragement of international co-operation, and in showing the dangers of isolationism and nationalism, that the war was to have its most important long-term impact.

2

Failure followed by success or success followed by failure? A re-examination of British economic growth since 1949

MICHAEL KITSON

Contents

INTRODUCTION

Economic growth has perplexed economic theorists, economic historians and policy makers.[1] Much of the theory of economic growth effectively

---

[1] This chapter is based on research supported by the Economic and Social Research Council (project L138251038). Earlier versions of this chapter were presented at conferences at

assumed away the issue by assuming that growth – like 'manna from heaven' – was not explicable by economic phenomena. Others believe that growth does respond to economic factors – but there is much disagreement about what these factors are and how big their impact may be (see Temple 1999 for a review of the vast literature).

Understanding economic growth may be difficult but it is important – not least because, if policy makers can create the right conditions to improve growth, then prosperity and welfare may increase. The goal of the current Labour government is to improve the UK's long-term growth rate and the benchmark that it is using is whether the productivity gap between the UK and the leading countries, especially the USA, is closing (DTI 2002, Treasury 2000). In 1999, the average American worker produced 30 per cent more per hour than the average British worker. If the UK economy grew faster and closed this gap, this would allow some combination of higher consumption of goods and services (or more leisure time), more investment, a better trade balance and more resources for government to spend on public goods.[2]

The existence of the productivity gap – and policy makers' preoccupation with it – suggests that the UK economy has underperformed or 'failed'. This contention is, however, subject to debate and a wide variety of interpretations. First, there are those who argue that the issue of 'decline' is largely a misnomer and a pessimistic misinterpretation as the level of prosperity in the UK is much higher now than ever before (Supple 1994a and see also chapter 8 below). This argument often fails to address adequately the key issue of 'relative decline' – that the UK position compared to many other advanced countries has deteriorated. Second, there are those who acknowledge that the UK position has declined but suggest that this does not reflect 'failure' but is the outcome of the dynamics of growth (countries that were behind the UK in prosperity had the potential to catch up) or advantages that some other countries, such as the USA, had or have in terms of resources (Feinstein 1994). Although this argument can explain why the USA maintains its lead and why many countries have caught up with the UK, it is weaker in explaining why some of these countries have subsequently overtaken the UK. Third, there are those who believe that the UK economy did fail during the 1950s and 1960s, but that it has subsequently been successful in reversing relative decline or, at the very least, halting the decline (Crafts 2002). Finally, some argue that the UK performance has been consistently poor during the period since the Second World War, although the causes of such underperformance have changed over time (Coates 1994).

London Guildhall University and at Wake Forest University, North Carolina. I am grateful to participants at both conferences for comments and suggestions. I would also like to thank Hussein Abbasbaiki-Varamin, Laura Webster and, especially, Nicholas Fawcett for research assistance and advice. I am responsible for errors and omissions.

[2] National income comprises consumption, investment, government spending and the trade balance (exports minus imports).

This chapter evaluates the evidence and analysis of the UK's growth performance. It does not address the issue that decline is a misnomer, because a wide variety of indicators show that the UK has a lower level of prosperity than many other countries. The first section of the chapter considers why economic growth is important. The second section evaluates the UK's relatively poor growth performance. The third section considers some of the insights from the economics of growth. The fourth section evaluates the various explanations for the growth performance of the UK economy.

WHY ECONOMIC GROWTH IS IMPORTANT BUT DIFFICULT TO MEASURE

Economic growth is important because it shows whether economic activity is expanding or contracting and it provides an indicator of the prosperity and well-being of a nation. But it is an imperfect indicator: there are empirical problems in measuring it accurately and difficulties in interpreting what it means for the standard of living.

Economic growth is normally conceived as the change in the real level of national output as measured by the percentage change in real Gross Domestic Product (GDP). Obtaining reliable measurements of GDP are problematic for a number of reasons. First, it is very difficult to measure the output of services (such as banking, health, education and so on) which are increasing in their contribution to GDP in the UK and in other advanced countries (see chapter 10 below). Second, it is increasingly difficult to measure the output of manufactured products because as they become more sophisticated their attributes are more difficult to quantify – e.g. the power of computers has changed so rapidly that many perceive that the statistics underestimate the contribution of Information and Communication Technology (ICT) to national output and growth. Third, there is the 'apples and pears' problem: how to combine the outputs of a variety of different goods and services (say, computer games and haircuts)? The answer is by creating index numbers of output and weighting the items together depending on the relative size of production, expenditure or income – but such weights change over time and this creates the problem of whether to use base-year weights or current-year weights – and there are strengths and weaknesses in either approach.

To use GDP as an indicator of the standard of living some account has to be taken of the size of the economy in terms of its population or workforce – in 2001 the GDP of China was more than 10 times greater than that of Ireland but the average income of a citizen of the latter was 33 times greater than the former. One of the most common measures of growth – although strictly it is a productivity measure – is the change in output per worker. And a variant, to take into account the difference in hours worked across sectors and, more importantly, between countries, is changes in output per hour worked.

GDP and its various derivatives are the most commonly used measures of growth and they are, in many ways, the best and most comparable – but care is required in their interpretation as GDP may not adequately reflect the standard of living when the latter is broadly defined. First, some components of GDP (investment and some parts of expenditure by government and on imports) are postponed consumption which will (hopefully) benefit future generations but do not have a direct impact on the current standard of living although they will indirectly benefit those who earn income through such expenditures. Second, having the financial power to purchase more goods and services may improve well-being but other factors may be more important (health, education and so on). An alternative measure of growth and development that helps to capture such factors is the Human Development Index (HDI) which combines GDP per capita with life expectancy and literacy levels.[3] Third, GDP and related measures do not take into account economic activity that does not involve a legitimate financial transaction – so they ignore the black economy but also many other forms of legitimate activity such as home improvement and some child-care. Distortions may arise over time when types of activity move from the informal economy (where they are not recorded) to the formal economy (where they are). For instance, if parents decided not to look after their child themselves but to employ a nanny or child-minder, measured national output would increase even if there were no real change in the level of activity. Such changes may be important in the UK, especially since the 1970s, due to increased female participation in the workforce and because of changes to lifestyle. Fourth, GDP includes many items that may not be good indicators of the standard of living. For instance, deteriorating health that is treated may be shown as higher output of health care, and a high crime rate may lead to a high output of policing and legal services. Fifth, GDP takes no account of the environmental impact of economic activity. Sixth, there is no account taken of the distribution of income.

UK GROWTH PERFORMANCE

The UK has been in relative economic decline since the latter part of the nineteenth century. Since the 1970s, the UK growth rate has been consistently less than that achieved by the other major capitalist countries. The norm has been for the UK growth rate to be approximately two-thirds of that achieved by the other industrialised economies and only during

[3] The United Nations measures the HDI by combining life expectancy, educational attainment (adult literacy and combined primary, secondary and tertiary enrolment) and adjusted income per capita in purchasing power parity (PPP) US dollars.

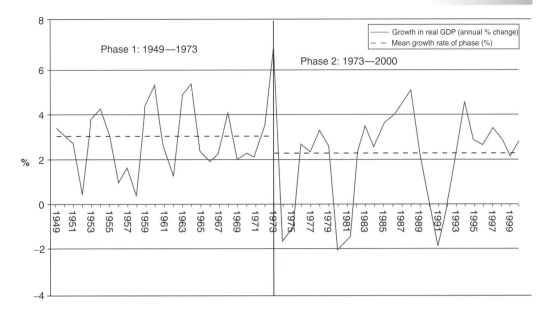

Figure 2.1 UK GDP growth, 1949–2000 (annual % change)

Source: ONS, *Economic Trends.*

the 1930s was this norm disrupted. The UK's fastest period of sustained growth was from the end of the Second World War up until the early 1970s. This period has often been described as the 'golden age of capitalism' as growth rates were much higher than previous or subsequent periods. Yet, even during the golden age, the UK's growth rate of 3.0 per cent compares with an average growth rate of 4.6 per cent achieved by the other leading capitalist countries (Kitson 1997).

The path of UK economic growth is shown in Figure 2.1. During the first major phase, from 1949 to 1973, the UK economy grew at an average of 3.0 per cent per annum with regular and (with hindsight) mild cycles. In the subsequent phase from 1973 to 2000 – following the collapse of Bretton Woods and the rise of free-market economics and policies – the growth rate slowed to 2.3 per cent per annum with more pronounced and irregular cycles. The post-1973 phase was characterised by a number of external and internal shocks which generated deep recessions, including the 1973 oil shock, the 1979 shock following the introduction of a new policy regime by Prime Minister Thatcher, and a 1989 shock which followed the collapse in the price of houses (which influenced householders' wealth) and problems of exchange rate management.

An analysis of the growth of key variables in various (peak-to-peak) sub-phases is shown in Table 2.1. Since 1964, the growth of GDP had fallen in each sub-phase – from 3.1 per cent in 1964–73 to 2.2 per cent in 1990–2000. This slowdown in growth reflected both a lower utilisation of resources – reflected in high and mass unemployment during much of the latter period – and a slowdown in productivity. As shown in Table 2.1 the growth in output per worker was significantly lower in

Table 2.1 Growth of key variables in various phases

	Phase 1: 1949–1973		Phase 2: 1973–2000		
	1949–64	1964–73	1973–9	1979–90	1990–2000
Average annual growth in real GDP (%)	3.0	3.1	2.3	2.3	2.2
Average annual growth in consumption (%)	2.5	3.0	1.9	3.2	2.5
Average annual growth in output per worker (%)	na	3.1	1.5	1.6	2.1
Average annual growth in total factor productivity (%)	na	1.8	1.2	1.3	1.3
Average annual ratio of current account surplus to GDP (% of GDP, current prices)	0.5	0.2	−1.2	−1.1	−1.7
Average annual ratio of balance of trade in goods and services to GDP (% of GDP, constant (1995) prices)	−0.1	−0.8	1.0	−0.3	−2.5

Sources: Office of National Statistics and National Institute of Economic and Social Research.

the post-1973 phases than it was in the earlier period although the rate of growth in the 1990–2000 phase was higher than that achieved in the 1970s and 1980s. Output per worker may increase because workers use new technologies or because they have more capital to work with. A measure that seeks to take account of this is total factor productivity (TFP) which attempts to quantify the productivity of both capital and labour. As shown in Table 2.1 there has also been a fall in TFP growth since the 1964–73 period, although the lowest growth rate was during the 1973–9 period. The growth of TFP tends to be lower than labour productivity as some of the latter is driven by investment and the growth of the capital stock and this difference is most noticeable during the 1964–73 period. There are limitations to the TFP concept. First, TFP is particularly difficult to measure and estimates are prone to error. Second, it is difficult to know what it is measuring: technological progress, entrepreneurship, managerial abilities or something else?

The consumption component of national income has increased its growth rate since 1973 – rising from 2.7 per cent in the 1949–73 phase to 2.9 per cent in the 1973–2000 period. As shown in Table 2.1, however, there have been variations with sub-phases with the fastest growth of consumption being in the 1979–90 period. Overall, there has been a shift from the economy growing at a faster rate than consumption, to consumption growth outstripping the growth of the overall economy. This may not be a problem if the economy grows more rapidly in the future but if it does not then consumers may have to save more in the future in order to service and repay their accumulated debt.

Table 2.2 shows the variability (using the standard deviation (SD) as a measure) of the key indicators. The issue of whether there are advantages or disadvantages to economic variability is subject to debate (see below) although the aim of the New Labour government is to reduce 'boom and bust' as it believes that such variability can harm the economy. During the 1949–73 phase the economy was relatively stable with low levels of

Table 2.2 Variability of key variables in various sub-phases *(standard deviations)*

	Phase 1: 1949–1973		Phase 2: 1973–2000		
	1949–64	1964–73	1973–79	1979–90	1990–2000
SD of annual growth in real GDP (%)	1.7	1.8	2.9	2.3	1.7
SD of annual growth in consumption (%)	1.7	1.8	3.1	2.5	1.9
SD of annual growth in output per filled job (%)	n.a.	1.1	2.0	1.8	1.1
SD of annual ratio of current account surplus to GDP (% of GDP, current prices)	1.2	1.1	1.4	2.2	1.0
SD of annual ratio of balance of trade in goods and services to GDP (% of GDP, constant (1995) prices)	0.7	0.7	1.3	2.0	1.5

Sources: Office of National Statistics and National Institute of Economic and Social Research.

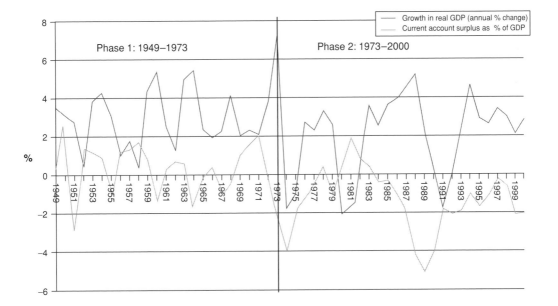

variability of the key indicators. This changed from 1973 when variability increased – with significant increases in variability during the 1973–9 and the 1979–90 sub-periods. In the most recent period (1990–2000) there is evidence that variability has fallen back to the levels prevailing during the 1950s and 1960s although the sources of this relative stability and whether it will continue are subject to debate.

As shown in Table 2.1, during the 1964–73 sub-phase the average current account balance was in surplus – this changed in the subsequent phase when the average balance was in deficit. The path of the current account is shown in Figure 2.2; during the first phase there were periodic but relatively small deficits, but since the early 1970s the current account has been in almost persistent deficit with the exception of the

Figure 2.2 Growth and the balance of payments, 1949–2000

Source: ONS *Economic Trends*, various years.

Table 2.3 The relative productivity performance of the UK – total economy output per hour (UK = 100)			
	USA	France	Japan
1953	195.7	75.5	39.5
1960	200.1	91.5	47.0
1970	180.7	112.6	70.1
1980	158.8	134.5	83.8
1990	137.6	139.6	92.0
1999	130.3	129.4	88.7

Source: O'Mahony and de Boer 2002.

early 1980s. The irony is that during the first period the balance of payments did 'matter' – both economically and politically. As Feinstein (1994) observed: 'The recurrent fear of actual and progressive deficits, together with speculation against the pound meant that there were repeated sterling crises, during which the currency was sold heavily by foreign holders and – if they could – by British residents.' Since the 1970s, the balance of payments apparently no longer matters: 'history offers no real precedent as to how long a country with good access to capital markets can run a balance of payments deficit before it starts to matter' (Pain, Riley and Weale 2001; see also chapter 8 below).

The UK's relatively poor growth rate has been associated with many industrialised countries catching up with the UK level of GDP and with some countries overtaking that level. For the past 180 years the UK has been slipping down the GDP league table. In 1820 the UK was the richest of the capitalist countries as measured by GDP per head (Maddison 2001). By 1870, per capita output of the UK remained greater than that of the USA and that of all the European countries and was only exceeded by Australia's. By 1913, the UK had also been overtaken by the USA and New Zealand, and by 1950 two European countries – Switzerland and Denmark – had also overtaken the UK. During the next twenty years the UK position continued to fall as it was overtaken by other European countries: by 1973 the UK had slipped to twelfth and five of the six countries that formed the European Economic Community had higher levels of output per capita. By 1999, the UK had been also overtaken by more European countries (Austria and Ireland) and by the leading Asian countries – Singapore, Hong Kong and Japan (rankings taken from Crafts 2002[4]). Although prosperity in the UK had been transformed in the period since the end of the Second World War – output per person in 1999 was 176 per cent greater than it was in 1950 – the UK's relative position had significantly deteriorated indicating that other countries had higher living standards and suggesting that the UK may have failed to realise its full growth potential.

Further evidence of the UK's relative performance is shown in Tables 2.3 and 2.4 and Figures 2.3 and 2.4 which provide data on labour productivity for the UK relative to the USA, France and Japan.[5] From 1960 the UK economy partially closed the productivity gap with the USA – whereas the US economy was twice as productive as the UK in 1960 it

[4] The UK has had a similar (although not identical) relative decline in terms of GDP per hour worked (see Crafts 2002: tab. 2.4).

[5] Germany has been excluded due to the empirical problems of adjusting for unification.

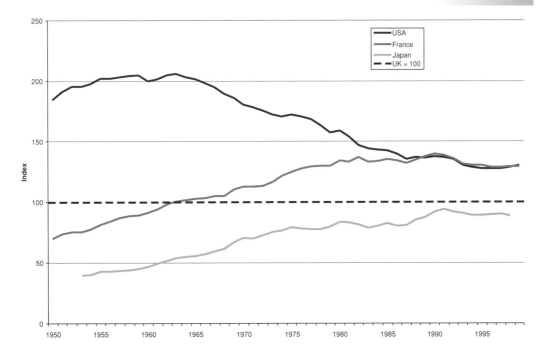

Figure 2.3 Total economy productivity, 1950–1999 (Output per hour, UK = 100)

Source: O'Mahony and de Boer (2002).

was only 30 per cent more productive by 1999 (measured by output per hour worked). In manufacturing, the gap narrowed from 121 per cent in 1960 to 38 per cent in 1990 – although the gap then widened to 55 per cent mainly due to the strong growth in US manufacturing productivity in the latter part of the 1990s. Despite the narrowing of the gap there are a number of issues of concern. First, other advanced countries have been much more successful in improving their position relative to the USA and have had much higher rates of growth. Thus, as shown in Figures 2.3 and 2.4, by 1999 France had achieved similar levels of output per person hour to the USA in the whole economy and in manufacturing. Output per person remains higher in the USA, because American workers work longer whereas the French take advantage of economic growth in terms of increased leisure time. Second, for many sectors in the UK, productivity has been associated with stagnant output and falling employment and this is most apparent in manufacturing. Since the 1960s the UK productivity level in manufacturing has remained significantly lower than that of the USA and manufacturing output growth in the UK has been very low and employment shedding has been

Table 2.4 The relative productivity performance of the UK – manufacturing output per hour (UK = 100)			
	USA	France	Japan
1953	267.5	86.3	55.9
1960	221.1	93.8	63.2
1970	185.8	116.9	115.2
1980	174.0	147.5	158.0
1990	137.5	125.9	148.1
1999	155.0	132.4	147.1

Source: O'Mahony and de Boer 2002.

Figure 2.4
Productivity in manufacturing, 1950–1999 (Output per hour, UK = 100)

Source: O'Mahony and de Boer (2002).

rapid (Rowthorn 2001; see also chapter 3 below). During the 1964–99 period UK manufacturing only grew at an annual average rate of 1.1 per cent compared to 2.9 per cent in Italy, 2.3 per cent in France and Germany, 3.7 per cent in the USA and 4.5 per cent in Japan (Kitson and Michie 2000).

EXPLANATIONS OF THE GROWTH PROCESS

Analysing the growth process has occupied much of the effort of academic economists, economic historians and policy makers. This section considers some of the key insights although consensus, not surprisingly, is not a dominant feature of much of the debate (on which see Grossman and Helpman 1991; Barro and Sala-i-Martin 1995; Aghion and Howitt 1998; and the symposium in the *Journal of Economic Perspectives* 1989).

Neoclassical perspectives

Neoclassical models of economic growth assume that in the long run the economy will settle at some steady state where the level of output will be determined by the availability of resources and will not be constrained by insufficient demand. The traditional starting point is the Solow–Swan model[6] which is designed to show how growth in the capital

---

[6] Often simply called the 'Solow model' in the literature – which is disingenuous to the Australian economist Trevor Swan.

stock, growth in the labour force, and advances in technology interact and how they affect a nation's total output. In such neoclassical models the long-run growth of per capita income is dependent on technology – which is exogenous, that is, it is not explained by the model itself – and in some models is universally accessible.

The implication of the traditional neoclassical approach is that economies with similar savings rates and population growth rates will converge to the same level of income per person. Thus, if, for whatever reason, the initial conditions of countries are such that per capita income levels differ, then subsequent growth rates will be inversely related to the level of output per person, with the scope for catching up being dependent on the extent of the productivity gap.

The evidence presented in Tables 2.3 and 2.4 and Figures 2.3 and 2.4 suggest that there has been some catch-up and convergence.[7] This is also confirmed by an analysis of a wider group of Western countries. In 1950 the per capita income of the leading European economy (Switzerland) was 5.7 times greater than that of the lagging economy (Greece); by 1973 the gap had fallen, with Swiss per capita GDP being 2.9 times greater than that of Greece; and by 1999 there had been a further reduction in the gap with Swiss per capita GDP being 1.9 times greater than that of Greece. These results are consistent with Abramovitz's (1986) view that the period from the end of the Second World War was one of rapid growth by catching-up. The processes of catching-up and convergence, however, are erratic across time and space. Crafts (1992, 1993) shows that traditional neoclassical models fail to predict post-war convergence accurately and he suggests that convergence rates differ substantially. Furthermore, the pattern of world-wide economic growth during the post-war period suggests that although there has been some convergence *within* groups of countries (such as Europe), there have been widening disparities *between* groups (Dowrick 1992).

Overall there is limited evidence of 'conditional' convergence, with catch-up processes being one of many forces that drive the growth process.[8] This, however, is certainly not evidence of a Solow-type growth process whereby technical progress, the engine of growth, was universally accessible, being an 'exogenously determined, fortuitous and costless occurrence – descending like manna from the heavens' (Shaw 1992: 611). Increased globalisation of the world economy, itself an uneven

---

[7] Gordon (1992) makes a distinction (which he attributes to Abramovitz) between convergence and catch-up. Convergence relates to a reduction in the variance of productivity amongst a group of countries, whereas catch-up concerns a reduction in the gap between a leader and its followers.

[8] Empirical evaluations of the convergence hypothesis provide a range of contrasting results (see Baumol 1986; De Long 1988; Dowrick 1992; Dowrick and Nguyen 1989; and Barro 1991). Mankiw (1995) has attempted to re-establish support for a Solow–Swan type model by arguing that the empirical limitations of the traditional neoclassical approach were due to a failure to estimate human capital correctly.

and variable process, has created the potential for follower countries to borrow and adopt new technologies and management techniques from leading countries. Increased trade integration, the rise of multinational enterprises and, up until the early 1970s, a stable international payments system all facilitated technology transfer between countries. Yet, the ability to exploit such technologies is dependent on domestic economic conditions, which in turn will reflect the historical legacy, the policy regime and the investment record.

The existence of persistent differences in growth rates, and in some cases, evidence of divergences in growth rates, cannot be easily accommodated within traditional neoclassical growth theories. New neoclassical growth theories, such as those developed by Romer (1986, 1994) and Lucas (1988), have attempted to resolve this deficiency by incorporating increasing (or non-decreasing) returns to capital. The major contrast between 'new' and traditional neoclassical models is that the former treat technical progress as an endogenous element of the economic system – an element that can be influenced by corporate strategies, investment behaviour and public policies.

Thus policies which promote investment, or at least certain kinds of investment (such as research and development (R&D) expenditure and investment in education), may be able to influence the long-term growth rate. The proximate sources of growth vary in the different vintages of these endogenous growth models. The models of Arrow (1962) and Lucas (1988) suggest that there is 'learning by doing' where technological progress is a result of the act of producing. In such models all firms collectively benefit from a higher level of aggregate capital stock because there is more 'learning' but there may be little incentive for individual firms to increase investment, as the gains will accrue to all firms not just the one making the investment. In Lucas' (1988) model it is investment in human capital (i.e. people – on this see chapter 5 below) that generates spillover effects to the rest of the economy. The role of human capital is stressed in many endogenous models but also in variations of the traditional Solow–Swan model. The augmented-Solow model divides labour input into two components, so that labour's contribution to output depends on both the number of workers and their skills (often referred to as human capital). Although 'education, education, education' is seen by many as central to economic growth there is, as yet, little empirical evidence to support such a contention – this may, in part, reflect the problem that while 'human capital' may be a useful concept in abstract models it is very difficult to measure (see Crafts 1995).

The importance of knowledge as an input into the growth process is emphasised in many endogenous growth models (Romer 1986). Some stress the importance of investment in R&D and the spillover effects to the rest of the economy and internationally through trade and technological collaboration (see chapter 12 below). In some approaches R&D may have bigger effects on productivity in sectors that are not undertaking the R&D (Scott 1989). An important implication of many such models is that firms require incentives to engage in research. For instance, public access to knowledge may have to be restricted (through patents or licences) to allow researchers to make monopoly profits on their discoveries.

Whereas many endogenous models stress the importance of one narrow aspect of capital (such as education or R&D), others stress the importance of a broader concept of capital – both physical and human (Frankel 1962). In such models all types of capital exhibit constant returns to scale and so a rise in the investment rate leads to rise in the growth rate, so growth is fully endogenous.

The limitations of endogenous growth models are both empirical and theoretical. That they have little empirical support may reflect the long lag before growth increases following a change in conditions. Although the new growth theories provide a more useful insight into the growth process than traditional neoclassical theories, they are limited by the usual neoclassical methodology. The models assume full employment and the competitive process is reduced to alternative specifications of market structure – monopolistic competition, oligopoly and so on. Furthermore, as noted by Skott and Auerbach (1995), the new theories largely ignore the importance of historical and institutional structures. Also, such models ignore the inter-relatedness of many forms of investments – the case that it is not just about 'ideas' but having the equipment and know-how to exploit such ideas.

Endogenous growth: a Keynesian approach

Although increasing returns have relatively recently been incorporated into neoclassical models of growth, they have been integral to many alternative approaches to growth, stretching back through the work of Kaldor, Myrdal, Young and Marx to Adam Smith. These approaches, however, do not depend on the assumptions of the neoclassical approach: full employment is not normally assumed and the economic growth is not determined by exogenously given factor endowments.

For Kaldor (1972), manufacturing acts as an engine of growth as it exhibits increasing returns whereas services are characterised by constant returns. This proposition may be too simplistic as increasing returns are likely to exist in services (although there are problems of measurement: see chapter 10 below). The existence of economies of scale means that a nation that is successfully competing in foreign trade can expect that the advantage of expanding demand will increase its competitiveness – including cost competitiveness and other non-price factors, such as product quality, customer service and technological development. Growing economies, for instance, will be able to invest in capital and skills, thus enabling them to improve processes and products. Conversely, a nation with poor performance in international trade can expect a trend of deteriorating competitiveness and declining market shares – with a lack of investment and a dwindling skill base likely to constrain future growth. Thus, while not explaining why initial imbalances occur, the existence of economies of scale indicates why such imbalances may generate virtuous (fast) or vicious (slow) circles of growth.

In neoclassical models divergences from 'equilibrium' can be rectified through price adjustment and/or the correction of market failures. A Kaldorian approach suggests that economies do not behave like this. First, history is important (as recognised by economic historians and, increasingly, economists who use path dependent models) such that the quantity and quality of factors of production accumulated from the past determine what can be produced in the immediate future. This is inconsistent with much conventional equilibrium theory which asserts that an economy is constrained by exogenous variables (with the exception of technology in the new growth theories). Additionally, it implies that it is difficult and expensive to reverse many economic decisions. If a factory is closed or if a market is lost it is difficult to regain the status quo ante. Second, the impact of economic shocks may not only have a once and for all impact on long-run capacity, but may lead to cumulative changes.

A cumulative causation approach may be taken to suggest that economies may be permanently locked-in to a slow or a fast growth path. This would be misleading, as well as being inconsistent with the 'stylised facts' of growth. Although cumulative processes may generate forces that encourage divergences in growth, other forces may temper or ameliorate such effects. As noted above, the international transfer of technology may allow the adoption of new techniques – improving the performance of weak economies. Furthermore, successful countries and regions may find that they are 'locked-in' to certain techniques of production or become overcommitted in certain sectors (Setterfield 1992) – factors which will constrain their future growth performance. Additionally, a change in policy regime may improve the growth path of a relatively weak economy, and if particularly successful may create the conditions for a virtuous cycle of growth. Thus, although a cumulative causation approach indicates the forces that generate divergences in growth, such divergences will be affected, and probably bounded, by the institutional, policy and technological regime.

Cycles, shocks and growth

Until recently the phenomenon of economic growth and the business cycle were analysed independently in the economics literature: business cycle theorists analysed detrended data and considered the trend as exogenous, whereas growth theorists focused on characterising a long-run deterministic growth path. Developments in economic theory since the

1980s, however, called into question this traditional division. There has been a re-evaluation of previous approaches, such as those of Schumpeter (1934) and Goodwin (1967), which view growth and cycles as unified phenomena and there has been the development of the concept of hysteresis, where short-term shocks have persistent impacts.

The rapid advances in economic theory have produced a rich variety of economic models and the relationship between growth and the business cycle can now be analysed from two directions: the impact of the cycle on growth and the impact of growth on the cycle. For instance, a temporary boom may not only increase output in the short run but it may also increase R&D and 'learning by doing', which in turn will put the economy on a higher growth path. In other models, however, a temporary recession may be a 'virtue' as organisational inefficiencies are reduced and inefficient firms are bankrupted, thereby freeing resources for newer and more efficient firms – a process of 'creative destruction' to use Schumpeter's (1934) terminology.

Other factors

Growth, like most economic phenomena, is influenced by social, political, geographic and institutional factors. Abramovitz (1986) and Abramovitz and David (1996) stress the role of social capability in the growth process. Social capability is a society's ability to assimilate technology and realise its potential and is determined by institutional and social structures as well as market structures. A lack of social capability can be due to perverse incentive structures which dissuade agents (such as workers, producers and government) in the economy from engaging in the most efficient and productive ways and to vested interests hindering the growth process. Olson (1982) has suggested that vested interests can create 'institutional sclerosis', leading to a resistance to the changes that are necessary for an economy to realise its growth potential.

A related concept is 'social capital' which has some similarities with social capability, although it has emerged independently. Social capital is a broad concept which consists of norms, networks and relationships that help determine society's social interactions (Putnam 2000). It is a difficult concept to quantify but the most commonly used measures are indicators of trust in other people (Performance and Innovation Unit 2002). Changes in social capital vary from country to country: evidence for eight developed countries indicates that it is declining in the USA and Australia; stable in two (the UK and France); and increasing in four (Germany, Sweden, the Netherlands and Japan) (OECD 2001). Social capital may improve economic growth by improving the efficient operation of markets through improved information flows and lower transaction costs. Within firms, networks and norms may improve the working environment and enhance the relationships between employers and employees. Fukuyama (1995) argues that private sector business depends on high degrees of social trust. The studies of Knack and Keefer (1997) and Whiteley (1997) found a significant relationship between measures of social capital and the rate of economic growth. Social capital is a contentious topic: it has been argued that it is a fuzzy concept and that the term 'capital' is inappropriate as it is not a tangible asset on which returns are earned.

The role of networks is also an important element in the analysis of industrial clusters. Clusters are geographic concentrations of interconnected companies, specialised suppliers, service providers, firms in related industries and associated institutions (such as universities) that collaborate with one another as well as compete (this is a concept that can be traced back to Alfred Marshall's notion of industrial districts). It is argued that clusters can increase economic growth by promoting knowledge spillovers and interactions; by increasing innovation and technological advance; and through promoting higher rates of new firm formation (Porter 1998). Thus countries that have fostered cluster formation will have higher rates of technological advance and higher economic growth. Successful clusters that are cited include Silicon Valley in the USA and the concentration of high-technology activities in and around Cambridge in the UK (see chapter 13 below).

The theoretical attempts to explain economic growth are vast and, increasingly, there are new insights from disciplines other than economics, including history, geography and sociology – these alternative lenses provide additional perspectives upon a complex phenomenon.

EXPLAINING THE UK'S GROWTH PERFORMANCE

> The list of explanations which have been advanced during the past forty years to explain Britain's failure to match her competitors is truly vast. It includes a divisive class system, an innate cultural hostility to industrialisation, the domination of government and industry by the financial interests of the City of London, lack of venture capital, excessive taxation, too much government spending, too little planning, insufficient expenditure on education and training, an adversarial two-party electoral system, restrictive labour practices and over-manning, incompetent managers and obstructive trade unions.
>
> Feinstein (1994: 116)

Explaining Britain's poor economic performance has been, and continues to be, a growth industry: since Feinstein's (1994) assessment, new – or in most cases newly resurrected – culprits include poor entrepreneurship, low levels of innovation and in particular a failure to commercialise science, a paucity of high-technology clusters and low levels of social capital (Treasury 2002; DTI 2002; and chapter 12 below). These explanations may be new to some but many will seem very familiar to those who have studied the literature on Britain's 'decline' since the 1870s.

As Feinstein (1994) pointed out, not only are some explanations of poor performance more persuasive than others (although economists disagree on which these are) but also countries at different stages of development are likely to experience different growth rates. Thus, an assessment of the UK's relatively poor growth rate performance must be evaluated in the context of different stages of development in advanced countries and the potential for catch-up: as discussed above, countries with relatively low income levels *may* have relatively higher growth rates as they have the potential to appropriate technologies and organisational techniques from the leading countries.

The growth of the UK economy was much faster in the period 1949–73 than it was in earlier periods (Feinstein 1994) or in subsequent periods (see Table 2.1 and Figure 2.1). Although this is prima facie evidence that post-war growth can be characterised as success followed by failure, analysis must take into account the potential for faster growth during this period. The process of catch-up may help to explain why the UK had higher growth rates in the 1950s and 1960s than previously as it exploited the potential to catch up with the technological leader – the USA. And it may help to explain why the growth rate fell from the early 1970s – as the gap narrowed, there was less potential for the UK to appropriate overseas technologies and know-how. There is, however, evidence to indicate that the forces of catch-up cannot simply explain the UK growth path; there is evidence of a weak performance and a failure to reach potential. Although the UK has been catching up with the USA it still lags behind – in 1999 the average American worker produced 30 per cent more per hour than the average UK worker (Table 2.3). Second, the UK's poor growth rate has not just been associated with other industrialised countries catching up with the UK GDP level, but with those countries overtaking that level. As shown in Figure 2.3, France, which lagged behind the UK in output per hour in the 1950s, not only caught up but also overtook the UK in the mid-1960s.

In the literature that seeks to shed light on the UK's poor growth performance since the 1950s a contrast can be drawn between those who emphasise the importance of market forces in ensuring efficiency and maximising growth and those that emphasise a more active role for the state in intervening in the economy to provide the appropriate macro-economic and industrial conditions. The role of the market and that of the state vary by country – there are 'varieties of capitalism'. Hall and Soskice (2001) distinguish between liberal market economies where firms co-ordinate their activity primarily via hierarchies and competitive market arrangements (on this, see also Williamson 1985) and co-ordinated market economies where firms depend on non-market relationships to co-ordinate activities and to develop their capabilities. Although Hall and Soskice consider that the UK is and has been a 'typical liberal market economy', the operation of markets and the role of the state in the UK have evolved and changed since the Second World War.

The tarnished 'golden age': a lack of competition?

From the end of the Second World War to the mid-1970s the state took an active role in demand management of the economy (see chapter 8 below) and industrial policy was characterised by state ownership of leading industries and state intervention to 'pick winners' (see chapter 4 below). For those who emphasise the efficiency of unfettered market forces this level of intervention created a 'lethal cocktail of weak competition, pervasive agency problems and deleterious industrial relations' (Crafts 2002: 9). Crafts (2002) argues that the origins of the UK's post-war malaise reflected the legacy of the excessive government intervention in the 1930s. During the post-war period the UK economy failed to realise its full potential due to a combination of market and government failures which had adverse effects on investment, innovation and policy making. Industrial policy focused on excessive interventionism such as nationalisation rather than improving the competitive environment.

In the corporate sector there were agency problems where the managers (the 'agents') of companies had few incentives to behave in the best interests of their owners leading to 'low effort equilibria' and slow growth. Competition is supposed to improve corporate productivity by providing a range of checks on managerial behaviour, including increased risk of bankruptcy, greater focus on profitability and increased work effort (Nickell 1996). Within this framework interventionist industrial policies can act to reduce competitive pressures upon managers allowing them to delay or postpone innovative activities. Industrial policy in the UK, however, was informed by a contrary belief that concentrated markets with a few big companies provided the stability and the economies of scale that would promote innovation and growth. Empirical studies by Geroski (1990) and Broadberry and Crafts (2001) suggest that this view was mistaken as market concentration and associated restrictive practices dampened innovative activity and productivity performance.

Even in the absence of a high level of competition, managers may face the threat of a takeover, but in the UK the threat of takeover failed to act as an effective 'market for corporate control' which disciplined poor managers. Although there was a rapid growth in mergers and takeovers during the 1950s and 1960s this primarily reflected managers pursuing their own interests, such as the desire to take control of a bigger business, rather than efficiency, the interests of shareholders and ultimately economic growth (Singh 1975).

A lack of competition in the labour market, and the state of industrial relations in the post-war period have been frequently identified as key weaknesses in the UK economy. The UK system of industrial relations evolved during the post-war period from a centralised system in the 1950s to a more decentralised system based on workplace bargaining from the early 1960s (see chapter 15 below). An unco-ordinated multi-union system with plant level bargaining may have led to high real wages which reduced the demand for labour and reduced the share of profits in national income. The system could have created a free-rider problem in the bargaining process as there was no incentive for any single wage negotiator to exhibit wage restraint, so all workers through their unions competed for a bigger share of national income. Denny and Nickell (1992) argue that union recognition had a significant negative impact on corporate investment. This may have been due to a number of mechanisms such as a fear that workers would have tried to appropriate the fruits of such investment through higher wage demands, or that unions created restrictive practices which reduced the profitability of some investment possibilities. There were weaknesses in industrial relations in the 1960s and 1970s but these are not sufficient in themselves to explain the poor growth record. Nor do they provide support for the naïve view that strong trade unionism always harms economic performance. In the Denny and Nickell study it was shown that union recognition raises investment if all workers can be efficiently organised behind an investment programme.

Broadberry and Crafts (1996) and Crafts (2002) have argued that the lack of competition in product and labour markets was due to a failure of government to implement supply-side reforms. Once again, inappropriate incentive structures are seen to be at the heart of the problem as governments increasingly adopted vote-winning strategies which involved trading off long-term supply-side opportunities for a better short-term macroeconomic climate. The informal post-war settlement between government, trade unions and employers resulted in an inappropriate policy framework including widespread nationalisation, the support of 'lame duck' companies, a failure to implement an effective competition policy and a gradualist approach to trade liberalisation. Additionally, for some (see Bacon and Eltis 1976), the growth of the public sector squeezed or 'crowded out' resources that could have been more productively used by the private sector. According to Crafts (2002) the UK lacked the appropriate institutional framework to ensure that the managers of companies maximised long-run profitability, that workers stuck to wage bargains, and that governments remained committed to long-run growth.

The tarnished 'golden age': structural change and low investment

For those who argue for an active role for the state, the poor growth of the UK economy was due to macroeconomic policy being repeatedly blown off-course by periodic economic crises combined with a failure to implement a coherent long-term industrial policy (Kitson and Michie 2000; Coates 1994). The world economy grew rapidly during the post-war period reflecting a stable international monetary system, the reduction of trade barriers and the initial boost to growth of the recovery from

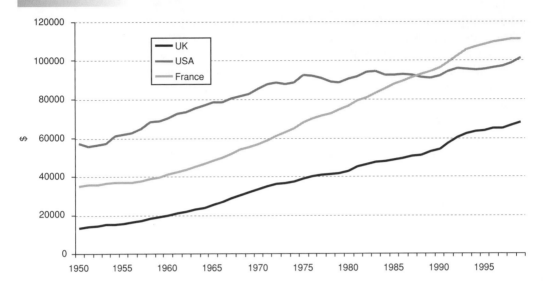

Figure 2.5 Whole economy capital per worker, 1950–1999 ($, constant prices)

Source: Calculations from O'Mahony and de Boer (2002).

the devastation of the Second World War (Feinstein 1994). Although this provided a demand boost for the UK economy, the UK's share of world trade was falling and its propensity to import was rising and some have argued that the UK's deteriorating trade performance – which was dominated by manufacturing – acted as a brake on growth. In analysing UK post-war economic policies Kaldor (1971, 1972) argued that the UK had a relatively slow growth of demand because it was suffering from a balance of payments constraint due to an excessive propensity to import relative to the ability to export. Thus the UK's poorly performing manufacturing sector and the process of deindustrialisation locked the overall economy into a 'vicious cycle' of slow growth (Singh 1977).

Additionally, the sluggish growth of demand interacted with poor investment. Output grew slowly because demand for British products was relatively low and investment was poor. Poor investment reduced competitiveness, which in turn depressed demand, which in turn reduced the incentive to invest. In addition investment remained depressed because of the distorted structure of the British economy, combined with inappropriate economic and industrial policies. The growth of the UK capital stock has been slower than that experienced in the other major industrialised countries and has left a legacy of a relatively low level of capital. As illustrated in Figures 2.5 and 2.6, capital per worker in the UK was significantly below that of the USA and France. Kitson and Michie (1996) argue that the UK's inadequate capital stock was a major cause of Britain's indifferent growth performance, constraining technological progress and the expansion of demand. The cumulative effect of this record resulted in British workers lacking the quantity and quality of capital equipment used by workers in many other advanced countries.

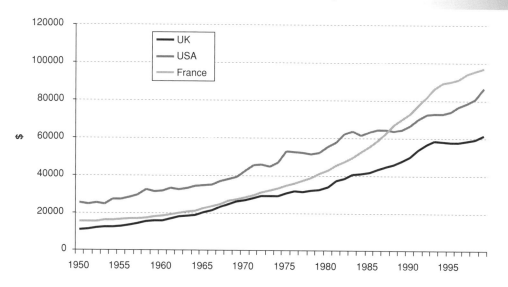

Figure 2.6 Capital
per worker in
manufacturing,
1950–1999
($, constant prices)

Source: Calculations
from O'Mahony and
de Boer (2002).

The poor investment performance has also been attributed to a number of additional factors. First, short-termism in financial markets and biases against the industrial sector created limits on long-term investment (Hutton 1995). Second, companies were reluctant to invest in R&D and products and processes with long gestation periods. Third, labour markets failed to develop and upgrade the skill base. Fourth, macroeconomic instability dampened 'animal spirits', reduced business confidence, increased uncertainty and contaminated the climate for investment. UK macroeconomic policy during the 'golden age' lurched from one crisis to another: there were periodic balance of payments crises and politically inspired business cycles leading to exchange rate, and monetary and fiscal, instability (see chapters 11 and 14 below). Such macroeconomic volatility led to another major problem for investment – the lack of a coherent industrial policy. An attempt was made in the early 1960s to improve long-term growth by establishing the Department of Economic Affairs (DEA) to co-ordinate economic policy and plan the use of resources. The credibility of the DEA was, however, destroyed by a sterling crisis and since then there has been no serious attempt to introduce indicative planning in the UK.

Many of those who argue that the UK suffered from a lack of investment and excessive deindustrialisation believe that UK growth would have been greater during the golden age if there had been a stronger manufacturing sector within the UK economy (Cosh, Hughes and Rowthorn 1994). This may have required a more active industrial policy to promote long-term investment. This contrasts with those arguments discussed above that emphasise that the UK's main problems reflected a lack of competition in product and labour markets.

The 1970s transition to Thatcherism

The 1970s witnessed a transformation in economic performance and sub-sequently economic policy. For the major industrialised countries, GDP growth rates in the 1973–9 period were only half what they had been in the golden age (Feinstein 1994). The international monetary system collapsed and in the UK, as in many other industrialised countries, there was the emergence of rising inflation and rising unemployment – so-called 'stagflation'. The causes of this are controversial. One school emphasised that inflation was driven by rising costs creating a cost-price-cost spiral. Wage costs were rising due to strength of trade unions and the pressure during the late 1960s for rising real wages. Additionally, in 1973 there was a fourfold increase in oil prices following the response of the oil cartel (OPEC) to the Yom Kippur War in Israel. This quickly increased energy costs which fed the inflationary spiral. At the same time, in a misplaced attempt to control inflation, the government introduced an incomes policy under which wages were permitted to rise in direct proportion to increases to the cost of living above a strict threshold. This helped to strengthen the inflation spiral. For the cost-push school, inflation and unemployment can increase at the same time because they are driven by different factors: rising costs drive inflation but unemployment is determined by aggregate demand. And demand was constrained during the 1970s by a series of factors. First, world trade collapsed and remained low. Second, the oil crises raised the incomes of the oil exporting countries, which they failed to re-inject into the world economy. Third, the decline of demand management ushered in a tightening of fiscal and monetary policy.

Monetarism, which provided an alternative explanation of stagflation, was a major influence on the shift in UK economic policy during the 1970s. For monetarists, governments (or the monetary authorities) cause inflation if they print too much money, and trade unions, and any other forces that impede the operation of the labour market, cause unemployment in the long run. Within this framework stagflation emerged due to an irresponsible and inflationary monetary policy, over-powerful trade unions and an excessively generous welfare state. The conquering of inflation was considered a necessary condition for economic success and economic growth would be raised by supply-side policies that decreased the role of the state and promoted the role of the free market.

Although, for many, the election of the Thatcher government in 1979 started the monetarist experiment in the UK, there were important earlier shifts in policy. In April 1975, the Labour chancellor, Denis Healey, announced that although unemployment was high he did not intend to use the budget to attempt to reverse this. This marked the end of demand management in the UK. This shift was confirmed the following year when the prime minister repudiated the key element of demand management:

he told the Labour Party Conference that a nation could not 'just spend its way out of recession . . . by cutting taxes and boosting government spending' (quoted in Feinstein 1994: 114).

Thatcherism: a successful experiment?

The Thatcher government elected in 1979 focused on inflation as the overriding priority and on reducing the role of the state in the economy to allow markets to operate more efficiently. Despite the government's official adherence to monetarism, the strategy that was implemented was a mixture of libertarian economic ideology and inherited policy instruments. The foundation of macroeconomic policy was the Medium Term Financial Strategy (MTFS) which identified targets for money supply growth. Monetary policy went through a number of transformations during the 1980s and early 1990s with different targets (the money supply or the exchange rate or both) and different instruments (interest rates, fiscal policy, exchange rate targeting). However, this did not accord with orthodox monetarism which advocated that the money supply should be controlled directly.[9]

As shown in Figure 2.1 and Table 2.2, UK growth was more volatile during the 1980s and 1990s with major recessions in 1979–81 and 1988–92. As discussed above, the impact of economic downturns on long-run growth is subject to debate. Some emphasise the positive effects of 'creative destruction' while others emphasise the negative effects of increased uncertainty and the loss of capacity. According to Oulton (1995) macroeconomic instability harmed growth performance by depressing 'animal spirits' and discouraging investment. Kitson and Michie (1996) argued that the depth of the UK recessions harmed the long-run growth potential of the UK economy because they led to the large-scale scrapping of capital and contributed to the UK's poor investment performance.

The other key economic strand of Thatcherism was the improvement of the supply-side of the economy by decreasing the role of the state and promoting the operation of the free market. Among the key elements of this policy shift were privatisation and deregulation, reform of industrial relations and weakening of trade union power, and restraint on public expenditure. Crafts (2002) has argued that these initiatives have improved incentive structures and have helped to halt relative decline.

---

[9] In his evidence to the House of Commons Treasury and Civil Service Committee, Friedman (1980) argued that: 'Trying to control the money supply through' fiscal policy and interest rates 'is trying to control the output of one item (money) through altering the demand for it by manipulating the incomes of its users (that is the role of fiscal policy) or the prices of substitutes for it (that is the role of interest rates). A precise analogy is like trying to control the output of motorcars by altering the incomes of potential purchasers and manipulating rail and airfares. In principle, possible in both cases, but in practice highly inefficient. Far easier to control the output of motor cars by controlling the output of a basic raw material, say steel, to the manufacturers – a precise analogy to controlling the money supply by controlling the availability of base money to banks or others.'

Privatisation was a central element of government economic policy during the 1980s and into the 1990s (see chapter 4 below). It was argued that the privatisation programme would improve efficiency, widen share ownership and generate government revenue which would help reduce public borrowing. There is, however, conflicting evidence that the programme has achieved these objectives. Although profits per employee improved, the evidence on the effect of privatisation on efficiency is, at best, ambiguous – there were productivity improvements in some privatised industries and not in others (Parker 1993). Moreover, the productivity improvements that were observed may not have been a result of the privatisation process. Bishop and Kay (1988) concluded that: 'The privatised industries have tended to be faster growing and more profitable, but it seems that the causation runs from growth and profitability to privatisation, rather than the other way around.'

The deregulation of financial markets was seen as central to the efficient allocation of capital (see chapter 7 below). One of the first measures was the abolition in 1979 of exchange controls over capital movements. This led to a large cumulative net outflow of capital (Coakley and Harris 1992). On the domestic front the main developments were, first, the reforms of the London Stock Exchange known as 'Big Bang', and second, the set of reforms which abolished the principal distinctions between banks and building societies. The former did improve the efficiency of the equity market although it led to excess capacity in security dealing which was to prove unsustainable. The latter was of greater concern as the increased competition in the banking system, in particular in the mortgage market, led to a credit explosion and rapid house price inflation. Although in the immediate short term this fuelled rapid consumption-led growth (throwing the government's monetary targets into turmoil) it created the conditions which would hinder growth in the medium term. The credit explosion – house price spiral fed on itself – easily available credit stimulated house prices thus increasing private sector wealth which in turn increased the demand for consumer credit. The situation was unsustainable – this speculative boom was no different from any other. When the housing market collapsed the spiral went into reverse – falling house prices led to declining wealth, increased indebtedness, reduced demand for credit and stagnant consumption. Furthermore, the property crash particularly affected new entrants to the market who were left with high mortgages and negative equity.

The other 'market' to feel the brunt of deregulation was the labour market. The government approach to tackling unemployment was to 'price workers back into jobs' and, by squeezing benefits, to force people off the dole queues. Reducing the power of trade unions was central to this strategy (see chapter 15 below). This took the form of expanding, rather than reducing, the role of law (Deakin 1992). A series of Acts reduced immunities, increasing the scope of common law regulation of strike activity. The 1982 Employment Act removed immunity of unions from liability in tort, narrowed the 'trade dispute' formula which had protected many forms of industrial action and strictly regulated the closed shop. Additional Acts, such as the Trade Union Act of 1984 and the Employment Act of 1988, added to this regulatory framework, undermining the basic rights of trade unions.[10]

It has been argued that the reforms to industrial relations were good for growth as they improved the competitiveness of the labour market. This led to a reduction of overmanning and restrictive practices (Metcalf 1994) and also reduced the equilibrium rate of unemployment (Broadberry 1991). There are, however, alternative perspectives to this: others have suggested that the policies impaired the operation of the labour market and the observed productivity gains were temporary and reflected harsher working conditions (Nolan 1989). Furthermore, the decline in trade union power was not solely due to policy as it also reflected changes in industrial, locational and occupational structures.

Another aspect of Thatcherism was the encouragement of an 'enterprise culture' to encourage new firm formation and the expansion of the self-employed. Yet, the developments in the small business sector do not suggest that government policy had a significant positive impact. Although the increased number of the self-employed was a phenomenon of the 1980s, the growth of small firms reflected a trend that started in the 1960s (Storey 1994). Moreover, much of the growth of the self-employed was a response to 'negative' factors – workers pushed into 'entrepreneurship' by unemployment and the contracting-out strategies of large firms (Kitson 1995).

Thatcherism: a new regime but continued failure?

Although the conventional wisdom is that reforms pursued since 1979 improved the UK's long-term growth performance and growth potential, there are those who remain both sceptical of their positive impacts and critical of their long-term implications. The improvement in productivity is one key piece of evidence presented in support of Thatcherism (Crafts 1996, 2002; Eltis 1996; and, for an opposing view, Kitson and Michie 1996). Certainly, labour productivity in manufacturing grew in the 1980s, although it has been argued that published figures tend to overestimate the extent of the increase,[11] but this growth was largely due to job cuts rather than increased output, and these jobs were not being lost in a period of full employment when the labour would be taken up productively elsewhere. Additionally, as shown in Table 2.1, labour productivity growth

[10] Regarding the more general claim that deregulation is required to promote the sort of flexibility necessary for a dynamic economy, see Tarling and Wilkinson (1997).

[11] See Kitson and Michie (1996) for a discussion of alternative measures of productivity growth during the 1980s.

in the 1979–90 period was only half the rate achieved in the 1964–73 period. Looking at the output performance of the whole economy, GDP grew at a rate of 2.3 per cent between the peak years of 1979 and 1990. Thus, despite the potential for growth through continued catch-up, the benefit of North Sea oil and the impact of an unsustainable consumption-led boom fuelled by asset price inflation and financial deregulation, the UK economy could not match the growth rate achieved during the golden age after the Second World War.

Of additional long-term concern for some was the stagnation of the manufacturing sector, particularly as it made a major contribution to UK exports (Rowthorn 2001). The relative decline of manufacturing may have been exacerbated by UK macroeconomic policy during the 1980s and early 1990s. 'The overriding priority' of controlling inflation led to periodic overvaluation of the exchange rate which was particularly damaging during the initial monetarist policies in 1979–80 and during the UK's membership of the Exchange Rate Mechanism. Furthermore, the prosperity of the private sector was hindered by the retrenchment of the public sector. The government's attempts to reduce the size of the public sector and public borrowing reduced investment in infrastructure and education (Kitson, Martin and Wilkinson 2000).

Post-Thatcherism: New Labour, post-monetarism and the Third Way

The election of New Labour in 1997 saw a continued focus on market orientated policies nuanced with a sprinkling of other influences including: the 'Third Way' (Giddens 1998), the importance of location especially for high-technology activities (Porter 1998) and, most recently, emphasis on social capital (Putnam 2000). There have been subtle shifts in policies with some redefined roles for the state: Coates (2002) has argued that New Labour sees the state as the 'lubricator' of the market. The role of demand management has been relegated to providing low and stable inflation. In the new monetary framework, there is an inflation target and one instrument – the interest rate – which is used to hit this target (see chapter 6 below). Importantly, the policy is implemented by an independent monetary authority, the Bank of England, as this has credibility with global capital markets. According to the chancellor, Gordon Brown, New Labour's economics is 'post-monetarist' (Brown 2001). The hollowing out of Keynesian economic policy represents a continuity of Thatcherism, although the chancellor's fiscal rule, which allows the budget to balance over the business cycle, has resonances of Keynesianism.

In terms of growth, the focus of New Labour's policies is to enhance 'competitiveness, productivity and entrepreneurship' through improvements in the supply side that will create a knowledge-based economy and improve employability. The theoretical case for a knowledge-based economy rests on the notion of endogenous growth (as discussed above) – Brown has stressed the importance of 'post-neoclassical endogenous growth theory' and the Prime Minister, Tony Blair, has stated that his priorities are 'education, education, education'. In the early part of its first term New Labour's commitment to the previous Conservative government's spending limits, and the overriding concern with inflation, meant that policies for growth took second stage. Subsequently there has been more activity; in particular the Regional Development Authorities (RDAs) have been tasked with building knowledge-based local economies. Following the work of Porter (1998) on 'clusters' the RDAs are seeking to identify and foster high-technology clusters in their regions. This is a particular challenge to the most depressed regions, especially the North-East and North-West, whose economic structures have depended on 'traditional' industries.

As for employability, the policies – the New Deal, the Working Families Tax Credit, skills training – are all concerned with improving the readiness for work or the supply of labour and not with the demand for labour. According to Gordon Brown (Brown 2001) the employability policies are aimed at reducing the equilibrium rate of unemployment and increasing economic growth.

During New Labour's term of office, economic growth generally has been above its historical trend (see Figure 2.1), unemployment has been falling and inflation has remained within its target range. In terms of productivity the performance has, at best, been modest (Nickell 2002). Looking at the government's key growth benchmark – the productivity gap with the USA – there has been very little change in the relative performance of the overall economy (see Figure 2.3) and for manufacturing the gap has widened (see Figure 2.4). The latter probably reflects the very rapid growth of US manufacturing productivity in the latter part of the 1990s which was responsible for a significant element of overall economic growth in the USA (Solow 2001).

Assessing the impact of New Labour's policies on growth is complicated by a number of factors. First, it will take a long time before it is possible to assess whether policies that focus on knowledge-based activities have increased economic growth. Second, the growth record of the second half of the 1990s may reflect the policy initiatives of earlier periods. Third, some of the growth performance may have been partly due to favourable external conditions – a buoyant US economy for most of the period and low import prices. Globalisation – particularly of capital markets – has also facilitated UK economic growth in the 1990s. Global capital markets have allowed the UK economy to consume much more than it produces, leading to rising balance of payments deficits (see Figure 2.2). In the 1950s and 1960s small deficits would generate balance of payments and exchange rate crises. For much of the 1990s onwards, deficits persisted and the exchange rate *appreciated*. This appreciation helped to keep inflation low and within the government's target band and the beneficial terms of trade also helped consumption growth. The behaviour of global capital markets has significantly changed exchange rate determination – in the distant past the value of sterling would reflect trade flows, and subsequently it reflected interest rate differentials, but now sterling is driven by unpredictable 'herding' behaviour in global capital markets.

There are a number of issues which will influence the future path of UK growth. First, there have been significant variations in performance within the national economy – by sector and by location. Imbalances in the macroeconomy – high levels of domestic demand combined with low levels of net export demand due to an overvalued exchange rate – have created a 'multi-speed economy'. The sector most disadvantaged is manufacturing, which, in turn, is having an adverse impact on many regions. In the three years between 1997 and 2000 the UK trade balance in manufactured goods deteriorated by £18 billion, whereas during the same period the surplus on knowledge-based services only increased by £10 billion. The damage to manufacturing capacity and to the regions that are highly dependent on manufacturing is likely to persist as it is difficult – and in some cases impossible – to rebuild capacity and competences.

Second, policy is narrowly focused on 'knowledge-based activities'. These activities are currently a relatively small part of the national economy and tend to be concentrated in the south and east of England. Furthermore, the notion of such activities being an independent development block ignores the important intersectoral linkages between 'new' and 'old' industries and the importance of technology and innovation in the latter. Also, some argue that the focus on clusters is a concept lacking in coherent content as there are a bewildering variety of ways of conceptualising clusters (Martin 2002).

Third, and related to the previous point, there is uncertainty about the impact of information and communication technology (ICT) on economic growth. The Solow Paradox – 'that you can see the computer age everywhere except in the productivity statistics' – seemed to have been contradicted by the surge in US growth in the 1995–2000 period (Stiroh 2001). There remains controversy, however, about the size of the impact of ICT and whether US growth was due to cyclical factors rather than a breakthrough in technology that has increased the long-run growth rate (Gordon 2000). Eltis (2002) suggests that ICT has the potential to raise the UK growth rate by around 0.5 per cent per annum. Crafts (2002) suggests that ICT provides an excellent test of whether the post-1979 economic reforms have provided the flexibility required to exploit the growth-inducing advantage of the new technology. The long-run impact of ICT on growth is subject to conjecture and many of the estimates seem overoptimistic in light of the business failures in the ICT sector and declines in global stock markets since 2000. Additionally, the policy regime that is most appropriate for exploiting new technologies is also open to debate. Crafts (2002) stresses the importance of reducing regulatory barriers to entrepreneurship and business start-ups, and of educational standards. But the economic environment conducive to growth of another new technology sector – biotechnology – suggests that other policies and institutions are required. Biotechnology has the potential to make a significant impact on health, well-being and growth and the UK has the second largest biotechnology sector in the world, albeit one that is much smaller than the sector in the USA. Biotechnology is a sector that is characterised by high risk (only one in 10,000 compounds becomes a drug), high cost (the average cost of developing a drug is £500 million) and a long product gestation period (the average drug takes fifteen years to get to market). Market forces alone will not ensure the optimum level of drug development – it is too risky and too uncertain for the private sector to develop drugs on its own. If this sector is to make a major contribution to economic growth what is also required is a strong science base, effective mechanisms to commercialise science and available finance to fill the gaps in private sector provision.

CONCLUSION

The level of national output and prosperity in the UK has increased rapidly in the post-war period – GDP per person in 1999 was 176 per cent greater than it was in 1950. But the UK has fallen down the international performance league and the issue of relative economic decline remains at the centre of the policy debate. During the golden age of capitalism in the 1950s and 1960s the UK growth rate exceeded that of earlier and later periods. But this is insufficient to argue that the immediate post-war period was successful and that failure was evident during the later period. After the Second World War, the UK had the potential to grow rapidly by using technologies and practices from the USA, which was, and remains, the world's technological leader. That it failed to catch up quickly and that other countries overtook the UK during this period suggest that that economy underperformed. In the post-1973 period the growth rate of the economy slowed to two-thirds of that achieved in the 1950s and 1960s. Despite this slowdown many have argued that this was a comparatively successful period because relative decline (on some measures) halted and the scope for catch-up growth was more limited than in earlier periods. The most common and widely accepted view is that the shift to more pro-market policies which started in the 1970s improved the UK's growth performance. But this view is not universally accepted;

there remains a body of analysis that believes that fundamental problems remain in the UK, most notably a small and uncompetitive manufacturing sector with a record of underinvestment. These structural imbalances have been masked by the forces of globalisation which have allowed the UK economy to maintain persistent balance-of-payment deficits since the late 1970s, allowing the economy to spend collectively more than it earns.

3

The performance of manufacturing

STEPHEN BROADBERRY

Contents

INTRODUCTION

By historical standards, British manufacturing enjoyed a very high rate of productivity growth during the period 1951–73. Nevertheless, this was still a relatively low rate of growth compared to most West European countries, so that Britain was slow in catching-up with the United States, the world productivity leader in manufacturing (and the economy as a whole). Since 1979, much of the manufacturing productivity gap that opened up with other West European countries after the Second World War has been eliminated, but this has occurred through a decline in employment rather than an acceleration in output growth.

The slow growth before 1979 can be explained by difficulties associated with the shift of markets away from the Empire towards Europe and by industrial relations problems associated with attempts to apply US-style mass production technology (Broadberry 1997c). Attempts to avoid deindustrialisation during this period led to the adoption of highly interventionist industrial policies, which contained deindustrialisation but did not really solve the underlying problems. After 1979, government support for ailing industries was drastically reduced and legislative reform transformed industrial relations. At the same time, there was a move away from US-style mass production technology and a revival of flexible production, a traditional British strength. Also, the adjustment to European markets was by this stage largely complete.

In considering the performance of British manufacturing since the Second World War, it is important to avoid the excessive pessimism of the 'declinists', who undoubtedly dominated the literature of the 1980s (Wiener 1981; Kirby 1981; Dintenfass 1982; Pollard 1984; Elbaum and Lazonick 1986; Barnett 1986; Alford 1988). When all is said and done, Britain has narrowed the manufacturing productivity gap with the United States since 1945, and the gap with Germany that opened up during the 1970s has largely been reversed. And, as Broadberry (1998) notes, manufacturing cannot be held responsible for the performance of the economy as a whole. Indeed, given the share of services in post-war economic activity, and Britain's declining relative productivity position in this sector, it is clear that more attention needs to be paid to services (see chapter 10 below).

However, some of the more recent literature surely goes too far in rehabilitating the post-war performance of British manufacturing and the British economy as a whole. This seems to ignore the fact that the structure of economic activity as well as comparative productivity performance in each sector matters for overall comparative productivity performance. This is because value added per person differs between sectors, and a successful economy must transfer resources to high value-added sectors. Booth (2001), for example, fails to note that Britain ceded its position as the major manufacturing nation in Europe to Germany, despite the trends in comparative productivity performance. And it surely goes too far to suggest, as Rubinstein (1993: 43) does, that the figures of aggregate economic performance are somehow not capturing Britain's exceptionally vigorous economic performance during the post-war period and that anyway Britain never had a comparative advantage in manufacturing (Rubinstein 1993: 24). This chapter aims to give a balanced overview of Britain's manufacturing performance since the Second World War.

PRODUCTIVITY PERFORMANCE

Table 3.1 sets out average annual growth rates of output and productivity in British manufacturing during three sub-periods since the Second World War. Figures are provided for a six-sector breakdown within manufacturing, which will be useful in understanding the disaggregated picture, but we begin by focusing on total manufacturing. During the period 1951–73 output, labour productivity and total factor productivity (TFP) in manufacturing all grew rapidly by historical standards. During the period 1924–37, for example, output grew at an annual rate of 3.2 per cent,

Table 3.1 Growth of output and productivity in British manufacturing, 1951–1999 (% per annum)

	1951–73	1973–9	1979–99	1951–99
A. *Growth of output*				
Chemicals & allied	7.4	−1.1	2.0	4.0
Metals	3.0	−5.2	−1.5	0.1
Engineering	4.1	−0.9	0.5	2.0
Textiles & clothing	2.6	−1.3	−2.0	0.2
Food, drink & tobacco	5.6	−2.0	0.4	2.4
Other manufacturing	4.6	−2.4	1.3	2.3
Total manufacturing	4.4	−0.8	0.8	2.2
B. *Growth of labour productivity*				
Chemicals & allied	6.8	−0.5	3.4	4.4
Metals	2.7	−3.4	2.5	1.9
Engineering	3.5	−0.1	3.1	2.9
Textiles & clothing	4.7	1.9	2.0	3.2
Food, drink & tobacco	5.1	−1.1	2.0	3.0
Other manufacturing	4.1	−1.8	2.7	2.7
Total manufacturing	4.3	0.4	3.3	3.3
C. *Growth of total factor productivity*				
Chemicals & allied	4.4	−1.0	2.7	3.1
Metals	1.6	−3.8	2.2	1.0
Engineering	2.8	−0.4	2.5	2.1
Textiles & clothing	3.2	1.7	1.6	2.2
Food, drink & tobacco	2.6	−2.1	1.0	1.4
Other manufacturing	1.9	−2.2	1.8	1.2
Total manufacturing	2.9	−0.1	2.6	2.2

Note: Labour productivity defined as output per person engaged; total factor productivity based on persons engaged and capital stocks weighted by shares of labour and capital in value added.

Source: Derived from O'Mahony (1999, 2002).

labour productivity at 1.8 per cent and TFP at 1.9 per cent. Output growth of 4.4 per cent per annum, combined with labour productivity growth of 4.3 per cent and TFP growth of 2.9 per cent per annum during 1951–73 thus represented a considerable acceleration of growth. The period between the business cycle peaks of 1973 and 1979 saw a dramatic setback, however, with output and TFP actually falling, and labour productivity growing only very slowly. The period since 1979 has seen a return to the rapid productivity growth of the 1950s and 1960s, but more through a shake-out of labour than through an acceleration of output growth, which has remained relatively modest.

The sectoral breakdown within manufacturing reveals faster-than-average output growth in chemicals and in food, drink and tobacco, with metals and textiles and clothing shrinking in relative importance over the period 1951–99 as a whole. Engineering and other manufacturing saw output growing at around the average rate for manufacturing as a

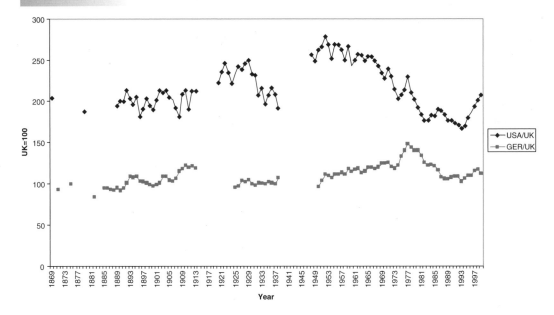

Figure 3.1

Comparative labour productivity in manufacturing

Source: Broadberry (1997).

whole. However, there was no simple relationship between output growth and productivity growth. For although chemicals experienced the fastest rate of productivity growth, the productivity growth performance of food, drink and tobacco was below average. Furthermore, although metals experienced the slowest rate of productivity growth, textiles and clothing had one of the fastest productivity growth rates.

Figure 3.1 puts the performance of British manufacturing in comparative perspective for the period since 1870. Perhaps the most striking result is the long-run stationarity of comparative labour productivity levels in manufacturing for both the USA/UK and Germany/UK comparisons. Nevertheless, during the period after the Second World War, faster labour productivity growth in Germany meant that Germany was faster in closing the gap with the United States. The sharp deterioration of British manufacturing productivity performance during the 1970s led to the opening of a substantial productivity gap with Germany by 1979. The acceleration of productivity growth in Britain during the 1980s then led to the closing of much of the gap that opened up with Germany, although the United States retained a substantial labour productivity lead over both Germany and Britain. The strong productivity performance of US manufacturing during the 1990s means that the USA/UK comparative labour productivity ratio in manufacturing has returned to its long-run two-to-one level.

Table 3.2 complements this picture of comparative productivity performance in manufacturing as a whole with information at a more disaggregated level for a number of benchmark years. This helps us to identify sectors where British performance has been above or below average. Data are provided for the six broad industry groups identified in Table 3.1, covering three heavy sectors (chemicals and allied industries; metals;

Table 3.2 Comparative output per person engaged by manufacturing sector, 1907–1987 *(UK = 100)*

	1907	1935	1950	1968	1987
A. *USA/UK*					
Seedcrushing	77	105		277	
General chemicals			372	258	174
Pharmaceuticals				305	
Soap and detergents	221	285	249	259	
Plastics and synthetics				216	128
Matches		336	376		
Total chemicals & allied	143	227	356	281	152
Iron and steel	283			259	
Blast furnaces		362	408		
Steelworks and rolling mills		197	269		
Total metals	288	192	274	261	166
Mechanical engineering	203	268			
Machine tools			221	162	
Electrical machinery			239	255	209
Radio & electronic components				193	
Electronic tubes			355		
Broadcast receiving equipment				288	
Radios		347	400		
Household appliances			412	239	
Electric lamps		543	356		
Shipbuilding	95		111	185	
Motor vehicles	435	294	466	438	
Machinery/transport equipment					176
Total engineering	203	289	337	294	186
Spinning & weaving	151	150	249	214	
Woollen & worsted	112	131	185	208	
Hosiery	230	156	187	209	
Boots & shoes	170	141	171	173	
Clothing					198
Total textiles & clothing	151	145	198	225	174
Grain milling	178	173	183	255	
Biscuits		345		349	
Sugar	110	102	148	169	
Margarine		152		405	
Brewing	146	201	300	294	
Tobacco	108	160	251	371	182
Total food, drink & tobacco	144	204	215	246	233
Bricks	217	132		169	
Glass		264	274	218	
Cement	219	99	116	191	
Paper & board	262	247	338	290	
Miscellaneous	227	211	285	276	208
Total manufacturing	209	218	273	276	187

(cont.)

Table 3.2 *(cont.)*

	1935	1968	1987
B. Germany/UK			
Seedcrushing	50		
Coke	174	102	
General chemicals		120	89
Soap	110		71
Total chemicals & allied	123	124	88
Steelworks	116	149	81
Blast furnaces	148		
Iron foundries	112		
Non-ferrous metals	85	113	144
Total metals	116	137	96
Mechanical & electrical engineering	112	111	109
Electrical engineering		94	91
Motor vehicles	141	141	111
Total engineering	120	117	112
Spinning	100	133	133
Weaving	69	149	84
Leather	99	97	117
Boots & shoes	121	85	82
Clothing		100	
Total textiles & clothing	97	108	109
Grain milling		65	82
Sugar	33	50	
Margarine	52		96
Brewing	62	105	70
Tobacco	26	114	83
Total food, drink & tobacco	41	94	114
Bricks		182	134
Cement	87	150	81
Paper & board		140	180
Miscellaneous	102	141	132
Total manufacturing	102	119	113

Note: Dates refer to UK census years; US data based on the following years: 1909, 1937, 1950, 1967, 1987; German data based on the following years: 1935, 1967, 1987.

Sources: Broadberry (1997c: 28–31); van Ark (1992); Smith *et al.* (1982); O'Mahony (1992).

engineering) and three lighter sectors (textiles and clothing; food, drink and tobacco; other miscellaneous industries). In addition, information is provided on comparative productivity performance in more disaggregated product areas, which will be useful in the case histories later in the chapter. For most of the twentieth century, between 1907 and 1968, British productivity performance was better in the lighter industries, especially textiles and food, drink and tobacco. This is apparent from both the USA/UK and Germany/UK comparisons.

To what extent does this variation in comparative labour productivity performance across industries reflect comparative advantage? Clearly, there is no one-to-one mapping between variations in comparative labour productivity and comparative advantage, since labour is not the only factor of production. However, in manufacturing as a whole, labour's share of value added has varied between about two-thirds and three-quarters over the twentieth century. Clearly, it would have been difficult for an industry with below average labour productivity performance to have thrived, because the existence of a national unified labour market severely limited the extent to which low wages could have been paid to offset low labour productivity (Salter 1960). Hence, it is not surprising to find a correspondence between industries in which a country had a relatively good labour productivity performance and those with a relatively strong export performance. Broadberry and Crafts (1992: 542), for example, note that for the 1930s, there is a strong relationship between comparative labour productivity performance in Rostas' (1948) sample and revealed comparative advantage as measured by Crafts and Thomas (1986).

Table 3.3 Persons engaged in manufacturing and the whole economy, United Kingdom, 1951–1999 *(thousands)*				
	1951	1973	1979	1999
Chemicals & allied	636	717	700	542
Metals	1,075	1,105	989	422
Engineering	2,602	3,017	2,883	1,771
Textiles & clothing	1,640	1,037	854	325
Food, drink & tobacco	689	763	722	540
Other manufacturing	1,239	1,353	1,277	1,035
Total manufacturing	7,880	7,993	7,424	4,635
Whole economy	22,971	24,824	25,495	26,592

Source: Derived from O'Mahony (1999, 2002).

The German productivity strength and export success in heavy industry, especially chemicals, in the mid twentieth century is also apparent in Table 3.2. The US productivity advantage before the 1970s was also strongest in heavy industry, especially engineering. Since the 1970s, however, there seems to have been a change in comparative advantage, accompanied by a reduction in the dispersion of comparative productivity ratios around the aggregate manufacturing ratio. Most notably, British performance has improved dramatically in heavy industry, with very rapid productivity gains in chemicals, metals (especially steel) and engineering (notably motor vehicles).

One point which needs to be emphasised in assessing the performance of manufacturing and its contribution to Britain's overall productivity performance is its declining share of employment. This can be seen in Table 3.3, which shows the share of manufacturing in total employment declining from 34.3 per cent in 1951 to 17.4 per cent in 1999. In 1966, the peak year of manufacturing employment, the share of manufacturing in total employment was 34.9 per cent. It is clear that most of the decline in manufacturing employment has occurred since 1979, which emphasises the point that Britain's labour productivity gap with Germany has been eliminated largely by shaking-out employment rather than by increasing output. This is consistent with the rapid productivity growth but slow output growth apparent in Table 3.1.

Table 3.4   Average annual hours per person engaged in manufacturing, 1951–1999

	1951	1973	1979	1999
United Kingdom	2,243	2,027	1,903	1,835
United States	1,995	1,949	1,909	1,991
Germany	2,327	1,833	1,736	1,495
France	1,991	1,874	1,718	1,614
Japan	2,349	2,169	2,124	1,889

Source: O'Mahony (1999, 2002).

Table 3.5   Shares of world exports of manufactures, 1937–1999 (%)

	1937	1950	1964	1973	1979	1999
United Kingdom	22.3	24.6	14.0	9.1	9.2	6.9
United States	20.5	26.6	20.1	15.1	16.3	17.8
Germany	16.5	7.0	19.5	22.3	21.6	14.2
France	6.2	9.6	8.5	9.3	10.0	7.4
Japan	7.4	3.4	8.3	13.1	13.1	12.2

Note: Total for world exports excludes exports from small manufacturing countries.

Sources: Matthews *et al.* (1982: 435); United Nations, *International Trade Statistics Yearbook*, Geneva: United Nations.

The disaggregated data in Table 3.3 also emphasise the shift within manufacturing away from textiles and clothing and metals towards chemicals and food, drink and tobacco. Whereas in 1951 textiles and clothing accounted for 20.8 per cent of employment in manufacturing, this had fallen to 7.0 per cent by 1999. Similarly, the share of metals fell from 13.6 per cent to 9.1 per cent over the same period. By contrast, chemicals increased its share from 8.1 per cent to 11.7 per cent, and food, drink and tobacco increased its share from 8.7 per cent to 11.7 per cent. Engineering and other manufacturing also increased their share of employment.

Table 3.4 suggests that we need to be careful about the definition of labour productivity when making international comparisons, particularly since 1973. For whereas in 1951 the average British manufacturing worker worked substantially longer hours than his American counterpart and slightly shorter hours than his German counterpart, by 1995 British hours were decisively shorter than American hours and German hours were substantially shorter still. Germany now operates the relatively short working week that is common in continental Europe, while the United States and Japan continue to operate long working weeks. Britain is now somewhere between these two positions. Allowing for this lowers Britain's productivity gap with the United States but increases it with Germany.

Table 3.5 sheds further light on the performance of British manufacturing from an international perspective, quantifying the changing shares of world manufactured exports accounted for by Britain and the other major industrial exporting nations. Whereas Britain still had a larger market share than Germany and the United States in 1937, the United States had a larger share by 1950 and Germany had decisively replaced Britain as Europe's major manufacturing exporter by 1964. Since the 1970s Britain has been roughly on a par with France. The other major gainer since the Second World War has been Japan.

CASE HISTORIES

We shall now examine post-war experience in a number of industries, being careful to cover a range of experiences, since it is all too easy to draw misleading conclusions on the basis of an unrepresentative sample of industries. In the recent literature, this has tended to mean looking only at British failures and ignoring successes (Elbaum and Lazonick 1986). The reader is referred to Broadberry (1997c) for a more complete picture, based on a detailed study of twenty-nine industries in the post-war period, covering all six of the broad groupings identified in Table 3.1. Here we examine one industry from each of the broad groupings apart from the heterogeneous 'other manufacturing' sector, plus another industry from engineering, the largest grouping. The particular industries have been chosen to highlight the central themes of markets and technology.

Britain emerged from the Second World War heavily dependent on Commonwealth markets, a legacy of imperial preference between the World Wars as the liberal world order disintegrated. A continued belief in the importance of the Commonwealth was an important part of the business environment in post-war Britain, colouring the attitudes of businessmen, who were keen to return to the pre-war cartels and to avoid direct competition with the United States and Germany. It also coloured the attitudes of politicians, who remained ambivalent about British participation in supra-national European institutions. Thus until Britain joined the EEC in 1973, British industry was to some extent shielded from international competition, while the rather hesitant use of anti-trust policy ensured that domestic competition was also relatively restrained. The strengthening of competitive forces in Britain on both the international and domestic fronts during the 1970s and 1980s represented a major change in the business environment. The difficulties of the adjustment 'from Empire to Europe' have been emphasised recently by Owen (1999).

The Second World War also left its mark on technology in British manufacturing, with many British industrialists seeing at first hand the much higher labour productivity achieved in American industry, as the two economies were integrated in the Allied war effort. War-time visits by British industrialists to the United States were followed up after the war by the Anglo-American Council on Productivity (AACP), which sponsored visits by productivity teams made up of managers and trade unionists from a wide range of industries (Hutton 1953). However, attempts to adopt American 'mass production' technology in British conditions were not very successful. As well as meeting the inevitable opposition of skilled craft workers, who saw the value of their skills being eroded, American technology was unpopular with managers, who were not used to exercising the degree of shopfloor control needed to make it profitable (Broadberry and Wagner 1996). The antagonistic industrial relations that emerged during this period of technological upheaval formed an important part of the post-war British industrial culture, and came to be seen as one of the major symptoms of the 'British disease' in the literature on economic decline.

These two issues of markets and technology came to a head in the 1970s. Although imperial preference had been removed and tariffs reduced under GATT during the 1950s and 1960s, EEC entry in 1973 produced a severe competitive shock. Industrial relations, which had been simmering throughout the post-war period, exploded in a wave of militancy. The situation was exacerbated by the oil shocks of 1973–4, when the price of oil was quadrupled, and 1979–80, when it was doubled again. The increase in the price of a major input inevitably hit manufacturing profitability, already reeling from the effects of increased competition within the EEC. Furthermore, the second oil shock had an additional damaging effect through exchange rate appreciation. Since Britain was a net exporter of oil by the end of the 1970s, the increase in the price of oil improved the current account of the balance of payments and hence put upward pressure on the pound, thus making British exports more expensive and imports cheaper (Bean 1987).

After the recession of the early 1980s, British manufacturing emerged substantially reduced in size, but, as the decade progressed, it became clear that much of the deterioration in comparative labour productivity that had occurred in the 1970s was being reversed. By the end of the 1980s, labour productivity in British manufacturing was once again approaching German levels. Rather than looking to American 'mass production' technology, with its emphasis on standardised production and unskilled shopfloor labour, British firms now returned to a more European 'flexible production' technology, using skilled shopfloor workers to produce customised output. The shake-out of labour that occurred during the recession of the early 1980s was largely unskilled. However, although there was a renewed emphasis on shopfloor labour force skills, Britain still lagged behind much of continental Europe in the provision of intermediate skills (Prais 1995). This has remained the case during the 1990s.

Motor vehicles

Data on registrations, production and trade are shown in Table 3.6. In the immediate post-war years, the increase in production was export-led. This was a part of the government's post-war export drive, needed to shore up the fragile balance-of-payments position. The predominance of exports was ensured through controls over steel supply, with allocations channelled to firms exporting at least 50 per cent of output, rising in 1947 to 75 per cent (Church 1994: 43). Britain's share of world motor exports rose from 15 per cent in 1937 to 52 per cent in 1950. However, this position could not be sustained once US production was no longer held back by the steel shortage and as production in continental Europe recovered (Dunnett 1980: 34). Britain's share of world car exports fell back to 24 per cent during 1957–62 and 19 per cent during 1963–7. From 1974, for the first time since 1914, car imports exceeded car exports (Church 1994: 44). By the end of the 1970s, imports were roughly equal to production, and continued to grow during the 1980s and 1990s. Although exports also grew rapidly during the 1990s, Britain remained a substantial net importer of cars at the end of the twentieth century.

During the period 1951–73, output of motor vehicles grew at an annual rate of 5.2 per cent, with labour productivity growing at 3.5 per cent per annum (Broadberry 1997c: 316). Nevertheless, the comparative data in Table 3.2 show the USA maintaining a roughly four-to-one labour productivity lead between 1950 and 1968, at the height of the Fordist era. During the period 1973–9 the output of motor vehicles in Britain began to decline and productivity stagnated. Although rapid labour productivity growth has occurred in British motor vehicles since 1979, this has been a result of massive labour shedding, with output still below its 1968 level at the end of the 1990s despite some recovery from the sharp recessions of the early 1980s and early 1990s.

Table 3.6 British registrations, production and trade in cars, 1946–1999 *(thousands)*

	Registrations	Production	Exports	Imports
1946	122	219	84	0
1951	138	476	368	4
1958	566	1,052	484	11
1968	1,144	1,816	677	102
1973	1,688	1,747	599	505
1979	1,716	1,070	410	1,061
1986	1,882	1,019	201	1,072
1989	2,300	1,299	339	1,371
1995	1,945	1,532	769	1,160
1999	2,198	1,787	1,159	1,671

Source: Society of Motor Manufacturers and Traders, various years.

Markets and technology were the fundamental factors underlying these dramatic trends. The British failure in the volume production of cars epitomises the general British poor performance in mass production. This conclusion is further underlined by the success of British producers in the smaller niche markets for luxury cars and 4-wheel-drive vehicles (Adeney 1989: 127–41). There was also British success in sports cars during the early post-war period, before the companies were absorbed in the ailing volume producer, British Leyland (Whisler 1995). The failure in mass production was rooted in the difficulties of switching away from the domestic and Empire markets traditionally served by British producers and the industrial relations problems brought about by attempts to reorganise production in ways which wrested control away from the shopfloor labour force.

Dealing first with the issue of markets, a mass market along American lines had not developed in Britain between the wars. Thus the post-war British industry inevitably inherited a structure which was more fragmented and produced many more models than its American rival (Dunnett 1980: 21; Political and Economic Planning 1950: 129–39). Furthermore, exports during the interwar period had been heavily oriented towards Empire markets because of protection in Europe and imperial preference. Whisler (1994) is nevertheless very critical of the marketing policies of the companies – in particular, their failure in the immediate post-war years to invest in an effective distribution system in Europe, which he sees as the outstanding potential market. However, it was by no means clear at the end of the war that Europe would be the outstanding growth market of the next two or three decades; indeed, the experience of the 1930s pointed in precisely the opposite direction. Furthermore, there were difficulties caused by the introduction of currency exchange restrictions and British government prevarication over participation in European supra-national bodies such as the EEC (Whisler 1994).

The concentration on Empire markets meant that British producers could avoid head-to-head competition with foreign producers in overseas markets, and these attitudes towards competition also spilled over into domestic markets. Thus although there was undoubtedly strong rivalry between firms, this did not lead to price competition in the early post-war period. Rather, competition tended to take the form of quality improvements, which took longer for competitors to match than price cuts (Cowling and Cubbin 1971).

Remaining with problems of markets, Dunnett (1980: 61–5) emphasises the role of stop–go policies, particularly changes in hire purchase restrictions, in creating an environment of uncertainty, thus hindering investment. However, as Prais (1981: 160) notes, it is now clear that the early post-war period was one of outstanding stability compared with what was to come during the 1970s and 1980s. Furthermore, the German and American car industries showed much the same variability around a trend as the British car industry over the period 1955–75 (Prais 1981: 356).

Even if all demand-side problems could have been overcome, however, there remained on the supply side serious barriers to the successful introduction of mass production techniques in the British car industry. For Lewchuk (1987), the central problem of the British car industry after the Second World War was a movement in the direction of American technology in an atmosphere of mistrust between management and unions. The deterioration of industrial relations showed up in an increase in the number of strikes, the number of workers involved and the working days lost (Durcan et al. 1983).

As the British firms made a switch to Fordist methods, all kinds of problems and anomalies cropped up. The British system of craft unionism meant that there was a huge multiplicity of unions to deal with (see chapter 15 below). Thus, for example, in the early 1970s British Leyland had to deal with 36 unions, and Ford with 22 (Rhys 1972: 445). The scope for inter-union disputes inherent in this structure was exacerbated by the two-tier nature of bargaining, with conflict between shop stewards and central union officials. Lewchuk (1987: 214) focuses on the difficulties caused by a shift from payment of piece rates under the British system to payment of fixed day rates under the American system. Under piecework, workers had a strong incentive to ensure that the plant ran smoothly, that parts were available when needed, that machinery was kept going, etc., otherwise they lost pay. Under measured day work, that direct incentive was removed, and management was ill prepared to fill the co-ordination gap. As Prais (1981: 161) notes, industrial relations problems were concentrated in large plants, and this was particularly serious in the volume car industry, where large plants were essential.

The adoption of American production methods required a major reorganisation of the British motor vehicle industry, since economies of scale could only be reaped if many of the smaller producers merged and rationalised their range of models. A series of mergers among the British-owned motor vehicle producers culminated in the formation of British Leyland Motor Corporation (BLMC) in 1968 (Turner 1971). The general verdict on the effects of these mergers has been highly negative, however, with the British-owned producers continuing to see their share of UK production decline (Cowling *et al.* 1980: 170–90).

One issue raised by the above emphasis on technology is the much poorer performance of Britain relative to Germany. To some extent this can be explained by Britain's traditional emphasis on Empire markets compared with Germany's historical presence in European markets. It can also be noted that Germany's success tended to be at the higher-quality end of the market, with companies like BMW and Mercedes. However, it must also be noted that during the early post-war years the success of Volkswagen was based on standardised mass production of a single cheap model, the Beetle. The difference between Britain and Germany here lies in the supply of unskilled labour from the countryside and overseas. Rather than persuading an established skilled labour force to accept dramatic changes in their working practices, Volkswagen could rely on rural migrants and guest workers who were more prepared to accept whatever working conditions were required to underpin relatively high earnings, since they did not intend to stay (Bardou *et al.* 1982: 247–9).

The British attempts to switch to Fordist production methods ended disastrously. With losses at British Leyland mounting, in December 1974 a rescue package was agreed between the government and the company involving nationalisation of British Leyland and the injection of substantial sums of public money (Adeney 1989: 281). The nationalisation of British Leyland was followed by a bail-out of Chrysler UK in December 1975 (Young and Hood 1977: 287).

Most writers see American-style mass production techniques in the motor vehicle industry as encountering difficulties since the late 1960s (Womack *et al.* 1990; Juergens *et al.* 1993). The emergence of modern flexible or 'lean' production techniques in the car industry is usually associated with Japan. However, it is also possible to see in modern flexible production techniques a return to some of the key features of the older British craft based flexible production system: in particular, the use of skilled workers to produce differentiated products.

In this changing environment, after a disastrous 1970s and a traumatic early 1980s, car production in Britain began to revive from the mid-1980s. This partly reflected inward investment from Japan, with Nissan, Toyota and Honda establishing plants in Britain (Juergens *et al.* 1993: 388). However, it also partly reflected a revival at British Leyland, which began under the leadership of Michael Edwardes, who was appointed chairman and managing director in 1977. Although the newly renamed Rover Group had some success at the higher-quality end of the market, it was reluctant to give up competing in the volume business, where success remained elusive.

Steel

Steel, as a mature industry, grew relatively slowly during the post-war period. The tonnage of crude steel, shown here in Table 3.7, grew at the relatively modest rate of 2.3 per cent per annum between 1951 and 1973. In the metals sector as a whole (including non-ferrous metals), where figures are available in Table 3.1, output grew at 3.0 per cent per annum during 1951–73 so that, coupled with only a slow decline of the labour force and a fairly rapid rise in the capital stock, labour productivity and TFP also grew slowly, at 2.7 and 1.6 per cent per annum, respectively. The steel industry was adversely affected in most countries by the first oil shock in 1973, which plunged the industrialised world into recession and encouraged substitution away from energy-intensive products like steel (Cockerill 1988: 70; Hudson and Sadler 1989: 18). However, the period 1973–9 was particularly disastrous for the British steel industry, with output slumping from 26.2 to 21.1 million tons, and with strongly negative growth of labour productivity and TFP in the metals sector. O'Mahony and Wagner (1994) chart the dramatic decline in Britain's labour productivity position relative to Germany during the 1970s in the steel industry, with German output per hour at 125 per cent of the British level in 1973, but 263 per cent of the British level by 1979. This was followed by a remarkable turnaround during the 1980s, with German output per hour at just 89 per cent of the British level by 1989. However, as is apparent from Table 3.1, the rapid productivity growth achieved after 1979 was the result of labour shedding rather than output growth.

Clearly, such dramatic trends in productivity are bound up with changes in organisation and the large literature on the post-war steel industry reflects this. However, as in many other industries, these changes in organisation can be related to technology, with the performance of British industry improving as the emphasis shifted away from the production of bulk steel in large integrated plants to the production of more differentiated special steels and the production of common grades in smaller-scale mini-mills (Cockerill 1988: 79).

The major technological changes were the shift from open hearth furnaces to Basic Oxygen Steelmaking (BOS) from the 1960s and the growth of continuous casting during the 1980s and 1990s. The diffusion path of both innovations can be seen in Table 3.7. BOS drastically raised the

Table 3.7	British crude steel production, 1951–1995					
	Total output (000 tons)	Production process (% of output)				Continuous casting (% of output)
		Open hearth	Bessemer	Oxygen	Electric	
1951	15,639	86.6	7.1	0.0	5.2	0.0
1958	19,566	87.6	6.0	0.0	5.8	0.0
1968	25,840	54.9	3.9	25.0	16.1	1.6
1973	26,173	31.8	0.9	47.3	19.9	3.0
1979	21,124	5.4	0.0	60.1	34.4	16.9
1986	14,492	0.0	0.0	71.7	28.3	60.5
1989	18,444	0.0	0.0	72.7	27.3	80.2
1995	17,325	0.0	0.0	74.3	25.7	86.6
1999	16,026	0.0	0.0	77.6	22.4	95.9

Source: Mitchell (1988: 289–90); Iron and Steel Statistics Bureau, various years.

minimum efficient scale of production in an integrated steel plant (Ray 1984: 6–8). The poor performance of the British steel industry during the transition from open hearth to basic oxygen production during the late 1960s and the 1970s is thus consistent with the difficulties experienced by many British industries attempting large-scale production at this time. It may also be seen as one of the factors explaining the relatively slow diffusion of BOS in Britain compared with other major steel producing countries (Ray 1984: 16). By contrast, continuous casting has drastically reduced minimum efficient scale, and, in combination with electric arc furnaces for the production of liquid steel, has allowed the growth of 'mini-mills' (Schenk 1974; Ray 1984).

The need for rationalisation of the British iron and steel industry was recognised in the Anglo-American Council on Productivity (AACP) reports on *Iron and Steel* (AACP 1952) and *Steelfounding* (AACP 1949). The existence of a large productivity gap at this time is confirmed by the figures in Table 3.2, which show large USA/UK labour productivity gaps in blast furnaces and in steelworks and rolling mills in 1950. Nevertheless, rationalisation was effectively achieved only during the 1980s, and much of the literature on the post-war industry is concerned with the barriers to change, which allowed the persistence of failure on such a grand scale. This is a story of political economy, with nationalisation in 1950, denationalisation in 1953, renationalisation in 1967 and privatisation in 1988. However, before the 1980s, public ownership failed to secure effective reorganisation and private ownership failed to inject effective competition.

Despite the election of a Labour government in 1945, nationalisation of steel was delayed until after the 1950 election because of divisions within the party (Vaizey 1974: 125–8). Since the Conservatives were returned to office in the autumn of 1951, the nationalised Iron and Steel Corporation of Great Britain (ISCGB) made little impact before it was given a standstill order, and the industry prepared for return to the private sector (Vaizey 1974: 150). This was facilitated by the form which nationalisation had taken, with the ISCGB acting as a holding company and leaving the companies as the major operating units (Vaizey 1974: 127).

Although for all but a brief period during 1951–3 the iron and steel industry was in private hands until 1967, it seemed almost to operate as part of a planned economy, with a series of five-year plans (Vaizey 1974: 148, 162). The plans generally aimed to patch up existing plant where possible and were heavily influenced by political factors when recommending new investments. Thus, for example, when a decision came to be taken on the location of a new strip mill in 1958, to be financed by public money, cabinet intervention ensured that two mills were built, at Newport in South Wales and Ravenscraig in Scotland. Since there were insufficient funds for two mills, both were starved of resources and neither turned out to be very satisfactory (Vaizey 1974: 169–76).

During the period of private ownership between 1953 and 1967, the industry remained largely shielded from competition. On the international front, the protectionist policies of the interwar years were retained, and imports and exports of iron and steel remained low relative to output (Rowley 1971: 71–3). Britain also remained outside the European Coal and Steel Community (ECSC) (Vaizey 1974: 168). On the internal front, the industry operated a system of uniform delivered prices, sometimes known by economists as the postage stamp system, since the price did not vary with distance to delivery, as in a national postal system (Rowley 1971: 91; Scherer 1980: 326).

When the industry was renationalised in 1967, the British Steel Corporation (BSC) took control of the fourteen major firms in the industry. Initially there were four regional groupings, but in 1970 BSC eliminated the old company structure more completely by reorganising on a product basis (Vaizey 1974: 181–3). In 1973 a Ten-Year Development Plan was unveiled, which envisaged a further expansion of capacity (Hudson and Sadler 1989: 62). The new structures were soon put to the test when Britain encountered intensified competition from European producers upon EEC entry at the beginning of 1973. Then at the end of 1973 the first oil shock plunged the industry into crisis. As the industrialised world moved into recession and as the development of less energy-intensive substitutes hit the demand for steel, BSC began to make heavy losses and were forced to change their policy from expansion to savage retrenchment (Hudson and Sadler 1989: 65). Although the trade unions in BSC had co-operated over plant closures during the early 1970s, within an environment of planned expansion, by 1977 union policy had become firmly opposed to closures within an environment of general contraction (Hudson and Sadler 1989: 64–5). There followed a period of bitter industrial relations, with campaigns to contest closures at Corby and Consett in 1979 and a national strike over wages in 1980 (Hudson and Sadler 1989: 66–72).

The capacity reductions of the early 1980s took place within the context of a quota system introduced by the European Commission under the Treaty of Paris, which established the ECSC (Hudson and Sadler 1989: 33). Once introduced, this crisis measure proved difficult to remove, and continued to operate until 1988, when much-improved demand conditions finally allowed the withdrawal of quotas. Cockerill (1993: 73) concludes that on balance the European Commission's intervention in the steel industry hindered rather than helped the process of adaptation to the structural crisis.

Along with the cut-backs at BSC, there emerged in the early 1980s plans for a rejuvenation of the steel industry in the private sector. The 1981 Iron and Steel Act exempted BSC from its previous statutory duty to provide the full range of steel products, permitted joint ventures between BSC and private companies and allowed for the eventual liquidation of BSC. The joint ventures were code-named 'Phoenix' to designate an industry rising from the ashes (Hudson and Sadler 1989: 78). These Phoenix companies, such as Allied Steel & Wire and Sheffield Forgemasters, were concentrated in particular in special steels, leaving BSC to concentrate on its core business of bulk steels. As BSC moved back into profit from the mid-1980s, the issue of privatisation moved onto the political agenda, and BSC returned to the private sector in 1988 as British Steel (Cockerill 1993: 68). After a merger with Hoogovens of the Netherlands in 1999, the old British Steel name was replaced by Corus (Owen 1999: 148).

As Aylen (1988: 3) notes, the remarkable turnaround of the British steel industry occurred while it was in public ownership. However, his conclusion that privatisation was therefore unnecessary does not follow, since it is highly unlikely that the changes in the structure of incentives faced by the management and workforce, which he sees as responsible for the improved performance, could have been implemented without the threat of an end to public ownership. As in many industries, the intensification of product market competition during the early 1980s was crucial in forcing managers and workers to address inefficient work practices. However, the fact that technology had changed to favour smaller-scale production methods also undoubtedly helped the British industry.

Chemicals

The growth pattern in chemicals is in many ways typical of manufacturing as a whole, with a period of very rapid output and productivity growth to 1973, followed by stagnation during 1973–9 and a strong recovery after 1979 (Table 3.1). However, output growth has been rather faster in chemicals than in total manufacturing, apart from during the troubled 1970s. Hence, as noted earlier, the chemicals industry has increased its share of manufacturing output over the post-war period as a whole.

The post-war British chemical industry continued to be dominated by ICI, which still accounted for 35 per cent of output during the early 1980s (Grant and Martinelli 1991: 81). Pettigrew (1985) characterises ICI in the early post-war period as an under-performing large company, badly in need of a shake-up. First, with the break-up of the international cartels that dominated the industry between the wars, ICI needed to shift the distribution of its assets from the UK and Empire and confront international competition directly in North America and western Europe. Second, the company needed to become more market-oriented in general, after years of captive markets, rationing and excess demand. Third, technology needed to be improved to best-practice levels, with the United States having emerged from the Second World War with a decisive technological lead. Fourth, there was a perception of the need to improve labour productivity in the British operations, particularly as a result of exposure to American methods via war-time economic co-operation and the early post-war Anglo-American Council on Productivity reports on *Heavy Chemicals* (AACP 1953) and *Superphosphate and Compound Fertilisers* (AACP 1950). Nevertheless, the backwardness of the British chemical industry after the Second World War should not be exaggerated. Indeed, if the comparison is made with the rest of Europe, the position does not look nearly so bleak. As Chapman (1991: 85) notes, the first petrochemical plants in western Europe were all established in Britain.

As Pettigrew (1985: 82) notes, by the early 1960s the ICI Board had evolved a corporate strategy to deal with the four problems of dependence on British markets, poor marketing, technological backwardness and low labour productivity. Nevertheless, progress was not always rapid; sales remained concentrated in the UK and Australasia into the 1970s, and the company remained dominated by distinguished scientists with little in the way of marketing skills until the emergence of John Harvey-Jones as chairman in 1982. However, progress was made in closing the technological gap, with Kennedy (1986) painting a picture of successful innovation in a number of areas, including fibres (Terylene, the first polyester), plastics (polythene), dyestuffs ('Procion' reactive dyes), paints (Dulux alkyd-based paints), pharmaceuticals (fluothane anaesthetic, beta-blocker heart drugs, Nolvadex cancer therapy) and agricultural chemicals (diquat and paraquat herbicides, 'Pruteen' artificial protein).

Labour productivity problems persisted throughout the 1960s, however, and worsened during the 1970s. Attempts were made during the 1960s to improve the utilisation of labour through the Manpower Utilisation and Payment Structure / Weekly Staff Agreement (MUPS/WSA). This was an example of productivity bargaining, following on from the famous 'Fawley Agreement' at Esso (Flanders 1964), where attempts were made to raise productivity by offering higher wages in return for agreement to new working practices. The inspiration for MUPS/WSA came from the United States, and it was seen by its advocates within ICI as holding out the prospect of attaining American levels of labour productivity, which the figures in Table 3.2 suggest were about three times the British level. The company relied largely on American social scientists brought in as external consultants. The scheme met strong resistance, particularly from the craft unions at the large Wilton and Billingham sites. The problems which plagued large-scale plants in other British industries at this time also occurred in chemicals (Prais 1981). Craft unions were suspicious of reforms to working practices, seen as an attack on their skills and high earnings, while many managers were wary of assuming detailed supervision of the workforce (Pettigrew 1985: 229–31). It may even be that the attempts to impose MUPS/WSA had by the 1970s increased the resistance of the workforce and management to change (Pettigrew 1985: 115). Given the productivity outcome reflected in Table 3.2, it is not surprising that most writers have concluded that MUPS/WSA was not very successful (Pettigrew 1985; Roeber 1975).

The improvement of Britain's comparative productivity position in chemicals during the 1980s, noted by O'Mahony and Wagner (1994), wiped out the deterioration of the 1970s. Undoubtedly, one factor here was the change in the external environment. Faced after 1979 with a sharp domestic recession, a steep rise in the price of oil, rapid sterling appreciation and excess capacity in European petrochemicals, ICI moved into loss for the first time in its history (Pettigrew 1985: 377). Rationalisation was clearly called for. Nevertheless, there were also technological trends favouring the British chemical industry during the 1980s and 1990s. As in other industries, British chemical companies found it difficult to compete in large-scale production of standardised items. The size of newly commissioned plant in petrochemicals, which had risen slowly during the 1960s and then increased very sharply during the early 1970s, stabilised in the mid-1970s and even began to fall during the 1980s (Chapman 1991: 123). More importantly, though, as the market for industrial chemicals matured, with the end of the major thrust of chemical substitution for natural products such as wood and paper, further growth depended on speciality products (Pettigrew 1985: 411). In these areas, where large scale was less important, British firms were not hampered by industrial relations problems. Accordingly, ICI has reduced its presence in commodity chemicals and strengthened its presence in speciality chemicals (Grant and Martinelli 1991: 62).

One other aspect of the chemicals sector worth commenting on is the success of British companies in pharmaceuticals. This has been one of the major growth industries of the post-war world, accompanied by a revolution in health care. Despite relatively low levels of per capita consumption of (legal) drugs in Britain compared with other rich industrialised countries, Britain has sustained a position as one of the four major pharmaceutical exporting nations, as can be seen in Table 3.8. Despite its relatively good performance, however, the British pharmaceutical

Table 3.8   National shares of world pharmaceutical exports, 1938–1988 (%)

	1938	1955	1963	1975	1980	1988	1995	1999
United Kingdom	12	16	14	12	12	11	11	10
United States	13	34	25	12	14	14	9	11
Germany	39	10	15	16	16	15	14	14
Switzerland	7	14	14	14	13	12	11	11

Sources: Cooper (1966: 249); Balance et al. (1992: 64–5); United Nations, International Trade Statistics Yearbook, Geneva: United Nations.

industry has suffered from a poor image, along with drug companies the world over, portrayed as parasitic, making huge profits out of the misfortune of others. Teeling Smith (1992) attributes this to a misunderstanding of the workings of competition in a high-risk business, where the possibility of high profits on a successful drug is needed to justify the huge research expenditure on products which may never come to market.

Note, finally, that British success in high-technology sectors such as pharmaceuticals is difficult to square with the characterisation of British society provided by many declinists. It seems clear that British society has not been anti-scientific or anti-technological, as writers such as Wiener (1981) and Barnett (1986) allege. The figures in Table 3.2 on labour productivity in pharmaceuticals, however, do suggest a production problem along the lines noted in the bulk chemicals sector. However, this was not an obstacle to British success in the pharmaceutical industry, where success depends rather more on prowess in research and development than on high labour productivity in production.

Electrical and electronic engineering

The British electrical and electronic engineering industry experienced rapid expansion during the period 1951–73. The data in Table 3.9 show output growth of 5.1 per cent per annum over these years, with labour productivity and TFP growing at annual rates of 3.1 per cent and 2.4 per cent respectively. This performance is nevertheless usually seen as disappointing when compared with other countries, particularly the United States, which came to dominate world markets (Owen 1992: 1; Cowling et al. 1980: 191–7; Morris 1990: 111). Output stagnated between 1973 and 1979, but, with employment falling substantially, labour productivity grew at 0.9 per cent per annum. Employment continued to fall during

Table 3.9   Output and productivity growth in the British electrical and electronic engineering industry, 1951–1999 (% per annum)

	1951–73	1973–9	1979–99
Output growth	5.1	−0.1	2.9
Employment growth	2.0	−1.0	−1.9
Capital growth	4.7	2.5	3.5
Labour productivity growth	3.1	0.9	4.8
TFP growth	2.4	0.3	3.9

Source: Derived from O'Mahony (1999, 2002).

the 1980s and 1990s, leading to a recovery of labour productivity growth to 4.8 per cent per annum between 1979 and 1999. TFP continued to grow rather more slowly than labour productivity from the 1970s as the capital stock continued to expand rapidly.

International comparisons in Table 3.2 suggest a substantial labour productivity gap between Britain and the United States in 1950, particularly in consumer products such as household appliances, radios and electric lamps. The economies of scale associated with mass production of standardised products for the large home market gave American producers a huge advantage in these product areas. However, in the more customised capital goods sections of the industry, such as electrical machinery, the productivity gap was somewhat smaller. Although the figures for 1968 suggest some closing of the gap in the consumer goods and components sectors, a substantial productivity gap remained. However, the figures in Table 3.2 suggest that the German industry was also constrained by a small home market, with labour productivity below the British level for most of the period.

The key problem faced by British producers in the early post-war period was one of markets. The traditional markets served by British companies, i.e. Britain and the Commonwealth, were not big enough, rich enough or homogeneous enough to allow volume production of standardised products on anything like the scale achieved by American producers. The situation was exacerbated by a hankering after the return of pre-war international cartel agreements, which meant that opportunities to enter new markets, particularly in western Europe, were forsaken (Jones and Marriott 1970: 172). These defensive attitudes to international competition were also carried over to domestic competition, where there was a reluctance to abandon restrictive agreements between companies. Only after the Restrictive Practices legislation of 1956 and pressure from the Monopolies Commission did the domestic rings begin to break up (Jones and Marriott 1970: 173).

The difficulties caused by growing international competition in the 1960s led to the round of mergers that occurred in many other industries, as an attempt was made to produce a national champion. The General Electric Company (GEC) took over Associated Electrical Industries (AEI) in 1967 and also absorbed English Electric (EE) in 1968 (Jones and Marriott 1970: 265–313). The merger was generally seen as a success, improving profitability and increasing efficiency (Cowling *et al.* 1980: 198–209). However, the company concentrated on sectors with captive domestic customers such as defence electronics, telecommunications equipment and electric power plant. In other sectors, in which GEC chose not to compete, the proportion of output produced by foreign-owned firms rose. In particular, Japanese firms were highly successful in consumer electronics during the 1970s and the 1980s (Morgan and Sayer 1988: 66).

Although there were some difficulties concerning redundancies after the GEC mergers with AEI and EE in 1967–8, the industrial relations

problems that plagued many of the more traditional engineering industries were much less severe in electrical and electronic engineering
(Cowling *et al.* 1980: 238–66). This can be attributed at least partly to the
orientation of the British industry towards the more customised capital
goods and defence equipment sectors, where skilled workers continued
to enjoy a high degree of autonomy (Morgan and Sayer 1988: 128, 205). In
consumer electronics, where volume assembly of standardised products
with unskilled or semi-skilled labour accounted for most of the employment, recruitment of a largely female workforce avoided many of the
problems encountered by deskilling in the traditional engineering industries (Morgan and Sayer 1988: 133). However, the potential for conflict
remained in an environment of boring, repetitive work. Thus, for example, Owen (1992: 17) mentions bad industrial relations as one factor in
the closure of Thorn's Skelmersdale tube plant in 1976. During the 1980s
and 1990s, the working environment in consumer electronics improved
as Japanese firms introduced flexible production techniques, such as autonomous work groups, job rotation, training, and quality circles, but,
even here, the problem of assembly line boredom was not eliminated
completely (Trevor 1988: 192, 209).

The policy of a single national champion in electrical engineering,
pursued by GEC under Lord Weinstock from the 1960s, was abandoned
during the second half of the 1990s. Weinstock's successor from 1996,
Lord Simpson, has sold GEC's defence electronics interests to British
Aerospace, focusing on telecommunications (Owen 1999: 288). As with
British Leyland and British Steel, the new strategy has been accompanied
by a change of name, from GEC to Marconi. The dramatic collapse of
Marconi's share price during 2001 suggests a lack of investor confidence
in this strategy.

Owen (1999: 289–94) argues that British performance in electronics
during the post-war period has not been as poor as is often suggested.
His assessment of Britain as a moderately successful niche player fits
broadly with the interpretation offered here of Britain being 'locked out'
of mass production because of the legacies of traditional markets and
craft skills. Thus, for example, given the difficulties of other European
electronics companies in television production, Owen (1999: 276–82) is
surely right to conclude that the decision of British companies to exit
this sector was rational. Similarly, in semiconductors, the failure of the
state-funded Inmos, conceived as a national hi-tech champion, can be
seen as a vindication of the strategy of niche specialisation pursued by
other British producers such as Ferranti, Plessey, GEC and Mullard (Morris
1990: 112–23).

Owen's work is a welcome counter to the pessimism of much of the
literature on the British electronics industry. Nevertheless, care must be
taken not to give too favourable an impression of the industry's performance. Given the importance of standards, network externalities and

learning curves in many electronic products, a clear investment strategy based on the exploitation of a technological breakthrough can transform the fortunes of a company or a country (Arthur 1989). Whilst it is true that all European countries experienced similar problems in competing with the United States and Japan, Germany did somewhat better than Britain. Thus by the end of the 1980s, West Germany accounted for 7 per cent of world electronics production, compared with 4 per cent in Britain and France and 3 per cent in Italy (Owen 1992: 48).

Textiles and clothing

Although output in the British textiles and clothing industry grew relatively slowly during the post-war period, labour productivity growth was more rapid than in manufacturing as a whole. Figures in Table 3.1 show that textiles and clothing output grew at an annual average rate of 2.6 per cent during 1951–73, compared with 4.4 per cent in total manufacturing. Over the same period, labour productivity grew at 4.7 per cent per annum in textiles and clothing compared with 4.3 per cent in total manufacturing. During the period 1973–9 textiles and clothing output began to fall in absolute terms but labour productivity continued to grow more rapidly than in total manufacturing due to the rapid shedding of labour. Labour shedding continued to deliver respectable labour productivity growth after 1979.

In the economic history literature, there has been much discussion of the cotton industry during 'Lancashire's last stand' (Singleton 1986, 1991; Higgins 1993; Lazonick 1986). In fact, however, distinguishing between different branches of the textile industry on the basis of fibre makes much less sense after the Second World War than in earlier periods, as man-made fibres have increasingly been used together with natural fibres on the same machinery (Anson and Simpson 1988: 7). This is important because looking at the industry as a whole yields a less pessimistic picture than concentrating only on cotton.

Changes in raw materials and technology were accompanied by organisational changes that led to the emergence of a British textile industry that was highly concentrated by international standards (Anson and Simpson 1988: 44). The high degree of concentration arose from a strategy of forward integration pursued by Courtaulds, the dominant supplier of rayon (Coleman 1980). Lazonick (1986: 39) claims that because the process of integration originated with raw material suppliers, it did not go far enough downstream to stem the decline of the British textile industry. However, this seems highly doubtful, since, with the introduction of computer technology and automation, and the need for quick response by producers and retailers to rapid changes in fashion, smaller-scale flexible production techniques have become increasingly important in textiles and clothing (Anson and Simpson 1988: 252). As in many other

British industries, a merger boom in the 1960s led to the adoption of high throughput methods at just the wrong time, when flexible production methods were about to become more important. The most successful European country across the full range of textiles and clothing has been Italy, where a large number of small firms have offered flexibility and large integrated groups have been internally sub-divided (Anson and Simpson 1988: 231).

The Anglo-American labour productivity comparisons in Table 3.2 suggest that the external economies of scale, so famously based by Marshall (1920) on the example of British textiles at the turn of the century, had largely disappeared by 1950. Whereas earlier in the century, labour productivity in the major British textile industries had been close to American levels, by 1950 there were sizeable productivity gaps even in cotton and woollen and worsted. However, relative to Germany, British labour productivity performance in textiles has remained good.

Whereas, in textiles, output began to fall from the 1970s as comparative advantage shifted to low-wage countries in line with the product cycle model, in clothing output continued to grow during the 1970s and merely remained stable during the 1980s. The decline in clothing has been less severe than in textiles because of the growing importance of flexible production methods, which have improved the competitiveness of clothing firms producing in developed countries (Anson and Simpson 1988: 252).

It should be noted that although the clothing industry shared in the general trend towards mass production methods during the 1950s and 1960s, with greater standardisation and deskilling mechanisation, the volatility of fashion and the instability of limp cloth as a working material set limits to the achievement of production economies of scale (Zeitlin and Totterdill 1989: 156; Wray 1957: 105). Hence the Anglo-American labour productivity gaps in the clothing industries in Table 3.2 were rather smaller than in many other sectors. Similar arguments apply in leather and footwear, where fashion set limits to the adoption of standardised mass production methods in the 1950s and 1960s, and where the application of flexible production methods since the 1970s has created opportunities for producers in developed countries (Organisation for Economic Co-operation and Development 1976; Flaherty 1985).

Food, drink and tobacco

The food, drink and tobacco sector is often neglected in assessments of the performance of British manufacturing. This is unfortunate, because it has been a relatively good performer in Britain, achieving high levels of labour productivity and providing a base for a number of successful multinational companies. One of the most successful British industries in the post-war period has been that of Scotch whisky, fuelled by a dramatic growth of exports (Moss and Hume 1981: 168). The huge success of the Scotch whisky industry in world markets during the period to 1973 was based on a strategy of producing a wide variety of highly differentiated brands in small distilleries, rather than attempting to mimic American production and marketing methods (Moss and Hume 1981: 190). This approach was threatened by the linking of distilleries through mergers and acquisitions during the 1970s, but after Guinness acquired Distillers in a keenly contested takeover battle in 1986, renewed emphasis was placed on product differentiation and the marketing of premium brands. By 1990, Weir (1994: 159) notes that the bad strategy of the early 1980s, when Scotch was sold at a low price in the quest for volume, had been reversed.

The brewing industry provides another example of the problems that could arise with the application of American production and marketing methods in inappropriate circumstances. A merger boom in the 1950s and 1960s led to the emergence of a concentrated structure and a narrowing of the range of choice available to consumers (Cowling *et al.* 1980: 223–36). As in so many other industries, brewers during the 1960s attempted to realise economies of scale through standardisation, and the attempt to establish national brands of keg beer was the most obvious manifestation of this trend. The concentration of production at larger sites and the consequent rationalisation of working practices led to the same pattern of labour unrest that characterised so much of British industry at this time (Gourvish and Wilson 1994: 519). However, more importantly, the standardisation process met growing resistance from consumers, and was widely seen as having gone too far. One symbol of the change was the strong consumer resistance to Watney Mann's ill-fated 'Red Revolution', an attempt to promote a uniform brand of bitter, Red, and to create a brand out of its tied houses by painting them red (Gourvish and Wilson 1994: 566). Another symbol was the establishment in 1971 of the Campaign for Real Ale (CAMRA), a consumer group which stressed the virtues of traditional draught ales and championed the cause of local and regional diversity. As well as bolstering the fortunes of a number of smaller regional brewers, CAMRA ultimately helped to bring about a reorientation of the marketing strategies of the Big Six away from national products (Gourvish and Wilson 1994: 567–8). Figures on comparative labour productivity in Table 3.2 suggest that, in brewing, the United States was able to reap greater economies of standardisation than Britain. However, the figures for Germany suggest a similar persistence of local small-scale brewers serving traditional markets (Prais 1981: 114).

Table 3.2 contains comparative labour productivity data for a number of food processing industries. In grain milling, although the US productivity lead increased between 1950 and 1968, it remained below the average for manufacturing as a whole. Furthermore, it can be seen that Britain retained a sizeable labour productivity lead over Germany in grain milling, which had not been eliminated by 1987. The performance of the British sugar industry also looks impressive in terms of the comparative productivity levels in Table 3.2. The US labour productivity advantage was one of the smallest in manufacturing for 1968, while German productivity was only half the British level at the same time. The British company, Tate and Lyle, pursuing a strategy of vertical integration since the 1930s, had become an international player in the global sugar economy (Chalmin 1990: 257).

The Anglo-American productivity gap was rather larger in biscuits, where American companies benefited from a greater degree of standardisation. Nevertheless, Prais (1981: 126) suggests that demand conditions were not the only factor here. Performing some additional productivity calculations for the period 1967–72, Prais finds German labour productivity at 101 per cent of the British level in biscuits. Since standardisation had clearly proceeded further in Britain than in Germany, Prais (1981: 137) attributes this puzzling failure of the British industry to reap economies of large-scale production to the weakness of product market competition in Britain at this time. The rapid productivity improvements experienced in the British biscuit industry during the fierce competitive battles of the 1980s would tend to support this view. Huntley and Palmer Foods was acquired by the American National Biscuit Company (Nabisco) in 1981, while British firms have extended their interests overseas, as food processing has become increasingly multinational (Sutton 1991: 467–83; Maunder 1988: 197).

The Anglo-Dutch firm Unilever has a strong presence in margarine through its subsidiary van den Berghs and Jurgens. Margarine output declined during the period 1951–73, as consumers favoured butter. With production already concentrated in two plants by 1949, there were no further large productivity gains available to Unilever, and a large Anglo-American productivity gap opened up by the late 1960s, as can be seen in Table 3.2 (Wilson 1968: 161). However, the British margarine industry enjoyed a strong revival from the 1970s, based on product innovation and a marketing campaign to exploit the growing medical consensus in favour of a low-fat diet (Sutton 1991: 440). British firms undoubtedly gained an advantage over their continental European and North American counterparts from a more permissive legal framework, since margarine has always been a highly regulated product (van Stuyvenberg 1969: 281).

CONCLUSION

British manufacturing undoubtedly faced serious difficulties between the 1950s and the 1970s, during the era of standardised mass production. Opposition by craft workers to a technology which undermined their skills and took away control of the labour process from the shopfloor, coupled with a hesitancy among managers to assume the responsibilities required to operate the American methods profitably, led to a deterioration of industrial relations, one of the most visible aspects of what came to be labelled as the 'British disease'. There were also problems in securing markets to accept the high volume of standardised output produced by the new methods. Constraints imposed by the size and variability of the British market were compounded by fundamental changes in the world economy, leading to a decline in the importance of Britain's traditional Commonwealth markets and requiring a reorientation towards continental Europe, traditionally seen as Germany's natural market. Adjustment to these trends, which would inevitably have been difficult, was delayed by a reluctance to allow competitive forces to affect the allocation of resources, a reluctance which was not fully overcome until the 1980s.

By the time that the corporatist approach was finally abandoned after 1979, technological trends had moved back in Britain's favour. American mass production techniques were no longer seen as appropriate, and manufacturing technology moved back in the direction of customisation and skilled shopfloor labour. By the end of the 1980s, British manufacturing was once again achieving labour productivity levels close to the European norm. Nevertheless, the decline of shopfloor labour force skills during the Fordist era meant that Britain had a large skills gap to make up compared with most European countries, and this gap remained substantial at the end of the 1990s.

The difficulties with standardised mass production should not be allowed to overshadow all achievements during this period, however. Some industries, such as pharmaceuticals, Scotch whisky or other food and drink industries, were extremely successful throughout the period. Although the defence sector has been shielded from competition, this has also been the case in other countries, and Britain has been relatively successful in these industries where customised production has remained the norm. In other industries, some firms were successful in niche markets even if the mass-production-oriented national champion failed. Thus even in the most widely cited British disaster, the car industry, there were successful niches such as the sports car during the 1950s and 1960s or the 4-wheel-drive vehicle during the 1980s and 1990s.

4

A failed experiment: the state ownership of industry

LESLIE HANNAH

Contents

> Of forms of ownership let fools contest, What e'er is best managèd is best.
> (M. V. Posner (1987), former Labour government economic adviser
> on nationalised industries, with apologies to Alexander Pope)

INTRODUCTION

The nineteenth century saw a few utopian socialist experiments, and Victorians uncontroversially resorted to municipal ownership in a wide range of public utilities. In the twentieth century, a remarkable series of political experiments with nationalisation has given applied economists and historians an even richer variety of material for investigation and encouraged systematic empirical investigation of the record of different systems of ownership. In the communist bloc, whole economies were

transformed from semi-feudal or capitalist market economies to socialist planned economies, of many varieties. They
shared the common characteristic that
the material means of production were
largely owned by the state and many
basic allocative decisions – on consumer
choice as well as allocations of investment – were made centrally. By the
end of the 1980s the economic inefficiency and political bankruptcy of
such socio-political systems precipitated
their widespread collapse and/or extensive marketisation.

Table 4.1   The share of state-owned enterprises in some OECD economies, c. 1980

	% of output	% of employment
France (1982)	16.5	14.6
Austria (1978–9)	14.5	13.0
Italy (1982)	14.0	15.0
Sweden (1982)	–	10.5
UK (1978)	11.1	8.2
Australia (1970–4)	10.7	–
West Germany (1982)	10.7	7.8
Portugal (1976)	9.7	–
Spain (1979)	4.1	–
Netherlands (1971–3)	3.6	8.0
Canada (1970–4)	–	4.4
USA (1983)	1.3	1.8

Sources: Pathirane and Blades (1982: 271, 273) for Canada and Australia; Milanovic (1989: tabs. 1.4 and 1.7) for the remainder.

Yet experience of state ownership has
not been confined to the totalitarian
socialist countries. Among the liberal
democracies, there was a wide range of
state ownership, though their powers were usually somewhat less than
in Soviet central planning. There are considerable problems in measuring the size of the state-owned industry sector in different economies,
not least because of the variations in national statistical definitions of
these industries (Pathirane and Blades 1982). Nonetheless, it is clear that
Britain did not have an unusually high degree of public ownership, by
European standards, even at the peak of public ownership before the
1980s privatisation programme began.

Table 4.1 suggests, for example, that Britain should be placed well
below France or Italy, and at about the same level as Germany, in the
degree of state ownership. This might seem surprising. West Germany's
post-war denationalisations and espousal of the *Sozialmarktwirtschaft* are
commonly supposed to have concentrated state interest in the market
economy on welfare rather than state industry. But government ownership in Germany was often on a *Land* (state), rather than a federal, level
and technocratic espousal of mixed public and private control had long
given legitimacy to government involvement (for example, in electricity supply) in Germany. There were also new German state investments
after the war (for example, in the aircraft and banking industries). Some
enterprises that were mutually owned by depositors and borrowers in
Britain – like savings or mortgage banks – were partially state-owned
in Germany. Together these forces led to high German levels of public
enterprise.

Britain built up levels of state ownership more slowly than continental
European countries in the first five decades of the twentieth century and
ran them down faster in the last two decades. France, for example, had
for long had an efficient state tobacco manufacturer (an industry never

nationalised in Britain), nationalised its railways in the 1930s (a decade before Britain), nationalised three-quarters of its banks in 1945 (again never nationalised in Britain) and further nationalised a wide range of its leading industrial companies in the 1980s (when Britain was actively denationalising). France retained one of the largest state-owned sectors in the closing years of the twentieth century (6 per cent of the employed labour force) at a time when Britain had reduced its state-owned sector to US and Japanese levels (i.e. with around 1 per cent of employees in state industries) (Pryor 2002: 314).

There is no simple relationship between the levels of public ownership shown in Table 4.1 and levels of development. The lowest share of public enterprise occurs both in rich countries, for example the USA, and in relatively poor ones, for example Spain. There is, then, no *prima facie* case to see the degree of commitment to state enterprise (as opposed to the *quality* of state enterprise and its alternatives) as a major determinant of poor economic performance in industrialised democracies. The late twentieth-century vogue for privatisation might suggest otherwise, but the question of the performance of state-owned enterprises in Britain is worth approaching with an open mind.

DEFINITIONS

There is no generally agreed economic definition of state-owned enterprises. At their core in the UK were the statutory public corporations of the kind that were referred to in the UK as 'nationalised industries': enterprises such as the BBC or the National Coal Board. In common parlance, the sector also includes businesses like the Post Office even when (before 1969) it was run as a civil service department rather than as a separate, publicly owned corporation. It seems sensible to include also those joint-stock companies – like the car manufacturer British Leyland (the Rover Group) between 1974 and 1988 – in which a majority of the voting shares were owned by the government. The economic essence of a 'nationalised' or 'public sector' enterprise is that it is owned by the state rather than by private interests.

How do such enterprises differ from the rest of the public sector? Essentially, it is that their output is not provided free, as, for example, the tax-financed output of the National Health Service or state education largely is. Even in that respect, however, there is scope for ambiguity: water authorities once financed their activities from local taxation but then charged separately for water. It is not obvious that this change (as opposed to their privatisation) fundamentally altered their nature as state-owned, public utilities. Contrariwise, British municipal rented housing, though locally managed, was (substantially) financed by the Treasury and (substantially) paid for by the tenants. It thus operated in many respects like a state-owned industry rather than a free public service, and indeed dominated other industries in the size of its capital stock. New council house building in the mid-1970s accounted for as much as 2 per cent of UK GDP, but then fell sharply to negligible levels today. The 1 million council houses sold between 1979 and 1987 alone were valued at £20 billion and (because of the discounts offered to tenants) produced £15 billion, more than any other privatisation (Bishop and Kay 1988: 3). Yet conventional discussions of nationalised industries exclude housing. This is essentially a matter of convention not of logic. Table 4.2 shows the main industries which were at some time nationalised in Britain, and their dates of entering (and, where appropriate, later leaving) the state sector.

In what follows, a broad definition of state-owned enterprises is used. Some of the studies which are referred to are confined to public utilities like gas, electricity, railways and telecoms; sometimes water is excluded, but non-utilities like coal or steel and, more rarely, other manufacturing industries are often included.

ARGUMENTS FOR NATIONALISATION

The 'core' of public utilities in the state-owned sector largely comprised industries that, despite being subject to the consumer disciplines of marketed output, have often been considered unsuitable for unfettered capitalist ownership. Many of the constituent elements in this core – telecommunications, railways, electricity, gas and water – were network natural monopolies in which a free market might be expected to lead to suboptimal output and high prices because of monopoly problems. This led to profits or prices in these industries being regulated, even in countries like the USA, where they were in private hands. Moreover, when in the 1980s and 1990s they were privatised in Britain, they required varying degrees of public regulation.

Yet the rationale for public ownership extended far more widely than such network monopolies. Industries such as coal, steel, oil, cars, aeroplanes, aero-engines and shipbuilding, which figure in Table 4.2, were far from being natural monopolies: indeed they were often subject to vigorous domestic and international competition. The motives for their nationalisation were varied and nebulous. The nationalisation of coal in 1947 was seen as a way of resolving the deep-rooted labour problems of the industry, though there was talk also of gaining economies of scale in operating coal mines (Supple 1987). Much was heard in the Labour Party of the need for the state to control the 'commanding heights' of the economy, for example in the context of the 1951 and 1967 nationalisations of steel. By the 1970s, politicians of both parties nationalised

Table 4.2 The main UK state-owned industries and firms with their dates of nationalisation and privatisation

Industry/firm	Date of nationalisation[a]	Date of privatisation[b]
Post Office	–	–
BBC	1926	–
London Transport	1933	–
Bank of England	1946	–
British Waterways	1948	–
Britoil/Enterprise Oil	–	1982
Amersham International	–	1982
Royal Ordnance Works	–	1986
Airports (BAA)	–	1987
Girobank	–	1990
Dairy Crest (Milk Marketing Board)	–	1994
Nuclear Power (British Energy)	–	1996
Telecoms	1912	1984
British Petroleum	1914	1979
National Electricity Grid	1927	1990
Airlines	1946	1987
Cable and Wireless	1947	1981
Coal	1947	1995
Electricity generation	1948	1991
Scottish Electricity	1948	1991
Electricity distribution	1948	1990
Road haulage	1948	1953
Buses	1948	1983 (NBC)
Ports	1948	1983/4
Railways	1948	1996
Gas	1949	1986
Steel (1st)	1951	1953
Steel (2nd)	1967	1988
Rolls Royce	1971	1987
Water	1973	1989
Jaguar	1974	1984
British Leyland (Rover Group)	1974	1988
British Aerospace	1977	1981
Royal Dockyards / British Shipbuilders (warships)	–/1977	1997
British Shipbuilders	1977	1985

[a] The date of 'nationalisation' is usually that of vesting, not of the decision to nationalise (e.g. steel in 1951 not 1949). Many industries (e.g. gas, water, electricity) had a substantial degree of public (mainly municipal) ownership prior to nationalisation. Where no date of nationalisation is given, the enterprises began in the public sector or had mixed ownership which was changed at various dates.

[b] The date of 'privatisation' is that when substantial assets were first transferred to the private sector, whether by public issue, tender offer or other means. Sometimes not all the assets were transferred: e.g. the first steel privatisation which began in 1953 was substantially complete by 1955 but one of the big fourteen firms – Richard Thomas & Baldwin – was still in the public sector when the industry was renationalised in 1967. Only about half the nationalised road haulage lorries were sold after the 1953 Act, and the public sector declined consistently until its rump was sold off to a successful de facto workers' co-operative in the National Freight privatisation of 1982.

failing companies on the grounds that they were too 'important' to be allowed to go bankrupt in the face of international competition. The state, it was argued, must act as the residual source of new capital for what opponents described as 'lame ducks'. The only common factor in nationalisation is that politicians wanted to nationalise, usually because they believed – not always correctly – that it would increase efficiency or promote equity (Millward and Singleton 1995).

State ownership usually implied state control, but there were exceptions. British Petroleum (BP) had majority state ownership from 1914, because Winston Churchill felt that it was important to secure naval fuel supplies. The dominant government shareholding in BP outlived memories of this rationale, but British governments were passive shareholders and exercised no more effective control over it than over other oil companies; BP's privatisation from 1979 thus had almost exclusively financial implications. Contrariwise, Keynes (1927), when asked whether the British clearing banks should be nationalised, replied (only half-jokingly) that they already were; and indeed they were in some respects mere adjuncts of the state's financial apparatus between the 1920s and the 1960s (Griffiths 1973; Ackrill and Hannah 2001). By the same token, in the 1950s politicians somewhat ruefully reflected that governments had more effective control over the (private enterprise) chairman of ICI than they had over Lord Citrine, the ex-trade-unionist chairman of the (publicly owned) electricity authority (Crosland 1956). British universities are all technically private non-profit institutions (though before 1992 some were municipally owned). Yet the British government is now so heavily involved in financing them, fixing their prices and rationing their output that their status is nearer to that of a 1950s nationalised industry than that of a US private university.

More generally in the post-war period, the case of a country like Japan has been held to show that, even though the state may have had a small share in industrial *ownership*, the *control* of its Ministry of International Trade and Industry over the economy's development was considerable (Johnson 1982). Ownership is in fact only one of the levers influencing industrial corporations available to democratic governments. In some respects it may be weaker than the alternatives, which range from sticks (e.g. rationing key resources and legal compulsion) to carrots (e.g. government purchasing and subsidies) (Foreman-Peck and Federico 1999). Ownership may in some circumstances be weaker than moral suasion based on coalitions of mutual interest and shared values, which were important levers with which governments influenced British clearing banks or Japanese and French industry in the post-war era. Problems of agency, information flow, and transaction costs – both in state ownership and in the many varieties of market-based, capitalist systems of decentralised decision making in firms – complicate the evaluation of the economic efficiency of alternative economic systems. This chapter focuses on the economic efficiency implications of state ownership[1] and its alternatives, not on broader issues of government planning and control in capitalist or mixed economies.

NATIONALISATION BEFORE AND AFTER 1945

Labour's election victory in 1945 inaugurated the largest ever transfer of ownership between the private and state sectors in Britain, measured by

---

[1] This chapter frequently discusses efficiency, measuring changes over time and differences between countries. There are three quite distinct concepts of efficiency. The central concept is productive efficiency: the level of inputs (principally, here, capital and labour in the industries studied, though land is also important in agriculture and mineral extraction) used to produce outputs. Labour productivity is a measure of total output divided by labour inputs (ideally a worker-hour, though, in practice, data are often only available for a worker-year; a working year now typically consists of rather fewer hours than historically, thus understating gains in labour productivity per hour).

A worker using a machine will typically be more productive than one without, and this is particularly important in highly capital-intensive industries such as electric utilities. Combining capital and labour inputs in the denominator of a productivity measure introduces more sources of possible error: both in measuring the machine's annual input (How long is it active? How are its depreciation and interest charges calculated?) and in determining its contribution to output relative to the complementary workers (Are there economies of scale or other factors making the contribution different from the relative average costs of workers and capital in national income accounts?). Total factor productivity is a measure of total output divided by a weighted average of labour and capital inputs.

Other things being equal, it is clearly better to produce more output with less labour and less capital. But it is possible for an economy to be very efficient in using both capital and labour, yet to be producing the wrong things: such an economy is productively efficient, but allocatively inefficient. (Allocative inefficiency can also arise from using the wrong combinations of capital and labour: a man can shovel snow with extreme efficiency, but the economy might be better off if he used a snowplough.) Such allocative inefficiencies typically arise because of mis-pricing of inputs or outputs. Because the state has a potentially powerful influence on relative prices (especially of nationalised industry labour and its outputs) and is also frequently involved as owner or regulator of industries with inherent monopolistic pricing problems, the issue of allocative efficiency is a key one for nationalised industries. The state may use this power to improve allocative efficiency (e.g. producing outputs for which the market price does not reflect the true social value) or to decrease it (e.g. producing outputs which no one wishes to buy without subsidy but which have no compensating social value).

A third kind of efficiency is dynamic efficiency: the capacity to generate new ways of doing things. This is arguably the most significant advantage demonstrated in the twentieth century by capitalist relative to communist economies. British state industries have not obviously been less innovative than private ones; for example, in the 1930s the BBC produced the first broadcast television service in the world; in the 1950s the state-owned Calder Hall power station was the first civil nuclear power station in the world; and in the 1990s British Rail produced the first high-speed tilting train capable of operation on conventional tracks. The advantage of invention has been less clear: war-time austerity forced the abandonment of the BBC experiment, nationalistic favouring of British nuclear technology made the nuclear programme a burden rather than an advantage, and Britain's tilting train was ineffective and was later replaced by an Italian model. In modern OECD economies, invention is critical to economic progress, but technology is easily purchased by countries that fail to generate it. There is, moreover, no clear evidence of superior performance overall – in invention or the more important optimal adoption of innovation – by the state sector.

the number of employees transferred; the privatisations of the 1980s and 1990s were larger in the sense that they covered a wider range of industries, but the transferred firms then employed fewer people than their counterparts of 1945–51. After allowing for the firms that were already municipally owned, the 1945–51 nationalisation programme – which included coal, electricity, gas, transport, and iron and steel – increased public sector employment by 2 million (Chester 1975: 38), that is by more than 8 per cent of the contemporary workforce.

In the following decades, employment in the labour-intensive industries like coal and railways fell, but other industries were newly nationalised and capital-intensive sectors like electricity and telecommunications for a time boosted the share of national fixed capital formation in the public sector (Pryke 1971: 289). The share of the public enterprise sector in total output peaked in 1977 at 13 per cent of GDP (Brech 1985: 774), though this was probably below what it had been in 1951.

The post-war state-owned industrial sector in Britain was not only quantitatively but also qualitatively different from what had gone before, though it is tempting to see earlier parallels and precursors. As Table 4.2 shows, some industries (like the Post Office) have always been state-owned, while other nationalised industries (like telecommunications, the BBC or the National Grid) dated from the first three decades of this century. There was also significant municipal ownership in the local network monopolies of gas, electricity and water, dating back to the nineteenth century; as well as industrial civil service organisations such as the Royal Dockyards and Royal Ordnance factories, which were each among the dozen largest manufacturing employers at the beginning of the century (Shaw 1983).

A common factor in early public ownership had been a perception by politicians of market failure, often buttressed by early cases of regulatory failure. In gas and water, for example, the need to avoid wasteful duplication of mains led to mergers and monopolies, requiring public ownership or at least public supervision. In telegraphs a price cartel of competitors was clearly inefficient, so a Post Office takeover was agreed in 1868, though merger and public regulation might have done just as well (Foreman-Peck 1989). In telephones inefficient attempts at regulated competition were replaced by a full Post Office takeover in 1912. In electricity, a full state takeover was avoided, but in 1926 the government decided on a new form of regulatory control of generation which compelled existing private and municipal generators to achieve economies of scale. The unusual (but well-directed) reorganisation of electricity wholesaling by a new, state-controlled national grid company, the Central Electricity Board, reduced bulk electricity prices to a third of their former level within a decade (Hannah 1979).

The methods of public ownership adopted before 1945 were more varied than the reasons for intervention: they included civil service departments with direct ministerial control (telephones, telegraphs, munitions, mail), municipal ownership (gas, water and electricity) and public corporations (the National Grid, the BBC, London Transport). The nearest precursors to the post-war nationalised industries were the industries under civil service departments, rather than the superficially similar public corporations. Before the war, in marked contrast to their general post-war experience, such public corporations had an unusual amount of freedom from government intervention.

Public sector business leaders before 1945 used their freedom to develop positive and successful corporate strategies with little ministerial interference. While contemporaries referred to nineteenth-century 'municipal socialism', it has been correctly pointed out that 'municipal capitalism' might have been a more accurate designation (Waller 1983). Much the same can be said of early nationalised corporations. For example, the Central Electricity Board, which ran the National Grid and controlled generation, raised its capital directly from the public, without using the Treasury guarantee, and paid its staff salaries well above civil service levels. Although its board members were appointed by a minister, they could not be removed by him, and hence they routinely ignored ministerial requests for policy changes where there was no clear statutory authority for such direction. They lacked any strong motive to maximise profits, which (with their monopoly of grid transmission) would have been easy for them, though socially undesirable. Otherwise, however, their behaviour was indistinguishable from that of privately owned companies.

Most 'municipalisations' and 'nationalisations' before 1945 had been undertaken by Conservative or Liberal local and national governments; Labour's 1931 legislation which survived to create London Transport in 1933 was the exception. This perhaps explains why they were less politically controversial than later nationalisation initiatives. There were criticisms of public enterprise: Post Office control of the telephone system, for example, led to Treasury restriction of capital spending to below economic levels and this retarded telephone use in Britain. Yet by the 1930s a wide range of middle opinion accepted the public corporations as a legitimate and efficient solution to the problems of running many areas of the British economy, where the need for public control was perceived. 'Gas and water socialism' at the municipal level had also initially been equally uncontroversial, though the electoral success of Labour and the politicisation of the municipal trading debate at the local level had destroyed that early consensus by the beginning of the twentieth century. Conservative rhetoric against the much more far-reaching nationalisations of 1945–51 followed the new trend of polarised opposition rather than the 1930s consensus of middle opinion. Yet Conservative ministerial policies did not conform to the party's rhetoric, and it was not until the

1980s and 1990s that extensive Conservative privatisation brought the British experiment with state 'socialism' to an end.

THE PERFORMANCE OF NATIONALISED INDUSTRIES

The diverse range of nationalised industries in the post-war period and the changing political and economic regimes led to highly variable performance. The industries' managerial development can be traced in corporate histories, notably of coal, London Transport, the BBC, railways and electricity (Ashworth 1986; Barker and Robbins 1974; Briggs 1979; Gourvish 1986; Hannah 1982).

A major objective of nationalisation was the improvement of the efficiency of the industries. The improvements in labour productivity over the post-war decades (see Table 4.3) show some clear patterns. There were nationalised industries, such as the airlines or telecommunications, in which a high rate of technical progress underpinned consistently high rates of productivity increase. The room for such productivity gains in industries like buses or coal mining, or (at least before the advent of North Sea supplies) gas, was considerably less. Taking this diverse public sector as a whole, however, the labour productivity gains were particularly feeble in the 1950s, picked up to a peak in the 1960s, fell again in the 1970s and were revived in the 1980s. The labour productivity gains registered in the post-war decades were better than those achieved by the same industries (under more diverse ownership regimes) in the first half of the twentieth century (Foreman-Peck and Waterson 1985). Supporters of public enterprise might take comfort from this, seeing in it a justification of Labour Party hopes in 1945–51 that they were inaugurating a programme which would fundamentally transform the efficiency of a large sector of the economy. However, such a productivity spurt was registered after the war throughout the economy (see chapter 3); indeed productivity growth was better – by nearly half a percentage point higher – in the (largely privately owned) manufacturing sector.

Labour productivity is, of course, affected by the capital intensity of production. It is not a very good indicator

Table 4.3 Labour productivity growth rates in the core nationalised industries, 1948–1985

Sector	1948–58 (% p.a.)	1958–68 (% p.a.)	1968–78 (% p.a.)	1978–85 (% p.a.)
Steel	–	–	−0.2	12.6[a]
Airlines	14.0	8.9	6.4	6.6[a]
Electricity	4.6	8.0	5.3	3.9
Gas	1.6	5.5	8.5	3.8
Road freight	0.8[a]	4.9	–	–
Coal	0.9	4.7	−0.7	4.4
Railways	0.3	4.3	0.8	3.9
Buses	−0.6	−1.4	−0.5	2.1
Post Office	–	–	−1.3	2.3
Telecoms	–	–	8.2	5.8[a]
Manufacturing[b]	1.9	3.7	2.7	3.0

[a] Data relate to slightly different years from those indicated at head of column.
[b] 'Manufacturing' includes some publicly owned companies, particularly in the 1970s.

Sources: Pryke (1971: 104) for cols. 1 and 2; Molyneux and Thompson (1987: 57–9), for cols. 3 and 4.

Table 4.4   Total factor productivity growth rates in the core nationalised industries, 1948–1985

Sector	1948–58 (% p.a.)	1958–68 (% p.a.)	1968–78 (% p.a.)	1978–85 (% p.a.)
Steel	–	–	2.5	12.9
Airlines	7.8	9.1[a]	5.5	–
Electricity	3.6	3.1	0.7	1.4
Gas	0.7	3.7	–	3.3
Coal	0.4	3.0	−1.4	2.9
Railways	–	2.4	−1.4	1.3
Post Office	–	–	–	3.7
Telecoms	–	–	–	2.4
Airports	–	–	–	1.6
Manufacturing[b]	1.5	2.4	1.7	2.6

[a] Data relate to slightly different years from those indicated at head of column.
[b] 'Manufacturing' includes some publicly owned industries, particularly in the 1970s; while in the 1980s some of the nationalised industries were privatised (see Table 4.2 for dates).

Sources: Pryke (1971: 112) for cols. 1 and 2; Molyneux and Thompson (1987: 57–9) for col. 3; Bishop and Kay (1988: 45) for col. 4.

of efficiency in highly capital-intensive industries like electricity supply, or in industries like gas, which are highly dependent on natural resource discoveries and consequential changes in technology and capital intensity. A better, though less reliably measured, indicator of productivity changes is total factor productivity, shown in Table 4.4. Taking into account the productivity of capital as well as labour, as this does, the performance of the electricity industry looks less impressive throughout than on the labour productivity indicator. However, steel after 1979 is impressive on both indicators: capital productivity clearly was increasing as rapidly as labour productivity in this industry. The 1980s recovery in public sector total factor productivity performance is especially marked.

There are no obvious general reasons for these variations in public sector performance between industries and over time. The explanation for them must be sought in specific historical changes.

1945–1958

Nationalisation involved, in most cases, managerial reorganisation on an unprecedented scale, though little thought was given by politicians to the managerial problems which they created. The National Coal Board merged 800 mines: on formation it was the largest business unit in Europe, with a workforce of 716,500 men at its peak in 1948. The British Electricity Authority merged 550 firms, the new gas boards 1,000 and the road haulage merger brought together as many as 3,800. Much smaller multi-firm mergers in the private sector had a uniform record of failure, except where there were effective core firms capable of absorbing the managerial shock (Hannah 1974). This condition was only satisfied in a minority of nationalised industries: in most cases they had to create new central organisations from scratch. In only one utility, water, was consolidation allowed to go at a more leisurely pace. About 20 per cent of the industry was supplied by private companies, the rest by municipalities or joint committees and water boards: the 1,055 separate water suppliers still in existence in 1956 were voluntarily reduced to 198 by 1970, making their final consolidation into regional boards in the eventual nationalisation of 1973 rather simpler than the earlier nationalisations of gas, electricity and coal (Hassan 1998).

The newly nationalised industries of the 1940s initially attracted much ill-informed political criticism for being over-bureaucratic, but it is now clear it was a lack rather than over-abundance of administrative and managerial resources that fatally compromised their early productivity performance (Pryke 1971: 26–7). The task of replacing the 'invisible hand' of the private market by the 'visible hand' of corporate management under state control posed severe problems for a British economy which already had acute shortages of managerial skills (Chandler 1990). Some potential gains from centralised control were simply never achieved: co-ordination of transport, for example, was minimal in Britain, especially when compared with that achieved between bus, rail and air in the Federal Republic of Germany. Yet eventually the managerial resources to improve productivity in the core businesses were assembled. By the mid-1950s, recruitment and development of administrators (helped in some cases by their enthusiasm for the principle of public enterprise) created a capacity for organisation which had initially been lacking (though low public sector salaries remained a major barrier to recruitment of senior management).

This new managerial capacity developed with little political intervention to change its direction. On returning to office in 1951, the Conservatives denationalised steel and road haulage (reducing the managerial strains in the public sector somewhat) and they generally encouraged more decentralised management structures. In electricity, for example, two Scottish boards were hived off, and in England and Wales generation was separated from the distribution and sales activities of twelve, loosely federated, area electricity boards. Like their Labour predecessors, however, Conservative ministers initially tended to leave the boards to act in the 'public interest' without closely defining what that meant.

The contemporary conception of the nature of public ownership did not differ very much from that advanced by R. H. Tawney (1919: 127), when advocating the nationalisation of coal. The advantages, he said,

> are of a kind which a public and representative body, of its very nature, possesses, and which private ownership (whatever its other merits) cannot pretend to cultivate. Such a body can organise the problem of organising production and distribution as a whole, instead of piecemeal. It can wait, and need not snatch at an immediate profit at the cost of prejudicing the future of the industry. It can enlist on its side motives to which the private profit-maker (if he is aware of their existence) cannot appeal. It can put the welfare of human beings, worker and consumer, first.

Those who ran the nationalised industries were perfectly willing to accept this generous view that they represented the public interest. Yet it did not take politicians long to see the flaws in Tawney's rosy, but naïve, image of public-spirited managerial discretion. Given the nationalised industries' monopoly position, there was a strong temptation for managers to take out their monopoly profits in what economists have long recognised as the favoured way: a quiet life. At first, the formal constraints on management were few. They were expected to break even financially ('taking one year with another'), though initially post-war price controls and rationing left such objectives in the government's rather than the managers' hands. The boards were also generally required not to discriminate in pricing (not to show 'undue preference' was the phrase used), a directive which usually led to more uniform prices and an increase in uneconomic cross-subsidies (for example to rural electricity consumers and bus travellers).

There was some debate on whether prices should be raised – particularly in industries like coal and electricity where demand clearly outstripped supply – but governments and managers showed a reluctance to finance new investment by unpopular price rises. Governments increasingly realised that, although they controlled the 'commanding heights', they really had very little idea about what commands they should be issuing, or the strategic principles on which such commands might be based, or the way that managers could be given an incentive to meet government objectives.

1958–1968

The catalyst for change was the Treasury's fear that the public sector was 'crowding out' investment in the private sector (see chapter 2). Cheap capital from the Treasury, it was argued, set too easy a target rate of return for nationalised industry management, a rate well below that required by new private sector investments with equal risks. Thus, too much investment was being undertaken by the nationalised industries: there were, for example, substantial demands for new investment in railway electrification and an extensive nuclear power station programme, both with strong political support.

The White Paper on the *Economic and Financial Objectives of the Nationalised Industries* (HM Treasury 1961) raised the target rate of return for the public corporations. In 1967 it was supplemented (HM Treasury 1967) by the rule that prices should be set at long-run marginal cost and new investments were to be subjected to discounted cash-flow analysis consistent with the target return. The problem of individual ministerial reluctance to accept such rules was to be overcome by cost-benefit analyses of any non-commercial responsibilities that ministers explicitly imposed on the nationalised industries: if industries agreed to shoulder social responsibilities at ministerial behest, they would be paid a commercial subsidy for doing so.

This policy was bipartisan: Conservative and Labour ministers were less impressed by the economic theory of allocative efficiency behind these prescriptions than by the improved productivity performance they hoped the higher financial targets would squeeze out of management. Under the Labour government of 1964–70 such pressures for efficiency were made more explicit by the audits undertaken by the Prices and Incomes Board. There were new managerial appointments from outside the industries to signal the need for policy changes. In 1961, Dr Beeching (formerly an ICI director) took over as chairman of the railways, with the task of closing down unprofitable branch lines and targeting investment more effectively. Total factor productivity in railways, which in the early 1960s fell below 1948 levels, was more than 50 per cent higher by the end of the decade (Gourvish 1986: 612). In electricity supply, Ronald Edwards (an LSE economist) was brought in as chairman to force more economic pricing techniques on to the area electricity boards (Hannah 1982: 193–217).

Profitability in the economy generally declined markedly in the 1960s (Matthews *et al.* 1982: 188), but the nationalised industries did not follow this trend: profits rose with improved productivity. Richard Pryke (1971), the leading academic investigator of the industries at the time, could soon confidently state that productivity gains were more rapid than in the past, and than in the manufacturing sector. He concluded that, by the 1960s, the management problems of reorganisation had been largely overcome by the nationalised industries (Pryke 1971). The new methods of public sector management were, he thought, such as to guarantee the continuation of superior performance into the future.

1968–1979

Tables 4.3 and 4.4 suggest Pryke was wrong. Ten years later he wrote a much more pessimistic book (Pryke 1981), reflecting the experience of the 1970s. The record was particularly bad in the steel industry (newly renationalised in 1967) and in the Post Office, but other sectors as different as coal and airlines also saw low rates of productivity increase. Their financial performance also deteriorated, as both Conservative and Labour governments in the 1970s capped prices, in further attempts to 'control inflation' by restraints on the public sector. Faced with economic depression, governments of both parties also nationalised more firms, though Labour proved the more enthusiastic. A remarkably high proportion of these 'lame ducks' proved to be dead ducks, whose factories and workers ultimately faced closure and redundancy after a brief subsidised half-life in a terminal care hospice, not the intended convalescence and recovery. If the productivity measures in Tables 4.3 and 4.4 had included such cases as British Leyland, the Meriden motor cycle factory or British Shipbuilders, the record would have looked even worse. The core nationalised industries by 1975 required more than £1 billion in revenue support for losses, as well as borrowing an equivalent sum to finance their capital expenditure (Pryke 1981: 261). While in the 1960s the good labour relations that had developed in many nationalised industries yielded productivity gains and desirable structural adjustments (such as the controlled run-down of employment in coal mining), by the 1970s labour practices became increasingly ossified and blocked required changes.

Critics pointed to the absence of accountability (by either nationalised industry managers or civil servants) as the root of the failure to achieve the objectives of the 1960s White Papers. Managers felt rather that they were *too* accountable to politicians, but often for the wrong things. In truth there were more fundamental problems behind the attempts to establish coherent pricing and investment rules and financial targets. Essentially the 1967 rules required the nationalised industries to behave *as if* they were private firms operating in competitive markets. There was a paradox here: politicians were bound to ask why, in this case, they were in the public sector at all. These questions became more persistent with the economic troubles of the 1970s, when politicians were searching for any lever to control 'stagflation', and intervened repeatedly in the management of the industries.

By the end of the 1970s, the consequences for morale and efficiency in the nationalised sector were clear, and a renewed attempt was belatedly made to re-establish financial control. The White Paper on *The Nationalised Industries* (HM Treasury 1978) implicitly recognised the impracticability of the 1967 rules, and made financial targets (rather than economic pricing and investment rules) again the centre-piece of government strategy (Heald 1980). Soon, however, more radical solutions to the problem of public sector management were being contemplated.

Since 1979

Mrs Thatcher's Conservative government, hesitantly in the first term to 1983, but with increasing confidence thereafter, privatised most of the nationalised sector. Between 1979 and 1990 some £33 billion was raised for the public purse by privatisations (*Economist* 1990), roughly the same (after allowing for thirteen-fold inflation) as the £2.64 billion which had been paid in compensation for the nationalisations of 1945–51. The government also substantially ran down employment in the industries which remained nationalised, and a few new infrastructure projects such as the Channel Tunnel were also private from the start. The result was a substantial transformation of the size and nature of the nationalised industry sector. The privatisation policy was a radical new departure, which even right-wing think tanks did not dare to contemplate seriously a few years earlier (Papps 1975).

Yet the successful preparations for privatisation required immediate productivity gains. Thus, a paradoxical achievement of the Thatcher years was that, by conventional aggregate productivity growth measures, they represent the most successful post-war experiment in the state management of industry. Contrary to popular impression, the substantial productivity gains of the 1980s (see Tables 4.3 and 4.4) were mainly achieved while the industries were still state owned, and not *after* they were privatised (Bishop and Kay 1988). The threats and opportunities of privatisation no doubt played a part in this achievement, but it clearly had other components too: clear financial objectives were set for the nationalised industries, and the commitment to support cost-cutting (even when it meant painful redundancies in marginal constituencies) was fully accepted by politicians. Politicians and industry leaders interacted in a way which bore more resemblance to the 1960s (when there were also favourable productivity achievements) than it did to the 1970s. New managers – such as Ian MacGregor at British Coal and British Steel – were, as in the 1960s, brought in to impose policy reforms. The pressure for efficiency was also consistent and serious: it was publicly symbolised now by referrals to the Monopolies Commission (which had previously only investigated the private sector).

The consequences for productivity of the revised policies in the new environment were remarkable. The British Steel Corporation's turn-round is one of the most impressive on record in any business in any country at any time. After nationalisation, in 1968, the performance of the already weak British steel industry deteriorated further in relation to its continental competitors. In 1980/1 it cost the Corporation £4 billion to produce steel worth £3 billion. Despite this £1 billion loss, they were rapidly yielding domestic markets to more efficient producers abroad. Yet, within several years, more than half the workforce were dispensed with and labour productivity more than doubled. By the late 1980s, British Steel overtook both US and German productivity levels for the first time since Britain's loss of leadership in the industry a century earlier. Before it was privatised, British Steel became the lowest-cost steel producer in the world, alongside POSCO of South Korea, having overtaken the USA, Japan and all its European rivals (Aylen 1988 and chapter 3 above). In 1990/1, the privatised steel corporation was profitable and had a turnover of £5 billion.

TECHNOLOGY AND PRODUCTIVITY IN THE NATIONALISED INDUSTRIES

This account of productivity gains by the nationalised industries has focused on changes in managerial organisation and incentives, largely determined by the industries' changing relationship with the government. Such an approach seems to fit the contrasting productivity experience of the industries, decade by decade, and the exceptionally good performance of particular sectors at particular times, for example, railways in the 1960s, or steel in the 1980s. The model of economic behaviour which seems best to fit what we have described is that which postulates a degree of 'X-inefficiency'. There is a certain managerial or organisational slack which leads to firms performing within their production possibility frontier unless they are prodded sharply to do better (Leibenstein 1966, 1976). High productivity is, however, more than a matter of organisational efficiency. It may have its roots in the development of human resources or in technical progress, rather than in a specific management strategy imposed by a strong business leader or a systematic government efficiency campaign.

In the case of technological innovation, the underlying rate of productivity increase may be boosted by factors which have very little to do with the nationalised organisations running the industries. The great efficiency increases in gas in the 1970s and 1980s, for example, derived from the shift from the old coal gas technology to natural gas from the North Sea: although it required investment in reorganisation, it was essentially a gift from the North Sea oil explorers. The telecommunications industry has also been the beneficiary of forces mainly beyond its own control: modern microwave transmission and electronic switching technology were not pioneered by British Telecom; they were principally the result of a series of world-wide technical innovations.

Of course, technology is not simply something exogenous to the British economy: it is partly generated by research and development expenditure by British nationalised corporations and their suppliers, and partly imported from the international stock of technology generated in a variety of ways by a range of nations. The speed of adoption is vitally affected by the policy of the nationalised industries. For example, by ordering its own rival 'system X', rather than buying on the international market, British Telecom both delayed and reduced the benefits to be derived from the new switching technology. Nationalisation seems generally to have reinforced such technological nationalism (the 'not invented here' syndrome). Where Britain attempted to go-it-alone, the results varied from the troublesome to the disastrous. The best example of the latter, imposing substantial social costs on the British economy, was the British nuclear power station programme. Britain's Magnox gas-cooled reactors, developed in the 1950s, were the first effective commercial nuclear power stations; by 1965 half of all the nuclear electricity generated in the world had been generated in Britain. With falling oil and coal prices, however, the pioneering technology proved uneconomic: most nuclear stations had been ordered with rash optimism after the 1956 Suez crisis created false expectations of imminent oil shortage. By the early 1960s American water-cooled reactors seemed to have a better chance of competing with cheap alternative fuels.

Nonetheless from 1965 the nationalised electricity industry was cajoled by the Labour government into buying a series of new (and, as it proved, either unworkable or excessively expensive) British advanced gas-cooled reactors. The first, Dungeness B, had to be substantially re-built, was two decades late in operation and cost three times as much in real terms as the initial contract price. British electricity consumers had to forgo not only much of the benefit of cheap oil in the 1960s but also the promised cheap nuclear power in the 1970s and 1980s. Electricity was cheaper in Japan and Germany, whose smaller, private or mixed ownership electric utilities reacted quickly to minimise costs with a flexible array of oil, coal and nuclear capacity, or in France which bought American pressurised water reactor designs and built a set of reactors more cheaply than Britain (though France's nationalised industry also over-reacted to its success and over-ordered reactors – thus eroding this advantage). The cost of building British nuclear power stations exceeded £50 billion but in the 1990s the state had to underwrite decommissioning and fuel processing costs before they could be privatised; within a few years it became clear that even with these guarantees, the stations were virtually worthless. The losses by the state – virtually the whole of Britain's nuclear investment – exceeded those by any private British corporation at any time.

Attempts to provide broader seed-corn funding to new technologies have been cheaper, but generally they, too, have not typically been effective in the public sector. The state-owned National Enterprise Board, established by the Labour government in 1975, was correct in spotting high growth markets (e.g. microchips and electronic office equipment) but the offshoots it established to exploit them (INMOS, NEXOS) did not become effective competitors. The state was more successful in a few high-technology industries (e.g. through shareholdings in Ferranti and Fairey), but these benefited from the rather special conditions of the defence industries, where the state itself generated a highly specialised demand. The nationalisation of Rolls Royce (between 1971 and 1987) enabled the state to finance the successful development of the company's organisational and technical capabilities, preserving its role as one of the three leading aero-engine makers in the world, which the private sector had been unwilling to finance, following temporary financial difficulties unrelated to long-term viability. The National Coal Board also successfully supported British manufacturers who were at the forefront of innovation in mining technology (Kramer 1989). Such cases do not, however, appear to have been sufficiently numerous to offset the losses from state failures in the attempt to promote technical change and increased efficiency.

NATIONALISATION AND BRITISH ECONOMIC PERFORMANCE

Did the nationalisation of large sectors of the British economy improve its overall performance – as was intended – or did nationalisation on balance intensify the problem of relative British economic decline? Such a question implies a counterfactual, and it is not easy to choose one, for few of the industries which were nationalised would have been likely to have retained their pre-nationalisation structure intact if they had not been nationalised. Some – as in the British-owned car industry – might not have existed at all.

Where new entry and competitive markets prevail, the 'survivor technique' is a reasonable approximation to answering the counterfactual historical question. For example, in the car industry, British demand is now met by a variety of commercial organisations: long-established foreign subsidiaries (e.g. Ford), imports from abroad (e.g. Volkswagen) and new overseas subsidiaries operating on green field sites in Britain (e.g. Nissan). All have certain advantages, they compete in the same markets, and, if, after several decades of such competition, their market share does not decline, it seems reasonable to suppose that they provide consumer value. Yet there may be market distortions (e.g. government subsidies to Nissan for opening in a depressed area) which render the survivor test suspect. Moreover, the survival of the Rover Group tells us nothing about whether the cost of temporary subsidy under nationalisation outweighed the benefits derived. Clearly unemployment would have been much higher in cities like Oxford if such firms had been allowed to go bankrupt. Yet it seems highly likely that the subsidies (both direct in government handouts to the Rover Group's predecessors, and indirect through the higher car prices 'conceded' to keep Rover alive by Japanese importers) reduced British national income. Such exercises demand their own counterfactual analysis, and typically reveal the very large opportunity costs of intervention to preserve jobs.

However, to judge the broader merits of public ownership – as opposed to the myopia of politicians and their short-term objectives – from particularly bad cases is not appropriate. Attempts to make more general judgements have therefore concentrated on the other (very few) industries where both public and private enterprises have competed in the same markets and been broadly subject to the same constraints, as well as open to the same opportunities. Historically, municipal enterprise sometimes performed as well as or better than private enterprise (Foreman-Peck and Waterson 1985; Millward and Ward 1987). However, comparisons of the few cases in which dual-ownership structures remained by the early 1980s were less supportive of public enterprise (Pryke 1982). British Airways was (before privatisation) overmanned compared with the private British Caledonian. The Sealink cross-channel ferries operated by the British and French national railways were slower, less fuel-efficient and less profitable (especially when they fixed similar prices for their inferior services) than the private Townsend-Thoresen ferries. Appliances from the shops of the nationalised electricity boards were more expensive to the consumer but less profitable to the boards than from private chains like Currys.

Moreover, where consumers had the choice of buying from nationalised or private enterprises, the market share of private enterprise was rising, except where subsidies or government favours kept the nationalised firms 'competitive'. In the few cases where such direct comparisons were possible (and consumers were, of course, making them all the time), public sector managers simply were not surviving the market test.

We can also compare the performance of the industries that were entirely nationalised and then privatised in Britain with the same industries in other advanced industrial nations, where they could be state-owned but were also sometimes in the private sector, in whole or in part. Such comparisons are most interesting in the network utilities such as electricity, gas, railways and telecommunications. These were mainly state-owned in the three major European countries in the second half of the twentieth century and privately owned in the USA, with Japan occupying the middle ground (with mainly private utilities, both state and private railways, and state-owned telecoms). At the time of the major mid-century British nationalisation programme, all four countries' utilities had fallen substantially behind the USA. This was partly a reflection of the remarkable overall economic performance of the USA, and particularly its service industries, in the first half of the twentieth century, but in utilities generally the relative productivity performance of the countries that relied more on state or municipal enterprise than the USA had been worse than their economy-wide performances in the period to 1950. In the latter year, as Table 4.5 shows, labour productivity in transport and communications in the UK, France, West Germany and Japan lagged productivity levels in the USA by about the same degree as in the economy as a whole. In gas, electricity and water, however, productivity levels in the UK, France and Germany lagged behind those in the USA by an even greater degree. This had, moreover, not been so generally and strikingly true in the nineteenth century (Broadberry 1997a, 1997b).

How did the state industries meet the challenge of catching up with the huge American mid-century productivity lead? All four countries found it harder to do this in the utilities than in the economy generally. There are only two cases where the utilities of these four countries more nearly approached US productivity levels than the rest of their economy, in the overall process of catch-up to US levels shown in Table 4.5. The

Table 4.5 Catching-up with US labour productivity levels, 1950–1996 *(US output per man hour = 100 at all dates)*					
	USA	UK	France	West Germany	Japan
Gas, electricity and water					
1950	100	24	15	26	36[a]
1979	100	33	55	52	77
1996	100	61	62	52	88
Transport and communications					
1950	100	53	36	34	16[a]
1979	100	55	73	60	39
1996	100	88	104	88	49
All market sectors[b]					
1950	100	49	35	39	18[a]
1979	100	63	77	88	46
1996	100	78	94	102	63

[a] 1953.

[b] I.e. whole economy, excluding health, education, public administration and housing.

Source: Derived from O'Mahoney (1999).

Japanese gas, electricity and water sector (which was already ahead of Europe in the 1950s and forged further ahead, doing better than the Japanese economy overall) was largely privately owned. However, French railways and telecoms (a sector which also did better than the French economy overall after 1979) were state owned in the relevant periods. Thus efficient management is clearly possible in both private and state sectors by this indicator. A favourable view of British nationalised industry management, is, however, extremely difficult to sustain from this evidence: the 1950–79 period of committed nationalisation generally saw slower increases in labour productivity in the utilities than in the wider British economy *and* than in the same industries in other countries. The highly centralised French gas and electric utilities (which started out behind Britain) and the mixed private, municipal and regional utilities of Germany (which started out in 1950 just ahead of Britain) both by 1979 attained productivity levels of half the American level, while Britain still languished at only one third of American levels. Since 1979, when the British utilities sectors were being prepared for privatisation or actually privatised, the story is different. The rate of improvement in labour productivity in Britain's utilities was more rapid in comparison both to the British economy generally and to the same industries in the three other large industrial nations. These international comparisons reinforce the views that, while state industries can be effectively managed, the British ones in general were not, and that efficiently regulated private ownership is more likely to result in good performance in the network utilities.

ALLOCATIVE EFFICIENCY

The emphasis on productive efficiency and technological progress in earlier sections of this chapter ignores the central concern of much economic analysis with allocative efficiency: that is the question of whether the right outputs are being produced (and with the right combination of inputs). Some analysts have suggested that removing allocative inefficiencies is a less important source of welfare gains than productivity growth (Pryke 1971), but others have seen serious allocative inefficiencies (Molyneux and Thompson 1987: 75) and the 1960s White Papers were principally aimed at removing them. Government policy initiatives to improve allocative efficiency were successful in some areas: for example, in developing off-peak pricing of electricity to reflect the cost structure of the industry. This was possible because the chairman of the industry, the economist Sir Ronald Edwards, shared the objective of improving allocative efficiency, and was successful in implementing change in collaboration with managers and civil servants (Hannah 1982). The results he achieved were clearly earlier than and superior to those of US regulators of private electric utilities (Papps 1975: 52; Hannah 1990).

Too often, however, attempts by government departments to promote discussion of this kind with nationalised industries foundered on asymmetries of information between them and the boards, which made intervention ineffective. In telecommunications, for example, where long-distance calls were priced well above costs to cross-subsidise local calls, the resultant welfare losses were considerable (Ergas 1984). The most effective solution proved to be, not the 1967 public sector pricing rules which worked for electricity, but the post-1983 licensing of competitors, which soon forced more economic pricing of British Telecom's long-distance calls.

OTHER OBJECTIVES OF NATIONALISATION

It is sometimes argued that the nationalised industries should have been judged not primarily by efficiency, but rather by their success in pursuing other objectives. A wide range of objectives has been proposed – ranging from the specific (a cleaner environment) to the general (equitable distribution of the just fruits of labour). Politicians were usually sensitive to the power of such objectives; but, where ministers shared them, they (often reluctantly) were led to conclude that the objectives were practically attainable in alternative ways. If equality is defined as an objective, it is generally more effective to give the poor more money, education, opportunity and incentives than, grotesquely, to nationalise industries which give them more high-speed trains and nuclear power stations. Even if it is concluded that the poor really require more of the latter, it can be more effective to subsidise private provision than to nationalise providers. Other objectives (e.g. good human resource practices) were often best pursued on a broad front by legislation rather than by setting an example in state-owned businesses, though in areas like gender equality of pay, state industries did generally lead the field.

For purposes of macro-economic management, it was sometimes argued that the state needed to accelerate domestic investment or overseas borrowing by the nationalised industries. Yet it might have been cheaper or more effective to offer general tax incentives than to instruct nationalised industries to implement these changes directly. It was certainly easier for the government to do some things – for example, forcing nationalised electric utilities to buy uneconomic British coal – than if they had been dealing with private sector enterprises, but this was largely because politicians did not wish the costs and effects of their policies to be transparent. The original intention had been that ministers should provide general guidance on objectives to the managers of the nationalised industries, abstaining from detailed intervention in operational matters. In practice the opposite happened: general guidance came through Treasury-inspired but politically insignificant White Papers, while ministerial enthusiasm propelled specific interventions to the forefront (House of Commons 1968). It is far from clear that such policies were in the long run successful in enabling the protected suppliers to create sustainable long-run competitive advantages, though they may have been temporarily effective in buying votes in marginal constituencies.

There developed, therefore, a wider appreciation that, while there may have been market failures which the state could intervene to correct, there was also a strong potential for state failures. It was, for example, simple for the initial advocates of nationalising electricity to suggest that private enterprise generators had only weak incentives not to pollute the environment, but the experience of eastern Europe (and, on a lesser scale, the nationalised electricity industry at home) showed that state ownership did not guarantee the absence of polluting behaviour. Both public and private ownership required some form of regulation (or pricing) of pollution.

For the issue of public ownership to be strictly relevant to any political objective, a case had to be made that the objective could best be achieved by nationalisation rather than by alternative means. Yet arguments of this kind frequently rested on a confusion of logic or a misunderstanding of facts. The case was frequently advanced, for example, that nationalising and subsidising railways would benefit the poor; yet empirical analysis showed that the main beneficiaries of rail subsidies were those on above-average incomes: overwhelmingly the poor travel either by bus or not at all (Beesley *et al.* 1983; Pryke 1971: 428). The state is frequently the tool of powerful pressure groups other than the poor.

The argument that nationalisation directly equalised British wealth distribution was equally flawed. If adequate compensation were paid, as it generally was (Chester 1975), then the distribution of wealth remained unaffected: the acquisition of the physical assets by the state was counterbalanced by the acquisition of financial assets (in the form of freely tradable compensation stock) by the private shareholders. Privatisation – the reverse process – could have had similarly neutral effects, though this was complicated by substantial initial discounts on the market value of the assets sold (Bishop and Kay 1988). The population of taxpayers (who probably lost) and that of new shareholders (who gained from the discounts) overlapped, and, since both were concentrated in the middle of the wealth distribution, there was probably little net effect on inequality.

It is more difficult than it first appears to calculate whether the British state has been a net accumulator of collective wealth for the average citizen through nationalisation (Hills 1989). The role of both nationalisation and privatisation in the changes has probably been small, relative to the state's accumulation of housing assets and collective provision of pension savings in the post-war decades. Certainly it was taxation and borrowing, rather than nationalisation, which ultimately determined the extent of collective savings administered by the British state on behalf of its citizens.

THE AFTERMATH: SUCCESSES AND FAILURES OF PRIVATISATION

By the turn of the twenty-first century there were only six 'nationalised industries', as conventionally defined, left in the UK public sector. The two biggest were London Transport (which already subcontracted its bus services to private bidders and was developing public–private partnerships for its underground railways) and the Post Office (just escaping privatisation, though increasingly subject to competition from private delivery companies and foreign post offices for express and bulk services). The others were small: BNFL (the residuary legatee of unprivatisable nuclear power), the Bank of England (given more monetary policymaking freedom), the British Waterways Board (as much an environmental service as a commercial business) and the BBC (still providing a distinctive public service, but subject to increasing competition from private channels and cable). The Labour government, elected after an unprecedented period of Conservative rule and privatisation, made no significant move to reverse the decisions of its predecessor, and nationalisation had been removed from the party's constitution as a policy objective. It was the belief of its leaders that the abandonment of this policy was essential to electoral success. The ownership of business was no longer a mainstream political issue in Britain. The interesting debates were now on the extent and nature of regulation; the direction, objectives and conditions of subsidy; competition policy; and the creation of level playing fields nationally and within the European economic space for capitalist businesses and the few remaining state-owned players. There was also increasing discussion – for example, in relation to rail infrastructure and hospitals – of new forms of non-profit enterprise, which bore more resemblance to the state corporations of the 1930s than to later nationalisations. The wisdom of this refocusing of political energies cannot seriously be questioned by the student of post-war experience.

Privatisation was sometimes seen as in itself sufficient to produce a cultural change that would improve performance (Leadbeater 1990). In some respects this proved true: after many decades of declining rail traffic, for example, improved marketing by the privatised train operating companies achieved a 25 per cent rise in passenger traffic. The quality of financial management and investment appraisal also markedly improved in the privatised companies. Yet most economic commentators suggested that efficiency gains would be sustained only if a more competitive structure was created (Bishop and Kay 1988; Bishop *et al.* 1994). Where national monopolies had been privatised as one – such as British

Gas – it eventually proved necessary to split the company and the regulator strove to encourage new competitors. Later privatisations such as electricity introduced more competition from the start: the largest generating company was split into three and its small Scottish counterparts and new entrants were encouraged to sell both to the National Grid and to large (and eventually to small) consumers. Technological progress also made competition more effective than it had been in earlier years. This process had perhaps gone furthest within the railways, where competition from road and air transport became the major restraint on pricing. Indeed it was clear that the railways were sustained by political support as much as by their economic contribution: for example, low-cost airlines (despite heavy new taxes placed on UK departures) offered cheaper and faster transport for national and cross-channel journeys above 200 miles than trains (which received substantial state subsidies). In telecommunications too, monopoly power was considerably reduced by competitor technologies to the old network: long-distance microwave transmissions, mobile phones and retail service lines from cable TV companies.

Nonetheless, new public agencies were established to regulate the network monopolies or oligopolies when they were privatised, since competition remained an ineffective control on pricing and performance (Vickers and Yarrow 1988; Bishop *et al.* 1995). Debates on regulation had, of course, been vigorous in countries like the USA, which long ago adopted regulated private enterprise as their preferred organisational form for network monopoly industries. The British legislation reflected some of the lessons of that experience. In particular, US profit controls were perceived by economists as introducing distortions similar to those that critics had identified in British nationalised industries. US utilities were, for example, accused of excessive use of capital, in the sense of using more capital-intensive technology than would be required by cost minimisation. Rate of return regulation encourages this because increased capital expenditure, even if it is not strictly necessary, permits the regulated company to declare higher profits (Averch and Johnson 1962; Stelser 1988). Regulatory failures were perceived in the USA as commonly as state ownership failures in Europe.

Mindful of this experience, the regulatory formula adopted in Britain for network monopolies such as gas, telecoms, water and electricity emphasised price not profit limitation, a focus that was also attractive to consumers and voters. It took the general form of limiting price rises to RPI-X, where RPI was the retail price index, and X was a fixed amount determined by the (somewhat arbitrary) view of each industry's underlying potential for efficiency improvement. This meant that, at least in the short and medium term, shareholders and managers in the private corporations gained the full benefit of any overall efficiency gains above the level implied by X, and thus had a strong performance incentive. Sceptics did, however, point to the fact that periodic re-setting of X introduces *de facto* profit controls: desirable to limit monopoly profits, but with undesirable incentive effects. In most regulatory reviews the X target was raised in response partly to the success – and great profitability – of the privatised companies. For example, X was initially set at 3 in telecoms, but was raised to 4.5 in 1988 and 6.25 in 1991. In gas, the initial X of 2 was raised to 5 in 1991. These were significantly higher improvement targets than the Treasury had been able to set for the same industries when they were under state control.

The first regulator to decide that competition was sufficiently advanced for retail price regulation to be abolished (in 2002) was the regulator of gas and electricity. In the period since privatisation, price regulation and market liberalisation had resulted in a 37 per cent reduction (in real terms) in household gas bills since privatisation in 1986 and in electricity a 28 per cent reduction since 1990. Of course, regulation of the 'common carrier' function of the national gas and electricity grids and local distribution networks (which remained monopolies) were still required. Other industries varied in the degree of competition that could be introduced: retail price regulation was still necessary but becoming less relevant in telecoms; it remained the fundamental restraint on prices in water.

Privatisation and competition were important not just in bringing prices to the consumer down at a faster rate than the state industries had been able to achieve. The new regime also fundamentally changed the nature of decision making and technical choice, forcing, for example, the cessation of nuclear power station building. In the 1980s, at a major public inquiry on the Sizewell B power station in Suffolk, the state-owned electricity industry made a strong case for building a pressurised water reactor (finally abandoning its support for British nuclear technology in favour of an American design). The public inquiry came to the (wrong) decision to allow that project to go ahead: electricity from the station now costs far more than electricity produced by conventional technologies in the new power stations built later by privatised companies. At the Sizewell inquiry the industry's leading witness revealingly spoke of 'closed expertise' – matters on which only they were qualified to pronounce – as opposed to 'open expertise' (that which the rest of us have). This arrogance determined the result: for the expert witness failed to foresee that the coal industry would become smaller and more productive, that gas would be the cheapest power station fuel, and that improved technology would increase the efficiency of conventional power stations generally. For years, politicians of both parties had told half-truths to parliament about the true costs of nuclear power and had not renewed the contracts of electricity industry leaders who showed a penchant for telling something nearer the whole truth (Hannah 1982). Pressure groups like Friends of the Earth were spectacularly ineffective at the Sizewell inquiry, because their opposition was independent of any facts or analysis: they preferred to rely instead on generalised objections to the modern world (Kay 2001). What changed this was not a change in political attitude – indeed, Mrs Thatcher was a strong supporter of nuclear power and originally made that and privatisation a cornerstone of her objectives for the electricity industry reform of 1990. Yet privatisation required the issue of a prospectus and lying to the stock exchange had more serious consequences than the past practice of lying to parliament or a public inquiry: individuals could be held criminally responsible. The ministers and businessmen involved were not willing to take that risk. Nuclear stations were, for a time, kept in the public sector, the newly private power companies shelved all further nuclear plans in favour of cheaper technologies, and, when eventually privatised, the nuclear company, British Energy, confined its activities to operating existing stations (with the necessary continuing state subsidy). The state electricity industry's monopoly on slanted knowledge was decisively broken by privatisation and by competition among generators.

Despite such successes, the privatisation programme was not entirely a story of progress. The most problematic case was the railways, where there had been excessive hopes of gradually reducing public subsidy in an industry which was fundamentally uneconomic and unlikely to survive against competition unless serious road pricing were introduced and rail subsidies increased. There were, of course, some key intercity and suburban rail routes that could be economic, but the government's ten-year transport plan, published in 2000, recognised that the private sector would be unwilling to fund much of the investment needed to upgrade the whole system. The financing and organisation of the rail infrastructure remains controversial, because it has no serious prospect of delivering social objectives without the significant involvement of government beyond the norms established by regulators elsewhere. Passengers are not willing to pay the full cost of providing rail services, so, as the government had no wish to see the railways disappear, it was obliged to underwrite the infrastructure company, Network Rail, as a non-profit company. In nuclear power too, the fall in wholesale electricity prices compromised the viability of British Energy and additional government support was again required. These outcomes showed, unsurprisingly, that private companies could not provide services that customers were not willing to pay for. Government was, however, now forced to be transparent about its subsidies so that they could be sensibly and critically discussed, while the private sector managers had no reason to conceal the true costs of large infrastructure projects (such as the West Coast main line) from government. The current transport plan envisages, over ten years, £2.9 billion public and £2.2 billion private spending on railways, compared with £1.8 billion total spending on roads (which account for far more passenger miles in buses and cars). The reaction of the travelling public to such a skewed pattern of spending away from their favoured transport modes remains to be assessed when the consequences – likely to be sharply deteriorating road conditions and only slightly improving train services – are experienced.

In other areas, there have been gains and losses from privatisation, but gains seem clearly to dominate. There was a learning process both for regulator and regulated, a process accelerated latterly by foreign takeover of British utilities. British firms in areas like electricity, water, gas and telecoms also attempted to use their expertise abroad, though they found it much more difficult to add value to foreign acquisition than they had anticipated. The quest to go further in productivity and price improvements also stalled after some time. After massive early gains to shareholders – caused by underpricing of initial share offers and unusually high structural levels of initial inefficiency that could be squeezed out – the majority of privatised companies have in recent years offered a poor return. Consumers' rates of gain now have also plateaued (Kay forthcoming). It remains to be seen whether any of the privatised companies will develop the capabilities to do more in the future, but, BP aside, the 'once public' sector still has to produce a world player comparable to long-term private sector industrial firms like Shell, Unilever and Diageo among leading British multinationals on the world business stage.

5

Employment, education and human capital

MARY O'MAHONY

Contents

INTRODUCTION

This chapter considers employment and human capital in post-war Britain. It begins with a look at trends in the labour force, employment and unemployment, taking account of the age distribution of the labour force, female participation, trends in participation in full-time education, part-time working, self-employment and the industrial composition of employment. Following this the chapter devotes most attention to the skill composition of the labour force, contrasting the position in the UK with that in the United States and Germany. Low investment in human capital has frequently been seen as a weakness of the British economy, and has been identified as a major cause of Britain's relative economic decline during the twentieth century, particularly by writers in the period from the end of the Second World War (Landes 1972; Levine 1967; Aldcroft 1992). The chapter first considers human capital accumulation in Britain from the Second World War to 1979, examining data available from a range of sources. This period also coincides with British productivity levels falling behind those in other European countries. This is followed by a consideration of the two decades since 1979, when more detailed data on labour force skills are available.

The final section considers the implications of human capital accumulation for Britain's relative productivity position. It is important to realise that at the end of the Second World War, although the United States had a substantial lead over Britain in aggregate labour productivity, Britain still had high aggregate labour productivity by European standards, and was not overtaken by most west European countries before the late 1960s (Maddison 1995). The growing concerns as Britain fell behind other European countries during the 1970s can be seen as preparing the ground for the large changes in the education and training system that have occurred during the 1980s and 1990s.

LABOUR FORCE, EMPLOYMENT AND UNEMPLOYMENT

Figure 5.1 shows trends in the labour force and employment (workforce jobs) from 1950 to 1999, with the difference between the two being unemployment. Labour force growth was moderate up to the mid-1960s, stagnated until the mid-1970s and then rose considerably. These trends can be explained in terms of both demographic factors and participation rates. Population growth occurred at a steady rate of about 0.5 per cent per annum from the end of the war to about 1966 (Mathews *et al.* 1982). Changes in the age distribution, with a rising population of children and elderly, depressed the positive effects from increased participation by some population groups, in particular female participation. In the following decade, increased participation in education by 15- to 24-year-olds, coupled with slower population growth and continuing increases in the proportion of young and elderly in the population dampened labour force growth. Many of these trends continued after 1974, but the effect on the age distribution of the post-war 'baby boom' dominated, outweighing the dampening effects from continuing increases in education participation and early retirement.

Employment was virtually stagnant across the decades of the 1960s and 1970s, following a small rise in the 1950s. Employment began to rise following a sharp dip in the early 1980s and again in the mid-to-late 1990s so that the 1999 level was about 6 per cent higher than in 1979. The trend in aggregate employment hides considerable variation in a number of dimensions. First, there has been a major change in the sex composition of employment, with females now accounting for about 45 per cent of total employment against 34 per cent in 1970 and under 30 per cent in the 1950s. Both male and female employment rose steadily to the mid-1960s (Matthews *et al.* 1982) but male employment declined by roughly a quarter from then to 1993 before rising marginally again in the later 1990s. In

Figure 5.1 Trends in the labour force and employment, UK, 1950–1999

Source: ONS *Economic Trends Annual Supplement* (2000).

contrast female employment increased throughout the post-war period, with the exception of a small dip in the recession years of the early 1980s. However, in the 1990s female employment growth was no greater than that for males. These differences in the employment experiences of males and females were partly due to the increased participation rate of married females but also reflected changes in the industrial composition of employment as discussed below.

Two additional changes in the composition of employment are worth mentioning. First is the trend increase in part-time working from about 12 per cent of employment in the early 1970s to nearly 25 per cent by 1999. In the late 1990s about 45 per cent of the female labour force worked part-time so that the trend increase largely reflected trends in female participation. But there was also a small increase in male part-time working up to the beginning of the 1990s and, since 1993, male part-timers have been increasing more rapidly than male employment as a whole. Male part-time workers now make up about 9 per cent of male employment.

The second change in employment composition is the rise in the proportion of self-employed in the workforce after 1979. Department of Employment data show that the self-employed proportion remained fairly static in the first three decades of the post-war period at about 7–8 per cent of total employment but rose sharply in the 1980s to reach 13 per cent by 1990. This can be explained by the low demand for labour in the recession of the early 1980s leading to laid-off workers setting up their own businesses. In the 1990s, however, there was little change in the number of self-employed leading to a decline in their employment share.

Finally it should be noted that trends in labour input, as measured by total hours worked, followed similar trends to employment in the early post-war period and again since the 1980s but declined sharply in the 1970s following a decline in the annual average number of hours per worker (O'Mahony 1999). This was due both to an increase in the average number of weeks paid leave and the increase in part-time working. Since the 1980s, while part-time working continued to rise in importance there was a slowing in the time lost due to holidays and sickness reinforced by the rising proportion of self-employed who typically work longer hours than employees.

One of the greatest changes in the composition of employment in the post-war period has been in its distribution across industrial sectors. In 1950, production industries, which in addition to manufacturing includes mining, public utilities and construction, accounted for over 40 per cent of UK employment. By the end of the twentieth century this share had fallen to just over 20 per cent. The share of employment in agriculture also continued to decline although this share was already small by 1950. In contrast there was a very large increase in the importance of service industries, both market services (transport, communications, distribution, financial and business services, and personal services) and non-market services (public administration, education and health). The share of employment in market services increased slowly in the 1950s and 1960s but took off rapidly from the mid-1970s. There was a big expansion in employment in non-market services in the 1970s but very little change thereafter and a slight falling off by the end of the 1990s.

This pattern of deindustrialisation is mirrored in other countries. Thus manufacturing's share declined from 25 per cent in the USA in 1950 to 19 per cent in 1995 and a similar rate of decline was experienced in France (O'Mahony 1999: 12, tab. 2.1). But deindustrialisation occurred at a faster pace in Britain than in these two countries. On the other hand Germany showed little decline in its manufacturing employment share throughout most of the post-war period. In fact West Germany's manufacturing employment share in 1950 was about equal to that in Britain, at about 33 per cent of total employment, but declined only to 27 per cent by 1995 against 19 per cent in Britain in that year. For a further discussion of the UK industrial structure, see chapters 10 and 15 below and the debate on the welfare implications of faster deindustrialisation in Britain since the early 1970s (Crafts 1996; Kitson and Michie 1996).

Finally in this section it is important to discuss trends in unemployment, the difference between the labour force and employment implicit in Figure 5.1. For the purposes of comparison it is useful to present UK unemployment rates relative to those in major competitor countries. Hence Figure 5.2 shows the unemployed as a percentage of the labour force for

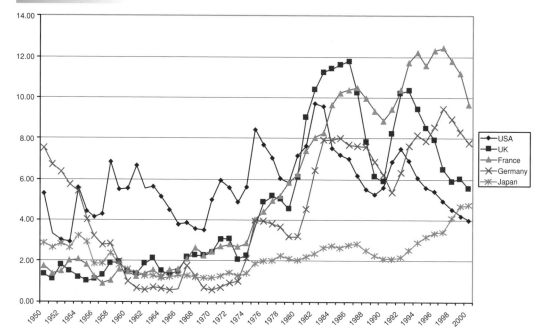

Figure 5.2 Unemployment rates, 1950–2000, selected industrial nations

Sources: From 1960 to 2000, OECD. From 1950 to 1960, USA: US Bureau of the Census (1960); UK: ONS, *Economic Trends* (various years); Germany: Federal Statistical Office (various years); France prior to 1965: Mitchell (1980) for numbers unemployed, combined with employment numbers from O'Mahony and de Boer (2002); Japan: 1953–60 from Economic Planning Agency *Economic Survey of Japan*; 1950–3 from Mitchell (1982).

the USA, the UK, France, West Germany and Japan. UK unemployment rates were historically low in the post-war boom of the 1950s and 1960s. This was true also in France and Japan and in Germany from the end of the 1950s. During the 1970s and 1980s UK unemployment rose above 3 million persons to levels similar to those experienced during the 1930s. Although unemployment rates also rose in competitor countries the increase was more pronounced and sustained in the UK. From the early 1990s unemployment rates fell in all countries other than Japan. But in a reverse to the previous experience, Britain performed better than the two continental European countries so that by the end of the twentieth century unemployment rates in Britain were significantly below those in France and Germany.

The large rise in unemployment in the 1970s and 1980s generated a substantial literature setting out a general framework to explain these trends. The models which emerged used the concept of the Non-Accelerating Inflation Rate of Unemployment, or NAIRU (see, e.g., Layard and Nickell 1986). If unemployment is low, inflation will tend to rise as firms are able to pay higher wages to attract workers and unions are in a strong position to press for high wage settlements. On the other hand if unemployment is high, trade unions will be in a weaker position and employers will not be trying to attract workers. Hence there is a critical level of unemployment at which inflation will be stable, the NAIRU. In these models the NAIRU is given by the intersection of the feasible real wage (what firms can afford to pay given that they must make profits) and the target real wage (resulting from wage negotiating behaviour of unions). If the target real wage is greater than the feasible real wage then inflation results. Workers press for higher money wages in an attempt to raise real wages, but firms respond by increasing prices. An increase in unemployment is then needed to moderate the target real wage and to stop inflation from accelerating.

The target real wage is affected by the extent to which unemployment benefits compensate for lost wages (the benefit replacement ratio), labour unions raise wages above non-union rates (the union wage mark-up), the unemployed are unsuited to available vacancies following rapid structural change (mismatch); and by incomes policies. Real import prices and employers' labour taxes affect the feasible real wage. There is evidence that all these factors may have had an influence in explaining the rise in unemployment in the 1970s and 1980s – see references in Layard *et al.* (1991). A discussion of the low unemployment rates in the early post-war period is presented in Broadberry (1994b). He argues that in the 1950s and 1960s wage restraint was the important factor which allowed the simultaneous achievement of low unemployment and stable inflation. But the post-war settlement which underpinned this wage restraint also allowed the entrenchment of over-manning and other restrictive practices which slowed the growth of labour productivity and hence the feasible real wage.

In the 1990s unemployment declined to rates not seen since the mid-1970s, reaching a level of just over 1 million persons in 1999. Recent research suggests a wide range of factors have contributed to this decline. These include moderate wage growth in the 1990s, the decline in trade union power, more flexible labour markets and changes to the benefit administration system (Nickell and van Ours 2000; Riley and Young 2001).

Coincident with this decline in unemployment has been a rise in inactivity or non-employment rates among adult males. The inactive population are those who are not currently seeking employment but who are potentially available to work if circumstances change. Nickell and van Ours (2000) show that inactivity has risen dramatically in the UK in the 1990s among non-student men, most of whose status has changed from being unemployment benefit recipients to being classified as disabled or long-term ill. An examination of the educational background of the inactive population also shows a high and increasing concentration of inactivity among unskilled males with low educational qualifications. Hence employability is intrinsically tied in with the skill levels of the labour force. This, together with increasing evidence that technical change has moved in a skill-biased direction (see below), implies that the educational qualifications of the workforce are important in understanding post-war trends in employment and unemployment.

HUMAN CAPITAL FORMATION FROM THE SECOND WORLD WAR TO THE 1970S

Individuals invest time and effort in education and training to increase their stock of knowledge. Since knowledge is used in production after it is acquired, and depreciates slowly, this investment is frequently termed human capital. Just as firms invest in physical capital to carry out tasks more effectively, investment by individuals in time spent on education and training facilitates their ability to produce additional output. Individuals get a return to this investment in the form of higher remuneration reflecting the increased marginal productivity of more educated workers. In addition, society in general may also benefit if increases in this stock of knowledge generate external benefits which raise the productivity of all workers. Hence investment in human capital is an important element in driving economic growth. The impact of human capital accumulation on productivity is discussed in more detail below.

We begin with a consideration of the available data up to 1979, contrasting the position in Britain with that of two major competitors, the USA and Germany. We then look at the position in the 1980s and 1990s when considerably greater detail is available from labour force surveys. There are essentially two methods of acquiring skills. The first is through formal education and training systems, the second is through informal 'on the job' training and experience. The figures presented below consider the former channel since informal training is difficult to quantify. The data relate mainly to certified qualifications, although time-served apprenticeships that are not certified are also included.

Schooling

Comparative data on formal school enrolment per head of population aged under twenty years are set out in Table 5.1, distinguishing primary and secondary from tertiary levels. The breakdown between primary and secondary education is affected by differences between these countries in the age at which transfer from primary to secondary education occurred, and by differences in the age structures of their populations. The table shows somewhat smaller school enrolment rates in the two European countries in the early post-war period with Britain catching up to US levels by the 1990s. The German figure remains lower throughout but this partly reflects the dual nature of the German educational system whereby traditional academic subjects are also taught in vocational schools (Prais

Table 5.1	Educational enrolment rates per 1,000 population under age 20, 1950–2000						
	Britain		USA		Germany[a]		
	Primary and Secondary	Higher	Primary and Secondary	Higher	Primary and Secondary	Vocational schools	Higher
1950/1	487	9	525	52	363	78	6
1960/1	533	14	575	63	409	100	14
1970/1	595	26	630	112	389	107	23
1980/1	654	31	638	167	569	145	63
1990/1	612	79	647	191	569	145	124
1990/1					*518*	*148*	*103*
1999/2000	672	123	658	188	*579*	*152*	*103*

[a] West Germany from 1950 to 1990, Unified Germany in italics 1990 and 1999.

Source: UK and USA from Broadberry and Ghosal (2002), updated using original sources, i.e. UK: ONS (2001) and CSO, *Annual Abstract of Statistics* for population; USA: US Bureau of the Census (2001); Germany: Federal Statistical Office (various years).

1995). If enrolment rates in German vocational schools, as shown in Table 5.1, are added to primary and tertiary then Germany looks more like the UK and the USA in the 1990s. There is little difference in the post-war period in primary school enrolments since education is compulsory for all children in the relevant age groups. Both Britain and Germany lagged behind the USA in secondary enrolments in the early post-war period with a greater degree of catching-up to the USA in Germany than in Britain up to 1981. The earlier development of mass secondary education in the USA has been emphasised by historians such as Goldin (1998).

The main vehicle for bringing about the development of mass secondary education in Britain was the 1944 Education Act, under which Local Education Authorities became responsible for providing free education to all children in their area (Vaizey and Sheehan 1968: 16). Although the Act made no mention of specific types of secondary school, this was commonly implemented through a tripartite system of grammar, technical and secondary modern schools, based on selection (Armytage 1970: 241). A commitment was made to raise the school leaving age to fifteen, and despite difficulties with the availability of both teachers and premises, the commitment was honoured with the help of an Emergency Training Scheme and a Hutting Operation for the Raising of the School Age, known as HORSA (Dent 1970: 126–8). The school leaving age was raised further to sixteen during the academic year 1970–1, following a decision taken in 1964 (Gosden 1983: 36).

Much political attention at the time was focused on the quality rather than the quantity of secondary education. Concerns were increasingly raised over the unfairness and rigidity of selection at the age of eleven via the 'eleven-plus' examination. After an initial expansion, the number of technical schools fell from 319 in 1948 to 266 by 1960, about the same level as in the 1930s (Sanderson 1988: 44). Hence for most of the country there was a bipartite rather than a tripartite system, with an academic minority in grammar schools receiving a better education than the majority in secondary modern schools, and with little transfer between the two (Gosden 1983: 30–1). Following the election in 1964 of a Labour government committed to equality of opportunity, legislation was introduced in 1965 to introduce comprehensive schools to replace grammar and secondary modern schools. By 1970, 32 per cent of all secondary pupils were in comprehensive schools, and despite the return of a Conservative government in that year, this had risen to 62 per cent by 1974. By 1979, the proportion of secondary pupils in comprehensive schools had reached more than 86 per cent (Gosden 1983: 42).

The main divergence across countries in Table 5.1 is the extent to which both Britain and Germany lagged behind the United States in the provision of mass higher education after the Second World War. Given the difference in the average time taken to obtain a degree in Germany (five years) compared to the UK (three years) it is not surprising that the UK enrolment figures are below those for Germany for most of the period. The 1990s was a period of very rapid expansion of higher education in Britain, so that the gap with the USA was narrowed but by no means eliminated. Trends in higher education are discussed further below.

Vocational training

For the European countries it is important that school enrolments are augmented with data on vocational training. An important distinction is between higher-level and intermediate-level vocational training. Higher-level training is taken to cover vocational qualifications at the standard of a university degree, including membership of professional institutions, while intermediate-level training is taken to cover craft and technician qualifications above secondary level but below degree level, including non-examined time-served apprenticeships (Prais 1995).

Table 5.2 shows patterns of apprentice-to-employment ratios in both manufacturing and the whole economy up to the early 1980s. Although Germany had a higher ratio of apprentices to employees in industry during the first half of the twentieth century, Britain narrowed the gap between the Second World War and the late 1960s. In fact, it is apparent from Table 5.3 that the biggest increase in industrial apprenticeship training in Britain after 1951 was in mineral extraction and the utilities, particularly in the newly nationalised coal and electricity industries. In manufacturing and construction, by contrast, the increase in apprenticeship between 1951 and 1966 left the apprentice-to-employment ratios below their 1925 levels (Broadberry 2003).

Broadberry argues that in manufacturing the relationship between human capital and labour productivity should be understood in the context of the distinction between 'mass production' and 'flexible production'

Table 5.2 Apprentices as % of employees in Britain and Germany, 1950–1988

	Great Britain		Germany	
	Manufacturing	Whole economy	Manufacturing	Whole economy
1950/1	3.0	1.9	4.6	4.8
1960/1	3.0	3.6	5.5	4.6
1970/1	2.7	3.3	4.4	4.9
1980/1	2.3	2.6	6.8	6.3

Sources: Derived from data presented in Broadberry and Wagner (1996) and Broadberry (1998b).

Table 5.3 Apprentices and articled trainees as % of employees, by sector, Great Britain, 1951–1981

	1951	1961	1966	1971	1981
Agriculture, forestry, fishing	0.17	1.41	1.34	1.11	0.56
Mineral extraction	0.94	3.19	3.83	4.25	3.38
Manufacturing	2.83	4.18	4.38	3.62	3.19
Construction	7.15	7.72	8.48	5.96	5.60
Utilities	2.63	3.79	5.57	4.61	3.58
Transport & communications	0.37	0.87	1.56	1.72	1.51
Distribution	0.68	1.98	2.30	1.94	0.99
Finance, insurance, real estate	0.21	0.23	1.57	1.53	1.86
Professional & personal services	0.83	4.82	4.92	4.11	2.88
Public administration & defence	0.26	0.65	1.37	1.31	1.13
Whole economy	1.87	3.56	4.01	3.28	2.58

Note: 'Employees' includes self-employed.

Sources: 1951: *Census of England and Wales, Industry Tables*, tab. 4.
1961: *Census of England and Wales (10% Sample), Industry Tables, Part I*, tab. 2.
1966: *Census of Great Britain, Economic Activity Tables, Part I (10% Sample)*, tab. 14.
1971: *Census of Great Britain, Economic Activity, Part II (10% Sample)*, tab. 16.
1981: *Census of Great Britain, Economic Activity (10% Sample)*, tab. 9.

technology, an issue explored in more detail in chapter 3 above. Mass production involves standardised products substituting machinery for skilled workers. Flexible production involves customised output utilising skilled labour. In countries such as Britain and Germany, with an orientation towards flexible production, one would expect to observe high demand for intermediate-level skills. In contrast, in the mass-production techniques more common in the United States, there will be a greater emphasis on higher-level skills, with the relatively unskilled shopfloor workers supervised by highly skilled managers.

Broadberry and Wagner (1996) show that the failure of British apprentice-to-employment ratios to regain the levels of before the Second World War was sharpest in engineering, the most important sector for the application of Fordist production methods involving a deskilling of the workforce. This is consistent with a demand-side explanation for the declining stock of skilled workers in post-war Britain, with British industry following a strategy of attempting to imitate American mass-production techniques (Broadberry 1997c). If Americanisation is accepted as a deliberate strategy of British industry, then it becomes easier to explain the narrowing of UK skill differentials with Germany as noted by Prais and Wagner (1988), drawing on the estimates of Routh (1965). The compression of skill differentials became greatest during the late 1960s and early 1970s, the high-point of the drive towards Americanisation, before the revival of flexible production technology under the stimulus of developments in information technology, particularly during the late 1970s and the 1980s (Broadberry 1997c).

Although it is sometimes suggested that the quality of training received by British apprentices left something to be desired, it should be noted that contemporary enquiries from the 1920s to the early 1960s generally concluded that Britain was not out of step with other European countries in this regard (Ministry of Labour 1928; Williams 1957, 1963; Liepmann 1960; Organisation for European Economic Co-operation, 1960). In fact, this ties in with the findings of later research for the 1980s, which, as discussed below, suggests that Britain's skills gap has more to do with the quantity rather than the quality of trained workers, at least in industrial sectors (Prais 1995).

Nevertheless, as Sheldrake and Vickerstaff (1987: 26–42) note, there was much criticism of Britain's vocational training system during the 1950s and 1960s, continuing a long line of critical commentary dating back to the late nineteenth century (Pollard 1989: 115–213). However, it should be noted that the most vociferous criticisms came from the education and training lobby, with employers and trade unions remaining unconvinced that there was a major problem (Sheldrake and Vickerstaff 1987: 31). To some extent this should not surprise us, since advocates of reform had vested interests as much as those they sought to reform, and the case against the voluntarist status quo would only seem convincing when productivity performance was decisively higher in countries with a more interventionist approach to training, such as Germany. Although the Industrial Training Act of 1964 introduced an element of compulsion with a training levy, which was then paid out in the form of grants where firms provided approved training, the system remained decentralised via a system of Industrial Training Boards (Gospel 1995). Protests from small firms, which all too often failed to qualify for grants, led to a growth in exemptions, and by the early 1970s it was clear that the system had failed to stem a steady decline in apprenticeships (Sheldrake and Vickerstaff 1987: 33–42). The 1973 Employment and Training Act, which established a tripartite Manpower Services Commission (MSC), also failed to reverse the downward trend in apprenticeships, and with unemployment trending upwards during the 1970s, the MSC became increasingly entangled in a series of ad hoc special measures to counter youth unemployment (Sheldrake and Vickerstaff 1987: 44–52).

Perhaps the most striking difference between Britain and Germany in the field of intermediate-level vocational training was in the service sectors. Whereas in Germany the apprenticeship system was extended from industry into services on a large scale after the Second World War, service sector apprenticeships remained at a much lower level in Britain. The much greater scale of service sector apprenticeships in Germany by the end of the 1950s was commented upon by Williams (1963: 22). Nevertheless, British training policy during the 1960s and 1970s remained firmly focused on industry, despite the growing importance of services in the economy and the loss of Britain's productivity lead over European countries in service sectors (see chapter 10 below).

Differences in the extent of vocational education in Britain and Germany reflect the underlying systems of provision. In Germany some training after the age of sixteen is largely compulsory so that a substantial period of vocational education is virtually obligatory for the majority of young Germans (Prais 1995). In contrast the onus on providing vocational training in Britain lies with either the employer or the individual. Hence the British system suffers from 'free-rider' problems whereby trained employees might be poached by competitor firms, leading to levels of provision that are socially sub-optimal.

Higher education

The early post-war expansion of higher education is usually associated with the Robbins Report of 1963, which set targets for an expanding student population into the 1970s. In fact, however, student numbers had been increasing throughout the post-war period, and the Robbins Report led merely to an acceleration of the rise (Gosden 1983: 137). The Robbins Report is thus best seen as an important step on the road towards mass higher education, which nevertheless remained another two or three decades away from achievement. Table 5.4 presents figures on the stock of employees with higher-level qualifications in Britain from 1961, decomposed by sector. The 1961 Population Census provides data on scientific and technological qualifications only, but, from 1966, figures on all higher-level qualifications, including membership of professional institutions, are also available. Employees with higher-level qualifications, particularly non-scientific, have increasingly made up a high proportion of the labour force in the service sectors, particularly finance, insurance and real estate; professional and personal services; and public administration and defence.

Professional qualifications were the major form of higher-level training prior to the development of mass higher education (Broadberry 2003) so that in the years immediately after the Second World War, members of the major professional bodies remained an important part of Britain's stock of employees with higher-level qualifications. This gave Britain a

Table 5.4   Percentage of employees with higher-level qualifications, by sector. Great Britain, 1961–1991

| | Great Britain, 1961–91 (%) | | | | | |
| | Scientific and technological qualifications | | All higher-level qualifications | | | |
	1961	1966	1966	1971	1981	1991
Agriculture, forestry, fishing	0.55	0.48	0.77	0.89	2.02	2.87
Mineral extraction & utilities	1.41	1.76	2.47	3.42	6.34	11.94
Manufacturing	1.15	1.30	1.81	2.39	3.92	6.30
Construction	0.58	0.80	1.26	1.70	2.95	3.11
Transport & communications	0.32	0.39	0.74	1.12	2.53	4.23
Distribution	0.15	0.19	0.93	1.33	2.18	3.36
Finance, insurance, real estate	0.43	0.49	2.44	4.06	14.05	19.43
Professional & personal services	1.99	2.30	8.42	9.53	19.30	16.78
Public administration & defence	1.70	1.48	4.06	5.35	6.75	16.56
Whole economy	1.08	1.26	3.15	4.01	7.22	10.01

Note: Includes qualifications at the standard of a university degree, including membership of a professional institution; 'employees' includes self-employed.

Sources: 1961: Census of Great Britain, Scientific and Technological Qualifications, tab. 1.
1966: Sample Census of Great Britain, Scientific and Technological Qualifications, tabs. 1, 2; Sample Census of Great Britain, Qualified Manpower, tab. 3.
1971: Census of Great Britain, Qualified Manpower (10% Sample), tab. 7.
1981: Census of Great Britain, Qualified Manpower (10% Sample), tab. 5.
1991: Census of Great Britain, Qualified Manpower (10% Sample) I, tab. 5.

human capital advantage over both Germany and the United States in the service sectors where these professionals were concentrated. However, the massive expansion of higher education, first in the United States and a generation later in Britain and Germany, has eroded this British advantage by providing an alternative route to higher-level qualifications.

This concentration of professionals with higher-level qualifications in the service sectors is consistent with the findings of a large number of surveys of industrial management during the period just after the Second World War, which consistently found few managers with professional qualifications or degrees (Broadberry and Wagner 1996: 257–8). For example, the Acton Society Trust (1956: 5–12) found that in a sample of 3,327 British industrial managers, only 18 per cent had professional qualifications and 19 per cent had degrees. Furthermore, whereas only 30 per cent of 'top managers' had been to university, 63 per cent of 'higher Civil Servants' were graduates (Acton Society Trust 1956: 9).

HUMAN CAPITAL SINCE 1979: THE EXPANSION OF EDUCATION AND TRAINING

The existence of more detailed data on labour force qualifications from labour force surveys since the end of the 1970s allows a more precise

Table 5.5 Stocks of qualified persons as % of employees, by sector and skill level in the UK, the USA and Germany

	Higher level			Intermediate level		
	UK	USA	Germany	UK	USA	Germany
A. 1978/9						
Agriculture	2.0	5.6	0.7	11.3	6.9	31.5
Minings & oil refining	4.5	12.0	4.7	20.9	11.7	62.6
Manufacturing	4.3	8.9	3.2	23.2	8.8	56.6
Construction	3.8	5.1	2.6	38.0	10.1	66.2
Utilities	7.8	12.6	5.9	31.6	12.5	75.9
Transport & communications	3.2	8.5	3.1	19.8	13.1	70.7
Distribution	2.3	9.1	2.1	11.0	12.8	67.3
Finance & business services	16.7	24.7	12.2	9.6	14.1	68.3
Miscellaneous personal services	6.1	45.4	8.3	19.4	9.2	58.5
Non-market services[a]	14.3	34.5	21.5	27.7	13.0	53.0
Whole economy	6.8	15.8	7.0	21.8	11.4	58.5
B. 1998						
Agriculture	6.1	14.6	4.8	29.1	13.3	67.5
Mining & oil refining	14.7	19.2	2.9	46.1	16.8	69.8
Manufacturing	10.9	20.7	9.9	39.5	16.7	68.4
Construction	6.0	10.6	7.0	55.8	15.7	73.6
Utilities	19.1	23.2	14.8	47.8	22.0	70.3
Transport & communications	7.9	19.8	8.6	33.8	20.6	71.8
Distribution	6.2	15.6	5.8	28.8	19.1	70.7
Finance & business services	27.5	33.0	24.1	23.1	20.2	58.4
Miscellaneous personal services	15.6	19.3	17.6	31.4	19.4	59.7
Non-market services[a]	25.9	46.0	27.5	34.4	19.1	56.5
Whole economy	15.8	27.7	15.0	33.9	18.6	65.0

[a] Comprising public administration, education and health.
Note: German figures refer to unified Germany in 1998 and the former West Germany for 1978.

Sources: 1978/9, O'Mahony (1999); 1998, unpublished data from: USA, Current Population Survey, US Bureau of the Census; UK, Labour Force Survey; Germany, Mikrozensus.

comparison of the UK experience in international perspective from that date. Table 5.5 shows proportions of the workforce with higher-level and intermediate qualifications in 1978/9 and 1998 by broad industrial sector. There have been definitional changes both in the types of skills allocated to each group and in industrial classifications over this period and the table compares total unified Germany in the later year with the former West Germany in earlier years. Hence these figures are not strictly comparable over time but nevertheless are a reasonable approximation to broad trends.

The data for 1998 in Table 5.5 show clearly the US dominance in higher-level skills. Thus for the total economy the proportion of the workforce with higher-level skills was around 70 per cent higher in the USA than in Britain and Germany. Both European countries had improved their position relative to the United States since 1979 but not sufficiently to narrow the gap to any great extent. There are similarities in the patterns of attainment of higher-level skills across industries. Hence these proportions are generally higher in the aggregate economy than in market sectors, reflecting the very high utilisation of graduates in non-market services, in particular in education. Graduate utilisation is very high also in financial and business services, the utilities and mining but tends to be much lower than average in manufacturing and is particularly low in agriculture and distribution.

Table 5.5 also shows clearly Germany's dominance in intermediate skills – in 1998 the proportion of intermediate skills in the aggregate economy in Germany was around twice that in Britain and the United States and this was true also for most broad sectors, in particular in service industries. To some extent this directly compensates for German deficiencies at the higher level since that country has a long tradition of providing qualifications through the vocational education system which are on a par with university degrees in the other two countries.[1] But the larger part of the German advantage in intermediate skills derives from that country's greater emphasis on workers obtaining craft-level qualifications.

Overall, then, Table 5.5 shows that Britain's workforce skill position falls between the two countries with a large gap relative to the United States in higher-level skills and a large gap relative to Germany in intermediate-skills. Also Britain's skill deficiency is apparent in all sectors of the economy. This is less pronounced in those sectors such as financial and business services where graduate utilisation is high but even in these sectors Britain's skill gap remains substantial.

A detailed comparison of the educational and training systems in Britain relative to those in other European countries is provided in Prais (1995) where the focus is largely on their impacts on intermediate-level skills. At the higher (degree and above) level, Prais also notes little difference between Britain and Germany. But he suggests that this is also true for skills at the upper intermediate level, i.e. those qualifications which involve long periods of full-time study for vocational qualifications. The big difference is in the lower intermediate vocational qualifications which generally involve some part-time study.

Persons acquiring vocational skills in Germany generally enrol on part-time vocational courses, which involve equal time spent studying vocational subjects specific to the person's job and general subjects such

---

[1] In Britain, membership of professional organisations is considered to be equivalent to university degrees and these are included in the proportions with higher skills. In Germany the equivalent are not generally separately identified in the data – a division of intermediate qualifications into higher and lower levels suggests that including persons with professional qualifications in the 'higher' group would bring Germany closer to Britain in this respect while retaining a large gap with the United States.

as mathematics, languages, etc. The German students are required to pass both written examinations and practical tests, both of which are set and assessed externally. A similar system is found in the traditional apprenticeships in engineering and construction trades in Britain. But Germany has extended this system to all sectors of the economy. Prais and his collaborators examined the subject material covered in the standard vocational training courses in the two countries and concluded that, generally, mechanical, engineering and construction skills were broadly equivalent in Britain and Germany with the main difference being the numbers pursuing these qualifications. In office work and retailing the courses pursued by British workers were, however, found to be of shorter duration and narrower in their subject matter than the courses undertaken by German workers. Also in these trades the German advantage in terms of numbers qualifying was considerably greater than was the case for those in engineering and related trades.

Prais (1995) also notes the general decline in numbers of workers pursuing apprenticeships in Britain. In many cases these were substituted by students gaining vocational qualifications such as City & Guilds and BTECs which combined written exams and practical tests. In recent years these have been increasingly replaced by national vocational qualifications (NVQs). The NVQs generally involve a testing procedure where the practical competence of the student is demonstrated to normal workplace supervisors and written tests are not usual. In continental Europe centrally set, externally marked tests are the norm. Prais suggests that the movement to NVQs has lowered the average quality of intermediate skills acquired in Britain and renders them less comparable with the skill levels reached by workers in continental Europe.

There is less evidence on the comparability of standards reached in higher-level qualifications in the three countries. But Mason (1995) suggests that the German basic degree, which takes an average of six years to complete, is more akin to the Masters than the Bachelors degree in Britain and the United States. Hence it is likely that graduates in Germany reach, on average, higher standards than graduates in Britain or America. However, when considering higher-level skills, the primary difference has been the substantial gap in the proportions of the workforce qualified to this level in the two European countries relative to the United States.

In Britain in the 1990s there has been a significant expansion of young persons gaining qualifications at both the higher and intermediate levels. Since new qualifications are generally gained by young persons who make up only a part of the workforce, a considerable period of time can elapse before an expansion of education and training translates into large increases in the stock of skilled workers. Table 5.6 compares graduate qualifications by age group in the UK and USA. In the youngest age group (18–24 year olds) the UK graduate share now exceeds that in the USA, partly reflecting the emphasis of the UK system on channelling

Table 5.6 Graduates as % of total workforce, 1998, by age group		
	UK	USA
18–24 age group	11	9
25–34 age group	20	31
35–44 age group	18	29
45–64 age group	14	31
Total 18–64 age group	16	28

Source: Labour Force Survey (UK), Current Population Survey (USA).

young school-leavers through relatively short first degree courses but also partly reflecting the relatively high proportion of Americans who study for degrees (often part-time) at later stages of their lives. In age groups above the age of 25 the UK still has some way to go to catch up with the USA. Mason (1995) shows that the annual British output of first degree graduates is higher now than in other European countries such as France and Germany but lower than in the United States or Japan. Following the launch of NVQs there has also been a large expansion in young persons gaining intermediate qualifications although it is doubtful if qualifications below NVQ level 3 are comparable to intermediate qualifications in other European countries.

In summary this section has shown that in the post-war era there were serious deficiencies in the skill position in Britain relative to both the USA and Germany. There is also evidence that this shortfall extends to other European countries such as France (Steedman et al. 1991; Crafts and O'Mahony 2001). There has been some progress since 1980 in the provision of both intermediate vocational and higher-level skills in the UK. Nevertheless Britain still falls short of the higher-level skill proportions in the United States and the intermediate-level skill proportions in Germany.

HUMAN CAPITAL AND PRODUCTIVITY

Broadberry (1998a) presents evidence that, between the end of the Second World War and the late 1960s, Britain retained an aggregate labour productivity lead over Germany and most other major West European economies, largely as a result of higher productivity in services. This can be linked, in turn, to higher-level training, particularly through the professional institutions. Furthermore, although there was a substantial US labour productivity lead at the aggregate level, this was largely the result of higher US productivity in industry, which owed more to natural resources and scale effects from mass-production technology than to human capital.

To what extent does this skill gap impact on Britain's relative productivity performance? O'Mahony and de Boer (2002) present traditional growth accounting estimates of the impact of labour force skills on relative labour productivity levels, which are shown in Table 5.7. Lower workforce skills in Britain are more important in explaining Britain's labour productivity deficits in 1979 than in 1999. But in both years the proportion of the productivity gaps accounted for by skills is considerably smaller than that due to physical capital or residual productivity. But the growth accounting calculation is likely to be misleading as it does not take account of external benefits from skill acquisition whereby the productivity of all workers is raised and not captured by any group of workers in the form of higher wage payments.

Details of the links between productivity and skills are shown in a series of studies, carried out over a number of years at the National Institute of Economic and Social Research (NIESR), London, comparing matched samples of production plants in Britain against those in competitor countries. Initially

Table 5.7   Relative total factor productivity, total economy

	US	France	Germany[a]
	(UK = 100)		
1979			
Labour productivity	154	131	130
TFP after adjusting for			
Physical capital	132	114	121
Physical capital and skills[b]	129	108	116
1999			
Labour productivity	130	129	117
TFP after adjusting for			
Physical capital	115	106	103
Physical capital and skills[b]	115	102	100

[a] Figures for 1979 refer to the former West Germany and for 1999 to the total unified Germany.
[b] Relative skill proportions from Table 5.5 were weighted by their relative remuneration and then multiplied by labour's share of value added.

Source: O'Mahony and de Boer (2002).

the studies compared British performance relative to that in continental European countries in branches of manufacturing including metalworking (Daly *et al.* 1985), woodworking (Steedman and Wagner 1987), clothing (Steedman and Wagner 1989) and food processing (Mason *et al.* 1994). These were also extended to cover a service sector, hotels (Prais *et al.* 1989) and to include comparisons with the United States (Mason and Finegold 1995, 1997). The comparisons were designed to reflect a range of industries with different average skill levels.

The mechanisms by which higher vocational skills in continental Europe raised productivity included a general ability to meet customers' specialised needs involving a considerably lower turnover time when changing production methods or changing to new product areas. Also higher skills among workers involved in machinery maintenance led to a lower rate of machinery breakdown and better adaptation of machinery to a plant's particular products. Better training amongst foremen and supervisors in continental Europe implied these workers took a much greater responsibility in many areas of production including work scheduling, stock control and selecting the most appropriate equipment. Generally, the greater amount of training enjoyed by workers in these countries led to greater flexibility and an altogether smoother operation of the production process than was found to be the case in British plants. In summarising the findings of the matched plant studies, Prais (1995) concludes that production today requires firms to produce a greater range of specialised products to meet the specialised needs of customers (flexible specialisation) and to do so on specialised machinery appropriate for small batches of variants. This requires greater skills in the choice of machinery, operating it effectively and maintaining it in good working order.

The matched plant comparisons involving European countries and the United States showed different mechanisms by which productivity is affected by skill. Production methods in the United States involve a largely unskilled general workforce combined with utilising a large proportion of graduates in managerial and technical roles. The matched-plant comparisons bring out some of the important mechanisms through which US productivity performance is indeed enhanced by the relative abundance of high-level skills. In particular, graduate manufacturing engineers play a key role in instigating incremental process innovations and improvements in US plants and, more generally, they represent key components of the traditional US mass-production system with prime responsibility for planning, assisting and improving the work of semi-skilled employees. Also the comparisons point to significant complementarities between physical capital and human capital assets which serve to raise productivity, as reflected in the role of highly qualified American engineers in selecting, installing and co-ordinating the use and maintenance of machinery (Mason and Finegold 1995, 1997).

There is evidence that the recent expansion of higher education in Britain has led to new ways of using graduates in directions approaching those employed in America. Mason (1995) examines the issue of the recruitment and utilisation of graduates, basing his observations on detailed studies of two sectors: steel production within manufacturing, and banks and building societies within financial services. The demand for graduates has been increasing in both sectors, partly reflecting a rising employment share of jobs which traditionally employed persons with high-level skills, such as those associated with the design and development of new products and information systems. But firms also have incentives to make use of the greater supply of graduates, creating new 'high-level' jobs.

In the steel industry, Mason (1995) found that graduates account for about one-third of new recruitment, which is large by historical standards. Most graduates employed by this industry have degrees in vocationally oriented subjects such as engineering, technology and business studies. He finds little evidence of under utilisation in this sector. New jobs were created to use the increased supply of graduates, and these involved graduate engineers more closely with day-to-day production either as production supervisors or with responsibility for the operation of highly specialised machinery. Clerical staff were also replaced by graduates who could 'take decisions' rather than mechanically follow procedures. Most graduates in steel continue to be employed in 'traditional' technical support functions such as product development but these jobs have also been changing in response to competitive pressures to diversify product mix and raise quality. The day-to-day contact between technical support and production departments has been increasing.

Hence in this one area of manufacturing the new graduates have been absorbed in a manner that has enhanced productivity. But manufacturing only uses a small proportion of graduates, the bulk of whom are employed in service activities. In the service sector examined by Mason, banks and building societies, the utilisation of the increased supply of graduates was less encouraging. Here there were essentially two streams of graduate recruitment, to traditional graduate jobs and some newly created jobs on the one hand, and on the other hand recruitment to jobs where a degree was not a formal requirement. Deregulation of the banking system has led banks and building societies to expand into more diversified financial services. This has led to an expansion of demand for graduates in traditional roles but has also increased the range of jobs where degrees are required.

On the other hand, many of the enterprises in the financial services sample reported that graduates make up an increasingly large share of applicants for jobs which have not traditionally required a degree and for which no salary premium is on offer. The larger banks and building societies were willing to take advantage of these new recruits, since they believed they worked more effectively than those with only high-school education, but did not feel that this extra productivity should be rewarded by higher pay. Smaller firms expressed more concern about the willingness of such graduates to stay in their firm in the long term. Mason estimates that as many as 45 per cent of new graduate recruits in financial services fell into the category of employees underutilising their skills, but recognises that this underutilisation was in some cases a temporary phenomenon.[2] Firms were looking increasingly at ways to utilise these skills and the graduates themselves were happy to get a foot in the door. In the steel sector, Mason finds little evidence of underutilisation of graduates.

In recent years a literature has emerged on the impact of new technology on demand for skilled workers. This stemmed largely from the observation that, throughout most of the 1970s and 1980s in the USA, the relative remuneration of workers with high-level skills (graduates and above) was increasing rapidly even though the supply of highly educated people was rising fast (Bound and Johnson 1992). Simple economic analysis suggested that demand must have been rising faster than supply at that time.

---

[2] Underutilisation as defined by Mason (1995) satisfies the following three requirements: (1) the job for which the graduate was employed was one where graduates had not traditionally been employed; (2) the job had not been substantially modified to take advantage of graduate-level skills; (3) there was no salary premium on offer to graduates relative to non-graduates.

The above observation induced researchers to examine more closely developments in technology which in turn led to a large number of papers which supported a skill-biased technological/organisational change explanation as the main determinant of changes in the skill structure (Autor *et al.* 1998; Berman *et al.* 1994; Machin and Van Reenen 1998). This hypothesis suggests that technological change can be more effectively implemented with the greater knowledge incorporated in a highly skilled labour force. Many studies have documented both skill-upgrading and the decline in employment of unskilled labour (e.g. Steiner and Mohr 2000). Much of the evidence for the skill-biased technical change hypothesis was based on industry-level data but micro/firm-level studies also supported these general findings (e.g. Bresnahan *et al.* 1999; Krueger 1993).

Over time the research in this area has linked the skill-biased technical change argument more tightly to developments in ICT technology. For example, based on evidence for the USA, Morrison, Paul and Siegel (2000) conclude that investments in computers increase the demand for workers with at least some college education while simultaneously reducing the demand for unskilled workers. In the UK, Haskel and Heden (1999) found that computerisation increased the demand for skilled workers in manufacturing.

In conclusion there are important channels through which differences in skill levels across countries impact on relative productivity levels and on Britain's ability to catch up with its competitors. This has been made all the more important in recent years with the possibility that fully embracing the new information technology is likely to require greater attention to human capital formation.

CONCLUSION

Since the late nineteenth century, education and training has been repeatedly cited as a weakness of the British economy. And yet, Britain still had high aggregate productivity by European standards at the end of the Second World War, and was not overtaken by most West European countries before the late 1960s. This apparent paradox is explained by the fact that Britain's aggregate productivity lead did not reflect high productivity in industry, but rather a smaller agricultural sector and high productivity in services (Broadberry 1998a). This meant that until the 1970s, when Britain began to lag in terms of overall productivity, calls for the reform of the education and training system, based largely on evidence from industry, could be resisted.

The reforms of the 1980s and the 1990s have led to a massive increase in education and training in Britain, at both intermediate and higher levels. However, because education and training is concentrated on the young, it will take a generation or more to make up the shortfall in higher-level skills with respect to the United States, and the shortfall in intermediate-level skills with respect to Germany. Although Britain's productivity performance during the 1980s and the 1990s has stemmed relative decline, it has not led to a dramatic improvement. This is understandable, however, once it is recognised that it takes a long time even for large increases in the flow of trained workers to affect the stock of human capital. It will therefore be some time before Britain compensates for decades of under-investment in human capital.

6

Money and monetary policy since 1945

SUSAN HOWSON

Contents

INTRODUCTION

In the years since the Second World War the role of money, and the use of monetary policy, has been peculiarly subject to the whims of intellectual fashion in economic thought, in Britain as elsewhere. At the outset the most commonly held view among British economists was that 'money does not matter (much)' for maintaining high employment, fostering economic growth or controlling inflation. By the 1970s, however, monetary policy had become a major issue in public policy debate; under Mrs Thatcher in the 1980s it became front page news. The 'monetarist' view that money matters a lot especially so far as inflation is concerned had come to dominate among economists and policy makers. The objectives of monetary policy have also changed, from facilitating government borrowing at low interest rates to supporting a fixed exchange rate and then to combating inflation with a floating exchange rate, to exchange-rate stability and back to price stability.

The monetary history to be described here runs from the nationalisation of the Bank of England by the first majority Labour government in 1945–6 to the restoration, by another Labour government, of operational independence to the Bank in 1997–8. For the purposes of this chapter it is divided into four periods: (i) the immediate post-war policies of the 1945–51 Labour governments under Prime Minister Clement Attlee, when the 'Keynesian' downgrading of monetary policy was still in the ascendant; (ii) the 1950s Conservative governments' 'revival' of monetary policy which, in spite of confused aims and uncertain methods, effectively reassigned it to the preservation of external balance with a fixed exchange rate; (iii) the 1970s and early 1980s, which saw new attempts at monetary control in 'competition and credit control', the adoption of monetary targets (that is, announced targets for the rate of growth of the money supply somehow defined) and the medium-term financial strategy of Mrs Thatcher's first government; and (iv) another reorientation of monetary policy after the abandonment of monetary targets, first towards exchange-rate stability and then back to price stability by means of inflation targeting. In each period the major policy changes reflected, with a lag, changes in Britain's external monetary arrangements: the increasing openness of the UK economy after 1947, in spite of the failure of that year's attempt to restore convertibility of sterling into dollars, and the adjustment to post-war realities in the devaluation of the pound from US\$4.03 to \$2.80 in 1949; the achievement of general convertibility of previously inconvertible European currencies in 1958 which ushered in the operation of the Bretton Woods system; the mounting difficulties of Bretton Woods which included a second post-war devaluation of the pound (to US\$2.40) in 1967 and its floating in 1972; the abolition in October 1979 of the remnants of the comprehensive exchange controls introduced in 1939; and the UK's short-lived membership of the exchange rate mechanism of the European Monetary System in 1990–2.

The next section of this chapter provides a simplified description of the changing theoretical views lying behind the conduct of British monetary policy since 1945. It also uses a simple model to illustrate the external factors that impinge upon domestic monetary policy and often restrict its operations. The section first briefly discusses the definition of the money supply and the methods of controlling it. The following section outlines the conduct of British monetary policy in the four periods mentioned above. The final section suggests some conclusions, especially in relation to Britain's experience of inflation since 1945.

THEORY

In a modern capitalist economy the supply of money, used for making payments and in final settlement of debts, consists of currency (notes and coin) in circulation with the public and bank deposits. (Credit cards provide credit, not money, because they do not finally extinguish debts.) The money supply can be defined in different ways depending on the categories of bank deposits included. A narrow definition, M1, covers currency and demand (sight) sterling bank deposits held by the private sector. In the years of monetary targets the preferred official definition was M3, which included 'all deposits, whether denominated in sterling or non-sterling currency, held with the UK banking sector by UK residents in both the public and private sectors, together with notes and coin in circulation with the public', or £M3, which was the same aggregate minus residents' foreign-currency deposits. In 1987 these were renamed M3c and M3 respectively. Since 1987 the preferred measure has been M4, which along with notes and coin includes the sterling deposit liabilities of all UK banks and building societies to other private sector UK residents (Bank of England 1970: 320–1, 1987c: 212, 214).

The monetary base (M0) is the total of currency in the hands of the non-bank public and the cash reserves of the banking system (partly currency but mainly deposits with the Bank of England). In *principle*, the central bank (Bank of England) controls the supply of reserves to the banks, and if the supply is increased (decreased) then, since banks hold reserves equal to only a fraction of their deposits, this will have a multiplier effect on bank lending and hence bank deposits and the money supply. In practice, the Bank of England has always disliked the idea of 'monetary base control' and preferred to influence banks' behaviour by altering short-term interest rates (on, say, Treasury bills) and the rate at which it is prepared to *lend* cash reserves to the discount houses and hence the banking system, a rate traditionally known as 'Bank rate'. (Discount houses were specialist financial institutions, who borrowed at very short term (on call) from UK banks and invested in short-term bills, especially British government Treasury bills.) If the Bank raises these rates then banks' willingness to lend should be reduced given the increased cost of acquiring additional reserves to support deposit expansion. Monetary *policy* includes all central bank attempts to influence the money supply directly (e.g. by controlling the monetary base) or indirectly (i.e. via changing those interest rates which the central bank can easily influence). 'Open-market operations' by the Bank, such as purchases of Treasury bills from the public, will reduce the supply and hence lower the interest rates on Treasury bills, as well as increasing bank reserves. The monetary authorities' intervention in the gilt-edged market – purchases or sales of marketable British government securities as distinct from Treasury bills which are part of the 'floating debt' – whether undertaken for monetary policy reasons or as part of the management of the national debt, will also alter interest rates and the supply of money.

The monetarist–Keynesian debate over the effectiveness of monetary policy can be described in terms of the well known IS-LM model, in which the debate was initially, though unrealistically, conducted. Until the 1960s many (but not all) 'Keynesian' economists assumed domestic monetary policy had little impact on aggregate demand and hence output and employment. This followed from their view of the 'transmission mechanism' of monetary policy: that a change in monetary conditions engineered by a central bank would influence demand through nominal interest rates on bank advances and on financial assets which were alternatives to investment in real assets. This meant that monetary policy primarily influenced firms' investment rather than consumers' expenditure, and investment decisions were also thought to be rather insensitive to changes in interest rates. Thus the demand for money was fairly elastic with respect to the nominal rate of interest and investment relatively interest-inelastic, making for a flat LM curve and a steep IS curve.

An increase in the nominal money supply, shifting the LM curve to the right, produces a large fall in nominal interest rates but only a small rise in income (Figure 6.1). An expansionary *fiscal* policy, on the other hand, which increases aggregate demand either directly by increasing government expenditure or through reduced taxation, has a large impact on income and employment in this framework (Figure 6.2).

A more realistic variant, to be found implicitly in the Radcliffe Report (Radcliffe Committee 1959), argued that the Bank of England did not control the money supply which accommodated itself to money demand generated by the level of economic activity and nominal income and the level of interest rates (which were influenced by the Bank's actions). Then the LM curve was essentially horizontal. Again, this made for relative ineffectiveness of monetary policy compared with fiscal policy.

In the 1960s the monetarists led by Milton Friedman of the University of Chicago challenged the 'Keynesian' view as seriously underestimating the potency of monetary policy, by taking too narrow a view of the transmission mechanism and by neglecting the contribution of monetary expansion to price inflation. Whereas the Keynesians described the demand for nominal money balances as a function of nominal income and a representative interest rate on those *financial* assets regarded as alternatives to money, the monetarists argued that the demand for money was a demand for real balances (M/P), dependent on real income (Y), wealth and the expected rates of return on a wide range of financial and real assets (including housing and consumer durables, for instance). The rates of return would themselves depend on, amongst other things, the expected rate of price changes. The proportion of real income held as real money balances was fairly stable in the short run, so that the elasticity of money demand with respect to interest rates could be regarded as low. A change in the real money stock could therefore affect firms and household demands for real assets 'directly' rather than just through changes in interest rates on financial assets. In the IS-LM model the IS curve is then relatively flat and the LM curve relatively steep; monetary policy is a more powerful instrument for influencing aggregate demand than fiscal policy (Figures 6.3 and 6.4).

Moreover, expansionary monetary policy can only increase real income and employment when unemployment is above the 'natural' rate of

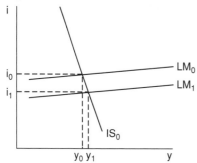

Figure 6.1

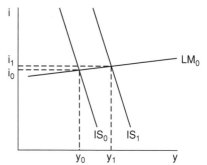

Figure 6.2

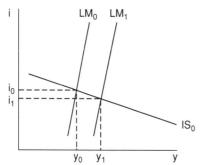

Figure 6.3

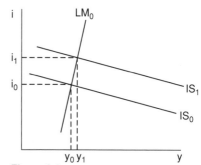

Figure 6.4

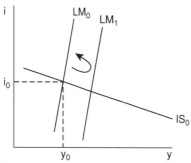

Figure 6.5

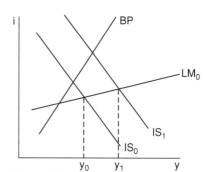

Figure 6.6

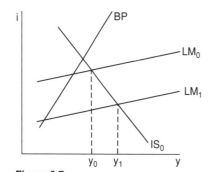

Figure 6.7

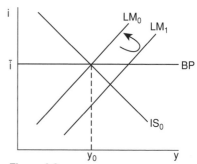

Figure 6.8

i interest rate   y real income

Figures 6.1 to 6.8 Different formulations of the IS-LM model

unemployment determined by demographic and social factors and in-stitutional arrangements in the labour market. If aggregate demand is boosted too much it will raise prices rather than real output; and if the authorities persist in trying to raise output the inflation will not only per-sist but will come to be anticipated, to be reflected in wage bargains, and to accelerate. (The so-called natural rate of unemployment is thus better known as the non-accelerating inflation rate of unemployment, NAIRU; see chapter 5 above). In IS-LM terms, rising prices caused by an increase in the nominal money supply when the natural rate of unemployment prevails and real output cannot be increased other than temporarily, will reduce the real value of the money supply, shifting LM leftwards (Figure 6.5) – unless there is a continuous and accelerating expansion of the nominal money supply, when inflation will also continue at an accelerating rate. (Fiscal policy can also not reduce unemployment other than temporarily above the NAIRU, but if an expansionary fiscal policy is *not* accompanied by monetary expansion the inflation cannot continue indefinitely.)

This is a crude characterisation of the monetarist–Keynesian debate in the 1960s and early 1970s. It is crude for at least two reasons: (1) as the debate itself implies the IS-LM model is inadequate for discussing the causes and consequences of inflation; (2) the external constraints on domestic monetary policy have been ignored. The model can, however, be used to illustrate the external constraints.

The balance of payments (B) of a small open economy can be written as

$$B = pX(ep^*/p) - ep^*M(Y, ep^*/p) + K(i, i^*)$$

where p and p^* represent domestic and foreign prices and e the nominal exchange rate (domestic currency, e.g. pounds, per unit of foreign cur-rency, e.g. dollars), so that ep^*/p is the *real* exchange rate; X and M are the volumes of exports and imports of goods and services, so that $pX - ep^*M$ is the current account of the balance of payments; and K stands for net capital flows, whose short-term behaviour is largely determined by interest rates at home and abroad (i, i^*). The combinations of real income and domestic interest rates which produce 'external balance' (B = 0) given the levels of the other variables can be added to the IS-LM diagram; the line will be flatter the freer international capital movements are to respond to changes in relative interest rates.

This expanded IS-LM model, usually known as the Mundell–Fleming model after Mundell (1962, 1963) and Fleming (1962), implies the effec-tiveness of domestic monetary and fiscal policy depends on the exchange rate regime as well as the degree of international capital mobility. With fixed exchange rates, which the UK enjoyed from 1945 to 1972, and a low degree of capital mobility (which may have prevailed until the later 1950s), the use of monetary policy to increase income would have the disadvantage of producing a larger balance-of-payments deficit than a fiscal policy with the same effect on income (Figures 6.6 and 6.7; the vertical distance of the intersection of IS and LM from the external balance line BP measures the increase in domestic interest rates necessary to bring about external balance and hence the size of the deficit).

A balance-of-payments deficit with fixed exchange rates will oblige the monetary authorities to sell foreign currency in exchange for pounds in order to maintain the value of the pound; hence UK official international reserves (of US dollars and other foreign currencies) will decline. The exchange-market intervention will reduce the money supply unless the Bank takes offsetting action by, for instance, buying Treasury bills from the non-bank private sector. If international capital mobility is high the running down of international reserves necessary to maintain a fixed exchange rate will be large and may be unsustainable, since reserves are not infinite. Also the size of the reserve changes may be too large for the authorities to 'sterilise' their effects on the money supply. In the limit, with 'perfect capital mobility', monetary policy is powerless to influence income (Figure 6.8). If interest rates fall below i, because of an expansionary monetary policy, there will be a massive capital outflow and fall in official international reserves: the money supply would fall back, interest rates would return to i, and income would be unchanged at y_0.

With flexible exchange rates, which the UK resorted to in 1972, monetary policy independence can be regained. A balance-of-payments deficit does not require a fall in reserves or sterilisation of the effect of a fall in reserves on the money supply. Furthermore, with high international capital mobility as we have had since the 1960s, monetary policy becomes *more* powerful than fiscal policy in its effects on the domestic economy, regardless of Keynesian–monetarist considerations. A fall in interest rates due to an expansionary monetary policy will both directly increase aggregate demand and depreciate the exchange rate. Unless domestic prices rise immediately a fall in the real exchange rate (ep^*/p) will increase exports of goods and services and reduce imports of goods and services, thus further increasing aggregate demand as well as offsetting the balance-of-payments deficit caused by the capital outflow. (This statement ignores lags in the response of the current account to exchange-rate changes but the principle nonetheless holds.)

The increased effectiveness of monetary policy under floating exchange rates is not an unmixed blessing: expansionary monetary policy can be particularly damaging to the domestic economy because of the increased possibilities of generating inflation if output and employment cannot respond sufficiently to increased demand. By the same token, however, restrictive monetary policy becomes a more powerful anti-inflationary weapon under floating exchange rates when an exchange-rate appreciation will reduce aggregate demand and reduce the domestic-currency price of imports, a major item in the retail price index.

Discussion of inflation goes beyond the confines of the essentially Keynesian Mundell–Fleming model. On the other hand the original monetarist attack on the Keynesian model ignored the external sector of the economy. The 'monetary theory of the balance of payments', developed in the early 1970s, by Harry Johnson (of the University of Chicago and the London School of Economics) among others, rectified this shortcoming. A small open economy in a global financial and trading system has to adapt to both interest rates set in international financial markets and the world prices of internationally traded goods. Under fixed exchange rates domestic interest rates will have to be kept in line with foreign interest rates (for otherwise capital flows would, through their impact on the domestic money supply, bring them back in line) and domestic prices will also largely reflect world prices. An unduly expansionary monetary policy will show up not in increased inflation but in a balance-of-payments deficit until the rate of monetary expansion is cut back (hence the '*monetary* theory of the *balance of payments*'). As the Mundell–Fleming model with perfect capital mobility also implies, there is no scope for an independent monetary policy under fixed exchange rates.

The monetary theory also implies that if a country with a balance-of-payments deficit under fixed exchange rates devalues its currency to try to eliminate the deficit, any improvement will only be temporary without a reduction in the rate of monetary growth. Older, more 'Keynesian' theories, such as the absorption approach (Alexander 1952; Johnson 1958), would agree that devaluation, in conditions of high employment such as the late 1940s and the 1960s, would not cure a deficit without a reduction in domestic demand, but they did not imply that the instrument of demand reduction would have to be monetary.

Other developments in macroeconomic theory in the later 1970s were to bear fruit in UK monetary policy only in the 1990s. Following the rational expectations revolution, formal recognition of the problem of time inconsistency in optimal policy led to new arguments for rules versus discretion in monetary policy, from Kydland and Prescott (1977) onwards. Friedman (1967) had argued for a consistent policy of maintaining a steady rate of growth of a specified monetary aggregate largely on the grounds of ignorance and uncertainties in decision-making, especially of the long and variable lags in the effect of monetary policy. Now it could be shown that even if the government and the public knew the structure of the economy, shared the same objectives and preferences, and formed expectations rationally, discretionary monetary policy could generate excessive inflation (Kydland and Prescott 1977; Barro and Gordon 1983). More realistically, it can be assumed that the public have *some* knowledge of policy makers' likely reactions to changed circumstances and that they will build this into their expectations of future economic variables, such as inflation rates, on which their own behaviour depends. Governments may often be tempted to exploit the short-run trade-off between unemployment and inflation and to boost aggregate demand to increase output and employment, and they can succeed temporarily while inflation is higher than anticipated. But when people are aware of this pattern of behaviour the gaps between actual and expected inflation will be short-lived. A government that regularly tried to maximise employment in the short run would on average produce more inflation but no more employment than one that did not yield to temptation; hence the optimal policy for each short period is not the best policy over the longer run. One way out of this inconsistency is for the monetary authorities to pre-commit to a policy of price stability. The problem then becomes how to make that commitment credible.

With these theoretical considerations as background, we can turn to the monetary policy practised by the UK monetary authorities (the Treasury and the Bank of England) since 1945.

POLICY

The monetary policies of the 1945–1951 Labour governments

The Second World War left Britain with a balance-of-payments deficit on current account equivalent to over one-sixth of her national income (which was just under £10,000m), a central government budget deficit of about the same size, and a national debt more than double national income (Feinstein 1972: tabs. 3 and 12; Pember and Boyle 1950: 447). With wartime exchange controls in force, the UK economy was *financially* closed, with low international capital mobility. This had allowed the government to maintain cheap money (that is, low nominal interest rates) throughout the war, with Bank rate at 2 per cent, the rate of interest on Treasury bills fixed at 1 per cent, and nominal yields on gilt-edged government securities ranging from $1\frac{3}{4}$ per cent for bonds with five years to maturity to 3 per cent for those with maturities of twenty years or more (see Sayers 1956: chs. 5 and 7). The money supply (M3) had doubled during the war and there had been a large increase in the amount of short-term government debt held by the banks and the non-bank private sector, but direct controls had prevented serious open inflation. In 1945 government officials and economists, including Lord Keynes, James Meade and Lionel Robbins, recommended the retention of cheap money and direct controls for at least a transitional period after the war. Their advice reflected widespread anticipations of a post-war slump like that which followed the First World War, recognition that relying on high nominal interest rates (dear money) to restrain inflation without controls would substantially increase the interest cost of the large post-war national debt, and, to a lesser extent, scepticism as to the influence of interest rates on private sector expenditure (Howson 1987: 438–41, 1993: 45–54).

The first post-war Labour chancellor of the exchequer, Hugh Dalton, tried, however, to go further and to *lower* nominal interest rates on government debt after the war. He lowered the fixed Treasury bill rate to $\frac{1}{2}$ per cent in October 1945 and then during 1946 issued two long-term securities yielding only $2\frac{1}{2}$ per cent at the time of issue. (The second issue, $2\frac{1}{2}$ per cent Treasury Stock 1975 or after, has always been nicknamed 'Daltons'.) Success in this extraordinary endeavour was short-lived. Nominal yields on long-term government securities returned to their war-time 3 per cent during 1947, once the authorities stopped buying in long-term government securities to keep up their market prices. This intervention caused a very rapid expansion in bank deposits (and hence the money supply: Figure 6.9), creating expectations of higher nominal interest rates. The 'cheaper money policy' was effectively abandoned early in 1947, well before the 'convertibility crisis' of the summer (Howson 1987: 441–50, 1993: 121–45).

The Labour government had attempted to cope with the balance-of-payments problem by seeking large-scale financial assistance from the US and Canadian governments. Under the Anglo-American Financial Agreement of December 1945 it was committed to restore convertibility of sterling into US dollars (in principle only for current transactions) by 15 July 1947. The crisis erupted when it tried to fulfil the commitment. The loss of international reserves which prompted the suspension of convertibility after less than six weeks on 20 August was caused by an increased UK current account deficit, by a current account deficit in the rest of the sterling area and by capital movements permitted by the exchange controls (Cairncross 1985: ch. 6). The cheaper money policy contributed, however, to the excessive domestic demand which produced the deterioration in the UK current account in 1947 (Howson 1993: 176–90). (This view differs from the earlier views of, say, Kennedy 1952: 193–5, and Dow 1964: 21–2, that the cheap money policy had little effect because it was short-lived and because investment was subject to controls; they reflect the Keynesian view of the transmission mechanism which relies on the interest-elasticity of investment.)

The reason for the 'cheaper money' policy was not so much a belief that monetary policy was unimportant as the choice of a particular assignment of policy instruments. Dalton thought that immediate post-war inflation could be kept at bay by controls and was more concerned to prevent unemployment in the anticipated post-war slump. He believed the current balance-of-payments problem could be contained by the US Loan and that the existing exchange controls *completely* insulated the domestic monetary system from external influences. His Treasury and Bank of England advisers also feared a severe post-war slump and saw the advantages to the budget of low nominal interest rates on government debt (Howson 1987, 1988, 1989, 1993: ch. 3).

Dalton resigned as chancellor in November 1947 after inadvertently leaking the contents of an autumn budget. By then he had begun a 'disinflationary' budgetary policy which his austere successor,

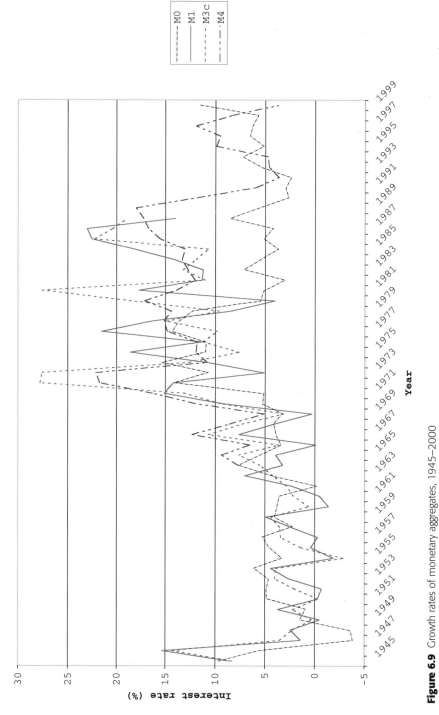

Figure 6.9 Growth rates of monetary aggregates, 1945–2000

Source: M0 1945–69: calculated from Capie and Webber (1985: tabs. I(1) and III(2)).
M0 1970–99: Bank of England, *Statistical Abstract*, various years.
M1 and M3c 1945–62: Capie and Webber (1985: tabs. I(2) I(2) and I(3)).
M1 and M3c 1963–90: *Bank of England Quarterly Bulletin*, various years.
M4 1964–99: Bank of England, *Statistical Abstract*, various years.

Sir Stafford Cripps, retained for the next three years. Monetary policy was a relatively passive accompaniment (Dow 1964: 48–9, 227–30). While Bank rate stayed at 2 per cent and the fixed Treasury bill rate at $\frac{1}{2}$ per cent, nominal yields on longer-term government bonds crept up to 4 per cent by 1951. The money supply (M3) grew slowly (at about 2 per cent a year instead of the annual rates in excess of 10 per cent experienced in 1946 and during the war: Figure 6.9), so that with prices rising slightly faster real money balances were declining. Since rising bank lending tended to offset the effect of government budget surpluses on the money supply, the clearing banks were from time to time ineffectually 'requested' by the chancellor of the exchequer via the governor of the Bank of England to moderate the growth of their advances.

Behind this inactivity lay a prolonged dispute between ministers, Treasury officials and the Bank of England about the use of monetary policy. The government side wanted in one way or another, but preferably without raising *short-term* interest rates and hence the cost of the floating debt, to control the growth of bank deposits as a contribution to the policy of disinflation. The Bank wanted to restore the traditional weapons of monetary policy, especially the variability of Bank rate and short-term money market interest rates, and hence its own pre-war position in the UK monetary system (Howson 1991, 1993: ch. 5; Fforde 1992: ch. 5(g) and (h)). The new governor of the Bank, C. F. Cobbold, opened his campaign during the balance-of-payments crisis which preceded the devaluation in September 1949. (On the devaluation see Cairncross 1985: ch. 7; Fforde 1992: ch. 4(e).) Although some government officials, especially Robert Hall, the director of the Economic Section, were prepared to see higher nominal interest rates, Cobbold lost his opportunity – partly because he also wanted large government expenditure cuts as a way of avoiding a devaluation and partly because he could not convince the Treasury that a small rise in the rate of interest on Treasury bills would produce a reduction in monetary growth sufficient to justify the increased interest cost to the budget (Howson 1991, 1993: ch. 4; Fforde 1992: 373–7; see also Hall 1989). There was no significant change in monetary stance to accompany the 30 per cent devaluation, merely another call for the bankers to restrain their lending.

After Hugh Gaitskell succeeded the ailing Cripps as chancellor in October 1950, the dispute over monetary control was rekindled, fanned by the inflationary pressures arising out of British rearmament and worldwide commodity price inflation during the Korean War. Gaitskell wished to pursue a more deflationary policy but he was reluctant to increase the cost of the floating debt and Cobbold would countenance no tightening of monetary stance without some movement in the fixed Treasury bill rate (Howson 1993: ch. 6; Fforde 1992: 387–94). The Bank rejected quantitative direct controls on bank assets or liabilities as administratively impossible. The authorities began, however, to 'fund' the floating debt,

Table 6.1   Market holdings of UK national debt, 1945–2000, selected dates, by maturity, as % of total market holdings[a] at 31 March

	1945	1952	1957	1969	1979	1990	2000
Treasury bills[b]	26.1	12.5	12.9	13.4	3.4	5.9	1.2
Stocks							
Up to 5 years to final maturity	7.6	15.6	18.1[c]	19.9	26.7	20.3	24.7
Over 5 years and up to 15 years	15.5	11.1	19.4[c]		15.5	30.3	30.5
				42.2			
Over 15 years and undated	33.4	44.8	34.6		36.3	19.7	20.5
Other[d]	17.3	16.0	15.0	24.5	18.1	23.8	23.1
Total market holdings	100.0	100.0	100.0	100.0	100.0	100.0	100.0

[a] Market holdings = total outstanding *minus* official holdings by Bank of England, government departments and the National Debt Commissioners; hence they include holdings of overseas residents, including overseas official holders.
[b] Includes Treasury Deposit Receipts in 1945.
[c] Includes holdings of Exchange Equalization Account and Banking Department of Bank of England.
[d] Includes national savings securities.

Sources: Calculated from: ONS, 'Exchequer financing and national debt, 1945–51', *Economic Trends*, December 1961, tabs. 2b, 3 and 4; Radcliffe Committee on the Working of the Monetary System (1960: I, 56, 111, 125); 'Distribution of the national debt: March 1969', *Bank of England Quarterly Bulletin* 10 (March 1970), tab. C; 'Distribution of the national debt at end-March 1979', *Bank of England Quarterly Bulletin* 19 (December 1979), tab. B; 'The net debt of the public sector: end-March 1990', *Bank of England Quarterly Bulletin* 30 (November 1990), tab. H.

that is, to replace it by longer-term securities, a habit that persisted for three decades (Table 6.1).

In the 1940s the Bank of England exercised no control over the monetary base. It supplied the banks with sufficient reserves for them to take up each week the quantity of floating debt desired by the government while maintaining a constant ratio of reserves to deposits (8 per cent for the London clearing banks from December 1946). If the Bank had not done so the banks could have replenished their reserves anyway for the fixed Treasury bill rate was maintained by the authorities' willingness to buy in bills from the discount houses at that rate. Bank rate was ineffective and the banks were always able easily and cheaply to acquire additional reserves to support additional lending. Any serious attempt to limit monetary growth would have to close the 'open back door' to the Bank of England as well as to allow more movement in interest rates.

The revival of monetary policy

A Conservative government was elected in October 1951, during another acute balance-of-payments crisis. The new chancellor of the exchequer, R. A. Butler, announced a rise in Bank rate to $2\frac{1}{2}$ per cent on 7 November in a package of emergency measures (mainly cuts in imports which were still subject to controls). Although most economists now favoured higher interest rates (Dow 1964: 67–9; Howson 1988: 562–3; Hall 1989: 168–221), it is not clear that the new administration knew what to expect from higher short-term rates. (The remarks about official intentions in the next seven paragraphs are based mainly on unpublished papers in the Public Record Office.)

From the Bank's point of view what was important was the introduction of a new rate of 2 per cent at which the discount houses could borrow from the Bank against Treasury bills, the closing of the Bank's 'open back door', and a special funding issue of £1,000m short-term bonds to replace outstanding Treasury bills (which totalled £5,000m), which reduced the clearing banks' liquid assets from 39 to 32 per cent of their deposits. The Bank hoped that the banks, which had kept their liquid assets ratio around 30 per cent before the war, would not let the ratio fall significantly below 30 per cent, but for most of the 1950s it was comfortably above that conventional minimum. There was also a further request to the banks on their advances in late November 1951. A new instrument, restrictions on the terms of hire purchase lending, which had been in preparation for some months, was added in February 1952. (For details see Johnson 1952 and Fforde 1992: 398–411.) The governor of the Bank told the permanent secretary of the Treasury, Sir Edward Bridges, that these measures would 'necessarily be experimental'.

The Bank rate increase had little impact on the exchange rate, and a 'crisis' rise to 4 per cent, with a corresponding rise in the operative lender-of-last-resort rate to $3\frac{1}{2}$ per cent, was announced in March 1952. The balance of payments turned round dramatically thanks to an improvement in the terms of trade as import prices fell and to the beginnings of recession at home (Dow 1964: 73–4; Cairncross 1985: 255–6, 266–7). The recession also reduced the private sector's demands for bank loans, but the authorities succumbed to the temptation to attribute the rapid fall in advances to their monetary measures and thus overestimated the impact of changes in short-term money market interest rates (Cairncross 1987: 11–13).

In September 1953 Bank rate was reduced to $3\frac{1}{2}$ per cent and the special rate for borrowing against Treasury bills introduced in November 1951 was merged with it, so that Bank rate became again the effective rate for last-resort lending to the discount market. (For a list of changes in Bank rate up to its abolition in 1972 see Table 6.2.) When the balance of payments went into deficit again, the authorities hoped to repeat their favourable 1952 experience with monetary policy. A 'package' of measures in February 1955, intended both to curb domestic demand and to support sterling externally, included a 1 per cent Bank rate rise (following a $\frac{1}{2}$ per cent rise in January) and the reimposition of hire purchase restrictions which had been lifted in July 1954. Since Butler went on to introduce an expansionary budget in April 1955, 'To a cold eye it may seem that he was relying on monetary policy to work wonders' (Dow 1964: 79). Further measures had to be taken: in July 1955 a request to the bankers for a 'positive and significant reduction in their advances over the next few

Table 6.2 Bank rate changes, 1951–1972					
Date of change	Amount of change	New rate, %	Date of change	Amount of change	New rate, %
1951 8 November	$+\frac{1}{2}$	$2\frac{1}{2}$	1962 8 March	$-\frac{1}{2}$	$5\frac{1}{2}$
1952 12 March	$+1\frac{1}{2}$	4	22 March	$-\frac{1}{2}$	5
1953 17 September	$-\frac{1}{2}$	$3\frac{1}{2}$	26 April	$-\frac{1}{2}$	$4\frac{1}{2}$
1954 13 May	$-\frac{1}{2}$	3	1963 3 January	$-\frac{1}{2}$	4
1955 27 January	$+\frac{1}{2}$	$3\frac{1}{2}$	1964 27 February	$+1$	5
24 February	$+1$	$4\frac{1}{2}$	23 November	$+2$	7
1956 16 February	$+1$	$5\frac{1}{2}$	1965 3 June	-1	6
1957 7 February	$-\frac{1}{2}$	5	14 July	$+1$	7
19 September	$+2$	7	1967 26 January	$-\frac{1}{2}$	$6\frac{1}{2}$
1958 20 March	-1	6	16 March	$-\frac{1}{2}$	6
22 May	$-\frac{1}{2}$	$5\frac{1}{2}$	4 May	$-\frac{1}{2}$	$5\frac{1}{2}$
19 June	$-\frac{1}{2}$	5	19 October	$+\frac{1}{2}$	6
14 August	$-\frac{1}{2}$	$4\frac{1}{2}$	9 November	$+\frac{1}{2}$	$6\frac{1}{2}$
20 November	$-\frac{1}{2}$	4	18 November	$+1\frac{1}{2}$	8
1960 21 January	$+1$	5	1968 21 March	$-\frac{1}{2}$	$7\frac{1}{2}$
23 June	$+1$	6	19 September	$-\frac{1}{2}$	7
27 October	$-\frac{1}{2}$	$5\frac{1}{2}$	1969 27 February	$+1$	8
8 December	$-\frac{1}{2}$	5	1970 5 March	$-\frac{1}{2}$	$7\frac{1}{2}$
1961 26 July	$+2$	7	15 April	$-\frac{1}{2}$	7
5 October	$-\frac{1}{2}$	$6\frac{1}{2}$	1971 1 April	-1	6
2 November	$-\frac{1}{2}$	6	2 September	-1	5
			1972 22 June	$+1$	6

months', an autumn budget, another Bank rate rise in February 1956, and further requests to the bankers (Radcliffe Committee 1959: paras. 415–22; Cairncross 1987: 14–17; Fforde 1992: ch. 10; see also Smith and Mikesell 1957).

The Treasury was now disillusioned with the Bank's claims for traditional monetary policy. One consequence was the resort to quantitative direct controls which the Bank had previously rejected. The July 1955 request to the bankers has been seen as the first step (Radcliffe Committee 1959: para. 417), but it was only a little one. The Treasury wished the chancellor's request to include a figure of 10 per cent for the desired reduction in bank advances, but the governor of the Bank refused. After his conversations with the bankers' representatives, however, they agreed amongst themselves to aim for a 10 per cent reduction by the end of the year. Bank advances fell by about 8 per cent in the second half of 1955, but rose again by a similar amount in the first half of 1956 (Cairncross 1987: 16–17; Fforde 1992: 637–40). In July 1956 and again in March 1957 (after a reduction in Bank rate in February!) new requests were made to the bankers, this time in person, by new chancellors of the exchequer (Harold Macmillan and Peter Thorneycroft respectively) but they did not include specific amounts, again because of the Bank's objections.

On 9 April 1957 Thorneycroft announced the setting up of the Radcliffe Committee on the Working of the Monetary System. During its deliberations another sterling crisis blew up: Bank rate jumped in one step from 5 to 7 per cent (its highest rate for thirty-six years) on 19 September 1957 and the chancellor asked the banks explicitly to reduce their advances to the 'average level of the last twelve months'. Thorneycroft wanted to go further and call for a 5 per cent cut in advances. He was frustrated by the governor's refusal to ask this of the banks and annoyed by his officials' apparent acceptance of the resulting limited possibilities of monetary control (Hall 1991: 124–8; Fforde 1992: 676–86). In January 1958 he resigned over his Cabinet colleagues' unwillingness to take stronger deflationary measures, and there was a subsequent cautious easing of monetary policy under his successor Heathcoat Amory (Dow 1964: 96–106). Thorneycroft, advised by Lionel Robbins, has been seen as an early convert to 'monetarism'; whether or not this is true, his resignation showed that official opinion was not yet ready for it, as the Radcliffe Report soon demonstrated. (To add to the excitement there were allegations of a 'leak' before the September Bank rate change and an official inquiry into them.)

The Bank of England claimed in its evidence to the Radcliffe Committee that existing techniques of monetary control were adequate since the banks voluntarily adhered to a cash reserve ratio of 8 per cent and a conventional minimum liquid assets ratio of 30 per cent (Radcliffe Committee 1960: I, 9–10). It considered some 'alternative techniques', however, one of which it found less objectionable than the others; in light of the previous few years' experience, the Treasury supported this 'special deposits' scheme (Radcliffe Committee 1960: I, 38–42, 120–1). The chancellor announced the new scheme, under which the Bank could call for special interest-bearing deposits from the clearing banks to reduce their liquidity, on 3 July 1958, without waiting for the Radcliffe Report. The first calls for special deposits were made in April and June 1960 (Dow 1964: 240–2).

Since 1951, monetary policy had been influenced at critical points by the authorities' gradual but hesitant movements towards the convertibility of sterling. Monetary policy was also constrained by their preoccupation with the problems of debt management. In February 1952 the Bank of England and the Overseas Finance Division of the Treasury launched their notorious 'ROBOT' plan, under which the pound would be made convertible immediately but with a floating exchange rate and blocking of some of the large sterling balances held by Britain's overseas official creditors. Although ROBOT was effectively shot down by Robert Hall and his allies in Whitehall (Cairncross 1985: ch. 9; MacDougall 1987: ch. 5; Plowden 1989: ch. 14; Hall 1989: 202–33; Fforde 1992: ch. 6(b)), its advocates, especially the governor of the Bank, continued to urge early convertibility, usually with a floating exchange rate. In the 'collective approach' to convertibility discussed at several Commonwealth conferences from December 1952 and with the American administration in 1953, the major currencies would have become convertible simultaneously with the help of a support fund from the USA. The only short-term result was to feed rumours which weakened sterling in the foreign exchange markets and obliged successive chancellors to disclaim all intentions of letting sterling float (Dow 1964: 80–90, 97–8, 106–8; Fforde 1992: ch. 7). It is not surprising that Bank rate changes were directed increasingly towards external balance. Sterling became freely convertible – but only for non-residents – in December 1958.

The governor of the Bank told the Radcliffe Committee that 'it has been the continuous need to raise finance to meet overall Government requirements . . . which, coupled with the refinancing of maturing Government loans, has made the monetary situation so difficult' (Radcliffe Committee 1960: I, 3–4, see also 22–32). The Treasury pointed to 'the perennial possibility of conflict in the aims of monetary policy' created by the need to fund the debt (Radcliffe Committee 1960: I, 95). There were three related aspects of the debt problem. First, there was the need to sell debt to cover both new borrowing, by nationalised industries and local authorities as well as by central government, and the repayment of maturing debt. Second, there was the funding of floating debt, which was desired mainly for monetary policy reasons, specifically to keep down the liquidity of the banks (Radcliffe Committee 1960: I, 105–12). The Bank believed that it could not control the banks' cash reserves (and hence the monetary base) because the banks held so many Treasury bills which could readily be discounted at Bank rate or allowed to run off as they matured each week (even if they could not obtain cash for Treasury bills quite as easily and cheaply as before November 1951). Hence the authorities' desire after 1951 to keep the banks' liquid assets ratio down to 30 per cent. Both problems provided reasons for wanting *low* nominal interest rates on government debt, which might conflict with the needs of monetary policy, but they also meant the authorities wanted to sell a sizeable amount of long-term debt all the time, which might require quite *high* nominal interest rates to persuade the private sector to hold such debt.

The debt problem was, thirdly, compounded by the Bank's belief that it could not sell bonds on a falling market, because investors would expect bond prices to fall and hence capital losses on bonds – as had happened under the 'cheaper money policy' in 1947. High interest rates would make gilt-edged borrowing expensive but rising interest rates could make it impossible. Hence the Bank concentrated sales of government bonds in periods of declining interest rates and also tended to be 'entirely passive, indeed fatalistic' about long-term interest rates (Radcliffe Committee Committee 1959: paras. 521–2). (Although the Radcliffe Committee swallowed the Bank/Treasury line about the importance of funding, it was critical of the Bank's view of the demand for government bonds.) The Bank's view also affected the timing and movement of short-term interest rates: when Bank rate was raised the Bank often wanted the market to be convinced this was the 'top' and hence anticipate falling interest rates; the Bank was also often anxious to lower Bank rate quickly but in small steps so as to encourage a rising gilts market.

The Radcliffe Report is best known for its statements of the unimportance of the money supply compared to 'the whole liquidity position' – such as 'spending is not limited by the amount of money in existence ... [but] related to the amount of money people think they can get hold of' – and its recommendation that the authorities operate on 'the structure of interest rates' rather than the supply of money, whose control was '[found] to be no more than an important facet of debt management' (1959: paras. 389–97, 514). In the short run the report provided an intellectual rationale for the authorities to continue their 1950s practice in the 1960s. In the longer run it brought about a permanent improvement in the availability and quality of UK monetary and financial statistics and eventually encouraged UK monetary economists to reconsider their views about the efficacy of monetary policy and to test them empirically.

Monetary policy in the 1960s was a continuation of the aims and methods of the 1950s (Bank of England 1969; Tew 1978a; Artis 1978). Hire purchase restrictions were reimposed in April 1960 and changed on twelve occasions in the next ten years. The special deposits scheme, supposed to substitute for direct controls on bank lending, was in operation through the 1960s except for about $2\frac{1}{2}$ years between 1962 and 1965, and from July 1961 was always accompanied by requests to at least some banks to limit their advances. (The scheme only applied to the clearing banks; since the deposits of other banks had been growing very rapidly since the restoration of convertibility in 1958 and the rise of the euro-dollar market, the authorities invented a 'cash deposits' scheme to apply to them but did not bring it into operation 'because it has continued to be necessary to exercise tighter control through ceilings' – Bank of England 1968, 1969: 226.) The requests to the banks became explicit quantitative ceilings from May 1965 and applied to commercial bills as well as advances.

The management of the national debt continued to restrict the ambitions of monetary policy. Since 'the chief purpose of debt management ... is to maintain market conditions that will maximise, both now and in the future, the desire of investors at home and abroad to hold British government debt', the Bank operated to stabilise bond prices, buying government securities to slow down price falls and selling them in large quantities when prices were rising (Bank of England 1984a: 75–82; see also Tew 1978a: 229–33; Artis 1978: 274–6). Since this made gilt-edged securities almost as liquid as Treasury bills, the maintenance of a minimum liquid assets ratio, even reinforced by special deposits, was not an effective constraint on bank lending: hence the renewed resort to advances control.

Bank rate changes were dictated by the fixed exchange rate, with the pound under severe pressure in 1961 and 1964–9. They were most frequent during the period (1964–7) when the Labour government under Harold Wilson was trying to maintain the pound at US$2.80. As in the 1950s the increases came in 'packages' intended also to deflate domestic demand. Although there was almost no conflict between internal and external balance, the measures were not successful in achieving either. The Labour government eventually decided to devalue the pound to US$2.40 on 18 November 1967 – when Bank rate went up to 8 per cent for the first time since August 1914. (On the devaluation see Tew 1978b: 310–15, 354–6, and Cairncross 1983.)

By the end of the 1960s British monetary economists were coming under the influence of the 'monetarist' ideas associated with Milton Friedman and, nearer to home, Harry Johnson. The Money Study Group was founded in 1969, in order to encourage both discussion of monetary issues and empirical research. (For some of the more notable empirical work, especially on the demand for money, see Walters 1969a, 1969b; Goodhart and Crockett 1970; Laidler and Parkin 1970; Laidler 1971; Price 1972; Artis and Lewis 1976.) The Bank of England began to publish money supply series (for M1 and M3) (Bank of England 1970). In spite of a spirited rearguard action by 'Keynesians' attached to Radcliffean ideas (see for instance Kaldor 1970), it was gradually accepted in the 1970s that any successful anti-inflationary policy must include control of the rate of growth of the money supply, which the Bank of England had so far failed to achieve. At the same time, since international capital mobility was now obviously higher than in earlier post-war decades, more economists favoured flexible exchange rates (which Friedman had always advocated) to overcome the external constraints on domestic monetary policy.

New approaches

The first new approach of the 1970s, *competition and credit control* (CCC), was formally announced in May 1971. It turned out to be the most spectacular failure to control monetary growth, which accelerated rapidly after the floating of the pound in 1972 (see Figure 6.9). The adoption of *monetary targets*, which were introduced more quietly in the mid-1970s, was more successful, but even as they were pursued more single-mindedly under the *medium-term financial strategy* of the early 1980s, doubts of their usefulness in combating inflation were growing. In the mid-1980s explicit targets for the rate of growth of the money supply were abandoned as the UK monetary authorities cautiously began to concern themselves again with exchange-rate stability.

CCC was intended to encourage greater competition among UK banks and other financial institutions and to make it easier to control monetary growth by interest rate changes. Quantitative lending ceilings would be abolished; the cash and liquid assets ratios which applied only to the London and Scottish clearing banks would be replaced with a single reserve assets ratio applying to all banks; the clearing banks would abandon longstanding collusive agreements on their deposit and advances rates of interest; and the special deposits schemes would apply to all banks. Reserve assets comprised banks' balances with the Bank of England (except special deposits), Treasury bills and government securities with a year or less to maturity, call loans to the discount houses, and bills eligible for rediscount at the Bank, but not till money. The new reserve asset ratio was set at $12\frac{1}{2}$ per cent of sterling deposits or 'eligible liabilities' (Bank of England 1971a, 1971b).

The London clearing banks also agreed to hold as part of their reserve assets non-interest-bearing balances equal on average to $1\frac{1}{2}$ per cent of their eligible liabilities, to be used for clearing cheques. They gave up their interest-rate cartel and ceased to tie their lending and deposit rates to Bank rate in October 1971; a year later the Bank replaced Bank rate with a *minimum lending rate* (MLR) which was to move automatically with Treasury bill rate (Bank of England 1984a: 114; Tew 1978a: 238–45). There were parallel changes in regulations governing the discount houses, who agreed to invest at least half of their borrowed funds in public sector debt as well as to continue to tender for the government's weekly issue of Treasury bills (Bank of England 1971a). (When the former regulation turned out to keep down the Treasury bill rate at times of rising interest rates, it was replaced in July 1973 by the requirement that a discount house's other assets not exceed twenty times its capital and reserves (Bank of England 1973).) A prerequisite for the variation of interest rates for monetary policy purposes was that the authorities reduce their intervention in the gilt-edged market. This they had already begun to do in 1969 when they ceased to announce the prices at which they would sell government bonds from their own holdings and purchase bonds nearing maturity (Bank of England 1969). In 1971 they reduced their commitment to only buying bonds with a year or less to maturity.

The overall aim of CCC was 'a system under which *the allocation of credit is primarily determined by its cost*' (Bank of England 1984a: 40). Monetary control would operate through the effect of interest-rate changes on bank lending. The subsequent 'troublesome and at times unhappy' experience (Goodhart 1975: 91) included a rapid rise in bank lending and hence the growth of the money supply, with M3 running at nearly 30 per cent in 1972 and 1973. M1 grew more slowly, but at double-digit rates, while nominal interest rates also rose to double-digit levels in 1972. With a lag the rate of price inflation moved into double digits in 1974–5 (Figure 6.10). The housing market boomed, and so did the commercial property market, whose collapse caused a banking crisis among secondary banks at the end of 1973 (see Gowland 1978: chs. 3–6, 1982: chs. 6–7; Reid 1982; and chapter 7 below).

Bank lending rose rapidly partly because of the ending of the ceilings and the interest-rate cartel – an effect which was anticipated although

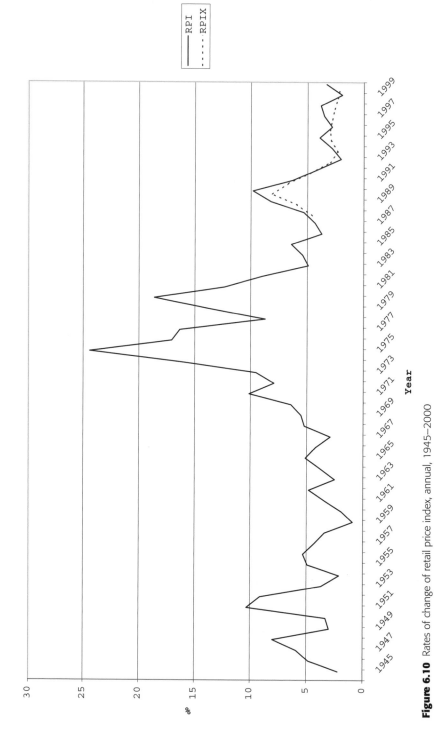

Figure 6.10 Rates of change of retail price index, annual, 1945–2000

Source: Calculated from Feinstein (1972: tab. 65); ONS, *Economic, Trends*, various years.

its size was not known or estimated – and partly because of the growth of 'liability management', which the authorities did not foresee. With greater competition the banks could react to strong loan demand by bidding for funds in the 'wholesale' money markets. They were not constrained by the reserve asset ratio, which was anyway subject to several loopholes (Goodhart 1975: 98–106; Gowland 1982: 96–100; Spencer 1986: 37–44). Hence the 'new approach' failed to control monetary growth because it continued the old practice of trying to control bank lending without controlling bank reserves.

In 1972–3 macroeconomic policy was designed to stimulate demand, with Anthony Barber, chancellor of the exchequer in Edward Heath's Conservative government, pursuing a highly expansionary budgetary policy. When the pound came under pressure the government decided to let it float from 22 June 1972 in order to remove the external constraint on domestic economic policy. When capital outflows reduced the banks' deposits and reserves the Bank lent them reserves (by temporarily buying government securities from them) after the Bank rate had been raised to 6 per cent on 22 June. In August the Bank resorted to requesting the banks to cut down their lending for property and stock exchange speculation – with little effect. In November and December it called for special deposits and the newly introduced MLR rose with Treasury bill rates to reach 9 per cent on 22 December. This had little immediate impact on the growth of M3, which was being increased by 'round tripping': high money-market interest rates made it profitable for bank borrowers to use overdrafts to invest in certificates of deposit (CDs) and other money-market instruments (Tew 1978a: 249–54; Gowland 1982: 104–11; Spencer 1986: 39–42).

There was no further restrictive action in the first half of 1973, when interest rates were allowed to *fall* (MLR was 7.5 per cent by June), perhaps because the rapid growth of M3 was regarded as 'artificial', inflated as it was by round tripping (Goodhart 1975: 104). When the floating pound depreciated sharply in July (against the US dollar as well as the Deutschmark: see Figure 6.11), the authorities at last reacted vigorously. As Gowland (1982: 111–12) remarks, a 'cynic with a long memory would have commented that the UK authorities had always responded . . . with higher interest rates when there was a foreign exchange crisis'. They made further calls for special deposits in July and November, and pushed up MLR, in July to 9 per cent by reducing the supply of reserve assets and in November to 13 per cent by administrative action.

The increase in money-market rates provoked a new bout of round tripping, to which the Bank reacted with a device quite contrary to the spirit of 'competition and credit control': Supplementary Special Deposits (SSDs) or the 'corset' (Bank of England 1974). The banks now had to make non-interest-bearing deposits with the Bank whenever their interest-bearing eligible liabilities (IBELs) grew at more than a specified

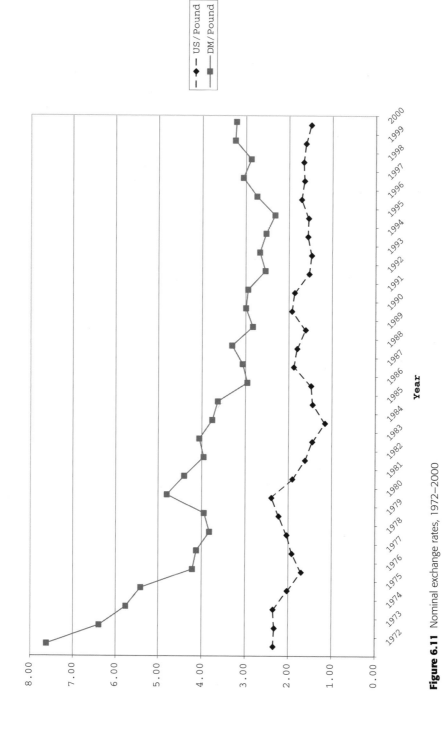

Figure 6.11 Nominal exchange rates, 1972–2000

Source: Bank of England, *Statistical Abstract*, various years.

rate, initially 8 per cent over the next six months; the SSDs required increased with the amount by which the specified rate was exceeded. Direct quantitative controls on bank activities had returned, this time on liabilities rather than assets.

The SSD scheme was used three times: December 1973 – February 1975, November 1976 – August 1977, and June 1978 – June 1980. Until the end of 1979 it did not involve the banks in making large payments to the Bank (Bank of England 1984a: 117–27). Its major and predictable weakness, especially when used for long periods, was disintermediation, the shifting of borrowing from instruments included in banks' IBELs to those which were not, such as commercial bills. While it helped to reduce monetary growth, especially in 1974 when the demand for bank lending was lowered by recession and the aftermath of the secondary banking crisis (Gowland 1982: 145–8; Spencer 1986: 44–5, 98–103), it was only an adjunct to other methods of monetary and credit control, including the old standbys of requests to banks to restrict their lending to certain types of borrowers and hire purchase controls, which were reimposed in December 1973.

The second 'new approach' of the 1970s, *monetary targets*, had been waiting in the wings for some time. It could not be seriously adopted until the government had given up the commitment to a fixed exchange rate, since in an open economy becoming smaller in an increasingly financially integrated world economy there was little scope for an independent monetary policy. It also assumed a stable money demand function, that is, that the estimated demand for some (controllable) monetary aggregate is related to income and interest rates in a sufficiently predictable way to be used to set monetary policy instruments.

From 1973 the Bank adopted an unpublished target rate of growth for M3. It chose this aggregate over M1 because of two 'somewhat fortuitous factors': the behaviour of M3 could be arithmetically related to, and hence analysed in terms of, its 'credit counterparts' (the public sector borrowing requirement (PSBR), government debt sales to the non-bank private sector, bank lending to the private sector, and net external flows) and the current statistical series for M1 was less reliable than that for M3 (Bank of England 1984a: 3, 45). Although the Bank's estimated demand-for-money functions for M3 were beginning to show signs of instability (Bank of England 1984a: 172–87), the Bank retained its preference for a broad aggregate through the 1970s. One reason was the credit counterparts analysis, the other was the acceleration of inflation in 1974–5: 'following closely on the heels of the monetary expansion in 1972–73, [this] led to even greater emphasis being placed on the need for a financial anchor in the form of a monetary target applied in order to constrain and control the rate of inflation'. In 1976, following another sterling crisis when the pound fell to a record low against the US dollar, the chancellor of the exchequer announced a target for M3 of 12 per cent for the 1976–7 financial year (Bank of England 1984a: 45–7; see Table 6.3).

Table 6.3	Monetary targets, 1976–1986			
Period	Announced	Variable(s)	Target (%)	Actual (%)
1976–7	July 1976	M3	12	10
1977–8	March 1977	£M3	9–13	16
1978–9	April 1978	£M3	8–12	11
1979–80	June 1979	£M3	7–11	10
1980–1	March 1980	£M3	7–11	18.5
1981–2	March 1981	£M3	6–10	13
1982–3	March 1982	£M3	8–12	11.5
		M1	8–12	11
		PSL2	8–12	9
1983–4	March 1983	£M3	7–11	11
		M1	7–11	11
		PSL2	7–11	12.3
1984–5	March 1984	£M3	6–10	12
		M0	4–8	5.5
1985–6	March 1985	£M3	5–9	15
		M0	3.7	3.5
1986–7	March 1986	£M3	11–15	20
		M0	2–6	2

Source: Dow and Saville (1988: Tab. 7.1).

The general election in February 1974 had produced a minority Labour government which obtained a majority in another election in October. It was therefore a Labour chancellor, Denis Healey, who announced the conversion to a 'monetarist' policy, or at least the acceptance that control of the rate of growth of the money supply is a necessary condition for control of the rate of inflation. The 1974–9 Labour government's monetary (and fiscal) policies were a continual struggle against inflation and unemployment and, in the early years, a current account balance-of-payments deficit and depreciation of sterling. At first monetary growth helpfully declined following the December 1973 measures, but inflation, in the wake of the first oil price shock, accelerated through 1974 and 1975 to reach an annual rate of over 25 per cent in the second half of 1975. The pound fell during the first half of 1975 (against both the US$ and the DM), prompting increases in interest rates (MLR reached 12 per cent in October); it fell even more in the first half of 1976 despite large-scale exchange-market intervention (Bank of England 1976). In spite of additional support from other central banks, public expenditure cuts, and the adoption of an M3 target, calls for special deposits and SSDs, and sharp rises in interest rates, including a 2 per cent jump in MLR to 15 per cent in October, the government had to apply to borrow from the International Monetary Fund in December. As with earlier IMF borrowings, the strings attached to the loan included a target for domestic credit expansion (DCE), which is roughly equivalent to the growth of M3 less the balance-of-payments deficit, but the Labour government nonetheless stuck to its money supply target in the following two years. At the beginning of 1977 the target was set in terms of £M3 (that is, excluding residents' foreign-currency deposits) and as a range (9–13 per cent for the financial year 1977–8) rather than a single number (Gowland 1982: 154; Bank of England 1977).

The Labour government was generally successful in keeping £M3 within the announced target ranges, except in 1977–8 (see Table 6.3). In the summer and early autumn of 1977 the authorities intervened in the foreign exchange market to prevent a rapid *appreciation* of sterling against the US dollar; in early 1978 they underestimated the actual rate of monetary growth (Gowland 1982: 171–4; Bank of England 1984a: 68).

In the spring of 1978 they raised MLR and abandoned its 'automatic' link with the Treasury bill rate (which had already been overridden on several occasions), and reintroduced the SSD scheme. But although monetary growth was brought under control, and the target range reduced to 8–12 per cent, inflation continued to be a problem, especially in the winter of 1978–9 after the second oil price shock.

The Bank's activities in the gilt-edged market in the later 1970s also reflected the new 'new approach'. In the early years of CCC it had not sold much gilt-edged to the market. Once it was concerned to control monetary growth it had to sell government bonds more aggressively. (If nothing else the credit counterparts analysis of M3 demonstrates that an increase in debt sales to the private sector will reduce monetary growth, other things being equal, and, more usefully in practice, will offset rising bank lending.) It began to manipulate MLR as it had Bank rate more tentatively in the 1950s so as to encourage gilt-edged sales, pushing it up sharply to foster expectations of future falls in interest rates and only gradually lowering it while selling large quantities of gilt-edged securities. This 'Duke of York' strategy was based on the Bank's belief that the gilt-edged market was dominated by asset holders with short holding periods and extrapolative expectations. According to Gowland (1982: 149) it was used successfully eight times between January 1974 and August 1980 in spite of the apparently irrational behaviour it assumes on the part of gilt-edged investors. Empirical studies of the demand for gilts (Goodhart 1969; Norton 1969; Spencer 1981; 1986: ch. 8) seem surprisingly to support the Bank's view. In the 1970s and 1980s the authorities also tried to facilitate long-term government borrowing by varying the types of securities issued and the methods of issuing them, such experiments including index-linked stocks and auctioning new issues (Bank of England 1984a: 88–104, 1987b, 1988a).

The early 1980s witnessed the 'high tide of monetarism' in Britain and several other countries which had tried monetary targeting in the 1970s (Foot 1981; Goodhart 1989: part I). They also saw a rerun in modern dress of the earlier debates about methods of monetary control. The general election of May 1979 returned a Conservative government under a prime minister (Margaret Thatcher) determined not to repeat the monetary mistakes of 1972–3. Her first chancellor, Geoffrey Howe, reaffirmed the commitment to achieve a monetary target defined in terms of £M3 and reduced to 7–11 per cent for 1979–80, but he made its achievement more immediately difficult by raising value added tax (VAT) from 8 to 15 per cent in June 1979 and abolishing exchange control in October. With inflation accelerating towards a peak of almost 22 per cent in May 1980, MLR was raised from 14 to 17 per cent on 15 November, partly to set off a 'Duke of York' manoeuvre and encourage gilts sales (Gowland 1982: 190–2; see also Bank of England 1980: 20–2). The chancellor also announced in November that the authorities were reviewing their monetary control methods and would be issuing a Green Paper, which was published the following March. The debate on monetary base control already underway continued for about a year (Bank of England 1984a: 129–49; below).

The March 1980 budget announced a medium-term financial strategy (MTFS), invented by Nigel Lawson, then financial secretary to the Treasury, and intended to commit the government both to reduce the (target and actual) rate of monetary growth steadily year by year and to subordinate fiscal policy as well as interest rates to this anti-inflationary aim. The SSD scheme was abolished as from June 1980, an inevitable consequence of the abolition of exchange control which increased the opportunities (and the practice) of avoiding direct credit controls by disintermediation. The 'bill leak' (bank bills held outside the banking system) is estimated to have reached £2,700m in the second quarter of 1980; it fell dramatically after the ending of the corset (by £1,000m in the first month), while the money supply soared well out of its target range in the second half of 1980 (Bank of England 1984a: 65–73, 117–27).

Meanwhile the combination of record high interest rates and North Sea oil had dramatically raised the nominal and real foreign exchange value of sterling (see Figure 6.11) and Britain entered a particularly severe recession. Industrial production fell by 10 per cent in 1980 and unemployment, already over 1 million, rose to over 2 million. (For a sample of the vigorous debate over the relative contributions of contractionary monetary policy and North Sea oil to the appreciation of sterling see Eltis and Sinclair 1981.) It was politically difficult for the authorities to raise interest rates to keep monetary growth on target, and short-term interest rates were in fact reduced to 16 per cent in July and 14 per cent in November 1980 (Goodhart 1989: 303–4). In spite of the overshooting of the target for £M3 (which was growing at an annual rate of nearly 25 per cent in the autumn of 1980: see Figure 6.9), Howe announced in his March 1981 budget a new target of 6–10 per cent for February 1981 – April 1982, while reducing MLR further to 12 per cent (Bank of England 1981: 3–4). A year later, when £M3 had grown by about 14.5 per cent in 1981–2, the target range was raised again to 8–12 per cent and this time encompassed *three* aggregates, M1, £M3 and a new, even broader one, PSL2. Goodhart (1989: 306) remarks: 'Outside commentators complained that this would give the authorities a greater chance to hit at least one target; insiders worried that the markets would concentrate on whichever indicator/target was currently doing worst.'

In 1983 and 1984 the government continued to set targets which in line with the MFTS were lowered each year in the budget, but the range of aggregates considered useful as targets or as indicators of the stance of monetary policy widened further. In 1983 the targets for 1983–4 were 7–11 per cent for M1, £M3 and PSL2. In 1984 the £M3 target was duly lowered to 6–10 per cent, but a new target (4–8 per cent) was set for M0, and 'attention will also be paid to other monetary indicators . . . in interpreting monetary conditions', including M2, PSL2 and the exchange rate. This reflected the increasingly divergent behaviour of the different monetary series (see Figure 6.9) and the chronic difficulty of controlling bank lending.

In the 1950s the Bank had rejected monetary base control (MBC) because it wanted a stable Treasury bill rate (Radcliffe Committee 1959: para. 376). In 1980 it rejected MBC for a similar reason, as did other central banks, namely that strict control would 'continually threaten frequent and potentially massive movements in interest rates' – a fear to some extent borne out by the US Federal Reserve's experience of operating a modified form of MBC in 1979–82 (Bank of England 1984a: 129–36; Goodhart 1989: 322–6). The Bank and other central banks generally preferred to try and control the rate of growth of the money supply by means of setting and maintaining very short-run (week-to-week) targets for short-term interest rates which were decided upon in accordance with the currently favoured estimated demand-for-money function.

The authorities did, however, make changes in their practice of monetary policy in 1980–1 which brought that practice closer to the economists' model of central bank control of the money supply. In November 1980 the Chancellor announced that, as the Green Paper on *Monetary Control* proposed, the reserve assets ratio would be eliminated and replaced with a low cash requirement, similar to the 1.5 per cent of eligible liabilities required of the clearing banks since 1971, on all banks and other deposit-taking institutions above a minimum size. The Bank was also to change its money-market intervention so as to rely more on open-market operations in bills than on discount window lending and use them to keep short-term interest rates within a narrow unpublished band consistent with the current desired rate of monetary growth. The 12.5 per cent reserve assets ratio was reduced to 10 per cent in January 1981 and abolished in August, when non-interest-bearing cash deposits at the Bank of England equal to 0.5 per cent of eligible liabilities were required of all 'eligible banks'. The Bank also abandoned MLR in August but retained the right to call for special deposits (Bank of England 1984a: 148–9, 152–64).

There were further developments in the Bank of England's intervention techniques in both the short-term money market and the gilt-edged market in response to structural and regulatory changes in the UK financial system. The most striking change was the 'Big Bang' of 27 October 1986 which eliminated the distinction between brokers and jobbers in the stock market and their fixed commissions for stock transactions; as a result the Bank now deals directly with a wider group of financial institutions than it used to (see Bank of England 1987a, 1988b, 1989a 1989b).

Since 1945 UK bank lending has always proved difficult to control by interest rates. In the 1980s it became even more so in a period of widespread financial innovation and deregulation (which both increased the supply of loans and made estimated demand-for-money functions unreliable for policy purposes: Goodhart 1982, Bank of England 1986). The problem was aggravated by the recession which maintained the demand for bank lending (and the PSBR). The Bank resorted, not for the first time, to 'over-funding', that is, selling more gilt-edged debt than was needed to finance the PSBR (Bank of England 1984a: 165, 1984b). This kept £M3 within its target range at the cost of producing other problems, both technical and economic. Whereas previous overfunding allowed the authorities to re-deem short-term government debt mainly held by the banks, this time the Bank had to buy private sector commercial bills from the banks since their holdings of Treasury bills and other short-term public sector debt were already low. The resulting 'bill mountain' was inconvenient (since a large volume of maturing bills had constantly to be replaced) and also reduced interest rates on commercial bills relative to other short-term as-sets. It also meant that the resulting reduced growth of bank deposits was largely artificial, raising doubts as to whether this was consistent with the objectives of controlling monetary growth: 'More fundamentally . . . was a technique that allowed bank credit expansion to continue roaring ahead, but restrained the growth of bank deposits, achieving any proper purpose, or was it just another "cosmetic" device?' (Goodhart 1989: 327–8).

During 1985 the doubts prevailed over the determination to maintain a £M3 target. With weakening sterling the Bank not only intervened to raise short-term money-market interest rates but also reintroduced MLR (at 12 per cent) on 14 January. In the budget in March the government retained targets for M0 and £M3, but in October the chancellor (now Lawson) suspended the £M3 target for 1985–6 and announced that he would now aim at fully funding the PSBR rather than overfunding. Over the year the authorities drew less attention to £M3 and more to M0 which was 'probably least affected' by financial innovation (Bank of England 1985a: 362–3, 1985b: 518–20; see also 1987d). Although a £M3 target was reinstated in the March 1986 budget (11–15 per cent for 1986–7 compared with 2–6 per cent for M0), no formal target for it or any other measure of broad money was set in 1987.

Inflation targeting

The structural changes in the UK banking and financial system led the Bank of England – in common with other central banks, such as the Bank of Canada, whose experiments with monetary targets in the late 1970s and early 1980s were also undermined by financial innovation and deregulation – to review its measures of the money supply (Bank of Eng-land 1990a, 1990b). In 1989 it ceased publishing estimates for M1 and M3, having already begun to publish figures for its new measure of broad money, M4, in 1987. However, there had been steadily increasing concern about the low foreign-exchange value of the pound after its fall from the heights of the early 1980s. The main occasions when interest rates had been jerked upwards all coincided with sterling weakness (Goodhart 1989: 307). In 1987–8 the pound was held in a narrow range against the

Deutschmark by exchange-market intervention or interest-rate changes, but this 'shadowing' of the DM was not sustained when monetary growth and price inflation increased in 1989 (see Figures 6.9 and 6.10). In the eyes of financial journalists, the authorities 'desperately need[ed] a credible monetary framework' (*The Economist*, 10 June 1989).

Of the available alternatives, exchange-rate stability was first chosen. Under Lawson's successor as chancellor, John Major, Prime Minister Thatcher's notorious reluctance to allow the exchange rate to be tied to other European currencies was overcome. Britain joined the Exchange Rate Mechanism of the European Monetary System on 8 October 1990 and committed itself to maintaining sterling within a ± 6 per cent band around a central rate of £1 = DM 2.95 (Bank of England 1990c). But the commitment was not wholehearted: in the summer of 1992 the UK authorities tried to avoid following Germany's post-unification rise in interest rates, only to land themselves in the crisis of 'Black Wednesday', 16 September 1992, when a frantic chancellor (Norman Lamont) twice announced massive increases in MLR during the day and announced the suspension of membership of the ERM in the evening (Cobham 1997: 1128–30; Bank of England 1992a: 392–3).

The government, of which John Major was now prime minister, moved quickly to try and restore credibility. Stating that the ultimate objective of monetary policy *remained* the achievement of price stability, which was now defined as an underlying inflation rate of 2 per cent or less, the chancellor in October announced an *inflation target*: a target range of 1–4 per cent per year for the twelve-month change in the retail price index excluding mortgage interest payments (RPIX). Later the same month he 'invited' the Bank 'to provide a regular report on the progress being made towards the Government's inflation objective' (Bank of England 1993a, 1993b). The governor warmly welcomed the government's recognition of the time inconsistency problem and its pre-commitment to a policy of price stability; his blunter successor admitted that 'in practice we really had nowhere else to go once we'd been driven out of the ERM' (Bank of England 1992b: 447, 1997a: 100). The Bank issued its first Inflation Report in February 1993. (For the progress see Figure 6.10.)

When the inflation target was first announced the intention was to aim for the lower half of the range by the end of the current parliament in 1997. Although a target range was set for M0 and a monitoring range for M4, these aggregates were to be used as indicators, not targets, of monetary policy. The inflation target was restated in June 1995 as 2.5 per cent or less for the longer term beyond 1997. By this time there had been several important changes in the relation between the Treasury and the Bank of England: the monthly meetings between the governor of the Bank and the chancellor of the Exchequer had been regularised and formalised; the minutes of the meetings were being published, usually about six weeks later; and the Bank had been given some discretion over the timing of interest-rate changes decided by the chancellor (Bank of

England 1997a; Cobham 1997: 1130–1). An underlying tension remained, however, in that the Bank remained under the control of the chancellor, who also controlled the instruments of monetary policy (Bernanke *et al.* 1999: 159–71).

Pre-commitment to a policy of price stability can only work to solve the time (in)consistency problem if the commitment is credible and widely believed by the public. The 'New' Labour government elected in May 1997 therefore went further and introduced the most important institutional and operational changes at the Bank of England since its nationalisation in 1946.

Four days after taking office the chancellor of the Exchequer, Gordon Brown, gave the Bank *operational independence*, handing over the responsibility for interest-rate decisions to a new Monetary Policy Committee (MPC), composed of the governor, two deputy governors and two executive directors of the Bank, and four members appointed by the chancellor (Bank of England 1997b, 1997c). The Bank of England Act 1998 provided a statutory basis for the MPC, reformed the governance and finances of the Bank, and transferred responsibility for the supervision and surveillance of banks from the Bank to the new Financial Services Authority. At the same time the task of managing the national debt was transferred from the Bank to the Treasury (Bank of England 1998a, 1998b).

These changes can be interpreted as providing 'incentive-compatible' institutional arrangements capable of enforcing appropriate behaviour on the monetary authorities. The duty of the MPC is to maintain price stability; the Treasury has to define and publish its price stability objective each year: in other words the government sets the inflation target and the Bank takes the operational decisions to reach it. The Bank has to explain its decisions by publishing the minutes of the monthly MPC meetings as well as its quarterly Inflation Report. (For details see Budd 1998.)

Central bank independence is currently widely regarded as the best way of achieving credibility in monetary-policy making. But ultimately credibility has to be built by establishing a reputation for matching actions to professed intentions (Blinder 1998: 64–6). The announcement of the strategy and the communication of the reasons for the tactical decisions of the MPC can be seen as a means to this end. Even more helpful to the Bank of England's current reputation is its five years of success in keeping inflation within a hair's breadth of the government's target, which has been 2.5 per cent (for RPIX) since June 1997.

CONCLUSIONS

There have been striking continuities in British monetary policy since 1945: an ambivalence about the role of monetary policy and whether it should be assigned to domestic or external objectives; until recently a preoccupation with the management of the national debt; and a chronic difficulty in controlling monetary growth. The previous section emphasised the authorities' problems in controlling interest rates, bank lending and monetary growth, and the contribution of the perceived needs of debt management to these problems. By way of conclusion it is useful to look at the outcome for monetary growth in relation to Britain's inflation experience since 1945 and the behaviour of the exchange rate (see Figures 6.9, 6.10 and 6.11).

Figure 6.9 shows three periods of rapid monetary growth: the immediate post-war period, where Dalton's cheaper money policy shows up as a blip in the growth rates of M1 and M3c in 1946; the 1970s, where there is a rapid acceleration in the growth of all the aggregates after the floating of the pound in 1972; and the 1980s, where the growth rates of M0 are modest while M1 and the broader aggregates are still growing rapidly. Figure 6.10 shows that the acceleration of monetary growth from 1972 was followed, with a two-year lag, by an increase in the rate of inflation, which persisted as long as, and for about two years after, the period of rapid monetary growth. In the 1980s the inflation rate gradually fell back to the levels of the 1960s, though it rose again at the end of the decade. Financial deregulation and innovation show up in the divergence of the growth rates of the different monetary aggregates both in the early 1970s, following the Competition and Credit Control reforms, and in the mid-1980s, when they also disrupted the previously observed correlation between the rate of monetary growth and the rate of inflation. Figure 6.11 shows the fall of the pound sterling against both the US dollar and the Deutschmark in the 1970s, its sharp appreciation in 1979–81 followed by renewed decline and then relative stability, particularly against the US dollar, till the end of the 1990s.

In a small open economy with a fixed exchange rate and internationally mobile capital the rate of domestic monetary growth will under a fixed exchange rate tend to reflect the (world) rate of inflation rather than the other way round. In the early post-war years, with comprehensive exchange controls still in place, the UK financial system was fairly closed, but as capital mobility increased in the late 1950s and the 1960s it became increasingly difficult for the UK monetary authorities to control the UK money supply, although it took time for them to recognise this. When it was recognised, the opportunity to pursue a sensible independent monetary policy given by a floating exchange rate was squandered – under the Thatcher administration as well as its predecessors – by the authorities' lack of determination to keep monetary growth under control. However Keynesian one's preferred approach to economic problems may be, it is foolish to try to ignore the conclusion implied by monetary theory that if monetary expansion proceeds significantly faster than the growth of real output the rate of price inflation will accelerate a year or two later. The floating exchange rate will itself exacerbate the inflation by increasing import prices as the currency depreciates.

The reasons for the lack of control over monetary growth in the floating rate period have varied: at first the Conservative chancellor wanted to accommodate expansionary fiscal policy and avoid politically unpopular high interest rates which would adversely affect home owners (Laidler 1976: 492); in the later 1970s the Labour governments were caught with the aftermath of the oil price shocks, with inflation accelerating world-wide, and their own attempts to keep the pound relatively stable. The Conservative governments of the 1980s had to struggle with the consequences of their predecessors' problems, the immediate consequences of some of their own actions, such as the abolition of exchange control, and the severe recession which followed the simultaneous attempts of the major industrial countries to reduce inflation from its 1970s levels. The UK government and central bank were not the only monetary authorities to be convinced of the need to fight inflation with a tight monetary policy just at the time when monetary targets were beginning to be undermined by financial innovation. When monetary targeting became unworkable, the UK monetary authorities first flirted with exchange-rate targets and then followed New Zealand and Canada in adopting inflation targets.

The strenuous anti-inflationary efforts undoubtedly succeeded, with UK inflation rates in the 1990s reaching and maintaining the announced targets. It is nonetheless too soon to predict that the new strategy of inflation targeting will remain consistently successful – or fashionable. As perceptive commentators have noted, the UK adopted inflation targets at a time when inflation had already fallen significantly over the previous decade (Bernanke *et al.* 1999: 148). The new monetary arrangements implemented in 1997–8 giving the Bank of England more independence have also not yet been seriously tested. As Marvyn King, the deputy governor of the Bank, commented in 1999, 'A true test of the MPC [the Monetary Policy Committee] is not whether it hits the target when the sea is calm, but how it reacts to the storms, or economic shocks, that will inevitably arise' (Bank of England 1999: 301). A larger uncertainty is whether the UK will decide to enter into European Monetary Union and adopt the single currency, the Euro. If that were to happen, UK monetary policy would no longer be determined by the Bank of England or the Treasury but by the Governing Council of the European Central Bank.

7

The financial services sector since 1945

KATHERINE WATSON

Contents

INTRODUCTION

Since 1945, Britain's financial services have been subject to considerable change, both in the scale of their contribution to the domestic economy, and in their character and operation. It is no surprise that the expansion of this sector and its success in relation to other key sectors has attracted the attention of economic historians. Dynamism within financial services seems to offer fertile ground for those seeking to explain the pattern and pace of recent economic development within the British economy, especially given its contrast with continued de-industrialisation in Britain during the last quarter of the twentieth century (see, for example, Clarke 1986: 186; Rybczynski 1988; Hutton 1995).

The most significant developments in this sector were concentrated in the 1980s and 1990s, these years seeing a wave of regulatory re-form, increased fluidity of institutional functions, and a large growth in the scale of financial business undertaken. During the 1960s there had been increasing pessimism regarding the durability of Britain's role as a dominant player in international financial markets, with financial services being seen as another casualty of Britain's supposed relative economic decline. Yet, for much of the 1980s, London's position as a financial centre seemed, once again, to be secure. Deregulation appears to have provided a strong positive impetus to the sector, augmenting expansion already evident within it. Business increased significantly, but economic recession during the late 1980s and early 1990s combined with various 'financial scandals' (including, for example, the Guinness, Barlow Clowes, and Maxwell pension fund crises) to deepen concern that liberalisation of the regulations governing financial services might have gone too far, and was in fact creating new sources of instability. A process of 're-regulation' ensued, in part motivated by concerns relating to European interests and the foundation of the single European market, but also prompted by the desire to reduce the scope for financial crises in order to maintain a more stable level of investor confidence. Notwithstanding revisions to the regulatory framework governing the sector during the 1980s and 1990s, financial services have continued to increase in significance to the British economy, becoming the dominant contributor to UK Gross Domestic Product by the end of the twentieth century.

This chapter seeks to outline first the key structural features of the financial services sector, indicating the changing scale and character of its business. We then consider the factors which have contributed to these changes and seek to evaluate their relative importance. This entails reviewing briefly the international and macroeconomic context in which Britain's financial services have developed, the institutional arrangements within which the sector operates (i.e. the principal features of deregulation and re-regulation policies during the 1980s and 1990s), and the importance of technological changes affecting the practice and delivery of financial services. The third task for this chapter is to examine the implications of developments in financial services in the context of principal consumers of these services such as households and individuals, businesses, and the economy more generally. Our aim is to assess here in greater detail the character and significance of changes within the financial services sector and to consider the implications which these have had for Britain's economic development since 1945.

THE SCALE AND CHARACTER OF FINANCIAL SERVICES SINCE 1945

It is important to begin by trying to define what we mean by the financial services sector. Our primary concern is with financial intermediation, namely the process by which the demands of potential borrowers are matched with the supplies of funds offered by savers. Amongst the principal functions of financial intermediaries is the aggregation of saved funds which can then be invested jointly in order to pool risk and reduce transaction costs. A particular benefit of aggregation is that it permits savers who prefer to store funds on a short-term basis collectively to supply capital which can be loaned on longer terms, thereby permitting a greater range of capital projects to be funded than would be possible by direct interchange between borrowers and lenders alone.

This process of intermediation is achieved by the transaction of a variety of financial instruments including, for example, equities, money deposits, bonds, mortgages, insurance policies and pension funds. A helpful initial classification of financial institutions was offered by the Wilson Committee which identified three broad categories according to purpose (Wilson Report 1980: 40). First, there are deposit-taking institutions such as banks and building societies which collect deposits that are usually highly liquid and convert these resources into long-term investment portfolios. A second group comprises those institutions, such as insurance companies, which collect savings committed to them for long periods and seek to secure the highest returns possible with the funds they manage in order to offer competitive returns to their policy holders at maturity. The third group consist of the specialised financing agencies developed at various times, such as, for example, Finance for Industry (established in 1973 from a group of agencies including the Industrial and Commercial Finance Corporation and the Finance Corporation for Industry). Typically, commentators on financial services tend to classify institutions more broadly as either banks or non-banking financial intermediaries. All of these definitions have limitations given the dynamism of the sector. As we shall see later in this chapter, since the early 1980s, the activities of individual institutions have become more varied, and this distinction between banks and 'non-banks' has become less sharp.

In examining the significance to financial and economic development of each type of financial institution engaged in intermediation, it is important to be aware of the distinction between the primary and secondary markets in which financial instruments are exchanged. In primary markets funds are issued directly between lenders and borrowers, such as, for example, when a bank or a building society records deposits for savers, and issues loans directly to borrowers, e.g. in the form of a mortgage contract. In secondary markets, institutions trade in the securities of other institutions, so, for example, insurance companies collect premiums from those maintaining a policy and then manage and invest these sums in a portfolio of securities. These distinctive markets create considerable scope for interaction between the different sectors of the financial services industry. The nature of these transactions and their significance within the financial services sector itself can have important repercussions for the rest of the economy: they may imply a shift in the balance of power between individual and institutional investors within the financial services sector which may, in turn, affect the character and price of financial instruments available and hence their accessibility to different consumers seeking funds within the market. It is for this reason that it is important to establish a sense of the changing scale of the sector as a whole and also of the individual institutional groups within it, as well as discuss in more depth the kinds of operation in which key agents within the financial markets are engaged.

In 1948 the banking and finance sector comprised about 3 per cent of Gross Domestic Product at factor cost. Between 1960 and 1975, the scale of output from this sector almost doubled, achieving a rate of growth in excess of other key sectors and of the economy as a whole. In 1975 it contributed about 7 per cent of GDP at factor cost. This pace of change was far outstripped during the 1980s and 1990s: by 1980 financial services comprised about 11 per cent of GDP at factor cost, but this had grown to 14 per cent by 1985, 18 per cent by 1990, and had reached 20 per cent by 1995. By the end of the century, Britain's financial services sector was responsible for about a quarter of GDP (ONS, *National Income Accounts*, Blue Books', various years). In 2001, Britain's net export income from financial services amounted to £13.2 billion, a more than threefold increase on the net exports achieved in 1991, and an important source of income which could partially offset the overall trade deficit facing Britain (International Financial Services 2002: 1).

Financial services also increased in significance in the employment opportunities offered. In 1950 the sector accounted for about 3.5 per cent of the total employed in the UK, contrasting with around 13 per cent by the mid-1990s and 18 per cent at the end of the twentieth century. By the 1990s there was growing disquiet regarding job security within the financial sector, especially in the wake of technological change in service provision in banking in particular, but, even so, employment in this sector was less acutely affected by recession than in most other sectors, and it had become a dominant employer of Britain's workforce.

If we turn now to considering the structure of the financial services sector itself, we can get some indication of the scale of composite groups within financial services from the distribution of assets of UK financial institutions (see Table 7.1). First, the significant post-war expansion of the sector as a whole is evident. The pace of growth is particularly rapid during the 1980s with a slightly slower, but continued, expansion during the 1990s. The banking sector has remained the dominant force within financial services, enjoying a general expansion in assets during most of the post-war period, with growth being particularly rapid during the 1980s and slowing in the 1990s. In general, about half of the assets of the financial services sector were placed with banks, with a large proportion of these being held in the form of highly liquid financial instruments.

Table 7.1 Assets of UK financial institutions, 1955–2000 *(£m current prices)*

	Banking sector	Building societies	Insurance (long-term)	Insurance (general)	Pension funds	Investment trusts	Unit trusts	Source
1955	7,905	2,075[a]	1,750		1,870	620		(1)
1960		3,183	4,820			1,989	191	(2)
1965	15,808	5,577	8,826	1,041	5,380	3,119	500	(2)
1970	33,727	10,940	13,781	1,671	7,644	4,469	1,316	(2)
1975	107,682	24,364	23,342	4,548	13,589	5,651	2,537	(2)
1980	233,392	54,317	53,746	11,516	51,555	8,352	4,629	(2)
1985	589,880	121,239	130,122	27,117	156,395	18,085	18,433	(2)
1990	1,031,245	221,974	232,314	44,216	302,670	19,108	41,617	(2)
1995	1,476,769	297,294	483,301	69,719	519,270	43,062	104,069	(2)
2000	1,467,943	158,703	932,686	89,025	765,199	60,499	222,824	(2)

[a] This figure for building societies' assets is a revised estimate offered in a later edition of ONS, *Financial Statistics* (i.e. source (2)).

Sources:
(1) CSO evidence given to Radcliffe Committee on the Working of the Monetary System (1960). CSO evidence in volume I, part III.
(2) ONS, *Financial Statistics*, various years (latest estimates).

However, following deregulation of the banking sector, banks have increased markedly their involvement in longer-term transactions such as, for example, the mortgage market. Equally clear is the challenge to bank dominance of financial intermediation since 1945 as other financial institutions have expanded (for elaboration of these issues, see, for example, Rose 1986: 27–9).

Building societies expanded their activities through to the 1990s, reflecting the improvement of British post-war living standards and the growth in home ownership. Relative to other financial institutions, the 1960s and 1970s were particularly buoyant years for building societies with between 80 and 90 per cent of mortgage business being undertaken by them (Building Societies Association, *Facts and Figures*, various years). Importantly, the market demand for mortgages was increasing: whereas in 1938 just 32 per cent of dwellings in England and Wales were owner-occupied, by 1960 this had grown to 44 per cent and it reached 50 per cent in 1970. By the mid-1980s more than 60 per cent of the population owned their own houses and this continued to increase, slowing during the early 1990s recession, but still reaching almost 70 per cent owner occupation by the end of the twentieth century (Building Societies Association, *Facts and Figures*, and Council of Mortgage Lenders (CML), *Housing Finance*, various years). However, in the wake of financial liberalisation, by the early 1990s, the virtual monopoly in private mortgage finance enjoyed by building societies for much of the post-war period, was under threat, in particular from the banking sector. Moreover, the easing of restrictions governing building societies permitted many to demutualise and convert to banks, thereby transferring their assets to the banking sector (hence the decline in building society assets from 1995 shown in

Table 7.1). By 2000, banks accounted for about 70 per cent of outstanding loans and building societies less than a quarter (CML, *Housing Finance* 2002 (54): 66).

The role of the insurance sector has also grown significantly, motivated by greater adoption of life cover (long-term insurance) as well as the delivery of ancillary services associated with the purchase of private property. This has created a large growth in institutional investment in long-term financial instruments, initially in the form of fixed-interest mortgages and loans which guaranteed a given income at a terminal date, but also in equities and property which can command greater returns and, it is hoped, enhance the 'with-profits' reward for investors. Scott (2002: 103) has recently argued that the origin of this trend towards equity investment by insurance companies was already evident during the interwar period, but that the interwar years essentially formed a transition phase, with the most significant adoption of equities taking place after 1945.

Greater ownership of consumer durables, including cars, has added to the market for general insurance too which has also been boosted by greater home ownership. Here a greater proportion of the assets accrued tend to be held in more liquid financial instruments in order to secure the cover for claims, the timing of which cannot be anticipated with certainty.

The market for private pension funds, investment trusts and unit trusts has also increased markedly, again responding to demographic and social change as well as economic and fiscal incentives. The most obvious example of this has been the rapid expansion in occupational and personal pension schemes during the post-war period. This growth was particularly acute from 1988 once individuals were allowed (and encouraged) to contract out of the State Earnings Related Pension Scheme. Combined with insurance providers, the developments in pensions and trusts have created a large cohort of institutional investors active within UK financial markets whose contribution to the financial services industry was significant by the 1980s. Whereas in 1958 institutional investors were estimated to hold no more than a third of the stocks and shares issued on behalf of British companies (Midland Bank, *Midland Bank Review* 1959: 8), by the end of 2000, UK financial institutions held ordinary shares valued at £855 billion, equivalent to 47 per cent of the total market value of equities; insurance companies and pension funds alone each hold around 20 per cent of the securities listed on the London Stock Exchange (ONS 2001: 520–1).

Having established the basic characteristics of the sector, we will now examine in greater depth the context in which financial services have been operating in order to understand more clearly why the sector has developed in the ways that it has.

EXPLAINING DEVELOPMENTS IN FINANCIAL SERVICES

The international and macroeconomic contexts

Many of the critical changes which have affected financial services since 1945 are associated with developments in the relationship between Britain and the international economy and also with the emergence of a monetarist economic strategy. The details of monetary policy, its motivation and effects are given in chapter 6 above, but it is important here to indicate the impact these policies had on the environment in which financial services operated as this provides a backdrop against which regulatory reforms can be understood.

An initial important act was the announcement of sterling's convertibility in 1958 (boosted subsequently by the abolition of exchange controls in 1979). Other European nations adopted convertibility during the same period, generating a significant increase in international capital mobility which encouraged the growth of the Euro-dollar and Euro-currencies markets.[1] Britain, particularly, benefited from this expansion, being favourably located geographically in a time zone which facilitated transactions in international markets, as well as having a stable political system, and a fiscal and regulatory framework which was largely favourable to overseas enterprise (Morison and Shepherdson 1991: 72–3).

The Euro-dollar market tripled in 1959 and doubled again in 1960. From 1959, tight credit conditions within the United States encouraged US companies to seek dollar loans overseas (Revell 1973: 295–307). Kennedy's attempt in 1963 to strengthen the dollar by restricting foreign borrowing in the United States also encouraged the Euro-dollar market, which was free from such controls. A further boost came with the oil crises of the 1970s: as oil prices spiralled, the foreign currency earned by oil-exporting nations provided huge deposits which were frequently invested with London and New York financial institutions (Wilson Report 1980: 68). Whereas in 1959 there were 45 overseas banks operating in London, this had risen to 351 by 1983, including 65 American and 25 Japanese banks (Clarke 1986: 20–1).

This growth in international banking made it increasingly difficult for the Bank of England to control bank lending since such a large proportion of business was now being conducted via institutions exempt from its regulation. In 1971 competition and credit control was introduced

---

[1] Euro-currency refers to currency deposited in and loaned from a bank operating outside the country from which the currency originates: thus Euro-dollars refer specifically to US dollars held as deposits by banks outside the United States of America and available for loan. The scale of the Euro-currency market therefore reflects the availability of financial assets denominated in overseas currencies. Its existence increases the opportunities for international financial intermediation and (at least initially) for financial trading outside the scope of domestic regulatory controls.

in an attempt to treat all banks in the same way and encourage competition: every bank was required to maintain a minimum reserve asset ratio of 12.5 per cent. This policy also saw the end of the clearing banks' interest-rate cartel: they now set interest rates individually in response to movements in the Bank of England's Minimum Lending Rate and market conditions (Wilson 1983: 101–5).

The inflation of the early 1970s exacerbated balance-of-payments problems and ultimately, from June 1972, sterling was allowed to float; this resulted in an effective devaluation of the pound which itself was inflationary as imports became relatively more expensive. The removal of lending ceilings in 1971 had also encouraged an inflationary expansion in credit, exacerbating the property boom. Periodically the Bank of England attempted to restrain monetary growth by implementing the 'Corset' – the Supplementary Special Deposit Scheme. This scheme operated by restricting the growth of banks' interest-bearing eligible liabilities, which meant that, in a period of credit restriction, borrowers would find it more attractive to draw on the services of non-banking financial intermediaries for loans. However, financial diversification served to undermine the credit restrictions: the impact of the Corset could be sterilised relatively easily by accessing alternative sources of credit, and it was finally abandoned in 1980 (see chapter 6). Banks were freed to enter the mortgage market, thereby challenging the traditional stronghold of building societies on loans secured by property.

Europe has also proved to be a significant source of pressure on the opportunities for Britain's financial services, especially since 1973 when Britain secured full membership of the European Economic Community. The Treaty of Rome in 1958 outlined the aim of securing freedom of movement of goods, services, labour and capital, but the process of achieving this in the face of disparate, and often conflicting, national economic and political aspirations proved challenging. During the 1980s and 1990s there was a growing perception that European economic performance was being impeded by a failure of member states to pursue complementary economic objectives. These problems were investigated by the European Commission, culminating in the publication in 1985 of a White Paper outlining a programme designed to 'complete the internal market' by 1992 and enforced in the Single European Act in 1987. A central objective of the European Union has been to achieve sustainable economic growth, price stability and high employment ultimately aimed at achieving Economic and Monetary Union.

As these reforms have been implemented, pressure has grown to create a single European financial market. Clearly, in order to achieve this, it has proved necessary to harmonise the regulations governing the provision of financial services within Europe. For those states, such as Britain, where regulation had previously been more restrictive, this has entailed a period of regulatory reform.

Several important directives have been instrumental in promoting change within European financial services. Foremost of these was the Second European Banking Directive, adopted in 1989 and implemented in 1993, which established a single banking licence allowing domestically authorised financial institutions of any European Union member country to operate freely within the European Union. Significantly for Britain, this directive also ruled that institutions from non-member states authorised to operate within a single member state should be treated as if they were 'home' institutions. This has encouraged competition between European financial institutions, but has also opened the market for financial services further: for example, US and Japanese financial institutions operating in London are now able to access European markets on equal terms with European Union financial institutions, thereby consolidating the attraction of a London base. From 1 January 1996, similar freedoms were granted under the Investment Services Directive to non-bank investment firms operating within the European Union. Combined with directives designed to enhance customer protection and financial stability, these reforms have done much to encourage the evolution of a single European market in financial services and create the pressure for further modification of the conditions governing financial institutions within individual countries in order to facilitate their own access to this trade.

A further important influence on the conduct of financial services worthy of brief mention is the provision by banks of loans to developing countries. This practice had grown during the 1970s as British banks recycled the deposits they had received from oil-exporting nations. The problems associated with international debt became increasingly apparent as the 1980s proceeded: the economic and political situation of debtor countries in Latin America and Africa increased their vulnerability to default. This pressure encouraged banks to reconsider their portfolios and re-emphasise domestic credit as a more sustainable avenue for development (Burton 1990: 575–6).

Although this section offers only a brief indication of key changes in the international and macroeconomic environment, three forces affecting financial service provision have been highlighted: first, during the last decades of the twentieth century, the opportunities for international financial intermediation increased significantly, expanding the market for financial services; secondly, the liberalisation of that market has encouraged competition between financial institutions both within the domestic arena and between nations; and thirdly, the globalisation of financial intermediation increased the scope for vulnerability to financial crises where control of business was distanced from the parent institution. We can now examine in greater detail the principal elements of Britain's regulatory response to these challenges to get a clearer sense of the specific context in which the British financial service sector has developed.

The institutional framework within Britain

In a chapter of this kind it is not possible or appropriate to indicate every single regulatory reform affecting financial services. Instead, the aim in this section is to highlight the most significant influences on the institutional framework operating within Britain and comment on their implications.

Many of the principal elements of what is often referred to as financial deregulation have already been mentioned: the lifting of foreign-exchange controls in 1979, and the abolition in 1980 of the Supplementary Special Deposits Scheme by the Bank of England, followed by the abolition of the Bank of England's reserve assets ratio in 1981. In July 1982 all government restrictions on hire purchase were removed, allowing suppliers of goods to set their own terms for loans. October 1983 saw the collapse of the building societies cartel on mortgage rates as the Building Societies Association ceased to recommend a rate (Sargent 1991: 77).

By the early 1980s, the regulatory framework was largely informal and self-regulating, with constraints focusing primarily on the prevention of fraud under the various Companies Acts and the Prevention of Fraud (Investments) Act of 1958 overseen by the Department of Trade and Industry (see, for example, Gowland 1990 and Hall 1987 for surveys of the regulatory framework in the early 1980s). The only sphere in which statutory prudential regulation had been established was banking, and that had only been achieved with the Banking Act of 1979 which, in order to satisfy European directives, provided a clear set of criteria governing the authorisation of a 'recognised bank' by the Bank of England (Balls and O'Donnell 2002: 117).

The benefits of financial liberalisation were already under challenge by the 1980s. First, the functions of the different financial institutions were becoming less distinct and this made it difficult to justify non-equivalence in the conditions under which bank and non-bank financial intermediaries operated. Secondly, the proposals for European integration and the growth of international competition made it more important that regulations were clearly defined in order that differences in local restrictions did not create artificial barriers to trade and competition. This motivation had already been reflected in the decision in 1983 to free Britain's securities markets from barriers to trade by removing immunity of the London Stock Exchange from the Restrictive Practices Act of 1956. This was to be implemented as 'Big Bang' in 1986, the immediate effects of which were that fixed commission charges would be abolished and demarcations between jobbers and brokers removed. In addition, it was agreed to admit corporate members to the Stock Exchange. The promise of 'Big Bang' itself intensified pressure for regulatory reform: as securities markets became increasingly international and the national barriers to competition were eroded, it became ever more important to ensure that financial confidence could be maintained and signalled, and that UK firms would not be disadvantaged in maintaining their business (Lawson 1992: 400). Finally, in the wake of several high-profile financial scandals, including, for example, the collapse of Johnson Matthey Bank in 1984, scepticism was growing as to the capacity of existing regulatory authorities, such as the Bank of England, the Council of the Stock Exchange, and the City Panel on Takeovers and Mergers, to cope adequately with the problems they faced.

The view that barriers to trade between institutions within the domestic market were no longer justified was being aired especially firmly in relation to competition between banks and building societies. Competition was seen to be stacked in favour of banks: banks had a wider range of deposit liabilities with a wider spread of interest rates, they could access wholesale money markets more easily, and they enjoyed a wider range of assets, again with a greater interest-rate spread. This enabled banks to 'cross-subsidise' and offer mortgages at a lower average rate than building societies, thereby enjoying a competitive advantage (Llewellyn 1987: 32).

The 1986 Building Societies Act permitted building societies to expand their activities beyond the savings and mortgage markets, enabling them to trade in insurance and investment products, engage in current-account banking activities, and foreign-exchange trading, as well as develop estate agencies. This Act contributed to a significant intensification of competition for banking services, resulting in the proliferation of varied banking products differentiated by terms and interest rates. Criticism continued of the remaining rigidities still evident in the Act, which established distinctive capital adequacy requirements for banks and building societies reflecting the greater restrictions necessary to maintain the status of building societies as mutuals should they choose to retain it. Llewellyn (1990) argued that the 1986 Act was ultimately self-defeating: if a genuine single market for financial services was to be created, and taking into account the significant overlap of banking and building-society business, it would be more efficient to establish a universal system of regulation which applied to all deposit-taking institutions.

Concerns about the adequacy of existing supervisory arrangements for financial services more generally were raised by the Wilson Report, especially in the context of the securities market, advocating reform and strengthening of the Council for the Securities Industry which had been established in 1978. The failure of the investment management firm Norton Warburg in 1981 provided a sharp challenge to confidence in investor security and the government responded by appointing the Gower Committee to review the protection of investors in securities (Balls and O'Donnell 2002: 118; Clarke 1986: 102–5). This committee's recommendations for a more clearly defined set of self-regulating bodies for the different branches of the financial services industry formed the basis for the reforms which ensued during the later 1980s.

The Financial Services Act of 1986, which became effective in 1988, established a new primary regulatory authority, the Securities and Investments Board (SIB), which was intended to supervise a number of self-regulatory organisations (SROs) which acted as overseers of their own markets, ostensibly operating from the informed perspective of engaged practitioners. Initially five SROs were established: The Securities Association (TSA); the Investment Regulatory Organisation (IMRO); the Financial Intermediaries, Managers and Brokers Regulatory Association (FIMBRA); the Life Assurance and Unit Trust Regulatory Organisation (LAUTRO); and the Association of Futures, Brokers and Dealers (AFBD). Gradually these authorities were reorganised to reduce costs and duplication of activity: the AFBD merged with TSA to form the Securities and Futures Association (SFA) in 1991 and in 1992 LAUTRO and FIMBRA merged to form the Personal Investment Authority (PIA).

Notwithstanding the formalisation of the regulatory arrangements, the Financial Services Act was subject to considerable criticism. Amongst the principal complaints was that self-regulation by 'insiders' to the industry weakened public confidence in their monitoring being open and objective; this fear was exacerbated by the apparent failure of these regulatory authorities to prevent scandals such as the Maxwell pension fraud revealed in 1991. A second criticism was that the self-regulatory system was inefficient: there were too many agencies and, with the diversification of firms' functions, many were forced to consult more than one authority. Initial conservative estimates put the cost of self-regulation at about £20 million a year (*The Economist*, 9 August 1986, 'Big Bang Brief': 69), with later estimates by 1994 putting the figure in the range of £169–£330 million, or about 9 per cent of the turnover of the life assurance industry (Harrison 2000: 19). Pressure was growing to simplify and unify the regulatory system to make it more effective.

One of the first announcements of the new Labour government in May 1997 was that there would be a single statutory regulatory authority governing financial services in Britain. The Securities and Investment Board changed its name to the Financial Services Authority (FSA) in October 1997 and became the designate sole regulator. The Bank of England Act of 1998 transferred supervisory responsibility for banking services from the Bank of England to the FSA. In June 2000 the Financial Services and Markets Act completed its passage through parliament and became effective from December 2001. This Act had four objectives: to maintain confidence in the UK financial system, to promote public understanding of financial services, to protect customers, and to reduce financial crime. The four objectives are to be pursued in a manner that does not jeopardise competition, which promotes the international position of UK financial services, and which is innovative and cost-effective (Balls and O'Donnell 2002: 120–2).

These measures have been supplemented by further legislation aimed at setting and maintaining standards for financial products. The launch of the Individual Savings Account Schemes (ISAs) in 1999 was accompanied by the introduction of the CAT standard which provides a benchmark set of criteria on Charges, Access and Terms for all financial services against which providers and consumers can compare their products. Lenders do not have to follow these standards, but can use the CAT standard as a marketing device if they wish (Balls and O'Donnell 2002: 126–7). This move towards regulation at product level is interesting since it reflects the disintegration of functional barriers between financial institutions which has gathered pace since the 1980s. If institutions are engaged in such a wide range of financial services, then the process of monitoring may be more effective if it focuses on the product rather than the intermediary.

Technological progress

Technological innovation has proved to be a very important factor influencing the development of financial services delivery and marketing. The greatest opportunities for change have been associated with the introduction of information technology. This has facilitated integration of international financial markets, a proliferation in the quantity of information being circulated, and a reduction in the relative cost of acquiring it. Inevitably this has also intensified the competition between individual financial institutions: it is now much easier for competitors and consumers to access the kinds of information on which to base an informed and more flexible business and customer strategy, and the barriers to entry have been reduced in the market for financial services as a result. This intensification of competition has encouraged product innovation in the areas of lending (such as, for example, in the mortgage market), but also in the areas of deposits as financial institutions have sought to ensure they secure the necessary capital with which to sustain their activities.

Technological progress has affected the industry at various levels. Initially computers were used largely for processing and storing information, thereby reducing the demand for semi-skilled staff. The development of automated teller machines (ATMs) has had a huge impact in extending the provision of banking services out of office hours and in reducing the demand for counter staff at banks. In 1985 the major British Banking Groups alone supported 7,702 ATMs, but the figure had grown to 13,283 by 1990 (British Bankers' Association, *Abstract of Banking Statistics: banking business*, 1996 (13): tab. 5.03). There has also been an increasing tendency for these machines to be located away from branches, reflecting the desire to make banking services accessible in retail centres as well as the reduction of branch banking offices. Of the 13,283 ATMs operated by the major British Banking Groups in 1990, 7.7 per cent were located away from branches; by 1995 they operated 15,385 ATMs of which almost 15 per cent were located away from branches, and, in 2000, they operated 24,170 machines, but 30 per cent of these were located away from branches (British Bankers' Association, *Abstract of Banking Statistics: banking business*, 2001 (18): 54).

Since the 1980s, a vast system of automated transfers has been created, so that most non-cash personal banking transactions are undertaken electronically, debit cards alone accounting for transactions worth £2.3 billion in 2000 (ONS, *Social Trends*, 2002 (32): 114). The growth of credit- and debit-card transactions has extended beyond banking services into the domain of non-banking financial intermediaries, as well as encouraging the growth of retail credit schemes. In 1990 about 35 per cent of women and 45 per cent of men possessed a debit card, 34 per cent and 43 per cent respectively had a credit or charge card and only 18 and 12 per cent respectively a store or retail card. By 2000 more than 80 per cent of both men and women had debit cards, 50 per cent of women and 57 per cent of men owned credit cards, and 40 per cent of women and 28 per cent of men possessed store cards (ONS, *Social Trends*, 2002 (32): 114, tab. 6.12).

Major initiatives such as 'telephone banking' were established in the UK initially in 1986 with the jointly operated Home and Office Banking Scheme of the Bank of Scotland and Nottingham Building Society, followed by the TSB Speedlink system in 1987, and, most notably, the launch of First Direct by Midland Bank (HSBC) in 1989. These services have been particularly successful, enabling customers to complete transactions from their own homes, and obviating the need for expensive delivery of financial services via local branch offices.

Whereas in 1985 only 13 per cent of UK households owned a computer, this had grown to more than 40 per cent by 2000–1, with the figure reaching more than 70 per cent for households headed by those in managerial or technical occupations. The National Statistics Omnibus Survey of July 2002 revealed that 40 per cent of adults had accessed the Internet in the month prior to the survey (ONS, *Social Trends*, 2002 (32): 218). As private access to computers has increased, financial institutions have extended their 'home-banking' provision further, offering Internet banking services (Taylor and Morison 1999: 64–8).

Increased use of computer-based service delivery systems has the added benefit for firms of providing access to information on customers. This allows them to manage more efficient customer databases, which, in turn, permits them to monitor the success of individual financial products and target their marketing of new products specifically. These benefits of technology have proved particularly attractive to supermarkets and other retailers such as Marks and Spencer, who have seized the opportunities to offer low-cost financial services, creating another source of competition for traditional banks and life assurance companies and prompting further product innovation on the part of established firms. In addition, the access to high-quality information about consumers has allowed firms to focus more intensively on customer relations in an attempt to increase consumer retention and target desirable customers with products which reward loyalty.

THE IMPLICATIONS OF DEVELOPMENTS IN FINANCIAL SERVICES

The most obvious implications of the developments outlined above have been reflected in the structure and delivery of financial services within the United Kingdom. More intense competition during the early 1980s increased the volume of banking business, but cut the profit margins associated with it, thereby making banks more vulnerable to bad debts. This has made small-scale retail banking business (i.e. the personal sector) relatively more attractive and encouraged securitisation as a strategy for reducing the risk associated with financial intermediation (Goodhart 1986: 93).

One of the consequences of financial reform has been increased concentration within the industry with each sector dominated by smaller numbers of larger companies. A series of bank mergers during the 1960s established the dominance of the major clearing banks still largely in existence today. Life assurance has also experienced similar patterns of concentration and rationalisation with the top ten companies having more than half the industry's assets by the end of the twentieth century. Post-war merger activity has been particularly significant in the building society industry. The number of registered societies has continued to decline, with the contraction being most rapid after 1960: in 1950 there were 819 registered societies, falling to 726 in 1960, 481 in 1970, 273 in 1980 and just 67 by 2000 (CML, *Housing Finance*). The average scale of the assets held by each society has increased commensurately, with the most marked increase in scale in nominal terms taking place during the 1970s and 1980s. Even after allowing for inflation, it is clear that the scale of building society enterprise was increasing notably and that trade was becoming concentrated in fewer hands. In 1950 the largest 10 societies held just less than half of the industry's assets, rising to 54.9 per cent by 1960, 64.3 per cent by 1970 and 71 per cent by 1980 (Drake 1989: 9; Boléat 1986).

Diversification in the nature of business undertaken by building societies has been reflected in the fact that mortgage assets generally declined as a proportion of the total assets of the industry from about 85 per cent in 1950 to 75 per cent by the end of the century (derived from CML, *Housing Finance*). This loss of demarcation between the activities of building societies and banks is similarly reflected in the changing contribution which banks have made to the mortgage market, noted above.

The principal feature of financial services provision at the end of the twentieth century is that institutions are much less segmented than they were during the 1950s both spatially and in terms of function. This has created a more intensely competitive market for most financial products putting pressure on firms to reduce the unit cost of their delivery, but has also increased the scope of operations which most financial intermediaries can access. The net effect of this has been for financial innovation to accelerate, reinforcing the impression of the sector as a dynamic force within the British economy. The next two sections seek to examine briefly how this dynamism has affected the relationship between the financial services sector and two key elements of the economy: the personal sector and the business community.

The personal sector

One of the interesting features of household economic activity since the war has been the fluctuations in the UK personal savings ratio. Figure 7.1 reveals the generally rising trend in the propensity of individuals to save during the third quarter of the twentieth century. By the end of the 1970s, personal sector saving comprised 41 per cent of aggregate saving in the economy as a whole and amounted to more than £17.6 billion (Wilson 1983: 16). Between 1975 and 1988, the savings ratio displayed a downward trend, before recovering again, to a slightly lower peak of about 12 per cent by the early 1990s, and then resuming its contractionary trend towards the end of the twentieth century. The pattern of savings behaviour is important for three reasons: first, savings behaviour is influenced by perceptions of personal wealth which may have real effects on the economy; secondly, savings clearly influence the supply of financial resources by determining the scale of deposits available for reinvestment by financial intermediaries; and thirdly, savings to some extent mirror consumption behaviour, which is closely associated with the demand for credit from financial institutions and may reveal important interactive effects between the demand- and supply-side forces in the financial services market.

These trends in personal saving reflect the trends in consumption which boomed during the 1980s and then collapsed in the early 1990s. In addition, the 1970s saw a period of high inflation and, it is argued, this caused precautionary savings to rise as individuals sought to restore the real value of their existing saving stocks, as well as perhaps seeking to increase savings in order to insure against the risks associated with recession. In addition, what we may be witnessing towards the end

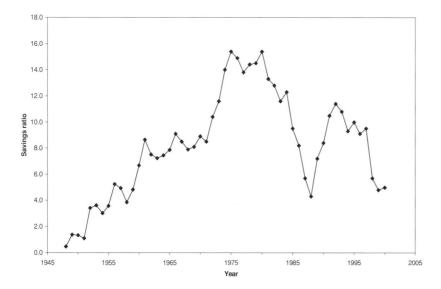

of the twentieth century is the consequences of positive wealth effects arising from the growth of home ownership combined with rising house prices, and the increased accessibility of pension funds and life-assurance schemes. In effect, households perceive their wealth to be sufficient to sustain their long-term needs, allowing them to replace precautionary savings with current consumption.

It seems plausible that the wealth effects associated with property ownership, which were positive for much of the late twentieth century (with the obvious exception of the early 1990s when house prices collapsed and many households were constrained by negative equity), consolidated the significance of financial institutions both as a source of personal credit, and as principal suppliers of investment funds. This trend has been reflected in the growth of equity withdrawal since the mid-1980s. As access to mortgage finance has eased with financial liberalisation, it has proved easier for households to borrow against the value of their property. Miles (1992) argues that financial liberalisation has therefore reinforced the underlying appreciation in property values as house prices have increased to reflect both their scarcity and their enhanced real value as a source of fungible wealth. Financial liberalisation may have been important in a number of ways: increased competition between mortgage providers encouraged a rise in the average loan–value ratio for first-time buyers, which permitted greater participation in the property market, but also created more risk of instability in the market once property prices became less buoyant; increased property ownership combined with customer nervousness during the early 1990s recession seems to have consolidated a shift in the way in which the personal sector interacts with financial services such that it provides a much more significant source of demand for

Figure 7.1 Personal savings ratio, 1948–2000

Source: Data derived from ONS (CSO), *National Income Accounts*, 'Blue Books', various years.

borrowing rather than supply of deposits. Although the 'excessive' burden of debt of the 1980s has been reduced, the personal sector does not yet seem to have returned to its former role as a significant net provider of funds (for more detailed discussion of some of these issues, see Sargent 1991, and Pain and Westaway 1994).

Business finance

The issue of how businesses have secured investment funds and the limitations which perceived financial rigidities ostensibly place upon them has been an issue of prevalent concern amongst policy makers and economic historians. Debate has focused on several themes including, in particular, whether the quantity of capital made available to British entrepreneurs was adequate for their needs, and whether it was offered under the right conditions in respect of price and term. The 'problems' facing 'small firms' have received particular attention as historians have sought to validate concerns expressed by the Macmillan Committee of 1931 about an 'equity gap' facing small businesses, which have been reiterated at various intervals since then, by, for example, the 1959 Radcliffe Committee, the 1971 Bolton Committee and the 1980 Wilson Committee. Notwithstanding the various post-war innovations in financial provision which sought to close the Macmillan gap (including, for example, the formation and subsequent expansion of the Industrial and Commercial Finance Corporation and the Finance Corporation for Industry in 1945, and of organisations such as Equity Capital for Industry formed in 1976), Wilson still drew attention to the inevitable limitations of a financial system relying on market forces alone to offer loans at a market clearing price and provide adequate support to firms of varying scale. Even in 2002, Britain's official yearbook was noting the importance of government intervention to alleviate difficulties small businesses can face in accessing finance, and commented on the formation of the Small Business Service in April 2000 as a major step forward in addressing these problems (ONS 2001a: 389).

Fears have frequently focused on the claim that the British financial sector operates with short-term objectives paramount, and that this has proved to have deleterious consequences for gross domestic fixed capital accumulation. This complaint has often been aired too in relation to an increased role for institutional investors where short-term fluctuations in returns are more likely to affect decisions than longer-term commitments to enterprise. Given the dynamism of financial services described above, it is clearly important to seek to provide some assessment of how this has affected industrial finance.

Internal finance, including reserves and allowances for depreciation of existing capital assets, remained the dominant source for industrial investment throughout the post-war period, although its significance was on a downward path falling from an annual average of 94 per cent of all funds 1952–5 to 80 per cent in 1971–6 (Thomas 1978: 315). On average, between 1949 and 1953 quoted manufacturing companies still relied on internal finance to support about three-quarters of their business and this reduced only slightly during the 1950s. Where external support was sought, reliance on bank loans was very limited (less than 3 per cent for 1949–53 and about 4 per cent for the remainder of the 1950s). The proportion of finance obtained by long-term loans and new issues of securities increased during the 1950s with fluctuations in the distribution of equity and fixed-interest securities apparently related to the business cycle (Paish 1965: 132–7). During the 1960s internal finance remained important for about 70 per cent of additional industrial investment, but this had reduced to just below 60 per cent during the 1970s, with bank lending increasing in importance, especially using the medium of short-term advances via overdrafts (Coakley 1988: 173). As the Bolton Report (1971: 160–2) observed, this made small firms in particular vulnerable to pressure from credit restrictions affecting both price and availability of funds.

For much of the 1980s and 1990s, the trend towards reduced reliance on internal finance was maintained, although fluctuations between years were quite marked: the typical ratio was that about half of industrial investment was sustained by internal finance. In general, bank lending consolidated its position as a significant supporter of industry, comprising on average about 18 per cent of industrial finance (ONS, *Financial Statistics*, various years). For small and medium-sized enterprises, the fluctuations in bank support were also notable, though banks remained the major source for external funds: banks provided about 60 per cent of external finance 1987–90, and 47.4 per cent between 1995 and 1997; much of this reduction in bank finance was filled by an increase in the contribution of hire purchase and leasing (Lund and Wright 1999: 196). The recession of the early 1990s had encouraged smaller businesses to reduce their overall indebtedness as well as their dependence on bank finance. This intention was reflected in the reduction in overdraft advances and a growth in term lending often at fixed interest rates. This shift has benefited small businesses by reducing their vulnerability to economic fluctuations: by 1998 70 per cent of bank finance for small businesses was in the form of fixed loans with two-thirds having maturities of more than five years (Harrison 2000: 295).

Sargent (1991) notes the large increase in corporate debt during the early 1980s, but suggests that the risks associated with this were diminished by the tendency for firms to rely more heavily than previously on banks. He argues that liberalisation of financial services has largely benefited industrial investment by permitting banks to broaden the range of services on offer and making it more attractive for firms to seek credit from them. The difficulties of the early 1980s did not represent

fundamental weakness in the new financial system, but rather transitional adjustment costs. These were fuelled by over-optimistic expectations of Britain's economic performance rather than a false conviction
that financial liberalisation could deliver sustainable economic growth.

Writers such as Hutton (1995) offer a far more pessimistic interpretation of the real effects of financial innovation. He argues that liberalisation of financial markets has increased reliance on market-based finance
to the detriment of British industrial investment. The turnover of Britain's
financial markets has increased, dividend payouts have accelerated, and,
whilst companies may find it easier to secure external support, they are
then saddled with maintaining debilitating rates of return on that investment at the cost of real expansion (Hutton 1995: 164–8). For Hutton, this
trend has been exacerbated by the growth of institutional investment
(especially with the expansion in pension funds). Fund managers have
become more willing to invest in equities, but cannot afford to maintain
portfolios in which dividend payouts are volatile. This creates pressure on
companies to maintain a corporate strategy in which financial returns are
high at the cost of longer-term investment considerations (Hutton 1995:
304–5).

This debate about the relative dominance of financial and industrial
interests and the significance of that relationship is difficult to resolve,
especially since, in the context of industrial finance, it is not easy to
be sure of the range and relative force of the different factors determining the supply and demand for loanable funds: does a given firm's
capital structure reveal its free or constrained preferences for business
finance? Capie and Collins (1992) suggest that the post-war expansion
in financial services resulted in industrialists having more choice over
their financial strategy and also that many of the constraints which had
faced business during the pre-1945 period had at least been eased. This
does not seem too controversial, but equally it does not really get us far
in understanding the complexity of the relationship between finance and
industry. As suggested in the context of our discussion of the personal
sector, the vast expansion in financial services and the merging of barriers between institutions may have created interactive effects which could
distort the market for industrial finance, increasing its volatility and undermining the efficiency of investment decisions. This suggests that it
is important for economic historians to develop a clear understanding
of the interdependence of different sectors of the economy and different components of individual sectors if they want to explain economic
development effectively.

Evaluating the contribution of financial services

It is not an easy matter to analyse the net contribution of the post-war
revolution in financial services to the economy. It is clear that they make

a major contribution in terms of employment, income generation and in relation to the balance of payments. However, the claim that Britain has consistently had a poor investment record in terms of its quantity, quality and productivity has been a persistent feature of post-war economic commentary. This criticism has inevitably led to the efficiency of growth of financial services being questioned.

Some of the concerns about the productivity gains from expansion in financial and business services are discussed by Millward in chapter 10 below. Using O'Mahony's (1999) study of Britain's productivity performance, Millward notes the low productivity growth for finance and business services compared to the overall performance of the economy. Productivity declined in this sector during the period 1950–73 and experienced only modest improvements between 1973 and 1995. Millward emphasises the measurement problems associated with service sector productivity estimates, but revised estimates still only bring productivity performance closer to the national average rather than indicating something spectacular. Interestingly Millward's discussion of O'Mahony's international comparison of capital intensity and productivity argues too that Britain's advantages in finance and business services during the 1950s had been eroded by the 1990s as the United States, France and Germany enjoyed superior productivity performances. Although the scale of this sector was more important to Britain than to the countries to which it was being compared, this suggests that the economic gains from rapid expansion of this sector were relatively less. Interestingly, O'Mahony's original data reported figures for Japan too, and, by comparison, productivity growth in the finance and business sector remained relatively strong for the UK in this case (O'Mahony 1999: tab. 2.10). This might be consistent with the notion that expansion of financial services generally, and the trend towards globalisation, favoured Europe and the United States more than Japan.

This commentary raises some interesting questions. Whilst this chapter has offered a survey of financial services which emphasises dynamism, growth and success, the prospects for enhancing economic growth at a rate comparable to other major economies seems limited unless productivity is improved in this key sector.

CONCLUSIONS

This chapter has sought to demonstrate the fundamental changes in Britain's financial services sector since 1945. During the post-war period the sector has become much larger and more competitive as institutional and regulatory reform has broken down some of the barriers between the various elements of the sector. The 1980s and 1990s have proved especially significant periods of expansion and change. Technological progress has revolutionised the delivery of financial services and facilitated innovation in financial products which has further helped to intensify competition. To some extent too, the dynamism of this sector during the post-war period has reflected the improvements in living standards which the majority of British people have enjoyed, and the social and demographic changes which have affected demand for financial products.

It is clear that this sector has outperformed and, at least to some extent, compensated for the decline in Britain's manufacturing sector and that Britain's economy is hugely dependent on performance in this sphere. Nevertheless, international productivity comparisons raise some doubts as to the long-term sustainability of Britain's reliance on this sector as the panacea for maintaining, or even enhancing, overall economic performance.

8

Economic policy

JIM TOMLINSON

Contents

INTRODUCTION

From 1931 the possibility of much greater management of the national economy was opened up by the departure from gold, the imposition of tariffs and, at the micro-economic level, the willingness of government to encourage cartels and price-fixing.[1] Together these policies enabled the pursuit of a loose-coupled strategy of raising prices in order to increase profits and hence, it was hoped, investment (Booth 1987). The war added a major impetus to this rise of national economic management (NEM). On the one hand, it greatly reinforced the political necessity for governments to offer economic security and betterment to their citizens, not least because the political support for a capitalist economy had been shaken by the interwar depression and now faced a potent ideological enemy in the Soviet system. Simultaneously, the war enormously enlarged the capacity of government, increasing the spending and taxing power, but also instituting a range of direct controls which meant that by 1945 we can sensibly talk about a semi-planned economy in Britain, albeit one in

[1] I am grateful to Alan Booth and Stephen Broadberry for helpful comments on the first draft of this chapter.

which the planning mechanisms were very much tied to the exigencies of wartime shortages (see chapter 1 above).

While there was some retreat from the intensive wartime controls in the later part of the Attlee period (1945–51), the belief that government's prime domestic purpose was to manage the economy persisted for the rest of the twentieth century, largely surviving even after the alleged 'retreat from economic management' of the late 1970s and 1980s. This high level of government activity has generated in its wake an enormous volume of scholarly comment and analysis. The great bulk of this commentary has been highly normative in character, commonly shaped by a perception of 'failure' in British post-war economic performance, with government policy in turn (through sins of both commission and omission) seen as a major culprit for this failure. It must be stressed that such notions of failure have affected not only commentators and historians: policy makers, both bureaucrats and politicians, have themselves commonly shared this analysis (Tomlinson 2000). However, recent work from a number of directions has undermined such blanket notions of failure, and this chapter gives an account of post-war policy which attempts to move away from a narrative of failure to one which suggests qualified success in the pursuit of a multiplicity of aims in a highly constraining environment.

The aims of post-war economic policy are conventionally described as fourfold. In the words of Harold Macmillan (chancellor of the Exchequer 1955–7, prime minister 1957–63): 'Full employment, an expanding economy, stable prices and a strong pound; these were the balls which the Chancellor of the Exchequer, like a new Cinquevalli was expected to keep in the air' (Macmillan 1971: 3).[2] To this list a fifth, reduction of poverty and inequality might be added, which is discussed in chapters 9, 14 and 15. In fact, governments have not normally given equal simultaneous weight to these objectives as Macmillan suggests. An important part of any account of policy in this period must be how and why at different times different objectives have been given greater weight than others. This is returned to in detail below, but in schematic form we may note here how in the 1940s and 1950s full employment and the balance of payments were given highest priority; that from the late 1950s growth became much more important; that inflation rose sharply up the agenda in the 1970s and 1980s; and how full employment came rather more to the fore in the late 1990s, albeit with a clear presumption that its achievement was conditional on sustained stable prices.

Before looking in detail at particular policy aims and the degrees of success in their achievement, it is necessary to look at the context in which British NEM was pursued. While versions of NEM appeared in almost all European countries in the post-1945 period, the British version had its own specific starting points and characteristics.

---

[2] Paul Cinquevalli (1859–1918) was a famous circus performer, known as 'the greatest juggler in the world'.

THE CONTEXT FOR NATIONAL ECONOMIC MANAGEMENT IN BRITAIN

The British economy was historically the most internationally integrated of all the major countries, and this is the single most important point of context for understanding post-war British economic policy (Tables 8.1, 8.2). This integration had been attenuated by events surrounding the depression of the 1930s, and even more by the war. But at the war's end few failed to accept that, in the long run, Britain's prosperity would require such integration to be re-built, certainly as far as trade was concerned. There were widely divergent views on the geographical scope of this policy and the pace at which the post-war economy could be opened up to international forces. But both the politics of the period and the structure of the economy told against any serious possibility of NEM implying movement towards a closed economy.

On the political side, successive post-war governments were determined to re-make Britain as a world power, and though the means to achieve this were matters of great contention, the strategy itself told against cutting ties (including economic ties) with the rest of the world. As far as the economic structure was concerned, Britain's evolution since the nineteenth century had been towards reliance on a relatively small range of staple export industries to provide the foreign-exchange revenues to pay for very large-scale raw material and food imports from abroad. Before 1914 these visible earnings had been greatly supplemented by invisible receipts, including from foreign investment, but two world wars had diminished and disrupted this earning potential. In consequence, foreign exchange now had to come to a greater extent from visible earnings, but at a time when the geographical and commodity patterns of visible trade were to undergo enormous shifts. The 'classic' nineteenth-century pattern of Britain trading its manufactured goods, many sold in primary-producer markets inside and outside the Empire, for imported foodstuffs and raw materials purchased largely from the same set of countries, was to be replaced by one in which manufactures were increasingly swapped for manufactures within the group of rich countries of the industrialised world.

The traditional trade pattern had been closely linked to important features of the internal economy which were also to

Table 8.1   Merchandise trade as % of GDP at current prices, 1913–1995

	1913	1950	1973	1995
UK	44.7	36.0	39.3	42.6
France	35.4	21.2	29.0	36.6
Germany	35.1	20.1	35.2	38.7
Japan	31.4	16.9	18.3	14.1
USA	11.2	7.0	10.5	19.0

Source: Hirst and Thompson (2000: 337).

Table 8.2   Net capital flows as % of GDP, 1890–1996

	1890–1914	1927–31	1947–59	1960–73	1990–6
UK	4.6	1.9	1.2	0.8	2.6
France	1.3	1.4	1.5	0.6	0.7
Germany	1.5	2.0	2.0	1.0	2.7
Japan	2.4	0.6	1.3	1.0	2.1
USA	1.0	0.7	0.6	0.5	1.2

Source: Hirst and Thompson (2000: 340).

be central to the British version of NEM. The international division of labour which underpinned these trade patterns had allowed Britain to lose most of its agriculture and more or less all its peasantry to become the most proletarian of major societies. The overwhelmingly working-class character of Britain, and the consequent reliance of the great majority of the population on wage labour, gave a political salience to security of employment unmatched by other major European economies with their large peasantries and more complex economic interests. The policy context was also affected by the fact that this working-class interest was represented by a unified trade union body (the TUC), undivided by religion or ideology, and closely allied to one of the two key political parties. Also important was the fact that the major staple export industries were highly regionally concentrated, so that structural change in the interwar period had created a regional problem which, after 1945, added another dimension to the complexity of managing a national economy in which spatial divergence in economic prosperity was a highly sensitive political issue (see chapter 13 below).

Finally, an important legacy of the war period for Britain was not only a bigger state, which was common across Europe, but a particularly centralised structure of that state. Not only did Britain have a unitary rather than a federal polity, but the pattern of public spending, especially on welfare, was much more concentrated at national government level than in other 'welfare states'. Added to on the tax side by the wartime development of PAYE, this structure gave a much greater perceived potential to fiscal policy than elsewhere, and helps to account for important and peculiar features of the British way of conducting NEM.

THE EVOLUTION OF THE INTERNATIONAL CONTEXT

Before discussing particular policy areas, we need to set out in more detail the international environment in which policy operated, this being, as suggested above, the key context for Britain's pursuit of NEM.

Britain was junior partner with the USA in the reconstruction of the institutions of the world economy at the end of the Second World War. The central thrust of US policy was to build a non-discriminatory trade system, coupled with an exchange rate system which at least discouraged competitive depreciations. This programme was seen by the USA as the way to prevent the recurrence of the economic and political breakdown of the 1930s, to make the world safe for American capitalism, and, according to some critics, to lessen the future economic strength of the UK (Dobson 1995: 81–90). Such a programme was highly problematic for Britain, with its legacy of Imperial Preference (a preferential tariff regime for British Empire and Commonwealth countries) and combination of commitments to both full employment and an overvalued currency sustained by exchange controls. Nevertheless, out of a combination of arm-twisting by the USA, great power pretensions relating to the value of the pound, and charismatic advocacy by Keynes, Britain committed herself in principle to such a regime (Pressnell 1986; Skidelsky 2000: chs. 6, 7, 9–12).

Britain's adherence to the Bretton Woods Agreement of 1944 committed her in broad terms to a regime of stable (but not unchangeable) exchange rates, and to the abolition of exchange controls. But in practice the transition to such arrangements was slow and painful, even with the eventual support of Marshall Aid from 1948. Exchange controls were lifted in 1947, a condition placed on the US loan to Britain in 1945, but such was the run on the pound that followed that after six weeks controls were re-imposed, not to be lifted again until the late 1950s. (Minor forms of exchange control were continued until 1979.) Despite such controls the pound was devalued in 1949, but then remained unchanged until 1967.

The attempt to establish a parallel body to the International Monetary Fund (IMF) created at Bretton Woods was unsuccessful. The proposal for an International Trade Organisation (ITO), designed to supervise multi-lateralism in trade, foundered. In the immediate conditions of the post-war world a general commitment to multilateral trade was contrary to Britain's concerns with employment and a continuing commitment to imperial trade links. The ITO charter was therefore never ratified (Diebold 1952). Nevertheless the non-discriminatory design was embodied in the General Agreement on Tariffs and Trade (GATT), which from 1947 onwards, in a series of rounds, moved much of the world towards freer trade, especially in manufactured goods (Van der Wee 1986: 349–51, 382–90). But as with currencies, so with trade, the movement towards the US ideal was halting in most European countries, including Britain. For example, vestiges of imperial preference, by which British goods received privileged access to Empire markets and vice versa, survived into Britain's entry into the EEC (1973) in the form of 'transitional arrangements' for privileged access of primary products such as New Zealand butter into the UK market.

Down to 1971/2 the international financial regime within which Britain conducted its policy is commonly seen as that laid down at Bretton Woods. Such a description needs to be qualified in a number of ways. As already noted, the full movement towards that regime cannot be dated before 1954 when *de facto* free convertibility of the pound into the US dollar was established. Second, the actual fixity of exchange rates under Bretton Woods was greater than its designers anticipated, in particular because political prestige became attached to a particular exchange rate in an economically irrational manner. Third, the Bretton Woods system relied for international liquidity on the free availability of dollars (and to a lesser extent on sterling), but from the 1960s the attractiveness of the dollar declined. While US deficits provided plenty of dollars in the 1960s, there were growing fears about the future sufficiency of international liquidity (James 1996: chs. 6, 7). Finally, and with especially direct implications for the management of individual economies, an unintended consequence of Bretton Woods was to encourage the expansion of international capital flows, though the upward movement began from a level which was hugely less than had existed in the pre-1914 years (Table 8.2).

Despite these significant qualifications, the designation 'Bretton Woods era' makes sense in distinguishing it from the sharply different years that followed, characterised by floating exchange rates and more generally by a much less stable economic environment. The new regime after 1971/2 was initiated by the declining capacity of the USA to act as the dominant power in the international economy. The comparative economic performance of the USA in the 1950s and 1960s was poor, and many other advanced capitalist countries caught up a considerable part of the gap between themselves and America. The Bretton Woods arrangements made it difficult for the USA to devalue its currency as the situation demanded, and the 1971 raising of the gold value of the dollar heralded the break-up of the system. However, that system was already under great strain from the acceleration of inflation from the late 1960s, the destabilising effects of which for exchange rates were transmitted and magnified by the increasing scale of capital flows.

The regime of floating rates was forced on the world but did not lack intellectual support. It could be seen not only as another case of allowing the market to determine prices, but, more particularly in Britain, as a way of resolving the perceived conflict between domestic and external policy objectives, between domestic growth and stability of the pound (Brittan 1971). The hopes entertained at the end of the Bretton Woods era about the effects of floating rates were cruelly belied by subsequent events. Nominal exchange rates have proved much more unstable than most anticipated, and real exchange rates fluctuated widely, with significant effects on output and employment (Dornbusch 1976; Krugman 1989). Since the 1980s the leading financial powers have periodically sought, with limited success, to re-stabilise exchange rates, through a variety of *ad hoc* arrangements (James 1996: ch. 13).

Multilateralism in finance has been accompanied by a parallel trend towards multilateralism in trade. This has always been qualified by an almost complete lack of application to agriculture, and a very qualified application to many services (at least down to the late 1990s), but the Uruguay Round of 1996 seemed both to symbolise and to encourage further liberalisation, especially with creation of the World Trade Organisation. However, the pattern has not been one of linear movement towards such liberalisation. Even in the most liberalised area, manufactured goods, there has been periodic 'regression'. In the crisis years of the 1970s, for example, significant expansion of trade restrictions was pursued, largely by European countries against Japanese producers. Other

Table 8.3 Geographical composition of British trade, 1955–1985 *(% of total)*	1955		1967		1972		1985	
	Imports	Exports	Imports	Exports	Imports	Exports	Imports	Exports
Sterling Area	39.4	27.4	47.0	30.4	23.3	24.4	–	–
USA	10.7	12.6	7.0	12.2	10.6	12.5	11.7	14.7
W. Eur.	25.7	36.4	28.1	38.0	43.9	42.9	63.1	58.3
(EEC)	(12.6)	(19.6)	(14.0)	(19.2)	(24.5)	(22.9)	(46.0)	(46.3)
USSR and E. Eur.	2.7	3.9	1.2	3.3	3.5	2.8	2.2	2.0
Japan	0.6	0.6	1.5	1.8	2.8	1.6	4.9	1.3

Source: Prest and Coppock (1986).

measures, such as the Multi-Fibre Agreement, have also until recently acted to reduce penetration of European markets by textile products from poor countries. But whatever the effects of such trade diverting policies, they have not been the main determinants of the shift in world trade patterns, which have increasingly seen trade concentrated in the swapping of manufactured goods between advanced capitalist countries. This pattern is evident in the changing geographical pattern of Britain's trade (Table 8.3).

Increasingly Britain's economic fortunes have been linked with the EU, and less with the old Sterling Area or Commonwealth, with which the Area was largely coterminous. The shift in pattern is partly linked with Britain's EU accession in 1973, but was already apparent before that date (see chapter 11 below). Trading links with Europe had grown rapidly, especially from the 1960s. The links with the Commonwealth and Sterling Area suffered from the erosion of imperial preference, but much more from the rapidity of growth of European markets. In addition, 'Europeanisation' of British trade was intensified by the agricultural protectionism introduced from the 1930s, further enhanced in the 1940s, and pressed even further under the Common Agricultural Policy. The extraordinary effect of this was to make Britain self-sufficient in agricultural products, reversing the trend of a century and a half and the underpinnings this provided to traditional trading patterns.

By the end of the twentieth century Britain was doing more than half its trade with western Europe and its government had committed itself in principle to the idea of joining the European Single Currency. While politically British governments still hankered after a world role, it was clear that Britain's economic fortunes were tied more closely than ever before to one region, that of Europe. Despite all the talk of globalisation, Britain was in most economic respects, and especially in trade, less globally and more European oriented than in 1945.

Within the environment sketched above the aims of economic policy have been both changing and controversial. The account below can only highlight developments in the four areas that have at times been deemed policy aims. Particular attention is given to how these aims relate to the idea of policy failure. Because of this focus, economic growth is given the most extended treatment, as it is 'failure' in this regard which has most shaped both policy and commentaries on that policy. This issue of failure also raises the question of an appropriate benchmark for British performance. There is no 'correct' benchmark, but it seems reasonable to make the comparisons with the other 'big three' western European economies, Germany, Italy and France, given their broad similarity in level of development and size (at least until German re-unification). In addition, these are also the countries with which contemporaries most commonly made comparisons.

POLICY ON THE BALANCE OF PAYMENTS AND THE EXCHANGE RATE

In the 1940s the balance of payments was at the top of the policy agenda, the war having left an enormous current-account deficit, especially with the USA. The Attlee government's propaganda, with such slogans as 'Export or Die' and 'England's Bread Hangs by Lancashire's Thread', concentrated attention on the requirement for exports to pay for food and raw materials, though the reality was that much foreign exchange was going to pay for government overseas spending and foreign investment (Cairncross 1986: ch. 4; Tomlinson 1997: ch. 3). Aided by diminished competition from Germany and Japan, the current account did recover markedly in the late 1940s, including that with the USA, helped by the 1949 devaluation. Whatever the underlying complexities of the balance-of-payments position, Labour had successfully conveyed the argument that full employment and economic security were crucially linked to export success. While in ministerial and official circles there was much debate about Britain's international economic policies, the public debate was largely dominated by this simple notion that the revival of export markets was a key underpinning of domestic stability; internal and external goals were neatly complementary.

In the succeeding two decades the balance of payments remained close to the top of the policy agenda. This reflected, in part, the structural fact noted above: that Britain was an unusually open economy in comparison not only with the USA but also with other major western European economies. This focus (or even obsession) also reflected the existence of a fixed exchange rate (down to 1972), which meant that payments difficulties were quickly translated into an exchange-rate problem, stimulating a rapid government reaction. Governments invested much rhetorical energy into making the external value of the currency an index of national strength (e.g. Blaazer 1999). In the 1950s and 1960s the determination to sustain the exchange rate alongside the concern with maintaining employment led to the 'stop-go' cycle, in which short-run deterioration in the payments position led to demand restriction at home, followed by renewed expansion when this restriction led to unacceptably high levels of unemployment. This stop-go cycle came to be invested with great significance because of the suggestion that it subordinated domestic expansion to international economic goals such as defence of the Sterling Area and the international role of the pound. This argument was first powerfully articulated by Shonfield in 1958, and, with variations, has provided a staple of negative judgements about British policy ever since.

However, this adverse judgement has in turn been the subject of powerful criticism. Schenk (1994) has shown that the defence of the Sterling Area in the 1950s was much less detrimental to the domestic economy than Shonfield and his successors supposed. She demonstrates that the sterling balances were *not* a highly volatile threat to Britain's reserves; that the Sterling Area did not provide a soft, uncompetitive haven for British exports; that the proportion of British GDP invested in the Sterling Area was almost trivial; and that, in any event, Britain's growth was not largely constrained by the supply of capital.

Bristow (1968) has shown that, for all the excitement generated by stop-go, fluctuations in the British economy in the 1950s and 1960s were no greater than elsewhere in Europe, so that the argument that British investors faced an unusually unstable investment environment seems ill founded. We may also note that the idea that the British economy up to the float in 1972 suffered from a chronically overvalued exchange rate is implausible. For most of the 1950s and 1960s the current account of the balance of payments was in surplus despite the high level of activity and trend towards liberalisation (briefly interrupted by the Temporary Import Surcharge in 1965/6). Indeed, a plausible judgement would be that Britain in these two decades adjusted well to the loss of invisible receipts during the Second World War and the need to adapt to the new pattern of post-war visible trade involving swapping manufactures with other (mainly European) countries, as opposed to exchanging manufactures for food and raw materials from the non-European world. Even the deficits of the mid-1960s and the forced devaluation of 1967 were as much to do with confidence and capital flows as with a fundamental misalignment of the currency (Middleton 2001).

The float of 1972 did not inaugurate a period of automatic current-account adjustment as some of its advocates hoped (Figure 8.1). Rather, the following decades saw sharp fluctuations in the exchange rate, and with significant real consequences for the level of activity, but with even larger deficits being generated than had occurred under fixed rates. The year 1974/5 saw a deficit of 4 per cent of GDP driven by the sharp deterioration in the terms of trade accompanying the OPEC and commodity price rises of the beginning of that decade, coupled to the trade

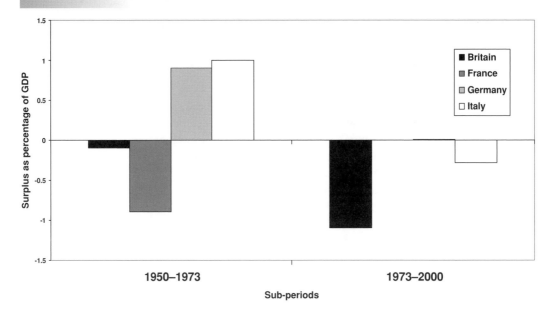

Figure 8.1

Balance-of-payments current-account surplus, 1950–2000

Sources: 1950–97: Middleton (2000: 34). 1998–2000: OECD, *Economic Outlook*, 2001.

liberalisation accompanying the completion of the Kennedy GATT round and entry into the EEC (Middleton 2000: 43). The late 1980s saw some even bigger deficits in the 'Thatcher boom'; up to 5 per cent of GDP in the worst year, 1989 (see chapter 14 below). Equally, the sustained expansion from 1992 until the end of the century saw persistent current-account deficits. What is striking is that, by the end of the century, these deficits had become almost ignored by policy makers and commentators. They were no longer regarded as a key index of successful economic management because they were no longer linked to an absence of 'confidence' in government policy. In a sense, the attachment of both Labour and Conservative governments to 'responsible' economic policies rendered the size of the current deficit almost invisible. The British obsession with the balance of payments in the 1950s and 1960s was replaced by an almost insouciant disregard by the turn of the century, though the message from the current-account numbers was clearly that there was a much more serious problem in the later period.

Success or failure is a very difficult judgement to make about post-war British balance-of-payments policy. In the 1950s specific objectives were given by the Treasury for surpluses on current account, which were not achieved (Radcliffe 1960). But these took it for granted that Britain's world role (political and financial) should be sustained, and that the commercial balance needed to be substantial to offset the cost of this stance. We plainly cannot treat this as an 'objective' test. There is no uncontestable value to maximise here, and many would say that the balance of payments is not an objective in its own right but a constraint on other objectives. In this light it can perhaps be said that up until the 1960s British policy was overly ambitious in terms of trying to sustain large overseas military commitments and large outward investment flows at a time when the economy had to readjust to the new realities of the post-war world (Manser 1971). But if one asks whether these ambitions led to major problems for the domestic economy, it is far from clear that this ever happened. The one time an external policy was proposed (the ROBOT float plan of 1952) which might have clearly repudiated domestic goals for the sake of such ambitions, it was not, ultimately, agreed. (For various interpretations of ROBOT see Schenk 1994: 114–19; Burnham 2000; Peden 2000: 458–62.)

By the end of the 1960s most of the government's excess overseas com-mitments had been (reluctantly) abandoned. Military spending east of Suez had ended, and the Sterling Area had been effectively dismantled. Floating was supposed to ensure that domestic policy was no longer inhib-ited by the 'external constraint'. Of course, it was never that simple, but it is right to say that under floating exchange rates the priority given to domestic goals (whether they be related to employment, growth or infla-tion) was clear. Governments gave up having balance-of-payments targets, and when they tried to revert to a target or fixed exchange rate (in the late 1980s and in the ERM, 1990–2) it was clear that the reasons were domestic, i.e. to secure an 'anchor' for anti-inflationary policy.

Finally, and most generally, Britain's broad support for a liberal in-ternational policy regime needs to be stressed. The British were junior partners in the design of that regime, and though they were slow to put those liberal principles into practice (Milward and Brennan 1996), the broad thrust of policy under both political parties was clear. In partic-ular, though both parties from the 1940s to the 1960s spoke much of the importance of the Empire and Commonwealth, the idea of an Em-pire/Sterling bloc as a strategic alternative to 'one-world' policy was never seriously pursued.

Qualified support for a liberal international regime could create ten-sions for policies of domestic stability and growth, but we should be wary of suggesting any simple external *versus* internal conflict in policy devel-opment. For a country like Britain the balance of advantage in trying to achieve domestic goals generally lay in simultaneously encouraging inter-national integration, whilst attempting to ensure that the international economy was in turn as stable as possible. Of course this argument can be pushed too far, and in the new century there are legitimate concerns about whether the extent of capital market integration in Britain (both financial flows and foreign direct investment) makes the economy exces-sively vulnerable to external events (Hirst and Thompson 2000). But that is far from proposing a fundamental and irreconcilable clash between 'in-ternationalisation' and maximising growth and employment at home.

INFLATION

Britain was an average-inflation country by European standards in the 1950s and 1960s, mainly because of the favourable international environment, but partly through both political parties' policy concern with this issue (Jones 1986; Booth 2000). However, the performance sharply deteriorated in the 1970s and early 1980s. Figures for the 1970s show that Britain's performance was part of a Europe-wide inflation surge, though with Britain at the top end of the distribution (Figure 8.2). The long period of slow growth relative to the rest of western Europe over the previous decades perhaps made it harder to sustain social agreement when the economy went into crisis. By the 1990s Britain was again a low-inflation country, and keeping it so was now treated as the bedrock of policy, illustrated most dramatically by the granting of independence to the Bank of England with a primary aim of low inflation.

The pattern in inflation is therefore straightforward. Britain has *not* been a country with a chronic inflation problem, but rather has been predominantly a low-inflation country with the exception of about a decade between 1972 and 1982. In an international context, Britain appears a better performer than Italy, but markedly worse than Germany, whose performance in this respect was remarkable by any standard. Apart from Germany, what stands out is the similarity of trends across countries; in a small, open economy, the capacity to control the rate of inflation is highly constrained.

Has Britain's predominantly good record been achieved at high cost to other policy objectives? This in turn raises the difficult question about how we understand the costs of inflation, and the extent therefore to which it makes sense to reduce its rate. Few would dispute the significant damage done by hyper-inflation, but it is far from clear at what rate inflation becomes a serious economic problem. What drove the growing policy concern with inflation in the 1970s was in any event not a clear identification of the economic damage incurred, but a belief in the social and political harm caused by prices consistently rising, a view expressed vividly by the Conservative chancellor of the Exchequer, Geoffrey Howe, in 1980: 'It is quite wrong to suppose that inflation is something with which only Treasury ministers need be concerned. So long as it persists, economic stability and prosperity will continue to elude us. Nothing, in the long-run, could contribute more to the disintegration of society and the destruction of any sense of national unity than continuing inflation' (House of Commons [26 March] 1980). Such rhetoric, while no doubt sincerely believed, served to license the downgrading of employment as a policy goal where this was seen as in conflict with low inflation. The idea of such a trade-off was most famously expressed by another politician,

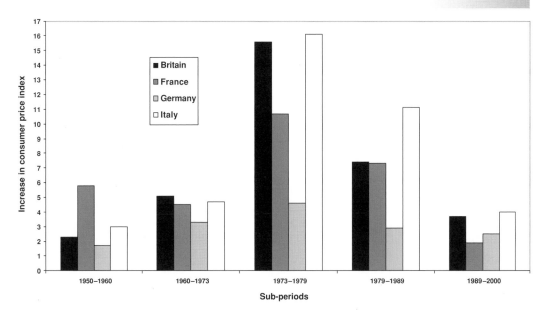

Figure 8.2 Inflation, 1950–2000

Sources: 1950–60: Maddison (1991: 185). 1960–2000: OECD, *Economic Outlook*, various years.

Prime Minister James Callaghan: 'We used to think that we could spend our way out of recessions, but I have to tell you that this option no longer exists, and that in so far as it ever did exist it only worked on each occasion since the war by injecting a bigger dose of inflation into the economy' (Labour Party 1976: 88). This, of course, was a highly political statement aimed at reassuring financial markets about the 'responsibility' of the Labour government. As a description of post-war economic events it was largely nonsense; full employment in the 1950s and 1960s had not been sustained at the price of 'higher and higher' inflation. But the politics of inflation of the last quarter of the twentieth century are suggested by Callaghan's speech. Thereafter both parties, either from ideological conviction or in order to secure international confidence, gave a high priority to that goal, though the constraints of confidence were felt more heavily by Labour than by the Conservatives.

FULL EMPLOYMENT

British post-war policy is often characterised as beset by excessive concern with employment levels. But in a comparative context it is important to note that our western European neighbours all had huge flows of labour from the countryside to the towns until the late 1960s, which made labour market conditions quite distinct. From the end of that decade they too faced problems with wage inflation that Britain had faced much earlier. The very low rates of unemployment of the 1950s and 1960s

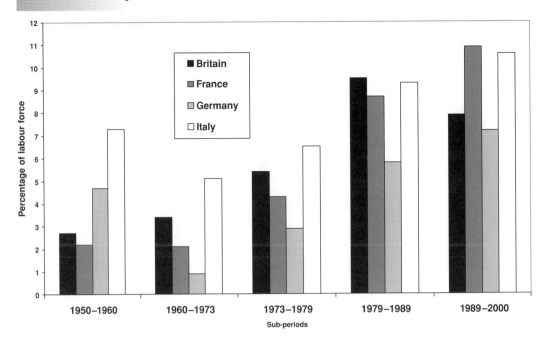

Figure 8.3
Unemployment,
1950–2000

Sources: 1950–89:
Maddison (1991:
192). 1990–2000:
OECD, *Economic
Outlook*, 2001.

(averaging under 2 per cent) had many favourable effects and few demonstrated damaging ones. First, to re-iterate, this was not a period of either high inflation or chronic lack of trade competitiveness, so full employment was not bought at the expense of failure in these areas. Second, the pursuit of full employment was not based on some sentimentality about the delights of work, but a hard-headed assessment of its consequences. Not only, of course, did it secure reasonable incomes for the great majority of the population (with significant effects on poverty and inequality) but also it meant high tax revenues to underpin expanding state expenditure, especially on welfare. Finally, full employment facilitated rapid structural change in the economy, the general buoyancy of the labour market greatly reducing opposition to the huge rundowns in employment in coal mining, railways and other staple sectors. While Britain did not have the possibility of shifting huge quantities out of agriculture as occurred in continental Europe at this time, the occupational pattern was far from static, and achieving these changes without serious conflict can reasonably count as a clear success of this period.

The focus of this chapter is policy aims rather than instruments, and the issues of fiscal policy and Keynesianism are taken up in detail in chapter 14. In the current context what is important is the degree of government responsibility for full employment in the golden age. What seems indisputable is that this was *not* the direct consequence of expansionary fiscal policy (Matthews 1968) and therefore was not achieved at the expense of financial 'irresponsibility'. Government expenditure was growing in the golden age (albeit slowly until the 1960s) from around

37 per cent of GDP in 1948 to 43 in 1973 (Middleton 1996: tab. 3.2). Plainly, this underpinned the effectiveness of fiscal policy, especially as expenditure was so centralised, so that the budget was usually balanced, not least because of the 'feedback' effects of high employment and growing tax revenues. This refutes the notion that budget deficits were characteristic of the 'Keynesian era' or that such deficits were spiralling out of control before the 1970s (Tomlinson 1981; Clarke 1998).

Table 8.4 Investment in the golden age *(gross fixed domestic capital formation as % GDP)*	
1950	13.0
1955	14.4
1960	16.6
1965	18.6
1970	18.4

Source: Feinstein (1972: tab. 5) for 1950–65; CSO, *Economic Trends*, 1970.

This is not to say that full employment happened entirely for reasons outside government control. The major causes of the buoyancy were the rapid expansion of world trade and investment. On the trade side we can say that British governments generally supported the international liberalisation which made this expansion possible, even if with some qualifications as outlined above. As regards investment, the reasons for the historically rapid growth rate of 3.3 per cent per annum (Matthews *et al.* 1982: 332) and 50 per cent rise in the share of investment in GDP (Table 8.4) include the pace of technological change and importing of new techniques, some of the latter via inflows of foreign, especially American, capital. All of these things were encouraged by government, notably by much greater government support for R&D and continuation of the policy of welcoming foreign firms (Edgerton 1996; Jones 1970). Golden-age governments also expanded direct financial incentives to invest from the small beginnings made by Cripps in the 1940s to the huge subsidies given by the Wilson government of the 1960s.

Eichengreen (1996) excludes Britain from his important thesis about the way in which, during the golden age, social pacts in European countries made possible acceptance by the workers of rising investment which was to their short-run disadvantage but long-run benefit. However, it is not clear that Britain should be seen in this regard as different from the generality of European countries, as investment rose sharply here too, and without the rapid wage inflation that might suggest the workers were trying to claw back the wages 'lost' in this way. Last, but far from least, the political commitment to full employment embodied in the 1944 White Paper on *Employment Policy*, and the evident high priority attached to this goal over the next two decades, can be seen as encouraging investment. Even the most cautious investor could be reasonably sure that in this new political world governments were going to fight hard to avoid the deflationary policies of the 1920s and 1930s.

In the 1970s full employment was downgraded as a goal, though this reversal should not be exaggerated for the Labour period (1974–9), as policy was often more concerned with this matter than the hawkish rhetoric, served up to maintain confidence in the financial markets, might suggest (Artis and Cobham 1996). Even under Thatcher the evidence suggests both that the horrendous increase in unemployment in 1979 to 1981 was unanticipated, and that the government felt itself extremely electorally vulnerable on this issue.[3] It was only when it became apparent that general elections could still be won with 3 million unemployed (1983 and 1987) that the government stopped worrying and felt able to celebrate the benefits for their policies (for example, on weakening trade unions) accruing from the reduction of labour's bargaining power. With the continuation of the long upswing into the late 1990s and the successful achievement of a reputation for 'prudence', New Labour felt able once again to speak of full employment as a goal for the new century.

Unsurprisingly, the rise in unemployment since the mid-1970s has been accompanied by increased poverty and inequality, a deterioration in the public finances, and greater resistance to structural change. This is precisely what would have been predicted from the experience of the golden age. How far was government responsible for the employment problems of these years? Plainly the international environment was less helpful, most obviously with the substantial shocks from the two OPEC crises of the 1970s, but also with the general instability in exchange rates that characterised the years that followed. Perhaps equally important were the consequences of the end of the once-and-for-all process of catch-up 'super growth' in continental Europe. Finally, the evident breakdown of the short-run Phillips relationship (the trade-off between the rate of unemployment and the rate of inflation) emerging in the late 1960s was bound to change government sensitivities about the priority to be accorded to inflation compared with employment, and this was especially so once the full fury of inflation was felt in the mid-1970s.

Nevertheless, while the Thatcher government can be acquitted of deliberately engineering 3 million unemployed, it cannot so easily resist the accusation of a damaging 'macroeconomic adventurism', of launching radical policy changes with little understanding of their likely consequences, and on an economy already suffering serious employment problems. Thus the medium-term financial strategy, and the accompanying monetary stringency, which were at the centre of Thatcher's economic policies seem to have been the key stimuli to the exchange-rate appreciation which was the immediate cause of the squeeze on cash flow which in turn lay behind the rise in unemployment. Yet no serious assessment of the effects of policy shifts in a regime of floating exchange rates seems to have been made (Dow 1998: 304–5).

---

[3] David Laidler, an economist supporter of the policy wrote later: 'Though some of us did expect the implementation of monetary strategy designed finally to bring the great inflation of the 1970s to an end, none of us expected the deep and prolonged depression that ensued' (1985: 36).

This adventurism was justified by a highly tendentious account of the alleged fundamental flaws of post-war economic policy and performance. A more sober reading of recent economic history would have suggested that the serious crisis of the mid-1970s was not the culmination of long-term trends (for example in public spending or deficits), and that the worst of the problems of the early and mid-1970s were already under control by 1979 (Figure 8.2, Table 8.5). (This general theme is returned to in the conclusion below.)

Table 8.5	Public spending and deficits in the 1970s	
	Public expenditure / GDP	Public deficit / GDP
1972	39.3	−1.3
1973	40.4	−2.7
1974	44.9	−3.9
1975	46.6	−4.6
1976	46.3	−5.0
1977	43.8	−3.4
1978	43.3	−4.4
1979	42.7	−3.3

Source: OECD, *Economic Outlook*, 47, 1990, tabs. R14, R15.

ECONOMIC GROWTH: THE BIG ISSUE?

By the late twentieth century it had become almost automatic amongst both policy makers and commentators to treat the rate of economic growth as the key measure of successful economic performance, and by extension the key judgement on economic policy. This status given to growth is highly political, being both the product of particular political circumstances (e.g. the downgrading of equality and employment goals) and with substantial political consequences (e.g. providing a rhetoric against allegedly growth-reducing policies such as state welfare). The intellectual status of growth as measured by the expansion of GDP, and particularly its ambiguous relationship to economic welfare, has long been explored, though other more plausible but less easily quantified measures have found it hard to get established (Crafts 1997b, 2000).

In Britain, the early concern with growth of the 1950s quickly became entangled with notions of decline, usually at that time measured by slow growth of GDP relative to near western European neighbours. (At other times other comparators have come and gone; most notably the USA, Japan and East Asia.) This ideology of 'declinism' was grounded in highly particular circumstances in Britain, including the availability of new comparative data on economic performance, changes in the rhetoric of the Labour Party towards a focus on economic 'modernisation' as a means of papering-over internal divisions, intensive inter-party competition on economic management, and a general cultural sense of 'failure' post-Suez (Tomlinson 1996). Two distinct narratives of failure became established at this time. One, broadly on the Left, by Shonfield (1958), located the source of 'decline' in low levels of physical investment, excessive overseas commitments, and the subordination of industry to the demands of the City of London. The alternative story, articulated by Shanks (1961) and more Rightist in character, emphasised inadequate competition, trade union obstructionism and a general culture of conservatism. In both these approaches government failure figured prominently; both accepted the wisdom of the age that governments both could and should largely determine economic behaviour, but indicted government for failing to carry out this role successfully.

Between them Shanks and Shonfield articulated most of the declinist accounts of Britain which, with extremely variable levels of sophistication, have predominated down to the present day. Major examples of those who have broadly followed Shonfield would include Pollard (1984) and Coates (1994). The arguments of Barnett (1986, 1998, 2001) and Broadberry and Crafts (see below) can be seen as having important affiliations with Shanks. There was a brief interlude in the mid-1980s when many people seem to have accepted the Conservative government's contemporary claims that decline was at an end and that a quite new era of economic performance was at hand, but this was soon seen to be a mirage, with the boom of the late 1980s replaced by the bust of the early 1990s. New Labour, both before and after 1997, deployed declinist rhetoric, and was only slightly discountenanced when the favoured East Asian comparators suffered serious difficulties after 1998 (Tomlinson 2000).

While declinism has dominated accounts of post-war Britain, there have always been dissenting voices. At the most general, McCloskey (1991) pointed out the bizarre perspective involved in an obsession with small differences in growth rates in a country which by world standards was unambiguously amongst the very rich. Supple (1994b, 1997) has emphasised the 'imaginary' basis of perceptions of decline, while Tomlinson (1996) has stressed its origins in very particular political circumstances. Edgerton (1991) has challenged the ubiquitous declinist notion that Britain has had an anti-industrial and anti-technological culture. Other recent work has also firmly 'historicized' declinism (e.g. Clarke and Trebilcock 1997; English and Kenny 2000), though the final stage, of declaring decline a 'myth', akin to the 'great depression' of the last quarter of the nineteenth century, has yet to find its bold proponent.

More concretely, the development of ideas of catch-up and convergence has put Britain's growth rate in a very clear perspective (Figure 8.4). The basic arguments from this framework relating to the golden age are clearly put by Feinstein: 'Our basic hypothesis is that the fundamental factor which served to constrain productivity growth in the US and Britain, and to boost that of their competitors in Europe and Japan, was the different levels from which they started in 1948'; and further, 'On this view comparable rates of growth were not attainable by Britain and the United States, precisely because they were already at a higher level of development . . . no doubt some improvement on the rates actually achieved was feasible, but the margin was very much smaller than most

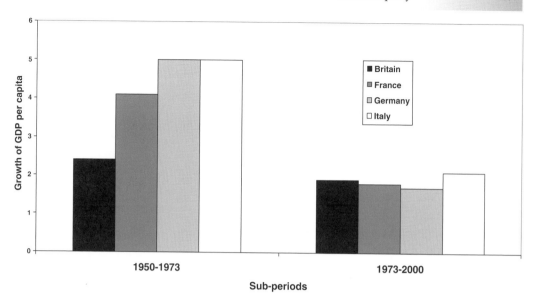

commentators suggested' (1990: 288, 291). This argument about aggregate comparative growth rates has been further refined by Crafts (1995), from whose data it can be calculated that Britain's growth 'shortfall' was less than 1 per cent per annum, with the real 'deviants' being Ireland and Norway. The convergence story is also compatible with experience since the golden age, when Britain's trend growth rate fell in absolute terms, but improved in comparison with western Europe as those countries exhausted the possibilities of catch-up (Figure 8.5).

Most declinism has focused its attention on the performance of industry. This focus has been partly the consequence of deeply felt views about the 'productiveness' of industry that have outlived the ineluctable rise of services to predominance in output and employment. Industrial employment peaked in Britain in the 1950s, and its decline since then is part of a Europe-wide pattern (Feinstein 1999). In the 1960s the selective employment tax was used to try and reverse this process, and in the 1970s ideas about 'de-industrialisation' informed policies pursued by the Labour Party. But while the data support the view that industry does indeed deliver faster productivity gains than services in aggregate (Feinstein 1999), the decline of the sector is a common feature of advanced economies precisely because it is the result of common features of economic and social development, rather than the characteristics of any one country.

This point means that popular stories of Britain suffering a unique 'anti-industrial' culture, and consequently anti-industrial policies (e.g. Wiener 1981; Barnett 1986) are fundamentally misguided. Britain in this respect cannot be distinguished from other advanced industrial countries. But even if this comparative data did not exist it should be apparent

Figure 8.4 Growth of GDP per capita, 1950–2000

Sources: 1950–97: Maddison (2001: 132). 1998–2000: OECD, *Economic Outlook*, 2001.

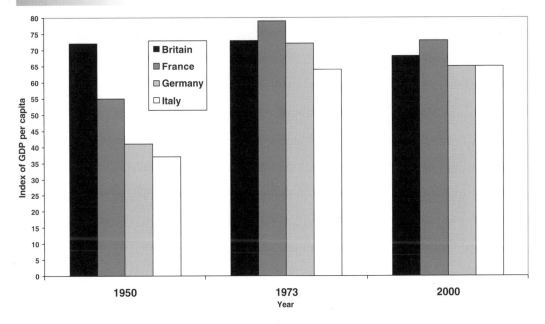

Figure 8.5 Level of GDP per capita

Sources: 1950, 1973: Maddison (2001: 185). 2000: OECD, *Economic Outlook*, 2001.

that such stories are highly implausible (Collins and Robbins 1990). Indeed it is more plausible to argue that Britain has had a highly technological culture, as this would amongst other things help explain why, especially in the golden age, it was one of the world's highest spenders on R&D (Edgerton 1996; chapter 12 below).

The growth performance of Britain has commonly been analysed with the use of data on comparative productivity, especially in manufacturing, and this has been most exhaustively investigated by Broadberry (1997c, and chapter 3 above). His data show that, far from a secular, deep-rooted problem of 'decline', British manufacturing had the same productivity level relative to Germany and the USA in 1989 as in the 1870s, the gap having widened against the USA in the 1940s and 1950s and then narrowed, and against Germany in the golden age, but especially in the 1970s, before also narrowing. Broadberry's data put British manufacturing performance in a light which makes much declinist discussion misdirected, though it still leaves a gap in performance in the golden age. Broadberry himself retains a qualified declinist approach, and uses a mass production / craft production dichotomy to try and explain post-war disparities in productivity, suggesting that in these years British firms were poor at producing goods requiring the use of mass-production techniques. However, this dichotomy appears too crude to deal with divergences in performance of British companies, even *within* sectors (Booth 2003).

These various re-assessments of economic performance leave the idea of a failure in growth highly qualified, since the performance of the British economy is represented by relatively small deviations around trends which are broadly European in scope. 'Relatively small' we may take, following Crafts, as a *maximum* of just under 1 per cent per annum in the golden age. Over twenty-five years this would still accumulate to a significant amount, but on the other hand it would hardly justify the cataclysmic stories of some declinists. Furthermore, as Figure 8.5 illustrates, by the end of the twentieth century all four countries enjoyed a strikingly similar standard of living; in this respect Britain is not significantly deviant from the western European 'norm'. In addition, in the context of the current discussion of policy, it must be noted that not all this 'failure' in the golden age is necessarily to be blamed on policy errors. Exogenous factors, such as the legacy of war, must be accorded some role. In sum, reassessment and down-grading of ideas of failures in performance logically leave notions of 'government failure' highly qualified.

As we have noted, the lagging growth rate of Britain in the golden age was largely based on the much greater scope for catch-up in continental Europe. Central to this process was structural change, especially the flight from agriculture (Feinstein 1999). British government was in no sense at fault in this process; indeed its policy of free trade had allowed these benefits to be captured in the late nineteenth century. Agricultural protectionism after 1945, while arguably perverse, did little to hinder redistribution of labour, given the smallness of the British agricultural sector at the beginning of the period.

As noted above, both Left and Right versions of declinism have found much fault in government policy. Setting aside the quantitative evidence that any failings must in any event have had limited impact on growth, how plausible are these accusations?

Taking first the 'Left' version, we have already noted that while the idea that British governments were slow to give up expensive global ambitions is plausible in regard to the period down to the 1960s, it ceases to be thereafter. Second, the idea of the interests of the City crowding out those of industry seems a very large generalisation from some very particular events, whose economic impact was in any case greatly exaggerated. Thus stop-go was not a big inhibition to growth in the 1950s and 1960s (and the stops of the early 1980s and 1990s were hardly due to a desire to defend the pound). Britain has not suffered from a chronically overvalued exchange rate. It is certainly arguable that the very high level of economic integration in Britain (which is the outcome of policy decisions) has inhibited policy, but not in any chronic, growth-reducing 'declinist' fashion (Hirst and Thompson 2000). Finally, investment statistics do not bear out the view that an over-powerful City has been allowed by government to undermine investment (Table 8.4). In the last decades of the twentieth century lagging investment levels in Britain have been most evident not in industry and commerce, where City 'short-termism' is usually criticised, but in the infrastructure, resulting either from public spending constraints or, where privatisation has taken place, from the terms of the sell-offs.

Turning to the 'Right' version of declinism it is obviously important to distinguish between the crude and sophisticated versions. Probably the declinism with the biggest political impact has been that of Barnett, but as academics we can only lament that this impact is inversely related to the quality of the argument. Barnett's work is characterised by sweeping generalisations and poor grasp of economic argument, and few academics have given his arguments much credence (Harris 1992; Edgerton 1991).

Quite different is the work of Broadberry and Crafts, who have employed new growth theory and formal models to tell a story of government failure. They diagnose failings in the provision of education and training, which to some degree would be accepted by all historians. More controversially, for both the 1930s and early post-1945 period they suggest that a high price in productivity and growth was paid for the government focus on macroeconomic stability (1992, 1996, 1998). For the postwar years in particular they argue that governments were over-concerned with full employment and with conciliating unions and employers, leading to cosy deals which restricted structural change, reduced competitive pressures on companies, and entrenched the powers of obstructive trade unions.

The persuasiveness of these arguments has been disputed (Tiratsoo and Tomlinson 1994; Tomlinson and Tiratsoo 1998). The matters in dispute range over the extent to which British companies were allowed by weak government policy to restrict competition either by monopolies and restrictive practices or controls on imports, and the existence of a 'cosy deal' in the labour market, which allowed restrictive practices by labour to be sheltered from competitive pressure. (On the general issue of the role of unions in Britain's productivity problem see the exemplary work of Nichols 1986.) These are matters of continuing dispute, partly because of the methodological issues about the extent to which the data available make econometric work entirely convincing.

The underlying theme of Broadberry and Crafts is one of a trade-off between macroeconomic stability and productivity enhancement. Their preference is clear when they suggest Britain would have gained from 'a somewhat more Thatcherite policy' in earlier years (1996: 86; see also Crafts 1998). This trade-off assumption is notably at odds with the traditional belief (especially in the critiques of stop-go) that investment levels and growth are encouraged by macroeconomic stability. Certainly, even if one accepts some productivity-enhancing effects from such an approach, a preference for Thatcher-style macro-policy as actually experienced in Britain is open to the strong riposte that 'you can get a heap of Harberger triangles in an Okun gap'.[4]

---

[4] That is, the benefits from full capacity working far outweigh the assumed increased output from greater competitive pressures when demand is slack.

CONCLUSIONS

Britain has not in any profound sense 'declined' economically over the post-war period, and we should avoid pathologising either performance or policy. Rejection of such 'declinism' does not mean embracing a Panglossian approach, but does mean that accounts of policy failures have to be much more nuanced than has often been the case.

Britain can be differentiated from other major European economies for much of the post-war period by its high degree of openness and/or concern with international economic relations, and consequently much of the story of post-war policy has been about trying to combine this openness with the domestic political imperative towards greater economic stability and security. This has had to be done when in one sense decline *was* unambiguously taking place, a decline in Britain's weight in the world economy. As Cairncross (1992: 286) summarised the position: 'The fundamental change was a loss of economic power: commercial power, bargaining power, financial power. Britain had become a much smaller fragment of the world economy with much less influence on the behaviour of that economy.' While the general idea of 'globalisation' seems much exaggerated (Hirst and Thompson 1999), the belief that the growth of international economic integration has put increased constraints on British policy seems a reasonable conclusion for the last quarter of the twentieth century. But such a view should not be used to imply that there is a simple conflict between domestic policy goals and greater integration. British NEM has always had to combine pursuit of those domestic goals with acceptance that they can only be realised by simultaneously pursuing stability and expansion in the outside world.

British NEM, especially up to the 1970s, placed more reliance on fiscal instruments than most other advanced capitalist countries. This followed both from the particular structure of the British state and the particular ideological form of discussion of NEM in Britain, i.e. 'Keynesianism'. However, to discuss Britain's post-war pattern of economic policy in terms of Keynesianism and its decline gives an over-parochial flavour to discussion of economic management. All major democracies had much more managed economies after 1945 than before 1939, and in all countries this management came under strain in the 1970s. In this sense Britain's 'Keynesianism' is best seen as one version of a much wider set of ideas about national economic management, rather than the key term for the whole phenomenon. The 'decline' of Keynesianism in Britain was matched by challenges to other characteristic forms of NEM in other Western countries.

The account of post-war Britain given in this chapter cannot escape the politics of either the policy makers or those who have commented upon those policies. We cannot even escape to political innocence in an uncontested chronology. The argument made here, that by any realistic assessment the economic policies of the 1940s to the 1960s were broadly successful, is at odds with the view of that period which sees it as one of disastrous decline. This, of course, was the view of Mrs Thatcher when, referring back to her period in office, she wrote that: 'everything we wished to do had to fit into the overall strategy of reversing Britain's economic decline, for without an end to decline there was no hope of success for our other objectives' (Thatcher 1993: 15; Cannadine 1997). But if the reality of that decline is disputed, the chronology which it supports, one of policy-induced failure followed in the 1980s by policy-induced success, also falls. An alternative chronology would see a sharp break in performance and policy efficacy in the 1970s, focusing attention on the 'conjunctural' problems of that decade, rather than seeing those problems as a culmination of failure over the whole post-war period. Equally, it would see the period since the late 1970s as years with some notable failures, especially on employment and inequality, compared with what went before.

9

The welfare state, income and living standards

PAUL JOHNSON

Contents

INTRODUCTION

In the fifty years following the end of the Second World War, the British people enjoyed the fruits of an unprecedented period of sustained economic growth. Real personal disposable income per capita (i.e. income after direct tax) grew at an average annual rate of 2.4 per cent over the period 1949–95. By the end of the twentieth century the average Briton was about three times better off than in the late 1940s, and in real terms earned and spent £2.95 for every £1 earned and spent in 1949. Yet despite the palpable economic achievements of the post-war period, there has been continuing concern about the failure to distribute the benefits of economic growth to all sections of the population. For example, if we define poverty in terms of having an income less than half the national average, then the number of people living in poverty rose from 5 million in 1979 to 13.5 million in 1990/1 (Hills 1993). If instead we look at physical indicators, the picture is no less depressing: between the mid-1970s and the late 1990s the difference in life expectancy at birth for men in professional and in unskilled manual jobs rose from 5.5 years to 7.4 years (Department of Health 2002).

This failure to eradicate, or even reduce, the level of economic and social inequality is all the more surprising given the significant expansion of public welfare expenditure in the post-war period. Between 1949/50 and 1996/7, real spending on social security benefits grew at an average annual rate of 4.5 per cent, more than 50 per cent faster than the rate of real income growth. In consequence, benefit expenditure as a proportion of GDP rose over this same period from 4.7 to 12.0 per cent (DSS 2000). It seems, therefore, that the British welfare state has been consuming an ever greater share of national income in order to achieve an ever diminishing degree of equality of income and life chances. This looks like government failure on a grand scale. But the failure could be even greater. A number of 'New Right' critics of state intervention, taking their lead from Hayek's (1944) critique of socialist planning, have argued that the public provision of welfare benefits restricts economic growth by directing resources away from their most productive use; thus the welfare state may actually have exacerbated, rather than ameliorated, poverty. According to one critic, Corelli Barnett (1986), the post-war commitment by both Labour and Conservative parties to a comprehensive welfare state is one of the prime reasons for Britain's long-run decline in international competitiveness and economic and political power.

Not surprisingly, other commentators disagree. In *The Future of Socialism* (1956), Tony Crosland, an Oxford politics don and subsequently a Labour politician, formulated a powerful intellectual justification of state welfarism as a set of policies which would both promote equality *and* stimulate economic growth by ensuring high levels of health, education and employment for all citizens (Sullivan 1999). A quite different justification for the public provision of welfare services is based on the fact that private insurance markets typically fail to provide optimal levels of cover against social risks such as unemployment and sickness (Barr 1998: ch. 5).

This chapter provides an evaluation of these divergent claims about the positive or negative impact of the post-war welfare state on economic growth and equality. The second part of the chapter examines the impact of the welfare state on economic performance. The following two sections consider how the welfare state has affected the distribution of income and the overall pattern of equality in Britain since the Second World War. But before turning to these different ways of assessing welfare state outcomes, we first need to consider why and how the welfare state has grown to its present size.

CREATION AND GROWTH OF THE WELFARE STATE

Concepts

All societies adopt strategies to provide for individuals in times of need – during childhood, sickness, old age, unemployment. These strategies can be entirely individualistic, such as when a person saves for their own old age; or family-based as when children are cared for by relatives; or collective, for example when all members of a community band together to provide care and sustenance for sick or injured compatriots. The twentieth century has seen a massive expansion in virtually all countries in collective support strategies organised at the level of the nation state, and these strategies together form what is commonly referred to as the welfare state. Only the state has the power to charge all citizens – via tax contributions – for support services that some will seek in times of need (a necessary power to prevent free-riding, in which the selfish seek to claim support from others without making any contribution to the common pool themselves). But in levying taxes to pay for social expenditure, the state reduces the ability of individuals to provide for themselves both by lowering disposable income and by restricting individual choice about the level and type of social support to be received.

There are many competing explanations for the twentieth-century growth of welfare states, and no consensus (see Pierson 1991 for a review of this literature). What is clear, however, is that in most places, and at most times, public provision of many (but not all) welfare services has been popular. Though nobody likes to pay taxes, on balance there has been collective support for a high and rising level of public welfare provision, at the cost of higher taxes and reduced disposable income. Public welfare provision exhibits the key characteristic of a luxury good – expenditure on the good increases at a faster rate than income rises. General welfare state expansion therefore reflects the increasing affluence of modern societies.

This expansion of welfare states has had important political as well as economic effects. It has created a close reciprocal tie between each and every citizen and the state. In Britain in 1900 most people lived their lives without any direct contact with public agencies unless they were poor or engaged in criminal activity. They paid no direct taxes, and received no benefits in cash or kind from the state, with the exception of elementary education for their children. Since 1945 the state has come to engage directly, and frequently, with almost every citizen. The British government now collects direct taxes and social security contributions from every worker's pay packet, and provides health care, an extended education system, and subsidised housing, together with cash benefits for children and for adults who are poor, unemployed, disabled, sick and retired. Welfare state expansion has created a new bond between citizenry and government, but has also created new political vulnerability as politicians compete to win votes by making unrealistic promises of more benefits for fewer taxes.

An examination of the development and functioning of the welfare state is, therefore, central to any analysis of the political economy of modern Britain. In 1997 welfare expenditure accounted for 25 per cent of total GDP; a weekly cash allowance from the government was paid for every pensioner and every child; every person visiting a family doctor or a public hospital could receive medical care without payment; almost one in five households lived in publicly owned accommodation. With such vast financial scale and such extensive coverage, the management of the welfare state has become a core function of government. Failure to use the resources devoted to public welfare in an efficient and effective way can jeopardise both the capacity of the economy to grow and the ability of any government to gain re-election.

Origins

As already noted, collective provision of welfare support for the poor and needy was not a mid-twentieth-century innovation, but the Second World War was an important watershed in the development of the welfare functions of government in Britain. Before 1914 most social expenditure in Britain was based on the concept of a *residual* welfare state, a system of physical and financial safety nets which prevented absolute destitution and relieved chronic ill health where it could be shown, on the basis of a means test, that the recipient was without alternative resources. The limited scope of this early twentieth-century welfare state is reflected by its cost – public expenditure on social services accounted for just 2.3 per cent of GDP in 1900, and 4.9 per cent in 1920 (Middleton 1996: 198, 332).

By 1948 the welfare state was very different in size and character. It accounted for over 10 per cent of GDP, and was both more centralised and more comprehensive in terms of the proportion of the population and the type of social contingencies covered (Glennerster 2000: 228). It had changed from being a *residual* to an *institutional* welfare system, integral to the structures of modern industrial society (Wilensky and Lebeaux 1958: 138–47). Some of the changes were a direct response to the unprecedented requirements that the waging of 'total war' placed on British society. Hospitals were reorganised to cope with the anticipated civilian and military casualties of war (Titmuss 1950: 55), and means-tested 'public assistance' payments (the old poor-law relief renamed) evolved into non-means-tested benefits payable to many thousands of households suffering financially from the effects of bombing, military conscription and war-time inflation. However, war-time welfare developments were not simply reactive, an official response to exogenous circumstances. British politicians and civil servants themselves generated, from the early years of the war, an ambitious and wide-ranging set of proposals for an extension of government involvement in many areas of social provision.

A multitude of advisory committees was established from 1940 to develop plans for post-war reconstruction and social reform, although they worked with little co-ordination or agreement over values and goals (Harris 1986: 238). Whilst education planning (culminating in the 1944 Education Act) followed administrative lines established in the 1930s and health proposals were conditioned by the practical achievement of running the war-time Emergency Medical Service, employment and social security proposals had more distinct ideological roots. The White Paper on *Employment Policy* (UK 1944) was an explicitly Keynesian document which committed post-war governments to 'the maintenance of a high and stable level of employment' through a conscious policy of economic management. And the report of a committee chaired by Sir William Beveridge on *Social Insurance and Allied Services* (Beveridge 1942), which advocated a comprehensive system of social insurance 'against interruption and destruction of earning power and for special expenditure arising at birth marriage and death', was a direct descendant of late nineteenth-century 'New Liberal' ideology which aimed at preventing destitution without undermining market structures and incentives (Harris 1977).

This 'Beveridge Report', as it came to be known, promised freedom from want for all citizens from the cradle to the grave in exchange for weekly insurance contributions (paid jointly by worker and employer) from all those in employment. Beveridge assumed that positive economic management after the war would prevent long-term unemployment and that medical services would be available through a comprehensive health care system: his insurance scheme was designed primarily to relieve the financial costs of temporary unemployment and sickness, long-term disability, and old age. The report attracted enormous publicity and public support, partly because its appearance fortuitously coincided with a wave of optimism following Britain's first major military victory at El Alamein, and partly because its ambiguity, breadth of vision, and overall optimism meant that almost everyone could find something in it with which they agreed (Harris 1986; Lowe 1993). It was, however, little more than one man's blueprint for the consolidation and extension of existing and overlapping schemes of social protection. It was also a blueprint for men: Beveridge based his proposals on an assumption that married women would be homemakers rather than paid workers, and that they would acquire welfare entitlements through the insurance contributions paid by their husbands.

The Beveridge Report was accepted only grudgingly as a policy document by the war-time government, with no immediate move made towards implementation. Although, according to Lowe's (1993: 134) assessment, the report was 'conservative, illogical, and ultimately impractical', it came, nevertheless, to take a central position in the plans for a post-war welfare state designed to destroy what Beveridge called the five giant evils of 'Want, Disease, Ignorance, Squalor and Idleness' (UK 1942: 6). In the general election fought at the end of the war in July 1945, the Labour Party readily adopted the major proposals of the report, together with commitments to better housing, greater educational opportunity and full employment, a strategy which undoubtedly contributed to Labour's electoral victory (Addison 1994). The new Labour government inaugurated a flurry of legislation which established the foundations of the post-war welfare state: in 1946 the National Insurance and National Health Service Acts, in 1948 the National Assistance and Children's Act, and in 1949 the Housing Act. Although there is disagreement among historians about the extent to which the specific institutions of the post-war welfare state reflected the novelty of war-time thought and action or the continuity of interwar developments (Titmuss 1950; Harris 1981; Smith 1986), there is little doubt that the impetus to legislative action came from a desire, shared by many Conservative as well as Labour politicians, to build a better and more equal Britain after the sacrifices of five years of total war. The idea of a residual welfare state that would do no more than respond to the economic and social problems of the destitute was superseded by a universal welfare ideology in which public social expenditure could be used to change and improve society. How much this universal welfare state would cost, how it would be funded or what impact it might have on economic performance was never fully considered.

Structure and finance

The structure of the welfare state that had emerged by 1948, and which has remained fundamentally the same since that date, is shown in Figure 9.1. There were two broad types of benefit, directly provided services and cash transfers. The cash transfers were themselves of two types, some being provided through the contributory system of National Insurance closely modelled on Beveridge's plan, and others being paid on a non-contributory basis from general tax revenue. National Insurance benefits were to be paid to individuals (and their dependants) who had made a sufficient number of actuarially calculated contributions to the National Insurance Fund, in the event that they succumbed to any of the contingencies most likely to lead to poverty – particularly sickness, unemployment, disability and old age. Membership of the National Insurance scheme was compulsory, and the contributions and benefits were flat-rate with benefits set at a subsistence level to encourage additional private saving for emergencies. The National Insurance Fund was to be managed as an independent account, ultimately to be self-financing and

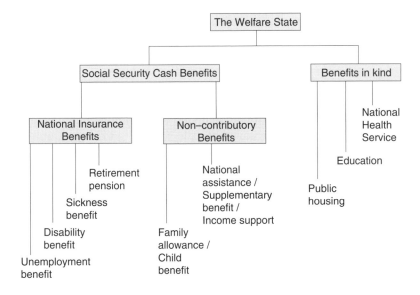

Figure 9.1 Main
welfare state benefits

entirely separate from all other government revenue. By contrast, non-contributory National Assistance benefits were intended to be a means-tested safety net for the few groups (for instance, vagrants) who did not have an adequate contribution record to qualify for, or whose needs were not sufficiently met by, National Insurance benefits. National Assistance was financed from general tax revenue and was intended to be a modern (and more humane) continuation of the residual welfare function performed in the nineteenth century by the poor law. In addition, families were to be assisted from central government revenue with the payment of weekly benefits (family allowances) to all parents with two or more dependent children, together with the granting to fathers of additional tax allowances related to family size.

The universal nature of the post-war welfare state needs to be stressed. Partly in reaction to the stigma associated with the Victorian Poor Law and the resentment towards the means test imposed on the unemployed during the interwar years, it was insisted that National Insurance benefits were a *right*, paid as a flat-rate benefit to everyone in exchange for their flat-rate insurance contributions. Furthermore, the centrally funded National Health Service (NHS) made medical attention available to everyone free of charge at the point of use, with access determined only by medical assessment of relative need. All school-age children were entitled (and required) to receive an education provided entirely without charge in state schools. Almost every household in the country was in regular, and in many cases daily, receipt of services and/or cash benefits from the all-embracing welfare state. But even as Clement Attlee, the Labour prime minister, was claiming in 1950 that 'the foundations of the Welfare State have been well and truly laid' (Pelling 1984: 117–18), substantial cracks were appearing in these foundations relating to the cost and adequacy of welfare benefits.

Beveridge had always held the vision of social insurance to be more important than the details of finance, and it was not until his 1942 report was in draft form that it was subject to careful financial scrutiny. This exercise revealed a number of immediate and longer-term problems with the plan. The Treasury calculated that after defence expenditure, remission of taxes and debt repayments, the post-war government would have surplus revenue of no more than £100 million, and thus it would be impossible to spend the £86 million needed to implement the Beveridge scheme (Lowe 1993: 129). Moreover, if National Insurance was to operate on true actuarial principles, pensions could be paid only after a full contribution period of around forty-five years, and the first National Insurance pensioners would not receive their pensions until the 1990s. Such a long delay was incompatible with the social and political goals of the social insurance scheme. The decision taken in 1946 to pay full pensions to all people above the qualifying age had the inevitable consequence of creating large and growing deficits for the National Insurance Fund.

Only by substantially raising contributions without offering any improved benefits for two or three decades could the long-run financial solvency of the National Insurance scheme be re-established, but political expediency demanded the reverse, an increase in benefits, which were falling behind earnings as real incomes rose in the 1950s. The solution to this difficulty was to abandon the idea of building up a fund which would cover future pension liabilities, and instead to use current contributions to pay current benefits. By 1958 National Insurance had changed from being a 'funded' to a 'pay-as-you-go' system, with the insurance 'fund' aiming merely to balance income and expenditure over the annual budgetary cycle. Future pension liabilities were to be financed not out of accumulated contributions, as the Treasury wished (UK 1954), but out of future economic growth. Dilnot *et al.* (1984: 13) have commented that 'the device of meeting yesterday's claims from today's premiums has been familiar to fraudulent and foolish financiers for millennia', and this was now to become the financial model for 'social security'. As the following section shows, in the 1960s and 1970s politicians took advantage of this opportunity massively to expand the generosity of the British welfare state.

Early concern about the overall cost of the post-war welfare state was matched by disquiet, from the very beginning, about the adequacy of benefits. Beveridge explicitly stated that the National Insurance benefit should 'provide by itself the income necessary for subsistence in normal cases', and although he intended that this subsistence level should be austere, it was supposed to be sufficient to ensure that members of the National Insurance scheme need have no resort to means-tested National

Assistance. But there is a clear contradiction between the goal of flat-rate cash benefits for all beneficiaries and the goal of providing a subsistence income for families whose size, needs and resources may vary enormously, particularly given that housing costs vary considerably by region. In 1948, at the outset of the National Insurance scheme, about 25 per cent of National Insurance benefit recipients had incomes so low that they also qualified for means-tested National Assistance (called Supplementary Benefit from 1966, and Income Support from 1986). Throughout the 1960s and 1970s over 20 per cent of benefit recipients continued to receive means-tested benefits, and this proportion rose further in the 1980s and 1990s as the scope of insurance entitlements was restricted, and more benefit payments were converted to a means-tested basis in a move designed to target limited resources towards those most in need (Dilnot *et al.* 1984: 22). Beveridge believed that means-tested poverty relief would wither away as the entire population was incorporated in the National Insurance scheme, but insurance benefits have always been set at too low a level to achieve this goal. The proportion of the British population receiving means-tested benefits has risen from just over 4 per cent in 1948 to 8 per cent in 1974, 16 per cent in 1986 and over 20 per cent in 1994 (Digby 1989: 68–9; Evans 1998: 302). As Figure 14.5 in chapter 14 below shows, means-tested benefits accounted for 42 per cent of total spending on cash benefits in 1948, a figure that had fallen to 26 per cent by 1965. Since then, however, their share has grown, and in 1998 they again accounted for 42 per cent of total benefit spending. This expansion of means-testing since the 1960s has required a corresponding growth of social security administrative complexity and has also reduced the incentive for some benefit recipients to work and save.

The disincentive effect of overlapping benefit systems has been exacerbated by changes to the structure of the income tax and National Insurance contribution systems. The decision to abandon the strict linkage between National Insurance premiums and the actuarial cost of the benefits provided allowed governments first to increase the level of contribution in order to pay for current benefits, then in 1961 to introduce graduated contributions, in 1975 to relate contributions to the level of earnings, and in the 1980s to increase contributions in order to gain additional general revenue rather than to balance the notional National Insurance Fund. Thus the National Insurance contribution came to resemble a general tax on employment income rather than a payment for insurance services. At the same time the threshold above which income tax is paid has fallen: in 1949–50 a married man with two children under the age of eleven began to pay income tax when his income exceeded 120 per cent of average manual earnings, but by 1980–1 an identical household began to pay tax when its income exceeded only 50 per cent of average manual earnings (Wicks 1987: 28). This development (which occurred with particular rapidity in the mid-1970s when tax thresholds were not adjusted to

take account of the high rates of inflation) has had the effect of making
more low-income families pay direct taxes for their own welfare. Many
households are thus regarded as being sufficiently rich to be taxed, while
at the same time being sufficiently poor to be eligible for means-tested
benefits. The failure to integrate personal tax and social security systems
created a number of 'poverty traps' in which poor households found that
a slight increase in income simultaneously increased their tax liability
and eliminated their benefit entitlement, thus effectively imposing very
high marginal tax rates (Field and Piachaud 1971), although the severity of these poverty traps has been systematically reduced since the late
1980s.

Expansion

Changes in the structure and finance of the welfare state have taken place
within the context of substantial long-run growth in the scale of public
expenditure and in the scope of government activities (see chapter 14).
Welfare expenditure doubled as a proportion of GDP in the three decades
after 1950, but it is not immediately obvious why this should have occurred, since economic growth over this period raised most incomes well
above the subsistence thresholds set by Beveridge in the 1940s. A preliminary view of the process of expenditure growth can be gained by
separating this growth into three constituent parts. First, demographic
change can alter the number of people in certain clearly defined benefit categories – such as children of school age, or pensioners. Secondly,
changes in coverage can alter the boundaries of benefit coverage, thus
increasing or decreasing the size of the eligible population. Thirdly, the
value of benefits, or the average level of expenditure on services, can
be changed. Governments have little control over the first of these factors, but coverage and benefit levels are directly determined by political
decisions.

Demography imposed consistent upwards pressure on welfare spending. The number of children under 15 rose gradually from 11.1 million
in 1953 to 12.9 million in 1970, although it has since fallen back to 11.7
million. The pensioner population, on the other hand, has expanded virtually without interruption since the Second World War: between 1953
and 2000 the number of pensioners rose by more than 50 per cent from
6.9 to 10.5 million (DSS 2000). Policy changes have also had some direct effects on the size of client groups. An increase in the school leaving age in
1972 from 15 to 16 added a further 780,000 15-year-olds to the 'children'
category, simultaneously increasing expenditure on education and reducing the income of the National Insurance system by removing 15-year-olds
from the working population. On the other hand, demographic change
has also added to the revenue side of the welfare state: in the 1960s there
was a considerable rise in the size of the working-age population as the

Table 9.1	Decomposition of the growth rate of social expenditure in the UK, 1960–1975 and 1975–1981					
	Education	Health	Pensions	Unemployment	Total of 4 programmes	Total social expenditure
Expenditure share in 1960 (% GDP)	3.7	3.4	4.1	0.2	11.4	13.9
Real growth 1960–75, % per annum	5.0	3.4	5.9	10.3	4.9	5.0
Of which						
Demography	0.6	0.4	1.6	6.5	1.0	
Coverage	1.1	0.0	0.9	−0.8	0.7	
Benefits	3.2	3.0	3.3	4.4	3.2	
Expenditure share in 1975 (% GDP)	6.8	5.0	6.3	0.7	18.8	22.5
Real growth 1975–81, % per annum	−2.0	2.0	4.5	14.2	1.8	2.5
Of which						
Demography	−0.4	0.0	1.0	19.1	0.9	
Coverage	−0.5	0.0	0.8	5.3	0.3	
Benefits	−1.1	2.0	2.6	−8.9	0.7	
Expenditure share in 1981 (% GDP)	5.8	5.4	7.4	1.4	20.0	23.7

Source: OECD (1985: 39).

post-war 'baby-boomers' moved into adulthood. This working-age population consisted of 31.2 million people in 1953, but by 2001 reached 36.1 million: it is, however, projected to decline over the next decade as the baby-boomers move into retirement.

Table 9.1 shows the relative role of changes in demography, coverage and real benefit levels in influencing the overall growth rate of social expenditure in the periods 1960–75 and 1975–81. In the first period real expenditure on the four specified programmes grew at an annual rate of 4.9 per cent, most of which (3.2 per cent per annum) was a consequence of increase in average real benefit levels. In the second period, however, the growth rate fell to only 1.8 per cent per annum, half of which was accounted for by demographic changes, with increases in real benefit levels playing only a minor role. The continued rise over 1975–81 in the number of elderly people and the fall in the number of children is reflected in the positive demographic impact on pension expenditure and negative impact on education. The large increase in the size of the unemployed population in the late 1970s accounted for a substantial 'demographic' boost to real expenditure on unemployment benefit. Since 1981, benefit expenditure has continued to grow slowly, driven mainly by the demographic pressure of an ageing population.

It is clear from Table 9.1 that the rapid growth in welfare expenditure that occurred between 1960 and 1975 came about largely because of positive decisions by governments, both Conservative and Labour, to raise the real level of welfare benefits. Table 9.2 shows that such decisions were not peculiar to Britain – most other OECD countries did the same, and in fact the UK had both the lowest overall growth rate of social

Table 9.2 International comparisons of education, health and pensions expenditure as a proportion of GDP (%)				
EDUCATION	1930s	1960	1980	1993–4
UK	4.0	4.3	5.6	5.4
France	1.3	2.4	5.0	5.8
Germany	2.7	2.9	4.7	4.8
Sweden	–	5.1	9.0	8.4
USA	–	4.0	–	5.5
HEALTH	1930s	1960	1980	1993–4
UK	0.6	3.3	5.2	5.8
France	0.3	2.5	6.1	7.6
Germany	0.7	3.2	6.5	7.0
Sweden	0.9	3.4	8.8	6.4
USA	0.3	1.3	4.1	6.3
PENSIONS	1920s	1960	1980	1993–4
UK	2.2	4.0	5.9	7.3
France	1.6	6.0	10.5	12.3
Germany	2.1	9.7	12.8	12.4
Sweden	0.5	4.4	9.9	12.8
USA	0.7	4.1	7.0	7.5

Source: Tanzi and Schuknecht (2000: 34, 38, 41).

expenditure and the lowest rate of growth of real benefit of the seven major OECD countries over the 1960–75 period (OECD 1985). Table 9.2 also shows that the growth rate of public social expenditure in the UK slowed after 1980, and in the case of education was even reversed. The slowdown was again a common feature across OECD countries, though with a fair degree of variation across the different spending programmes. However, the UK slowed more rapidly than most: in 1960 it was close to the top of the international public spending league for education and health, but by the mid-1990s it was at or close to the bottom. Only in the case of pension expenditure did the UK maintain its post-war ranking as one of the most miserly providers.

THE WELFARE STATE AND ECONOMIC GROWTH

The impact of the welfare state on economic efficiency and growth is difficult to evaluate, partly because the boundaries of the welfare state are imprecise, and partly because it is impossible to identify all the indirect effects welfare policy may have on economic activity. However, a strong belief among critics of public welfare expenditure is that the tax and benefit system reduces the incentive for individuals to work and save. The policy-induced restriction of labour supply, together with the employment taxes needed to finance the benefits, raise labour costs above their 'natural' level, thus reducing the international competitiveness of the economy. The reduction in savings that comes from people relying on the state for their pension rather than on accumulating their own assets, leads to a higher overall interest rate in the economy, which in turn produces a lower rate of net investment, and a lower rate of growth (Feldstein 1974, 1996). A different but equally powerful critique is that the direct supply of welfare services by the government is necessarily wasteful because government agents are not subject to the competitive pressures of the market. Both arguments point in the same direction – that a reduction in the role of government and the level of taxes will increase the efficiency of the economy, and will raise the overall growth rate.

This was a minority view in the 1950s and 1960s, although attempts were made within the Conservative Party and by the Institute of Economic

Affairs to develop an alternative approach which emphasised the virtue of private insurance and the means test (Macleod and Powell 1952; Seldon 1957). The election of a Conservative government in 1951 led to the establishment of a whole series of policy reviews which were designed to curtail the creeping universalism and rising cost of health and welfare provision. By the late 1950s, however, electoral and administrative discontent with welfare budgets that were static or declining as a proportion of GDP, and social investigations which revealed the extent of old-age and child poverty, spurred governments to expand welfare state expenditure and provision (Glennerster 2000: ch. 4).

In the 1960s Labour and Conservative administrations were equally lavish towards the welfare state, but the economic stagnation and high inflation ushered in by the first oil price shock of 1973–4 forced a reassessment of the economic consequences of a growing public sector. In a contemporary comment on this reversal, Glennerster (1980) noted that while in the 1960s social expenditure was viewed as the 'handmaiden' of a growing economy, by the mid-1970s it was labelled a 'burden'. Far from helping the government to manage the economy out of short-run difficulties in good Keynesian fashion, the welfare state was now seen to be hindering economic management because of the political and practical difficulty of cutting the welfare budget. Cuts were reluctantly imposed by the 1974–9 Labour government, particularly on the housing and education budgets, though expenditure on cash benefits rose with an increase in the unemployment rate. The result was that the growth rate of social expenditure fell abruptly, though it remained just above the growth rate of GDP over the period 1975–81 (see Table 9.1). What was reluctant retrenchment for Labour was a positive policy goal for the Conservative Party under Margaret Thatcher. The first policy statement on public spending issued by the Conservative government in 1979 was forthright: 'Public expenditure is at the heart of Britain's present economic difficulties' (UK 1979), and much effort and even more rhetoric in the following decade were devoted to 'rolling back the frontiers of the state', including, of course, the welfare state.

The economic logic that lay behind these policies was not always as clear cut as advocates of welfare retrenchment believed. It was argued, for instance, that the high taxes needed to pay for the welfare state reduce work incentives, and thereby retard economic growth. It is true that an increase in the marginal tax rate will lower the opportunity cost of leisure, so encouraging people to work less and play more (the substitution effect). But it also lowers people's income, and so may induce them to work harder in order to maintain their standard of living (the income effect). Which effect dominates is an empirical question, and evidence for the UK is inconclusive (Le Grand 1982: 148). In the case of cash benefits – for instance unemployment benefits or retirement pensions – there is no ambiguity in the direction of the effect, since an increase in non-labour income will reduce work incentives. What really matters, however, is the size of the effect, and again this is an empirical question which has proved difficult to resolve.

There may be more evidence to support the other strand of criticism – that the direct provision of services by the government involves ineffi- ciencies because of the absence of price signals and competitive market pressures (Minford 1991: ch 7). Although this argument can apply to the entire public sector, and seems to have had particular relevance to the nationalised industries (see chapter 4 above), within the field of social ex- penditure it can apply only to services provided directly by the state (pri- marily health, education, personal social services and housing) since cash transfers enable recipients to buy goods and services in the free market. In fact, social security cash transfers have consistently been the largest sin- gle element of welfare state expenditure since 1948, and have dominated the growth of expenditure since the mid-1970s (see below, chapter 14, Figures 14.4, 14.6 and 14.7). Public expenditure on directly supplied wel- fare services actually declined as a share of GDP over the decade from 1975 (Berthoud 1985: 7), and so any associated efficiency losses are likely to have declined in tandem. The magnitude of such losses is very diffi- cult to estimate. Bacon and Eltis (1976) believed that it was considerable both because public services were themselves inefficient and because they were too large, soaking up unproductive labour which the free market, if left to its own devices, would allocate to more productive uses. Their cri- tique relied on an overly simplistic accounting convention which viewed non-market activity as non-productive – thus producing nonsensical con- clusions such as that private education (marketed output) was of benefit to the economy while state education (non-marketed output) was not (Middleton 1996: 526–9). In fact the data in Table 9.2 suggest that, by the standard of other developed countries, public expenditure in Britain on welfare services, particularly health care, may have been too small rather than too large.

The enormous practical difficulty of identifying and measuring the overall disincentive effects and inefficiencies of the welfare state has led many critics to adopt a more *ad hoc* approach based on the association between rising rates of social expenditure in the 1960s and early 1970s and declining rates of economic growth. The idea that rising social ex- penditure was a *source* of the economic problems moved from extremist wings to centre stage of economic analysis: the OECD (1981) gave its offi- cial sanction to this view with the publication of a report on *The Welfare State in Crisis*.

This report was an immediate reaction to the perplexing economic downturn that affected all developed economies in the 1970s, but it was a profoundly unhistorical document. Although there was a clear temporal association between rising rates of social expenditure across the OECD economies from the late 1960s and a slowdown in economic activity, a longer-term analysis would have shown that the even faster rates of social expenditure growth from the 1950s to the mid-1960s were associated with the 'golden age' of post-war growth – the strongest and most sustained economic boom ever experienced by the developed economies (Johnson 1986). The OECD subsequently conducted a more thorough historical analysis which 'failed to reveal an inverse relationship between public sector size and economic performance as reflected in GDP growth rates, unemployment rates and inflation rates, or between public sector growth and inflation rates' (OECD 1985: 15). Between 1960 and 1981 the country with the highest growth rate of social expenditure, Japan, also had the highest annual growth rate of GDP, while the UK had the lowest growth rates of both GDP and social expenditure. Germany, the other stellar economic performer, had the highest share of social expenditure as a proportion of GDP of all the major OECD countries in both 1960 and 1981.

While the OECD has over time tempered its views about the negative effects of welfare expenditure, the International Monetary Fund has taken up the call for greatly reduced public spending. A recent study argues that between 1960 and 1990 there has been no consistent relationship – positive or negative – between the size of expenditure programmes on health and education and the resulting social indicators such as life expectancy, infant mortality or illiteracy (Tanzi and Schuknecht 2000). This leads the authors to conclude not that public provision is itself problematic, but that the scale of provision is not directly related to the quality – thus 'small government' can be as good as, or better than, 'big government'. What matters, they suggest, is the quality of public provision – the specific institutional arrangements and how they are operationalised. This is essentially an argument about the cost-effectiveness of alternative forms of service delivery. It is certainly true that the absence of explicit prices and markets in public services may lead to a sub-optimal allocation of resources. On the other hand, market allocation may produce socially sub-optimal outcomes, as is demonstrated by the fact that the mainly private-sector health care system in the USA consumes a larger proportion of GDP than in any other major industrial economy, yet produces worse results in terms of population-wide infant mortality and life expectancy (Propper 2001).

The argument that public welfare provision inevitably harms economic performance seems still to be unproven, although there is little doubt that a badly designed or a badly administered welfare system can have an adverse impact on the economy even if it meets some of its social targets. Since Britain has, for much of the post-war period, spent less on welfare state transfers and services than many of its major competitors (see Table 9.2), it is difficult to see how the welfare state could have been responsible for the relatively poor growth performance of the British economy. In fact high welfare expenditure financed by progressive taxation clearly has a positive macroeconomic impact in terms of automatic stabilisation of the economy. When the economy is booming and incomes and employment rising, welfare taxation will tend to dampen the upswing of the economic cycle. As a corollary, during a period of economic slowdown, welfare expenditure will cushion the decline in aggregate expenditure.

THE WELFARE STATE AND EQUALITY OF INCOMES

Supporters of the welfare state argue that its achievements should be judged not solely in relation to economic efficiency and growth, but also in relation to its impact on welfare. They suggest that it has scored a major success in reducing poverty and promoting a more equitable distribution of income in British society since 1945. The reduction – and ideally the eradication – of poverty was one of the explicit aims of Beveridge when he drew up his blueprint for social reform in 1942. However, the promotion of income equality through redistribution, although favoured by many members of the post-war Labour government, was not part of the 1942 plan. Beveridge proposed that benefits should be limited to a subsistence level and that contributions should be the same for all workers, meaning that redistribution would occur only to the extent that the incidence of insurance contingencies (sickness, unemployment, disability, old age) varied between income groups.

In the immediate post-war period it seemed that the welfare state had succeeded in preventing poverty. Seebohm Rowntree published a third poverty survey of York in 1951 which showed only 3 per cent of the population living in poverty, compared with 13 per cent in his interwar study and 30 per cent in his original investigation in 1899 (Rowntree and Lavers 1951). Beveridge had used the earlier poverty surveys of Rowntree to determine the level at which benefits should be paid, and the 1951 survey vindicated his hopes that social insurance and social assistance benefits would provide at least a subsistence income for all recipients. But this was a false dawn. In the mid-1960s social researchers discovered widespread poverty in many families with dependant children and among pensioner households, two groups who were specifically supported by the welfare state through the payment of family allowances and old age pensions (Abel-Smith and Townsend 1965).

The rediscovery of poverty coincided with a redefinition of what it was to be poor. For Beveridge, poverty was defined as having an income so low that it prevented the purchase of necessary food, clothing and shelter – this is commonly described as an *absolute* measure of poverty. As real incomes in society rise due to economic growth, absolute poverty should decline, as should the need for the welfare state to support families with incomes below this minimal absolute level. Abel-Smith, Townsend and other social researchers, by contrast, adopted a *relative* measure of poverty, which defined households as poor if they had incomes significantly below the national average. By this definition, a general growth of real incomes, and an increase of welfare state benefits in line with this income growth, would do nothing to diminish the proportion of the population living in poverty. In the 1990s the idea of relative poverty has been further extended to encompass the notion of *social exclusion*, which occurs when households lack the resources, financial and otherwise, to engage in a standard range of social, economic and political activities.

The shift in conception of poverty from an absolute to a relative definition underpins much of the apparent increase in poverty rates in Britain since Rowntree's 1951 survey. Studies throughout the 1960s and 1970s found that poverty continued to be a major social problem, despite the rapid growth of social expenditure (Townsend 1979; Fiegehen *et al.* 1977). A survey of evidence in 1987 concluded that 'the burden of poverty has increased grotesquely over the last eight years' (Piachaud 1987: 26). The number of people receiving means-tested benefits because of poverty doubled from 1 to 2 million between 1948 and 1966, and doubled again to reach over 4 million in the deep recession of the early 1980s, with many more living on incomes only marginally above this poverty threshold. Digby (1989: 68, 107) summarised the pessimistic view by concluding that, in 1983, almost one in three people in the UK – 16.3 million – lived in households on or just above the poverty line (defined as incomes of no more than 140 per cent of the supplementary benefit level). Little changed over the next two decades. Using the standard EU definition of poverty as people living in households with less than 60 per cent of the median income, the Joseph Rowntree Foundation found that in 2000 13.3 million people in the UK were in poverty, and that this figure had remained unchanged throughout the 1990s, though it almost doubled in the 1980s from just over 7 million in 1979 (Rahman *et al.* 2001).

This seems to suggest that the welfare state has failed in one of its primary goals. Yet, of course, the growth in average incomes, and in the real value of social security benefits, means that even those people entirely dependent on benefits today have a real income far above Beveridge's 1942 absolute poverty line. Nevertheless, the fact that so many people by the 1990s had incomes of less than 60 per cent of the median indicates a failure to meet the aim of the post-war Labour government to reduce inequality through redistribution of income. What accounts for this apparent failure?

Although *average* real disposable income has risen almost three-fold since 1949, not all groups in the population have benefited to the same extent. Figure 9.2 shows different, but overlapping, estimates of what has happened to overall income inequality between 1949 and 1999. The graph represents an index of inequality called the Gini coefficient, which ranges between 0 and 100. The closer the coefficient is to 0, the more equitably income is distributed across the population; conversely, as it

Figure 9.2 Trends in income inequality, 1949–1999

Source: Hills 1996; Goodman 2001.

tends towards 100, the distribution of income becomes more and more unequal with a small group of rich people taking an ever growing share.

The top lines (the Blue Book series) are based on Inland Revenue data relating to the disposable income of 'tax units' with no adjustment for household size. A 'tax unit' can refer to a single adult, a married couple, or a family with several dependent children. The middle line (*Economic Trends*) shows disposable income adjusted for family size, and the bottom line shows long-run estimates on a slightly different basis created by the Institute for Fiscal Studies (Hills 1996; Goodman 2001). There is significant variance in the level of income inequality identified by these different methods, but the trend is common to all three series.

Income inequality appears to have been more-or-less constant through the 1950s – people had never been having it so good in equal measure. It should be noted that this plateau represents a considerable change since the pre-war period. Comparing 1938 and 1949 (there are no Inland Revenue data for the intermediate years), the Gini coefficient on income after tax fell from around 43 to 35. This was due to a decline in the disposable income of the richest tenth of the population (their share fell from 35 to 26 per cent of total after-direct-tax income), and this was itself primarily due to a fall in the earnings and increase in the tax liability of the richest 1 per cent of the population, who saw their share of disposable income fall from 12 to 6 per cent of the total over this period (UK 1975: 36). This war-time curtailment of the income privileges of the very highest of earners was sustained through two decades of post-war economic and fiscal management, by both Labour and Conservative governments. In this respect, at least, a post-war political consensus is very apparent in the data (Rollings 1992).

From 1964 to 1970 there was little change in overall distribution of income, even though the Labour government was explicitly committed to creating a more equal society. Inequality rose slightly in 1971–2, then fell to the mid-1970s. It appears to have been increasing before the electoral victory of Margaret Thatcher in 1979, but it is clear that inequality increased very rapidly after that date. By 1985, according to the Blue Book series, income inequality was greater than at any time since 1949, and the income share of the richest fifth of the population – at 43.1 per cent of the total – was higher than at any time since the Second World War. From the mid-1980s to the early 1990s income inequality grew more rapidly than at any period since the war, and more rapidly than in any other OECD country with the possible exception of New Zealand. In fact many European countries – Italy, Denmark, Spain, Portugal and Ireland – experienced declining inequality in the 1980s (Atkinson 1996: ch. 2). This is significant because it shows that generic and international explanations for rising inequality, such as the globalisation of the international economy, the rise of new technologies, changes in relative prices, and the impact of European economic integration – are insufficient. If we are to look for causes, the search must begin at home.

Overall income inequality can change because of movements at the top (high pay) or bottom (low pay) of the income distribution. If the overall income distribution is divided into deciles, and each separate income group is examined over time, then over the period 1961–79 each income group enjoyed a growth of real net income very close to the mean for the entire population, with the exception of the poorest decile which experienced an increase in real income 50% above the mean (54 percentage points, compared with a mean growth over this period of 36 per cent) (Hills 1996: 4). The general decline in measured inequality over this period came through a considerable reduction in the relative poverty of the poorest tenth of the population, within a context of significant income increases for *everyone*. For the period 1979–92, however, the picture was very different. Although the average income of the entire population again rose by 36 per cent in this period, it was the richest fifth who enjoyed real income growth higher than the average, whereas the poorest one-tenth of the population enjoyed no real income growth at all over this thirteen-year period.

Much of this change can be attributed to deliberate decisions made by the Conservative government to change the impact of tax and benefit policies. Analysis by the Institute for Fiscal Studies concluded that half the rise in inequality could be attributed to the tax and benefit system (Johnson and Webb 1993; Goodman *et al.* 1997). Comparing the 1978/9 tax/benefit system with the 1994/5 system, it can be shown that the poorest one-tenth would have been 40 per cent better off in 1994/5 if the 1978/9 tax/benefit system had still been in place; only the richest tenth of the population gained unambiguously from the intervening tax and benefit changes. Since 1997 the New Labour government has stabilised the income distribution, but has not significantly reversed the trends of the previous two decades.

It is clear that discretionary changes to the system of taxes and benefits that constitute the welfare state can have a profound effect on the distribution of income in society, and it is also clear that the Conservative governments of the 1980s and early 1990s reversed earlier policy commitments towards actively using the welfare state and tax policy to reduce income inequality. But it is equally true that a broad range of concomitant changes in society – in the structure of employment, of earnings, and of households – also had a major impact on the distribution of income, accounting for half the rise in inequality through the 1980s. The rise in the number of unemployed from less than half a million through most of the 1960s, to 1 million after the first oil shock in the mid-1970s, to 2 million by 1981 and over 3 million throughout 1983–6, increased the burden on the tax and benefit system and helps to explain why income inequality rose even as total expenditure on cash benefits was also rising. Even more important was a growing inequality of earnings within the working population: between 1978 and 1993 real hourly wages for men in the tenth percentile of the wage distribution barely changed, whereas the median wage rose by 30 per cent and for men at the ninetieth percentile wages increased by over 50 per cent (Goodman *et al.* 1997: 279). Such changes are driven primarily by supply and demand in the labour market, rather than by government policy. And significant social developments – for instance the expansion of the pensioner population from 13 per cent to 18 per cent of the total between the late 1950s and the mid-1990s, or the more than doubling in the number of single parents over a twenty-year period to reach 1.3 million by 1991 – have created new demands on the welfare system which even rising expenditure cannot necessarily fully meet. Thus an initial judgement of welfare state failure, based on poverty rates and income distribution data, must be tempered by a realisation that many of the forces driving the distribution of income lie beyond the remit of the welfare state, and that part of the reason for continued high rates of relative poverty is the changing social and economic structure of the country that has resulted in more households – both young and old – being detached from the labour market, and thus dependent on benefit income.

THE WELFARE STATE AND EQUALITY OF OPPORTUNITY

The provision of income for poorer and older members of society is not the only function of the welfare state, though it is an important one, since it is income that gives people choice over consumption in a market economy. However, the post-war welfare state has also directly provided citizens with a wide range of services outside of the market system in the areas of health care, education, social care and housing. It is through the direct provision of services that the welfare state may be able to counter inequality, and provide similar opportunities for all. In the words of Aneurin Bevan, the minister of health in the post-war Labour government, 'a free health service is pure socialism and as such it is opposed to the hedonism of capitalist society' (Bevan 1952: 81). How has the welfare state performed in this role? This section examines two major areas of service provision which can have the greatest impact on life chances and equality of opportunity: education and health.

Education

Although state funding of education in Britain has existed since 1870, the 1944 Education Act was intended to provide all children with an equal right to education up to the age of 15 (extended to 16 in 1972). In the 1980s and 1990s there has been a further expansion of educational provision, particularly at post-18 level, so that by 2000 over 30 per cent of 18- to 20-year-olds were enrolled in some form of higher education, up from 9 per cent in 1960 (see also chapter 5 above). But the expansion of access to higher education has not been equitably distributed throughout the population. Among the pre-welfare-state cohort of children reaching age 20 between 1933 and 1942, just 1 per cent of working-class boys and 7 per cent of middle-class boys entered university. For the cohort reaching age twenty between 1963 and 1972 these figures had risen to 3 per cent and 26 per cent respectively; both the proportionate and the absolute increase was greater for middle-class children (Halsey *et al.* 1980: 188).

This inequality was to some extent a structural consequence of the post-war secondary education system, in which pupils were tested at age 11, with the 'bright' children going to grammar schools, and the 'non-academic' going to secondary-modern schools. Dissatisfaction with the rigidity and divisiveness of this system, together with a commitment to extending equality of opportunity, led the Labour government in 1965 to attempt to replace grammar and secondary-modern schools with non-selective 'comprehensive' schools. By 1986 almost all state school pupils in Scotland and Wales, and 85 per cent of those in England were being educated in comprehensive schools. These reforms did have some impact on educational performance, and a further raft of reforms in the 1980s and 1990s which have introduced more centralised control of the curriculum and of teaching standards have also helped to increase examination success rates. They have, however, done little to reduce the class divide in educational attainment.

Access to higher education is rationed by competitive examinations at age 18, and working-class children have a much lower chance of sitting these exams because of their low rate of continuation in school beyond the minimum school leaving age. In order even to have a chance of competing for university entrance at age 18, pupils must gain five or more higher-grade passes in examinations at age 16. In 1989 30 per cent of boys and 36 per cent of girls succeeded in passing five or more exams at age 16, figures which had risen to 43 per cent of boys and 53 per cent of girls by 1999. However, over this period the gap in attainment by social class widened. Children from managerial or professional households had a success rate that rose marginally from 22 percentage points above the national average in 1988 to 24 percentage points above in 1997. For children from unskilled manual households, on the other hand, the pass rate was 18 percentage points below the national average in 1988, and had declined further to 24 percentage points below by 1997 (Gilborn and Mirza 2000: 22).

The better educational performance of middle-class children is in part a consequence of choices made by their parents to purchase educational services in the market. Since the mid-1980s private schools have catered for more than 6 per cent of all school pupils, and about 18 per cent of 16–18-year-olds. Private schools achieve better examination results than state schools, partly because of greater resources per pupil, partly because they cream off academically gifted children and teachers, and partly because the fees they charge largely exclude lower-performing children from working-class backgrounds. However, the majority of children from middle-class homes are educated in the state sector, and their high level of educational attainment and high rates of university entry represent a clear case of 'middle class capture' of this part of the welfare state (Goodin and Le Grand 1987). Although all parts of the educational system are, in theory, accessible to all individuals, in practice universities continue to be dominated by students from middle-class backgrounds. Thus most of the 4 per cent or so of the total welfare state budget devoted to higher education (about £8 billion in 1996–7) represents a recycling of general tax revenue towards the middle classes.

Health

The National Health Service (NHS) came into operation in July 1948 to provide comprehensive health care and treatment which would be free at the point of use and financed from general taxation. The intention was to provide equality of access to health care and to promote equality of health outcomes. Although direct charges have been introduced for some minor parts of the health service (for instance charges for pharmaceuticals – 'prescription charges' – were introduced in 1951, abolished in 1965, and reimposed in 1968) medical consultation and treatment remains free at the point of delivery, so equality of access has largely been achieved. On the other hand, consumer demand has not been satisfied: queues for treatment, particularly for 'non-urgent' surgery, have been a constant reminder of health service 'failure'. Although spending on the NHS as a proportion of GDP has risen from just over 3 per cent in the early 1950s to over 5 per cent by the early 1980s and almost 6 per cent by 1999, this has not been sufficient to meet rising demand caused by the ageing of the population, the development of new and expensive medical interventions, and higher expectations of treatment and service. There has been a small expansion of private health care expenditure over time; this ran at about 0.5 per cent of GDP from the late 1950s to the mid-1970s, before gradually rising to just over 1 per cent of GDP by the mid-1990s (Propper 2001). As a proportion of total health spending, however, private health care expenditure represented much the same share in 1999 (16 per cent) as in 1960 (14.8 per cent). Despite the apparent failure of the NHS to satisfy demand, there has been no significant drift of the middle classes towards private provision, and the NHS remains the most popular element of the entire welfare state.

Success in providing equality of access (limited only by the tyranny of the consultants' waiting lists) has not been matched by success in achieving equality of health outcomes. Although life expectancy has continued to rise in the post-war period, class differentials in mortality and morbidity (sickness) rates appear to have widened rather than narrowed since the establishment of the NHS (Black 1980; Acheson 1998). Between 1972–6 and 1997–9 the difference in life expectancy at birth between men in social classes I (managerial and professional) and V (unskilled manual) widened from 5.5 years to 7.4 years; for women it widened from 5.3 years to 5.7 years. In 1998 the infant mortality rate among children in social class V was double that for social class I; the male death rate from chronic heart disease was three times higher in social class V than class I; the suicide rate was almost four times higher in social class V; the incidence of mental illness was 80 per cent higher in class V compared to class I (Department of Health 2002). Of course, these differences have little to do with the NHS itself, the primary function of which is to respond to symptoms of illness rather than to their underlying socio-economic causes. One major cause of health inequality is smoking, the prevalence of which in 1998 was 15 per cent among professional men and 42 per cent among unskilled men. This class gradient in smoking accounts for over half of the entire difference in risk of premature death between higher and lower classes. The effects are not restricted to men. Among women, smoking in pregnancy – a major indicator of low birth weight and excess infant mortality – is four times more prevalent in social class V than in social class I. Teenage pregnancy – again closely associated with a wide variety of poor health indicators – is ten times more likely among young women in social class V than in social class I.

These health indicators reflect a deeply rooted problem of multiple deprivation. Poor physical and mental health tends to be associated with low educational achievement, low income and low-quality housing. The welfare state ameliorates many of these problems through its multiple activities, but there are clear limits to the degree to which the various public welfare agencies can or should intervene with the choices that individual citizens make about how to allocate their time and money.

CONCLUSION

In 1950, expenditure on all the income transfers and services provided by the welfare state amounted to around 12 per cent of GDP; by 2000 this figure had risen to almost 25 per cent. There is little evidence that this expansion has had a significant negative effect on the overall performance of the economy. In fact, public expenditure on education has promoted growth by raising the skills base of the working population (see chapter 5 above), and the activities of the NHS have helped to improve the health and life chances of this population. On the other hand, this large increase in real expenditure has not prevented the distribution of income becoming less equal in the last quarter of the twentieth century (Figure 9.2). Since the mid-1970s a relative decline in the demand for unskilled workers and an increase in the number of single parents, together, have doubled the number of households that receive no income from employment. These households are almost entirely dependent on social security benefits which, despite their aggregate cost, provide a low standard of living for the recipients. Throughout the post-war period employment has been the primary route by which people have secured a claim on resources, and those unable or unwilling to work have consistently lived in or on the margins of poverty.

However, most welfare state outputs – whether direct services or cash transfers – are consumed not just by the very poor, but by people right across the income distribution. The most expensive of all the cash benefits – the old age pension – is an insurance benefit paid without regard to the income of the recipient. The same is true of child benefit. Education and health services are accessible to all, and, as noted above in the case of post-16 education, tend to be consumed more heavily by middle-class households. Falkingham and Hills (1995) have shown that more than 80 per cent of lifetime payments into the welfare state are effectively re-cycled across the life-course: people receive financial transfers and health and education services as children, and receive even more cash transfers and health care when old, in exchange for substantial tax payments and National Insurance contributions while they are of working age. In this respect the welfare state provides exactly the sort of 'cradle to grave' support that Beveridge intended. What it has not done is achieve the type of wholesale redistribution of resources and opportunities that was hoped for by Aneurin Bevan and many other members of the 1945–51 Labour governments. These redistributional hopes were always unrealistic: Beveridge's plan for flat-rate contributions and benefits was designed in part to prevent wholesale redistribution. The fact that everybody pays, but everybody receives, helps to account for the enduring popularity of the welfare state as a mechanism for providing social insurance and welfare services.

10

The rise of the service economy

ROBERT MILLWARD

Contents

INTRODUCTION

In the analysis of the structure of modern economies, it is common to identify three sectors: agriculture, industry and services.[1] The dividing line between services and industry is a rather grey area but services are usually taken to include, at a minimum, transport, communications, retail and wholesale trade, recreational activities, banking and professional services, as well as many activities directly financed by government like education, health and social services. For long seen as peripheral to economic development, services came by a quiet revolution to dominate the economies of the Western world by the end of the twentieth century. Services increased in the nineteenth and early twentieth centuries, but for many historians this was a feature of industrialisation, not the driving force. Technological developments in industry and the railways, along with increasing occupational and spatial specialisation, promoted the growth of separate sectors like wholesaling, insurance and telecommunications and increased the importance of education and training for the supply of technicians and scientific manpower. The rise in per capita

[1] The author wishes to thank Barry Supple, Paul Johnson, James Foreman-Peck, Katherine Watson and Peter Howlett for comments on the first draft and the Leverhulme Trust for financial support.

incomes generated a demand for better health and for wider access to recreation and the performing arts. However, it was the second half of the twentieth century which saw a truly remarkable rise in services. Specialist firms supplying professional services like accounting and computer support mushroomed and, in conjunction with the continuing rise in employment in health, education and retail trade, ensured that services became the dominant source of employment for Britain's labour force.

Precisely how important services have been for the British economy is a matter of some dispute. Some historians, like Rubinstein (1993), think that Britain's long-term economic strength has always been in services. With London as the main base, overseas trading and merchanting flourished in the seventeenth and eighteenth centuries. They were overshadowed in the middle of the nineteenth century by the spread of factory industry in the north of England, the Midlands, South Wales and the central belt of Scotland but, by the second half of the twentieth century, finance and business services, based very much in London and the south-east, had again taken the dominant position.

There was, on the other hand, a continuing worry that a strong economy could only be maintained if a large industrial sector existed. The dramatic decline in manufacturing during the 1960s and 1970s in some of the economically advanced nations caused alarm. During the lively exchanges before the 1984–5 House of Lords Select Committee on Overseas Trade, Lord Weinstock (chairman and chief executive of GEC, one of Britain's largest engineering companies) voiced the concerns of many industrialists about the apparent complacency of the Treasury:

> I have heard this argument about service industries going to replace manufacturing before, and asked myself what will the service industries be servicing when there is no hardware, when no wealth is actually being produced. We will be servicing, presumably, the Beefeaters around the Tower of London. We will become a curiosity. I do not think that is what Britain is all about; I think it is rubbish. What service industries are there going to be in Wigan, or in Bolton or at Smethwick? These are places where there are no tourist attractions at all. How are these people to live if there is to be no manufacturing industry? (House of Lords 1984–5: II, 474, question 1381)

There are some good questions here which were largely unanswered at the time. The counter arguments can now be more forcefully advanced. Indeed as early as 1985, in the USA where the trend to services was even more advanced, President Reagan was able to declare: 'The move from an industrial economy to a post-industrial service economy has been one of the greatest changes to affect the developed world since the Industrial Revolution. The progression of an economy . . . from agriculture to manufacturing to services is a natural change' (quoted in *Financial Times*, 22 May 1987, p. 16). Clearly, huge changes had occurred in Britain by the last quarter of the twentieth century when three-quarters of the labour force were in service sectors. Education, health and retail trade continued to be important but a major change had been that services like accounting, marketing, research and development, computer support and catering, which had traditionally been provided 'in-house' in large companies like ICI, Unilever and British Telecom, were being supplied, by the end of the twentieth century, by separate specialist firms. A new 'service economy' rooted in the proliferation of such producer services had emerged. The proportion of British national output that was exported as goods (rather than as services) remained buoyant and indeed was higher at the end of the twentieth century than it had been at the middle. Nevertheless it has become less useful to talk of 'the service sector'. In the modern economy the majority of transactions are measured as service activities – and some like Castells (2000) would even like to call it an informational economy.

   This chapter analyses the rise of services in the second half of the twentieth century and assesses how far the British pattern was mirrored in what was happening in other economically advanced nations like France, Germany and the USA. It does this in the following four sections by addressing four questions:

- was the rise of employment in services largely reflecting the expansion of sectors that were very labour-intensive, with low productivity growth?
- how and why did producer services associated with finance and the professions come to be organised in specialist firms separated from manufacturing?
- how successful was Britain in the growth of the international trade in services?
- what role did services have in Britain's economic growth performance?

THE EXPANSION OF LABOUR-INTENSIVE CONSUMER SERVICES

The three decades after 1945 were marked by a large expansion of employment of nurses, teachers, clerks, civil servants, supermarket assistants and shop workers. They were employed in sectors that, traditionally, were very labour-intensive and this raises the question of how far the rise in the share of services in the economy was mainly a rise in employment rather than a rise in the real volume of services supplied. In addressing this question it is useful, first of all, to see how this period fits in with long-term changes in the structure of the economy. In the seventeenth and eighteenth centuries Britain experienced a revolution in agriculture which raised productivity. This released labour and other resources for industry, a process that was already well advanced in Britain by the middle of the nineteenth century, and by 1913 a quite distinctive feature of

Table 10.1 Shares of resources and production in the UK economy, 1913–1995 (%)							
	Manufacturing, construction, oil, mining, agriculture			Services			Dwellings	
	Capital	Labour	Output	Capital	Labour	Output	Capital	Output[a]
1913	32.2	52.4	43.6	47.4	47.6	55.7	20.4	1.3
1951	31.2	51.3	49.0	39.9	48.9	50.4	28.9	0.6
1973	29.0	47.8	50.2	43.1	52.2	50.7	27.9	−0.9
1995	19.1	28.4	31.1	50.0	71.6	65.7	30.9	3.2

[a] Includes the deductions for financial services usually recorded separately in the national accounts.

Definitions: The labour entries relate to hours worked. Output is net output (value added); at 1924 market prices for 1913, at 1958 prices for 1951 and 1973 and the 1995 entry is at current prices. The figures for capital are gross capital stock at the replacement prices of the same years except that the 1995 entry relates to 1990 replacement prices.

Sources: The first three rows are from Matthews, *et al.* (1985: tab. 8.1). The output and capital figures in the last row were derived from CSO, *UK National Accounts*, 1997, and the hours-worked entries from the data on persons engaged and average hours worked in tabs. B and C of O'Mahony (1999).

Britain was that less than 5 per cent of its labour force was in agriculture. During the nineteenth century many different service sectors had seen a rise in employment but the most significant increases were in civil public administration, professional and scientific personnel, the distributive trades, domestic servants, postage, transport and communications. Two forces seem to have been at work. One emphasised by North (1981) was the scope afforded by the eighteenth- and nineteenth-century economic revolutions for spatial and occupational specialisation. The volume of transactions rose and they were increasingly taken out of the home, the village and the counting house into a market setting. Agencies to facilitate transactions therefore grew rapidly – in finance, law, policing, commerce, telecommunications. A second major force in Britain was urbanisation, carrying with it all the problems of health and planning; hence the growth of the utilities (water supply, trams, electricity, gas) and of civil administration at local and central government level.

Indeed, on the eve of the First World War, services already employed nearly one half of Britain's workforce, as may be seen in Table 10.1. The share of services in the economy is an issue running throughout this chapter and raises the question of how to define the boundary of the sector. Many services seem to be distinguished from manufacturing by being intangible (advice from an architect) or invisible (music over airwaves) or non-storable (a haircut). Water supply has the character of a manufactured good when it is used for washing and drinking but of a service when it is part of a central heating system. A useful method of differentiating services from goods lies in the cost of storage. The output of some production processes cannot always be readily stored (in contrast to oil and coal) and, as the cost of storage rises, outputs will tend to be classified more as a service (the music concert) than as a manufactured good (a CD). Clearly there are activities on the borderline like electricity supply, which can, at some cost, be stored in batteries. On this basis, the following sectors in British official statistical records, will be treated in this chapter as services: (1) transport and communications, (2) utilities (gas, electricity and water), (3) wholesale and retail trade, (4) finance and business services, (5) education, health and social services, (6) public administration, (7) other services including hotels, pubs, recreation, sanitation, domestic service and other mainly personal services.[2]

Services so defined saw little change in the first half of the twentieth century in their shares of resources or of output, the decline of domestic service offsetting increases in transport, communications, distribution, the utilities and public administration. Indeed, with Japan, France and Germany physically devastated, the first decade after the Second World War saw British manufacturing bathing in a sellers' market. The shares of output recorded in Table 10.1 for 1951 show a significant rise for manufacturing as compared to 1913 whilst the share of services actually fell. It was the second half of the century that witnessed the major surge towards a service economy. Part of that surge was a rise in those services linked to increases in living standards and to the increased role of government after the Second World War: education and health in particular. The 1940s, 1950s and 1960s saw the emergence of the National Health Service; compulsory education up to age sixteen; improved access to polytechnics, universities and other forms of higher education; and a new consumerism linked to household durable goods and leisure. The introduction of a nationally run pension fund and of social security payments, including National Assistance for the worst-off, all added up to new functions for the civil service in both local and central government. These services figured more as items of consumption for households and government than as intermediate inputs for industry, which were usually manufactured goods. Indeed final expenditure by households and government on services was only 33 per cent of all national final expenditure in 1951 but had risen to 55 per cent by 1975.

Such services appeared to be closely linked to the rising prosperity of the 1950s and 1960s. But there was at least one other competing explanation, which arose from what many observers saw as the essentially labour-intensive nature of the services that had been expanding. Labour had traditionally been a key resource in education and health and also in retail trade, tourism, public administration and banking. Whilst automation and mechanisation might provide some room for increases in output per employee, the scope was thought to be limited (before the advent of information technology). The extreme case was the Shakespearean play, with a specific list of characters, which could not readily be automated

---

[2] Dwellings yield housing services, the output of which take the form of income from renting or as the imputed income of owner-occupied property. These are sometimes recorded separately, as in Table 10.1.

if the performance was to be true to the text and which meant that labour-saving innovations were out of the question (notwithstanding the endless possibilities in Shakespeare for dual roles for actors). It was this employment dimension of services which came to attract attention in the USA and Britain from the late 1960s onwards. The sheer growth in employment seemed to creep into people's perceptions and several social scientists and historians started to talk about a revolution in the economy. Contemporaries struggled to put their fingers on the essence of this service expansion but more and more were wondering whether the rising demand occasioned by rising per capita incomes might be less important than the fact that they seemed to be very costly in terms of labour inputs (Fuchs 1968; Hartwell 1973; Channon 1976, 1978; Daniels 1982; Marquand 1983).

The implication, drawn out most explicitly by Baumol (1967), was that over time the cost of services would rise relative to manufactured products and that, even were the demand for services to increase at the same pace, they would account for a rising share of the national labour force and even of national money income depending on what happened to wages and salaries. Table 10.1 provides some support for this view in that the service sector's share of output fell in the first half of the century and remained constant 1951–73, while the labour input rose throughout – and this was not a mere chimera produced by increases in part-time employment since this Table records the labour inputs in terms of total hours worked. Indeed, looking over the long term, the growth rate of productivity in the service sector in Britain was 0.2 per cent per annum on average for the period 1856–73 as compared to 0.9 per cent for manufacturing. Thereafter the two figures were 0.3 and 0.6 respectively for 1873–1913, (−) 0.1 and 1.9 for 1924–37 and 1.8 and 2.5 for 1951–73.[3] A problem in gauging the size of the service sector is how to make allowance for this seemingly unavoidable slow growth of productivity. For example, the Treasury in Britain regularly reported government expenditure plans and outcomes. In addition to making allowance for any general rise in prices which occurred each year, they also estimated and made allowance each year for the rise in the relative cost (or 'price') of services (cf. chancellor of the Exchequer 1969: appendix II).

Three questions are suggested by these observations. Firstly, how far did the main growth areas for services in the 1950s and 1960s maintain their significance in the last part of the twentieth century? Secondly, how far was the pattern of service growth in Britain repeated in other advanced industrial nations? Thirdly, how much of service growth was actually due to rising demand, how much to its expensive use of labour and how much to the growth of specialisation in production and hence in services for other producing sectors.

---

[3] Millward (1990), referring to total factor productivity.

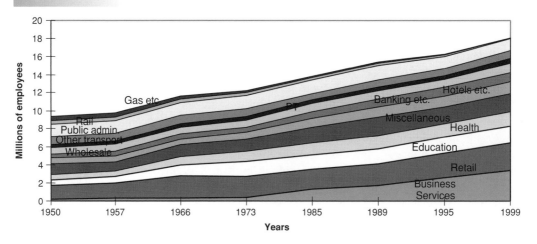

Figure 10.1

Employment in UK services, 1950–1999

Note: 'PT' means posts and telecom.
Sources: CSO (ONS), *Annual Abstract of Statistics*, 1958, 1972, 1975, 1991, 2000 with varying industrial classification.

Figure 10.1 partly answers the first question by showing how the composition of employment in service production changed over the period 1950–99. Up to the end of the 1970s employment was fairly constant in wholesale trade and finance. It fell in some of the key infrastructure industries, although in electricity and gas this was very much a substitution of capital for labour rather than a decline in output; so also for the railways, with the important qualification that the 'Beeching axe' of the 1960s heralded the pruning of the Victorian track and service network. The main growth areas for employment in these decades are confirmed as health, education and public administration, together with hotels, catering and other recreational and cultural services embraced in the miscellaneous category. However, this pattern (apart from recreation and cultural services) was not repeated in the last quarter of the century when the main growth areas were retail trade, financial services and especially business services, accompanied by a huge rise in part-time employment. Whereas in the 1950s and 1960s the big recruitment drive was for nurses, teachers and civil servants, by the 1990s it was computer programmers and operators, management consultants, accountants, word processors, check-out assistants, economists and financial analysts. Many of the new professionals in Britain were accountants by origin since, in the early absence of business schools, the traditional training in chartered and other accounting proved to be one of the best development routes for British managers. The labour force in finance and business services rose from 637,000 in 1951 to 1,472,000 in 1975, rocketing to 4,276,000 by 1998. In June 1999 there were nearly 1 million males and females working part-time in business services like engineering, advertising, architecture, accounting, surveying, research and development. A further 780,000 part-timers were in hotels, restaurants, pubs and other parts of catering. The rise in part-time labour was probably only a subsidiary factor in the rise of services in the second half of the twentieth century. Services did tend to use more part-time labour than manufacturing but this was as true in 1950 as in 1996. Annual average hours worked per person engaged fell by

Table 10.2	Sectoral % shares of employment: international comparisons, 1950–1995				
	UK	USA	France	West Germany	Japan
Agric., mining, oil, etc.					
1950	9.8	12.4	29.3	30.5	45.1
1995	2.3	2.1	4.9	3.4	7.4
Manufacturing & constr.					
1950	39.5	30.4	31.7	39.1	23.3
1995	23.6	19.0	24.7	34.0	33.0
Services					
1950	50.7	57.2	39.0	34.4	31.6
1995	74.1	78.9	70.4	62.6	59.6
of which: Electricity, gas & water					
1950	1.6	0.9	0.6	0.7	0.5
1995	0.8	0.7	0.7	1.0	0.7
Transport & comm.					
1950	7.3	6.4	4.7	5.4	4.6
1995	5.6	4.5	5.7	5.5	5.6
Distributive trades					
1950	18.8	19.8	12.0	10.9	11.2
1995	21.9	23.5	17.4	17.2	16.7
Finance & Business services					
1950	3.5	4.4	4.0	2.7	3.3
1995	13.4	12.2	11.9	8.5	9.3
Miscellaneous personal services					
1950	7.0	9.5	1.2	5.2	6.9
1995	12.2	12.4	3.4	10.5	18.5
Education, health, government, etc.					
1950	12.5	16.2	16.5	9.5	5.1
1995	20.2	25.6	31.3	19.9	8.8

Source: Derived from O'Mahony (1999, tab. 2.1).

15 per cent in manufacturing which was a smaller decline than in retail trade and personal services but actually the same as or greater than in all other service sectors.[4]

This pattern displays some similarities with what was happening in other countries. Table 10.2 shows the UK just behind the USA where the services' share of total employees rose from 57 per cent in 1950 to 79 per cent in 1995. France started from a lower base but had over 70 per cent of its employees in services by 1995 whilst Germany and Japan were

---

[4] See O'Mahony (1999: tab. C); Department of Employment, *Employment Gazette* 1987 and *Labour Market Trends*, October 2000. For discussion of the use of part-time labour in the modern British economy, see chapter 5 above (O'Mahony) and also Bower (2001), Daniels (1982), Robinson and Wallace (1984), Twomey (2001). For accountancy as a training ground for managers in Britain, see Matthews *et al.* (1997). For Lord Beeching's proposals see British Railways Board (1963).

at a distinctly lower level of about 60 per cent. An important feature of Britain's comparative position was the huge number of workers in manufacturing and construction after the Second World War, in part as a result of its favourable sellers' market – 40 per cent of the labour force in 1950. This was not only bigger than in the USA but well above the level in France and Japan and matched only by Germany which had a smaller service sector. The shift out of manufacturing was therefore most dramatic in Britain. In contrast France, Germany and Japan had very large agricultural sectors in the 1950s so that the shift, statistically, between the 1950s and the 1990s was from agriculture to services. The other distinctive feature of the British position was that by the 1990s it had a relatively high proportion of its employment in finance and business services – which raises the question of how far it could be seen as a sector where Britain had a comparative advantage. Both these matters will be addressed later.

How much of the observed growth in services' share of the economy's resources was simply due to low productivity growth? Early work by Baumol (1967) and Fuchs (1968) for the USA focused on changing shares of employment in 1929–65 which was hypothesised to be a function of:

a) the amount by which service sector productivity growth fell short of that in manufacturing,

b) the growth in the demand for services due to increases in income per head, less any offset from the rise in the relative price of services as a result of (a),

c) a residual amount attributed to the growth of services as intermediate inputs for firms and institutions.

Under certain assumptions about the response of the demand for services to increases in their cost and to increases in income levels, it is possible to show that, for the USA in 1929–65, the labour productivity effect was dominant.[5] These estimates do have weaknesses; as we shall see later, service sector productivity is difficult to measure and appears often to be

[5] See Inman (1985: 1–24). The equation used was $P = (M - S)(1 + b) + M (a - 1)$ where P is the growth rate of the service sector's share of employment, M is the growth rate of labour productivity in manufacturing, S is the growth rate of labour productivity in services, b is the price elasticity of demand for services (assumed to be −0.6) and a is the income elasticity of demand for services (assumed to be 1.05). The service sector's *share* of employment was growing at 0.8 per cent per annum in this period and the calculations suggested that the labour productivity effect accounted for 0.44 per cent (even after allowing for some demand offset by the rise in services' relative price), the income effect was 0.11 per cent, leaving only 0.25 per cent for increased specialisation and other dimensions of the expansion of producer services. Summers' (1985) cross-country comparison suggests that, once relative price effects are taken out, the demand for services did not rise proportionately more than income. For education, recreation and some government functions, the income elasticity of demand was less than 1. For medical services, housing and certain other consumer services it was above 1 but overall the best bet seemed an income elasticity of demand of 1. Put otherwise, service sector shares adjusted for price effects lay much more closely together around the 30–40 per cent range (Summers 1985: tab. 1.4). India emerged with a share of

understated. They can, however, shed some light on the UK – primarily in differentiating the 1950–73 period from 1973–95. In the first period the service sector's *share* of employment grew on average at 0.47 per cent per annum, in the second period at 1.23 per cent. Using raw data from O'Mahony (1999), these growth rates can be decomposed into that resulting from the slower labour productivity effect, and that due to rises in income levels, leaving a residual for producer services and other effects. The results were:

	1950–73	1973–95
Labour productivity effect	1.05	0.51
Income effect	0.23	0.13
Residual	−0.82	0.59
Total	0.47	1.23

In summary, and in answer to the first question posed in the introduction, the rise in employment in services in the period 1950–73 was accompanied by a significant rise in the real volume of services supplied. However the rise in services' *share* of employment was very much a result of the measured slow growth of labour productivity in services relative to manufacturing. Such growth was faster in the period from the mid-1970s onwards. This confirms the impression that the fourth quarter of the twentieth century was different from the third in that the balance of service provision moved away from the supply of labour-intensive services demanded by consumers and government, especially in health and education, to the supply of less labour-intensive services which played a much more active part in the production of manufactured goods and in the delivery of traded services for export.

THE RISE OF PRODUCER SERVICES AND THE LINKS WITH MANUFACTURING

It is clear from the employment figures in Figure 10.1 that a major feature of service growth in the last quarter of the twentieth century was the rise of finance and business services. The second question posed in the introduction was how and why such activities became organisationally separate from manufacturing. Table 10.3, which is derived from the UK input–output table for 1998, provides some idea of the way services related to other sectors. Reading horizontally, each row shows how much

28 per cent, USA 38 per cent and the UK 47 per cent suggesting that the opportunity cost of services in Britain was less than in the USA. This is the mirror image of the proposition that Britain was very good at services, relative to manufacturing. See Foreman-Peck and Hannah (1999) and also Bhagwati (1984a) and Green (1985).

Table 10.3 Flow of goods and services in the UK, 1998 (£ '000 million)[a]

| | Intermediate goods and services | | | | |
| | Used by: | | | | |
	Agric., oil, mining	Manufacturing & construction	Services	Final demands[b]	Total
Domestic supply and imports of:					
Agric., mining, oil	6	21	10	21	58
Manufacturing & Construction	7	213	114	547	884
Services	7	79	389	516	989
Total	20	313	513	1,084	1,931

Notes: [a] At purchasers' prices.
[b] Domestic consumption, government spending, capital expenditure and export demand. Note that deducting imports from the 1,084 total yields the figure of national income.

Source: Derived from CSO, *UK National Accounts 2000*, tab. 2.1.

of the supply from each sector went as intermediate goods to other pro-ducing sectors and how much to final demands. Taking the first row for illustration, the total value of agricultural goods and mining commodi-ties produced in the UK (or imported) was £58,000 million in 1998. Of this £21,000 million was sold as intermediate inputs to the manufacturing and construction industries (e.g. hops for breweries), a further £10,000 million went to the service sector (coal for gas supply) and £6,000 million was actually used within the agriculture and mining sector itself (manure as fertiliser). This left £21,000 million which went directly to final demands, which embrace the demands of households and government (for milk, coal), of exporters (for cattle, apples) and of firms buying capital equip-ment or adding to inventories (such as stocks of oil). Of course to gauge the role of each sector one has to recognise that the above is only a 'first round effect'. The coal input to the gas industry in 1998 is passed on in 1999 as gas supply to, say, the chemical industry, and so on. Turning now to the service sector, its major role in meeting final demands has not been in exports or inventories or capital goods (where manufacturing is dominant) but rather in meeting the final demands of households and government. Here all the different types of services recorded significant transactions, from health, education and public administration through financial services and retailing to transport, electricity, gas and water. As a supplier of intermediate inputs, the service sector was more im-portant than manufacturing, construction, oil, mining and agriculture combined. The particular service sectors supplying significant amounts of intermediate inputs to other sectors like mining and manufacturing were transport, telecommunications, finance and business services, and these were the sectors that figured most in exports. A striking feature was that a major user of services was the service sector itself. Table 10.3 shows that 80 per cent of services used in production processes went,

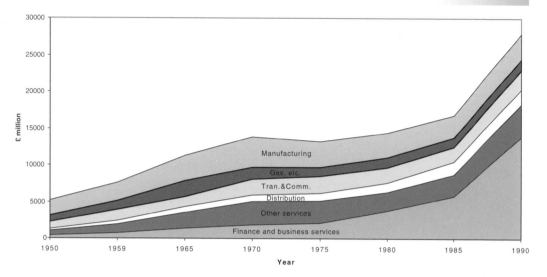

Figure 10.2 Annual investment expenditure in the UK, 1950–1990

Note: Data refers to gross domestic capital formation in £ million at 1975 prices; selected years, selected sectors. *Source*: CSO, *UK National Accounts*, 1960, 1967, 1971, 1979, 1986, 1992.

as 'first round effects', to service sectors (rather than to manufacturing, building, agriculture and mining). Thus accounting services were used by computer firms who advised banks who provided finance for manufacturing firms. The transaction started in 1998 by a service sector firm would eventually emerge embedded as part of an input to a manufacturing firm in, say, 2002.

Although the expansion in the number of professionals and support staff in business services such as accountancy, the law, engineering and computer services might suggest that producer services were labour-intensive, the case is not clear-cut. The increase in office buildings, computer hardware and software, new operating systems, automatic teller machines was huge. Service industries in general, and finance in particular, were disproportionately large investors in information technology (IT) in the last quarter of the twentieth century. By 1989 in the USA the service sector accounted for 85 per cent of the accumulated IT investment while IT itself accounted for 45 per cent of the banking industry's capital stock; by 1992 computer-related investment in finance, insurance and property amounted to 37.8 per cent of the annual total for all the US economy. Figure 10.2 sheds light on the British position by showing how capital formation from the early 1980s came to be dominated by acquisitions by the service sector, dwarfing that by manufacturing, and indeed capital formation in finance and business services alone exceeded that in manufacturing and the infrastructure industries combined. A large part of the capital stock was of course in dwellings – and many would class housing as a service. By the 1990s, as Figure 10.3 shows, the capital stock in services, measured at constant 1975 prices, had grown so much that, even with dwellings excluded, it exceeded that in the rest of the economy. More to the point was the amount of capital relative to labour. The capital stock per employee in manufacturing, construction and extraction,

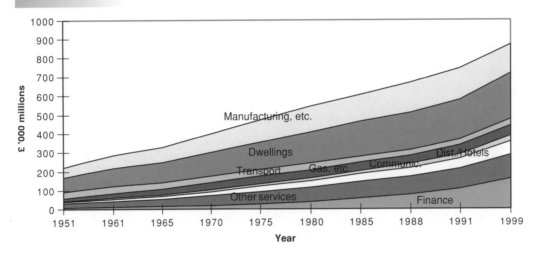

Figure 10.3 UK capital stock, 1951–1999, at constant cost

Note: Data refers to gross capital stock at 1975 replacement cost in £ mellion. 'Other services' includes business services throughout but excludes hospitals, universities and schools 1951–70. 'Manufacturing', etc., covers the rest of the economy.

Source: CSO, *UK, National Accounts*, 1967–2000.

for example, for 1991, was £23,000 at 1975 prices. Transport was slightly higher at £29,000. In finance and business services the figure was £34,000, communications £51,000 and the utilities £183,000. Only the distributive trades, recreation, education, health and related personal and government services came out at the bottom end – £10,000–15,000 – and even here an allowance for part-time work would raise the figures.[6]

Studies of the rise of producer services suggest it was linked to rising income levels, and hence a phenomenon closely associated with the experience of the economically advanced nations in the last part of the twentieth century. Some of this may simply have been activity once classed within the manufacturing sector but which was 'outsourced' to or 'splintered' into specialist firms. A key question is: how much was simply splintering without any efficiency gains to the economy? Some labour working within manufacturing firms may be classified as 'indirect' in that it is not involved on the shop-floor or assembly line, but rather in marketing, computer services, legal advice, carpentry, maintenance and repair. Much of this came to be contracted out, as were recruitment,

[6] The British figures are derived from the Figure 10.3 data on the capital stock and O'Mahony's data (1999) on persons engaged. For the US figures in this paragraph, see Haynes and Thompson (2000: 95). The issue of capital intensity is, however, more complicated than these figures imply. The proportion of the gross value of output which was devoted to wages and salaries was larger in services than manufacturing. The Table 10.3 data, when supplemented by information in the 1998 input–output table on value added, indicate that 20 per cent of the service sector's gross value of output accrued as profit (13 per cent for manufacturing), 49 per cent was spent on intermediate goods (manufacturing 62 per cent) and the rest on wages and salaries (CSO, *UK National Accounts*, 2001, tab. 2.1). Clearly, on the aggregate data, the wage share of service output was larger (31 per cent) than that of manufacturing (25 per cent) for 1998. A more sophisticated measure of capital intensity would decompose intermediate inputs into their labour and capital components. Greenhalgh and Gregory (2000: tab. 3.2) show that, tracing through the supply chain, service outputs emerge as a more labour-intensive component of final consumption than manufactured goods.

tax and accountancy services, to consultancies and specialist agencies. Some of the outsourcing of this kind of work reflected the British system of national employee insurance, which favoured sub-contracting and self-employment of, for example, taxi and lorry drivers, joiners and plumbers. The contracting-out of cleaning and catering in hospitals and schools was but one manifestation of the privatisation movement introduced by the Thatcher governments which affected all of the public sector in the 1980s and 1990s.

There are several reasons, however, for thinking that the rise of producer services was something more than simply outsourcing in response to government tax and economic policies. Many parts of business and finance were not directly affected by privatisation. In the middle decades of the century, much of the investment in manufacturing firms related to buildings and plant and machinery directly involved in the production line rather than to supporting services. Since the capital stock in finance and business services alone exceeded that in manufacturing by the end of the century, it seems unlikely that this was simply a process of outsourcing. A more searching test would be whether the rise in the service sector's supply of intermediate inputs was accompanied by a fall in the amount of 'indirect labour' within manufacturing. One piece of evidence against this was that 22.8 per cent of employees in British manufacturing were 'non-production workers' in 1964, a figure that increased to 28.8 per cent by 1984. More generally, a comparison in 1992 of countries with different levels of income and producer services – ranging from China and the Asian tigers to Latin America, the European Union and the USA – suggested that falling 'indirect' labour only accounted for a small part of the overall increase in specialist service firms (François and Reinert 1996; see also François 1990: 718, tab. 2, and Bhagwati 1984b).

The more positive explanation for the growth of producer services relates to the process of spatial and occupational specialisation which occurred as income levels rose. The phenomenon was not new but its scale was; why then was there such a spurt in the late twentieth century? One factor was the increased sophistication of both products and processes. The multitude of attributes which accompanied many manufactured products – ambience, style, location – incorporated much human capital imported from service activities: in the clean floors and youth culture found in McDonalds as much as in the technical properties of CDs and mobile phones. Services themselves acquired complex service inputs: witness the engineering and architectural soundness of the London Eye (the huge ferris wheel constructed in central London in 2000) and the quality of the financial advice from the local office of any building society. This suggests that the 'service content' of capital goods and of final consumption goods increased. A characteristic of all services is that delivery and consumption take place simultaneously. This is significant for many business and professional services which are fundamentally concerned with the supply of information. Modern IT then made dramatic changes to the speed with which this knowledge could be imparted and to the range of access. Where trade in services traditionally required providers to move around geographically (management consultants) or required users to be similarly mobile (for ship repairs, health care, airlines for airports), the geographic proximity became no longer vital for many professional and business services.

For example, the Paris branch of the US firm Dresser Industries, which was heavily involved in the 1980s in the construction of the Soviet pipeline to western Europe, relied heavily on up-to-the-minute design information, financial data, personnel files and inventory lists from the company's Dallas headquarters. A political difference between the USA and France prompted President Reagan in 1983 to order the Dallas HQ to cut off the computer lifeline to Paris, a classic example of how services were transmitted on-line. It may be expected then that countries like Britain would increasingly be found specialising in the production of manufactured goods with a high service content. Evidence for Britain for 1979–90 does show the service sectors were increasingly involved in supply to high-tech manufacturing firms and their output was incorporating a rising research and development (R&D) component. Manufactured products took on a greater service content in the form of marketing, software development and IT support while others, like videos, emerged as disembodied versions of service activity in film and TV. More generally, there was a shift, in the more economically advanced nations, to the export of services and of highly technical commodities with a high service content, like electronics and pharmaceuticals. More rudimentary manufactured products, such as machinery and transport equipment, came to be a key element in the exports of countries like Korea. At income levels higher than Korea's there was a definite shift to the export of services. More pointedly, while the exports of high-income countries, like Britain, were still dominated by goods rather than services, when one accounts for the full set of economy-wide intermediate linkages, it is found that the most important sectors for export performance were services. The exports of the economically advanced nations were still largely commodity exports but the leading cost component of these exports was actually service activities.[7]

TRADE IN SERVICES AND BRITAIN'S EXPORT PERFORMANCE

How successful was Britain in the growing international trade in services? From the 1960s, the decline in manufacturing focused attention on the

[7] See Bhagwati (1984b: 139–40); François and Reinert (1996: 18); Greenhalgh and Gregory (2000); Sapir (1991).

extent to which services could be a substitute, especially with respect to export earnings. As a great trading nation, Britain had always been a big exporter. It was even more active in imports of food and raw materials. Towards the end of the nineteenth century, it had a visible trade deficit of the order of 5 per cent of national income. This was offset by investment income, in the form of interest and dividends on British-owned overseas property and assets, of about the same order of magnitude. The net foreign earnings from shipping, finance and other services was also equal to about 5 per cent of national income so this was the size of the current account surplus, enabling Britain to engage in huge amounts of overseas investment. In the twentieth century, and especially since 1945, the relative magnitudes were about the same but accounted for smaller proportions of national income and hence the risk of balance-of-payments problems was greater. In the 1940s and 1950s, helped by a sellers' market, foreign trade in manufactures was in surplus such that the deficit on raw materials and agricultural products meant a visible trade deficit of about 1 per cent of national income. Services and overseas property yielded a net inflow of about 2 per cent of national income so that while the current account was in surplus the margin was less and with British overseas investment still very buoyant, the 1950s and 1960s were peppered with persistent balance-of-payments crises. Once France, Germany and Japan had fully recovered from the war, more competition arose in export markets. The signs were there in the 1960s and, by the 1970s, the manufacturing trade balance moved into deficit. The advent of North Sea oil provided some relief but this was expected to be temporary, so that there was much discussion of how far services could expand and meet the gap in the balance of payments. Because Britain was already strong in certain key services, few expected relief from that quarter (Singh 1977; Sargent 1979; the Clare Group 1982; Whiteman 1985).

In fact most observers of the time failed to anticipate the strong surge in the direct export of services, and, more importantly, the rising service content of manufacturing exports which we have already described. In the 1950s and 1960s the export of commercial services, especially travel and financial services, more than doubled their share of national output, offsetting in part the severe drop in earnings from sea transport. Imports of commercial services were not rising by anything like the same amount. Thereafter, as Figure 10.4 shows, the main expansion was in travel, and business and financial services, together with royalties from books, films and TV – a pattern very similar to that in the world's largest trader in services, the USA. Imports of services associated with transport and travel grew very rapidly as income levels rose and holiday resorts in Spain and Greece became popular, and by the 1990s these were the service areas where Britain registered a foreign-trade deficit. Nonetheless, as may be seen in Figure 10.5, the overall trend in the balance of payments in services was upward, averaging 0.3 per cent of GDP in the 1950s rising to

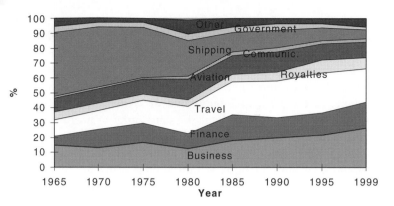

Figure 10.4 Export of UK services, 1965–1999 (% share of receipts)

Source: CSO (ONS), *UK Balance of Payments*, 1973–2000.

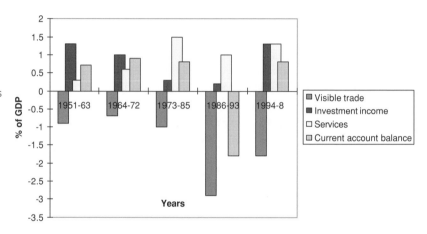

Figure 10.5 UK current account balance of payments as % of GDP, 1951–1998 (annual averages at market prices)

Note: Excludes government transfers. *Sources*: CSO (ONS), *Annual Abstract of Statistics*, 2000: tab. 18.10, and CSO (ONS), *UK, National Accounts*, 1971.

1.3 per cent by the middle 1990s. Indeed in the 1970s and 1980s income from services provided a useful offset to the drop in investment income. Overall, the rising direct trade in services had been enough, in conjunction with investment income, to more than offset the visible trade deficit (except for the disastrous commodity trade flows of the late 1980s). This good performance in services never proved strong enough to offset the declining balance in Britain's *traditional* industries such as cotton, steel, coal and motor cars. In this respect some of the pessimists were correct. However, they were not able to foresee the way services became embedded as knowledge inputs to manufactured products and also became disembodied into new manufactured products. Reinforcing this was the exporting propensity of UK manufacturing which showed a trend increase in the second half of the twentieth century. Exports of goods were averaging 16.6 per cent of GDP in the period 1951–63, holding that level or thereabouts at 16.3 per cent for 1964–72, surging to 23.2 per cent in 1973–85, falling to 18.3 per cent in 1986–93 but rising again to 20.9 per cent in 1994–8.

Are the British good at services? Did they have any marked comparative advantage in particular services? The main areas where imports exceeded exports were travel and transport, as already noted. The biggest net earners by the 1990s were financial and business services. By 1999 the receipts from the sale abroad of life insurance, pension funds, freight insurance and reinsurance yielded receipts, net of imports, of £3,500 million or about 10 per cent of the net surplus on all services. The activities of banks, fund managers, money market brokers, security dealers and the like yielded £6,900 million; computer and information services £1,400 million; film, television and other royalties and licence fees £500 million. Business services yielded £6,100 million which included the foreign-exchange earnings of institutions and individuals working in advertising, market research, accounting, surveying, engineering, architecture, research and development, as well as the Law Society and the Commercial Bar Association.

Economists prefer other indicators of comparative advantage, focusing more on a country's share of world trade. A common method of assessing whether the UK had a 'revealed' comparative advantage, for, say, freight transport services, would be to calculate the freight services' share of all UK service exports divided by a similar share for the world as a whole. For 1995 that figure was 0.71 whereas the figure for passenger transport was 1.55. When the ratio exceeds unity that country is deemed to have a comparative advantage. The UK earnings from passenger transport did account for nearly 10 per cent of all world trade in this sector – much bigger than our share of freight transport – though the surplus above imports of passenger services was quite small. Britain had no comparative advantage in other transportation (0.59) or in travel (0.84). But for other traded services (embracing all business, professional, financial and personal services) the figure was 1.21.[8]

SERVICES AND ECONOMIC GROWTH

What role did services play in the growth of British output and productivity? The answer, apparently, is a very important one, if not always to Britain's advantage. It appears that, from the nineteenth century onwards, productivity growth in British services was lower than in manufacturing; it was growing more slowly than in USA, France and Germany; and, by the late twentieth century when services were a large part of all economic activity, the level of productivity in British services was less

[8] See Hoekman (1994, 1995) for the general issues and Landefeld (1987) for the picture in the USA. For the British data on foreign trade in services see CSO and ONS, *UK National Accounts* 1979, 1986, 2000, and *UK Balance of Payments*, 2000. For the international data see International Monetary Fund, *Balance of Payments Yearbook for 1997*, tabs. B-2 to B-10.

than that in all these other countries. At the same time the output of services is not easy to quantify and indeed sufficiently difficult for leading authorities to assert that recorded differences in productivity between manufacturing and services are dwarfed by the issue of the measurable and unmeasurable outputs of the modern economy.[9] The question of measurement will be confronted in the course of trying here to ascertain what role services played in British economic growth since 1950, what can be deduced about the causes of growth, and how Britain's performance compared to that in the other economically advanced countries.

A common measure of productivity growth, across countries or over time, is *total factor productivity growth*, that is, the change in output less the change in resources (labour and capital usually aggregated by shares in total expenditure or receipts). The output of services is less easy to measure than manufactured goods. The biggest problems arise with services which are financed through general taxation and which are not charged for directly; there are no sales receipts for education, roads and health. The benefit of these services accrues to users in the form of higher earnings and savings in journey costs and human life. In the UK, indicators such as number of visits to hospitals and pupil-days for schools are sometimes used. Indeed, one study of higher education was able to demonstrate that Britain's performance, relative to manufacturing, was much better than in many other countries (Marris 1985). Unfortunately such measures of outcomes are not available on a routine basis, and in the official statistics of many countries changes in such outputs are proxied by changes in employment in the sectors in question which of course implies there is no growth in labour productivity. Even when services are marketed, as in banking and business services, outputs are difficult to define. The number of loans will be a crude indicator of the output of a bank if the number of customers is not included. The services of architects and other professionals are often of a one-off variety so that data on standard fees are not easy to come by.

Even when a detailed study of productivity is possible, there are often significant problems in capturing all the attributes of services, especially when comparisons are made across countries. For example, in a major study of the service sector in the USA, UK, France and Germany, Baily (1993) found that, in the late 1980s and early 1990s, labour productivity levels were significantly higher in the USA for airlines, banking, telecommunications and retailing and he attributed this to the more competitive environment in the USA. Baily's article was linked to a study by the McKinsey Global Institute (1992). Both studies identified various attributes to be measured (for example for airlines, hours flown; passenger-miles; number of cockpit, cabin, ramp and maintenance personnel; tickets issued; ticket staff; etc.). How these varied with factors beyond the control of the airline companies was quite crucial in judging performance.

[9] Griliches (1994); Ray (1986); Marris (1985); Levitt and Joyce (1986); Aanestad (1987).

In a blistering comment on the conclusions, Gordon (1993) said the authors had no controls: no control for proportion of flights which were international (compare Belgium to USA); no control for language problems, whereby Lufthansa needed more ticket staff in Florence than did US airlines, many of whose passengers would accept English. The development of the 'hub' system of airports, which Baily saw as important for US success was very much 'conditioned by lack of land, gates and runways' and this, said Gordon, was the 'basic reason why London Heathrow . . . and Frankfurt have spread-unit flight patterns' instead of the bunched patterns conducive to the effective development of hub airports (p. 140).

In the case of measurement of services in Britain, the official data used for routine national accounts purposes contain a reasonable if not ideal range of output indicators for evaluating changes in output over time for infrastructure services such as transport and communications. In other cases, as for hotels, restaurants and business services, the procedure has been to take a measure of total receipts (turnover) and allow for price changes over time. Even this is far from easy since the development of price indexes for producer services like courier and security services, sewerage, accountancy, consulting engineering, is an art which is still in its infancy. Where even turnover figures are not available, as in banking, employment figures are used as a benchmark and the same labour productivity growth is assumed as in the service sectors (like transport) where the output is more readily measured. In summary, while the estimates for distribution, hotels, catering, transport and communications are probably no worse than non-service sectors, the estimates for financial and business services can be misleading.[10]

These measurement problems may go some way to explaining some peculiar features of the pattern of productivity growth in the UK recorded in Table 10.4. Here the growth rate of total factor productivity (TFP) is shown in the middle column and the growth rate of labour productivity shown in the last column. The growth of labour productivity consists of the growth of TFP plus the growth in the capital–labour ratio (suitably weighted), as shown in the first column.[11] The figures for the whole of the UK economy display the familiar story of strong TFP growth of

[10] O'Mahony *et al.* (1998: 541); see also O'Mahony (1999: 4); Price (1996); CSO (1985: ch. 5); Mansell (1996); ONS (1998: chs. 12 and 13).

[11] Strictly speaking this holds true only under certain conditions. In the simplest constant returns to scale production technology, the growth rate of output may be written as

$$Q = Z + XL + YK$$

where Z is total factor productivity growth, L is the growth rate of labour, K is the growth rate of capital and where X and Y are weights (output elasticities) which add up to one. Hence labour productivity growth may be written as

$$Q - L = Z + Y(K - L)$$

For purposes of interpreting Table 10.4, a figure of 0.3 (that is, capital's average share of value added) could be taken as a rough guide to Y.

Table 10.4 Growth of productivity and capital intensity in the UK, 1950–1995 *(Annual average % growth rates)*

	Capital Intensity (K/L)	Efficiency (TFP)	Labour productivity (Q/L)
Agriculture, etc.			
1950–73	5.20	2.53	5.22
1973–95	1.58	2.92	3.66
Mining, oil			
1950–73	8.33	0.46	2.23
1973–95	12.73	−2.15	5.37
Manufacturing			
1950–73	4.39	3.28	4.69
1973–95	3.35	1.85	2.54
Construction			
1950–73	5.85	1.03	1.72
1973–95	1.45	2.15	2.60
Electricity, gas & water			
1950–73	4.78	3.36	6.09
1973–95	3.35	2.87	4.96
Transport & communications			
1950–73	3.64	2.31	3.22
1973–95	2.70	3.06	3.88
Distributive trades			
1950–73	6.79	0.78	2.76
1973–95	3.82	0.43	1.52
Finance & business services			
1950–73	5.80	−1.43	0.95
1973–95	2.80	0.98	2.07
Personal services			
1950–73	6.03	1.10	2.20
1973–95	2.01	1.21	1.57
Education, health, government			
1950–73	3.31	−0.27	0.04
1973–95	2.53	0.17	0.45
UK Total			
1950–73	4.73	1.74	2.99
1973–95	2.87	1.65	2.22

Note: Capital intensity is capital services (K) per employee hour (L). Labour productivity is net output (Q) per employee hour. Efficiency is total factor productivity (TFP) measured as output per unit of labour and capital weighted by their base year shares of value added.

Source: O'Mahony (1999: tabs. 2.2, 2.7, 2.9)

1.74 per cent per annum in the first few decades after the Second World War, better than in any period since the mid-Victorian boom. Myths to the contrary, the golden age also had a good record in capital accumulation – sufficient to account for a significant part of the 3 per cent growth in labour productivity. Manufacturing and agriculture show a TFP growth above the national average so that services as a group emerge as below average. There are, however, big differences within the services group. TFP growth in transport, communications, gas, electricity and water is above average and, since these infrastructure industries were mainly in the public sector in the 1950–73 period, this performance casts some doubt on the argument that the nationalised setting had a deleterious effect on productivity (see chapter 4 above). By the same token, the general decline in growth rates of TFP in all sectors in the 1973–95 period does not sit easily with those who see the later period of deregulation and privatisation as conducive to productivity growth, although all these issues need to be considered in relation to the fortunes of other countries and to this we shall turn shortly.

For the moment it is important to note the very low productivity growth figures for finance, business services, education, health and public administration – where productivity is actually recorded as declining in the first period. Indeed, productivity growth was quite low in the distributive trades and personal services. A *decline* in productivity may occur in any year if the physical environment changes (wars, etc.), if a series of long-term investments are being made (as in North Sea oil and gas) or if outputs and inputs are not being properly measured. There remains a strong suspicion that the apparently poor productivity record in services is, in part at least, a measurement issue. When outputs are not measured and are proxied by the growth of employment, this implies the growth in output per person was zero and TFP growth comprised simply the growth of output per unit of capital. In fact all the evidence suggests that the output increases were accompanied by processes like mechanisation and computerisation which actually used less labour and more (not less) capital per unit of output. If, therefore, a proxy has to be used for the change in service output it would be better as the change in capital not the change in employment. Doing this for the data for the last quarter of the century yields TFP growth rates for finance, the distributive trades, education, health, and other personal and social services much nearer to the national average of 1.7 per cent per annum. Does this not make more sense in relation to sectors which were expanding, and some very rapidly, in response to demand from business and individual customers? Moreover, if productivity growth were very poor, would this not be reflected to some extent in profits? The evidence suggests that the pre-tax rate of return on the capital stock at replacement cost in all UK industrial and commercial companies averaged about 8 per cent in the early 1970s, falling to 5 per cent in the mid-1970s, rising to 7 per cent up to the early 1980s, then rising again to about 10 per cent by the early 1990s. There was no trend decline in this economy despite it being dominated by investment in services. Similarly, whilst Table 10.5 shows that the rate of profit on turnover was less in financial services than in other sectors sampled by the Bank of England, it is not that far out of line, and the other service sectors (including

Table 10.5 Profitability of British industry and services, 1987–1992 *(Operating profit as % sales: selected sectors)*						
	1987	1988	1989	1990	1991	1992
Financial services	6.7	6.2	5.5	5.8	3.1	6.5
Utilities	n.a.	n.a.	n.a.	23.5	12.8	15.3
Telecommunications	22.9	23.4	23.6	21.7	24.9	23.6
Mining, oil, gas	9.4	10.7	11.8	10.9	8.1	3.7
Civil engineering & construction services	7.2	8.6	7.9	5.2	n.a.	0.5
Building materials	11.5	12.9	13.0	10.0	6.7	6.4
Engineering (manufactures)	7.6	9.1	8.4	7.4	5.9	4.0
Chemicals and pharmaceuticals	12.6	13.4	13.5	12.6	13.4	10.1
Food, drink & tobacco	8.3	9.0	10.0	9.4	9.1	10.5

Source: Bank of England, *Bank of England Quarterly Bulletin*, August 1993.

business services in civil engineering and construction) are comparable to manufacturing.[12]

To press the point further there is the so-called 'IT productivity paradox' – that 'computers are everywhere except in the productivity statistics'. The surge in producer services in the last quarter of the century was stimulated in part by the development of IT in which, as noted earlier, the service sector was a large investor. Most IT applications were neither pure process nor pure product. Unless the output and price data capture these dimensions, productivity will be understated in the official statistics. Consider Haynes and Thompson's study of the introduction of Automatic Teller Machines (ATMs, that is cash machines) in ninety-three UK building societies over the period 1981–93. How to measure output in this area is a much-debated topic and here they used the level of earning assets. Some societies adopted ATMs, others did not; some adopted them

[12] The implication of assuming labour productivity growth was zero may be seen from the equation in footnote 11. If $Q - L$ is assumed to be zero, Z becomes equal to $Y(L - K)$. See also Millward (1990). For a demonstration that productivity was very high in Britain in some service sectors, relative to manufacturing, see Marris' estimates (1985) for British universities. The data on rates of return on capital are from Bank of England, *Bank of England Quarterly Bulletin*, 1993: chart 3. The results concerning TFP, stated in the text for the last quarter of the century, rest on the following calculations. In the period 1977–99, the capital stock (at constant prices) grew at 2.18 per cent per annum on average whilst national output grew at 2.06 per cent. Over the same period, conventional measures record TFP growth of 0.19 per cent in finance, −0.51 per cent for the distributive trades, hotels and catering and 1.05 per cent for all other services (excluding the utilities, transport and communications which are not relevant to this issue). Using capital growth as the proxy for output growth yielded revised productivity growth figures of 4.38 per cent for finance, 2.71 per cent for the distributive trades, etc., and 1.66 per cent for the other services. Output here is measured as value added at 1975 constant factor cost and capital as gross capital stock at 1975 replacement cost. The sources were CSO and ONS, *UK National Accounts*, 1979, 1982, 1990, 1997, 2000. Labour is measured as full-time equivalent employment, treating part-time as one-half full-time and taken from Department of Employment, *Employment Gazette* (Historical supplement), 1987, and *Labour Market Trends*, October 2000.

intensively, others much less so. Differences in productivity growth in different building societies may have been reflecting variations in managerial enterprise as much as differences in the pace at which ATMs were introduced. Haynes and Thompson made explicit allowance for this and still emerged with the result that the more intensive the adoption of ATMs the larger was productivity growth. More generally, if one traces the use of producer services through the intermediate input chain, the service content of many production activities has exhibited a high labour-saving trend.[13]

Despite the problem with official measures, it is possible to draw some conclusions about the role of services in British economic growth by making comparisons with other countries, all of which have similar measurement problems. It is now well established that national income per head was growing faster in the USA than in Britain in the late nineteenth century and that Britain was overtaken around the turn of the century. The USA became the technology leader in the twentieth century and suffered nothing like the same devastation in the two world wars. Since 1945, Britain and other European countries have narrowed the gap – though, by the 1990s, US national output per hour worked was still 20 per cent higher than in Britain. The process of overtaking and convergence over the very long term varied across sectors. There was no catch-up or convergence in manufacturing. In the nineteenth century, US labour productivity in manufacturing was roughly double that in the UK and, setting aside short-term oscillations, that gap persisted to the end of the twentieth century. The availability and choice of different quantities of natural resources as well as product mix account for the stability in comparative productivity levels; mule spinning machines, skilled labour and fine cotton cloth in Britain; ring spinning machines, unskilled labour and coarser cloth in the USA. Germany showed labour productivity levels in manufacturing some 20 per cent above the UK level in the late nineteenth century, a gap that was still present at the end of the twentieth century.

If US economic growth exceeded Britain's, the proximate causes cannot therefore lie in manufacturing. There are two main candidates. One is agriculture, where we have already remarked on how small that sector was in Britain by the start of the twentieth century. The decline of agriculture's share of output, given its low productivity level in the USA and the continental European countries, played an important role in the catch-up with Britain. The other part of the story is services. The level of labour productivity in services in the USA and Germany in the late nineteenth century was less than in Britain. Table 10.6 shows that, from the 1870s, the levels in the USA and Germany grew and overhauled

---

[13] The IT productivity paradox is attributed to R. M. Solow, quoted in the study of UK building societies by Haynes and Thompson (2000: 93). See also Greenhalgh and Gregory (2000: 72).

Table 10.6 Labour productivity in the UK, USA and Germany, 1869–1990
(Output per employee: selected years: UK = 100)

	Agriculture		Industry		Services		Total economy	
	USA	Germany	USA	Germany	USA	Germany	USA	Germany
1871[a]	87	56	154	86	86	66	90	60
1911[a]	103	67	193	122	107	81	117	76
1935[a]	103	57	191	99	120	86	133	76
1950	126	41	244	96	141	83	163	74
1973	131	51	215	129	137	111	152	114
1990	151	75	163	117	129	130	133	125

[a] The US data relate to annual averages of 1869/71, 1909/11 and 1937.

Source: Broadberry and Ghasak (2001: tab. 1).

the UK in the twentieth century. This was a major source of the faster economic growth. Broadberry's thesis is that services were affected very much by changes in office technology (telephone, telegraph, typewriters, copiers, etc.) in which the USA and Germany performed better than Britain whose comparative advantage lay in networked services such as finance whose productivity level remained higher in Britain into the interwar period and, with respect to Germany, up to the 1970s (Broadberry and Ghasak 2001: tab. 2; Broadberry 1993, 1998, 2000; Abramovich 1986; van Ark 1996). The shift to mechanised techniques in other services had parallels in manufacturing where, however, competition across countries ensured that comparative productivity levels remained stable. Services, in contrast, were traditionally not traded so freely so that British productivity in services fell relative to the levels in the USA and Germany but without any major impact on the output of British services.

That story does not carry over so readily to the second half of the twentieth century. Britain started reducing some of the USA's lead in services as well as in industry. In addition there was the complication that the period from the 1940s to the 1970s is usually viewed as one where nationalisation and heavy regulation characterised many service activities in Britain and continental Europe, giving way to more competition as deregulation and privatisation took the stage from the late 1970s. Yet Germany's gains in services as a group continued through both these periods, while output per employee in British services rose relative to the USA in the first phase as well as the second (Table 10.6). The post-1945 picture is in fact quite complex. Economic losses during the war were much bigger in Europe than in the USA so an element of catch-up with the USA was involved, at least for the first few decades. We also have to allow for particular resource endowments, such as the discovery of North Sea oil and gas, to set against the USA's generally rich endowment of oil,

Table 10.7 International comparisons of levels of capital intensity and productivity, 1950/1973/1995
(Indexes based on UK = 100: selected sectors)

	USA			France			Germany		
	K/L	TFP	Q/L	K/L	TFP	Q/L	K/L	TFP	Q/L
Manufacturing									
1950	273	216	290	104	72	77	92	84	74
1973	173	159	186	142	89	101	152	102	115
1995	161	142	171	171	103	130	156	108	126
Electricity, gas & water									
1950	345	214	425	319	37	64	112	120	109
1973	228	219	370	220	88	143	121	119	134
1995	158	115	163	168	87	120	104	79	84
Transport & communications									
1950	338	141	189	157	66	68	223	56	65
1973	223	139	174	130	107	113	166	81	92
1995	121	111	113	135	110	117	156	85	100
Distributive trades									
1950	405	113	162	208	93	126	178	71	76
1973	188	119	146	172	116	139	182	90	106
1995	151	135	155	165	126	143	141	106	111
Finance and business services									
1950	245	136	194	77	104	92	57	73	55
1973	106	182	187	57	215	169	79	150	134
1995	87	122	115	75	134	112	119	141	169
Miscellaneous personal services[a]									
1950	254	172	200	167	170	141	116	43	40
1973	165	157	172	89	170	163	224	87	104
1995	119	135	133	114	131	132	263	115	145
Total economy									
1950	339	146	195	133	74	79	135	65	63
1973	193	138	168	120	109	116	168	104	119
1995	128	112	121	149	118	132	172	109	129

[a] Covers other 'market' services like R&D, leisure, domestic, etc. (not health, education, government).
Note: Capital intensity is capital services (K) per employee-hour (L). Labour productivity is net output (Q) per employee hour. Efficiency is total factor productivity (TFP) measured as output per unit of labour and capital weighted by their base year shares of value added. All the 1950 entries for levels (except for Q/L) were derived from the growth rate data for the different countries as were the 1973 level data. Note that some of the 1950 figures in tab. 1.4 of O'Mahony do not tally with her growth rate figures (e.g. total economy data for TFP in tab. 1.4).

Source: Derived from O'Mahony (1999).

coal and other minerals and France's strengths in hydro-electricity. As the second half of the century unfolded, competition and trade increased, not only in commodities, but also in services so that technological imitation and catch-up became common.

The broad message from Table 10.7 is that the British economy, taken as a whole, gained on the USA in both sub-periods with respect to both TFP and the investment record. France and Germany gained in both periods in both measures relative to the UK (except for the French investment record) so that they were more successful in closing the productivity gap with the USA than was Britain. In terms of productivity levels, Britain by the 1990s had the advantage, relative to France and Germany, only in agriculture, construction and the utilities, and in transport and communications with respect to Germany only. Whatever advantages Britain had, in these terms, in finance and business services in the 1950s had disappeared by the 1990s despite the fact that, as recorded earlier, these were (along with passenger services) the sectors where Britain's share of world trade was proportionately larger than that in many other countries. For services as a group, Britain's productivity performance does match the change in the total economy pattern in that productivity rose relative to the USA, with gains in capital intensity actually bigger than the national average. Investment in supermarkets, computer systems, roads, gas, electricity, research and development all allowed Britain to improve labour productivity in services relative to the USA. The French and Germans did even better, so that their productivity levels rose, relative to the UK, in all services except utilities in Germany and personal services in France. There are therefore some puzzles in Britain's performance in productivity when viewed against its success in foreign trade in services. One answer may be simply that the more rapid expansion of production and trading in services in the UK, relative to France, Germany and Japan, would, in the absence of massive technological breakthroughs, make for a relatively slower service sector productivity growth (Foreman-Peck and Hannah 1997: 50).

The impact of regulation and nationalisation is also far from clear. Some observers have argued that the shift to deregulation and privatisation in the last quarter of the twentieth century was the occasion for an improvement in Britain's productivity in some key service areas – especially transport, communications and utilities – which had been in public ownership in the first period. Table 10.7 does record that, in comparison to the USA, the British utilities show a deterioration in TFP in the first period whilst in the second period they show a large gain. But the 1970s saw the start of returns from North Sea oil and gas. Moreover, the trends were similar in financial services which were not nationalised. The distributive trades, which were not strongly regulated, declined relative to the USA in both periods. In the nationalised transport and communications sectors, British capital intensity, TFP and labour productivity all improved relative to the USA in the first period. Whilst it is possible to point to the healthy investment record of the privatised utilities and transport sector in the 1973–95 period, the same could be said about the 1950–73 period, as is clear from Table 10.7. Indeed if one looks more closely at the precise sectors which were nationalised in the 1951–73 period – that is, coal mining, gas, electricity, railways, airways, telecommunications – they all showed a superior TFP growth over the same sector in the USA with the one exception of the railways.[14] The picture of public ownership is also muddied once it is recognised that the German and French infrastructures were heavily regulated and also largely publicly owned in the 1950–73 period. If the big gains in productivity in the British utility sector relative to Germany in the period 1973–95 are attributed to privatisation, how is one to account for transport and communications where German growth was greater in both periods, perhaps because in terms of productivity *levels*, Germany was still behind Britain in the 1990s. Similarly whilst capital intensity in French utilities (electricity in particular) was two or three times higher than in Britain, the TFP level was still lower than in Britain in the 1990s. The sheer size of the investment programme in French electricity was reflected in big gains in labour productivity relative to Britain but one should recognise that Eléctricité de France was a nationalised enterprise and it dominated the energy sector for much of the second half of the twentieth century.

CONCLUSION

The second half of the twentieth century witnessed two surges of service activity. The first was a consumer- and government-led rise in health, education and leisure in the 1940s, 1950s and 1960s. Retail trading was a major source of employment throughout the twentieth century and it also featured strongly in the second surge from the 1970s onwards, headed by the growth of producer services, and especially of business, including professional, services.

Many of the traditional consumer services and retail trade were labour intensive and the scope for productivity advances seemed less than in manufacturing. As a result, the cost of services relative to manufactures tended to rise, especially in the first phase when the labour productivity effect accounted for a significant amount of the rising share of services in total employment. At the same time, technical progress in the last quarter of the twentieth century allowed the disembodiment of certain services into manufactured products like CDs and videos. An even stronger feature was the growth of services as intermediate inputs; that is, a rising amount of research and development, IT, software and marketing was supplied by specialist producer service firms and embedded

[14] Broadberry and O'Mahony are amongst those who argue that performance in the nationalisation period was worse than in the privatisation period (Broadberry 1997: 258; Broadberry and Ghasak 2001: 21; O'Mahony 1999: 20, 23). However, using the more detailed data in the tables of chapter 4 of O'Mahony (1999), annual average total factor productivity growth 1951–73 for electricity in the UK works out at 5.51 per cent while the comparable US figure was 3.93 per cent. For other British nationalised sectors the results were (USA in brackets): gas 4.71 (3.02), coal mining 1.34 (0.82), railways 1.60 (4.45), air transport 11.53 (9.55) and telecommunications 2.13 (1.73). See also Millward (1990, 1999), in conjunction with Kendrick (1987) and Griliches (1988).

in manufactured products. Specialisation and scale economies induced a growth of indirect labour groups within firms as well as the splintering of such labour into separate firms. Business and professional services (even when financial services are excluded) came to account for 15 per cent of all employment in Britain by the end of the century. The capital stock in business, professional and financial services was, by then, bigger than that in the whole of manufacturing while their exports accounted for nearly one half of all British exports of services.

Britain's international comparative advantage, on conventional measures, seemed to lie in passenger transport services and a group embracing business, professional, financial and personal services. Yet by the end of the century, productivity levels in these sectors were actually lower than those found in comparable sectors in the USA, France and Germany. In productivity terms Britain performed best in the infrastructure industries – electricity, gas and certain parts of transport and communications. The output of services, however, is difficult to measure. This and other dimensions of the development of services is a territory into which historians have as yet made few forays and scope for further historical insights is immense.

11

Impact of Europe

LARRY NEAL

Contents

INTRODUCTION

The outbreak of the Second World War drew Britain into a new phase of its historic, geopolitical and economic relationships with the European continent. Nazi domination of the continent completed the economic cut-off that began with the proliferation of exchange controls in the 1930s. Reliance on the United States as the 'arsenal of democracy' inserted US economic policy into the framework of imperial preference that had worked well for Britain's economic recovery in the 1930s. Mobilising the Empire's world-wide resources while co-ordinating America's military contributions throughout the Second World War, Britain's policy makers laid the foundation for the country's post-war relationships with its overseas Empire, the USA and Europe. Britain's relationships in these three world regions varied over the period 1939–99 in response to a succession of external shocks: first and foremost came the shock of the Second World War, but that was followed in rapid sequence by shocks from the disastrous effects of the temporary resumption of convertibility of the pound sterling into gold or dollars in 1947, then the outbreak of the Korean War in 1950, the Suez Crisis of 1956, the successive oil shocks of 1973, 1979 and 1986, and the German reunification shock of 1990.[1] Europe experienced the same shocks, to be sure, but in different ways, so the continental nations often responded with different strategies from those adopted by Britain.

One might think that Britain and Europe, comparing the relative results of different strategies that were taken in response to similar shocks, would gradually converge in economic policies by adopting in common whatever policy seemed to work best. Given the historical differences in economic structure and political institutions that had arisen between Britain and Europe over previous centuries, such an optimistic view would be premature, if not naïve. There were already deep-seated differences between Britain and Europe when the Second World War broke out on the European continent in 1939. Britain's relative economic success during the decade of the 1930s had rested upon creating the sterling area in which trade based on the common currency of the pound sterling was bolstered by imperial preference, compensating British traders for the decreased trade with the European continent caused by the widespread imposition of exchange controls. Deeper and more persistent sources of differences with Europe stemmed from dissimilarities in economic structure, political and economic organisation and policy imperatives.

Britain's economic structure differed radically from the major European economies in that agriculture was a much smaller part of its economy, whether measured in terms of value added to gross domestic product or as a share of the labour force. The difference was made up by a much larger share of the services sector in the British economy than in any of the European economies (see chapter 10 above). The agriculture–services difference also meant that Britain's population was more heavily concentrated in urban conglomerations and occupations than was true for the populations of continental Europe. For the manufacturing sector, roughly the same size in Britain as in Germany, France and Italy, the differences lay in the composition of product between capital goods and consumer goods or in the composition of foreign markets for the output of the manufacturing sector. The markets for British manufacturers lay mainly in the sterling area, while their continental counterparts concentrated on the European market. The organisation of labour unions in the manufacturing sector reflected these differences in composition of product and location of markets as well. Labour unions in Britain were organised more along craft lines for local manufacturing

---

[1] Economists consider 'shocks' as exogenous events beyond the control of policy makers that come as a surprise and require an immediate policy response. The result may be a permanent shift in the long-run development path of the economy, or a quick reversal to normal conditions, depending on the nature of the shock, the flexibility of the economy's institutions, and the policy response made.

specialities and focused more on maintaining high wages and good working conditions, while labour unions on the continent were organised more as industrial unions concerned with exercising national political power on behalf of their working class.

Contrasting with the fragmented power of labour unions, political power in Britain was firmly entrenched in an all-powerful Parliament where an effective two-party system meant that legislative, executive and even judicial power was concentrated in the hands of the majority party. Policy initiatives by the ruling party were only constrained by the threat of elections, which had to be held at least every five years. Continental efforts to establish parliamentary democracies while expanding the franchise after the First World War, by contrast, had led to multiple parties, weak governing coalitions, and, ultimately, in frustration, their replacement by more radical and authoritarian regimes, starting with fascist Italy, then Nazi Germany, and finally the Popular Front of France. Establishing legitimacy for the newly created democracies on the continent after the Second World War was much more of a challenge than in Britain. The stability of the political regime in Britain meant also that it could finance its war effort effectively by issuing debt, which was readily accepted and held by domestic individuals and institutions but also by their foreign counterparts, especially in the Commonwealth countries as well as in the imperial colonies. Increases in direct taxes on income and property were accepted in Britain as well to maintain the interest payments on the increased debt. By contrast, the Nazi government's war effort on the continent required increases in indirect taxes on sales, and its debt was unacceptable to foreign holders, so that areas occupied by Hitler's armies were forced to contribute in kind to the Nazi war economy.

The combination of differences in economic structure and political organisation was exacerbated by the differences in experience during the Second World War. Britain was not occupied by German forces, so its postwar political imperatives were quite different from those that emerged in Europe after the defeat of Nazi forces in 1945. The imperative of the newly elected Labour government in Britain, whose leaders had proved their patriotism in the war cabinet, was to make sure that the working classes of Britain, subjected to decreased standards of living during the war, would be compensated by the assurance of full employment and social safety nets protecting them from 'cradle to grave'. A secondary objective, but one still important for the long-run legitimacy of the Labour Party, was the effort to reclaim as much as possible of the past power and prosperity of the British nation, whose efforts, after all, had prevailed to win the war decisively. The leaders of the new governments on the continent, by contrast, were confronted not only with the challenges of rebuilding a war-torn economy, but also with establishing their own legitimacy with a demoralised electorate. While they were concerned as well to restore some measure of their past power and prosperity, European leaders were committed most of all to ensuring that war would never again devastate their land.

While the political imperatives of Britain and Europe had much in common, and were certainly compatible with each other, their priorities and their procedures for achieving them were quite different. It could have hardly been otherwise, given the underlying differences in economic structure and political organisation. Throughout the late twentieth century, the impact of Europe on the British economy has been to demonstrate the advantages or costs of particular policies in responding to common shocks. Over the sixty years covered in this volume the economic relationship of Britain with Europe has periodically deepened, so the demonstration effects have had increasing impact on British policy. Nevertheless, convergence in economic policies between Britain and Europe remains incomplete, and will likely continue so. To understand the continuing 'impact of Europe' upon the British economy and its limits, we have to start with the differences in the British and European roles in the Second World War.

THE SHOCK OF WAR

The first common shock to both Britain and Europe, of course, was the outbreak of the Second World War in September 1939 as Nazi forces invaded Poland. With the evacuation of British and French troops from Dunkirk in June 1940 after the Nazi conquest of France and the Low Countries, Britain remained the one country in Europe that avoided domination by the Nazi war machine during the Second World War. The impact of Europe on Britain then became a matter of military strategy. British leaders responded to the German bombing raids in the Battle of Britain first by relocating the armaments factories and then by retaliatory bombing. They responded to the pleas of General de Gaulle of the Free French by mobilising the world-wide resources of the British Empire and its American allies to liberate the continent. (De Gaulle's first speech broadcast to France on the BBC after arriving in London hailed this commitment of Britain in words now engraved under the Arc de Triomphe in Paris.) Britain served both as the supply depot for American material support and as the launching pad for Allied military forces against Nazi-occupied Europe. In this critical position, British leaders played an equal role with their American counterparts in formulating Allied policies, from high politics (Churchill and Roosevelt) to military strategy (Montgomery and Eisenhower) to international finance (Keynes and Morgenthau).

Mobilising Britain's overseas resources for the war effort was done most easily at first through the financial network of the sterling area – that group of countries and colonies whose currencies were fixed at par value with the pound sterling. For them, British government bonds were 'as good as gold' for backing their issues of domestic currency, and some £3.355 billion of sterling liabilities were outstanding at the end of the war, against £0.6 billion of foreign reserves in the form of gold and dollars. For the duration of the war, the 'lend-lease' arrangement with the USA was even more effective, amounting to $31 billion to Britain and the Commonwealth countries, £7.7 billion at the war-time rate of $4.03 for the pound sterling. Meanwhile, the conquered countries of Europe were forced to finance their own occupation and to provide the resources, including forced labour, for sustaining the German war machine (Milward 1977).

THE POST-WAR SHOCK

The special relationship forged between the USA and Britain during the war meant that Britain had a very different view of post-war economic reconstruction from that of the defeated European powers. Concern by British policy planners during the war about the implications of Europe's post-war recovery for Britain's economy had focused on avoiding a repeat of the problems that had arisen after the First World War. War-time planning for dealing with a defeated post-war Germany vacillated between either minimising the expense to Britain of reconstruction in Europe by using Germany's industrial capacity or minimising the competition of Germany's post-war industry with British exporters (Cairncross 1986). Following the war, however, Britain's overriding concern was to minimise the expense of occupying Germany. The problems of administering the British zone of occupation, which deliberately included the North Sea ports of Hamburg and Bremen, Schleswig-Holstein for access to the Baltic, and the industrial heartland of North Rhine Westphalia, could be considered theoretically in terms of whether it would be most efficient to extract reparations at once by expropriating German factories or over time by exploiting German manufacturing production. Given that the devastation wreaked by Allied bombing was most intense precisely in the British zone, because of the strategic importance of the Ruhr and the ports, either approach was costly, but the long-term expense of exploiting German production over time was beyond the immediate capacity of Britain's finances without continued 'lend-lease'. The political will to maintain a large military force in place to control production in its occupation zone was also absent, much to Britain's credit. The immediate policy, therefore, was to take reparations at once in the form of German capital equipment. The impracticality of this approach quickly became evident with the difficulties encountered while trying to dismantle the Herman Goering steelworks at Salzgitter and relocate them in mainland Britain. German operators proved as important as German machines for the production process.

Given the complementary nature of the occupation problems faced by the British and the Americans – Britain faced with rebuilding damaged infrastructure and replacing destroyed housing while the USA confronted the care and feeding of millions of refugees – it made increasing sense to both democracies to administer their two zones jointly and to enlist the co-operation of local authorities, provided they disclaimed their Nazi past. Over the next forty-five years, the Soviet Union was able to extract far more reparations from East Germany than the Western powers ever conceived of extracting before they shifted their policy to the Marshall Plan strategy of incorporating a democratic Germany into the reconstruction process of all Europe. In fact, continued repression of occupied Germany was never a viable option for Britain and when American occupation policy changed formally in 1947, so did British policy in its zone. This 'reality check' upon Britain's thwarted plans to extract reparations from a defeated Germany brought British policy toward Europe into closer harmony with that of America, while lessening the impact of Europe and its economic problems upon the formation of future British economic policy.

The first of many shocks to British foreign reserves that were to follow over the next twenty years also helped shift the British policy toward Europe. This was the run on sterling in July 1947 when convertibility into dollars of sterling balances held in London was established, conforming to the conditions set by the US when it extended a loan of $3.75 billion to Britain at the beginning of 1946. The background to this condition had arisen as British war finance, in order to maintain British forces around the world and to supply vital materials to the war effort in Europe, had created enormous debts, denominated in pounds sterling, that Britain owed to its sterling area trading partners. Offsets to the debts were arranged with Canada, Australia and South Africa. US aid came under the provisions of the 'lend-lease' agreement, but India and Egypt held large sums on account. Against total liabilities of over £3 billion (£1.7 billion to India, Burma and the Middle East) at the end of 1945, Britain had available less than £0.5 billion in gold and dollar reserves (Presnell 1986: 413). These reserves would have been lost immediately to Britain's creditors if the sterling balances could have been converted into gold or dollars at the exchange rate agreed on at Bretton Woods with the Americans and the independent countries in the sterling area.

Nevertheless, the American loan of $3.75 billion was granted in 1946 on condition that the pound resume convertibility at least on current account transactions by mid-1947 so that Britain could become a full voting member of the International Monetary Fund. When convertibility was allowed in June 1947, the proceeds were exhausted within weeks, by the end of July 1947. Britain was faced with a situation where it needed more imports from the dollar area than from the sterling area, while the sterling area also needed more imports from the United States than from Britain. So the result was that exporters throughout the sterling area turned in their sterling proceeds for dollars to pay for imports from the United States.

Scarred by this episode, British authorities became obsessed about exchange rate policy and available foreign reserves. They continued to block the sterling balances from being converted into dollars or gold, which meant keeping trade within the sterling area from becoming fully integrated within the multilateral trading system desired by the United States. Indeed, the blocked sterling balances were not fully eliminated until 1979, as part of the conditions for an IMF loan to Britain. It appears in retrospect that, by 1950, they were not sufficiently liquid in any event to have posed any further threat to British reserves (Schenk 1994). The bulk of them had already shifted from India and Egypt to Australia and South Africa, neither of which had cause to convert them to dollars. Nevertheless, the trauma of 1947 led to British reluctance to join the European Payments Union as originally designed by American and French planners. Not until Britain could be assured that sterling balances earned by Europe from exports to the sterling area would not be convertible into dollars, even indirectly through exchange within the European Payments Union, would she agree to become a member. Concentrating on creating an export surplus with the sterling area in order to draw down the overhang of sterling balances left after the war became a fixation with British policy makers, a fixation lasting long after the bulk of the problem had dissipated. As long as European exporters were not competitive with British exporters in the sterling area, European economic developments could be ignored.

The sterling problem was further complicated by the promise of the war-time government that British labour would be paid for its war-time sacrifices by payments deferred until the war was over. This created a monetary overhang domestically as well as internationally. Eliminating it in the French fashion by allowing rapid inflation would have caused a rapid devaluation of the pound on current account. This would have increased immediately the burden of the sterling balances, which had been pegged to the dollar and gold. Eliminating it in the Italian fashion by financial repression of the financial sector would have reduced foreign-exchange earnings by the City, which had been important for covering Britain's traditional deficit on trade. As a result, war-time measures of price controls and rationing, it was felt, had to be continued until the early 1950s, with some lasting until 1954. After all, they had worked remarkably well to maintain price stability throughout the war (Mills and Rockoff 1987). Ration cards were the domestic counterpart to the exchange controls on sterling balances held by overseas creditors. The constraints of ration cards on British consumers contrasted vividly with the buying splurges of West German consumers after the currency reform of June 1948 in the British and American occupation zones.

FROM GREAT POWER TO WITHDRAWAL FROM EAST OF SUEZ, 1945–1957

In fact, the immediate post-war strategy of blocking sterling balances externally and restricting domestic consumption with rationing worked well for its immediate purpose. Britain quickly removed its import deficit, which had continued for a couple of years after the war due to the need to restock its industrial and distribution system for civilian goods, but it did so mainly by increasing exports to the sterling area in the late 1940s. The export surplus with the sterling area, however, only partially reduced the overhang of sterling balances accumulated during the war and immediately afterward. It did nothing toward increasing Britain's reserves of gold or dollars. Without such reserves, it was in no position to play equal partner with the United States in the IMF or in financing the reconstruction of the rest of Western Europe. Britain did earn some dollars and gold from limited exports to the dollar area and received huge sums in the form of relief from the United Nations Relief and Rehabilitation Agency, the Anglo-American Loan of 1946, and the Marshall Plan. Britain, in fact, was the largest single recipient of Marshall Plan aid. But it offset all of this and more by capital exports. Some of the capital went toward reduction of the sterling balances through trade with third parties, some toward building up British military establishments overseas, and some toward restoring British direct investments abroad. Rather than applying American aid directly toward rebuilding export capacity as in the case of Germany and the Netherlands, or toward restoring basic industries such as energy and steel as in the case of France and Italy, Britain's ruling Labour Party applied it more toward attempting to restore Britain's great-power status enjoyed before the war. To the extent that Marshall Plan aid was directed to domestic investment, Labour's goal was to ensure employment of Britain's demobilised armed forces in the civilian economy, particularly in the newly nationalised basic industries.

In many respects, Labour was simply following the path marked out by its European counterparts for post-war reconstruction and rehabilitation of civilian life. Even more extensive and expensive welfare systems were established on the continent. Nationalisation of basic industries – steel, coal, airlines, gas, electricity – was also more extensive on the continent, especially in France and Italy. But British nationalisation proceeded on a different basis from on the continent. There, nationalisation was often a reaction against war-time seizures of industries by German firms or, in the case of Renault in France, against war-time collaboration with the Nazi occupiers. British nationalisation, by contrast, was driven by a perceived need to sustain the war-time controls over employment in basic industries in order to minimise the shock of converting from war-time to peacetime production. As a legacy of German bombing raids during the Battle of Britain at the outset of the Second World War, British government policy for many years following, whether directed by Labour or Conservative leaders, was to disperse the location of industrial plants and population centres. This policy, ultimately abandoned by the end of the 1970s, did little to enhance productivity. By the 1980s, under the privatisation projects of Margaret Thatcher, discussed below, much of the nationalisation carried out by Labour immediately after the war was reversed. The more pragmatic basis for British nationalisation in the first place, perhaps, made it easier to undo eventually than on the continent.

The sterling strategy – maintaining preferential trade arrangements between Britain and the former colonies while keeping sterling inconvertible with gold and the dollar – helped the British government maintain a sense of control over the twin processes of decolonisation abroad and peacetime conversion at home during the critical five to seven years after the war. Both decolonisation and conversion proceeded more gradually and with less political trauma for Britain than they could have done had it followed the French examples in Indo-China and Algeria. The pound sterling was maintained unchanged as the unit of account not only for the British economy, but for the entire sterling area as long as the sterling area lasted (until 1958). Currency reform along either the French or German models was avoided, as was Italian-style inflation. Colonies were lost, true, but without Britain suffering casualties on the order that had become all too familiar during the Second World War. On these terms, which after all were paramount to British politicians, the strategy has to be judged a success.

It did have unfortunate long-term consequences, however, in separating Britain economically and politically from both the United States and Europe. Figures 11.1 and 11.2 show the effect of British strategy on the pattern of trade it developed, concentrating both exports and imports in the sterling area. This meant cutting Britain's exports off from both the richest market – North America – and the fastest-growing market – western Europe. British leaders constantly found themselves holding fast to untenable positions against either American or European initiatives and then yielding with bad grace and limited reward for the concessions made. Finally taking the obvious step of devaluing the pound against the dollar in September 1949, for example, it had to devalue the pound fully 30 per cent, from $4.03 to $2.80. But with over one-third of its imports and nearly one half of its exports with the sterling area and with most of western Europe devaluing as much or more against the dollar, this translated into a mere 9 per cent overall devaluation against the currencies of its trading partners. The end result was a limited improvement in Britain's current account, which was offset in large part by an increased burden of dollar and gold-denominated debt on the capital account.

In coming into the European Payments Union at the insistence of the Americans at the beginning of 1950, Britain had to give up its network of

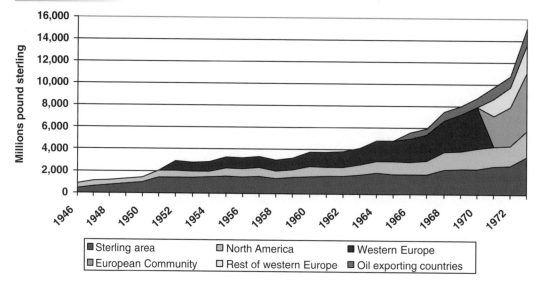

Figure 11.1 Value of imports by area, 1946–1973

Source: CSO, *Annual Abstract of Statistics*, various years

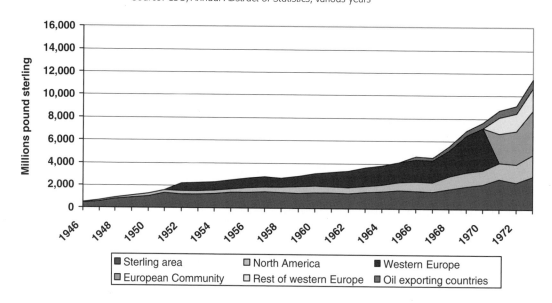

Figure 11.2 Value of exports by area, 1946–1973

Source: CSO, *Annual Abstract of Statistics*, various years

bilateral agreements with each European country in which trade deficits beyond certain agreed limits were paid off in sterling. Only when Britain, in effect, was allowed to act as the banker for the entire sterling area in its dealings with any of the European countries was it satisfied with the EPU arrangement. The British obsession with maintaining its preferred trading relationships within the sterling area meant continued resistance to American plans to liberalise trade patterns and reintroduce multilateral settlements of financial imbalances within Europe.

Britain's sterling strategy also meant that it resisted European initiatives for dealing with the dollar shortage. For example, the Schuman Plan was devised by the French and Germans without any thought of British participation.[2] The immediate casualty of British intransigence was the American proposal for an international trade organisation to oversee the removal of non-tariff barriers to trade and the reduction of tariff barriers. In its place, the makeshift arrangement called the General Agreement on Tariffs and Trade, begun in October 1947, had to be the framework for international trade negotiations until it was superseded by the World Trade Organisation in 1995. The Suez Crisis in 1956, when Britain led a joint French–Israeli scheme designed to regain control of the Suez Canal in Egypt, ended with a run on sterling that forced Britain to withdraw from the Suez venture (Klug and Smith 1999). Worse, it estranged Britain from the United States, which joined the Soviet Union in condemning the venture in the Security Council of the United Nations, and led France to pursue a continental strategy independently of Britain for the future. Britain was to pay a high price in later years for this estrangement from both America and Europe.

OPPORTUNITY KEEPS KNOCKING, 1958–1973

The next fifteen years, moreover, continued to shake British confidence in its post-war strategy. The war-torn economies of Europe had started their rapid recovery from a much lower base than in Britain, so it had been assumed that their pace of growth would slacken off as they regained pre-war levels of output and per capita income, perhaps falling to the British level. Instead, the members of the EEC continued to grow rapidly, enjoying what came to be termed the golden age of economic growth until 1973. Meanwhile, British growth continued at its sedate pace of the 1950s. The result is shown clearly in Figures 11.3 and 11.4. (Both use the OECD's base of 1995 US dollars in their purchasing power parity exchange rate with a given country, to compare Great Britain's level of gross domestic product and per capita income with that of Germany, France and Italy for the period 1960 to 2000.) In 1960, Britain's total output was already below that of Germany, then fell below that of France in 1970, and even that of Italy by 1979. The relative decline was even more dramatic in per capita terms, given Britain's relatively faster growth in population. Barely behind Germany in 1960, Britain fell below France in 1966 and below Italy for the first time in 1977. Britain then fell below all three from 1979 until the late 1990s, when it overtook Italy, which had sluggish growth after it made the political decision to rejoin the European Monetary System in

---

[2] The Schuman Plan (1950) proposed that the coal and steel industries of France and Germany be pooled under a common authority. The Plan formed the basis for the creation of the European Coal and Steel Community in 1952.

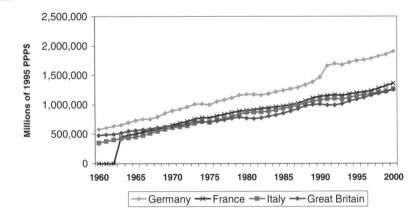

Figure 11.3 GDP compared: Great Britain, France, Germany, Italy

Source: OECD, 2002

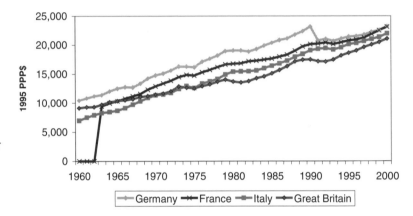

Figure 11.4 GDP per capita compared: Great Britain, France, Germany, Italy

Source: OECD, 2002

1996, and by 2000 British GDP had actually overtaken that of France. In per capita terms, Britain had actually surged to the front of the continental majors, if one took the existing exchange rate of the pound with the euro to make the comparison. Even by adjusting for purchasing power parity, however, by 2000 British per capita GDP was comparable to the continental levels once again.

Much analysis has gone into uncovering the reasons for Britain's relative decline during the period up to the first oil shock (Bean and Crafts 1996). The first suspect was the low level of investment relative to total output in Britain as compared with the growth leaders on the continent. This gave a very satisfactory explanation for Britain's relatively slow growth during the 1950s and continued to be the favourite villain for British policy makers through the 1960s, even as the close relationship between ratios of investment to output and the rate of growth of output among the OECD countries began to dissolve. Some policy makers even persisted with this explanation during the 1970s, when it entirely lacked empirical support.

The consensus in the most recent research is that Britain's rate of investment was not so much to blame as was the low productivity of its investment (see chapter 1). Low productivity of the new capital, in turn, has been attributed to the large proportion of it coming from the public sector, especially in housing and in the nationalised industries, which seemed more interested in maintaining large numbers of employees than in increasing productive efficiency. But even in the private sector, new investment proved less productive than in Germany or France. The conjecture here is that the fragmented structure of British labour unions and the ability of each small craft union to protect the jobs of its members by preserving out-of-date work rules prevented the new equipment from being used most efficiently. This made it difficult for even American or Japanese firms to achieve the same levels of productivity with their new plants built in Britain as they were able to reach in their home country. Economic historians have also drawn attention to the likelihood that investment in human capital in Britain was misdirected (Broadberry 1994a, 1997c). Lacking the intensive government- and business-supported apprenticeship programmes of Germany and the northern European countries, Britain could not match the productivity of their labour in specialised, small-scale production. Lacking the business training programmes that supply skilled managers to American corporations, Britain could not match the productivity of American and Japanese firms in mass production (see chapters 3 and 5 above).

Recognising the power of export-led growth in the cases of both Germany and Italy, France took the initiative to form the European Economic Community in 1958, in a bid to bind the emerging economic powerhouse of West Germany to the French economy. The earlier example of the benefits reaped by the Netherlands when it formed a customs union with Belgium and Luxembourg, both countries enjoying export surpluses in the reconstruction of continental Europe in the 1950s, combined with the revival of French industry under the aegis of the European Coal and Steel Community, persuaded France to take this major step. Economic conditions were propitious as well, as the European Payments Union was scheduled to be wound up in 1958 when all European participants allowed convertibility of their currencies on current account transactions at the fixed exchange rates agreed upon with the International Monetary Fund. Political conditions were ripe in France as well, with General de Gaulle returning to power as president of the newly constituted Fifth French Republic and determined to set a new, Europe-oriented rather than Empire-oriented, foreign policy for France. The Common Market that emerged with France, West Germany and Italy combining with Belgium, the Netherlands and Luxembourg (the six members of the European Coal and Steel Community) was a customs union – each country eliminated all tariffs on manufactured goods against the other members of the customs union while creating a common external tariff against imports of manufactured goods from any non-member country. Such was the basis for developing what became the European Union with a common currency by the end of the twentieth century.

In response to the possible loss of markets on the continent for its manufacturing sector, Britain took the initiative to found the European Free Trade Association (EFTA) to widen the European market for its own export industries (Ellison 2000). EFTA combined the traditional trading partners of Britain – Portugal, Denmark, Norway and Sweden – with the neutral countries in central Europe, Austria and Switzerland. A much looser combination of countries than the EEC, with four members of NATO and three neutral countries, EFTA had no ambitions for political integration arising from economic integration. Rather, each country agreed to remove its tariffs on industrial imports from any of the other member countries. But each maintained its own tariff schedule against imports from any other country, rather than working to establish a common external tariff. Each country then pursued its own negotiating strategy with the combined countries of the EEC, usually to the advantage of the EEC. Europe in the 1960s then became divided into the 'inner six', the member countries of the EEC, and the 'outer seven', the members of EFTA. Both groups, one a customs union with a common external tariff and one a free trade association with free trade only with each other, were clearly in violation of the articles of agreement in the General Agreement on Tariffs and Trade, which pledged member countries to work toward eliminating multiple tariffs as well as non-tariff barriers to trade in manufactured goods.

American policy makers were displeased at this obvious rebuff of multilateral trade relations by thirteen of the sixteen countries it had introduced to the advantages of multilateral clearing in the European Payments Union, following on the Marshall Plan. They had to be content with the restoration of convertibility of each country's currency based on fixed exchange rates, which by itself allowed multilateral clearing of trade imbalances regardless of the differences in trade barriers. Through another round of negotiations on tariff levels in the GATT, called the Dillon Round, the United States was able to extract the commitment by the members of each trade grouping that the average of their new tariff against the rest of the world would be no higher than the original average tariff. The hope remained, then, that reducing some of the tariff barriers within Europe would increase trade and lead to further tariff reductions as the advantages of more liberal trade became apparent.

Looking at a map, the seven countries formed an outer ring around the inner six countries constituting the EEC. All thirteen countries continued to be members of the Organisation of European Economic Co-operation, the European organisation for administering the Marshall Plan funds, and later the European Payments Union. The OEEC had little of its original functions left to justify its existence, but the United States was now left out of all European economic policy discussions. In 1960, the OEEC was formally dissolved and replaced by the OECD, the Organisation for Economic Co-operation and Development, made up of the sixteen European members of the OEEC plus the United States and Canada. It remains the main international organisation for policy discussions among the rich industrial nations of the world, some of which may lead to policy co-ordination. More likely, such discussions may lead to some degree of policy convergence as alternative policies to counter similar problems are compared regularly and systematically. In this context, the British could keep closely informed of the increasingly obvious success of the EEC participants and the relatively lacklustre performance of its own economy and that of its EFTA partners. Not only had the EEC countries caught up with Britain as anticipated in the 1950s, they were now moving steadily past.

Concern about the relatively slow pace of British growth had already started to influence British policy makers in the late 1950s, especially after the Suez débâcle. In addition to the 'fine tuning' of the demand side of the economy in the short run through fiscal policy, the Conservative government made an explicit effort to improve the long-run supply-side performance of the economy as well. Until the early sixties, however, these efforts were limited to more vigorous action against restrictive marketing practices that had become endemic in Britain since the rationalisation movements in British industry in the 1930s. The Restrictive Practices Court set up in 1956 managed to eliminate overt price-fixing arrangements throughout British industry. Instead of leading to price competition that might have forced increases in productivity, however, it appears the RPC simply encouraged the development of other means of market control. For example, trade associations were very effective in disseminating information on market shares of firms, which could be used to monitor informal agreements. A second form of supply-side encouragement came in the form of government finance of higher levels of research and development expenditures than in Germany, France or Italy. However, these were mostly for very expensive military projects in nuclear energy and supersonic aviation, which did nothing for industrial productivity.

Impressed by the evident French success in stimulating rapid industrialisation, the Conservatives initiated a British version of 'indicative planning' by setting up the National Economic Development Council (NEDC) in 1962. Lacking even the access to government-directed finance that the Commissariat du Plan enjoyed in France, however, the NEDC was unable to put any force behind its recommendations of how to raise the rate of economic growth. In fact, the first 'plan' proposed by the NEDC in 1963, calling for a target of 4 per cent annual rates of growth over the next three years, was quickly followed by a deflationary budget in 1964. This showed clearly that Conservative economic policy was still more focused on demand management to maintain the fixed exchange rate of the pound. Moreover, as achievement of this goal seemed to require keeping down the pressure of rising wages on the rate of price inflation, the indicative planning efforts of the NEDC were accompanied by calls for a stronger 'incomes policy'. The idea was that increases in wages might be held down but the share of wages in national income could remain the same by agreeing that non-wage incomes would not rise any faster. The Trades Union Congress naturally objected that while union contracts could enforce the wages part of the incomes policy, there was no comparable mechanism for keeping other incomes under control. Moreover, they wanted to increase the share of wages, not just keep it constant.

In 1964, the Labour Party came back to power determined to make economic planning a success and, like the Gaullist regime in France, raise real wages as part of the social dividend from achieving higher rates of growth. The policy was a failure, as growth rates, while positive, fell off and unemployment edged up. The basic problems that had confronted the Conservative government remained unsolved by the increased vigour of the Labour government. On the macroeconomic level, the problem was an increasingly overvalued exchange rate due to a fixed rate for sterling and higher rates of inflation in Britain than in its major trading partners.[3] This steadily reduced the market share for Britain's exports while increasing imports, so that the resulting adverse balance of payments became again the primary policy issue. On the microeconomic level, wage bargains struck with the Trades Union Congress had to be offset with increased entitlements or increased power for the individual unions. In the short run, this raised expectations in the financial markets of future inflation, inducing speculative movements out of sterling. In the longer run, this reduced incentives to raise labour productivity by reorganisation of shop floor practices and reduced the incentive to invest in more modern capital stock. In November 1967, the pound had to be devalued at last, from $2.80 to $2.40.

The delay in devaluation was due to a dangerous combination of pride, presumption and pragmatism. The pride lay in maintaining the role of the pound sterling as a reserve currency for the remaining countries staying in the sterling area, now reduced by the withdrawal of India and Argentina, but still including former African colonies, Hong Kong, Malaysia and Australia. As long as these countries and colonies maintained their deposits, Britain had a credible claim to maintaining a major

---

[3] The real exchange rate between any two countries is calculated by deflating each currency by the price index in that country. To find the real price of the pound sterling in terms of Deutschmarks, for example, one should divide the 'real' Deutschmark, DM/P_{DM}, by the 'real' pound, $£/P_{UK}$. Rearranging, one multiplies the fixed nominal exchange rate, $DM/£$, by the ratio of price indexes, P_{UK}/P_{DM}. Therefore, if the price level in the United Kingdom rises relative to that in Germany, the real exchange rate of the former has risen, making its exports less competitive compared with those of the latter.

role within the IMF, second only to that of the United States. If official holders of sterling thought it would be devalued, however, it was feared the deposits would be withdrawn quickly. Such a run on sterling also concerned the Americans, whose gold stock was now less than the sum of dollars held by foreign central banks. Because a run on sterling might have created a spillover run on the dollar as well, American support for the pound was often forthcoming.

Moreover, there was a presumption among British economists and politicians that monetary policy would have little or no effect on the economy, even if it were freed of the constraint to keep the exchange rate fixed. The Radcliffe Commission was set up in 1959 to examine the British financial system and to assess the benefits of adopting German- or Italian-style monetary policy. It reported that the complex British system of specialised banks, other financial intermediaries, and sophisticated capital markets made it impossible for the Bank of England to control domestic credit expansion in the way that the Bundesbank or the Banca d'Italia was able to do (see chapter 6 above).

Finally, the pragmatism lay in the realisation that devaluation would immediately raise the overhang of the remaining sterling balances, while any advantage in increasing exports or decreasing imports would take one to two years to be realised. As it turned out, the devaluation regained export competitiveness for Britain very quickly and the United States and IMF provided overwhelming credit lines to Britain to defend the pound at the new parity, so no adverse consequences occurred on capital account. The dangers of inflation breaking out with the devaluation were forestalled successfully by imposing wage and price freezes across the board at first, and only gradually relaxing them to allow wage increases in line with rises in the cost of living and in productivity. Pride was maintained, while the presumption was undermined, and pragmatists appreciated the value of capital controls.

Decolonisation continued to completion as Britain withdrew its forces first from east of Suez and then from Cyprus and Malta. (Gibraltar remained the last British base in the Mediterranean, much to the continued chagrin of the Spanish.) This helped reduce British military spending to more sustainable levels, a consideration that became increasingly important as the costs of the welfare state set up immediately after the war now began to mount. It also cast Britain clearly as a junior partner of the United States in the Western alliance, which did not bother the Labour government particularly when it came back into power in the elections of 1964. But dealing with the United States as supplicant during the successive balance-of-payments crises became increasingly expensive, especially as the expenses of the Vietnam War began to take their toll on the US balance of payments.

One way to offset the diminished role of sterling as an official reserve asset for foreign central banks was to encourage the development of the

Euro-dollar market in London. This helped restore the leading role of London bankers in the finance of international trade, even if most of that trade world-wide was now invoiced in dollars rather than in sterling. Euro-dollars were simply deposits of dollars made in non-US banks and kept on account as dollars. The advantage to depositors was that the accounts were free from restrictions placed by the US authorities on US bank practices, such as interest rate ceilings and withholding taxes on interest to be paid overseas. European banks, with tighter government regulations and much less contact with international capital markets, found London's financial markets attractive as well. The Euro-dollar market developed rapidly in London after 1964.

The other offset, pursued by both Labour governments in 1967 and Conservative governments from 1971 on, was to open up the European Economic Community market to British exporters, while subjecting British labour unions and management to healthy competition from the continent. The negotiations with the EEC were protracted and at times seemed destined to failure as Britain seemed determined to hold on to the advantages of the sterling area as it saw them, while France was determined to maintain the methods of operation that had been developed within the EEC. Eventual compromise was reached when Britain extracted commitment from the EEC to broaden its eligibility requirements for backward regions to receive community aid, so that regions with low per capita incomes as a result of an industry becoming uncompetitive and declining would be eligible for assistance in addition to regions with low per capita incomes as a result of having no industrial base. This would bring EEC aid, it was thought, into declining industrial regions in the north of England, especially Lancashire, and into southern Scotland and South Wales. The hope was that enough regional subsidies would be forthcoming to offset what clearly would be net payments to the rest of the community for food imports. These would now bear a high variable levy if imports continued from the sterling area and the United States or a high price if they came increasingly from within the Community. Other member states could see that they might also have regions that could become eligible for aid under the new, broadened criteria, and so the British proposals were accepted.

The other concession of sorts that Britain extracted was to broaden the membership of the African, Caribbean and Pacific countries, so that the poorest of the sterling area countries and colonies could continue to enjoy preferred access to the British market and now to the rest of the European market in addition. New Zealand, however, did not qualify as a low-income country, so final concessions were extracted to permit continued imports of New Zealand butter and lamb for the five-year transition period allowed for full compliance with the Common Agricultural Policy (CAP). The common external tariff, however, had to be imposed around the British market within four years. As it turned out, commitments of

EEC resources to the price support system of the CAP were allowed to expand over the next decade, which limited the possibility for expanding regional aid, much less foreign aid, to the less developed countries now included in the African, Caribbean and Pacific countries. All these concerns, however, were put aside over the next decade as much more pressing problems confronted Britain and the other members of the EEC than the distribution among them of the EEC's modest resources.

THE OIL SHOCKS, 1973–1985

The negotiations for entry into the Common Market coincided with the end of the fixed rate regime of the Bretton Woods era, which was terminated by the United States in August 1971, when President Nixon ordered the Federal Reserve System to stop selling gold to foreign central banks, especially those in France and Germany. At home, the Conservative government of Edward Heath was under constant challenge from the labour unions, whose strikes always seemed to bring a new round of pay increases. Drawing on the lessons of the 1967 devaluation, Britain let the pound float in 1972, assuming it would fall relative to the dollar and to the European currencies and so stimulate exports. It did fall, but exports did not rise, while prices and wages did. To keep imports from rising too rapidly, the Heath government tried its hand at an incomes policy. Unions agreed to keep wage demands moderate so as not to push up prices, but only on condition that if prices did start rising rapidly they would be free to catch up. The threshold chosen was 7 per cent; a rise in the retail price index greater than that would trigger a wave of wage increases greater than 7 per cent by an amount equal to the shortfall of wages behind prices that had accumulated to that point. The effect was that Britain entered the Common Market in 1973 pursuing much the same line of policy as Italy at the time, providing accommodative financing by the central bank to allow nominal wages to rise as much as the price level. As in the Italian case, this made Britain very vulnerable to the first oil shock, and made the shock of entering the continental system even harder.

The first-round effect of the 1973 oil shock was the same as in the other countries in Europe – a sudden, sharp rise in both unemployment and inflation. In the British case, however, the inflationary shock was exacerbated by the Heath government's incomes policy, because the threshold of 7 per cent was quickly exceeded. The Labour government that came to power in 1974, thanks to the support of the labour unions, naturally supported the catch-up wage increases that followed. Given the continued indifference of both Labour and Conservative governments to any thought of controlling the growth of the money supply, these wage increases were readily financed by the banking sector, supported by the

Bank of England's policy of keeping interest rates low. So the rise in inflation rates for Britain far exceeded that in the rest of Europe, reaching a high of 27 per cent in 1975. Fiscal policy was also lax, as first Heath and then Labour in the first election in 1974 had weak majorities in parliament, so they kept spending high and taxes steady. Accommodative monetary policy combined with loose fiscal policy in this case did nothing for unemployment rates, which also rose. The excessive inflation rates forced the floating pound to devalue even further relative to both the US dollar and the European currencies. This encouraged speculative attacks on the pound, forcing it lower. IMF assistance was limited in the amount it could offer and even then would be conditional on an anti-inflationary policy being imposed.

Even though Britain was formally a member of the EEC at this point, the conditions of entry had factored in four- to five-year transition periods for switching fully to the Common Agricultural Policy or to the common external tariff. The shocks of adjustment to the continental way of doing things were not yet a factor, but it was clear they would only make economic conditions worse in the short run. Consequently, Labour held a referendum in 1975 asking British voters whether they approved of Britain remaining in the European Community on the terms negotiated by the Conservative government. Two-thirds approved. So the remaining way out of the oil shock quandary for the Labour government was to stake everything on developing North Sea oil-producing potential as quickly as possible. To make this pay off, however, required that oil prices remain at least as high as the OPEC cartel had raised them; the costs of exploiting offshore wells in one of the stormiest seas in the world were enormous. Consequently, Britain's interests with respect to dealing with the OPEC cartel were directly counter to those of the European oil importers.

By the end of 1976, the costs of importing the construction materials for North Sea oil facilities had increased the pressure on the balance of payments and the value of the pound to the point that IMF assistance was required. The conditions, as foreseen and already anticipated by the British government, were to impose a more anti-inflationary budget but also to remove exchange controls on capital account transactions. This meant freeing up the blocked sterling balances that still remained from the end of the Second World War. As anticipated, they were rapidly withdrawn. Fortunately, North Sea gas exports began to appear in 1977 and oil exports in 1978. These helped reduce the deficit on current account that might otherwise have occurred, but deficits still existed. Nevertheless, the pound stabilised and even began to strengthen on the basis of strong capital inflows.

The cause of these gyrations in the exchange rate of the pound remains an interesting issue for economists (Britton 1991). A favourite explanation is that investors anticipated the higher interest rates and future export

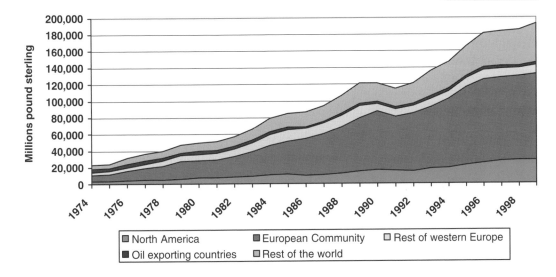

Figure 11.5 Value of imports by area, 1974–1999

Source: CSO, *Annual Abstract of Statistics*, various years

earnings from North Sea oil that in fact did occur in 1979–81. But economic historians emphasise that the root causes of these phenomena – the second oil shock in 1979 and the 'Volcker shock' in 1980[4] – could hardly have been anticipated in 1977 (Foreman-Peck 1991). A more plausible explanation is that removing restrictions on foreigners' deposits in the British financial system made the London capital market that much more attractive as a place for OPEC countries to deposit their excess profits. The Euro-dollar market was a natural focal point for this activity. The British government helped by putting a dollar guarantee on its new bonds. Even though denominated in sterling, their higher interest rates made them an attractive alternative to US government bonds. Only Switzerland, with its banking secrecy, provided any European competition to London's Euro-dollar market. The other European economies maintained controls on the export of capital – France and Belgium even imposed separate exchange rates for foreign deposits in their banks. Capital controls prevented Europe's banking sectors from establishing a continental counterpart to London's international banking market. Whatever the cause of capital flowing into Britain at this time, the pound strengthened and official reserves began to rise once again in the late 1970s.

Figures 11.5 and 11.6 show the course of British trade patterns over the period 1974–99. Joining the Common Market had the desired effect of increasing British exports to Europe. Even as the inflation of the late

---

[4] The term 'Volcker shock' refers to the decision in 1980 by Paul Volcker, head of the Federal Reserve System in the USA, to focus on restricting the growth of the US money supply to the exclusion of other monetary goals. The result was a sudden skyrocketing of US interest rates, which both strengthened the dollar on foreign exchanges (increasing the effect of the second oil shock on oil-importing countries) and plunged the US economy into a sharp, if short, recession.

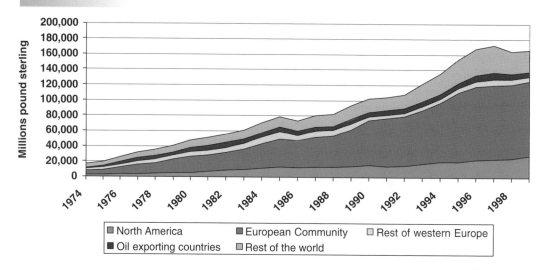

Figure 11.6 Value of
exports by area,
1974–1999

Source: CSO, *Annual
Abstract of Statistics*,
various years

1970s and early 1980s raised the total levels of both imports and exports of goods measured in current pounds sterling, the pattern of both
imports and exports shifted dramatically toward Europe. Given the magnitude of the oil shocks of the 1970s, which increased the proportion of
imports coming from the oil-exporting countries dramatically for continental Europe, it is surprising that so little change in British trade flows
with the oil-exporting countries shows up. Because the 'Rest of the world'
category includes most of what had been the sterling area, it is clear as
well that abandoning the sterling area as a target for British trade was
long overdue by 1973. Best of all, cutting loose from the European Monetary System in 1992 actually helped promote trade with North America,
a goal that had long since been abandoned as unfeasible by British policy
makers, but one that now seemed worth considering seriously again.

THE THATCHER REVOLUTION

The beginning of the Thatcher era was shocking, to say the least, and not
at all auspicious for the future of the government. Unemployment rose
sharply, soon hitting the unimaginably high figure of 2 million out of
work, and then moving on to put a full 3 million on the dole. The growth
rate of the economy was actually negative for two successive years, 1980
and 1981. Inflation rose to nearly a record high in 1980. Even the pound
began to decline relative to the dollar again in 1981. Every aspect of British
macroeconomic performance that had obsessed governments from 1945
on deteriorated in the first two years of the Thatcher era. Nevertheless, her
economic policy remained committed to reducing inflation by controlling
the rate of growth of the money supply (Buxton *et al.* 1994). True, her

economists dithered over how to measure the money supply, and the announced targets were regularly exceeded. But, as bad as things were, they seemed no worse than the travails being endured at the same time by the rest of Europe. North Sea oil was now in full production and contributing larger and larger amounts to the current account.

By 1982, the worst was over for Britain, and recovery began to show up in renewed rates of growth, while inflation seemed to stay under control. No progress was made in terms of reducing unemployment, which continued to rise, but in comparison with the continued slow growth in the rest of Europe, the British did not look so bad, and they certainly were not doing as badly as they had become accustomed to doing relative to France and Germany. The success of British forces in the Falklands/Malvinas War of 1982 renewed British pride and no doubt helped re-elect Thatcher and the Conservative parliament in 1983. Without this kind of extra-economic boost to Thatcher's popularity, it is likely she would have been defeated when the next mandatory election occurred in 1984. Then the effects of her reforms would not have had time to show up in increased rates of productivity and rising rates of growth. It was precisely this long lag time required for institutional changes to take effect, coupled with the requirement to have new elections at least every five years, that inhibited previous Conservative prime ministers from initiating fundamental reforms. It also explains why the Thatcher reforms have not been quickly imitated by other industrial democracies.

After Thatcher's re-election came the Trade Union Bill in October 1983, which was intended to break the power of trade union leaders by requiring them to subject their decisions on strikes or political contributions to direct vote by the union membership. The coal miners struck in 1984 to test the resolve of the Thatcher government and to rally other unions to their support. They failed on both counts, although the battle lasted for some months. The failure of the miners' strike meant that henceforth much of the ability of British labour unions in general to limit reorganisation of work practices and the effective use of labour-saving technology was dissipated. As British investment rates rose over the rest of the 1980s, so did the total factor productivity of British manufacturing. Overall, Britain stopped falling behind the rest of Europe and the level of income actually began catching up with France and Germany, as Figures 11.3 and 11.4 show.

This supply-side effect of Thatcher's economic policy was reinforced by a commitment to privatisation of as much of the nationalised industries and the public sector as possible, starting in 1984 (see chapter 4 above). Although this could not be done systematically or quickly, given the entrenchments of at least forty years, eventually gas and electricity were privatised, then waterworks as well as coal and steel, aviation, and telecommunications. In most cases, the revenues from the sale of the enterprises were used to reduce the government debt or income taxes, while expenditures in the future were no longer burdened by the need to subsidise inefficient and overstaffed operations. Unemployment rose as a result, but customers and taxpayers were satisfied with the results on the whole. Of course, objections were raised that regulators were allowing prices charged by the utilities to rise too much to benefit the new shareholders and penalise the customers, or, conversely, that prices were being kept too low to benefit customers at the expense of shareholders. As privatisation was usually carried out by giving the customers preferential purchase rights to the shares, however, the customers and shareholders tended to be the same people. Consequently, losses suffered in one role were offset on average by gains in the other. Overall, improvements in the quality of infrastructure encouraged private industry to increase its productivity further. It is arguable that the success of British privatisation, combined with the competitive spirit within Europe that was engendered by the European Commission's oversight of the Single Market and competition policy, helped encourage European governments to begin privatisation of the postal services and especially the telecommunications sector.

Thatcher's policy with respect to the EC, however, was always controversial. She fought incessantly with the other heads of government at the semi-annual meetings of the European Council over most initiatives being proposed. Eventually she won a sizeable rebate from the Community in recognition of Britain's substantial net payment into the Community's coffers despite its having a lower per capita income than some of the net recipients. In return, she allowed the Commission to expand in size by allowing each new member to have at least one commissioner. But she was also one of the prime movers in promoting the Single Market initiative in 1985, as it was consistent with her overall philosophy of reducing the amount of government regulations and imposition of additional transaction costs on the operations of markets. When the momentum from the Single Market initiative was carried on by the Commission to the Delors Plan, which eventually culminated in the Maastricht Treaty of 1993, she raised stern objections. Both the common currency and the additional responsibilities that would be given to the EC's supranational authority in foreign and social policy were anathema to her vision of revitalising the British economy by freeing its markets of excessive government regulation and interference.

ONLY PART OF THE EUROPEAN UNION, 1986–1999

Renewed vitality of the British economy in the early 1980s was achieved while Britain remained out of the European Monetary System (EMS). Initially, this made sense, because Britain had become a net oil exporter by the end of 1978. Since oil was invoiced in dollars, it would be to

Britain's advantage to see the dollar strengthen relative to the pound, because then the oil earnings in dollars would have more purchasing power for extinguishing British liabilities denominated in pounds sterling. The interests of Germany, France and Italy as large net oil importers were exactly opposite. As it turned out, the combination of the second oil shock and the Volcker shock greatly improved Britain's situation with respect to the balance of payments as reserves accumulated rapidly. The exchange rate, after strengthening relative to the dollar in 1978–80 as expected from the second oil shock, then weakened in common with the rest of the European currencies during the Volcker shock of the early 1980s, even as the export surpluses continued from North Sea oil. When the third oil shock occurred in early 1986, however, the price of oil fell sharply and the British balance of trade began to weaken. Initially, however, the pound strengthened relative to the dollar even as it weakened relative to the Deutschmark and the currencies of the rest of the EMS countries. As part of the US-led effort to stabilise exchange rates in the late 1980s, the pound stabilised with respect to both the dollar and the Deutschmark. By 1990, as the balance of trade began to improve, Britain seemed determined to try anything to keep inflation from cropping up again. This finally led Thatcher to agree to commit the pound sterling to a fixed parity with the Deutschmark and the rest of the participating currencies in the Exchange Rate Mechanism of the EMS. If this move had convinced foreign investors that Italy had a credible commitment to stable prices, surely it would convince them of Britain's commitment! Like Italy, however, Britain was now poised to participate fully in the economic shock caused by German reunification. After the German Economic and Monetary Union took place in July 1990, the Bundesbank tightened monetary policy in order to reabsorb the excessive amounts of East German marks that had been issued in anticipation of the promised exchange rate of 1 Deutschmark to 1 Ostmark. All participants in the Exchange Rate Mechanism of the European Monetary System had to follow the Bundesbank's lead, regardless of their own economic conditions. Both Italy and Britain were forced to leave the Exchange Rate Mechanism and the EMS in September 1992, as neither central bank was able to restrict the growth of its domestic currency to the extent achieved by the Bundesbank. After their departure from the EMS, the sharp devaluation of the two currencies relative to those of what were now their primary trading partners created an export-led recovery for both Britain and Italy. Both countries resumed relatively higher growth rates than in France and Germany.

The exit of Britain from the EMS occurred as the discussions over the ratification of the Maastricht Treaty were preoccupying Europe. John Major, who had brought Britain into the EMS in October 1990 as the chancellor of the Exchequer under Thatcher, was now her successor as prime minister. Reluctant to damage relations with the EU in the way

Thatcher had enjoyed doing, he argued for the British parliament to rat-
ify the treaty. In deference to his party's concerns that the supranational
goals of the Maastricht Treaty might undo or stymie Thatcher's reforms,
especially in limiting the power of British labour unions, he had negotiated agreement that Britain could opt out of the Social Chapter of the
treaty, which would have required Britain to harmonise its labour union
legislation with that of the rest of the EU. Moreover, by withdrawing
from the EMS in 1992 before ratification of the treaty, he was holding
open the options for Britain of whether and when to rejoin the EMS as
it progressed towards the treaty's objective of European Monetary Union.

Parliament approved, narrowly, and Major won re-election in 1992,
again narrowly. In the meantime, British unemployment rates began
to fall once again as the growth rate of the economy picked up. The
British had the best of the economic worlds available to members of
the European Union: full access to the markets of the fifteen-member
European Union for its exports, investors and work force – without bearing the economic costs they had had imposed on them by the shock of
German reunification. For foreign firms seeking access to the enlarged
Single Market and its possible extension into central and east Europe in
the near future, this meant that Britain was the preferred location for
setting up distribution and manufacturing centres. So Britain became
the fortunate recipient of increased foreign direct investment as well as
being able to maintain its attractiveness for foreign portfolio investment
in British securities. As the elections of 1997 came into view, both parties
seemed content to continue this state of affairs as long as possible. Even
with an overwhelming victory by the Labour Party's Tony Blair, Britain remained apart from the common currency. Gordon Brown, the new chancellor of the Exchequer, took one step immediately in the direction of
easing Britain's possible entry, however, by declaring that the Bank of
England would be solely responsible for monetary policy. Independence
of national central banks from their respective ministers of finance is a
requirement of the European Monetary Union, so Chancellor Brown's decision could be seen as a testing of the waters, perhaps leading to a legislative Act that would formalise the independence of the Bank of England.
In the meantime, its responsibility for monetary policy could be taken
from it at any moment, especially after the re-election of Labour in 2001.

OVERVIEW: BRITAIN'S ECONOMIC RELATIONS
WITH EUROPE, 1960–1999

Figures 11.7, 11.8 and 11.9 show the course of growth rates, inflation and
unemployment for Britain, France, Germany and Italy from 1960 to 2000.
They show clearly the effects of the changing economic policy regimes
of Britain and Europe over these forty years (Neal and Barbezat 1998). For

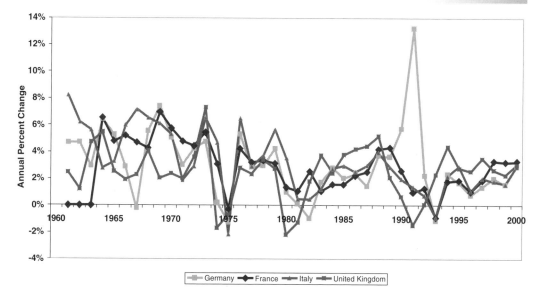

Figure 11.7 Growth comparison: Germany, France, Italy, UK

Source: OECD, 2002

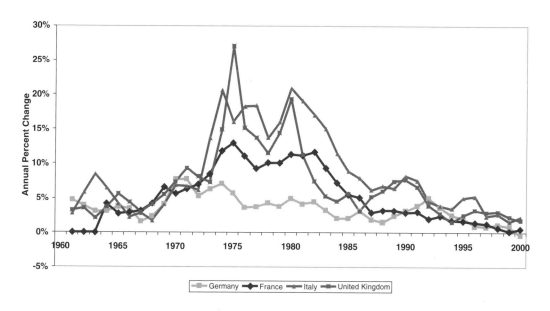

example, the growth rates of the 1960s were high by historical standards for Great Britain, but well behind those generally experienced on the European continent at the time. Unemployment rates in Britain likewise were low by historical standards but still above those in the economic miracle leaders in the EEC before Britain's entrance into the Community. Moreover, inflation was definitely more of a struggle for British policy

Figure 11.8 Inflation comparison: Germany, France, Italy, UK

Source: OECD, 2002

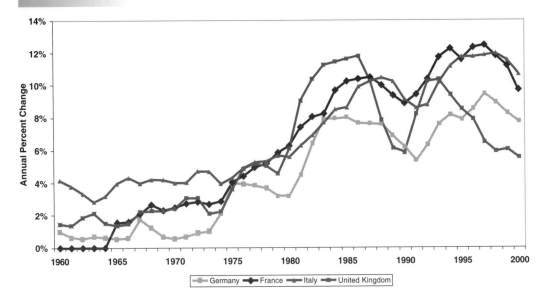

Figure 11.9
Unemployment
comparison: Germany,
France, Italy, UK

Source: OECD, 2002

makers than for Germany or France, approaching double digits even
before the oil shock of 1974. This first oil shock clearly hit Britain harder
than any of the other large countries in Europe. Unemployment rates
doubled, growth rates of GDP turned negative for two years running, and
the inflation rate peaked at a record 27 per cent in 1976. Small wonder
Britain was a supplicant to the International Monetary Fund and had to
meet stringent terms imposed at the insistence of both the United States
and Germany.

It is interesting that the economic indicators were all improving in
1977 and 1978, despite the worsening political situation for the ruling
Labour party. If the beginning of the Thatcher revolution was, in fact, the
prime mover for these macroeconomic indicators in the years 1979–81,
one would have to infer it was a disaster. Inflation shot up again close to
20 per cent, unemployment rates jumped, never returning to their pre-
Thatcher levels, and growth rates turned negative once again. Of course,
the full panoply of Thatcher economic reforms was not yet in place or
even begun as far as privatisation or monetary policy was concerned. The
second oil shock in 1979 and then the Volcker shock of 1980–1 were the
dominant forces acting on the British economy, as they were on the rest
of the European economies. The second oil shock, which doubled the
price of oil, did not affect Britain directly, since it exported as much oil
by then as it imported. However, it certainly reduced world-wide demand
in general and demand for British exports in particular.

In sum, the comparison of Britain's performance relative to the major
European powers in terms of the chief policy targets of modern governments – high rates of economic growth, low and steady rates of inflation, rates of unemployment – show clearly the to and fro movements

of Britain and Europe. The turnabouts were all associated with external shocks, felt by Europe as well as Britain, but responded to differently in each case. The results were sometimes in Europe's favour, sometimes in Britain's.

CONCLUSION

As Figures 11.10, 11.11 and 11.12 show, the long decline of the once proud pound sterling from a war-time level of $4.03 to a range of $1.45 – $1.55 at the end of the twentieth century had stabilised in the 1990s. Moreover, in the late 1990s, it began to rise significantly against the new common currency of its European Union partners. The exchange evidence in Figure 11.10 has to be read in conjunction with Figures 11.11 and 11.12, which track the respective levels of international reserves held by Britain, France and Germany over the period 1948–73 and then from 1974 through 1999. The first period, corresponding to obsession with the sterling balances and maintaining a primary role for sterling along with the dollar in international finance, saw Britain's reserves stay level while first Germany, and then France, surpassed it. By the 1980s, the Deutschmark and the yen were the main reserve currencies in the world other than the dollar. Since joining the European Economic Community in 1973 and redirecting its trade towards Europe, Britain's international reserves have risen overall at the same rate as those of France. By the end of the 1990s, with Britain following an independent monetary policy from the rest of the European Union, both France and Britain had reserves approaching those of Germany, still the dominant economy in Europe.

At the end of the twentieth century, as for most of its history, Britain was not really sure if it was better off as part of Europe or separate from Europe. Clearly it was part of the European economy to a much greater extent than it ever had been since the seventeenth century. But just as it had never been militarily allied with both France and Germany at the same time until the North Atlantic Treaty Organisation was established after the Second World War, and then only with the likelihood of a 'special relationship' with the American superpower, so Britain's leaders were unsure if they should support the Franco-German architectural design for the continent in the twenty-first century. This dichotomy between support for the economic goals of France and Germany and resistance to their political ambitions came out clearly in Britain's internal conflict over joining the European Monetary Union. There the economic gains seemed clear but minor, whereas the political gains or losses were not at all clear but could be major. Until this internal conflict is resolved, Britain will not be able to help determine the future course of Europe, save by setting an example of what can be accomplished by following alternative economic policies, for instance in privatising state-owned

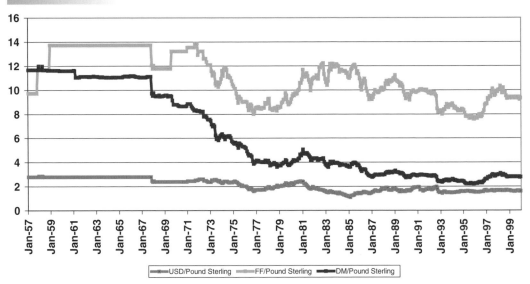

Figure 11.10 Exchange rates, 1957–1998: British pound vs USA, France, Germany

Source: International Monetary Fund, 2000

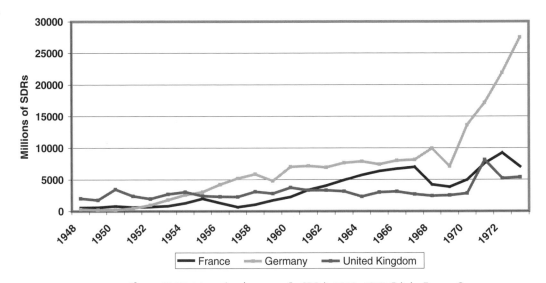

Figure 11.11 International reserves (in SDRs), 1948–1973: Britain, France, Germany

Note: The SDR (Special Drawing Right) is an international reserve asset created by the International Monetary Fund.
Source: International Monetary Fund, 2000

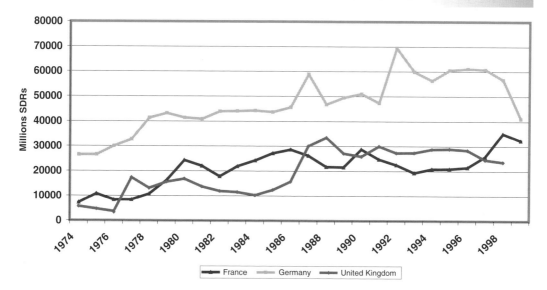

Figure 11.12

International reserves, 1974–1999: Britain, France, Germany

Source: International Monetary Fund, 2000

enterprises. Privatisation of certain state monopolies has been followed by much of Europe, especially in telecommunications. Electric utilities and airlines seem more doubtful examples to European states, as does the move toward more flexible labour force regulations, especially allowing firms to hire temporary workers for extended periods and for part-time work.

While insisting that its membership in the European Union is irrevocable and that it wishes to play a major role in its future development, Britain also insists that the EU should remain a flexible organisation capable of containing a wide diversity of nations with distinct national interests. More democratic procedures and attention to the will of the people within the separate nation states should be developed, so that it can continue to contribute to the peace of Europe, especially by enlarging its membership as quickly as possible to include the central and east European countries who became applicants after the 1995 enlargement of the European Union. But Britain feels that the EU contribution has been, and should remain, primarily in the economic sphere: this means expansion of trade by elimination of tariff barriers and reduction of non-tariff barriers, but not necessarily the co-ordination of national fiscal and monetary policies.

Reform of the Common Agricultural Policy is clearly one area where Britain differs from the original members of the European Community, who are much attached to maintaining those parts of the *acquis communautaire* that have served to deepen Franco-German co-operation over the years and fearful that any backtracking, once begun, will be difficult to halt in other domains as well. The British trauma with mad cow disease in the late 1990s could be taken, however, as an example to Europe showing the abuses to food safety that can arise in modern agri-industry that is geared towards reaping price supports rather than competing in the market on the basis of food quality. The lesson could have been made applicable to Europe with the dioxin scare in Belgian agriculture in 1999 and then the outbreaks of mad cow disease in Europe in autumn of 2000.

The impact of Europe on Britain's economic history since 1939 certainly increased greatly. But it did so not in a steady, incremental fashion, but rather erratically, whenever both Europe and Britain had to deal in their own ways with the recurring shocks of war, revolution, collapse of empires, and the emergence of the USA as the world's lone superpower. The economic successes of Germany and Japan after the Second World War, when both countries were freed from the expenses of colonies and military establishments, eventually led both France and Britain to accept decolonisation and reduced defence budgets by the late 1950s. In turn, both countries experienced improvements in economic performance as well, although the superior performance of the Common Market countries led Britain first to emulate, then finally to join the European Community in 1973. Thereafter, Britain only partly participated in the expanding functions of the European Union such as its Common Social Policy, its common currency, and its common external border, reserving to its national sovereign power the ability to manage these functions of government in its own tradition. At the same time, Britain, by pursuing alternative economic strategies in response to economic shocks that strike modern industrial economies from time to time, came to have an increasing impact on Europe as well.

12

Technology in post-war Britain

NICK VON TUNZELMANN

Contents

INTRODUCTION

Technology had been an area of sporadic governmental concern for several centuries, but after the Second World War it moved nearer the centre-stage of thinking in both public and private domains. This growth of interest in, and concern about, technology was driven by a number of factors, none of which was new but all of which were accentuated. First was the growing complexity of technology, associated in part with extending links with the science base and in part with the advent of new technological fields. Second was the impact of 'globalisation', which helped to place technology at the forefront of the 'competitiveness agenda' in the economic domain. And third were the intensifying public anxieties about unchecked technological proliferation and potentially adverse environmental impacts, which led to demands for tighter control and regulation. In various ways, each of these brought about a widening consciousness of technology among the people of Britain.

Though concerns and anxieties were to grow in the second half of the twentieth century, technology had emerged from the war with a high reputation: in the military, in government and in the public at large. Initial excitement over how atomic bombs had brought a speedy end to the war in the Pacific led not only to enlarged testing programmes for nuclear weapons, by the UK as well as other leading military powers, but also to General Eisenhower's call for 'Atoms for Peace', and nuclear power that would prospectively generate electricity that was to be 'too cheap to meter'. Computers that had been first developed to analyse the ballistics of rockets could be harnessed for a wider range of scientific calculations, and perhaps other purposes. Electronics in communication systems such as radar or code-breaking machines held out similarly high promise for civilian use. The pharmaceutical industry was beginning to offer antibiotics that would have a major impact on human health and the fight against disease.

These hopes propelled a vigorously positive view of technology in the UK through the 1950s and 1960s. Around the beginning of the 1970s, however, the growing awareness of Britain's apparently poor relative growth record in the post-war period when compared to rival countries led to growing scepticism in government about technology as a fix for prosperity. Frequent reorganisations of government ministers and ministries proceeded, to little effect. This scepticism spread to the public at large, first through specialised pressure groups, and later through a number of consumer rebellions. Alongside a sequence of public relations disasters associated with technologies such as nuclear power – which had proved far from being 'too cheap to meter' – and biotechnology, the public drew the conclusion that technology was by no means safe in the hands of scientists. The century ended with a stock-market frenzy in shares of high-technology companies which quickly turned into a dramatic collapse, so even in financial terms technology seemed to be failing to deliver. It is the task of this chapter to trace the evolution of technology in Britain in such a context, and assess its economic and social impacts.

ECONOMIC THEORY AND TECHNOLOGY

Economists and economic historians have for some time observed that countries have been performing consistently differently in terms of long-term growth patterns. According to conventional neoclassical growth theory, countries should 'converge' in terms of their long-run growth paths, subject to certain conditions being met ('conditional convergence'). This simply did not appear to be happening – as Abramovitz (1986) pointed out, a few countries were indeed catching up from initially low income levels, but some of the leaders continued to 'forge ahead', while many countries continued to 'fall behind'. The conventional view of Britain is one of a country that was long 'falling behind', even if its plight scarcely compared with many Third World countries.

These inconsistencies led to two kinds of outcomes so far as analyses of economic growth and technological change were concerned. First were attempts to reformulate growth theory within economics. The so-called 'new growth theory' or 'endogenous growth theory' argued against the neoclassical assumption that there would be diminishing returns to factor inputs such as capital. 'Broad capital' – defined so as to include not just the traditional investments in 'tangible' physical capital but also 'intangible' technology (R&D investments) and/or 'human capital' (educational investments) might be able to offset the conventional diminishing returns. Hence greater and greater investments in either intangible or human capital could yield more and more growth.

Some economic historians have found it useful to deploy the new growth theory to interpret post-war European growth (e.g. Crafts and Toniolo 1996). However, there are some serious limitations of the new growth theory on both theoretical and empirical grounds. First, it continues the economist's tradition of implying a purely supply-driven approach to growth: according to what is known in innovation studies as the 'linear model', more research generates more technology, which generates more diffusion of technology, which generates more economic growth. Although this was popular among post-war scientists as a justification for their research, it stands contrary to a long tradition of work on innovation studies, in which contributions by some economic historians have been notable (e.g. Schmookler 1966). The present consensus in this field is that, alongside the supply-driven effect of technology leading to growth, there is a parallel demand-pull effect of growth leading to technology. Empirical studies of the industrial countries demonstrate the demand effect to be at least as important as the supply one (von Tunzelmann and Efendioglu 2001). An equivalent case can be made for human capital – it seems just as plausible on *a priori* grounds that the post-war boom in education, emphasised by Crafts and Toniolo, could be explained by growing demand for raising levels of education as well as by a supply-push of greater educational provision. Naturally, if growth is (partly) responsible for technological capital or human capital, then we cannot simply explain growth by these factors.

Moreover, the notion that there were non-diminishing returns on intangible capital in the late twentieth century has been challenged on empirical grounds (Jones 1995). In practice the costs of innovation appear to have been rising rather than constant or falling over the last quarter of the century. This is an important part of our story, and will be developed at greater length below for the UK case.

A broader kind of response, from outside economics, extended the scope of the analysis to wider issues of entrepreneurial behaviour and 'social capabilities' (the latter being Abramovitz's term to account for why some countries grew but many did not). The analytical apparatus that has been developed for this purpose has come to be known as the study of 'national systems of innovation'. This will be the approach utilised in the present chapter.

In the 'national system of innovation', the 'national' term drew attention to sharply contrasting behaviours across countries, as well as to the point that many of the key decisions relevant to innovation were indeed made at the national level, especially if one were considering the whole framework of innovation rather than specific technologies (e.g. the impinging legal systems, labour markets, financial arrangements, etc.). The 'system' term emphasised the entire structure pertinent to innovation performance – the elements of the innovation structure (e.g. public and private sector laboratories, research institutes, universities and so on) were found to be fairly similar between countries, but their relative influence and power differed considerably, as, even more, did the presence or absence of effective links interconnecting them. Finally the 'innovation' term tended to be applied rather loosely, as the interconnections to the wider framework mentioned above were shown to be critical. It also came to be accepted that interactions took place not just at the national level but also at more local levels ('regional systems of innovation', including 'industrial districts'), more transnational levels ('global systems of innovation') and more sectorally specific levels ('sectoral systems of innovation'). However only the national level will be analysed at any length in this chapter.

TECHNOLOGICAL PERFORMANCE

By convention, indicators of technology are divided into those purporting to measure technological 'inputs' and those directed at technological 'outputs'. The former are normally assessed by figures on R&D expenditures or R&D employment, the latter by patents and publications. However, it is often inappropriate to see patenting as the termination of the technological development process; for example, a patent often triggers an upsurge of R&D by the company in question or by its competitors, so reversing the causal sequence between inputs and outputs (for critiques see Griliches 1990; Stoneman 1995).

Moreover, all the conventional measures are inadequate on grounds of both quantity and quality. R&D expenditures are usually assessed according to the 'Frascati' definitions provided by the OECD – definitions which themselves have changed over time. The Frascati breakdown of R&D into 'basic research', 'applied research' and 'experimental development' is known to leave much activity essential for technology accumulation out of account. For instance, it is known that most countries report relatively little R&D from SMEs (small and medium-sized enterprises), mainly because small firms tend not to have specialised R&D departments (their technological development is carried out within their ordinary production processes or 'after hours'). The UK has a relatively low proportion of SMEs in manufacturing and is thus less heavily underestimated than a country like Italy or Japan, where such firms are numerous. Equally, patents are widely recognised to be biased indicators of 'outputs': not all outcomes are patented and indeed many cannot meet the legal requirements; on the other hand, large numbers of patents are never followed through into practical use. 'Input' and especially 'output' indicators vary widely in quality – of the hundreds of thousands of patents taken out annually nowadays, only a small proportion probably represent significant advances, and similarly for the publication of scientific papers. It has become increasingly common to measure publications (and more recently patents) by 'citations' to them, as a way of gauging their relative impact, but the data have to be treated with considerable scepticism.

Theoretically preferable to any of these measures are the numbers and quality of actual 'innovations'. However, there are major barriers to compiling an acceptable list of innovations. The only annual series that has achieved any degree of acceptance is that constructed at the Science Policy Research Unit (SPRU), University of Sussex, for the UK between 1945 and 1983. This relied on the recall of several 'experts' in each field to establish the breakthroughs over the period in question, and therein lay its main limitation since their memories proved rather variable; moreover, the coverage of fields was somewhat unequal. Nevertheless, in conjunction with other indicators this has been used with some success in econometric studies (e.g. Geroski 1991; Greenhalgh 1994; Geroski *et al.* 1997; Wakelin 2001). Unfortunately, it has not proved possible to continue this series into more recent times.

R&D expenditures

Figures on R&D expenditures have become the most widely cited of national indicators pertaining to technological performance. As just noted, the attempt to construct a narrow consensual definition through the Frascati manual means that much developmental work aimed at the commercialisation of innovations is left out of the figure for R&D. It is widely believed that the UK is stronger at 'upstream' science and technology than at 'downstream' adoption and diffusion, so UK expenditures tend to overstate its relative international performance in technology. Internally, the UK figure is considered to have overstated the country's position for many years because the large element of (governmental) military expenditure on R&D is known to have included a high proportion of product development work that should not have been classified as R&D according to Frascati. As noted above, the UK has a small share of smaller enterprises – a rough estimation by Taylor and Silberston (1973: 55–7) reckoned they added no more than 6 per cent to the figure for large firms in 1967/8. Overall it seems reasonable to say that the published data do not underestimate the UK's relative standing.

Expenditures on R&D are divided into three categories: business expenditure on R&D (BERD), i.e. that performed by industrial businesses; government expenditure on R&D (GOVERD); and higher education expenditure on R&D (HERD), with the last-named usually supported by government as well. These add up to a total known as gross expenditure on R&D (GERD), which is the most commonly cited single figure. The ratio of GERD to GDP is often known as the country's 'R&D intensity'.

Estimates of R&D spending for the early post-war years suggest a rapid build-up of R&D intensity through the 1950s (Carter and Williams 1957: 44–5; Saul 1979: 125; Broadberry 1997c: 122). Data on funding imply a GERD intensity of from 2.4 per cent to 2.6 per cent from the late 1950s to the beginning of the 1970s when related to the data of Feinstein (1972) on GDP, a little higher than the results shown in Figure 12.1. Considering ten leading industrial countries, Patel and Pavitt (1989: 115) found that the UK stood second in terms of total R&D intensity in 1967, falling to sixth in 1983. After removing the large military component, in civilian R&D its position was fourth in 1967 and only ninth in 1983.

Figures 12.1 to 12.2 chart available data on expenditures in more recent times. Figure 12.1a sets out overall R&D intensity (GERD as a percentage of GDP) for the UK (black diamonds) as against its most obvious comparators – the USA, France and Germany. The comparisons are hampered by a lack of continuity of the series, especially for the 1970s in the UK. Aside from the USA, the UK starts with the highest R&D intensity, running at around 2.3 per cent in the late 1960s. The (more reliable) figures for the late 1980s show about the same level, with the scattered observations for the 1970s suggesting a dip to nearer 2.0 per cent in that decade. After allowing for improvements in collecting the data, we could draw the conclusion that the long-term performance was at best one of holding the position, and probably declining in the mid-1990s, despite the latter being a period of rising prosperity. The much stronger performance of France and Germany (the latter until reunification in the early 1990s), and also of the USA during the 1990s, is evident from the diagram. In the long term the UK thus failed to keep up with comparable countries in terms of R&D intensity.

Figure 12.1(b) gives R&D intensity in terms of BERD, i.e. business expenditure on R&D relative to GDP. In the long run there is again basic stability – from the late 1960s through to the late 1980s BERD sticks at

GERD % GDP

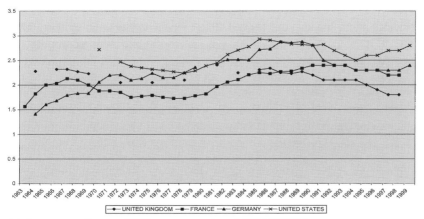

(a) Gross expenditure on R&D as a proportion of GDP (GERD)

BERD % GDP

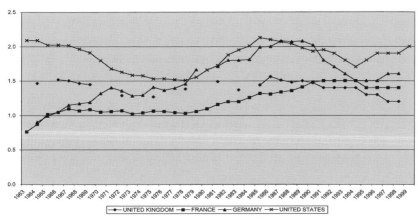

(b) Business expenditure on R&D as a proportion of GDP (BERD)

HERD % GDP

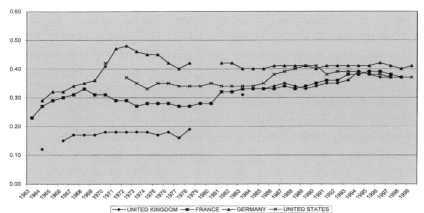

(c) Higher education expenditure on R&D as a proportion of GDP (HERD)

Figure 12.1 R&D intensity

Source: see text.

about 1.5 per cent of GDP. The cutbacks in government expenditure on R&D to be described below did little if anything to stir the business sector out of its torpor, and indeed BERD intensity declined in the 1990s. The figures from the mid-1980s get somewhat inflated because of the privatisation process, which transfers many government laboratories like the Atomic Energy Authority into agency status and then some into the private sector though they continue to do similar research (Beesley *et al.* 1998); so the 'true' business sector performance is actually rather poor. Again, the UK did relatively badly compared with its international rivals.

For the case of HERD as a percentage of GDP (Figure 12.1(c)) the story is very different – here a positive performance by the UK not only features in but almost dominates the picture. Until the cuts in university funding at the end of the 1970s the contribution of UK higher education institutions to the country's R&D was well below that in comparable countries, despite some growth in the 1960s. The cuts and the associated reorientation of university research towards applied objectives in order to secure non-governmental funding more than doubled the HERD contribution to UK GDP during the 1980s. By the mid-1980s the UK ratios were in the same ball-park as its rivals. By the mid-1990s there was strong convergence between the charted countries. It can reasonably be claimed that the UK was successful in steering its universities into industrially relevant research, though whether at a cost to basic research remains an open issue. Thus the pattern observed for the UK is rather different from most industrially advanced countries – instead of a slowdown in government R&D expenditure being more than offset by rising business expenditure, the UK witnessed a slowdown in business R&D expenditure, perhaps even a fall, and a rise in higher education R&D that was offset by a fall in government expenditure in other domains.

R&D funding

These figures on expenditures, reflecting amounts performed by the respective agents, must be clearly differentiated from the sources of funding. In the UK, as in most countries, the government funds considerably more R&D than it performs. For instance, industrial funding was under one-quarter of total R&D in 1955/6, but industry still did most of the performing, probably from 1945 and clearly from 1955 (Gummett 1991). In 1996 private business in the UK funded about 47 per cent of total domestic R&D but performed about 75 per cent (Diederen *et al.* 1999). In the UK most of this 'subsidy' to industry has reflected military R&D, where the government contracts out a substantial portion of defence-related R&D, especially in more 'downstream' developmental work, to private sector business to carry out. This will be studied in more detail below.

Figure 12.2 breaks down the funding of GERD in the UK. Figure 12.2(a) displays data assembled by Mottershead (1978: 450) from government

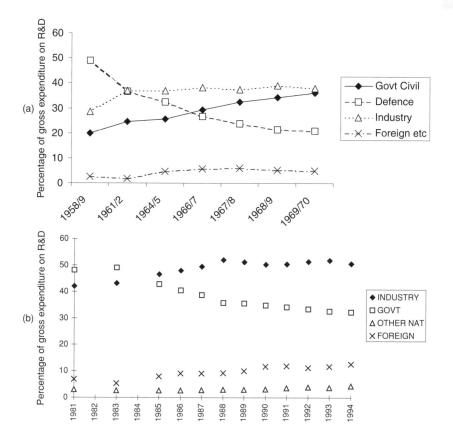

sources for the years from the late 1950s to the end of the 1960s. According to these data, defence accounted for almost half of the funding in 1958/9, though this had fallen to under a third by the mid-1960s and continued to drop proportionately. The compensating increase came more from private industry at first, though then levelled out for the rest of the period, with the fall of defence thereafter instead being offset by rising government funding of civilian R&D. A continuing rationale for such government activity through the 1960s was the poor performance of the private sector, especially outside defence contracting.

Large changes also occurred during the 1980s and early 1990s, as shown in Figure 12.2(b), which is based on OECD data. At the beginning of the 1980s government funded around half of the total R&D performed in the country, much as in 1970, but from 1983 this share dropped away; rapidly at first in response to government expenditure cuts, then more slowly after about 1988. Government investment in civil R&D fell from 0.72 per cent of GDP in 1981 to 0.43 per cent by 1996 (Georghiou 2001). Industry's share rose from just over 40 per cent in 1981 to a maximum about 10 points higher in 1988. Some part of the falling government

Figure 12.2 Share of funding of gross expenditure on R&D, 1958/9–1969/70 and 1981–1994

Sources: (a) Mottershead (1978: 450); (b) Georghiou (2001).

share was compensated by a rising share funded by foreign sources, i.e. by increasing reliance on foreign-based multinational companies, and by other national sources (e.g. charities), especially after 1988. Charities were especially important in funding basic scientific research.

These patterns were quite similar to what was later observed in the EU. In the USA, the trends over the whole period were similar but the cuts in government share occurred mainly in the early 1990s, as a result of the 'peace dividend'. The major difference between the USA and the UK was the higher proportion of government-funded research that was contracted out to industry in the USA, so there was a larger subsidy of government to industrial research there, contrary to much popular belief. Overall the experiment of cutting UK government spending on R&D in the hope of boosting private R&D can hardly be judged a success. The growth in the UK R&D stock was the slowest of the G6 countries (Canada, France, Germany, Japan, UK, USA) in 1972–89 and, especially, in 1990–4 (Buxton *et al.* 1998: 172). We return to this below.

Manpower

Another way of measuring the technological inputs is by counting numbers of people declaring themselves to be R&D personnel, or, more generally, the number of qualified scientists and engineers (QSEs) working in industry. Intermittent data from the 1930s have been collected by Broadberry (1997c: 124–5). Britain devoted less manpower than spending to R&D relative to competitor countries (Peck 1968). From 1981 to 1993, the numbers of R&D personnel as a proportion of the labour force can be obtained for some seventeen OECD countries. Over this period all of them (apart from Germany after reunification) show a sustained increase in this proportion, with the single exception of the UK, where the number of R&D personnel per thousand of the labour force fell from around 11.5 in the early 1980s to just over 9 in the early 1990s, by which time most advanced industrial countries had higher proportions than the UK. The picture for total QSEs (or university graduates) in the labour force is less gloomy, with the proportion in the UK rising from 4.7 per thousand in 1981 to 5.5 by 1998, with all of the increase coming in the mid-1990s. However, most of Britain's larger rivals registered more substantial increases over these years, while the OECD average rose from below Britain's to above it.

One of the factors retarding the expansion of qualified personnel in the UK has frequently been considered to be the low social valuation placed on engineers in the country, as compared with their standing in Germany, France, etc. (e.g. Albu 1980; Millward 1994). Britain employed about 5 engineers for every 4 scientists in 1959, whereas in its main competitors the ratio was about 3 to 1 (Peck 1968: 451; Broadway 1969: 140). The enduring scarcity of engineers relative to demand, which labour market mechanisms failed to redress, had a long history, dating back to the reluctance of universities to admit engineering into their faculties in the second half of the nineteenth century. Extensive research by Sanderson (1972), however, suggested that universities were responding rather well to the needs of industry by the early twentieth century, yet the problem did not go away. A succession of investigations, such as the Finniston Committee (1980), continued to produce further evidence of its longevity.

Even more concerning is the low proportion of British employees with qualifications. Extensive analyses by Prais (1988) found the output of skilled manpower in the UK lower at all levels except doctorates relative to France and Germany, with the greatest differences being in trade qualifications (see chapter 5 above). Broadberry (1997c: 111) provides data on the collapse of apprenticeship from 1964 to 1989. As noted earlier, the issue as to whether these patterns came about because of failings on the supply side (producing skills) or the demand side (wanting them) remains an open one. British companies were reluctant to train employees for fear of losing them in the competitive labour market to rival companies, but this led to general shortages of labour 'with five years of experience' even in times of high unemployment.

Publications

As a guide to the underlying strength of technology, the growth of the science base is an obvious pointer. Figure 12.3 gives data on the numbers of scientific papers and citations thereto, using data from the Science Citations Index for 1981–2000. The UK figures are expressed as percentages of the (1990) OECD totals. Despite the global spread of science the UK shares of both papers and citations remain at respectably high levels. The share of uncited papers – i.e. supposedly less significant publications – is lower than either papers or citations, though it does rise, possibly because of pressures to 'publish or perish'.

Overall, the data on publications when compared to the material covered above appear to indicate a much healthier state of British science than of British technology throughout the periods for which we have reasonable data. A government report in 1997 showed the UK carrying out 5.5 per cent of the total world's research effort, producing 8.0 per cent of the world's scientific publications and 9.1 per cent of all citations (May 1997; Diederen *et al.* 1999). The Office of Science and Technology thus showed a high 'productivity' of British science in terms of papers per amount spent on science, although it can be doubted whether like was being compared with like. Even if valid, to many this simply reflected the low amounts spent in the denominator rather than the high outputs achieved in the numerator of the productivity calculation (Georghiou 2001). The data do at the same time make the government attempts in the 1980s and early 1990s to blame universities rather than industry for Britain's economic woes implausible, as will be further argued below.

Figure 12.3 Scientific papers and citations for UK publications, as % of OECD totals, 1981–2000

Source: See text.

The universities for their part represented about 60 per cent of total government expenditure on civilian R&D by the early 1990s. For them, the main problem faced was how to deal with a gradual erosion of government sources of funding, whose usual strategy was 'selectivity', though this meant different things to different funding streams at different times. From the late 1960s the Research Councils tended to think of selectivity as concentration in particular areas of research or in particular laboratories or departments, implying a controversial tendency to concentrate in large and well-established departments, especially in the 'golden triangle' of Oxford, Cambridge and London. A different view was held by what was long entitled the University Grants Committee, which in the 1970s and 1980s developed formulae which weighted teaching numbers, Research Council and other income, and research 'excellence'. This led to the Research Assessment Exercises (RAEs) on a four- or five-year basis from the mid-1980s. By the beginning of the twenty-first century these had become discredited to the extent that, while they appeared to show marked improvement in research 'excellence' over time, governments refused to match this by increased funding (a situation which is under review at the time of writing). Moreover, the RAEs innately favoured pure basic research, directly contradicting government hopes for greater industrial 'relevance'.

By the 1980s research funding had reached a stage which John Ziman captured in the title of the report, *Science in a 'Steady State'* (1987). The report contrasted the sustained growth in science funding of preceding decades with the levelling off of the 1980s, which Ziman considered would continue. At the same time the need for science showed no sign of levelling off, and the costs of undertaking science were also on the rise. How could this situation be squared? Industry and government implored academia to adopt more business-like methods, which was partly

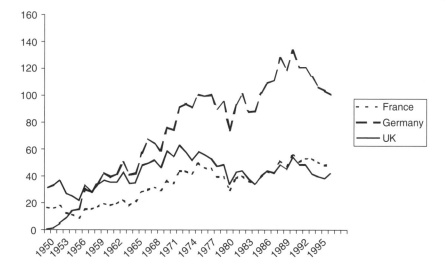

pursued; but to critics within academia this was imposing on them, undoubtedly still in the top echelon by international standards, the methods
of a UK business system that was equally undoubtedly nowhere near the
top echelon.

Patents

Patent figures are regularly, though for reasons given above somewhat
unadvisably, used as a measure of the output of technology. Despite these
reservations, most scholars are prepared to use them to gauge trends
through time, if used with due care. The data here are for patents in
the USA, chosen because it is the largest world market, and because the
standards for granting patents are well recognised. The figures are divided
by population, though in fact the populations of the three countries
included in Figure 12.4 are quite similar (the USA itself is not calculated
here because it is the home country and therefore likely to take out a
disproportionately large number of patents).

It can be seen that Germany shows a sustained increase almost
throughout, reaching its peak just before German reunification in 1990.
Having overtaken the UK in the late 1950s, at its peak the German level
was about two and a half times that of the UK. France shows a slower
rate of increase but still caught the UK by the early 1980s and rose somewhat above in the early 1990s. The UK instead shows only a very slow
trend increase, reaching its peak in the early 1970s. All of these patterns are in fact dwarfed by Japan, not shown here, which had dramatic
rates of growth of US patenting over these years. Relative to other advanced countries apart from the USA, UK patenting was declining in most

Figure 12.4 US
patents per million
population, for UK,
France and Germany,
1950–1995

Sources: US
Department of
Commerce, Patent and
Trademark Office,
1978, *Technology
Assessment and
Forecast*, Washington;
SPRU, 'Megatech'
database.

Table 12.1 Distribution of types of innovation in five countries 1953/73, % per country					
	UK	USA	France	Germany	Japan
Improvement of existing technology	4	41	12	36	38
Major technological advance	40	31	65	50	54
Radical breakthrough	56	27	24	14	8
No. of innovations covered	*45*	*237*	*17*	*22*	*26*

Source: Quoted in Pavitt (1981: 97).

periods from the 1880s onwards (when the data begin), except for the period between the two World Wars (Pavitt 1980: 38–44).

Productivity and growth

It is difficult not to come away with the impression that British technology underperformed during the later years of the twentieth century. All the referenced measures of 'technology' show Britain at best treading water while most of its leading rivals were swimming ahead. On the other hand, science – and indeed technology activities in higher education – continued to fare rather well by international standards, confirming the widespread impression that Britain was ineffectual at turning its science into industrial use.

A related proposition is that Britain was better at radical breakthroughs than persistent improvement. A study by the US National Science Foundation of 500 innovations between 1953 and 1973 appears to confirm this view. Table 12.1 gives percentages of the totals in the bottom row in each of these three categories, for 347 classified innovations; though no guarantee can be given that the data are representative.

This has been an area of contention for many years, dating back at least to the 'second industrial revolution' of the later nineteenth century. Economic historians contend that UK R&D was failing to deliver even in the post-war 'golden years' (Crafts and Toniolo 1996; for a contrary view see Edgerton 1996a). We need to widen the study to see how much all of this may have mattered.

It seems highly likely that the growth performance of the British economy since the Second World War has been shaped strongly by performance in technology, but there are many problems with identifying just how much. Spurts and setbacks in productivity growth show little correspondence with those in technology indicators. Across UK industries in the 1960s there was a weak positive association between R&D intensity and productivity growth, which, however, could largely be explained by both being influenced by output growth (Taylor and Silberston 1973: 66–78). Furthermore, Williams (1967) long ago showed that R&D intensities across some major countries were *inversely* related to their pace of development, so countries with relatively high R&D had slower rates of growth. Several factors probably explain this, but the main one is the 'diminishing returns' to additional R&D already noted – getting faster growth as GDP rises becomes more and more costly in terms of the R&D necessitated. Therefore both time-series and cross-sectional data appear to rule out crude 'growth accounting' exercises as ways of evaluating the contribution of technology.

Despite such difficulties, technology and its diffusion has been seen throughout as crucial to Britain's competitiveness, which in turn is usually proxied by productivity. Immediately following the Second World War, studies showed backwardness compared with US productivity (surveyed by Broadberry 1997c). 'Total factor productivity' (TFP) undoubtedly drives economic growth and welfare, but it should not be equated with technology, even as an approximation. The presumed association between the productivity gap on the one hand and backwardness in science and technology was never really proved and indeed often doubted (Allen 1979; Edgerton 1996a).

The pattern appeared to be rather one of brilliant science but poor exploitation by industry (Saul 1979). By and large, the productivity gap was in any event treated by British governments as a macro and not a micro problem, unlike in some of its main rivals (Shonfield 1965). This left productivity and growth performance wide open to the vagaries of macroeconomic disturbances.

While there is considerable doubt about the link between technology and growth, there is more evidence to support a link between technology and exports, at least at the industry level. A variety of analyses emanating from both innovation studies (e.g. Patel and Pavitt 1989; Cantwell and Hodson 1991) and economics (e.g. Hughes 1986; Greenhalgh 1990, 1994) demonstrated this association between sectors of comparative advantage in international trade and those in technology. This suggests the need to explore more deeply at the 'meso' level of particular technologies and particular industries.

THE RISE OF THE 'KNOWLEDGE-BASED ECONOMY'

As has already been observed, economic theorists refocused their attention somewhat from physical capital to intangible and human capital in the later years of the twentieth century. The data for the EU and for the OECD countries as a whole reflect this shift of emphasis: the ratio of physical capital relative to GDP trended upwards to about 1970 followed by a declining trend thereafter, albeit with some subsequent upsurges, while the ratio of R&D to GDP rose from the late 1970s (von Tunzelmann and Efendioglu 2001). It appears that the issue for the advanced industrial countries shifted from being one of 'more' machinery and equipment to one of 'better' machinery and equipment. It also needs emphasising that tangible and intangible capital are not just substitutes but that there are positive causal links between them in both directions (Pavitt 1980).

This relative shift from physical investment to investment in intangibles, and especially 'knowledge', is critical to interpreting the contribution of technology to growth in the second half of the twentieth century. It is evident that much of the growth in R&D intensity for the OECD countries as a whole in the 1980s is accounted for by electronics-related industries; however, Britain participated to only a limited extent in this rise of R&D related to electronics. Early attempts to stay in the race towards information and communication technologies (ICTs) soon foundered in both the private and the public sectors.

The consequences of the ICT 'revolution' for economic growth are widely regarded as rather paradoxical. Across the Western industrial countries the switch to ICTs as the new 'technoeconomic paradigm' (Freeman and Louçã 2001) at the heart of the 'third industrial revolution' appeared to coincide with a productivity 'slowdown'.

Various explanations were advanced as to why the payoff to ICTs should have been seemingly so weak, at least initially. From a historical point of view, however, there was nothing particularly paradoxical about what was happening in this early phase of the alleged 'third industrial revolution' in the last quarter of the twentieth century – the same had happened in earlier industrial revolutions (von Tunzelmann 2000). The initial period involves relatively costly outlays on technological development, especially on account of the high uncertainty about which directions to pursue. These costs tend to rise faster than output, thus leading to diminishing returns to 'R&D' (broadly defined) as opposed to the increasing returns promised by the 'new growth theory'. Subsequently these advances spread not just in their source areas but also over a much broadened range of production and consumption activities. At this stage the new technologies become 'pervasive'. In the terminology of a recent perspective, these radical advances may become 'general purpose technologies' (Helpman 1998). Robson et al. (1988) found a pattern of concentrated production of technologies but widening sectors of application from 1945 to 1983, using innovation data for the UK.

In contrast with the supposed 'productivity slowdown', the UK experienced its only significant period of faster productivity growth in manufacturing relative to Germany and the USA in the twentieth century (Broadberry 1997c), notwithstanding its comparatively poor showing in ICTs. Britain bypassed the rising costs of the new technologies by running down its domestic sourcing of ICTs and importing both the equipment and the technological knowhow. Thus in the 1980s British R&D and patenting continued to decline by international standards but its productivity growth was among the highest (Walker 1993; Broadberry 1997c). Wakelin (2001) found R&D intensity was significant for productivity growth only in the innovation-*using* sectors. But, in the long term, commercial expansion is difficult to sustain without technological underpinnings.

These patterns had significant consequences for welfare as well as for growth. The period of 'productivity slowdown' was also a period of widening inequalities in earnings. The most popular explanation for this era of greater inequality – which reversed half a century of progress towards greater equality up to the 1960s – is 'skill-biased technological change'. In this view, only the favoured few blessed with the appropriate skills of computer literacy were able to benefit from the new technological opportunities of the 1970s and 1980s; only with the widening of access and lowering of skill entry barriers in the 1990s and after could greater numbers hope to be rewarded. More recently, scholars have suggested that even command of ICTs is not sufficient to benefit from new technology; organisational change also has to be implemented alongside technical change (Caroli and van Reenen 2001).

Other causes have been advanced to explain the growth of earnings inequality in the last quarter of the twentieth century (Wood 1994). There is no space to deal with them here, except to state that in the long run over historical epochs, it is conceivable that many of these other factors are also interlinked with new technologies.

PUBLIC SECTOR R&D

The legacy of the Second World War was the envisaging of technology as primarily the responsibility of the public sector, especially in regard to 'Big Science'. With governments for long congregating close to the centre of the political spectrum, there was little disagreement about the public sector role. Moreover, technology was regarded in a generally favourable light by the public at large, with reservations about the military arena. This enthusiasm probably reached its peak in the time of Harold Wilson's Labour government, which came to power in 1964 after Wilson had made a widely reported speech about the 'white heat of the technological revolution' in 1963 (Edgerton 1996b). The organisational implications will be discussed below, but here we may note how technology, especially in the form of new processes, was construed as being part of a world advancing through a macro-level combination of Keynesian rationalism in economic policy, partnership in governance with both industry and trade unions (e.g. through the National Economic Development Council) and mass education (Buxton *et al.* 1998: 500–1). These macro-level perspectives were met at the meso level by an emphasis on the manufacturing sector (especially through exports), and at the micro level by the perceived virtues of scale economies especially through the creation of 'national champions' in selected industries.

In practice the Wilson government failed to bring this system together. The high hopes vested in the establishment of a specialist Ministry of Technology – for the only time in British history – were dashed by a combination of adverse macroeconomic conditions and political infighting. Even had the political strategy for technology succeeded, it would have been losing touch with the transition of the 1970s to new technologies, new modes of governance, and new circumstances of global competition and collaboration. The main thrust of policy in the 1970s became propping up old industries based on industrial concentration and high capital intensity. Attempts were made to construct forward-looking policies, especially in relation to microelectronics in the late 1970s and early 1980s, but these failed to incite sufficient momentum to match what was then happening in California or Japan.

The factors that were driving the technology itself were thus shifting from scaling up to scaling down, e.g. into more and more densely packed microelectronic circuits. The new UK policy agenda for the 1980s encouraging deregulation, privatisation and 'enterprise' captured part of this shift of emphasis, if inadvertently. This was justified as representing 'working with the grain of market forces . . . [assisting firms] without weakening their commercial responsibility for their own actions' (Barber and White 1987: 26), and as evidently preferable to working against the grain of market forces as in the 'lame ducks' strategies of the 1970s.

Less charitably, it represented policy by default and left the key positive aspects of a technology strategy out of the system. Despite a similar pro-business, anti-regulation governmental stance both in the USA and in the UK during the 1980s, the former saw a much more concerted effort towards new policy stances in which government proactively supported new technologies, their commercialisation and their diffusion (Branscomb and Keller 1998). In effect, there opened up a large gap between the rhetoric of 'hands off' and the reality of 'hands on' in US industrial policy. Much of the latter was directed at small businesses, local environments and universities, amounting to a major subsidisation of the activities of such groups. In the UK, the reality was constricted to meet the rhetoric. R&D by government departments was reined in, most substantially in the Department of Trade and Industry (DTI). Government support for industry was not only greatly reduced, it was displaced into consultancy activities in the second half of the 1980s. While some of this may have had positive value, it was chiefly driven by fear of government meddling in the affairs of business and an express attempt to shift out of commercial activities, together with the efforts to cut government spending in the large. Any government money for these purposes had to be justified on grounds of 'market failure' (the market sector would not do such things unaided), 'additionality' (government money could not simply replace private expenditures), and especially the criterion of consisting of 'pre-commercialisation' research. The latter could scarcely have been more different from what was happening – in reality if not in rhetoric – across the Atlantic.

Some useful programmes were developed in the UK under these auspices, the most noteworthy perhaps being the DTI's LINK programme to support industry–university partnerships in a number of defined areas, begun in 1986 and still actively pursued. However, the larger-scale programmes aimed at these laudable objectives, begun in the early Thatcher years – most notably the Alvey programme in IT (1981) and the Joint Opto-Electronics Research Scheme (1982) – were effectively wound up in the second half of the 1980s. On the other hand, then, the emerging need for taking technologies downstream from the research stage to the point of commercialisation and diffusion was hardly touched upon in the change of policy direction; indeed the policy reorientation went precisely the other way. Again the situation could not have been more different from what was actually taking place in the USA.

Technology policy had reached an impasse from the mid-1980s. The retreat from government involvement in any 'near-market' technological development was directly contrary to the shift in the phasing of emerging technologies described throughout this chapter, as well as to the prevailing view that the UK was good at invention but poor at commercialisation. We need to put this in a broader context.

Mission vs diffusion orientation

National technology strategies can be categorised as 'mission-oriented' or else 'diffusion-oriented', depending in the first instance on whether the primary emphasis was placed on the generation of technology or on its use. 'Mission-oriented research can be described as big science deployed to meet big problems' (Ergas 1987: 53). Typically, government funding would go predominantly into a select few highly concentrated projects chosen as 'missions' on a number of grounds. Implicit in this was the 'linear model' noted above, of big science feeding through to dramatic technological breakthroughs, and ultimately into international strategic leadership. Among the advanced industrial countries, Ergas nominated the USA, UK and France as the clearest examples of mission-orientation; contrasting with examples of diffusion-oriented countries like Germany, Switzerland or Sweden, with their profusion of technology transfer institutions and a decentralisation of decision making. Ergas accepted that each country he classified had programmes not fitting this simple division (for the UK, see, for example, White 1981), but overall there was a reasonably clear demarcation in the statistics of government funding of R&D: the diffusion-oriented gave relatively more to medium- and low-tech industries (see Table 12.2).

Ergas concluded from his studies that diffusion-oriented strategies were more effective and less costly than the mission-oriented; moreover, among the three mission-oriented countries the UK had fared worst from

Table 12.2 Share of industries in government R&D funding, 1980			
	High-tech	Medium-tech	Low-tech	Defence[a]
UK	95	3	2	49
USA	88	8	4	54
France	91	7	2	39
Germany	67	23	10	9
Sweden	71	20	9	15

Notes: [a] =1981.
OECD definitions of technology levels of industries.

Source: Ergas (1987: 54).

its mission-orientation. He attributed this to political-cultural factors: tangled decision-making processes, the formation of cosy clubs with suppliers, and the reluctance to include penalty clauses in contracts. By comparison, the mission focus in the USA led into much more dissemination, because of the larger scale of operations, the insistence on second-sourcing, and the greater provision of information even in defence work.

In a celebrated paper, the economist David Henderson (1977) called attention to the failure of big projects in the UK, referring specifically to the Advanced Gas-Cooled Reactor (AGR) in nuclear power and the Concorde aircraft. Both undoubtedly fell into the category of being mission-oriented projects, intended to gain international strategic and commercial leadership through the deployment of high technology. Like Ergas, Henderson related this primarily to obsessive governmental secrecy and lack of independent evaluation. While subsequent governments drew the inference that the state should keep out of commercial technological activities, the real message was perhaps that governments should be very careful in leading from the front through large missions – the diffusion-oriented governmental strategies in countries like Germany were arguably more 'commercial' than these, but rather successful. The subtlety of this distinction was unfortunately lost in the 1980s.

For a variety of reasons, perhaps as much fortuitous as intentional, UK policy in the 1980s in any case shifted away from the mission-orientation model and towards the diffusion-orientation model. A similar process was at work in the USA (less so in France), though, as already pointed out, the reorientation towards 'diffusion' was much more proactive in the USA, and far better resourced. Indeed the diffusion arm of UK government technological development somewhat contracted in the 1980s, in part through partial or full privatisation of former government laboratories. Devolution of political responsibilities to Scotland and Wales went with a more positive attitude in these regions in later years.

There had long been some intention that government research ought to be able to pay part of its way through commercialisation. Under the Wilson Labour government in 1967 and the temporary regime of the Ministry of Technology, government establishments facing reductions in the government's own demand for technology were permitted to contract for private work. The principle became enshrined in the Rothschild Report in 1971, which formalised the 'customer–contractor' principle for public sector R&D, whereby government or other public sector laboratories sought contracts with various ministries (or industry) acting as 'customers' for the item of research. For wider application in scientific research the notion of 'customer–contractor' was flawed in principle in assuming that the questions to be resolved were known *a priori* (Cunningham *et al.* 1998), a point made by Rothschild himself in his report. In practice very little money was earned back directly by government labs for their commercial activities. As noted below, the major social benefits of public sector research really accrue outside of commercial returns, yet questions of financial pay-offs continued to haunt governments even in the sphere of their military research.

Military R&D

It is no coincidence that the three Western countries most identified with 'mission-oriented' R&D programmes were also those most identified with expenditure on defence. Military R&D continued to be a giant arena for playing out all the themes associated with the country's R&D performance more generally. In 1955 as much as 63 per cent of total estimated R&D in the UK was spent on defence (Saul 1979: 125). From the late 1960s defence accounted for about half the total UK government expenditure on R&D, and even though it fell by a quarter in the early 1990s as a result of the ending of the Cold War it was still 36 per cent of the total in 1997–8 (Georghiou 2001). As already noted, the figures for R&D in the defence area were over-inflated for most of this period by the inclusion of much 'downstream' development and technology demonstrator programmes that fell beyond the Frascati definition of R&D, and indeed some of the reduction in the 1990s represented a cutback in this element of exaggeration in the published figures.

Two main issues dominated discussions of the role of military R&D. One was the arms race concept, which generated huge 'overkill' in the provision of systems in the efforts to maintain both response and strike capability. Opinions differ as to how far this oversupply of weapons of mass destruction itself helped prevent any actual recourse to their use, but this topic is too consequential for us to ponder on here.

From the economic and technological perspective this in turn raised a second issue. Military technology was, in the phrase of Mary Kaldor (1982), 'baroque'. It was baroque firstly in the sense that it was (over-) ornate – there were repeated allegations of 'gold-plating' and excessively wasteful flourishes in the products. It was baroque secondly, and more importantly, in the sense of being old-fashioned. Weaponry and the associated military technology are developed most rapidly under actual war-time conditions. Following a period of peace, the technology is almost invariably found to be inadequate when war breaks out again; partly because the military strategies and contexts change, partly because of the lack of practical testing under 'real' war conditions. This is even more intense for new equipment – the high-tech weaponry deployed in the battles in the Middle East and former Yugoslavia in the 1990s revealed a poor performance by the allegedly 'smartest' missiles and bombs.

The implication of both of these 'baroque' characteristics is that commercial opportunities for exploiting military technology in civilian markets tend to decline. Military and related mission-oriented conditions are often effective in launching new technologies, as was shown by integrated circuits during the 'space race', but competitive civilian markets generally catch up and overtake rapidly. Thus although military R&D turned its attention to civilian applications ('dual use') in the 1990s after the cessation of the Cold War, it found that it was now lagging well behind the level of technological achievement displayed in many of those civilian markets it was attempting to enter. Moreover, the lack of cost efficiency barred it from competing on price as well as quality grounds.

Like university research, military R&D therefore fell prey to government demands for 'value for money'. Schemes to increase spillovers into commercial use from 1985, however, achieved little and were steadily abandoned. The non-nuclear research was reorganised into the Defence Research Agency in 1991 (later DERA), and plans were drawn up for privatising much of it. However, the brief history of privatisation as at the time of writing indicates continuing problems with commercial success, notwithstanding the undoubted technical excellence of much of the research work.

Regulation

Issues of competitiveness and anti-interventionism equally permeated the other main role of government in relation to technology, that of regulation. New technologies are inherently risky, and the scale of many of the technologies being developed in this era posed risks for the community at large as well as for their originators. According to one line of thinking, the world had become a 'risk society' by the end of the twentieth century (Beck 1992), though whether this factor had really risen over the period is more contentious. Politicians were faced with a conflict between the desires of the public at large for greater regulation and industry's desires to be left to get on with it, and on the whole the latter better suited the attitude of 'hands off'.

Market mechanisms for regulation such as 'emissions trading' and fiscal disincentives achieved relatively little; direct standards setting and direct controls predominated. One of the most problematic areas was that of energy. In London in the early 1950s, severe 'smogs' arising because of the lack of dispersal of smoke led to many premature deaths. The blame was placed on industrial chimneys, and legislation to enforce 'tall chimneys' appeared to have a remarkable beneficial impact. In later years attention shifted to national and international concerns, first from 'acid rain' and later from 'climate change'. The UK's performance in meeting targets for reduced emissions was reasonable, even if as much because of independent changes in the fuel base and generating technologies as through any direct intervention.

No fuel was, however, completely 'green', and uncomfortable compromises sometimes had to be made. Nuclear power was favoured on grounds of being a low emitter of acids and carbon, but problems of nuclear waste disposal and 'back-end' costs of decommissioning old plants meant that the energy source that was intended to be 'too cheap to meter' failed to match the degree of cost reduction achieved by some of the alternatives. Fears also mounted of the vulnerability of nuclear reactors to explosion, in the wake of the Chernobyl disaster in the Ukraine in 1986 and of acts of 'terrorism'. Safety on this score could be enhanced by increasing the levels of 'containment', e.g. building thicker outside walls, but this too drove up the costs of constructing the plants. With rising public concern, by the 1980s each suggested new reactor was made the subject of a public inquiry, which raised costs still further and generally failed to arrive at any defensible conclusion. However, this did mark a change in the nature of decision making over technology.

Public faith in the autonomy of science was shaken by a series of scandals which did little to alleviate growing anxieties. A number of the best-known revolved around food, as a matter which affected all consumers. Scares over such everyday items of consumption as eggs (food poisoning from salmonella), milk (administering BST to cattle) and beef (large outbreaks of BSE and foot-and-mouth disease) fuelled public concern that scientists were either wrong-headed or incompetent, and it was the public who suffered. The problem lay to a large extent in the structure of policy making, in which the Ministry of Agriculture, Fisheries and Food (MAFF) was required to act on behalf of both producers and consumers. In a climate of civil service secrecy, constrained by the extraordinary scope of the Official Secrets Act in the UK, this led to repeated attempts to stifle information in order to protect producers, with outcomes that were often much more disastrous than the original problem. Although excessive regulation was seen as endangering the competitiveness of British industry, the power to protect consumers never became as great as in, say, US environmental regulation.

Such ineffective activity was of long standing. In agricultural pesticides, a number of deaths of agricultural workers reported shortly after the Second World War led to enquiries and eventually the Pesticides Safety Precautions Scheme, 1957 (Gillespie 1979). The voluntary and pragmatic basis of the standards imposed meant little real impact from any 'interference'. Cosy co-operative relationships developed between regulator (MAFF) and those being regulated (the suppliers and farmers). Within MAFF, the same laboratory was responsible for investigating safety as for disseminating the latest technology (Gillespie 1979: 210). Reports by the relevant Advisory Committee all tended towards public reassurance and self-justification – there was no independent evaluation.

In the area of genetic modification (GM), science was seen as more directly to blame. European consumers, including the British, rebelled against what they saw as an attempt to foist 'Frankenstein foods' on them without due warning, for which the scientists were held responsible. Again the regulatory system was deficient: despite an impressively early start to regulation in the UK (the GM Advisory Group, 1977, with a statutory requirement to report on all experiments), discussion was limited to an elite of molecular biologists, and many of the key issues surrounding risk were never adequately taken up (Yoxen 1979). All these examples point to the problems that followed from lack of provision of information, coupled with a lack of good governance to cope with its consequences.

International influences

As an indication of the growing internationalisation of economic activity, the UK accepted a wider international role in relation to technology, particularly from the 1980s. To fill the void created by the sharp decline of domestic firms in high-tech and medium-tech areas, inward foreign direct investment (FDI) was strongly encouraged and in many cases partially subsidised, to supply the deficiencies in technology, production processes and especially management. Reflecting the changing pattern of global activity, the sources of FDI broadened to include Japan and Korea as well as the more traditional western Europe and especially North America. However, outward FDI greatly exceeded inward FDI from 1979, so the net advantage is debatable; moreover, there were signs in the 1990s that the UK's perceived attractions of an active market for corporate control, comparatively low hourly labour costs and the English language were becoming less potent.

There were also more aggressive, as well as these somewhat defensive, lines of action. Most important here was the shift of focus in research and some areas of technology to Europe. Despite a somewhat ambivalent attitude of many UK governments to too close relationships with western Europe, new possibilities opened up by the European Economic Community (EEC) and its subsequent formats (now the European Union) were strategically seized upon.

Two areas stood out in this process. One was the involvement of British research scientists and particularly university-based scientists in 'pre-competitive' research, most extensively through the 'Framework Programmes' which began in 1984, spearheaded by the European Commission's ESPRIT programme for information technology. UK scientists were the largest of any national group represented in the First Framework Programme and continued to be strongly represented in its successors, despite some belief that other countries were more politically favoured. The second major area for European involvement by the UK was in aerospace. Despite the failure of the Concorde supersonic aircraft in narrowly economic terms, its Franco-British structure paved the way for more successful co-operation subsequently, most notably the Airbus family of jet aircraft. Similar collaboration arose in military aircraft and in the arena of space, where Britain shifted the locus of much of its activity to the European Space Agency, though it pulled out of the rocketry itself which in Europe came to be dominated by the French. Again, EU-based programmes such as EUREKA (1985) played a key role in fostering co-operation in technological development in such fields.

UK government attitudes were somewhat mixed. Intergovernmental collaboration on the part of the UK government was inspired by: (a) financial considerations (cost sharing in expensive fields like basic physics); (b) political factors (the rather pragmatic approach of UK scientists to European collaboration); (c) organisational issues (e.g. the absence for most of the period of any central ministry of science, unlike in many continental countries). But unlike most of Europe, the UK government insisted on the European spends coming out of existing budgets, so that the domestic spend of the government department in question would be reduced pro rata for any EU increase. Despite this evident discouragement, the EU spend did rise.

Contribution of public sector research to the economy

A view that spread widely in the 1980s, not least within government, was that public sector research 'crowded out' more desirable private sector research, as any government spending was alleged to do to private investment. In the R&D sphere it is important to distinguish between the impact of defence and of civilian R&D, since different schools of criticism are involved (Edgerton 1996a: 44). The attack on defence research followed from the points made above about its limitations. One view was that the 'crowding out' in the defence area was exercised less in money terms than in human resources, diverting scarce scientists and engineers from more productive employment in commercial activities (Peck 1968; Nicholson *et al.* 1991: 89). Neoliberal critics instead attacked state-funded civilian R&D as inherently non-commercial and a waste of taxpayers' resources (Kealey 1995). This proposition led to an acrid debate in the 1990s (David 1997; Kealey 1998). More detailed time-series analysis across all OECD countries drew the opposite conclusion to Kealey – that for nearly all of them there was probably a positive relationship between BERD and GOVERD, despite the inclusion of defence in the latter (for a survey, see David *et al.* 2000). There is little support for the notion of rising government R&D 'causing' a consequent fall in private R&D. The dramatic cutbacks in government R&D in the UK in the 1980s failed to elicit any noteworthy rise in overall BERD, other than through privatising public research institutions. It seems likely that the problem here was under-commitment by the private sector to R&D, together with an under-commitment by government to higher education.

There have been many attempts to measure the social rate of return from public sector research, most frequently in relation to agriculture where most of the R&D is actually carried out in the public sector. Typically the estimated rates of return are in the range of 30–40 per cent (Nicholson *et al.* 1991: ch. 7; SPRU 1996), far above the returns to physical investment, indicating that existing levels of public sector research fall well short of fully overcoming 'market failures'.

It may well be that these estimated returns, despite their consistency across many studies and several countries, are overstated, because the benefits are exaggerated or the costs are under-estimated (or both). Nevertheless, these outcomes are almost certainly too low, inasmuch as they aim to calculate the direct benefits in terms of new products and processes. According to surveys conducted at SPRU (1996; Salter and Martin 2001), much larger benefits to the private sector accrue from indirect gains. Probably the greatest of all the spillover benefits comes from training students to graduate levels, i.e. through the human capital formation in research capability, especially in a country like the UK which has a poor track record for training offered in the private sector. Aside from what these students learn directly, academic standing also permits engagement through international networks with foreign researchers, and thus opens up a much broader base of access to world-wide R&D activities at the scientific frontier.

It seems evident that the concerted attempts by a number of post-war governments to wind down technological research in the public sector are hard to applaud on economic grounds, quite apart from with regard to satisfying any scientific curiosity. But we need to consider also the counterpart in private sector research.

THE PRIVATE SECTOR

Determinants of private sector technology accumulation

The dominant popular image of technical breakthroughs was personified as the isolated tinkerer or 'boffin', even at the end of the twentieth century through such figures as Trevor Bayliss and his clockwork radio or James Dyson and his cyclonic vacuum cleaner. The reality was that the great preponderance of innovation had moved from the individual to the corporation in the course of the second and third industrial revolutions. Pursuing this line, American economic and business historians have contended that the UK's dilatoriness in copying modern corporate forms of organisation from the USA can account for the persistent weakness in its technology development in business. In particular the UK persevered too long with 'personal capitalism' at the expense of developing the 'multi-divisional' (M-form) corporate structure, in which diversified companies were organised into divisions each oriented to a specific line of business (Mowery 1986; Chandler 1990). Supporting this view is the observation that the UK fared better in industries characterised by well-managed giant firms based (at least partly) in the country, like Shell and BP in petroleum. However, the same authors have elsewhere found fault with the M-form as a means for developing new technologies, for instance because the boundaries between divisions restricted spillovers among them within a particular corporation. The M-form, at least in its pure guise, has been dissolving in the face of challenges from radical new technologies like ICTs.

More popular among British scholars has been the view that the kind of capitalism embraced in the UK over-stressed finance at the cost of technology. The need to meet financial goals imposed by a combination of accountant directors, shareholders and stock markets is said to have brought about excessive 'short-termism'. Technological accumulation inherently requires taking a long-term view, and uncertain and distant returns from exploring technological possibilities are tempting to sacrifice when immediate financial targets need to be attained. As noted below there are some important exceptions to this pattern, but equally clear is the record of companies like the General Electric Company (GEC) under Lord Weinstock for accumulating monetary reserves rather than developing new high-tech avenues. Even more inhibiting was the dominance of the 'market for corporate control' which led to aggressive takeovers and subsequent 'asset-stripping' in the form of disposing of research capabilities – the record of the Hanson Trust in eliminating patenting from the companies it acquired being a truly woeful example. Evidence to support the prevalence of short-termism in British industry has been supplied by Miles (1993).

Why such factors should have been especially potent in the UK – if indeed they were – is less clear. Lack of resources to carry out R&D does not seem to be an explanation – in the period when the UK fell behind, from 1979 to 1989, profits in British industry rose 44 per cent, dividends 73 per cent (Buxton *et al.* 1998: 511). The determinants of technology accumulation have been listed as a combination of opportunity, appropriability, cumulativeness and the knowledge base (Malerba and Orsenigo 1997, 2000). The first of these, opportunity, spans market opportunity alongside the kinds of technological opportunity (e.g. in new breakthroughs) noted previously. One view is that post-war Britain withdrew into largely captive but slow-growing home plus Commonwealth markets, for instance in vehicles, rather than confronting global competition; with these failing to exercise enough pressure to change, even they were lost to the global rivals in due course (Walker 1980; Owen 1999). On the other hand, the stability of 'organised' markets in relevant areas in the UK, such as that provided by the National Health Service, has been considered as one explanation for the relative technological strength of the British pharmaceuticals industry. But these organised markets were too few and too often under threat themselves.

Appropriability refers here to the ability to leverage returns out of technological advances or R&D. Patents, trademarks and copyright constitute the most evident form of 'intellectual property rights' (IPRs), but not necessarily the most important in actual industrial practice. Patents are, however, of overwhelming importance in the pharmaceuticals industry and to some extent in other chemicals branches, because it is straightforward to describe a new chemical entity in very precise form, whereas it is frequently comparatively easy to 'invent around' a patent in a field such as electronics. This suggests a second explanation for the very different pattern of British pharmaceuticals, when linked with stock market readiness to finance expansion when the future seemed well secured by patent rights. The equal and opposite reaction of financial markets in other sectors, where appropriability was so much harder to guarantee, may have underlain their converse fortunes.

Most attention has been paid to the consequences of the third factor – cumulativeness. There has been a long debate as to whether large and concentrated firms give rise to more innovation or not, or to incremental rather than radical innovation. Kamien and Schwartz (1982) established conclusively that the answer could be very different for large size and for high concentration, even though one would expect *a priori* that large firms would be found in concentrated industries. The general consensus is that, in terms of size, both small firms and large firms had advantages for innovation though of different kinds – small firms gained from organisational flexibility while large firms gained from cost economies (Rothwell 1995). R&D data are of limited use here since they are known to underestimate very seriously the amount of technological accumulation in small firms. The data on innovations for the UK 1945–84 from the SPRU database appear to confirm a proper U-shaped relationship, with both small and large firms more strongly represented relative to middle sizes (Pavitt *et al.* 1987; but see Tether *et al.* 1997). Other indicators, like patents, however, have been used to tell a different story. Moreover, when it comes to concentration the consensus is the opposite – medium firms gain from being neither too powerless (as small firms are) nor too complacent (as monopolies are), so the relationship is an inverted U. However, the empirical data generate very confused results (see Table 12.3).

Measured R&D is evidently more concentrated than either innovations or patenting. With more detailed data available in the late 1990s, the top 3 pharmaceutical companies were found to account for one quarter of total BERD and the top 20 companies of all kinds for two-thirds of it (Georghiou 2001). Over time the extent of this concentration has fallen, with the share of the top 100 companies dropping from 91 per cent in 1978 to 71 per cent by 1994 and their share of government funding falling from 99 per cent to 79 per cent over the same years (Buxton *et al.* 1998: 176), as small firms have come to play a larger role in the economy, and as sectoral shifts have diversified the location of innovative activities (see below). Unfortunately, our data on technological accumulation in small firms remain meagre.

This association of concentration with R&D should not be taken to imply that greater concentration will aid R&D, or innovation more generally. Such thinking was the most powerful driver of government policy under the Wilson government of the 1960s, via the Industrial Reorganisation Corporation (IRC) (Mottershead 1978). So long as intangible investment in R&D is positively linked with tangible investment in physical capital, innovation may come through obtaining scale economies in fixed capital, but as seen above this ceased to be the case from the 1970s. On balance, the concentrations forged out of mergers and takeovers with the assistance of the IRC during the late 1960s, such as GEC or International Computers Ltd (ICL), were not to be great advertisements for using concentration to boost innovation. In fact, industrial R&D fell in their wake (Edgerton 1996a: 36).

Finally, some consideration should be given to the fourth determinant noted by Malerba and colleagues – the type of knowledge base. After 1945 Britain fared rather badly in industries of the second industrial revolution era in which production skills were crucial, such as orthodox motor vehicles (see chapter 3 above). A much better performance was registered in industries like pharmaceuticals where laboratory skills were more significant. Thus a third explanation for the better achievements of pharmaceuticals may derive from the fact that the kinds of skills needed for success in the companies in this field were very similar to what their qualified scientists learned on the lab bench in universities – the transfer of people to the private sector involved relatively little disruption in their modes of working, unlike in the lagging sectors. Another area where Britain often did surprisingly well was in certain niche areas of specialist design, such as racing cars, architecture, offshore oil plant and portable microprocessors. This may perhaps be because organisational hierarchies are unsuited to such fields, and individual initiative is welcomed; again, (mass) production values count for less.

Table 12.3 Concentration of technology efforts in British firms %

Firms with largest share	Share of R&D, 1975	Share of innovations, 1970–9	Share of US patenting, 1969–84
Top 5	40	15	19
Top 10	52	22	26
Top 20	66	32	36
Top 50	83	48	48
Top 100	91	62	58

Source: Patel and Pavitt 1989: 125.

Sectoral composition

So far a number of assertions have been made about changes in the sectoral pattern of technologies without much evidence. A comparative study for 1962 indicated a very similar breakdown by industry for the UK

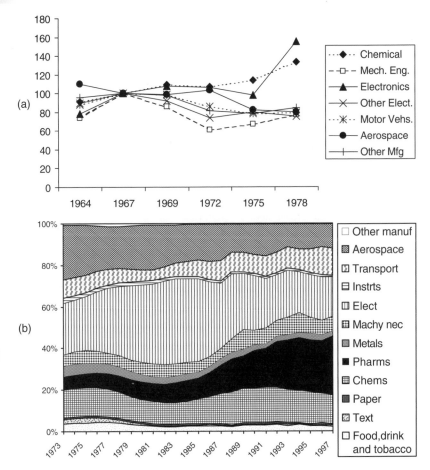

Figure 12.5 Sectoral shares of R&D expenditure in UK, 1964–1978 and 1973–1997

Sources: (a) Pavitt (1981: 93); (b) see text.

as for the USA, not differing greatly from that in France (Freeman and Young 1965). Thereafter, Figure 12.5(a) gives data on the changes in real R&D expenditure by sector in British manufacturing from 1964 to 1978, indexed to 1967 = 100 for each sector. What are usually regarded as high-tech sectors are marked by black shapes. Chemicals and electronics, as expected, showed rises, mostly confined to the final triennium in the case of electronics. Aerospace, however, trends downwards, as do most other sectors after 1967; though aerospace and chemicals are the only sectors that gain relative to other countries between 1967 and 1975 (Pavitt 1981: 94). Patents were also highly concentrated in these industries (Taylor and Silberston 1973: 61–6).

Figure 12.5(b) shows the percentage breakdown of BERD by manufacturing sector for later years, using OECD data instead. Over the years from 1973 to 1997 there are some very strong trends in the composition of UK BERD. The picture is dominated by the share of pharmaceuticals, which rises from under 6 per cent of the UK total in 1973 to over 28 per cent by 1997. There are two major fields that are squeezed out – the share of aerospace in BERD more than halves, while that of electrical and electronic equipment falls by about one quarter. In other west European countries for which the OECD has sectoral data on BERD, lumped together, the sectoral share shows little change over this period.

The British share of the European total therefore rises in pharmaceuticals but falls sharply in some other high-tech areas, like electronics and, even more, instruments. This pattern of BERD is in sharp contrast with data from the same OECD source on production, where the latter shows remarkably little change in the UK's share in European output, whether one is talking about electrical and electronic equipment, aerospace or indeed pharmaceuticals. Why should there be such a dramatic contrast between the marked trends and differences in R&D shares and the relative stability and consistency in production shares?

British electronics companies flourished from the late 1970s but failed to grow to large size on a par with their competitors in the USA or Japan. The relatively slow-growing British companies bifurcated into technically advanced specialists with limited markets, like Acorn (which later resurfaced as ARM in microprocessors), or market traders with little interest in R&D, like Amstrad. UK production activities were increasingly dominated by foreign-owned companies, which either took over the smaller British producers or set up their own manufacturing subsidiaries. The key to technological strength lies in possessing a domestic power base, usually in the form of the headquarters of multinational companies, because such companies do most of their R&D 'at home'. This probably accounts for the much stronger correlation of British technological strengths with British export strengths than with its overall production and growth patterns, as already noted.

However, the figures quoted here exclude R&D in services, which were arguably a stronger area of British comparative advantage, and a slowly rising proportion of total UK R&D. Over the years 1987 to 1995, services accounted for about one quarter of formal measured GERD by industry (Boden 1998), and possibly more if less formal definitions are used. While services continued to draw upon technology developed in the manufacturing sector, such as information technology, in order to propel major changes, manufacturing arguably warranted less special treatment over time as the driving force of economic development.

Interaction of the public and private sectors

It seems reasonable to claim that public involvement in R&D had a number of successes but failed overall through running counter to addressing the widely recognised problem that the UK was good at science and invention but poor at commercial development. As previously pointed out this generalisation has many exceptions, but public policy was not usually the source of those exceptions. Public corporations such as the National Research Development Corporation (NRDC), and its successor the British Technology Group (BTG), were aimed at the development and licensing of inventions, not full-scale commercial development (Johnston and Gummett 1979: 35).

In the commercialisation sphere, public policy to establish and protect firms that could act as 'national champions' often had perverse consequences, as in the long saga of ICL in computers (Stoneman 1976). In Computer-Aided Design (CAD), both the consolidation of the electronics industry in the late 1960s and the government support in the late 1970s to early 1980s mainly benefited American suppliers (Sharp 1985). Direct government efforts to create 'international champions', such as Celltech in biotechnology, deserve some credit, but suffered from a lack of government funding by comparison with their US counterparts and fell well short of expectations. 'Open door' policies of supporting all-comers made the creation of national champions barely possible in North Sea oil supplies, but proximity to the new resources coupled with access to 'international champions' in the oil industry like Shell brought some success (Sharp 1985). Commercially oriented industries were largely ignored in government funding of R&D; for example government supplied under 1 per cent of the motor industry's modest R&D by the early 1970s (Johnston and Gummett 1979: 123). In these and other fields, government thus turned increasingly in the 1980s to foreign direct investment into the country to bail out R&D as well as management and profitability.

Bridging activity between invention and commercialisation was also largely left to the private sector to handle. Even so, the UK had a long history in 'third way' activities. One of the most distinctive characteristics of the British scene was the early formation of research associations (RAs). These were sector-based institutions designed primarily to meet the needs of industries dominated by SMEs, and often though not invariably in industries that were not 'high-tech'. At the outset they were co-financed by government and their industry, beginning with scientific instruments in 1918, and peaking in terms of numbers in the early 1960s (Nicholson *et al.* 1991: ch. 12). Mowery (1986) argued that they failed to stand up to the challenge thrown down by corporate R&D as it was developing in the interwar period in the USA, but others believe that the principle was a valuable one in industries like scientific instruments that were never taken over by large corporations. Japan borrowed the concept with considerable success in its growth spurt after the Second World War, and in the UK itself there was a resurgence of RAs at this time. However, many evolved towards being independent contract research organisations, especially as government funding was wound down following the Rothschild Report, and competed for research contracts along with public sector labs, universities and other private sector organisations. While more competition probably did no harm, key interlinkages of the national system of innovation were being dismantled at the very time they were most called for.

CONCLUSIONS

In this light, the UK 'national system of innovation' fragmented from the 1970s and too little was done to assemble a new system thereafter. Technological performance in Britain from the end of the Second World War to the end of the twentieth century could be described as a 'game of two halves'. In the first half the commitment to spending on technology was strong in both private and public spheres, buoyed up by public support, even though much of the government spending may not have been well directed. In the second half, as public doubts spread, spending fell sharply in the public sector despite a vigorous effort by the higher education segment, and failed to show any overall rise in the private sector, unlike all the country's competitors. The underlying trend in technology development warranted the opposite pattern. The first half was a period in which established technologies were further developed, while in the second half the introduction of dramatic new technologies called for a rise in public spending and a redirection of business spending. In practice the government share in intramural R&D fell from 33 per cent in 1972 to just 12 per cent in 1994 (Sharp 2000), while the private reorientation was limited almost entirely to pharmaceuticals.

There is therefore some justification for taking a positive view of British technology until the 1970s (Edgerton 1996a) but less so thereafter. Explanations need to be couched in terms of where the failings emerged. As the biggest failings were in business R&D, arguments such as short-termism in capital markets and the undervaluing of engineering must be given some credence. The decline of government involvement at the time when more was called for can be seen mainly as driven by ideology (which British governments unlike their American counterparts took seriously), along with a drawn-out overcommitment to defence and under-resourcing of education and training. To this familiar litany, which may be somewhat oversimplified, Walker (1993) added the point that there was too little co-ordination across relevant spheres of activity; for instance between science and technology, between technology and product development, between producers and users of technology, between management and their organisations, and between banks and industry. Constant government efforts to overcome this lack of cohesion achieved little, mostly because the resources they provided came nowhere near matching the aspirations (Georghiou 2001). In effect, the national 'system' of innovation in the UK was just not sufficiently systemic.

13

Regional development and policy

PETER SCOTT

Contents

INTRODUCTION

One of the most enduring features of Britain's post-war economic development has been the persistence of the 'north–south divide'. Incomes, employment growth, job opportunities and even education expenditure have all remained substantially lower in the less prosperous regions of northern and western Britain than in the booming south. Such a pattern of uneven development has presented major problems for policy makers. In addition to the obvious disadvantages to the less prosperous regions, the south-east has also experienced difficulties from its boom conditions. For example, soaring house prices have acted as a formidable barrier to in-migration from less prosperous areas, have eroded local social services (as nurses, teachers and other public sector workers are priced out of housing markets) and fed back into employers' costs – as workers demand higher wages to meet their accommodation bills.

The costs of uneven regional development also have a national dimension. Macroeconomic stabilisation is made more difficult by the co-existence of labour shortages and inflationary pressures in the south and substantial unemployment in Britain's 'peripheral' regions. For example, during the boom of the mid–late 1980s tight labour markets in the south-east fuelled wage inflation that was in turn transmitted to other regions with higher unemployment through national wage agreements, inter-plant agreements for multi-plant firms, and wage-setting based on relative earnings in related occupations. The resulting national inflationary pressures forced government into deflationary policy, despite the persistence of substantial unemployment and unused capacity in less prosperous regions.

The next section examines the extent and persistence of regional disparities in employment and incomes. This is followed by a discussion of the policies pursued by successive governments since 1945 to combat the 'regional problem'. The types of policy instruments used by government to address regional disparities are then examined, together with their effectiveness. Finally the ways in which long-term patterns of regional development have contributed to these inequalities are assessed, together with the influence of government policy on such patterns.

REGIONAL PERFORMANCE AND DISPARITIES

Regional boundaries within the UK reflect inherited political and economic divisions. For much of the post-war period government data have been based on eleven Standard Economic Regions (SERs), illustrated in Figure 13.1. Some represent coherent entities from an economic perspective, such as the north-west, with its inherited textile base; the engineering- (and more recently motor-vehicle-) dominated West Midlands, or the 'metropolitan' south-east. Others are less economically consistent – for example Scotland includes some of the most densely populated industrial areas of Britain, while the vast majority of its landmass is made up of sparsely populated agricultural counties. Similarly, there are strong economic, cultural and even linguistic differences between South Wales and North/mid-Wales. Yet despite such imperfections, the SERs do constitute a convenient and useful means of classifying the broad geography of UK regional differences.

Analysis of regional disparities usually begins with unemployment. Unemployment is an important index of welfare; in addition to being a major cause of deprivation in itself, regional and local unemployment disparities are highly correlated with other indices of social deprivation, such as incomes, the quality of jobs available, the proportion of lone-parent families, crime, health and housing conditions (Armstrong and Taylor 2000: 166–7; Taylor and Wren 1997; Turok and Webster 1998). Table 13.1 examines regional unemployment since 1951. In 1951 unemployment was very low nationally, as had been the case since the Second World War. The three main assisted regions – Scotland, the Northern region and Wales – had unemployment rates several times the national average, but still low in absolute terms. During the mid-1950s unemployment remained low throughout the British regions, but was much higher in Northern Ireland. The late 1950s and early 1960s witnessed an increase in national unemployment, together with a marked widening of regional differentials. These trends continued during the mid–late1960s. National

Figure 13.1 The UK Standard Economic Regions

Source: CSO, *Regional Trends*, 29, 1994: 7.

unemployment rose sharply during the 1970s, while regional differentials further increased.

Table 13.2 provides a more detailed picture of the different labour market conditions experienced by the UK's largest assisted regions (Scotland, Wales, Northern Ireland and the Northern region) and by its other regions, over the three decades to 1981. Substantial employment increases in Britain's other regions during the 1950s were very largely met through increased labour force participation – mainly accounted for by the growth in female employment. During the 1960s the other regions' rise in labour force participation exceeded their (much more moderate) employment growth. Conversely the main assisted areas faced stagnating employment. Despite more moderate increases in labour force participation over the period as a whole and some out-migration (though at levels much lower than during the interwar years) their rising workforces – boosted by relatively high birth rates, especially in Northern Ireland – were provided

Table 13.1   Regional unemployment rates, 1951–1995

Unemployment rate	1951	1956–7[a]	1958–63[a]	1963–73	1973–9	1979–88	1988–95
South-east	1.1	1.0	1.3	1.7	3.2	6.5	7.0
East Anglia	1.9			2.2	3.8	6.9	5.9
South-west	1.8	1.6	1.9	2.7	5.1	7.8	6.9
West Midlands	1.3			2.1	4.5	10.8	8.6
East Midlands	1.2	0.9	1.5	2.1	3.9	8.3	7.5
Yorkshire & Humberside	1.6			2.7	4.6	10.3	8.8
North-west	2.2	1.5	2.4	3.1	5.9	11.7	9.5
North	3.1	1.6	3.3	4.9	7.1	13.4	10.7
Wales	3.5	2.3	3.3	4.1	6.3	11.6	8.9
Scotland	3.5	2.5	3.9	4.7	6.4	11.6	9.3
Northern Ireland	n.a.	6.9	7.8	7.7	9.1	14.8	13.3
United Kingdom	n.a.	1.5	2.1	2.8	4.8	9.1	8.2

[a] Disaggregated data are not available for the south-east and East Anglia, or for the West Midlands, East Midlands and Yorkshire & Humberside.
'n.a.' = not available.

Sources: 1956–63, CSO, *Regional Trends* (1966: tab. 2.7); 1988–95, CSO, *Regional Trends*, 31 (1996: tab. 5.18); other years – Lee (1995: 67).

Table 13.2   Main changes in UK regional labour markets, 1951–1961 to 1971–1981
(as % of labour force at start of each period)

	Four main assisted regions[a]			Other regions		
	1951–61	1961–71	1971–81	1951–61	1961–71	1971–81
Natural increase in labour force	2.5	3.0	3.0	1.0	0.6	1.7
Increase in participation	2.3	4.8	1.3	11.0	3.3	0.7
Increase in employment	−0.2	0.8	−2.4	12.9	1.9	−1.7
Net out-migration of labour force	3.8	4.3	1.8	−1.8	−0.4	0.4
Increase in unemployment	1.2	2.8	4.7	1.0	2.4	3.7

[a] Scotland, Wales, Northern Ireland and the Northern region of England.

Source: Moore et al. (1986: 77).

with insufficient job opportunities and unemployment thus rose faster than the national average.

During the 1970s employment levels fell both in the assisted regions and (to a lesser extent) elsewhere in Britain. A major cause was the on-set of 'deindustrialisation' – the decline in manufacturing employment, which fell by more than 40 per cent from its peak of 8.7 million in 1966 to around 5 million during the late 1980s. This process was common to all mature industrial countries, but was particularly rapid in Britain. An-other important trend was 'de-urbanisation': the movement of economic activity – particularly services – away from large urban centres to towns, suburbs and rural areas. Between 1961 and 1999 the number of manu-facturing employees in Britain's conurbations declined by almost 75 per cent (Rowthorn 1999: 16). This process again had a distinct regional dimension, as the south contains no conurbations other than London – which is to some extent exceptional as the nation's financial and administrative centre.

The mid-1970s also witnessed the start of an almost continuous decline in the North's employment performance relative to both the South and the countries of the EU fifteen (Regional Studies Association 2001: 11). This is partly the result of changes in the pattern of UK specialisation in the world economy that have disadvantaged the north's price-sensitive 'mature' manufacturing industries. Regionally concentrated non-manufacturing activities, such as North Sea oil, the expansion of the City of London's role as a world financial centre, and the more general growth of internationally traded services in the south, have formed a rising share of exports. Currency appreciation arising from the improving non-manufacturing trade balance has led to a deterioration in the UK's manufactured trade balance, depressing manufacturing exports and regions (Rowthorn 1999: 12). Thus the decline of the north is directly linked to the prosperity enjoyed by the south.

These trends were starkly reflected in employment changes during the 1980s. A quarter of manufacturing jobs disappeared between 1979 and 1989, while job creation was mainly in services concentrated around the south-east – particularly financial and business services and personal services (see chapter 10 above). This produced a substantial widening of the north–south unemployment gap, while the severely affected areas expanded to include the north-west and Yorkshire & Humberside. Meanwhile outer-Britain experienced a much heavier decline in manufacturing employment than the south. Its manufacturing base had a greater weighting of older, declining, price-sensitive industries such as steel and shipbuilding. Furthermore, the peripheral regions' heavy reliance on branch plants made them particularly vulnerable to plant closures. Analysis of plant closures by Fothergill and Guy (1990) found that the role of plants within the overall structure of the corporation was a key determinant of selection. Firms closed their smaller factories and those producing items in their product range facing the sharpest declines in demand – often 'mature' products manufactured in peripheral branches. Lack of specialist headquarter functions was another factor making a plant more likely to be selected. Many branch plants in peripheral regions had these characteristics.

The 1990s witnessed what appeared to be a remarkable reversal of the widening regional divide. The south-east and the service sector bore the brunt of the late 1980s – early 1990s recession, while in all Britain's peripheral regions unemployment actually fell, greatly reducing regional disparities. That this occurred during a period of recession is particularly surprising, as previous recessions had seen an expansion in regional unemployment differentials (which then contracted during subsequent booms).

Yet, despite claims that the regional problem had disappeared by the end of the century, looking at the number of people *in employment* paints a very different picture. While some 80 per cent of working-age people in the south-east were in jobs, this proportion averaged only 68–69 per cent in the north-east, 65 per cent in Merseyside, 63 per cent in Glasgow, and less than 60 per cent for large areas of South Wales (Regional Studies Association 2001: 1). The gap between regional employment and unemployment figures may be due at least in part to far-reaching changes during the 1980s in the ways in which unemployment rates were calculated and those out of work were treated by the benefit system. Unemployment can be defined in a number of ways. The International Labour Office and the UK's Labour Force Survey define it in terms of numbers seeking work. However, Britain's main published figures are based on 'claimant count unemployment'. This has been subject to major changes in definition – originally measuring those registered as unemployed, then, from October 1982, those in receipt of unemployment benefit. During the 1980s changes in the detailed definition became very frequent (their number running well into double figures over the decade, all but one revising the figures downwards). It has been estimated that had the method of estimation used in 1979 been left unchanged, unemployment in September 1986 would have been 14.3 per cent, rather than the official figure of 11.6 per cent (Jones 1988: 87–93 discusses how the figures were massaged).

One way in which this has impacted on regional unemployment differentials is through putting large numbers of, particularly older, unemployed workers on sickness-related benefits. Between 1981 and 1999 the number of working-age adults claiming Incapacity Benefit (or its predecessor Invalidity Benefit) for more than six months rose from just over 0.5 million to almost 2 million, at a time when the population's general standard of health was improving. When other sickness benefits are added, the number of working-age adults covered rises to almost 2.5 million; more than double the number officially unemployed. In many former coal, steel and heavy engineering areas some 15–20 per cent of working-age men are out of the labour market on sickness benefits (Regional Studies Association 2001: 8). 'True' unemployment is further hidden by people being otherwise ineligible for unemployment benefits (for example due to being a single parent, or by virtue of their partner's earnings; due to being on a government scheme; or through premature early retirement). Such 'hidden' unemployment is, in turn, highly concentrated in Britain's older industrial areas.

GDP per capita is another important indicator of regional disparities. This is examined, relative to the UK average, in Table 13.3. The table reveals a remarkable persistence in the ranking of regions. The south-east has the highest GDP per capita for all years for which data are available, while Northern Ireland, Wales and the Northern region maintain their places at the bottom of the table. The most striking change is the decline in the position of the West Midlands, which fell relative to the UK

Table 13.3 Regional GDP per capita, 1951–1994
(UK = 100)

	1951	1954	1958	1962	1966–73	1973–9	1979–88	1988–94
South-east					114.0	113.7	116.0	117.0
East Anglia					95.5	94.6	98.9	101.5
East Midlands					97.1	96.3	97.7	97.2
Scotland	92	90.4	87.9	87.7	91.1	96.0	95.5	96.8
South-west					92.9	91.8	93.8	95.0
West Midlands					104.9	98.7	91.9	92.9
Yorkshire & Humberside					94.8	93.9	93.1	90.9
North-west					96.4	96.6	94.5	90.7
North					86.6	92.6	91.7	88.9
Wales	84	91	90	88	86.6	87.2	85.2	85.0
Northern Ireland	65	62	61	63	71.1	76.7	78.5	79.9

Note: Data exclude UK continental shelf.

Sources: Scotland (1951), Wales and Northern Ireland (1951–62) – McCrone (1969: 159); Scotland (1954–62) – Lythe and Majmudar (1982: 22–3); 1966–94, CSO, Regional Trends, various years.

by some 12 percentage points between 1966–73 and 1988–94. Although GDP data for the English regions are not available prior to 1966, data on weekly household incomes indicate that a substantial decline in the West Midlands' ranking had already occurred during the 1960s – between 1961–3 and 1968–9 its average weekly household income had fallen from 113 per cent of the UK average to only 103 per cent (Beckerman 1972: 242). The West Midlands' decline is largely the result of the collapse of its key manufacturing sector – motor vehicles.

Yorkshire & Humberside and the north-west have also experienced relative declines in GDP since 1966. These regions, like the West Midlands, traditionally had more broadly based industrial structures than the coal-dominated Northern region, Scotland and Wales. Meanwhile, the two regions which are grouped with the south-east to make up the 'south' – East Anglia and the south west – have improved their relative positions. It thus appears that the main changes in regional GDP differentials since 1966 have been an improvement in the position of the 'south' and a decline for the 'manufacturing heartland' of the West Midlands, Yorkshire & Humberside and the north-west. The peripheral regions have generally maintained their ranking, with the exception of Scotland.

Scotland experienced declining relative GDP until the mid-1960s, though this was sharply reversed in the 1970s – largely as the result of North Sea oil. While oil revenues are attributed to the 'UK continental shelf', rather than British regions, in GDP data, employment income accrues to the region where the employment is based. Following discoveries in the 1960s, large-scale oil production commenced in the mid-1970s, making Britain self-sufficient in oil by the end of the decade and a significant exporter during the 1980s. The economic impact was strongly concentrated in Scotland, oil-related sales comprising 6 per cent of Scottish manufacturing gross output in 1989 (Lee 1995: 103). Scotland received a variety of benefits from North Sea oil, including employment in direct production and ancillary industries and local taxation revenues. Yet oil proved a volatile prize, subject to considerable price changes that have produced substantial variations in the sector's employment.

Another region for which long-term trends were disrupted was Northern Ireland, following the onset of the 'troubles' in 1968. Some companies pulled out as a result of the security situation and economic and political instability, while others were deterred from setting up in the province. Similarly, key managerial and technical personnel were deterred from moving there. Meanwhile, especially at the height of the troubles, doubts were raised by British firms regarding the reliability of supplies from Northern Ireland plants in an environment of industrial unrest and terrorist activity (Harris 1991: 79). The impact of the troubles is difficult to quantify as they coincided with a long-term downturn in international economic conditions, to which Northern Ireland as a small, open, economy was particularly exposed. One indicator is Northern Ireland's share of employment created by factory moves into the UK's main assisted regions (the Northern region, Wales, Scotland and Northern Ireland). Northern Ireland's share of such moves fell from 15 per cent over 1966–70 to less than 6 percent over 1971–5, recovering to 10 per cent from 1976 to 1980 (Fothergill and Guy 1990: 143). Given that government made particular efforts to attract firms to Northern Ireland during the 1970s, the true deterrent effect of the troubles, other things being equal, is likely to be greater than figures suggest. Furthermore, the data do not include the impact of firms already established in the province that decided to avoid further investment, or even to close plants.

While estimates of total job losses arising from the troubles are subject to serious methodological problems, studies concerning the 1970s indicate around 20,000–25,000 job losses over the decade, while those which extend into the mid-1980s produce a wider range of estimates, some putting overall losses as high as 40,000–45,000 (Fothergill and Guy 1990: 143). Northern Ireland's GDP has actually improved relative to the UK average since the onset of the troubles – largely due to heavy government expenditure to support the province – but it remains the poorest UK region. It is still too early to judge what impact the new 'post-Good-Friday' political agreement will have on improving the province's economic position (though the strong growth record of the Irish Republic gives grounds for optimism).

To what extent has government policy re-distributed funds between regions? Government income and expenditure data are inadequate for precise calculation of net revenue flows between even the four constituent 'countries' of the UK, let alone the English regions. For example, in 1989–90 the 'non-identified' category of government expenditure comprised 21.8 per cent of the UK total (Lee 1995: 140–1). Items such

Table 13.4   Estimates of regional taxation and public expenditure per capita, 1974–1978 (£)

	Expenditure	Tax revenue	Expenditure/revenue	Expenditure-revenue
South-east	725	852	85.1	−127
East Anglia	619	689	89.8	−70
South-west	618	675	91.6	−57
West Midlands	626	710	88.2	−84
East Midlands	622	680	91.5	−58
North-west	694	682	101.8	12
Yorkshire & Humberside	650	683	95.2	−33
North	790	676	116.9	114
Wales	768	648	118.5	120
Scotland	866	691	125.3	175
Northern Ireland	974	542	179.7	432
UK	708	730	97.0	−22

Note: Figures are averages for the four tax years 1974/5 to 1977/8.

Source: Short (1981: 44–71); summarised in Lee (1995: 147).

as defence, overseas expenditures and some industrial subsidies cannot be assigned to individual areas of the UK in any meaningful sense. The only detailed direct analysis of the inter-regional balance of taxation and expenditure is provided by Short (1981), for the mid–late 1970s. Short's estimates, summarised in Table 13.4, indicate substantial redistributions of income out of the south and Midlands. The main gainer was Northern Ireland, with expenditure almost 80 per cent in excess of tax revenue. Scotland and Wales also derived substantial gains, while the only English region to benefit substantially was the Northern region. However, the dramatic reduction in regional and industrial policy expenditures since the 1970s have greatly reduced the magnitude of regional income redistribution. Furthermore, Short's estimates may not reflect some less visible regional biases in government spending which disproportionately benefit the south-east. For example, a large proportion of the 'non-identified' element relates to national defence, while both armed forces bases and military suppliers are concentrated in the south-east. Subsidies to Network South East and the Channel Tunnel project have also disproportionately benefited that region (Lee 1995: 148).

How important are regional disparities to the lives of ordinary people? Table 13.5 examines differences in GDP per capita and their relationship with three indicators of living standards and welfare. Mortality is shown to vary substantially between regions, even after adjusting for age structure. The south-east and East Anglia have mortality rates significantly below the national average, while regions with less than 90 per cent of average UK GDP per capita all have above-average mortality (though the relationship is not always strong, as shown by Wales). One surprising

Table 13.5 A profile of British regional inequality in 1994 *(UK = 100)*[a]				
	GDP per capita	Mortality[b]	'Middle-class' employment[c]	Households on sickness, invalidity, or disability benefits
South-east	117	94	116	69
East Anglia	102	91	94	77
Scotland	100	115	93	123
East Midlands	96	99	91	92
South-west	96	89	98	85
West Midlands	93	101	91	100
North-west	90	108	95	138
Yorkshire/Humberside	89	102	87	123
North	89	110	86	146
Wales	84	101	94	146
Northern Ireland	82	108	87	N/A

[a] Except for final column, where Great Britain = 100 (no data are available for Northern Ireland).
[b] Standardised mortality ratio, i.e. adjusted for age structure of population.
[c] Percentage of economically active population in professional, managerial and technical occupations in spring 1995.

Source: ONS, *Regional Trends*, 31 (1996: tabs. 3.9, 3.15, 8.6, 12.1).

result is the high mortality rate in Scotland, despite a GDP per capita equal to the national average. This may reflect the large clusters of very severe deprivation in certain areas of Scotland – poverty having a greater impact on mortality than average prosperity.

The second indicator is the proportion of workers in 'middle-class employment' (professional, managerial and technical occupations). This shows a clearer relationship with GDP per capita. Such jobs are over-represented in the south-east by some 16 per cent, while in the Northern region and Northern Ireland they are under-represented by 14 and 13 per cent respectively. Differential access to such job opportunities has obvious implications for equality of opportunity. Finally, as discussed earlier, the proportion of households on sickness-related benefits shows considerable variation between regions, being 31 percent below the British average in the south-east and 46 per cent above in the Northern region and Wales.

Table 13.6 compares UK regional disparities with those for 'substantial' EU nations (with four or more regions). EU countries are shown to fall into two groups. Those which emerged as modern nations through unification or independence during the nineteenth century (Italy, Germany and Greece) have much greater regional unemployment disparities than Britain, while the older nation states of Europe have disparities of broadly similar magnitude. Britain compares well with most EU nations in terms of disparities in GDP per capita. Yet when the proportion of the unemployed in long-term unemployment is examined, disparities in the UK are shown to be relatively wide.

Table 13.6 UK regional disparities compared to those of other 'substantial' EU nations (with four regions or more), 1994

Country	Number of regions	Coefficient of variation[a] in:		
		Unemployment[b]	Long-term unemployed as % of total unemployed[b]	GDP per capita (1993)[c]
Italy	11	0.52	0.19	0.25
Germany	16	0.44	0.16	0.40
Greece	4	0.36	0.12	0.11
Spain	7	0.19	0.07	0.18
France	8	0.18	0.09	0.24
UK	11	0.18	0.17	0.10
Netherlands	4	0.12	0.07	0.09

[a] The coefficient of variation is a measure of dispersion: the closer to 0, the more equal is the dispersion across regions.
[b] Based on Community Labour Force Survey definitions.
[c] Based on the Purchasing Power Standard – a unit of measurement which expresses an identical volume of goods and services in each country, taking account of price-level differences.

Source: ONS, *Regional Trends*, 31 (1996: tab. 2.3).

Table 13.7 Wage indices for full-time employees on adult rates, April 1995 *(Great Britain = 100)*

	Average gross weekly pay	Average hourly pay[a]	Relative proportion earning less than £220 per week
South-east	115.8	117.4	70.2
North-west	94.4	93.9	110.9
South-west	93.3	93.4	116.1
Scotland	93.2	93.6	113.0
West Midlands	92.5	91.1	112.3
East Anglia	91.8	90.0	110.5
East Midlands	90.8	89.2	114.7
Yorkshire & Humberside	90.7	89.3	117.9
Wales	89.6	89.1	119.3
North	88.9	88.3	122.5

[a] Excluding overtime.

Source: CSO, *New Earnings Survey 1995* (1995), tab. AX 5.3.

High regional disparities in long-term unemployment and sickness-related benefits suggest that the effects of Britain's regional problem fall disproportionately on lower-income groups. This is confirmed by analysis of regional wage data in Table 13.7. Average gross weekly pay is shown to vary between 15.8 percent in excess of the national average, in the south-east and 11.1 per cent below it, in the Northern region. Average hourly wages show slightly more variation, though this may reflect the higher proportion of salaried employees (who do not receive formal overtime pay) in the south. However, the proportion of people on low wages (here defined as less than £220 per week) varies from almost 29.8 per cent below the national average in the south-east to 22.5 per cent above it in the Northern region. Thus, in addition to the long-term unemployed and those in disguised long-term unemployment through sickness-related benefits, workers in poorly paid jobs bear the brunt of Britain's uneven regional development. The main impact of regional inequality therefore appears to be the compounding of the general disadvantages faced by the poorer sections of the UK population.

THE DEVELOPMENT OF BRITISH REGIONAL POLICY

Neoclassical economics predicts that the free market would remove regional disparities, through adjustments in wages to reflect local labour markets, labour migration from high-unemployment to low-unemployment areas, and firm migration to areas of cheaper labour. However, as Armstrong and Taylor (2000: 209) note, 'This scenario does not accord with reality.' In fact these adjustment processes prove far too weak. Firm locations display strong geographical inertia, as movement would involve uncertainties regarding such important variables as costs, input–output linkages, and the recruitment and retention of key workers. Wages are also inflexible; for some classes of jobs they are nationally determined, while for others they are constrained by agreements and legislation (such as the minimum wage).

Meanwhile, the geographical mobility of labour has proved very limited, especially since the mid-1970s (Gordon and Molho 1998). This has been a particular problem for manual workers; analysis of their net inter-regional migration rates in the mid-1980s indicated that they amounted to less than 0.3 per cent of the manual workforce per year for most regions: just over half the rate for other workers. Furthermore, having examined the direction of this migration, it was found that: 'manual labour is not, on balance, flowing from high unemployment regions to areas of lower unemployment' (Hughes and McCormick 1994: 524). This is partly the result of the high cost of housing in the south, which prices many less well-paid workers out of its labour market. Harrison and Hart (1993: 32) estimated that during the 1970s and 1980s housing costs may have deterred some 300,000 potential in-migrants to the south-east. Had regional house price differentials maintained their 1977 level, in-migration would have raised the south-east's unemployment rate close to the national average.

While the problems of regionally immobile labour and industry are generally recognised, they give rise to two opposing policy solutions. The first is the 'market-based' strategy, of attempting to remove the impediments to market clearing by actions such as reducing the power of trade unions, abolishing public sector national wage agreements and removing legal constraints such as minimum wage legislation. Similarly, it is argued, policies aimed at reducing planning restraints on house building in the south, and encouraging the private rented sector, would lower the housing barrier to migration. However, such policies are generally viewed as having high social costs, both through depressing incomes in less prosperous areas and in creating congestion in booming districts (as revealed by the recent political backlash in the south against government proposals to expand housing development).

The alternative strategy is one of government intervention to 'take work to the workers'. Yet this raises substantial efficiency concerns. By distorting the free market in industrial location, intervention may increase the costs, and reduce the efficiency, of British industry, with potentially significant long-term impacts on productivity and economic growth. At the heart of this debate lies the 'structural versus locational controversy' (Keeble 1976: 34–5). The structural school argues that the poor economic performance of Britain's peripheral regions was, at least until the 1960s, basically due to their historical legacy of extreme specialisation in the declining staple industries of coal, iron and steel, textiles and shipbuilding. Conversely, the locational school argues that their problems do not merely reflect historical development, but are largely due to these regions' locational disadvantages, such as poor communications links with markets and suppliers. The importance of such links does not lie primarily in transport costs, which generally form only a small percentage of turnover, but in the need for close and frequent contact with customers.

If the structural view is correct, government merely needs to steer a sufficient volume of firms in expanding sectors to the depressed areas for them to become prosperous. If locational arguments are valid, such steering would damage the performance of British industry, unless accompanied by policies that reduced the peripheral areas' locational disadvantage. What the literature often fails to recognise is that inherited structure can influence locational advantage. An area with a legacy of rapid industrial expansion is more likely to attract infrastructure investment to improve its communications. It is also likely to have a better network of suppliers and a more appropriately trained workforce.

British regional policy was initiated during the interwar years, when severe depression in Britain's staple industries produced very high unemployment in Scotland, the north and Wales (establishing a 'north–south divide' which has proved remarkably durable over subsequent decades). After initially restricting its activities to encouraging labour migration from depressed areas, the government introduced a very limited, experimental, regional policy initiative under the 1934 Special Areas Act and 1937 Special Areas (Amendment) Act. A number of chronically depressed 'Special Areas' (located in the north-east, central Scotland, South Wales and west Cumberland) were designated for assistance. The main

initiatives involved the provision of government-sponsored industrial estates and financial assistance for firms establishing new plants. These
measures reflected widespread perceptions that the development of industrial estates and the greater availability of capital in the south had
given it important advantages in attracting industry and that publicly
assisted provision of such facilities in the north might correct this im-
balance. While the initiatives were on too small a scale to make any real
impact on unemployment in the Special Areas, analysis has indicated
that – when account is taken of savings in government welfare payments
and tax revenue generation – they proved a very cost-effective means of
generating employment (Scott 2000).

Regional assistance was given substantial emphasis in war-time planning for post-war recovery, reflecting a consensus that considerable government intervention would be necessary to ensure that Britain did not
revert to mass unemployment. These plans passed into legislation under
the coalition government's 1945 Distribution of Industry Act, which targeted a number of 'Development Areas' – based on expansions of the Special Areas, together with some additional localities that appeared likely
to experience high unemployment (see Figure 13.2(a)). The Development
Areas initially covered 15.7 per cent of Britain's population, while subsequent additions increased this to about 18 per cent by 1953.

The 1945–51 Labour governments developed an extensive regional policy programme. Chief among the incentives offered was the development
of government-financed factories for renting to industrialists. Meanwhile,
factory location was restricted via the continuation of war-time building
licence controls, supplemented in 1947 by the requirement for Industrial
Development Certificates (IDCs) – Board of Trade certificates stating that
the development was consistent with 'the proper distribution of industry'. This rather vague wording allowed the government to use IDCs for
a number of purposes, such as the promotion of New Towns, in addition
to regional policy *per se*.

Although the 1945 Distribution of Industry Act had contained provisions for regional expenditure on transport and infrastructure improvements, this did not form a significant element of regional policy until
the 1960s, despite the fact that many assisted areas suffered from poor
infrastructure, particularly regarding long-distance road links. Similarly,
another measure outlined in the 1945 Act – capital subsidies to firms
via loans and grants – played only a minor role until the 1960s, as is
shown in Table 13.8. Treasury opposition delayed the initial development
of activity in this area, while subsequent cuts in the regional budget,
together with the government's wider national policy of rationing industrial credit, led to its progressive curtailment from 1947 (Carnevali and
Scott 1999).

Labour's regional initiative was substantially scaled down following
the 1947 economic crisis, precipitated by the abortive American-inspired

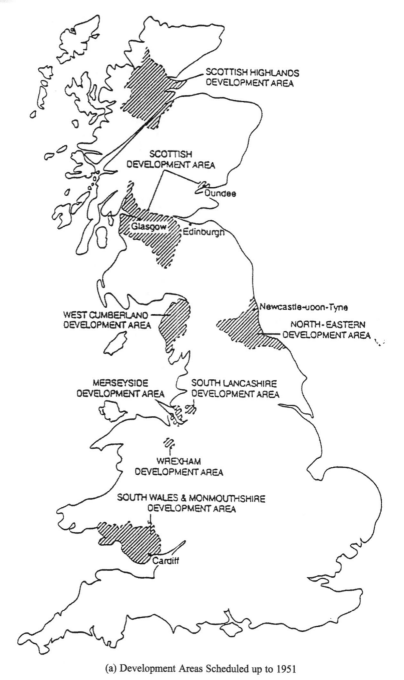

(a) Development Areas Scheduled up to 1951

Figure 13.2 The changing geography of British regionally assisted areas

Source: Scott (1997: 363); Moore *et al.* (1986: 20, 22).

(b) The Development Districts in 1966

Figure 13.2 *(cont.)*

move to sterling convertibility. Near-full employment throughout Britain, together with severe balance-of-payments problems, made regional policy less of a priority. Expenditure was reduced by around 45 per cent in real terms, while the proportion of new industrial building approvals granted for the Development Areas fell from 51.3 per cent of the national floorspace total in 1945–7 to 19.4 per cent in 1948–51 (Maclennan and Parr 1979: 8). Despite these cuts, by December 1951 some 230,000 jobs in the Development Areas had been created in factories newly built, extended or converted from war-time premises (Scott 1997: 381).

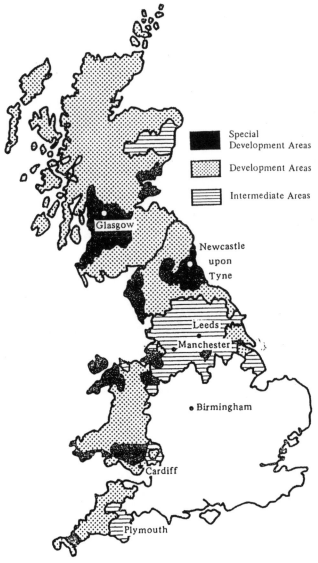

Figure 13.2 (*cont.*)   (c) The Assisted Areas as at June 1979

Northern Ireland faced similar problems of heavy dependence on industries in secular decline. The government of Northern Ireland sought to diversify its industrial base by selectively encouraging the growth of new industries, principally through attracting inward investment. Selective assistance was offered under the Industrial Development (NI) Act 1945, to encourage companies to locate branch plants in the province. The 1945 Act was very similar to Britain's 1945 Distribution of Industry Act. Yet the Stormont government proved much more willing to provide

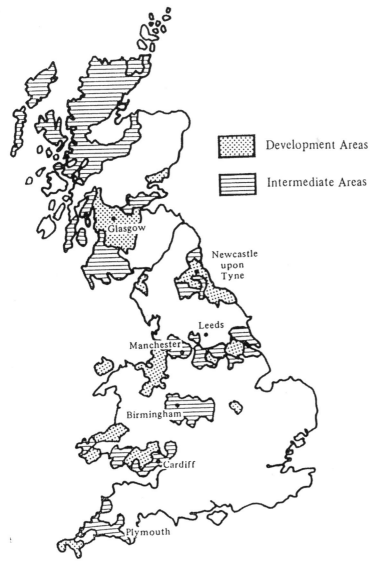

Development Areas

Intermediate Areas

(d) The Assisted Areas as at November 1984

Figure 13.2 *(cont.)*

grants (Harris 1991: 10). Meanwhile the poor productivity and technological backwardness of indigenous industry was addressed by offering
capital grants to manufacturers under the Re-equipment of Industry (NI)
Act 1951 and subsequent legislation (Harris 1990: 344).

The Conservative governments of the 1950s put regional policy
into abeyance, expenditure being limited to a few 'blackspot' areas
of unusually high unemployment, justified on social, rather than economic, grounds. Ministers pointed to the absence of significant regional

Table 13.8 The direct Exchequer costs of British regional policy (annual averages, £M) 1946/7–1983/4

Type of incentive	1946/7–48/9	1949/50–51/2	1952/3–58/9	1959/60–60/1	1961/2–63/4	1964/5–71/2	1972/3–75/6	1976/7–79/80	1983/4
Investment incentives									
Investment grants, RDGs and regionally differentiated free depreciation	–	–	–	–	–	71	193	408	440
Regional Selective Assistance	–	–	–	–	–	–	32	67	98[a]
Local Employment Acts									
(a) Government factory building/land[b]	9.7	5.5	3.8	6.3	8	12	17	84	105[c]
(b) Other loans/grants	0.3	0.7	0.9	3.9	12	35	34	–	–
Labour subsidies									
Regional Employment Premium	–	–	–	–	–	57	143	44	–
Other labour subsidies	–	–	–	–	–	9	8	8	–
Other assistance	–	–	–	–	1	3	6	15	–
Total expenditure at current prices	10.1	6.2	4.6	10.2	21	187	433	626	643
Total expenditure at constant (1975) prices[d]	36.2	19.6	11.6	22.2	55	383	578	407	261

[a] Estimate.
[b] Includes expenditure of Scottish and Welsh Development Agencies on land and factories.
[c] Includes land reclamation.
[d] GDP deflator used to obtain constant prices.

Sources: 1946/7–1960/1 – United States, Dept of Commerce (1965: 406); 1961/2–83/4 – Moore et al. (1986: 23).

unemployment, though Board of Trade officials continued to have strong concerns regarding the likely resumption of the staple industries' long-term decline and advocated the maintenance of an active regional policy to safeguard against this (Scott 1996a). Regional policy ran counter to the government's strongly neo-liberal economic philosophy. A further factor contributing to its down-grading was the competing demands of the new towns programme. New town development had been initiated by the previous Labour government, but was accelerated by the Conservatives in order to fulfil their election pledge to build 300,000 new houses (Cullingworth 1979: 118). The largest area of activity concerned eight satellite towns around London, which required considerable industrial development to provide employment for their growing populations. Over the decade to 1961 London's new towns increased their employment by over 100,000, while regional policy created only 73,435 new jobs in the Development Areas from November 1951 to March 1960 (Thomas 1969; Scott 1996a). Thus, rather than assisting Britain's peripheral regions, the bulk of government-sponsored factory development during the 1950s was actually located in the south-east. Northern Ireland, by contrast, retained its active regional policy.

By 1958 rising regional unemployment prompted the government to make a major U-turn. Such was the pressure to steer jobs to high unemployment areas that government made a series of major interventions in the location of large-scale projects, with unfortunate long-term consequences. For example, as a result of Harold Macmillan's 'judgement of Solomon', the steel industry's giant new strip mill was split into two smaller units, at Llanwern in South Wales and Ravenscraig in Scotland. This resulted in neither being sufficiently large to obtain the economies of scale of continental plants (see chapter 3 above). Similarly, government pressure resulted in several of Britain's leading car manufacturers announcing major expansions in the Development Areas during 1960 (Wilks 1984: 76). These interventions were also to result in long-term problems of sub-optimal capacity, eroding the competitive position of the industry. Meanwhile IDC controls were applied much more strictly: refusals (as a percentage of approvals plus refusals) in the Midlands and south-east rising from 0.5 per cent in 1956 to an average of 16.5 per cent from 1961 to 1963 (Scott 1996a: 55).

The government's continuing perception of the regional problem as one of localised unemployment was demonstrated by the Local Employment Act (1960), which replaced the Development Areas by 'Development Districts'. These were designated on the basis that they had unemployment rates of 4.5 per cent or over. Their coverage thus varied considerably over time, from 9.2 per cent of Britain's population in 1962 to 16.8 per cent in 1966 (Beckerman 1972: 226). The Development Districts excluded large parts of the old Development Areas, while adding pockets of relatively high unemployment scattered throughout the country (see Figure 13.2(b)). Their scope could be quickly changed, without parliamentary approval. The ease and speed with which this could take place and the single criterion used, unemployment, militated against long-term policies such as industrial estate development. Furthermore, by aiming for small 'Districts', rather than broad 'Areas', those parts of depressed regions with the greatest potential to act as growth points were removed from assistance.

Yet, within a couple of years of the 1960 Act, policy had begun to move towards the promotion of long-term regional growth. Concerns regarding Britain's poor post-war growth record, its continuing balance-of-payments difficulties, and the apparent failure of current macroeconomic policy, led policy makers to turn their attention to the long-run structural weaknesses of the British economy. This re-appraisal resulted in a new range of measures aimed at targeting Britain's supply-side difficulties to promote faster growth. Regional policy was to play an important part in this strategy, attention being concentrated on two regions, Scotland and the north-east. Their development was addressed in two White Papers published in autumn 1963, which advocated the promotion of 'growth points' within them through integrated programmes of infrastructure and factory development. By concentrating on areas with the potential for long-term self-sustaining growth, it was argued, a process of development could be induced which would eventually 'spill-over' to benefit the entire region.

The 1964 Labour government greatly expanded regional expenditure, which rose sixteen-fold in real terms between 1962–3 and 1969–70. Meanwhile, building controls were extended to the service sector, with the introduction of Office Development Permits (ODPs) for new office building in London and, later, other congested areas in the south and Midlands (Scott 1996b: ch. 7). The 1966 Industrial Development Act replaced the 165 Development Districts by 5 broad Development Areas which, unlike the Development Districts, were not designated only on the basis of unemployment. Designating large areas represented a compromise between an entirely employment-orientated policy and a growth point strategy. Growth points had proved politically unattractive on account of the implied lack of effort to help other parts of declining areas. Yet the broad Development Area approach did allow growth points to develop spontaneously, as a result of firms choosing those parts of the Areas that offered the best prospects for growth. The Act provided assistance through a system of investment grants. These were believed to promote economic growth strongly – Whitehall economists having noted a close correlation between investment and growth in industrialised countries (Pliatzky 1984: 65–6).

Regional policy had become an instrument of macroeconomic policy. The most important innovation was the Regional Employment Premium

(REP). This was viewed as an important means of preventing the pressure of demand for labour from building up in the south and midlands – with consequent inflationary effects and damage to the balance of payments – by subsidising labour costs in less prosperous areas. The REP produced an effective reduction in labour costs of about 7 per cent compared to non-Development Areas – equivalent, on average, to roughly 2.5 per cent of annual operating costs. The regional differential in investment grants was about 12 per cent of gross capital costs for plant and machinery, again reducing total operating costs by roughly 2.5 per cent. Together, these measures gave Development Area firms an average total subsidy of around 5 per cent, while the greater subsidy on capital gave capital-intensive firms a larger cost reduction (Beckerman 1972: 230).

Meanwhile two new classes of assisted areas were introduced. The first, announced in November 1967, were the 'Special Development Areas'. These were given more generous assistance than the Development Areas as they were otherwise expected to suffer high unemployment (over 8 per cent) from colliery closures. Concern was also growing, particularly following the introduction of the REP, that 'grey areas' on the fringes of Development Areas, such as the north-west and Yorkshire & Humberside, would face problems since they had neither the government support offered to the scheduled areas, nor the strong locational advantages of the south-east and Midlands (Parsons 1986: 217). To meet these fears the government created seven 'Intermediate Areas', encompassing 5 per cent of Britain's insured population, in which limited assistance was provided. By the time Labour left office in 1970, regional expenditure had reached unprecedented levels and some 40 per cent of Britain (encompassing 20 per cent of its population) was scheduled in some form (Parsons 1986: 225). Regional expenditure on roads and other infrastructure had also been substantially increased. Yet regional unemployment disparities remained wider than at any time since the Second World War.

Edward Heath's Conservative government set out its initial approach to regional policy in the October 1970 White Paper *Investment Incentives*. This stated that policy would be more selective and orientated towards areas of growth potential rather than merely aiming to alleviate unemployment. IDC controls were to be less stringently implemented, REP was to be phased-out, and the emphasis of policy shifted from investment grants to depreciation allowances on capital and plant (Parsons 1986: 241). Yet this return to a growth point approach was rapidly abandoned in the face of rising unemployment. In February 1971, with unemployment threatening to reach a million, government increased grant assistance to the Special Development Areas, while expanding their scope to include major industrial areas such as Glasgow and Clydeside, Tyneside, Wearside and additional parts of South Wales. This increased their coverage from roughly 1.8 per cent of the insured population to 8.5 per cent. In March the coverage of Intermediate Areas was also extended. Meanwhile the summer 1971 budget included £100 million worth of Development Area public works projects.

The government's new interventionist stance was typified by the 1972 Industry Act. This emerged from plans to prepare for EU membership by modernising Britain's industrial capacity and strengthening its regional infrastructure. Unemployment fears formed an important subsidiary motive (Ball and Selden 1996: 152–3). The Act had a strong regional element, offering up to £250 million a year in new Regional Development Grants for investment in plant, machinery and factory building. Furthermore the Secretary of State was given sweeping powers to provide any form of financial assistance to industry, providing he/she deemed it to be of likely benefit to the economy, in the national interest, and to constitute funding not available from any other source (subject to parliamentary approval for projects over £5 million). The Act also provided major additional assistance to the shipbuilding industry. Following the Act the government also granted substantial assistance to other industries concentrated in the Development Areas, including the nationalised steel and coal industries.

The only major changes introduced by the 1974 Labour government during its first two years in office involved doubling the value of the REP instead of phasing it out (the real value of its original flat rates having been severely eroded by inflation), and further extending the boundaries of the Development Areas and Special Development Areas (see Figure 13.2(c)). By 1976, assisted areas encompassed 43 per cent of Britain's workforce (Keeble 1976: 232). Yet the deteriorating economic situation forced the government to scale-down its regional assistance. The July 1976 budget introduced substantial regional expenditure cuts, while the December 1976 mini-budget brought more drastic cuts, including the termination of REP. Between 1975 and 1979 regional policy expenditure fell from 0.7 to 0.3 per cent of GDP (Martin 1988: 408). Like its 1945 predecessor, the 1974 Labour government had seen its ambitious regional programme come to grief on the rocks of economic crisis. Meanwhile the government's general policy of industrial intervention had led to large-scale assistance to some industries concentrated in the south-east and Midlands, such as British Leyland and the civilian aerospace industry, that threatened to counter the regional incidence of industrial assistance (Maclennan and Parr 1979: 31). The problems of the inner cities had also begun to compete with regional policy for government attention and finance. After initially rejecting additional expenditure specifically targeted at the inner cities, the government launched its first substantial initiative in 1977 in response to growing public pressure, further assistance being provided a year later under the Inner Urban Areas Act (Parsons 1986: 247).

By the end of Labour's term in office, with high unemployment having become a long-term national problem, a sea-change in government thinking away from active regional policy was evident. At the same time regional analysis and planning was suffering from what Parsons (1986: 261) described as a 'theoretical and professional crisis', with commentators beginning to suggest that regional planners were better at analysing problems than finding solutions. As McCallum noted, 'Enough of the traditional interpretations and prescriptions have been shaken to make the future of British regional policy fundamentally uncertain. A consensus, nearly fifty years in the making, is probably collapsing; it is unclear what will take its place' (Maclennan and Parr 1979: 37–8).

The advent of Mrs Thatcher's government in 1979 marked the start of a further downgrading of regional policy. Shortly after she came into office, a substantial programme of descheduling assisted areas was announced, together with a reduction of the Regional Development Grant to 15 per cent in the Development Areas and the abolition of its counterpart – the Building Grant – in the Intermediate Areas (see Figure 13.2(d)). The criteria applied to Regional Selective Assistance (RSA) were also tightened. Regional Policy underwent two major reviews during the 1980s, in November 1984 (March 1985 for Northern Ireland) and in January 1988. The first led to the abolition of Special Development Areas, the phasing-out of investment incentives, including free depreciation, and a tightening of the criteria for Regional Development Grants. These and a range of other changes reduced regional policy expenditure from a projected £700 million per annum to around £400 million (Harrison and Hart 1993: 255). The 1988 review led to the abolition of the Regional Development Grant, leaving discretionary RSA as the only significant regional incentive. This period also witnessed other policy initiatives that severely disadvantaged the peripheral regions, including macroeconomic and industrial policies that led to a dramatic decline in the staple industries. For example, from the early 1980s the coal industry alone shed more than 250,000 jobs, largely as the result of the government's decision to remove production subsidies (despite the fact that many of the industry's overseas competitors enjoyed similar subsidies).

During the 1980s regional issues became increasingly over-shadowed by the inner cities. In 1981, riots in several inner-city areas moved their plight sharply up the political agenda. Between 1980–1 and 1989–90 government regional policy expenditure (including payments to the nationalised industries, but excluding special arrangements for Northern Ireland) declined from £623 million to £540 million, while inner-city and other urban aid expanded from £142 million to £762 million (Harrison and Hart 1993: 271). The 1990s saw further emphasis on inner-city regeneration, encouraged by EU funding for 'community economic development initiatives'. Ministers were keen to point to the pockets of deprivation and high unemployment in inner London, together with the prosperity of some areas in the north such as Cheshire and North Yorkshire, as evidence that the 'regional' problem had been replaced by a local employment problem. Yet, while inner-city and other sub-regional problems were becoming increasingly severe, broad regional disparities remained an important feature of the British economy.

From the mid-1990s regional policy witnessed a very limited revival, as demonstrated in the 1995 White Paper *Regional Industrial Policy*, which recognised the importance of enhancing the competitiveness of depressed areas on both economic and social grounds. To some extent this reflected the availability of EU funds for such programmes, thus allowing government to offer support without incurring additional costs. Indeed in some cases EU funds enabled the government to reduce its own expenditure (Taylor and Wren 1997: 839). Yet regional policy remained virtually in abeyance compared to the scale of assistance during the 1970s and to that of most EU nations: over 1996–8 UK regional expenditure amounted to only 30 per cent of the EU average and half that of France, which had similar regional differentials (Regional Studies Association 2001: 17–18).

The year 1997 saw the election of a Labour government committed to regional devolution. Following referenda, a Scottish parliament and a Welsh assembly were established in 1999. The Scottish parliament had legislative powers, very limited tax raising powers, but wide-ranging government functions (excluding only macroeconomic stabilisation policy, regulation of employment and transport-related matters, plus specifically 'national' functions such as foreign policy, defence, border controls, etc.). The Welsh assembly had no legislative or tax raising powers and was given only those government functions previously exercised by the Secretary of State for Wales. Labour also created nine new Regional Development Agencies (RDAs) for the English regions and encouraged them to establish (non-elected) regional assemblies. This facilitated the attraction of EU funding (under its 'partnership approach' of working with regional organisations). However, the English RDAs remained firmly under Whitehall control, with Boards entirely comprised of ministerial appointments. Britain thus remains one of the most centralised large nations in the OECD.

Labour also shifted the focus of government regional analysis (and, to a very limited extent, policy), with new emphasis on knowledge, skills, innovation and enterprise. Rather than lacking appropriate transport, factories, and other infrastructure, the less prosperous regions were viewed as having failed due to under-investment in R&D, workforce training and policies designed to foster entrepreneurship. Yet in practice RSA has remained the key tool for steering footloose enterprises to high unemployment areas, while measures concerned with innovation and enterprise received relatively modest funding. Meanwhile, although Labour's shift in emphasis from physical to human capital partially reflects a sea-change in prevailing academic analysis, it also embodies a view that 'what is good for the UK economy as a whole is particularly good for the weaker regions' (Regional Studies Association 2001: 5). This echoes the Conservatives' 1950s policy that the best regional policy is a successful national economic policy. The eagerness of Labour ministers to emphasise the lo-calised nature of deprivation and deny the existence of a broad regional problem similarly mirrors 1950s Conservative policy. There is a real danger that, as then, national prosperity and employment growth will be allowed to by-pass Britain's peripheral regions.

REGIONAL POLICY INSTRUMENTS AND THEIR EFFECTIVENESS

Policy makers use evaluation techniques to answer a range of questions regarding the impacts and effectiveness of policy instruments. They may wish to know whether a policy measure produced the intended changes in the behaviour of the actors at whom it was targeted (for example whether IDC controls led firms to switch the location of new plants from prosperous to depressed areas); whether instruments had the intended regional impact in expanding employment or increasing manufacturing investment in targeted regions; and whether this regional impact was achieved at the cost of adverse impacts on the national economy. Finally, they may wish to know the cost-effectiveness of achieving these results.

Evaluating regional policy is complicated by the fact that many important government interventions do not fall under the formal heading of regional policy. For example, for much of the period under discussion government provided considerable support to the coal, steel and ship-building industries, one important reason being that they were major employers in high unemployment regions. Even the assessment of specif-ically regional policies involves considerable methodological difficulties. Policy expenditure will produce a *deadweight effect* – some assistance will merely fund investment and job creation that would have occurred (at least partially) even in its absence. Measures may also produce some *displacement effect*, creating jobs in assisted firms by displacing jobs which would have been provided to other local businesses. *Multiplier effects*, aris-ing from sales by local enterprises to new/expanded firms in receipt of assistance, and their workers, must also be taken into account. Even after allowing for these effects, job creation will not be matched by an equiv-alent reduction in unemployment, as it will reduce migration out of the region and increase labour force participation.

One means of estimating the impact of regional policy (and specific policy instruments) is analysis of aggregate data under different policy regimes. Such studies, pioneered by Moore and Rhodes (1973) generally compare the assisted areas' economic performance relative to national performance in periods of weak regional policy (or the absence of spe-cific policy instruments) with periods of strong policy (or their presence). Dissatisfaction with the reliability of such aggregate techniques has led to the increasing use of micro-based studies, using techniques such as interview surveys of the recipients of assistance, or analysis of micro-data sets covering particular groups of firms. Yet these methods are also not unproblematic. For example, it is difficult for surveyed managers to un-pick the precise influence of each of several policy incentives that they are receiving simultaneously. Meanwhile, their answers might be subject to bias, either due to beliefs that overstating the impact of assistance might encourage its continued provision and preserve eligibility for fu-ture grants, or, conversely, from a tendency to post-rationalise and claim that successful assisted projects would have been good enough to attract finance even in the absence of the assistance (Hart and Scott 1994). Such methodological differences and problems are important, as alternative methodologies can produce considerable variations in the estimated im-pacts of policy instruments (Wren and Waterson 1991).

Most regional policy instruments (especially prior to the 1970s) have been targeted at manufacturing industry. Manufacturing firms are viewed as being more mobile and less tied to local consumer demand than many service sector firms and as having greater local and regional multiplier effects on account of their typically higher wages and greater likeli-hood of contributing to 'industrial linkage chains' of intermediate, semi-processed production (Keeble 1976: 204–5). British regional policy initially concentrated on attracting manufacturers via the development of facto-ries for letting to industrialists at subsidised rents. Some of these, termed 'advance factories', were built before a particular tenant was found and thus offered firms ready-made plants in which they could rapidly estab-lish production. Factory building has assumed diminished importance in the government's regional policy portfolio, as shown by its declining share of total regional policy expenditure over the period 1960–76 (see Ta-ble 13.8). Yet available evidence suggests that it constituted a cost-effective means of creating employment (Law and Howes 1972; Scott 1996a).

While government attracted firms to assisted areas via factory devel-opment, it also impeded firms from building in more prosperous areas through IDC controls. One attraction of IDCs was that they were cost-effective from a Treasury viewpoint, in that the only public expenditure incurred was on their administration. They also proved extremely flexible in that they could be applied with varying severity to different sectors, or at different phases of the economic cycle, at the discretion of govern-ment. Furthermore, by compelling firms considering expansion to open up a dialogue with government regarding their plans, IDCs gave the Board of Trade and its successors an opportunity to inform each firm of the pos-itive inducements available in the scheduled areas (Armstrong and Taylor 2000: 239–40).

As Figure 13.3 shows, IDC refusals experienced a considerable long-term decline from the mid-1960s, controls eventually being abolished in 1981. While refusing an IDC might 'steer' the project to an area of greater employment need, it might have less desirable consequences. Analysis of

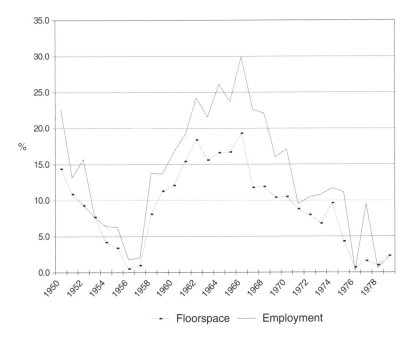

Figure 13.3 IDC
refusals as % of
approvals plus refusals
in the Midlands and
south-east 1950–1979

Source: Moore *et al.*
(1986: 28).

firms refused IDCs between 1958 and 1971 showed that 50 per cent of projects were undertaken in a non-assisted area in a modified form (such as using existing buildings or expansion below the minimum floorspace for IDC approval), which may have had a significant negative effect on scale and efficiency. A further 13 per cent were abandoned, 1 per cent located abroad, and 18 per cent had other outcomes not involving location in an area acceptable to government (such as the subsequent closure or reorganisation of the plant in question). In only 18 per cent of cases was the project diverted to an area that met with government approval (Wettman and Nicol 1981: 120). Furthermore, many of these merely went to less congested areas of the south-east, or to the south-west and East Anglia (Twomey and Taylor 1985; Ashcroft and McGregor 1989). Office development restrictions were also found to have mainly resulted in the dispersal of jobs to other areas in and around the south-east rather than to peripheral regions (Alexander 1979: 63–70).

Another important means of influencing firm location has been the provision of financial incentives such as various forms of capital subsidies. Capital subsidies encourage both *net investment* – additions to productive capacity – and *replacement investment* – where a firm's plant and machinery is modernised without increasing capacity. Both types of investment offer economic benefits, the first by expanding output (possibly including diversification into new product lines) and the second through increasing efficiency via the employment of more modern plant. Yet, given that technological improvements are known to be generally labour-saving, replacement investment can lead to a reduction in employment, at least

Table 13.9 The impact of individual regional policy instruments since 1960 in creating jobs in the Development Areas by 1971 and 1981

	Impact (000s manufacturing jobs)	
	At 1971	At 1981
Industrial Development Certificates	89	74
Investment incentives	157	307
Regional Employment Premium	63	27
Regional Selective Assistance	N/A	42
Total (net manufacturing jobs)	309	450

Note: N/A = not applicable.

Source: Moore et al. (1986: 9).

in the short term (though in the long term it will increase job security by enhancing competitiveness). Even where capital grants encourage net investment, they are likely to produce fewer immediate jobs per pound of government expenditure than labour subsidies, as they encourage production techniques that substitute capital for labour (Harris 1990).

Although the 1945 Distribution of Industry Act contained provisions for grant and loan assistance to industry, capital subsidies only became a substantial feature of UK regional policy from the late 1950s (with the exception of Northern Ireland which had made substantial use of them since the immediate post-war period). One means of providing assistance was 'free depreciation', introduced in the 1963 Finance Act. This enabled firms to write off, for tax purposes, new plant and machinery at whatever rate they chose. It was aimed at encouraging the modernisation of plant, amounting, in effect, to granting interest-free loans of varying periods. Other such assistance has included grants towards the cost of new plant and machinery and the provision of loan finance. Research by Harris (1990) regarding the impact of capital grants in Northern Ireland suggests that grants have been effective in boosting manufacturing efficiency and competitiveness (though their effectiveness ran into serious problems during the 1970s and 1980s, when economic growth in the province was low and often negative). Analysis by Wren and Waterson (1991) of two major British initiatives, Regional Development Grants and RSA, has indicated these also proved relatively efficient in terms of the cost per job created.

In addition to subsidising capital costs, government has also attempted to subsidise labour costs, principally through the Regional Employment Premium (REP). As Table 13.9 shows, REP is not estimated to have been particularly effective as an employment creation measure. This is partly due to its sudden abolition in 1976 and the fact that many of the jobs it had generated subsequently disappeared. Yet Moore et al. (1986) concluded that, even at its peak, REP was the least effective of the main regional policy instruments. It was also found to be the least cost-effective, with a gross Exchequer cost per job created as of 1981 of £73,000, compared to £25,000 for investment incentives or £17,000 for RSA.

The last two decades of the twentieth century have witnessed a move from general to selective regional instruments, aimed at projects where assistance is expected to achieve particularly favourable results. One class of enterprises on which funding has been concentrated are the branches and subsidiaries of overseas multinationals; by the early 1990s over 40 per cent of RSA was being paid to foreign-owned companies (Taylor and Wren 1997). Multinationals are regarded as being particularly 'footloose', often not having very strong existing ties to any particular British location. Furthermore, large projects, concerning, say, Japanese motor vehicle manufacturers, can create several thousand jobs at a stroke. There is also substantial international competition among governments to attract such projects; assistance can therefore be justified on the grounds that in its absence the corporation might locate overseas.

The emphasis on attracting multinationals has led to an increased concentration of multinational plants in Britain's peripheral regions. An extreme example is Northern Ireland, where intensive efforts to attract inward investment led to 23 per cent of manufacturing employment being provided by foreign-owned plants in 1978. By 1993 (largely as a result of the privatisation acquisitions of Shorts Aerospace and the Harland and Woolf shipyard) the foreign-owned sector had risen to 28 per cent (Stone and Peck 1996).

Empirical studies suggest that the direct effects of multinationals have been positive. Yet their 'spill-over' effects, especially with regard to local sourcing, have been very disappointing – as many plants do not enjoy autonomy in purchasing decisions and receive many of their inputs from their parent company (Young *et al.* 1994). These plants also appear particularly vulnerable to international recession, as companies generally select their geographically peripheral, rather than core, operations for closures. As such, the emphasis on multinationals, while creating a good deal of employment, appears to have accentuated problems associated with the 'branch plant economy' of Britain's peripheral regions.

Partly in response to these concerns, recent years have witnessed increased interest in fostering indigenous development by targeting aid at small firms – which had hitherto been generally neglected by British regional policy. Assisting small firms also proved politically popular to Conservative governments during the 1980s, as part of a wider policy of fostering the 'enterprise culture'. Analysis by Hart and Scott (1994) of grant assistance to small firms in Northern Ireland indicated that the cost per job created compared favourably with the province's other main employment programmes and appeared cost-effective in terms of savings in unemployment welfare benefits. Similarly, analysis by Wren (1994), concerning firms in north-east England, indicates that assistance to small firms is much more effective than that provided to large firms.

Another policy option that has been relatively neglected in Britain for much of the post-war period is the improvement of transport and other infrastructure in peripheral regions to reduce their locational disadvantages. Such assistance appears attractive on theoretical grounds since it produces enduring benefits, unlike grant assistance. Yet this very feature has often deterred policy makers looking for quick and easily identifiable results. Analysis of the impact of infrastructure development is particularly difficult, not least due to the counterfactual problem of assessing what expenditure would have occurred in the absence of regional assistance. Yet there is a great deal of evidence that the quality of the local environment and its communications exercise a strong influence over firm location. For example, private sector industrial estate developers generally concentrated their developments along Britain's expanding motorway network and only began to show interest in the peripheral regions when they developed motorway links (Bale 1974).

Following the UK's accession to the EU in 1973, the scope and character of regional policy has become increasingly influenced by EU regional programmes. Accession gave the UK a conduit to European Social Fund (ESF) grants towards the cost of training and worker mobility schemes. As a country with some of the poorest regions among the states that had then joined the EU, the UK rapidly became the recipient of one third of all ESF grants (Armstrong and Taylor 2000: 221). Britain also became eligible for European Coal and Steel Community assistance, including 'conversion loans' to help new industries establish themselves in former coal and steel areas, European Investment Bank loans for industrial and infrastructure projects in depressed regions, and support for depressed agricultural areas.

In 1975 the European Regional Development Fund (ERDF) came into operation. This provided grants and interest rebates for industrial investment projects and small firms, together with finance towards infrastructure projects. The ERDF gradually expanded during the 1980s and was substantially boosted in 1989 (to meet the expected adverse impact on depressed regions from the introduction of the Single European Market). As a result, in the 1990s the EU became the dominant partner in British regional policy, with much national government assistance taking the form of 'matching funding' for EU initiatives (Armstrong and Taylor 2000: 222).

Evidence indicates that government regional policy measures have been effective, in terms of job creation. A widely respected study by Moore et al. (1986) estimated that, over the period 1960–81, regional policy directly created 604,000 manufacturing jobs in the Development Areas – an average of almost 29,000 jobs per year. Of these, 154,000 were lost before 1981 (a rate of job loss not greatly different from that for manufacturing industry elsewhere in Britain), leaving some 450,000 surviving at 1981. These figures do not include the multiplier effects on service industry employment. Assuming a regional multiplier of 1.4, the 450,000 surviv-ing manufacturing jobs would generate a further 180,000 jobs in service industries, giving a total (direct and indirect) jobs gain of 630,000 at 1981. The cost per job to the Exchequer averaged about £40,000 in real (1982) prices. Yet, as noted earlier, regional disparities have proved remarkably durable. This has been linked to the pattern of British post-war regional development, which – it is argued – regional policy has reinforced rather than countered.

PATTERNS AND MODELS OF REGIONAL DEVELOPMENT

While neoclassical models have not proved successful in analysing the nature and persistence of uneven regional development, *new economic geography* theories have managed to capture many of its dynamic features. These take account of economies of scale, imperfect competition and the process of cumulative causation that characterises the path-dependent evolution of local and regional economies. Regions which gain a head-start in a particular industry benefit from the clustering of related plants producing intermediate goods or conducting ancillary processes. Close input–output linkages generate external economies of scale and foster in-novation and co-operative product development. Meanwhile regions lack-ing these advantages may become dominated by the sort of production for which they are not important – standardised, low-value-added, assem-bly and manufacture of 'mature' products.

Such patterns are evident within the UK. Massey (1984) and Heim (1987, 1988) have argued that during the twentieth century, and particularly after the Second World War, the UK witnessed a major change in the spatial division of labour, the nineteenth-century pattern of regional spe-cialisation by industry being replaced by a trend towards specialisation by function. R&D and management have become concentrated around the south-east, while standardised assembly work has moved to areas of inexpensive, adaptable labour. Regional specialisation in particular indus-tries, such as textiles in Yorkshire and Lancashire, or the metal trades in the West Midlands, still survives, but tends to be more characteristic of de-clining rather than expanding sectors and of those dominated by smaller rather than larger firms. Such a pattern of regional development would have important implications for incomes, welfare and economic opportu-nities, since domination by a 'branch plant economy' and the consequent low availability of 'white collar' employment damages the development of job skills, the quality of available work, the fostering of entrepreneur-ship and the prospects for new firm formation (Harris 1988). Peripheral branch plants producing well-established products are also more vulner-able to closure during recessions, as noted above. Furthermore, as many

Region	Non-production employment in manufacturing per 1,000 manufacturing employees[a]	Producer service industry employment per 1,000 total employees[a]	% of manufacturing workforce in plants over 100 miles from Head Office[b]	% of workers in previous column in firms employing over 10,000 workers[b]
Table 13.10 Indicators of regional divisions of production by function, c. 1981				
South-east	364	345	12.7	8.2
South-west	305	264	45.2	42.3
East Anglia	290	274	33.2	6.7
North-west	277	277	55.5	48.4
West Midlands	274	264	26.7	25.4
East Midlands	261	242	17.1	12.8
Yorkshire & Humberside	259	247	31.0	23.4
Scotland	259	244	65.9	50.4
North	254	223	53.7	27.4
Wales	232	214	68.1	55.0
GB Total	295	284	N/A	N/A

[a] Derived from 1981 Census data. Excludes producer service employment within primary industry, construction and utilities, due to classification problems.
[b] Derived from 1980 Workplace Industrial Relations Survey. Includes plants with no UK Head Office.
N/A = not applicable.

Sources: columns 2–3 – Marshall (1988: 64); columns 4–5 – Harris (1988: 337).

branches produce for national and international markets and have purchasing decisions made at Head Office (which also provides many of their business services), they generally demonstrate weak linkages with the local economy (Fothergill and Guy 1990).

Table 13.10 examines the accuracy of this 'spatial divisions of labour' model using four indicators. The first two show the extent to which employment in producer services (which is closely associated with headquarter functions) was unevenly distributed at the time of the 1981 Census. The south-east has an unusually high proportion of employment in this sector, in terms of both non-production employment in manufacturing – which represents 'internalised' producer services – and producer service industry employment – which represents specialist marketed services. R&D jobs have become even more concentrated in the south-east, which accounted for 54.9 per cent of Britain's R&D employment in 1984, compared to 7.2 per cent in Scotland, 3.0 per cent in the Northern region, and only 1.7 per cent in Wales (Martin 1988: 400).

The third column examines the extent to which manufacturing employment was dominated by firms headquartered more than 100 miles from the plants in question. This is important given the wealth of evidence that the further plants are from Head Office, the more likely they are to be used for assembly and other routine functions. Scotland, Wales, the Northern region and the north-west are each shown to have over 55 per cent of their manufacturing workforce employed by such plants, compared to only 12.7 per cent for the south-east. Regions dominated by enterprises headquartered more than 100 miles away were also found to have a considerable proportion of their employment in companies employing over 10,000 people. These characteristics of ownership by very large enterprises and remoteness from Head Office often went hand in hand, as is shown in the final column. Conversely, the peripheral regions generally had a relatively low proportion of large indigenous firms. They were thus subject both to a high degree of external control and to a high level of control by very large, distant, corporations.

Marshall (1988) has argued that these trends in manufacturing are paralleled in the office sector. 'Higher' headquarters, research and technical functions have become increasingly concentrated in and around the south-east to take advantage of economies of agglomeration and pools of skilled labour, while regional branches have become increasingly devoted to routine functions. These trends have been boosted by innovations in information and communications technologies that have allowed the decentralisation of data processing and similar routine activities to office 'factories' in areas with a plentiful supply of cheap, especially female, labour. There has also been a tendency for service sector firms to serve peripheral markets with a depressed manufacturing base from more central areas. While there has been substantial decentralisation of office activities from central London since the 1960s, this has mainly involved short-distance moves to other parts of the south-east, which accounted for three quarters of relocations over 1983–93. Meanwhile only 13 per cent went to destinations outside the south-east, south-west or West Midlands (Jones Lang Wootton 1994).

As Fothergill and Guy (1990: 170) have noted, government regional and other policies have mainly acted to reinforce, rather than redress, this trend towards 'regional dualism' – the progressive development of a successful 'core' around the south-east and 'periphery' in northern and western Britain. The government's overriding emphasis on employment creation resulted in a failure to shift firms' 'centre of gravity' to the assisted regions, white-collar, R&D and key production facilities remaining in the south-east. Instead the assisted areas received labour-intensive production that was marginal to the firms concerned, reinforcing an economic peripherality that mirrored their geographical peripherality.

The main features of British regional policy can be distinguished as: an overriding concentration on employment creation; concern with immediate problems rather than long-term development; a macroeconomic rather than regional planning focus; and (largely arising from these other factors) a heavy reliance on branch plants. Throughout the post-war period policy has mainly aimed to attract branches of national and international companies rather than foster indigenous development. Branch plants offered obvious advantages to policy makers, compared to indigenous industry; they diversified the regions' industrial base and, most importantly, enabled the rapid development of substantial factories, employing large numbers of people.

Yet by the early 1950s studies were already beginning to highlight the long-term problems that this emphasis on branch plants was producing. It was found that branch plants attracted to the Development Areas generally undertook the more labour-intensive, less-skilled, processes of the firms in question and employed an unusually high proportion of females. Their production was also found to be often marginal to the parent firms' activities and, therefore, extremely vulnerable to closure in the event of recession (for a summary of these studies see Scott 1997). Meanwhile the Board of Trade had allowed new R&D facilities (both corporate and government) to become concentrated around London (Heim 1987, 1988). Analysis by Heim (1987) of applications for corporate R&D plants from November 1944 to July 1948 revealed only one instance involving location outside a Development Area being ultimately rejected. Southern locations were justified on grounds of organisational links, intellectual and commercial contacts, and the preferences of skilled staff. Firms were often allowed to expand R&D or pilot production around London on condition that they undertook to disperse standardised production activities, thus reinforcing the functional regional division of labour. Similarly, firms in expanding, capital-intensive, sectors were usually able to avoid the Development Areas by arguing that efficiency considerations made their preferred locations essential (Rosevear 1998).

An alternative strategy, advocated by some experts and officials since the 1940s but generally rejected by government, involved basing regional development around 'growth points'. By selecting particular areas within high unemployment regions that had real potential to act as efficient and prosperous industrial centres, and concentrating resources on these, it was argued, a process of self-sustained growth might be initiated that could eventually stimulate wider industrial growth throughout the region. Some supporters of this strategy also advocated encouraging particular industries to locate in such areas, in order to foster economies of agglomeration. Yet growth points only formed a significant strand of British regional policy for a brief period during the early 1960s, which offered insufficient time for their advantages to be seriously tested.

In recent decades concerns regarding the increasing domination of peripheral regions by branch plants have led to renewed interest in the possibilities of fostering industrial clusters as a means of promoting self-sustaining local and regional development. This has occurred in the context of research into the success of agglomerations of small, sectorally specialised, craft and artisan firms in 'new industrial districts'. The use of computers for programmable assembly operations has, it is argued, radically reduced the cost of small batch production relative to mass production and thus fostered a resurgence of flexible, craft-based, production methods (Piore and Sabel 1984). Such districts have been identified in various regions of Europe, particularly north-eastern and north-central Italy. High-tech firms have also shown a notable tendency to form industrial clusters, famous examples including Silicon Valley in California and a cluster that has developed around Cambridge (fostered in part by the development of the Cambridge Science Park).

The Labour government has recently placed considerable emphasis on the support and development of regional high-tech clusters as a key strand of its regional policy, in the wider context of fostering a 'knowledge-driven economy'. However, given the extremely limited high-tech base of most peripheral regions, there is considerable doubt that government support would be sufficient to promote such clusters, which remain largely confined to the Oxford/Cambridge/London axis. The government's continued emphasis on localised pockets of deprivation, rather than broad regional problems, also runs counter to this strategy – as the areas within less prosperous regions that offer the best environment for industrial clusters are unlikely to coincide with the particularly deprived communities on which government assistance is concentrated. Meanwhile, analysis by the Regional Studies Association of policies aimed at indigenous growth through new firm formation, enterprise and competitiveness (both in Britain and elsewhere) has concluded that 'there have been modest successes but no-one has found the magic formula' (Regional Studies Association 2001: 12–24). The trend towards the concentration of 'core' functions in the south and more routine and marginal production in the north and west does not, therefore, show any clear signs of being reversed in the foreseeable future.

14

British fiscal policy since 1939

TOM CLARK AND ANDREW DILNOT

Contents

INTRODUCTION

This chapter covers the two distinct areas of public policy that can be described as 'fiscal'. It begins by looking at 'tax and spend', examining issues such as the proportion of the nation's output controlled by government, the evolution of the tax system and public expenditure trends over the period. It then considers the macroeconomic issue of government borrowing.

In spite of the apparent intellectual distinctiveness of these two aspects of policy, our chapter will reveal parallels in their histories. In particular, after the Second World War both 'tax and spend' and macroeconomic fiscal policies evolved fairly smoothly until the 1970s, when in both fields there was a significant change of direction. In the case of 'tax and spend', the trend in the first twenty-five years after the end of the Second World War was for growing government, and growing discretionary expenditure on the welfare state in particular. After the mid-1970s growth in state spending in the economy was checked, and ultimately partially reversed. Macroeconomic fiscal policy proceeded smoothly in the first half of the post-war period, being based on the view that discretion in setting the government's borrowing was invaluable in regulating economic demand. But it, too, changed course in the mid-1970s, and discretion was jettisoned in favour of a rules-based approach. In the final sections of the chapter, therefore, we try and analyse why it was that these changes were in parallel, and argue that it was more than a coincidence.

GOVERNMENT SPENDING AND TAXATION IN THE ECONOMY

The scale of the public sector

In 2000, government spending in the UK was a little less than £360 billion, and government revenues a little more than £370 billion[1]. Numbers like this are so large as to be hard to interpret, but equate to between £14,000 and £15,000 for each UK household – an amount equivalent to the post-tax income a childless couple would need to be in the middle of the income distribution.[2]

Looking back over the period since 1939, we have seen substantial growth in the size of government. There has been an increase by a factor of about 5.5 compared with 1938 in the real level of government spending. But while changes in the real level of spending provide some indication of the developments we have seen, they conflate the growth of the whole economy and the change in the role of government within that economy. Since 1938 the real level of GDP has grown by a factor of somewhat less than five. We therefore focus in most of the rest of this section on the share of the economy absorbed by government activity.

Figure 14.1 shows the level of government revenues and spending since 1900, so as to set our discussion of the period from 1939 in the context of the whole of the twentieth century.

Perhaps the most striking feature of Figure 14.1 is the role of wars. The twentieth century begins with relatively high spending reflecting the costs of the Boer War. The First and Second World Wars both lead to very large increases in public spending and rather smaller increases in tax. The Korean War (1950–3) may just have a discernible effect, but neither the Falklands (1982) nor Gulf (1991) conflicts seem to have had an impact on spending which is visible in Figure 14.1.

---

[1] This section of the chapter is based closely on the analysis in Clark and Dilnot (2002a). Consult this for more details on data sources and methods.

[2] A. Goodman (2001). The similarity of median income and Government spending per household helps give a rough feel for the scale of the latter. But for several reasons it implies little about the relative magnitude of private and public spending – for one thing because some items (like social security benefits) count in both.

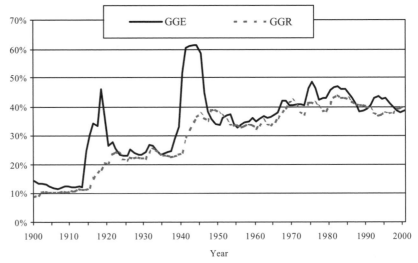

Figure 14.1
Government spending
and revenues as % of
GDP since 1900

Source: Institute for
Fiscal Studies (IFS)
data files.

GGE = General Government Expenditure; GGR = General Government Revenue.

More important than the short-run effect of the major wars on spending was the more enduring effect on the size of government. After both First and Second World Wars public spending fell back when hostilities ceased, but to levels much higher than those which had preceded the war. This failure of government to return to its pre-war role has been called the 'ratchet' effect.

Discussion of the size of the state activity typically focuses on public spending. A natural model of the activity of government is to think of politicians (or voters) starting with a set of desired objectives for state activity, and then raising tax to finance these. But if we look at tax as a share of GDP (the GGR series in Figure 14.1) another possibility also seems plausible. Whereas the spending share falls at the end of both wars, albeit not completely, the tax share barely does. Perhaps, then, electoral pressures check the ability of politicians to raise taxes as much as they would like in peacetime, but wars ease this constraint. If so, then the role of wars in allowing governments scope for higher levels of non-military spending once war is over may be important.

The wars dominate Figure 14.1 to an extent which dwarves any trends in post-war tax and spending. Figure 14.2 therefore focuses on the path of taxation and public spending for the period since 1948. In the early post-war years overall spending continued to decline for a period, although it was boosted temporarily by the Korean War in the early 1950s. From the mid-1950s until the mid-1970s there seems to be a trend to higher spending, although there is considerable volatility. From the mid-1970s until the end of the century the pattern is reversed, with an apparent tendency for public spending to decline as a share of GDP, although again with

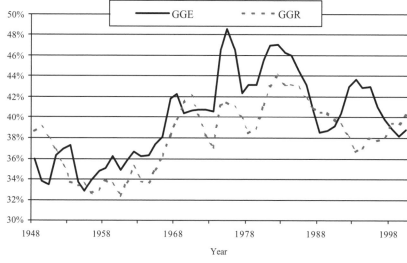

GGE = General Government Expenditure; GGR = General Government Revenue.

Figure 14.2
Government spending
and revenues as % of
GDP since 1948

Source: IFS data files.

some periods of growth. The two marked periods of growth in the last quarter of the century, in the early 1980s and early 1990s both coincided with downturns in the economy, which led both to shrinking GDP and to higher cyclical government spending as unemployment rose steeply. The first decline, from the mid-1970s peak, reflected substantial reductions in the real level of public spending, while the long declines from the early 1980s and mid-1990s combined spending restraint with economic growth.

The path of revenue fluctuates less than that of spending, and, far from falling smoothly after the war, actually rose as a share of GDP in 1948 and 1949. The tax share showed no clear and systematic sign of increasing until the mid-1960s, but did then rise substantially to 1970. The second half of the 1960s is striking as the most (or, perhaps, the *only*) significant and sustained increase in the tax burden seen over the twentieth century which did not reflect war or pre-war military build-up: between 1964 and 1970, General Government Revenue increased from 33.6 per cent of GDP to 42.1 per cent, an increase of 8.5 percentage points.

Over the following fifteen years, to the mid-1980s, the tax share fluctuated without any obvious trend up or down. In part the fluctuations were driven by the performance of the economy, in part by discretionary policy. In the last decade and a half of the twentieth century, Figure 14.2 shows that tax as a share of GDP declined, although far from smoothly – a sustained decline until 1993 was followed by a tendency for the tax burden to rise. The election of a Labour government in 1997 was followed by a small increase in the tax share, raising questions about whether a return to growing government might be seen, but it is as yet too early to judge this.

| Table 14.1 Number of income taxpayers by year, 1938/9–1998/9 |||
Financial year	Number of taxpaying families (thousands)	Number of taxpayers (thousands)
1938–9	3,800	n.a.
1948–9	14,500	n.a.
1958–9	17,700	n.a.
1968–9	20,700	n.a.
1978–9	21,400	25,900
1988–9	21,500	25,000
1998–9	n.a.	26,900

n.a. = not available.

Source: HMSO, *Inland Revenue Statistics* (1987, 1992 and 2001 editions).

Across the developed world, the evolution of the UK's tax burden is relatively distinctive. In the early post-war years the UK was a relatively high-tax country, and the large increases in the UK's tax burden that we have seen took place over the 1960s ensured that it remained so into the 1970s. But in most other industrial countries the state continued to grow at least into the 1980s and often beyond; by contrast, the absence of a trend in the UK's tax burden since the mid-1970s now leaves it as a relatively low-tax country, when compared to the G7 and EU averages. (See OECD 2000 for more details.)

The tax system

As we have already noted, the Second World War led to a substantial increase in taxation. In 1939 government revenue absorbed 23.4 per cent of GDP, while by 1945 it had reached 37.6 per cent, compared to the 9.0 per cent of 1900 and 40.2 per cent in 2000. The need for more revenue during the war led to increases in tax rates, increases in the coverage of existing taxes, and the introduction of wholly new taxes. Perhaps the most dramatic change was to income tax. Prior to the war, income tax had never been a 'mass' tax. First introduced in 1799, and permanently in place from 1842, there were still fewer than 4 million taxpaying families in 1938. By the end of the war the number had increased to over 12 million, an increase which was sustained into the following decades, as shown in Table 14.1. Indeed, over the post-war decades the number of taxpaying individuals tended to continue growing, so that by 1998–9 there were some 26.9 million. The other major sources of new revenue during the Second World War were an excess profits tax, increased excise duties and capital levies.

As Figure 14.2 showed, during the post-war period the overall level of tax first fell, then remained broadly stable until the mid-1960s, after which it rose to 1970, was broadly stable for a decade and a half, then declined somewhat after the mid-1980s. Figure 14.3 charts the relative

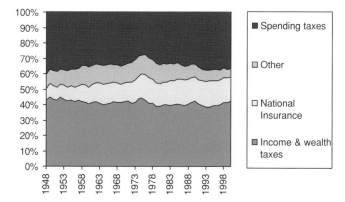

Figure 14.3 Breakdown of gross government revenue by source since 1948

Notes: 'Income and wealth taxes' includes local taxes directly paid by households, taxes on corporate incomes and capital taxes. 'Spending taxes' includes intermediate taxes on production, such as non-domestic rates.
Source: IFS data files.

importance of different types of tax in providing this evolving total of government income since 1948.

Looking at Figure 14.3 overall, the stability in the relative importance of the different types of government income is perhaps more striking than the changes over time. But some interesting trends are evident. The relative importance of taxes on income and wealth tended to decline a little over most of the post-1948 period, from 44.8 per cent of General Government Revenue (GGR) in 1949 to 38.9 per cent in 1980. Since this time, there has been a slight recovery in their relative importance, so that by 2000 they stood at 42.3 per cent GGR. By contrast, the role of National Insurance contributions, which should probably be thought of as more like a tax on income than anything else, increased in importance fairly smoothly between the 1940s (they represented 8.8% of Government revenue in 1949) and the mid-1980s (16.4% in 1986), since when their share has stabilised. Taken together, these trends mean that broadly defined 'direct' taxes (National Insurance and income and wealth taxes combined) have increased modestly in importance over the whole period, from having accounted for about 50–2% of revenue in the 1950s to reaching 58% in 2000.

The stability of the share of taxes on spending, as shown in Figure 14.3, masks shifts in the balance between excise duties on individual commodities and general sales taxes. Aside from National Insurance contributions, VAT is the only major source of revenue to have become much more important over the period. By contrast, for much of the period, product-specific excise duties failed to keep pace with inflation.

Indeed, the effect of inflation on the composition of the tax take is clearly visible in the first half of the 1970s, an era before indexation of the tax system for inflation was automatic. In these years, therefore, price increases reduced the state's real take from excise duties, while increasing its take from income tax, by eroding the real value of allowances. The share of spending taxes fell from 32.7 per cent of GGR in 1972 to 27.6 per cent in 1975, while those of income tax and National Insurance rose. After the mid-1970s inflation rates tended downwards, and it came to be expected that budgets would adjust the tax system for inflation, so trends in the price level become a less important determinant of the balance of revenues. (See Dilnot and Emmerson 2000, for further discussion of aggregate figures, and Clark and Dilnot 2002 for more detailed consideration of the development of the tax system.)

The composition of public spending

The first section of this chapter showed that the importance of overall government spending in national income tended to increase during the first half of the post-war era, and has tended to decrease since then. But this overall story masks considerable variation across different areas of spending, the issue to which we now turn. In particular, expenditure on the main pillars of the welfare state is seen to have grown in relative importance – reflecting changing demographic and economic conditions as well as increasing public expectations – at the expense of spending elsewhere.

The most substantial growth in spending share is seen in social security. Social security spending merely involves the government redistributing money between people, rather than deciding on what it should ultimately be spent. As such, one might expect that the former would have very different economic effects from the latter and (perhaps) that it could more easily receive public approval. In fact, however, the steepest rise in social security spending coincided with the cessation of growth in state spending in the economy overall.

As Figure 14.4 shows, at the beginning of the post-war period only 15 per cent of total public spending went on social security. A buoyant economy helped ensure that this grew fairly slowly to 20 per cent in 1975, despite significant increases in benefit levels and considerable growth in the numbers entitled to retirement benefits. From the mid-1970s to the early 1980s, however, spending grew much more rapidly, approaching 30% in 1986, reflecting huge increases in the numbers dependent on benefits – both because of a substantial increase in unemployment (and non-employment more generally) and because of changes in the demographic structure, such as the increasing numbers of low-income lone parents. Since the mid-1980s, in spite of cyclical fluctuation, the overall share has remained fairly stable.

The relative stability of social security spending since the mid-1980s might seem surprising given that demographic forces for increased

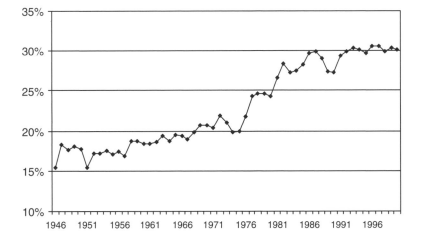

Figure 14.4
Government spending
on benefits as % of
General Government
Expenditure

Source: IFS data files.

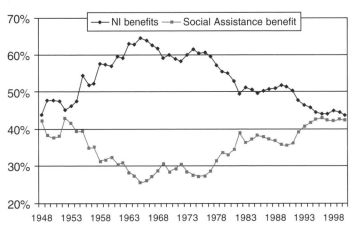

NI = National Insurance

Figure 14.5 Cost of
selected types of
benefit as % of total
benefit spending

Source: IFS data files.

spending (such as the aging population) have continued to operate. It reflects rather tight control of benefit rates, which have mostly fallen relative to earnings since 1979. But the move away from contributory benefits to those tested on incomes has also played a part. Figure 14.5 shows the changing relative importance of the two main types of benefit since 1948. The first class, 'National Insurance' benefits, are conditional on the claimant having made contributions out of earnings in the past but entitlement is not reduced if claimants have independent income or wealth. They are paid when the claimant stops working – for example, the state pension in the case of retirement. The second class, 'Social Assistance' benefits, have no link to past contributions, and are made dependent on 'need', which, depending on the benefit, is assessed by income, family size or health.

Figure 14.5 shows that in the first two decades after the war, the relative importance of National Insurance benefits increased, from 42.2 per cent of the total in 1948 to 65.6 per cent of the total in 1965. This reflected real-terms increases in the rates of these benefits, as well as an increase in the proportion of the population entitled to them. Over these years, the proportion of benefit spending represented by Social Assistance fell commensurately. In the fifteen years after 1965, these trends were slightly reversed, initially because of the introduction of new benefits which were not conditional on contributions and so counted as 'Social Assistance', notably a raft of new benefits for disabled people in the late 1960s and early 1970s and, from the late 1970s onwards, the universal child benefit.

After 1979 these trends continued, but for new reasons. In particular, National Insurance benefits were made less generous, through tighter time-limits, the abolition or reduction of earnings-related top-ups and the freezing in real terms of benefit rates. So the proportion of benefit spending they accounted for fell from 55.4 per cent of the total in 1979 to 43.5 per cent in 2000. To a degree, Social Assistance spending increased automatically as a result, because means-tested benefit entitlement was required to 'top up' the incomes of an increasing proportion of those in receipt of National Insurance benefits. But the overall effect of the shift away from the 'contributory' principle was to reduce benefit expenditure, as increasingly widespread means-testing targeted money away from all but the poorest.

Two other areas of spending, health and education, have seen their share of the total rise over the post-war period, although their growth paths have been very different. In health we see relative stability in the spending share until the mid-1970s, since when the spending share has risen by nearly a half (Figure 14.6). Demographic pressures may explain some of this pattern, as the number of the very oldest pensioners, who are particularly heavy users of healthcare, went up most rapidly in the last quarter of the century. But given that pensioners more generally (a far larger group) also use the health service disproportionately, and given that their numbers increased more rapidly in the post-war period than in the last two decades of the century it seems unlikely that demographics can offer anything like a complete explanation. Rather, it seems that some combination of rising relative costs in healthcare provision and rising public expectations must have been important.

In education, the pattern of increase is reversed – with a fairly steady rise until the mid-1970s followed by a quarter of a century of broad stability (Figure 14.7). The trend in education mirrors the demographics of post-war Britain, and may be partly explained by them. In the years up until the mid-1970s the 'baby boom' combined with increases in the school-leaving age to increase the school-aged population. Between the mid-1970s and the end of the 1980s, though, the total number of pupils

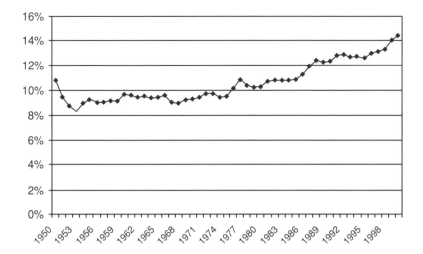

Figure 14.6 Health spending as % of gross government expenditure since 1950

Source: IFS data files.

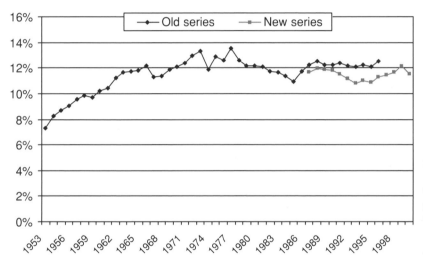

Figure 14.7 Education spending as % of gross government expenditure since 1953

Source: IFS data files.

declined in more years than it increased, which might have been expected to reduce the pressure on the education budget. Again, however, demographics are unlikely to provide a complete explanation, as, throughout the 1990s, the school-age population grew, but there was little sign of a recovery in education's spending share.

Overall, then, since the 1950s the proportion of government spending consumed by the three main pillars of the welfare state have tended to increase – social security by just under 15 percentage points of the total, health by around 5 percentage points, and education by around 4 percentage points. Corresponding to these increases in shares are reductions elsewhere.

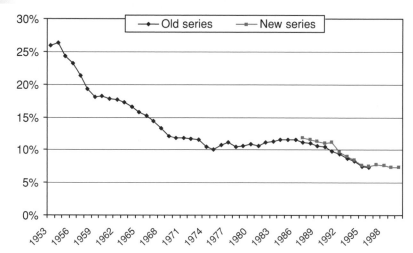

Figure 14.8 Defence spending as % of gross government expenditure since 1953

Source: IFS data files.

Defence is the single field of government activity which has seen the most dramatic decline. Figure 14.8 shows defence spending as a share of the total in the years since the end of the Korean War. In 1953 and 1954 defence spending constituted over a quarter of government outlays, but then fell very steeply throughout the remainder of the 1950s and 1960s. In these years National Service (i.e. conscription) was phased-out and imperial commitments were scaled back with decolonisation and the ultimate decision to withdraw from all bases east of Suez (in 1968). By 1975 defence spending had reached just 10 per cent of the total. At this point the decline was checked, and the defence share actually inched up for a period as Britain entered into a new NATO commitment to increase defence spending until the mid-1980s. But the thawing and then the end of the Cold War heralded a new decline – the defence share fell from around 12 per cent to about 7 per cent between 1986 and the end of the century.

The overall decline in the defence share since the 1950s thus approaches 20 percentage points, a decline so large that it could be thought of as offsetting the great bulk of the increase in the share for social security, health and education. The particularly rapid decline in defence spending between 1954 and 1964 (during which around half the total decline occurred) helps explain how it was that over these years welfare provision was expanded and demographic pressures were apparently met without difficulty, even while, as we saw in Figure 14.2, the tax burden was relatively stable: reduced defence commitments were freeing resources for the government to spend on the welfare state.

In later decades, another area of government activity to be squeezed was spending on capital projects. The investment done by central and local government fluctuated at around 10–12 per cent of GGE between 1956 and 1976. As Figure 14.9 shows for the years since 1963, if investment

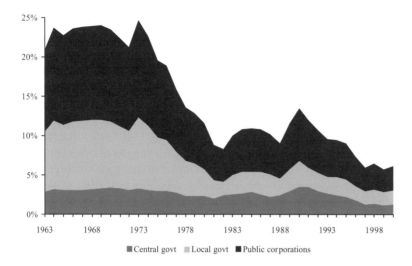

Figure 14.9 Different types of state investment as a share of gross government expenditure since 1963

Note: Public corporation investment does not count as part of GGE in the national accounts.
Source: IFS data files.

by the nationalised industries is taken into account, the scale of public investment until 1976 approximately doubles. After the mid-1970s, the relative importance of public investment declined very sharply indeed. It fell to represent less than 10 per cent of GGE by the early 1980s, since when, in spite of fluctuations, it has declined further, so that it represented just 6 per cent of GGE by 2000.

The decline breaks into three phases. First, between 1976 and 1982, as the chart shows, the decline is principally explained by the decline in local government investment. Housing explains most of this – council housing investment had fluctuated around 5.5 per cent of GGE in the two decades after 1956, but collapsed almost to zero between 1976 and 1982, and has never significantly exceeded 1 per cent since then. House building is one activity which the state withdrew from almost completely – the number of council houses completed in 1998 was less than 1 per cent of the 1976 level. Education investment, another responsibility of local authorities, also fell especially sharply between the late 1970s and early 1980s and has never significantly recovered.

The second phase of the decline in public investment as a share of GDP, which lasted for most of the 1980s, reflected lower public corporation investment. (Public corporation investment looks fairly stable in Figure 14.9 because it is given as a proportion of GGE, which declined as a share of GDP over most of this period.) This fall largely reflected privatisation, and so the majority of this investment has been substituted by private sector activity rather than discontinued – for example, when British Telecom was privatised in 1984, a significant amount of public sector investment was simply reclassified as being private.

After a modest recovery in the years 1987–92, public investment started falling again. The investment cuts in this third phase of decline were general across public services, and the figure shows that central government investment fell most sharply. Although the current Labour government has announced plans to increase public investment, they do not seem likely to be sufficient to reverse the trend seen since the 1970s. (For more on this, see Clark *et al.* 2001.)

The final type of Government spending with dwindling relative significance is debt interest payments. In 1955, interest paid out by the state to the private sector and the rest of the world was equal to 14.3 per cent of GGE, but had fallen to just 9.4 per cent of GGE in 1975, since when, in spite of fluctuations, it has tended to fall further, to just 7.2 per cent by 2000. But the extent to which indebtedness constrains the government's ability to engage in other types of spending will depend on the underlying strength of its financial position, rather than on the cash flow of interest payments it is making. We consider how the former can be assessed below.

MACROECONOMIC FISCAL POLICY: MEASURING THE FISCAL STANCE

In this section we start by sketching out alternative measures of macroeconomic fiscal policy since the Second World War.[3] In subsequent sections, we consider how these measures were influenced by the evolution of the policy making framework since 1939.

The macroeconomic 'fiscal stance' is usually assessed by looking at the scale of the public deficit – the gap between the state income and expenditure. High levels of borrowing increase demand and are therefore generally held to stimulate economic activity; low levels of borrowing (or, on occasion, actual repayment of debt) decrease demand, and so are generally thought to depress economic activity.[4] The strength of these effects will depend on the size of the surplus or deficit in relation to the economy as a whole, so they are best measured as a proportion of GDP.

Public borrowing can be measured in a number of ways depending (amongst other things) on treatment of one-off receipts like asset sales and on whether the borrowing that public corporations undertake is included. Over most of the post-war period, the different measures have followed similar paths.[5] We focus on Public Sector Net Borrowing (PSNB), which is designed to avoid one-off receipts having a dominant effect.

---

[3] This section of the chapter is based closely on the analysis in Clark and Dilnot (2002b). Consult this for more details on data sources and methods.

[4] The doctrine of Ricardian equivalence, revived by Barro (1974), lays down a theoretical challenge to the idea that expansionary fiscal policy will affect the real level of economic activity at all. In practice, except in peculiar circumstances, it is not contentious that there will be at least some short-term effect on output from a fiscal expansion or contraction.

[5] The notable exception is the late 1980s and early 1990s, when widespread privatisation revenues produced a number of one-off receipts which strengthened the public finances significantly on some measures but not on others, from which asset sales were excluded.

So how can the path of the deficit best be summarised? The immediate aftermath of the Second World War saw the closure of the huge wartime deficit over 1946 and 1947, followed by a few years of surplus as demobilisation reduced government expenditure. But in 1950 military commitments again arose in Korea, and the deficit reached 4 per cent in the final year of that conflict, 1953. After this, sustained peace began, and the fiscal stance stabilised. Although the 1950s and 1960s are associated with fiscal activism and macroeconomic 'fine-tuning' in policy making, as subsequent sections will show, it is apparent that the deficit followed a remarkably steady course over these years compared with what has occurred in more recent decades. The deficit fluctuated in the region of 2–3 per cent of GDP in every year after 1953 until 1967. The latter year saw the deficit increase to almost 4 per cent, but was immediately followed by a fiscal tightening visible from 1968, which eventually produced surpluses in both 1969 and 1970.

After 1970, fluctuations in the deficit become increasingly marked. The PSNB increased each year in the early 1970s, so that by 1973 the deficit was back to 1967 levels, in spite of an economic boom. It increased further when the first significant post-war recession struck in 1974–5, and in 1975 reached a post-war high, standing at 7.3 per cent of GDP on the old measure (6.9 per cent on the new measure). There then followed what can be seen as a very prolonged – if faltering – period of deficit reduction, culminating in the surpluses of 1988 and 1989.

Finally, the 1990s saw the most violent swings in this measure of the fiscal stance in the entire post-war era. The decade started with an extremely rapid rise in borrowing, so that in just a few years the surpluses of the late 1980s had turned into a deficit of unprecedented peacetime proportions – in 1993 the PSNB reached 7.8 per cent of GDP. The subsequent tightening of the fiscal stance was almost equally dramatic – borrowing dropped every year until in 1998 a surplus was once again recorded, and by 2000 the surplus reached almost 2 per cent of GDP – a level not even approached since the late 1940s.

In general, the graph suggests that the fiscal stance has been expansionary since the war. The government has engaged in borrowing in most years since the war, repaying debt only in a few brief periods.

How useful is the deficit as a measure of discretionary fiscal policy? One obvious problem concerns the economic cycle – even where there are no discretionary changes in policy, an economic downturn depresses government receipts (as falling incomes reduce the tax base) and at the same time increases expenditures (notably, on unemployment-related benefits). These effects mean a downturn will produce a deficit under policies that would previously have achieved balance; conversely, a boom can produce a surplus where policies previously implied balance.

On these grounds, if the aim is to isolate the stance of *policy*, then perhaps fluctuations in the fiscal stance should be discounted to the extent

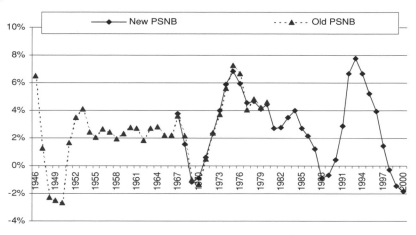

Figure 14.10 The public sector deficit as a proportion of GDP, 1946–2000

Note: The 'old' series is based on official estimates of the public sector deficit; the 'new' series is based on official estimates of public sector net borrowing.

Source: IFS data files.

PSNB = Public Sector Net Borrowing.

that they merely reflect variation in actual economic growth rate around its trend.[6] How does this insight colour our interpretation of Figure 14.10? The absence of a serious recession in the UK over the 1950s, 1960s and early 1970s means that over these years the picture is not dramatically changed. Estimates of a cyclically adjusted General Government Deficit for this era suggest a slightly more volatile pattern than the 'raw' numbers, but the required adjustment never reaches 1 per cent of GDP, so the pattern seen over these years barely changes (Allsopp and Mayes 1985).

After the 1970s, however, cyclical adjustment does produce marked effects as economic growth became more volatile. In Figure 14.11, the official estimate of the cyclically adjusted deficit is shown alongside the 'headline' measure of Figure 14.10. The adjustment does not hugely change the picture over the 1970s, but in the 1980s its effect is pronounced. In particular, once adjusted for the cyclical effect of the severe recession of the early 1980s, the discretionary fiscal stance of the time appears contractionary. The total contribution of policy was to impose a cyclically adjusted surplus that approached 2 per cent of GDP in 1982. In the late 1980s boom, the opposite is true. In spite of the surpluses achieved in the years 1988 and 1989, the effect of budgetary policy was actually expansionary. Once allowance is made for the excess of output over trend in these years, the fiscal surplus becomes a deficit, which by 1989 was 2 per cent of GDP.

Over the 1990s, the two measures diverge less, especially in the second half of the decade. Over the years 1992–5, output remained below

---

[6] The 'cyclically adjusted' deficits, which we refer to in this section, are calculated by assuming that the economy follows a particular long-run growth path. This allows estimation for each year of what the policies in place during it would have meant for the tax burden and for aggregate expenditure had the economy been on its long-run growth path. The difference between these magnitudes gives the adjusted deficit.

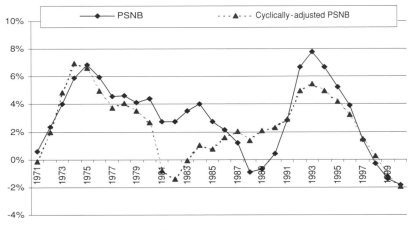

Figure 14.11 The
public sector deficit as
a proportion of GDP
since 1971

PSNB = Public Sector Net Borrowing.

Source: IFS data files.

trend as the economy recovered from the 1991 recession. As a result, the deficits appear more modest than on the unadjusted count. The adjustment leaves the deficits of these years looking somewhat smaller than the peak reached in the 1970s. Still, there can be no doubt that the effect of discretionary policy was significantly expansionary – an adjusted deficit worth 5.5 per cent of GDP is shown for 1993, a degree of discretionary expansion unmatched at any point in the post-war era except the mid-1970s.

The cycle aside, another potential objection to relying on the PSNB as the only measure of fiscal policy is that it ignores the level of the stock of outstanding government debt. Figure 14.12 shows this for the whole twentieth century.[7] The dominant effect of the two world wars is immediately obvious: in each, vast borrowing massively increased the debt burden. The Second World War took the debt burden to its highest point in the era: it reached over 252 per cent of GDP during demobilisation. But the story in the aftermath of the two wars is strikingly different. The debt burden left by the First World War was not rapidly reduced. Indeed, in 1934, sixteen years after the Armistice, the debt burden stood at 182 per cent of GDP, higher than in the immediate aftermath of war. By contrast, the large debt run up during 1939–45 started declining almost as soon as demobilisation was underway: the debt burden fell in each of the thirty

[7] The National Debt is the chosen measure of public debt because it has been recorded over a long period: Public Sector Net Debt (PSND) is now the officially preferred measure of debt position, but is unavailable for earlier years. In practice, the two series have followed very similar courses. From 1970 to the mid-1980s PSND and the National Debt were consistently extremely similar; in the late 1980s, privatisation transferred much debt from the former nationalised industries to outside the public sector, which reduced PSND but not the National Debt, so the PSND fell faster as a share of GDP in these years. Since the early 1990s the two series have run roughly in parallel, with PSND representing around 5–10 fewer percentage points of GDP than the National Debt.

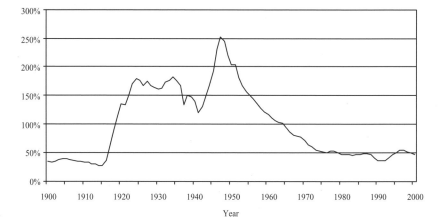

Figure 14.12

National debt as a proportion of GDP over the twentieth century

Source: IFS data files.

years after 1947, after which it stabilised at around 50 per cent of GDP, a fifth of its 1947 peak.

This way of looking at the fiscal stance, then, radically changes the picture of the post-war period from that obtained by looking at a measure of the cash flow of borrowing, such as PSNB. The 1950s, 1960s and even the 1970s are now revealed as years during which the government steadily but very substantially improved its financial position. And the comparison with the interwar years suggests that policy may have been important in this – as it is not necessarily something that happens automatically in peacetime. The century's last two decades look rather different, with debt being generally stable as a share of GDP. The only exceptions are the late 1980s, during which there was a visible reduction, and the early 1990s, when the debt burden rose appreciably for the first time in the post-war world.

Why, then, did the debt burden fall continuously over the first thirty years after the war, and why did it stop trending downwards after that point? The decline reflects a number of factors working in the same direction. First, the very high level of the debt ratio left by the Second World War meant that significant borrowing was required to avoid eroding it, given that national income was growing (and especially as it was growing rapidly).[8] Secondly, post-war inflation persistently turned out to be higher than anticipated. As a result the real value of the (cash-denominated) stock of debt eroded.[9] Finally, as we have seen, measured by comparison with what came next deficits tended to be modest in these years.

[8] For any rate of nominal national income growth, the greater the debt ratio, the higher the level of borrowing which is consistent with a stability in this ratio.

[9] The fact that the rate at which the government could borrow remained low right through the 1960s even once inflation started rising may seem surprising. It could be taken as indicating a delay in expectations of investors adapting to inflation but may also have followed from government intervention in the gilt market, which was widespread until 1971.

The debt ratio stopped declining when all these factors ceased to operate as they had done earlier: the debt ratio had fallen and economic growth slowed, making a lower rate of borrowing compatible with the ratio's stability; expectations had adjusted to higher inflation; and borrowing was, on average, higher. The increasing debt ratio of the early 1990s reflected all these things, but especially the fact that sustained disinflation was finally achieved, leaving inflation lower than had been expected during the (mostly high inflation) years when the National Debt stock was sold. This meant that the interest on the outstanding debt was now more than compensating for the inflation, increasing the real debt burden.

Is there anything we can take away from all these alternative measures aside from having learnt that measuring the fiscal stance is complicated? Whether we assess the fiscal stance through trends in the National Debt burden, the actual deficit or the cyclically adjusted deficit, it seems that fiscal policy was tighter through most of the 1950s and 1960s than it has tended to be since. This is, perhaps, in contrast to what might have been expected, given that the 1950s and 1960s are often associated with especially expansionary (and perhaps unsustainable) policies. We shall see below that in the early post-war decades policy makers were indeed far more focused on economic expansion and far more willing to use fiscal policy to achieve it than were their successors.

One possible interpretation of this apparent puzzle is that the autonomous and underlying strength of the economy in the so-called 'golden age' was sufficiently robust to ensure healthy public finances in spite of expansionary policies, and that since that time its underlying weakness has had the opposite effect. Another view would be that the strength of the economy itself in part flowed from the fact that the government was committed to expansion, an interpretation which could have the curious implication that the government's willingness to countenance substantial borrowing actually helped contain the scale of borrowing actually required.

THE EVOLUTION OF POLICY

The Second World War and its aftermath: activism gains a foothold

In the 1920s and later 1930s, as Britain struggled through two slumps (1920–1 and 1929–31) and protracted unemployment, the idea of using fiscal policy to 'pump-prime' the economy gained advocates. At the 1929 election Lloyd-George famously advanced the idea of loan-financed public works. But these ideas never took hold: the goal, if not the outcome, of interwar fiscal policy remained what it had traditionally been in peacetime – an annually balanced budget.

It is not hard to see why the active use of fiscal policy to regulate demand did not take hold before the Second World War. During Britain's (relatively mild) interwar depression, the theoretical argument for fiscal expansion had not been articulated – Keynes' *General Theory* was not published until 1936, and the basic concept of the multiplier was barely formulated. By the time the theory was established, it had little obvious practical bearing: Britain was well into recovery, and indeed, from 1937, the government was already boosting demand in the depressed heavy-manufacturing regions by deficit-financed rearmament which the rest of Whitehall forced on a reluctant Treasury.

The absence of theoretical foundations, though, was only half the story; the other half was institutional resistance. After the UK left the gold standard in 1931, the Treasury dominated policy making. The famous 'Treasury view' of unbending economic orthodoxy was in many ways a caricature – mandarins appreciated the need to manage actively both sterling and interest rate (Howson 1975, 1980; Howson and Winch 1977). But in fiscal policy the Treasury did indeed remain conservative – the priority remained 'sound' national finances.

Total war made an increased fiscal deficit unavoidable. This meant that, after 1939, the principal economic threat was no longer insufficient demand and unemployment, but inflation caused by excessive demand. In *How to Pay for the War*, Keynes argued that fiscal activism could help to check inflation without threatening military expenditure or necessitating tight money (Keynes 1940). In practice, compulsory savings were imposed on a relatively small scale, with much of the anti-inflationary work being left to rationing and price controls. But Keynesian ideas had for the first time changed the terms in which the Treasury thought about fiscal policy and gained real influence over its formation. This became evident, for example, when the government constructed the first serious national income tables to help it prepare the 1941 budget – previously macroeconomic information would have been seen as irrelevant to the budget judgement, but from this time on records and forecasts of economic performance became central to it.

At the same time, official views of what economic policy could and should achieve expanded. In particular, full employment came to be viewed as a necessary goal. The official and hugely influential Beveridge Report (Beveridge 1942) argued 'the place for direct expenditure and organisation by the State . . . in maintaining employment of the labour'. Two years later, the government appeared to embrace this view in the 1944 employment White Paper, in which it accepted responsibility for securing 'high and stable levels of employment', through ensuring that: 'total expenditure on goods and services must be prevented from falling to a level where general unemployment appears'. In this way, the post-war commitment to demand management was effectively established; and, according to the ascendant Keynesian view, this would necessarily involve fiscal activism – interwar experience was taken as showing that, in slump conditions, monetary policy was like 'pushing on a piece of string'.

In fact – in spite of the new consensual willingness to countenance fiscal expansion – in the immediate aftermath of war, as in the war itself, fiscal activism played a secondary role in economic policy. As reconstruction got underway, cheap money proved sufficient to sustain it; and when inflation threatened, price controls and rationing continued to be used to keep it at bay. During Dalton's chancellorship (1945–7), fiscal policy was free to focus on finding the revenue that the Attlee government's ambitious schemes required, as well as on redistribution.

Under Cripps (1947–50), fiscal policy did play a (albeit supporting) macroeconomic role, but not in an expansionary manner; rather, it helped rein in demand. Surpluses were achieved by the maintenance of high wartime taxation together with an increasingly tight grip on public spending. So it was only really from the early 1950s that an active fiscal policy began to focus on maintaining the 'right' level of output.

1950–1967: 'Butskellism' and fiscal fine tuning

The 1950s and 1960s can be seen in retrospect as the high point of the 'Keynesian' approach to fiscal policy making. Regardless of whether the policies produced were ones that Keynes himself would have approved of, it is certainly true that policy exhibited certain tendencies which have since been associated with him. In particular, the fiscal stance in these years came to be regarded to an unusual degree as a matter of *discretion*, something to be set by policy makers with a view to controlling the performance of the economy overall, in particular in avoiding recession.

In the later years of the Attlee government, the 'bonfire of controls' began the removal of the many quotas, regulations and rations which the war had necessitated. The surrender of most direct economic controls meant that the government came to rely on fiscal and monetary policy to steer the economy.

Whereas interwar advocates of active fiscal policy had tended to argue for public investment schemes, in practice the fiscal fine tuning in Britain's 'Keynesian age' was mainly attempted through manipulating tax rates. Counter-cyclical tax changes were regular – as they were announced both in regular budgets and 'emergency' statements, they could sometimes take place several times a year.

Considerable attention has been given to the allegation that demand was regulated in line with the political, rather than the economic, cycle in the 1950s. Certainly, it is true that policy took an expansionary turn before each of the general elections in these years – in 1955, 1959 and 1964. The example of 1955 is perhaps particularly striking. The April budget cut income tax rates and boosted allowances, even though unemployment was close to 1 per cent (low even by the standards of the day); in July, with the May election out of the way, a mini-budget then tightened policy. Whether or not electioneering dominated the fiscal stance in these years, the perception that it might have had a bearing eventually proved significant; for if politicians were seen as using their ability to manipulate demand for non-economic reasons, then the expectation would be that policy could actually be destabilising, indicating that a policy based on rules might do better.

Throughout the 1950s, though, such thoughts were some way off. There was agreement between the two parties on this basic strategy of fiscal activism. Indeed, the resulting continuity of policy between Gaitskell, the Labour chancellor in 1950–1, and his Conservative successor, Butler, inspired the term 'Butskellism'.[10]

But from the start of the 1960s strains emerged on the Butskellist consensus. Focus shifted from favourable comparisons of contemporary economic performance with the interwar era to much less flattering contrasts with the UK's competitors. The feeling grew that fiscal policy alone was inadequate to secure rapid, steady growth. But the initial response was to supplement fiscal activism, rather than to abandon it.

In the last years of the Conservative government, Selwyn Lloyd's 1961 'pay pause' signalled the beginnings of incomes policy; and a new willingness to engage in corporatist macroeconomic management was reflected in the founding of the NEDC (National Economic Development Council). On its arrival in power, in 1964, the Labour administration tried to go further in extending the number of economic tools available to complement fiscal policy by announcing an indicative National Plan. Balance-of-payments crises and low growth persisted, though, and by 1967 the failure of economic management became transparent with the forced devaluation of sterling.

1967–1979: inflation and disillusion

From the late 1960s onwards the fiscal agenda gradually moved away from that of the post-war era. The shift was gradual and faltering – not being completed, perhaps, until 1979. There were two aspects to it. First, a shift in the relative priority attached to the various goals of policy – in particular, a new stress on inflation – which had implications for the fiscal stance. Secondly, policy makers' conception of the appropriate role of

---

[10] 'Butskellism' refers to the style of economic policies that British governments pursued over the 1950s, based on Keynesian demand management, an acceptance of significant welfare spending and a reasonably *laissez-faire* approach to most labour market and microeconomic issues. The term derives from a journalist who argued continuity between Labour and Tory policy meant the economy was effectively run by 'Mr *Butskell* . . . a composite of the present Chancellor and the previous one' (article in *The Economist* referring to R. Butler and H. Gaitskell, 13 February 1954).

fiscal policy in reaching economic goals changed. Ultimately, the framework of policy was to move a long way from the discretionary approach back towards the rule-based approach of the interwar era.

Arguably, the first significant shift can be dated to the 1967 devaluation. The government had for years tried to ward this off, but, once it became inevitable, policy became geared to ensuring that devaluation 'worked' – in other words, that the gains in competitiveness were sustained, rather than being rapidly eroded in price and wage increases. This meant keeping inflation low, something the new Chancellor set about doing by instigating a major fiscal tightening. The hope was that, in restraining domestic demand, the government would create the conditions under which the foreign sector would ensure full employment by demanding more British goods. So, in contrast to the Butskellist era, over the next several years, fiscal policy was focused in a sustained way on restraining demand rather than maintaining it. Figure 14.10 shows how the PSNB of 3.8 per cent of GDP in 1967 gave way to a surplus of 1.2 per cent and 1.3 per cent of GDP in 1969 and 1970. These were the first surpluses since 1950.

The 1970 Conservative platform expressed a new conviction that postwar governments had tried to do too much in the economy, stating 'there has been too much government: there will be less' (Conservative Party, 1970). Although there was no explicit abandonment of fiscal activism, this attitude combined with the high priority the Heath government initially claimed to attach to controlling inflation to suggest that they no longer believed that the first sign of recession should be met by fiscal expansion. Although the fiscal stance was actually loosened modestly almost from the outset (the basic rate of income tax being cut 2.5 percentage points in 1971) this proved insufficient to prevent an economic slowdown, and unemployment was allowed to approach and then exceed the 1 million mark in 1972. At this point, the government retreated from its bold rhetoric.

In the March 1972 budget, Chancellor Barber restated the commitment to demand management, and public spending increases as well as substantial tax cuts followed. The eventual reflation was all the larger because the traditional restraining mechanism on excessive expansion – the onset of a balance-of-payments crisis which threatened sterling's fixed parity – was lost when, in June 1972, the government decided to let the pound float freely. It proved possible to increase the PSNB to 6 per cent of GDP in 1974, a deficit on a different scale from those of the 1950s and 1960s. Barber's expansionary measures put the public finances significantly into *structural* deficit. As this occurred at a time when the first serious recession since the war was about to begin, the effect on the headline public finance figures was especially dramatic, which helps explain why for the next few years policy was framed in an atmosphere of fiscal crisis.

In late 1973, the government realised the loosening had been excessive (due to forecasting error) as the inflationary 'Barber boom' took hold. But at this point the policy decision was complicated by the first OPEC shock, which simultaneously threatened increased inflation *and* recession. From late 1973 to mid-1975 fiscal policy followed an uncertain course in a series of budgets and mini-budgets. The Conservatives attempted a modest deflation in late 1973, but lost power in February 1974, after which the Labour administration alternated between announcing deflationary tax increases (as in March 1974 and April 1975) and expansionary measures (as in July 1974).

The year 1976 proved to be a watershed. In spite of unemployment at 5 per cent and rising, fiscal policy was tightened on a number of occasions. First, in February the Public Expenditure White Paper replaced the proposed growth path of spending announced in 1975 with proposals for real-terms cuts in each financial year up until 1978–9. Secondly, in July a mini-budget announced further spending cuts as well as increased National Insurance contributions. Finally, at the end of the year, a sterling crisis enforced recourse to the IMF, which extracted a 'Letter of Intent' from the chancellor which pledged to still more fiscal tightening. James Callaghan's speech to the 1976 Labour Conference indicated that he no longer believed that fiscal policy could – or should – prevent unemployment at all costs. He announced the death ('insofar as it ever existed') of 'the cosy world . . . where full-employment would be guaranteed by a stroke of a chancellor's pen'.

In 1977 restraint continued even whilst unemployment was allowed to remain at around 6–7 per cent. Even so, the post-war fiscal approach was not yet completely abandoned: the 1978 budget provided a fiscal loosening aimed at 'setting the level of economic activity so that unemployment [would be] reduced'. As the crisis of the mid-1970s receded, then, the government appeared to be reverting to the fiscal policy it regarded as 'normal', suggesting it did not agree with the radical critics of the post-war approach who argued that it was demand-management policies themselves which were responsible for the crisis in the first place. Only with the election of Mrs Thatcher, in 1979, did a government with this view assume power.

1979–1999: a return to rules-based fiscal policy

Several important ministers within the 1979 Conservative administration were influenced by Milton Friedman's 'monetarist' school. The school criticised fiscal demand management on two counts. First, fiscal policy was held to be secondary to monetary policy, because it was effective only where accompanied by an appropriate policy towards the money supply. Secondly, the real effects of fiscal expansion were seen as temporary and contingent on its ability to raise prices. Expansionary policy increased

inflation and so could temporarily (through 'money illusion') lead workers to lower their real wage demands.[11] This encouraged firms to hire
more workers and so boosted output. Eventually, however, workers came
to expect higher inflation, so real wage demands recovered and unemployment tended back to the 'natural rate'. This could only be prevented
if policy became even more expansionary, meaning even higher inflation
had to be tolerated. In essence this is what post-war governments were
seen as having repeatedly done.

The Thatcher government's adhesion to the monetarist view that fiscal policy would not be inflationary if accompanied by sufficiently tight
monetary policy was arguably evident in its 1979 budget. For in spite of
its declared intention of prioritising the battle against inflation it substantially increased VAT, rejecting concerns over the inflationary consequences of this fiscal move. Even so, it did immediately reduce the public
deficit through expenditure cuts. But it was only really from 1980 that
it became clear how central a tight fiscal policy was to the Thatcherite
anti-inflationary approach. The budget in that year set out the 'medium-
term financial strategy' (MTFS), which proposed a path of reduction in
the cash deficit (the public sector borrowing requirement) as a share of
GDP.

The declared intention of the fiscal tightening was to 'support' the disinflationary monetary policy, by removing a possible source of monetary
growth (the monetisation of the public deficit). The same policy could
instead have been advanced as disinflationary in Keynesian terms – a fiscal tightening would reduce aggregate demand, and so would directly
reduce output and employment, putting downward pressure on prices
and wages. Politically, the monetarist rationale was the more attractive
to emphasise, as it did not necessitate appearing deliberately to plan large
increases in unemployment. But the more traditional view doubtless also
had influence in Whitehall.

In the event, the determination to stick to the rules was tested extremely hard by economic depression. By 1981 the economy was in a
severe downturn as the fiscal tightening already in place, a tight monetary policy, depressed world trade (in the aftermath of the second OPEC
oil price increase) and an extremely high pound combined. But even in
these circumstances, the government (or at least the 'drys' within it, most

---

[11] The 'new classical' school augmented the monetarist approach with fully forward-looking
rational expectations. This saw them go further than the Friedmanite monetarists, and
deny the efficacy of macroeconomic policy on real quantities, even in the short run. This
followed for two reasons. First, money illusion was ruled out even in the short term;
secondly, forward-looking agents would realise that higher government borrowing would
eventually produce higher taxes, so the demand effect of fiscal expansion would be offset
as private agents cut down on spending in order to save to meet these future tax bills
(a view known as 'Ricardian equivalence'). Perhaps because there is considerable evidence
that in practice policy can have real effects the impact of these more extreme views on
government was more limited.

significantly the prime minister and Chancellor Howe) was determined to stick to the MTFS. As the recession had increased the 'headline' deficit, this meant that a further tightening was required. In 1981, for the first time since 1931, in spite of rapidly falling output, budgetary policy was tightened. In particular, taxes were sharply increased through the non-indexation of allowances. This helps explain why the 'cyclically adjusted' deficit, shown in Figure 14.11, tightened dramatically, by almost 4 percentage points of GDP, in the single year between 1981 and 1982.

By 1982 inflation seemed to be coming under control – it had fallen substantially, and was still declining. At the same time, the beginnings of economic recovery in terms of output (although not unemployment) helped contain the 'headline' deficit and so reduced the fiscal tightening that fulfilment of the MTFS demanded. The role of fiscal policy continued to be downplayed by the government, but, over the next few years, as unemployment continued to rise, a modest loosening brought about through tax cuts was allowed.

In the later 1980s, the onset of a boom combined with privatisation to ensure that government revenues increased until borrowing turned negative (debt was repaid). In this context, given the continued focus on the unadjusted deficit it was possible to combine a significant fiscal loosening with the continued balanced-budget rhetoric. In both 1987 and 1988 the 'headline' strength of the public finances rationalised expansionary tax cuts which soon contributed to the onset of an inflationary boom. In the 1988 budget Chancellor Lawson could simultaneously boast that he had restored as a 'hallmark of good government' the 'simple and beneficent rule' of a balanced budget *and* make large tax cuts which loosened the fiscal stance. But by 1989, rising inflation caused a slight retreat, as Lawson saw that the additional fiscal expansion required to return to balance would be disastrous. He argued that 'the path of prudence and caution must be to return to balance not overnight, but gradually, over a period of years'.

In other words, after 1989 aggregate demand was once again being allowed to have at least some bearing on the public finances. This development was little noticed at first, as it implied a tight fiscal policy, but its effects became clear with the onset of a new economic downturn, as large increases in the deficit were tolerated on the grounds that the economy was below trend. Under Chancellors Lamont and Clarke the rhetoric of the MTFS gave way to the mantra of 'balancing the budget over the medium term', and the focus of fiscal policy shifted away from headline measures towards those which accounted for the economic cycle. The move in the direction of fiscal activism may have been further encouraged in the early 1990s because of the unavailability of other macroeconomic instruments. From 1990 until autumn 1992, the over-valued pound was locked into the exchange-rate mechanism. This directly prevented the manipulation of the exchange rate, but also ruled out the counter-cyclical use of interest rates, as they had to be kept high to resist speculative pressure.

The effect of the modest shift in policy after 1989 was exaggerated, because in these years the cyclically adjusted public finance measures which were the focus of the new approach were especially flawed. By the later 1980s there had been several years of rapid growth. This fact, in combination with the government's belief in the productivity benefits of the microeconomic policies that they had introduced (in terms of curtailing trade union influence, and reducing direct taxation), encouraged them to increase the estimated 'trend' rate of growth, in various budgets between 1984–5 and 1988–9, from 2.25 per cent to 3.0 per cent (HM Treasury 2000). As 'cyclical adjustment' of the fiscal stance depends upon the position of national income relative to what is reckoned to be its sustainable trend, such a change allows a looser fiscal stance to be employed.

At the end of the 1980s the first effects of these errors arose. In 1989 and 1990 non-fiscal instruments (the exchange rate and the interest rate) were used to cool the economy, while fiscal policy remained loose. Although this may have been partially because fiscal policy's importance continued to be downplayed, it largely reflected the erroneous view that the economy was close to sustainable potential (rather than well above it), so a fiscal stance that looks expansionary in retrospect was seen as tight at the time.

In the early 1990s the effects of the miscalculation became far clearer. The monetary tightening of the late 1980s and early 1990s finally combined with exogenous recessionary pressures in the world economy (such as a rising oil price) to push the UK into recession in late 1990. The fiscal response was in very sharp contrast to that to the (rather deeper) recession of the early 1980s. Figure 14.10 shows that between 1990 and 1992 the PSNB was allowed to loosen by 6.3 per cent of GDP, whereas between 1980 and 1982 the PSNB was actually tightened by 1.6 percentage points.

In part, the contrast reflected the moderation of policy implied by the move to target cyclically adjusted – rather than headline – measures: in the early 1990s the automatic stabilisers were allowed to run their course without offsetting retrenchment, and high headline deficits were not seen as worrying as long as they were credibly seen as temporary. So, when the government finally decided that it needed higher taxes to reassure the markets that its finances were sound, it announced some of the increases with a delay so that the recovery had time to gather strength first. The 1993 budgets therefore announced tax increases that were effective with a delay of a year and more. Yet again, policy was guided by the excessively optimistic estimates of potential GDP. They implied the economy was much further below trend than it really was, leaving the government underestimating the structural deficit and so leaving it unconcerned at high borrowing.

During the 1990s, official assumptions about the trend rate of growth were revised downwards, and in the July 1997 budget they were finally cut back to the early 1980s rate, 2.25 per cent. This change made it clear that the economy had been far closer to trend throughout the early 1990s than had previously been thought, and the cyclically adjusted deficit appeared more serious as a consequence. The fiscal stance was therefore tightened in a series of steps, by a mixture of tax increases and spending restraint, until eventually the public sector turned a surplus at the turn of the century.

The final change in fiscal policy seen in the twentieth century occurred in 1997, when Labour returned to power. Chancellor Gordon Brown announced two explicit fiscal rules that would form the constraint on government discretion. First, the 'golden rule', that over the economic cycle borrowing should only cover investment. Secondly, 'the sustainable investment rule', which stated that net public sector debt should never exceed a 'stable and prudent' level, fixed by the chancellor at 40 per cent of GDP. Taken alone, the golden rule allows more discretion than the previous policy of 'balance over the cycle', as it leaves net borrowing over the cycle as an option as long as its scale is smaller than government investment spending. But the addition of the 'sustainable investment rule' curtails the extent to which this freedom can be used, unless the debt ratio is well below 40 per cent of GDP. (See Emmerson and Frayne 2001.)

Neither rule, nor any of the other rules applied in the post-1979 era, is economically optimal from a theoretical point of view. The golden rule is justified by the notion that investment spending benefits future generations. But in practice it is clear that some spending not counted in the national accounts as investment does benefit future generations of taxpayers, perhaps most obviously education. And there is no obvious economic argument why a debt ratio of 40 per cent – rather than 30 per cent or 50 per cent – is optimal. As had been the case throughout the 1979 era, however, the government seemed to find it advantageous to bind itself through some commitment, rule or target not to engage in excessive fiscal expansion. The main positive effect of surrendering discretion in this way is on the confidence of investors in government stock (through a reduction in inflation-expectations and the perceived risk of default), and through these expectations on the long-term interest rate.[12]

Since 1979, therefore, governments have moved away from the post-war view that the best fiscal framework is that which allows maximal discretion. In the early 1980s, the government moved to the opposite extreme and made central the pre-Keynesian target of planning towards an annually balanced budget, irrespective of the economic cycle. Subsequently, the experience of that time saw the position moderate, and in

---

[12] There may be a more general disinflationary advantage – wage-setters may reduce inflationary expectations in the light of a credible commitment to fiscal restraint, and so reduce their demands.

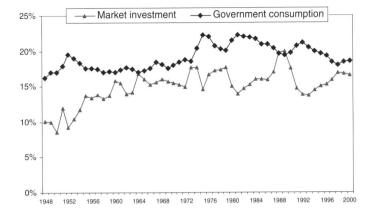

Figure 14.13 Market investment and final government consumption as % of national income, 1948–2000

Source: IFS data files.

various ways adjustments for the fiscal cycle were re-introduced. But the preoccupation with rules remains, and any rule that constrains behaviour will incur costs when shocks do arise. It seems that governments have come to believe, though, that these costs are worth paying.

ECONOMIC LIMITS ON THE USE OF FISCAL POLICY

We have seen that, both in terms of macroeconomic policy and in terms of tax and spend, the direction of policy changed markedly after the 1970s: discretionary manipulation of the deficit was curtailed, and the growth of the state was checked. This section briefly investigates whether particular economic constraints that have been hypothesised necessitated either change.

One economic argument which implies that the growth of the state could give rise to problems is 'resource crowding out': i.e. the idea that high government spending (specifically government final consumption, rather than spending on transfers) denies resources to the sales-financed 'market-sector' which ultimately funds non-market activity through tax (Bacon and Eltis 1976). The alleged risk was that market investment would suffer as a result, which would ultimately hurt output. One mechanism by which the effect could result would occur if unions offset high tax with wage demands, leaving profits squeezed and thereby hurting investment.

In fact, however, as Figure 14.13 shows, over the post-war period investment as a share of GDP has tended, if anything, to vary positively with government consumption. It might be objected that investment in the nationalised industries should be excluded, on the grounds that this sector is not fully 'market'. But even if this is done the data do not support the crowding-out hypothesis.

If investment did not suffer as government consumption and investment grew, then what did? Figure 14.14 provides the answer. As final

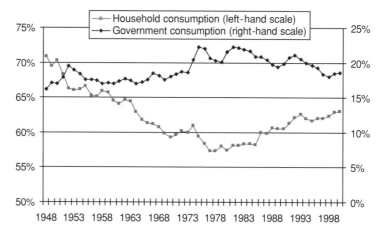

Figure 14.14
Household consumption and final government consumption as % of national income, 1948–2000

Source: IFS data files.

government consumption trended up, household consumption fell from 70.9 per cent of GDP in 1948 to 57.3 per cent in 1977. Once the relative share of government consumption started falling, after the mid-1970s, household consumption recovered – increasing to 63.0 per cent of GDP by 2000. Perhaps falling levels of private consumption relative to total output eventually produced electoral resistance. If so, the lesson taken from examining the changing composition of GDP since the Second World War would seem to be that the growth of government up until the 1970s ran into political rather than economic limits.

Even while rejecting the 'resource crowding out' argument as an explanation for the end of the growth of government, it is possible that we could maintain that the move towards a rule-based macroeconomic fiscal policy reflected economic constraints. In particular, it is often argued that expansionary fiscal policy is ultimately self-defeating because of 'financial crowding out' – a growing supply of public debt forces the government to offer a higher interest rate to persuade investors to hold it. The increased interest available on government bonds makes holding productive assets less attractive, as their relative return is reduced. This leads to a decrease in investment, perhaps to the extent that the expansionary effect of increased government borrowing is fully offset.

The argument has been applied to many countries outside the UK, and it has been argued that increasing interest rates did indeed follow on from expansionary fiscal policies after the 1970s (Barro and Sala-i-Martin 1990). In Britain, however, the force of this argument is lessened by the fact that real interest rates were low during the early post-war era, when (as Figure 14.12 revealed) Britain had a high debt burden. And in the 1970s, just before macroeconomic fiscal policy was to move away from the toleration of discretionary borrowing, real interest rates fell. Since that time, in spite of the debt burden being far lower than in the 1950s or 1960s, interest rates have risen to be relatively high.

These simple observations are not conclusive, for they tell us nothing directly about what would have happened to real interest rates in the last two decades of the twentieth century *vis-à-vis* the counterfactual in which a high stock of debt was maintained. A full evaluation of the effect of government borrowing is a difficult task, and certainly one that is beyond the scope of this chapter. (See Chada and Dimsdale 1999 for an attempt at addressing this difficult issue.)

But it is, perhaps, worth noting that, on the surface at least, the story of Britain's real interest rates since the war does not suggest that financial crowding out enforced the change in policy. Perhaps in the case of macroeconomic policy, as well, it would be at least as useful to look at changing political priorities and ideas as it is to look at economic constraints, in seeking to explain why it is that policy changed direction in the 1970s.

CONCLUSIONS

We have seen that the Second World War fundamentally altered the course of both aspects of fiscal policy. It dramatically increased government's share in the economy, and it enabled an activist approach to the fiscal stance to gain a foothold in Whitehall. The twenty-five years following it were characterised by the continuation of big government and fiscal activism into peacetime. Indeed, the state continued to grow. At the same time, pressure mounted to supplement macroeconomic fiscal policy with other types of activism. In all respects, then, in these years, fiscal policy reflected a strong and growing faith in the capacity of the state.

In the 1970s, suspicion of government activism developed. The rhetoric of 'rolling back the state' took hold, and the last quarter of the twentieth century did indeed see a trend for government to decline as a share of national income. Simultaneously with this, the macroeconomic argument that the state could and should manipulate its borrowing to protect full employment ceased to convince policy makers. In the early 1980s politicians deliberately sought to bind themselves to particular plans for the public deficit, and so committed themselves not to manage the economy actively. Since that time, tolerance of cyclical fluctuations in the fiscal stance has returned, but the preoccupation with rules continues, limiting the scope for demand management.

There is little evidence that 'crowding out', of either the resources or the financial variety, enforced the policy change in either aspect of fiscal policy after the mid-1970s. Of course, crowding out is far from being the only potential economic constraint facing politicians in these years – inflation, for example, was undoubtedly important, for macroeconomic fiscal policy at least. Still, the fact that the policy changes of the mid-1970s have largely been sustained in spite of significant variation in economic conditions seen in the last quarter of the twentieth century suggests that non-economic explanations are something historical research could usefully investigate. Such a story might be able to explain why it was that both aspects of fiscal policy changed simultaneously.

One possibility is that there was a change in the intellectual mood and that this encouraged policy makers to be suspicious of government activism, both in terms of the state controlling a high proportion of the economy, and in terms of policy attempting to regulate the level of output. Another is that social groups who were ascendant in the electorate from the 1970s onwards for some reason particularly tended to favour low taxes and/or prioritising of the battle against inflation.

A final way in which the history of the two aspects of fiscal policy could be linked would be if change in one aspect of policy *caused* change in the other. For example, it could be that Britons never really had been willing to pay for the big state through high tax, but that the bastardised Keynesianism popular until the 1970s gave the impression that it was possible, through expansionary borrowing, to increase state provision without raising taxes. Inflation in the 1970s could then have forced a change in macroeconomic policy, which, in turn, could have made clear to the public that state provision meant higher taxes, something they were unwilling to countenance. This story might draw some support from Figure 14.1 which showed that the only really large increase in peacetime taxes in the twentieth century was introduced by the (ultimately electorally unsuccessful) Labour government of 1966–70. Another story would be that the high unemployment following on from the macroeconomic 'reckoning' of the 1970s reduced most people's willingness to pay taxes, by making it increasingly clear that state finance was being spent disproportionately on the poor.

Whether any of these stories hold is clearly an issue requiring future research. But if support is found for any, then it might begin to look as though the parallels in the history of the two distinct aspects of fiscal policy since 1939 are more than a coincidence.

15

Industrial relations and the economy

WILLIAM BROWN

Contents

INTRODUCTION

Organised labour entered and left our historical period like a lamb, but for the central decades it dominated the political and economic scene like a lion. Managing trade unions was seen by government at times to be central to the task of managing the economy. Changes in the economy were to transform trade unions and, over the course of the period, the conduct of British industrial relations changed beyond recognition. This chapter is concerned with this change and with its economic implications.

The account begins with a brief discussion of the basic features of industrial relations and with an overview of how they changed. The chronological narrative is then broken into three twenty-year periods. The first takes us through the years of war-time regulation to the end of the relatively calm 1950s, a period during which Britain was widely perceived to have a settled (and even superior) system of industrial relations based upon collective bargaining. The second period was one in which this system began to break up, and in which governments, forced to abandon a *laissez-faire* approach, became embroiled in attempts at reform. The final twenty years witnessed irreversible changes, with collective bargaining undergoing substantial contraction.

Table 15.1 Trade unions and trade union membership in Great Britain: 1939–1999

	Number of trade unions registered	Number of union members (000s)	Union density: membership as per cent of employed
1939	1,019	6,206	31.9
1949	742	9,077	44.7
1959	668	9,257	43.3
1969	561	9,999	44.2
1979	454	12,639	53.4
1989	309	10,158	44.2
1999	237	7,898	32.8

Note: These data are from those obtained by the Certification Officer; from 1989 additional data from the Labour Force Survey suggest the CO's membership figures to be approximately 10 per cent overstated.

Source: Wrigley (1996: 63); Department of Employment. *Employment Gazette* and *Labour Market Trends* (various years).

THE BASIC FEATURES OF INDUSTRIAL RELATIONS

It is uncontroversial that the relationship between employer and employee is of profound economic significance. The way labour is managed determines its productivity, its cost, its welfare and its skills. What *is* controversial is how best labour might be managed, and who should be the beneficiaries. Employment is at heart a most unusual economic transaction, impossible to contain within a normal contractual arrangement because of the difficulties of monitoring and motivating workers, usually over continuous periods of many years. As a result the employment contract is generally contained and protected by complex institutional arrangements intended, with varying degrees of success, to uphold chosen standards of effort, expertise, fairness, flexibility, security, discipline, decency and so on. Because these are inherently controversial, and because the employer is generally in an overwhelmingly strong position with respect to the individual employee, two particular means of employee protection have been developed. These are, first, trade union involvement through collective bargaining and, second, the statutory protection of individual employment rights.

There was substantial change in the proportion of employees in trade union membership in Britain over the period. As Table 15.1 indicates, it rose during the war and 1940s before levelling out for three decades, then rising to a peak at the end of the 1970s before falling back sharply to much the same level in 1999 as it had been in 1939. It will also be evident that the number of unions declined steadily over the whole period, as unions merged in response to structural and technological change.

From an international perspective, as Table 15.2 suggests, Britain's trade unions were distinctive in that they experienced substantial growth through the 1970s, and a particularly sharp collapse afterwards.

Trade unions fulfil a number of functions for their members, ranging from protecting the vested interests of their skills through to defending their individual rights. Their capacity to do the former depends to a substantial extent upon how far the competitiveness of the product market in which the employer operates permits the accumulation of rents, of which the union might be able to extract a share. For this reason most western European countries tend to have highly unionised public services. As will become clear, a fundamental influence on industrial relations over the 1939–99 period was the changing competitive context in different industries, imposing increasing constraints on both rents and access to them.

Table 15.2 Trade union density in Britain, USA, Germany and France, 1940–2000				
	Great Britain	USA	Germany	France
1940	33	27	n.a.	25
1950	45	31	41	30
1960	44	31	39	19
1970	48	27	38	21
1980	54	22	41	17
1990	38	16	38	9
2000	30	13	30[a]	9

[a] German data for West Germany up to and including 1990.
n.a. = not available.

Sources: USA from Kochan *et al.* (1986); Bureau of Labor Statistics. Great Britain, Germany and France from Waddington and Hoffman (2001); Bain and Price (1980); Visser (1989); EIRO (2001). The GB figures differ from those in Table 15.1 partly as a result of differences in definition of potential membership.

Trade unions attempt to influence the employment contract by engaging with employers in what is generally called collective bargaining. This covers a spectrum of influence. It ranges from, at one end, detailed agreements that regulate not only pay and working time but also all manner of aspects of the conduct of work. At the other end of the spectrum there may be no more than weak opportunities to be consulted and to represent individual members. To different extents and with different timing in different industries, collective bargaining moved over the course of our sixty-year period first towards the strong influence end and then far back over to the weak influence end of this spectrum. As will become clear, there are substantial microeconomic implications in the extent to which collective bargaining constrains employer discretion in the management of labour.

The conduct of collective bargaining has strong macroeconomic as well as microeconomic implications. One aspect of this is the overall coverage of collective agreements, in terms of what proportion of employees – regardless of whether or not they are individual members of trade unions – have their wages and hours of work regulated by a collective agreement. It will be evident from the rough estimates in Table 15.3 that for most of the period this was the great majority of employees, but that such coverage grew rapidly during the war and collapsed in the 1990s. The effect of this collapse, concentrated within the private sector, was augmented by the abolition in 1993 of all but one of the statutory wages councils, which provided legally binding minimum wage rates for a limited number of low-paying industries.

Another feature of collective bargaining that underwent substantial change over the period was whether employers bargained as a group or

Table 15.3   Estimates of the coverage of principal pay fixing arrangements for all employees in Great Britain: 1940–1998 (%)

	1940	1950	1960	1970	1980	1984	1990	1998
Collective bargaining and wages councils *of which:*	50	80	80	80	75	73	55	40
Industry-level agreements (multi-employer)	40	55	50	50	35	30	25	20
Wages councils	10	25	25	15	15	13	10	0
Enterprise/factory agreements (single-employer)	0	0	5	15	25	30	20	20
No collective bargaining or statutory support	50	20	20	20	25	27	45	60

Source: Public and private sectors; estimates derived from: Flanders (1954); Beatson (1993); Millward *et al.* (1992); Milner (1995); Millward *et al.* (2000); Brown *et al.* (2000). Public sector review bodies (from 1970) counted as multi-employer collective agreements.

as individuals. The bargaining strategy that had developed in Britain as elsewhere in Europe since the nineteenth century was that employers' associations would be formed industry by industry, initially on a regional but later on a national basis, in order to present a united front to organised labour, to prevent individual employers being picked off one by one. It can be seen from the rough estimates provided in Table 15.3 that from the mid twentieth century this strategy broke down. Employers in the private sector increasingly broke ranks to continue to bargain, but on their own, at enterprise or sub-enterprise level. If, indeed, they chose to bargain with trade unions at all. The result was a massive increase in the decentralisation or fragmentation of bargaining, especially in the private sector, a factor of profound macroeconomic importance in those decades when the avoidance of wage inflation became a paramount government objective.

The strength of trade unions depends ultimately upon their capacity to organise effective industrial action. Here again there have been substantial changes over the period. Table 15.4 provides five-year averages of two basic measures of industrial action: the number of strikes, and the number of working days lost, which incorporates the numbers of workers involved and the duration of strikes. But the economic significance of strikes lies less in their immediate cost than in the threat they pose to the employer. Put simply, an employer's backing down in the face of a strike threat may have far costlier implications for them in the longer term than their taking on the action. Thus, from the employer's point of view the crucial question is the credibility of the strike threat. In the third and fourth columns of the table we have accordingly calculated measures that are crude indicators of the propensity of union members to strike and to bear the costs of strikes: the number of strikes per million members, and the number of working days lost per thousand members. It will be seen that the average propensity to take strike action was fairly stable until collapsing sharply from the 1980s. For reasons that will be evident when the sub-periods are described separately, the number of working days lost had a more dramatic climax in the 1970s before again falling in the 1980s to unprecedented low levels in the 1990s.

Table 15.4 Industrial disputes in the UK: 1939–1999				
Years	Average number of strikes p.a.	Average working days lost through strikes p.a. (000s)	Average number of strikes per 1,000,000 trade union members p.a.	Average working days lost per 1,000 trade union members p.a.
1935–9	863	1,977	152	349
1940–4	1,491	1,813	197	239
1945–9	1,880	2,235	211	251
1950–4	1,701	1,903	179	200
1955–9	2,542	4,601	261	473
1960–4	2,511	3,180	251	318
1965–9	2,380	3,929	231	382
1970–4	2,885	14,077	253	1,237
1975–9	2,310	11,663	181	914
1980–4	1,350	10,486	115	890
1985–9	895	3,940	85	376
1990–4	334	823	37	90
1995–9	213	495	27	63

Sources: Wrigley (1996: 135); Department of Employment, *Labour Market Trends*, June 2001: 302.

Table 15.5 Working days lost through industrial action per 1,000 employees in UK, USA, Germany and France, 1940–2000				
	United Kingdom	USA	Germany	France
1940–4	96	296	n.a.	n.a.
1945–9	119	1,298	n.a.	1,306
1950–4	89	669	61	501
1955–9	207	610	34	130
1960–4	117	305	19	150
1965–9	145	532	5	127[a]
1970–4	441	551	48	169
1975–9	477	235	43	177
1980–4	244	144	44	75
1985–9	123	80	2	35
1990–4	37	43	18	47
1995–9	21	38	3	105

[a] Excluding 1968.
n.a. = not available.

Sources: for 1940–9 – Ross and Hartman (1960); for 1950–74 – Clegg (1976); for 1960–89 – Edwards (1998); Edwards and Hyman (1994); US Department of Labour (various years); for 1990–9 – Department of Employment, *Labour Market Trends*, April 2001; National Statistical Office (2002). Note that these relate to days lost per employee, whereas Table 15.4 relates to trade union members.

How far did the British experience reflect broader international patterns? An attempt at comparison is made in Table 15.5, although definitional differences demand extreme caution. It is apparent that over the whole period, strike propensities generally differed greatly between the UK, USA, Germany and France, with Germany relatively dispute-free throughout. Britain's experience of working days lost through strikes rose to be relatively high, although below the USA until the mid-1970s, before falling faster and further from the early 1980s.

No overview of the basic features of industrial relations would be complete without mention of the law. This has two aspects: collective labour law and individual labour law. The first provides the framework within which trade unions can operate – rights to strike, rights to organise, and rights to employer recognition. These became a major focus of policy debate by the end of the 1950s and led to largely aborted legislation in the 1970s before settling into a series of legal restrictions on trade union power in the 1980s and early 1990s. While leaving most of these restrictions in place, in 1999 New Labour provided unions with new organising rights. The second aspect of the law has been in the provision of employees with a growing range of individual rights on such matters as minimum wages, protection against sex discrimination, and maternity rights. Although normal elsewhere in Europe, such rights were unknown in Britain until the 1960s after which, at an accelerating pace, they have come to play a major part in improving and protecting the employment contract.

One final point in this introductory overview concerns neither trade unions nor government, but the employers. Although employers are less obvious in industrial relations because they neither take strike action nor introduce legislation, they are in reality the key actors. It was, for example, their lack of solidarity that led to the break-up of industry-level bargaining, and their inadequate controls that encouraged unprecedented workplace bargaining in the 1960s and 1970s. It may be too trite to say that employers get the trade unions that they deserve, but an understanding of trade union behaviour certainly requires an understanding of the conduct of management. Above all it requires an understanding of the competitive pressures faced by employers in their product markets, and of their skill in responding to these pressures through the more effective management of labour.

THE SETTLED SYSTEM, 1939–1959

Writing in 1937, in the second edition of the first systematic description of the British system of industrial relations, J. Henry Richardson felt able to say:

> During the five years since the first edition of this study was written, industrial relations in Great Britain have shown remarkable stability, combined with a high standard of industrial peace. This stability has been maintained in a period of great change in economic conditions; . . . The stability of British industrial relations is the more noteworthy when it is contrasted with the almost revolutionary changes during the last five years in the United States, Germany and France.
> (Richardson 1938: vii)

Despite the crisis of the General Strike of 1926, it was a view shared by government, with the official *Industrial Relations Handbook* published in 1944 asserting that 'Collective bargaining between employers and workpeople has for many years been recognised in this country as the method best adapted to the needs of industry, and to the demands of the national character, in the settlement of wages and conditions of employment' (Davies and Freedland 1993: 42).

Great weight was placed on the benefits of what was seen as a 'voluntary' system. What this meant was that, since the 1875 Conspiracy and Protection of Property Act, reinforced by the 1906 Trades Disputes Act, employers and trade unions could not sue each other for damages arising from a strike or lock-out 'in contemplation or furtherance of a trade dispute'. This provided in an elliptical way a partial substitute for what in other countries would be specific rights to strike and to organise. The beauty of it for its many British admirers lay in the fact that the courts were effectively excluded from collective bargaining and industrial disputes. If you could not get a court to give you financial compensation for a broken agreement or an unconstitutional strike, there was no point in going to the law. Collective bargaining thus developed in its own way, eased through sticky patches by practical people familiar with the world of work and its underlying power struggles. If by chance a question relating to an individual's contract of employment did come before a court, it was dealt with on the basis of the implied rights in any relevant collective agreements and of reported precedent (Kahn-Freund 1954).

There were, however, problems inherent in this 'tradition of voluntarism' that were to emerge as major policy issues later in our period. The first of these arose as a by-product of the fact that agreements were unenforceable in court. Because this reduced the incentive to write agreements down, the British system became characterised by a messy mass of half-remembered understandings, unwritten 'custom and practice', and odd notes of meetings. The second problem arose because, since the law did not specify which 'agent' was responsible for upholding agreements on each side – whether union district secretary, company personnel director or whoever – there was further ambiguity as to who was the person on each side who had the procedural right to decide on points of dispute. The third problem arose directly from this. Because the law provided no scaffolding on which responsibilities could be determined, people on each side would choose to deal with the person most likely to be able to cope with the dispute in hand, and that was typically based on an assessment of the current exercise of industrial muscle. As a result, over the course of the twentieth century, to different extents in different industries, the locus of decision making swung to and fro between workplace and national bargaining, depending on the level at which market circumstances permitted union strength to be most effectively mobilised. The fourth problem with the 'tradition of voluntarism' proved to be of profound importance for those who were in mid-century its most enthusiastic supporters, the trade unions. Having no legal rights to organise was no problem for them when the economic tide was flowing with trade unionism. But it proved to be a fatal flaw when that tide began to ebb.

The war was of profound importance for organised labour. With it came, by stages, all the draconian emergency measures of a managed labour market. There was the direction of labour to essential work, the dilution of traditional skills, guaranteed minimum wages and, through Order 1305, the banning of strikes and lock-outs (Wrigley 1996). It would be reasonable to suppose that this might break the old mould and force the British system of industrial relations into new structures. In fact, it did the reverse, so that, with the coming of peace, the pre-war system was reaffirmed and extended.

Much of the explanation for this lies in the role played by the trade union leadership in the conduct of war. From the early 1930s the Trades Union Congress (TUC), under its general secretary, Walter Citrine, and the towering general secretary of the Transport and General Workers Union, Ernest Bevin, had campaigned hard against the rise of Nazism and Fascism. When the war came they were ready and able to mobilise the trade union movement. In May 1940 Bevin was made the minister of labour and became one of the most powerful members of the War Cabinet (Taylor 2000). Quite apart from winning acceptance for the emergency measures, Bevin sought to extend collective bargaining. As he put it himself, he hoped that 'by the time that hostilities cease, there will not be a single industry of any kind in the country that has not wage-regulating machinery of some kind or another' (Taylor 2000: 38). No less than forty-six new 'joint industrial councils', as the national bargaining bodies were called, were created during his ministry, as well as a number of new wages councils for industries where unions were still poorly represented. Even Order 1305 (which, as is evident from Table 15.4, did not stop strikes, most of which were in coal mining) became a means of enforcing the terms of national collective agreements and of providing individual members with rights to trade union representation with reluctant employers. The trade union movement thus emerged from the war greatly strengthened, both politically and industrially.

With this fresh authority, the trade union movement was able to argue for a substantial role in the newly nationalised industries. Unions won members and recognition not only in poorly organised industries such as civil aviation and road haulage, but also among hitherto unrepresented white collar and managerial employees in industries such as coal, electricity and railways among whose manual workers they were already strong. During the later 1940s, trade union leaders, with fewer than 100 joint industrial councils and a few score more national agreements, presided over a remarkably centralised national bargaining system. The degree of their control over it was successfully tested when, between 1948 and 1950, they and their employer association counterparts were able to deliver a substantial period of wage restraint.

In these circumstances, it was forgivable that, when in 1954 Alan Flanders and Hugh Clegg published the successor to J. Henry Richardson's textbook, they were able to describe a system of collective bargaining and statutory wage boards that appeared to be largely controlled, almost comprehensive and apparently institutionally stable (Flanders and Clegg 1954). And yet, within their analysis, one can discern the seeds of the problems that were to tear that system apart. There was the problem of reconciling the authority of the union with that of the elected grass-roots activists, commonly called 'shop stewards', who in practice were increasingly called on to deal with management. There were the strains placed on the TUC in trying to maintain unity in delivering their part of an incomes policy. And there was the fact that elaborate structures for 'joint consultation' established during and after the war were melting away as trade unionists discovered that they achieved far less through passive consultation than they could through negotiations backed by the threat of industrial action.

Later in the 1950s these problems became more evident. With continuing low levels of unemployment, labour shortages were placing severe strains on local managements. They were especially vulnerable to these pressures in industries where product market competition was non-existent or weak, such as the nationalised industries, public services and the defence industries. In many of these it became commonplace to try to retain labour and win its compliance by adding surreptitiously to pay, over and above what was permissible through their industry's national agreement. Thus it was that, following the reduction of the standard working week from 48 to 44 hours in the late 1940s, and from 44 hours to 42 in the late 1950s, the actual working hours of manual men increased, with overtime working effectively becoming institutionalised, padding out pay packets whether or not it was actually required for production (Flanders 1964). Thus it was also that piecework payment systems were often allowed to degrade in order to deliver the pay rises that would retain skilled labour. A phenomenon termed 'wage drift' developed, whereby earnings consistently rose at a faster pace than nationally agreed wage rates (Phelps Brown 1962).

The growing willingness of employers to bargain at the workplace, outside the scope of industry-level agreements, created substantial problems for the trade unions. With the Labour Party out of power, the trade union movement had lost much of its influence nationally. It had also lost its more visionary leaders. Union rule books did not recognise the shop steward's role. If it was not bad enough that local managers were choosing to negotiate with shop stewards, activists at the grass-roots were being encouraged to exceed their limited formal authority by an energetic industrial wing of the Communist Party. Although the great majority of strikes in the 1950s were in the coal mining industry, they accounted for a small minority of working days lost. More important was an increasing tendency for strike action to become a routine in other industries, especially those such as engineering, shipbuilding and the docks which, like coal mining itself, had archaic and poorly controlled piecework payment systems. To add to the leadership's concerns, politicians were becoming restive. A Conservative Party pressure group published a pamphlet entitled *A Giant's Strength* in 1958, questioning the monopoly powers of trade unionism. There was also a growing concern about inflation that led, in 1957, to the appointment of a three-person expert body, the Council on Prices, Productivity and Incomes, with the intention of educating public debate. For the more reflective trade union leaders it was plain that a golden age was coming to an end.

Looking back over this twenty-year period, however, it can be argued that trade unions made a positive, if diminishing, contribution to Britain's economic performance. After playing a crucial role in the mobilisation of the war economy, they helped to establish highly centralised wage regulation that permitted a period of price stability and low unemployment. They supported an apprenticeship-based system of skills training that largely met the economy's needs (Gospel 1992). This was, as Broadberry demonstrates (chapter 3 above), a period of relatively high labour productivity growth in highly unionised manufacturing industries. The spread of collective bargaining probably contributed to the general narrowing of the national pay distribution that occurred during the 1950s (Routh 1980). The spread of trade union membership to less skilled workers during the 1940s and 1950s encouraged a narrowing of skill differentials at both national and workplace level as a result of electoral pressures within trade unions and their shop steward committees (Turner 1952). The longer-term problem for labour lay in the way it was managed. As an authoritative study of management concludes: 'In most firms managerial and supervisory systems remained weak: personal management often persisted at senior levels; managers were poorly educated and trained; and levels and functions were inadequately integrated. Labour management was left to line managers and foremen within the firm and was delegated to employers' organisations outside the firm' (Gospel 1992: 178).

THE COLLAPSE OF THE SYSTEM, 1960–1979

A recurring source of conflict, beginning and ending with this twenty-year period, was the efforts of governments to control inflation by means of incomes policies. As Britain's international competitive position began to deteriorate, and the international balance of payments became more adverse, there were increasing pressures on the exchange rate for sterling. These dominated the lives of governments. Because wage bargaining pressures were widely perceived to be central to the domestic inflationary process, governments repeatedly tried to persuade or coerce trade unions to moderate wage claims. Since what little influence trade union leaders might have had over the process was diminishing rapidly over the course of the period, this proved to be a political nightmare. It continued up to and until North Sea oil came on stream at the end of the 1970s, which effectively removed the balance-of-payments problem, and removed also the need for politicians to seek trade union support.

The first attempt at incomes policy was unilateral government action. In July 1961 the Conservative government announced a 'pay pause' for all public sector wages and asked the private sector to follow suit. Nine months later it proposed that all pay increases should be kept within the 2 to 2.5 per cent annual rise that was expected in overall productivity. As for the future, the prime minister, Harold Macmillan, proposed that the government would lay down 'norms' but that difficult cases would be dealt with by a new body, to be called the National Incomes Commission (NIC). Boycotted by the TUC, this was ill equipped to tackle the few cases handed to it. It did not survive the next election. It was overshadowed by Macmillan's creation of the National Economic Development Council (NEDC) in February 1962. This consisted of representatives of the TUC General Council and senior industrialists, as well as government ministers, and had a substantial specialist secretariat. Against all the odds, NEDC was to survive for thirty-one years, albeit in increasing obscurity. But it started well. In 1963 it agreed to propose a 'guiding light' of permissible pay increases of between 3 and 3.5 per cent, thereby offering the possibility of a tripartite approach to the wage inflation problem.

This spirit of tripartism was seized by the Labour government taking office in October 1964. The TUC and the central employers' organisations (shortly to be merged into the Confederation of British Industry) were persuaded to sign a joint 'Declaration of Intent' acknowledging the need for pay and price restraint. Guidelines were to be kept under review by the NEDC, but particular cases were to be investigated by a new body, the National Board for Prices and Incomes (NBPI). This enjoyed the full commitment of both TUC and CBI and had a substantial research and investigation team. It was able to roam beyond individual price and wage references and to explore broader issues such as the wage drift implications of payment by results, and the newly popular practice of productivity bargaining. By getting its staff out into the poorer-managed workplaces of Britain, talking to the junior managers and shop stewards who kept things moving, the NBPI was to gain an unprecedented understanding of the complexity of Britain's worsening industrial relations problem. Use of this knowledge was, however, increasingly restricted by the Wilson government's incomes policy.

In late 1965 the government introduced a voluntary 'early warning' system in the belief that advanced notification might temper wage claims. The TUC had itself earlier instituted a similar policy for its members. However, mounting inflation and a strike of merchant seamen in the summer of 1966 led to an exchange rate crisis to which Harold Wilson responded by declaring a complete and compulsory standstill to all pay and price increases. The statutory freeze was partially relaxed at the end of 1966 and the NBPI was given the additional task of determining the criteria for exceptional treatment in the phases of incomes policy that followed. Pay settlements once again exceeded the 'ceilings' proposed, and in late 1969, as political expedience came to dominate the government's selection of cases referred to the NBPI, its chair resigned. The NBPI itself was abolished after Edward Heath's victory in the election of 1970.

In parallel with these manoeuvrings over incomes policy, the Wilson government had been forced to tackle the question of industrial relations reform. An increasing number of non-mining strikes, typically short, unofficial and unconstitutional, was widely perceived as damaging Britain's international trade reputation. In 1965 a Royal Commission was established under Lord Donovan to investigate all aspects of the problem, especially the scope for substantial alteration to the law. The Commission reported in March 1968, informed by the findings of a substantial programme of research. Like its nineteenth-century predecessors, it favoured collective bargaining as the best means of industrial government, and it saw no reason to abandon the 'tradition of voluntarism'. It considered that the formal system of industry-level agreements was failing because employers were subverting them by preferring to deal with their employees' shop stewards at workplace level. It was up to individual employers to come off the fence and decide whether they wanted to make their industry-level agreements effective, or whether they should face up to what they were doing and commence formal bargaining at enterprise or sub-enterprise level. The law could play little role in achieving this, but an advisory body, the Commission on Industrial Relations (CIR), should facilitate the process of change. So far as strikes were concerned, these were seen as symptoms of chaotic procedures and poor management, and there was no point in penalising strikers so long as these underlying problems remained unreformed. All this was a deep disappointment to the Wilson government, which wanted clear interventions and fast results. It introduced the CIR, but it also tried to introduce what were called by their opponents 'penal clauses' – compulsory strike ballots and 'cooling off' periods before strikes – which had been rejected by the Donovan Commission. These proposals were thwarted by a back-bench revolt in the Labour Party and time ran out with the 1970 election (Jenkins 1970). The next attempt at reform was left to the Conservatives.

The reforming legislation introduced by Edward Heath's government – the 1971 Industrial Relations Act – was far more radical than the Donovan Commission's proposal. Behind it lay the belief that something was fundamentally wrong with the voluntary system enshrined in the 1906 Act. It therefore set up a completely new machinery, including a National Industrial Relations Court, supported by the CIR in an investigative role, whereby written collective agreements would be enforceable in law. It specified rights to organise for registered trade unions, and the procedures whereby strike action could or could not be legal. This bold new departure was never put to the test. The TUC boycotted it by insisting that its own member unions deregistered, and it expelled the few unions that refused. Employers were at best unenthusiastic, and proved willing to go along with union requests that collective agreements should be specified to be 'not legally binding'. Particularly damaging politically was a series of disputes concerning small employers whose attempts to apply the new law resulted in complex legal proceedings and massive protest demonstrations. From 1972 Heath's government was drawing back from the legislation, anxious lest it should damage his efforts to rebuild bridges with the unions whose co-operation he now sought as events dragged him reluctantly into his first incomes policy.

Strike action was a constant feature of Heath's period in office. Both the location and the nature of strikes were changing. The coal mining industry, once the major source of strikes, had calmed down substantially since the introduction of the Power Loading Agreement in 1966, which replaced piecework bargaining at pit level with a national pay structure. In other strike-prone industries there was a shift from the small spontaneous stoppages associated with disputes over manning, piecework, overtime and so on, to larger and longer disputes encompassing whole workplaces, as companies, for example in the car assembly industry, moved towards more formal workplace bargaining along the lines suggested by the Donovan Commission. But a willingness to take strike action was also spreading to industries where it had been largely unknown, perhaps encouraged by the almost obsessive attention given to strikes in the news media. The once virtually strike-free public services were affected. Local government, the health service, the civil service, teachers, postal workers and the fire-fighters all took substantial industrial action in the 1970s, in some cases provoked by managerial efforts to improve their efficiency. The most dramatic action of Heath's period in office was, however, taken by the coal miners, re-entering the fray with the greater unity offered by their new national bargaining arrangements. A coal strike in early 1972 hit the power generating industry so severely that an official state of emergency was declared, with much of British industry reduced to working for only two or three days a week before it was settled. Another massive unofficial strike the following year saw the development of what were called 'flying pickets', mobile bands of activists who organised blockades of coal storage depots.

In 1972 inflationary pressures, partly fuelled by a rise in international commodity prices, drove Heath to seek TUC support in voluntary wage restraint. The CBI launched its own policy of voluntary price restraint. But the TUC was too alienated by the Industrial Relations Act and refused to co-operate. The government then unilaterally introduced a statutory pay freeze, with subsequent intricately drafted phases intended to facilitate productivity-linked pay rises and to provide some protection against rises in the Retail Price Index over a certain limit. But this was insufficient to placate the miners, buoyed up by soaring petroleum prices as a consequence of another Arab–Israeli war. They called for a coal strike for February 1974. Heath announced a general election in the same month on the platform that the miners were challenging the authority of parliament. He lost the election.

The political impact of what was seen to be Heath's 'defeat by the miners' was profound. For the Conservative Party it meant that great resolve and careful planning were devoted to defeating the miners ten years later. More immediately for Labour it meant that the Wilson government returned to power in 1974 desperate to win trade union support for its policies. This showed in its approach to labour law reform, in its approach to incomes policies, and in its approach to public sector employment. Before taking these in turn it is worth noting more generally how much in this twenty-year period Labour Party policy was influenced by trade unions on matters quite unrelated to industrial relations and employment. Through their substantial voting power in the Party they played an energetic role in some of Labour's most divisive internal struggles – over nuclear disarmament, the Vietnam War, and membership of the European Community. Bitter memories of these arguments remained fresh when New Labour distanced itself from the union movement both constitutionally and financially during the 1990s.

The 1974 Labour government used legislation as an inducement to win trade union support for pay restraint in what came to be called 'the Social Contract'. It was by any standards an ambitious programme. The first element of it was to abolish the 1971 Industrial Relations Act and reinstate the *status quo ante*. The 1974 Trade Union and Labour Relations Act did this, reasserting the provisions of the 1906 Trades Disputes Act and preserving only the Industrial Tribunal procedures providing protection for individuals against unfair dismissals. No thought was given to salvaging some of the positive rights for trade unions to organise that were in the 1971 Act. The second element of the legislative programme was the Employment Protection Act that replaced the NIRC and the CIR with several new legal and quasi-legal bodies of which the most important was the Advisory, Conciliation and Arbitration Service (ACAS), all of which continue, although with somewhat altered powers. The purpose of these innovations was to ensure that industrial relations disputes remained in the hands of industrial relations specialists and out of the normal courts. A third element introduced new individual rights – maternity rights, and rights against discrimination in employment through the 1975 Sex Discrimination Act and the 1976 Race Relations Act – which proved broadly effective and continue. A fourth element was piecemeal measures to assist trade unions in their work – time off for trade union duties, protections for union activism, rights to consultation on redundancies and on health and safety matters, and a distinctly confused and confusing right to invoke arbitration to get pay up to the 'general level' of the locality. Most of these innovations were abolished by the Conservatives in the 1980s. As was a fifth element, a right to call on ACAS to investigate and make a recommendation if an employer refused to recognise a trade union. This ran into substantial problems, most notoriously with a two-year conflict over recognition at a London photographic works called Grunwick, where mass picketing and conflicting court judgements almost brought an early end to ACAS. Finally, the sixth element was an attempt to introduce a step towards industrial democracy in the form of elected worker representatives on boards of directors. The committee established to decide the details of this failed to agree on anything, however, and the idea was abandoned.

Since Labour took over power in 1974 at a time of rapidly rising inflation it was inevitable that it would have to re-engage with the problem of incomes policies, of which the trade union movement was now deeply suspicious. Part of the problem was that there was very little restraint that the TUC, or anyone else, could deliver, because the national bargaining structure was becoming ever more fragmented as employers increasingly concluded pay deals within their own enterprises in the frenetic atmosphere induced by double-digit inflation. In 1975, as domestic price inflation rose to an annual rate of 25 per cent, the government was forced to seek support from the International Monetary Fund in its efforts to protect the sterling exchange rate. At this point it was the TUC itself that delivered an incomes policy that was, in effect, used as surety. Called the 'Social Contract', the deal proposed a statutory ceiling on pay rises, embodying a substantial redistributive element, in return for the package of rights described above. The architect of this policy was Jack Jones, the general secretary of the Transport and General Workers Union. It was remarkable that Jones, whose reputation had been built on his championing of shop steward involvement in decentralised bargaining, should be the force behind one of the most centralising policies in labour history, but his motive was explicit and political. He feared that if inflation continued out of control it might lead to a more authoritarian government whose first act would be to cripple the trade union movement (Taylor 2000).

The Social Contract pay policy, backed by strenuous efforts of the TUC, did, by stages, see inflation fall. But there were adverse consequences because it was adhered to most carefully in those sectors where bargaining was least fragmented, notably the public services, whose pay thereby fell substantially behind workers in the private sector and in the nationalised industries. Two groups that looked after themselves were the police and the fire-fighters, whose agitation and, in the case of the latter, strike action, won them a coveted arrangement whereby their pay was index-linked to a measure of average earnings. But those in the health service and local authorities were not so lucky. When in 1978 James Callaghan, then prime minister, proposed an ambitiously low target for pay increases in the run-up to the next general election, the public service union activists rebelled, and although the ensuing strikes in what became mythologised as 'The Winter of Discontent' were not substantial, they had a political potency that did much to lose Labour the election. Callaghan tried to salvage the problem by establishing a Pay Comparability Commission to restore public service pay. The TUC and CBI announced that they would be willing to engage in what was called an 'agreed economic assessment' and a 'national economic forum' as a basis for a bipartite approach to incomes policy. But the electorate was weary of both the actors and their plays.

Before considering the upheaval that was to follow Labour's defeat in 1979, it is important to note one dog that did not bark. The 1974–9 Labour government was notably inactive in its policy towards its own employees, a public sector that amounted to about 30 per cent of all UK employment and almost half of all trade union members. Wilson's first governments in the 1960s had used the NBPI, the NEDC and the Ministry of Technology as catalysts of innovation in labour management in, for example, local government, coal, electricity and steel. Heath had reorganised health and local government and had introduced Review Bodies to advise on the pay of doctors and dentists, armed forces and top public sector salaries, and Thatcher was later to add further Review Bodies for the nurses and for teachers. But when Wilson returned in 1974, his government seemed fundamentally inhibited by fear of further industrial conflict and the need at all costs to retain trade union support for incomes policies. No attention was given to the manifestly poor labour management in state-owned industries, especially the recently nationalised British Leyland, British Steel, British Shipbuilders and British Aerospace, which continued the same poor management practices with regard to training, payment systems, and bargaining procedures that had forced them into public ownership in the first place. No doubt both managers and politicians would have blamed trade union resistance for this; the short-term costs of the strike action associated with breaking this resistance were not considered worth the long-term gains of more efficient labour utilisation. But the unions could see that their industries were being allowed to drift into competitive annihilation, and were in no position to initiate change themselves. Had government provided the combination of product market pressures and managerial competence, the unions could have learnt from strike defeats and responded positively. As it was, Labour demonstrated that it was incapable of managing an efficient public sector. It thereby condemned that sector to the far less sympathetic treatment of the Conservatives.

What of the economic consequences of industrial relations in this increasingly tempestuous twenty-year period? At the macroeconomic level there can be little doubt that the root of much of the inflationary pressure with which successive British governments struggled during the 1960s and 1970s was the fragmented, and highly strike-prone, bargaining system. Britain's labour market had become, in international terms, particularly vulnerable in its propensity to amplify external inflationary shocks (Bruno and Sachs 1985; Flanagan 1999). At the microeconomic level this was a period during which the national income distribution narrowed again, from the mid-1960s until the mid-1970s. The renewed growth of trade union membership probably contributed to this, certainly the introduction of equal pay legislation between men and women in 1970 did, and also the incomes policies, which typically responded to trade union pressure by applying floors and ceilings to permissible pay rises (Brown 1976). Productivity growth, as Broadberry demonstrates (chapter 3 above), suffered a substantial setback. But while there is a general acceptance that Britain's system of industrial relations constrained productivity growth during the period, there is more disagreement over whether the prime responsibility for this lay with trade unions or employers, or both (Metcalf 1993; Nolan 1996). It is a question best addressed by means of contrast with the remarkably changed circumstances of the following years.

COLLECTIVE BARGAINING IN RETREAT, 1980–1999

Although Margaret Thatcher's government came in on a wave of anti-union sentiment, it had no grand strategy to address the problem. Almost immediately confronted with what turned out to be the last nationwide strike action in the engineering industry, it passively watched the employers collapse in disunity and concede a shorter working week. Its initial legislation in 1980 offered some constraints on picketing, secondary action and enforcement of the closed shop, but nothing to cause trade unions particular alarm.

Quite quickly, however, the position began to change, both in terms of the economic context and in terms of the government's perception of what could be done. The new government's fiscal policy, and an exchange rate influenced by the arrival of North Sea oil, provoked a sharp recession that hit manufacturing particularly hard. Unemployment doubled sharply to levels unprecedented since the war, from 5 per cent in 1979 to 10 per cent in 1980, and was not to fall below that level until 1988. The daily reports of factory closures and redundancies had a growing effect on the self-confidence of trade unions and of their members. In 1980 management precipitated a three-month strike in the still nationalised steel industry that brought the defeat of the unions and cleared the way for plant closures. The government began to give more public support to employers willing to face up to trade union action. A dispute over trade union membership at a small Cheshire printing firm in 1983 was doubly significant. When the union ignored a court order to stop now unlawful secondary actions, it was fined for contempt of court and, when the fines were not paid, its assets were sequestered and its head office taken over by the court authorities. A divided TUC decided not to support the union's unlawful actions. The union had no option but to pay its fines and stop the picketing. The message to the government was clear. Contrary to prevailing assumptions, trade unions could be forced to obey the courts, and they could not expect wider union support if they resisted.

The most politically significant trade union defeat was that of the coal miners in a strike that started in 1984. The government had planned carefully for such an eventuality by ensuring, for example, that coal-fired power stations could be switched to oil and that refurbished wharves could take barge traffic. In the event the National Union of Mineworkers (NUM) walked into the trap by announcing that a rolling strike, that had started in Yorkshire over pit closures, should become an official national strike. The question of the legitimacy of this decision split the union, with a sizeable section based in Nottingham refusing to take part and eventually breaking off into a separate union, but not before it had inflicted substantial legal costs on the NUM for acting unconstitutionally. The government, meanwhile, declined to use its own legislation against the union, knowing that the union's leader might win sympathy if imprisoned for contempt of court. Instead it permitted a large police presence to be mobilised to suppress picketing and disruptive action. After eleven months of violent confrontation in the coalfields and bitter recrimination within the union movement, the strikers returned to what was to be a greatly reduced number of pits. Over the course of the 1980s the NUM saw its membership fall from over 250,000 to under 10,000. So great had been the damage to the confidence of industrial users of coal that within a few years the once vast mining industry had almost disappeared.

There were many highly publicised and bitter trade union defeats during the 1980s, with increasingly confident employers, backed by a supportive government, typically responding to a sharp change in product market circumstances. Some of these came from technological and other changes within the industry. Thus, for example, the legendary strength of the printing unions was broken in a series of defeats, most notably in 1985 when a major newspaper company, threatened by new technologies, moved suddenly out of Fleet Street to a fortified site on the Isle of Dogs where the print unions were not recognised. In 1988 the merchant seamen's union was broken when its local activists in Dover resisted initiatives by the cross-Channel ferry companies to reduce costs before the Channel Tunnel was opened. In 1989 the once powerful unions covering commercial television suffered a fatal defeat by an employer anticipating the competitive impact of cable and satellite television. All these unions were so damaged that they had no option but to merge with others.

A more calculated product market upheaval achieved radical change in the highly unionised public sector. The privatisation of telecommunications, gas, buses, the airports, steel, aerospace, water, electricity, docks, railways, British Airways and British Leyland was achieved, sometimes without any disruption. More often there was local industrial action around the time of transition as union members sought to stave off the new competitive pressures and the new styles of management that were to transform most of their working lives and remove many of their jobs. In the public services the unprecedented competitive pressures came from the requirement to compete for activities that could be out-sourced. This led to a steady growth in employees from private, often non-unionised, contracting companies working alongside the public sector employees. There was also a general erosion of the control over working practice exercised by the professions and supported by their trade unions and professional associations throughout government, health and education. The use of league tables as a guide to government discrimination in resource allocation undermined the once substantial solidarity of these groups.

At the time, much was made of the importance of the Conservative governments' industrial relations legislation in changing trade union behaviour. That legislation emerged by stages, roughly every two years from 1980 until 1993, with disparate measures bundled rather untidily together, sometimes amending or even cancelling earlier measures. It had no radical objective, such as Heath's ill-fated 1971 Act had. It accepted the 'tradition of voluntarism' as given, seeking instead broadly to make striking and trade union organisation more difficult. The anti-strike measures narrowed the definition of a lawful strike primarily by banning secondary action, and banning action that could be considered 'political'. It restricted picketing, required union leaders to repudiate unofficial strikes, permitted the selective dismissal of strikers, and prevented unions from disciplining members who refused to take part in official action. Perhaps most important of all, a precise balloting procedure was established which subsequently gave rise to the routine use of strike ballots as a normal part of bargaining procedure. The outcome has been that, while almost all ballots go in favour of strikes, very few strikes actually take place; the balloting legislation has in effect facilitated the bargaining process.

The other legislative measures were intended to increase the accountability and representativeness of trade unions. The enforcement of any closed shop was made illegal, and employees were given the right to join any union or none. Trade unions' national executives had to be directly elected by the membership. Ballots had to be held if a union wished the employer to collect membership dues, or if the union wished to conduct a levy of members for a fund for political campaigning. Any member could inspect unions' financial and membership records, and a new commissioner was created to carry out enquiries into suggested abuses of trade union internal authority. With the exception of this commissioner and the requirement for balloting on the deduction of union dues (both to be abolished later by Labour), these measures, if not welcomed, helped the unions to modernise their internal arrangements and to justify to their members a long overdue increase in membership dues.

There can be no doubting the symbolic impact of the legislation. Nor can it be doubted that it made striking more difficult and increased the authority of trade union leaderships over their grass-roots activists. It encouraged greater procedural care at all levels, and ballots improved the information available to employers. The role of ACAS conciliators became more important – for example, the proportion of ACAS-conciliated disputes that led on to strike action fell fivefold during the 1990s. But the law was not the main driver of these changes. It is true that some unions suffered crippling costs as a result of the new legislation, but arguably what mattered far more was simply the fact that employers were facing up to the challenge of strikes. And the bolstering of the employers' resolve to see disputes through to victory owed more to their facing a competitive crisis in their product market than to governmental encouragement and legislative support. It was tightening international competition and the break-up of the public sector that transformed British industrial relations in the 1980s and 1990s.

The 1990s were, as Table 15.4 makes plain, a period of unprecedented industrial peace. What few disputes occurred were increasingly confined to the public sector and, in particular, to those parts of the public sector faced with reorganisation or the prospect of privatisation, such as the postal service and the London underground system. Employers felt increasingly free to do without trade unions or to confine their influence to a narrower range of issues. With greatly reduced inflation, for example, a substantial proportion of employers who recognised unions for consultation and individual grievances ceased to allow them to negotiate over pay (Brown *et al.* 2000). Perhaps particularly notable was the fact that firms with trade unions were able to achieve improvements in working practices and manning levels at least as good as comparable firms that had excluded or rejected trade unions (Brown *et al.* 1998).

In part this was because the character of trade unionism was undergoing a profound change. Increasingly confined to bargaining within individual enterprises, unions came to act more like company unions. They were more dependent upon the employer for resources, of which the most important was recognition itself. They were less able to mount effective industrial action, partly because their members were aware of the increasingly hostile product markets in which their employers operated, but also because union leaderships were aware that a reputation for taking strike action would not help in winning recognition from other employers. In the late 1990s the TUC encouraged what was called 'workplace partnership' agreements, aimed at promoting co-operative rather than confrontational bargaining. It was an acknowledgement that employers were, in effect, 'rerecognising' trade unions for their employees, but doing so on their own terms.

Another important trend that had been gathering pace since the 1970s had been the growth in statutory individual rights: against unfair dismissal, various forms of discrimination, and a range of minimum entitlements. A substantial force behind this had been Britain's membership of the European Union, with the direct or indirect impact of its directives, and of established continental European practice, including the assumption that such issues should be resolved through the involvement of the 'social partners', the employers and unions. By 1999, ACAS was conciliating almost 100,000 individual rights cases each year and the number was growing rapidly. Trade unions were also finding a valued role in helping their members benefit from these new legal rights.

The policies of the Labour government of Tony Blair that took power in 1997 reflected these trends. Committed by its trade union supporters to unravel the Conservative labour legislation and to introduce a National Minimum Wage, it turned to the 'social partners', the TUC and CBI. On the latter the government and its social partners worked closely through an independent advisory Low Pay Commission to produce a result that settled in with little controversy. On the former they bargained out the basis of what became the 1999 Employment Relations Act. This barely touched the Conservative restrictions on strike action. It eased some of the constraints on union organisation and gave union members an important individual right to be represented by unions even if employers did not recognise them. Most controversially, it introduced a procedure whereby, if unions can prove that they have substantial membership support, employers can be obliged to grant them recognition. Although the symbolic significance of this should not be under-rated, its effects were only as great as trade union power could bring about. While trade union membership was once again starting to grow in 1999, after eighteen years of contraction, there was no reason to expect a return to any semblance of past trade union influence.

What have been the economic effects of this turnaround in industrial power? Whether or not changed industrial relations played a part, the evidence certainly suggests that Britain's relative productivity performance improved over the period (see chapter 3 above). The post-war gap between productivity growth in Britain and other European economies did not re-emerge after 1979 (Crafts 1997a). We can, however, say much more about the causative influence of labour management for this than for previous periods, because of a series of large workplace surveys in 1980, 1984, 1990 and 1998 that provided repeated and representative statistical data on a number of key variables. They show that the extent of negotiation at the workplace over work organisation declined substantially between 1980 and 1998 (Millward *et al.* 2000). One illustration will suffice. The 1980 and 1998 surveys allow us to compare directly the experience of managers of workplaces of twenty-five or more employees where unions had workplace representatives. The proportion of managers who said they negotiated with these representatives over recruitment fell from 43 per cent in 1980 to 3 per cent in 1998 (Brown *et al.* 2000). There is clear evidence that, on a wide range of labour management issues, and over most sectors where unions had once been strong, their influence had been greatly reduced.

If the evidence is clear that management became less constrained by trade unions during the 1980s and 1990s, was this reflected in economic outcomes? Let us consider first 'mark-up' of the wages of unionised employees over non-unionised, bearing in mind that this is a flawed indicator of union impact since many firms which are opposed to trade unions pay above market rates as a defensive measure. A union wage premium of up to around 10 per cent in the presence of a closed shop was evident in 1980 (Stewart 1987). This appears to have declined in the late 1980s (Stewart 1990, 1991, 1995) and by the late 1990s a number of studies showed no general workplace-level union mark-up, although there remains some evidence of a small mark-up for women and in workplaces where union membership is high (Hildreth 1999; Booth and Bryan 2001; Machin 2001; Bryson 2002).

What of the productivity of labour? Had unionised labour also become more productive? The linking of productivity with pay negotiations became more frequent in the 1980s (Marsden and Thompson 1990), and during the 1990s it became the norm (Brown *et al.* 1998). At the start of the 1980s, a positive association between trade unionism and productivity growth appears to have emerged. Productivity growth in unionised employment increased relative to that in its non-union counterpart between the 1970s and the early 1980s, by when, by most accounts, it had become absolutely higher (Wadhwani 1990; Oulton 1990; Nickell *et al.* 1992). While there was evidence that union presence was associated with lower *levels* of productivity in 1990, a comparable study found no evidence of this by 1998 (Fernie and Metcalf 1995; Addison and Belfield 2001). This would support the case study evidence that unionised workplaces had tended to catch up with the productivity levels of non-unionised workplaces during the 1990s.

This combination of changing union wage and productivity effects has been reflected in firms' financial performance. Although the main studies rely upon managers' subjective assessments of their firm's performance, the trend appears clear. In the 1980s there was evidence of unions having a negative association with firm performance. By 1990 these effects had diminished, especially in more competitive markets (Machin and Stewart 1990, 1996; Menezes-Filho 1997). By 1998 a number of studies could detect no association at all between various measures of union presence and the firm's financial performance (Addison and Belfield 2001; Bryson and Wilkinson 2002). By the end of the period unions had ceased to be associated with adverse effects upon profitability.

What about union members? The evidence is clear that employers came to find unions easier to work with in the later 1980s and the 1990s. But was this at the expense of their members? It should be noted, first, that unions have continued to have a substantial effect on the equality of pay structures, narrowing differentials across gender, ethnicity and occupation (Metcalf *et al.* 2001). Secondly, there is evidence that unions continue to protect 'public goods' in employment. Positive associations with trade union presence have been found in studies of training (Green 1993). There is evidence that union presence has a benign effect on labour turnover (Elias 1994). There is a similar association with health and safety at work, although the weakening of union influence since 1979 appears to have been associated with some erosion of this (Dawson *et al.* 1988; Sandy and Elliott 1996). Thirdly, unions appear successful in upholding individual rights. For a number of statutory individual rights, a trade union presence in 1998 was associated with higher employer conformity – and, indeed, with improvement on those rights (Brown *et al.* 2000). Despite the general decline that has been described in union influence over the control of work, in the late 1990s their influence appeared still to offer their members substantial benefits in terms of improving the working environment and the defending of rights at work.

Declining union influence may, however, have been reflected in income distribution. The contraction of collective bargaining in Britain since 1980 was accompanied by a marked growth in wage inequalities, reversing moves towards greater equality in the distribution of earnings that characterised the post-War period up to the late 1970s. In the twenty years after 1978, real hourly earnings of employees in the bottom decile of the wages distribution rose by 20 per cent, compared with 66 per cent for those in the top decile (Low Pay Commission 1998). If unearned incomes are taken into account the picture becomes starker. The top 1 per cent of income recipients saw their share of total income in the UK, which had been falling steadily since the 1910s, double from about 5 per cent to about 10 per cent between 1980 and 1998 (Atkinson 2001). If one takes the broadest perspective, in 1994 the share of employment income in national income was the lowest since 1950, and more than 10 percentage points below its peaks in 1975 and 1980 (Ryan 1996). In international terms, Britain's experience of widening earnings inequality was extreme. An analysis of male wage inequality from the late 1970s to the mid-1990s suggests that the dispersion of earnings widened much more in Britain and the USA than in continental Europe (Machin 1999).

Although there will have been many contributory factors, including changes in the supply of and demand for skills and the abolition of wages councils, an analysis of the British Household Panel Survey from 1983 and

1991 attributed between 20 and 37 per cent of the rise in wage inequality to falling unionisation (Machin 1997). It also suggested that while
wage inequality among individuals rose within both the union and the
non-union sector, the spread of earnings increased at a faster rate in
the non-union sector. It thus appears that both the weakening of unions
in the unionised sector, and the diminution in size of that sector, contributed to the substantial increases in incomes inequalities during the
1980s and 1990s. Compounding this diminishing union impact, there
is evidence of a further collapse among the unorganised. Gosling and
Machin (1995) found a widening of the gap in the spread of earnings
across union and non-union plants between 1980 and 1990, estimating
that around 15 per cent of the rise in the dispersion of semi-skilled earnings between 1980 and 1990 was attributable to the decline in unionisation. In short, the sharp increase in income inequality in Britain at the
end of the twentieth century is in part a consequence of the weakening
of trade unions.

CONCLUSION

Anyone scanning the newspaper headlines over our sixty-year period
could be forgiven for concluding that industrial relations lay at the heart
of Britain's economic performance. Trade unions, it might be conjectured,
were the root of the country's economic problems. Certainly they featured
prominently and often noisily throughout much of the period, whenever governments strove to defend exchange rates by restraining pay, and
whenever employers tried to meet new competitive pressures by changing working practices and shedding jobs. But it would be misleading to
see the explanation as ending there. Trade unions are fundamentally reactive organisations. They can act to defend their members' jobs and pay
and skills, but there is little they can do to create new structures or to
innovate employment practices. The failures and achievements of trade
unions in terms of the performance of the economy unavoidably reflect
those of the employers with whom they deal.

Trade unions emerged from the Second World War stronger, more
united and closer to government than ever before, able to deliver what
was generally considered to be appropriate for a mixed economy of that
era. In the private sector this began to crumble in the 1950s as a tight
labour market encouraged employers to subvert their sectoral collective
agreements, thereby nurturing workplace union activism and fragmented
ad hoc management that led to a loss of control in many key industries.
Rising strike propensity and defensive, short-term management fed off
each other with grave consequences for economic performance. It was
not to be until the 1980s and 1990s that tightening competitive pressures forced appropriate improvements in management control, assisted

to some extent by government action that further weakened trade unions. There is ample evidence of improved competitiveness in those industries that survived. For the public sector the crisis came a decade or so later, and again it was product market pressures, but here primarily through privatisation, that brought about an upheaval in the way labour was managed. Still unclear at the end of the period were the consequences for the quality, as opposed to the cost, of public services.

As the period ended it was becoming evident that the diminished influence of trade unions might be generating new problems. Deepening interpersonal inequality and the denial of representation for the weaker employees were creating an increasingly stratified labour market. The wider societal consequences of poverty and divided communities might create new demands on the economy and new constraints on economic performance. Additional individual employment rights were unlikely to be sufficient to deal with this prospect. A key question was whether trade unions might be encouraged to develop new and more inclusive forms of collectivism.

References

Place of publication is London unless otherwise stated. All references to the *Economic History Review* are to the second series, unless otherwise stated.

AACP. *See* Anglo-American Council on Productivity.

Aanestad, J. M. 1987. Measurement problems of the service sector. *Business Economics* 22: 32–6.

Abel-Smith, B. and Townsend, P. 1965. *The Poor and the Poorest.*

Abramovitz, M. 1986. Catching up, forging ahead and falling behind. *Journal of Economic History* 44: 385–406.

Abramovitz, M. and David, P. 1996. Convergence and delayed catch-up: productivity leadership and the waning of American exceptionalism. In Landau *et al.* 1996.

Acheson, D. 1998. *Independent Inquiry into Inequalities in Health.*

Ackrill, M. and Hannah, L. 2001. *Barclays: the Business of Banking 1690–1996.* Cambridge.

Acton Society Trust 1956. *Management Succession.*

Addison, J. T. and Belfield, M. L. 2001. Updating the determinants of firm performance: estimation using the 1998 UK WERS. *British Journal of Industrial Relations* 39: 3.

Addison, P. 1994. *The Road to 1945.*

Adeney, M. 1989. *The Motor Makers: the Turbulent History of Britain's Car Industry.*

Aghion, P. and Howitt, P. 1998. *Endogenous Growth Theory.* Cambridge, MA.

Albu, A. 1980. British Attitudes to engineering education: a historical perspective. In Pavitt 1980.

Aldcroft, D. H. 1992. *Education, Training and Economic Performance, 1944–1990.* Manchester.

Alexander, I. 1979. *Office Location and Public Policy.*

Alexander, S. S. 1952. The effects of devaluation on a trade balance. *IMF Staff Papers* 2: 263–78.

Alford, B. W. E. 1988. *British Economic Performance, 1945–1975.*

Allen, G. C. 1951. The concentration of production policy. In Chester 1951.
   1979. *British Industry and Economic Policy.*

Allen, R. G. D. 1946. Mutual aid between the US and the British Empire, 1941–1945. *Journal of the Royal Statistical Society* 109: 243–71.

Allsopp, C. J. and Mayes, D. G. 1985. Demand management in practice. In Morris 1985.

Anglo-American Council on Productivity 1949. *Steel Founding.*
   1950. *Superphosphate and Compound Fertilisers.*
   1952. *Iron and Steel.*
   1953. *Heavy Chemicals.*

Anson, R. and Simpson, P. 1988. World textile trade and production trends. Special Report No. 1108, Economist Intelligence Unit, London.

Arestis, P., Palma, G. and Sawyer, M., eds. 1997. *Markets, Unemployment and Economic Policy.*

Armstrong, H. and Taylor, J. 2000. *Regional Economics and Policy*, 3rd edn. Oxford.

Armytage, W. H. G. 1970. *Four Hundred Years of English Education*. Cambridge.

Arrow, K. J. 1962. The economic implications of learning-by-doing. *Review of Economic Studies* 29: 155–73.

Arthur, W. B. 1989. Competing technologies, increasing returns and lock-in by historical events. *Economic Journal* 99: 116–31.

Artis, M. and Cobham, D., eds. 1991. *Labour's Economic Policies, 1974–79*. Manchester.

Artis, M. J. 1978. Monetary policy, part II. In Blackaby 1978.

Artis, M. J. and Lewis, M. K. 1976. The demand for money in the United Kingdom 1963–1973. *Manchester School of Economic and Social Studies* 44: 147–81.

Ashcroft, B. and McGregor, P. G. 1989. The demand for industrial development certificates and the effect of regional policy. *Regional Studies* 23, 4: 301–14.

Ashworth, W. 1986. *The History of the British Coal Industry*, V, *The Nationalised Industry, 1946–1982*. Oxford.

Atkinson, A. B. 1996. *Incomes and the Welfare State*. Cambridge.

2001: Top incomes in the United Kingdom over the twentieth century. Mimeo, Nuffield College, Oxford.

Autor, H., Katz, L. and Krueger, A. 1998. Computing inequality: have computers changed the labour market? *Quarterly Journal of Economics* 113, 4: 1169–213.

Averch, H. and Johnson, L. 1962. Behavior of the firm under regulatory constraint. *American Economic Review* 52: 1052–69.

Aylen, J. 1988. Privatisation of the British Steel Coproration. *Fiscal Studies* 9: 1–25.

Bacon, R. and Eltis, W. 1976. *Britain's Economic Problems: Too Few Producers*.

Baily, M. 1993. Competition, regulation and efficiency in service industries. *Brookings Papers in Microeconomics* 2: 71–159.

Bain, G. S. and Price, R. 1980. *Profiles of Union Growth*. Oxford.

Bale, J. R. 1974. Towards a geography of the industrial estate. *Professional Geographer* 26: 291–7.

Ball, S. and Selden, A., eds. 1996. *The Heath Government 1970–74: A Reappraisal*.

Balls, E. and O'Donnell, G., eds. 2002. *Reforming Britain's Economic and Financial Policy, Towards Greater Economic Stability*. Basingstoke.

Bank of England 1968. Control of bank lending: the cash deposits scheme. *Bank of England Quarterly Bulletin* 8: 166–70.

1969. The operation of monetary policy since the Radcliffe Report. In Croome and Johnson 1969.

1970. The stock of money. *Bank of England Quarterly Bulletin* 10: 320–6.

1971a. Competition and credit control: the discount market. *Bank of England Quarterly Bulletin* 11: 314–15.

1971b. Reserve ratios: further definitions. *Bank of England Quarterly Bulletin* 11: 482–9.

1973. Competition and credit control: modified arrangements for the discount market. *Bank of England Quarterly Bulletin* 13: 306–7.

1974. Credit control: a supplementary scheme. *Bank of England Quarterly Bulletin* 14: 37–9.

1976. The balance of payments and the exchange rate developments in the first half of 1976. *Bank of England Quarterly Bulletin* 16: 308–13.

1977. DCE and the money supply – a statistical note. *Bank of England Quarterly Bulletin* 17: 39–42.

1980. Financial review. *Bank of England Quarterly Bulletin* 20: 19–32.

1981. Economic commentary. *Bank of England Quarterly Bulletin* 21: 3–18.

1984a. *The Development and Operation of Monetary Policy 1960–1983*. Oxford.

1984b. Funding the public sector borrowing requirement: 1952–83. *Bank of England Quarterly Bulletin* 24: 482–92.

1985a. Operation of monetary policy. *Bank of England Quarterly Bulletin* 25: 361–70.

1985b. Operation of monetary policy. *Bank of England Quarterly Bulletin* 25: 517–25.

1986. Financial change and broad money. *Bank of England Quarterly Bulletin* 26: 499–507.

1987a. Changes in the Stock Exchange and regulation of the City. *Bank of England Quarterly Bulletin* 27: 54–65.

1987b. The gilt-edged market: auctions. *Bank of England Quarterly Bulletin* 27: 203.

1987c. Measures of broad money. *Bank of England Quarterly Bulletin* 27: 212–19.

1987d. The instruments of monetary policy. *Bank of England Quarterly Bulletin* 27: 365–70.

1988a. The experimental series of gilt-edged auctions. *Bank of England Quarterly Bulletin* 28: 194–7.

1988b. Bank of England operations in the sterling money market. *Bank of England Quarterly Bulletin* 28: 390–409.

1989a. The gilt-edged market since Big Bang. *Bank of England Quarterly Bulletin* 29: 49–58.

1989b. Bank of England operations in the sterling money market. *Bank of England Quarterly Bulletin* 29: 92–103.

1990a. Monetary aggregates in a changing environment: a statistical discussion paper. *Bank of England Discussion Papers* 47: 1–44.

1990b. The determination of the monetary aggregates. *Bank of England Quarterly Bulletin* 30: 380–3.

1990c. The exchange rate mechanism of the European Monetary System. *Bank of England Quarterly Bulletin* 30: 479–81.

1992a. Operation of monetary policy. *Bank of England Quarterly Bulletin* 32: 382–98.

1992b. The case for price stability. *Bank of England Quarterly Bulletin* 32: 441–8.

1993a. Inflation report. *Bank of England Quarterly Bulletin* 33: 3–45.

1993b. Operation of monetary policy. *Bank of England Quarterly Bulletin* 33: 59–67.

1997a. Evolution of the monetary framework. *Bank of England Quarterly Bulletin* 37: 98–103.

1997b. Changes at the Bank of England. *Bank of England Quarterly Bulletin* 37: 241–3.

1997c. Reforms to the UK monetary policy framework and financial services regulation. *Bank of England Quarterly Bulletin* 37: 315–17.

1998a. The Bank of England Act. *Bank of England Quarterly Bulletin* 38: 93–6.

1998b. Inflation targeting in practice: the UK experience. *Bank of England Quarterly Bulletin* 38: 368–74.

1999. The MPC two years on. *Bank of England Quarterly Bulletin* 39: 297–303.

Bank of England Quarterly Bulletin, various years.

Bank of England Statistical Abstracts, various years.

Barber, J. and White, G. 1987. Current policy practice and problems from a UK perspective. In Dasgupta and Stoneman 1987.

Bardou, J.-P., Chanaron, J.-J., Fridenson, P. and Laux, J. M. 1982. *The Automobile Revolution: The Impact of an Industry.* Chapel Hill, NC.

Barker, T. C. and Robbins, M. 1974. *A History of London Transport*, II, *The Twentieth Century to 1970.*

Barnett, C. 1986. *The Audit of War: the Illusion and Reality of Britain as a Great Nation.*
1998. *The Lost Victory: British Dreams, British Realities 1945–1950.*
2001. *The Verdict of Peace: Britain between her Yesterday and the Future.*

Barr, N. 1998. *The Economics of the Welfare State*, 3rd edn. Oxford.

Barrell, R., ed. 1994. *The UK Labour Market.* Cambridge.

Barrell, R., Mason, G. and O'Mahony, M., eds. 2000. *Productivity, Innovation and Economic Performance.* Cambridge.

Barro, R. J. 1974. Are government bonds net wealth? *Journal of Political Economy* 82: 1095–117.
1991. Economic growth in a cross section of countries. *Quarterly Journal of Economics* 106: 407–44.

Barro, R. J. and Gordon, David B. 1983. A positive theory of monetary policy in a natural rate model. *Journal of Political Economy* 91: 589–610.

Barro, R. J. and Sala-i-Martin, X. 1995. *Economic Growth*. New York.

1990. World interest rates and investment. In Blanchard and Fischer 1990.

Baumol, W. J. 1967. Macroeconomics of unbalanced growth. *American Economic Review* 57: 415–26.

1986. Productivity growth, convergence and welfare. *American Economic Review* 76: 1072–85.

Bean, C. 1987. The impact of North Sea oil. In Dornbusch and Layard 1987.

Bean, C. and Crafts, N. British economic growth since 1945: relative economic decline . . . and renaissance? In Crafts and Toniolo 1996.

Beardwell, I., ed. 1996. *Contemporary Industrial Relations*. Oxford.

Beatson, M. 1993. Trends in pay flexibility. *Employment Gazette* September: 405–28.

Beck, U. 1992. *Risk Society: Towards a New Modernity*.

Beckerman, W., ed. 1972. *The Labour Government's Economic Record 1964–1970*.

Beesley, A. E., Cunningham, P. and Georghiou, L. 1998. Convergence of research: the government, public and independent sectors. In Cunningham 1998.

Beesley, M. E., Gist, P. and Glaister, S. 1983. Cost-benefit analysis in London's transport policies. *Progress in Planning* 19: 171–269.

Bernanke, Ben S., Laubach, Thomas, Mishkin, Frederic S. and Posen, Adam S. 1999. *Inflation Targeting: Lessons from the International Experience*. Princeton.

Berthoud, R. 1985. *Challenges to Social Policy*. Aldershot.

Bevan, A. 1952. *In Place of Fear*.

Beveridge, W. H. 1942. *Social Insurance and Allied Services*. Cmd 6404.

Bhagwati, J. N. 1984a. Why are services cheaper in the poor countries? *Economic Journal* 94: 279–86.

1984b. Splintering and disembodiment of services and developing nations. *World Economy* 7: 133–43.

Bishop, M. and Kay, J. 1988. *Does Privatisation Work? Lessons from the UK*.

Bishop, M., Kay, J. and Mayer, C., eds. 1994. *Privatisation and Economic Performance*. Oxford.

1995. *The Challenge of Regulation*. Oxford.

Blaazer, D. 1999. 'Devalued and dejected Britons': the pound in public discourse in the mid-1960s. *History Workshop Journal* 47: 121–40.

Black, D. 1980. *Inequalities in Health: Report of a Research Working Group*.

Blackaby, F. T., ed. 1978. *British Economic Policy 1960–74*. Cambridge.

1979. *De-industrialisation*.

Blanchard, O. and Fischer, S., eds. 1990. *NBER Macroeconomics Annual*. Cambridge, MA.

Blinder, Alan S. 1998. *Central Banking in Theory and Practice*. Cambridge, MA.

Boden, M. 1998. Science and technology in the private sector. In Cunningham 1998.

Boléat, M. 1986. *The Building Society Industry*.

Booth, A. 1985. Economists and points rationing in the Second World War. *Journal of European Economic History* 14: 297–317.

1987. Britain in the 1930s: a managed economy? *Economic History Review* 40: 499–522.

1989. *British Economic Policy 1931–1949: Was There a Keynesian Revolution?* Hemel Hempstead.

2000. Inflation, expectations, and the political economy of Conservative Britain, 1951–1964. *Historical Journal* 43: 827–47.

2001. *The British Economy in the Twentieth Century*.

2003. The manufacturing failure hypothesis and the performance of British industry during the long boom. *Economic History Review* 56: 1–33.

Booth, A. and Bryan, M. L. 2001. The union membership wage premium puzzle: is there a free rider problem? Working Paper, Institute of Social and Economic Research, University of Essex.

Booth, A. and Coats, A. W. 1980. Some wartime observations on the role of the economist in government. *Oxford Economic Papers* 32: 177–99.

Bound, J. and Johnson, G. 1992. Changes in the structure of wages in the 1980s: an evaluation of alternative explanations. *American Economic Review* 82, 3: 371–92.

Bower, C. 2001. Trends in female employment. *Labour Market Trends*: 93–106.

Branscomb, L. M. and Keller, J. H., eds. 1998. *Investing in Innovation: Creating a Research and Innovation Policy that Works*. Cambridge, MA.

Brech, M. J. 1985. Nationalised industries. In Morris 1985.

Bresnahan, T., Brynjolfsson, E. and Hitt, L. 1999. Information technology, workplace organisation and the demand for skilled labour: firm-level evidence. Working Paper 7136, NBER.

Briggs, A. 1979. *The History of Broadcasting in the* UK. IV, *Sound and Vision*. Oxford.

Bristow, J. 1968. Taxation and income stabilisation. *Economic Journal* 78: 299–311.

British Bankers' Association, various years. *Abstract of Banking Statistics*: banking business.

British Railways Board 1963. *The Reshaping of British Railways*. (The Beeching Report)

Brittan, S. 1971. *Steering the Economy*.

Britton, A. J. C. 1991. *Macroeconomic Policy in Britain 1974–1987*. Cambridge.

Broadberry S. N. 1988. The impact of the World Wars on the long run performance of the British economy. *Oxford Review of Economic Policy* 4: 25–37.

  1991. Unemployment. In Crafts and Woodward 1991.

  1993. Manufacturing and the convergence hypothesis: what the long-run data show. *Journal of Economic History* 53: 772–95.

  1994a. Technological leadership and productivity leadership in manufacturing since the industrial revolution: implications for the convergence thesis. *Economic Journal* 104: 291–302.

  1994b. Why was unemployment in post-war Britain so low. *Bulletin of Economic Research* 46: 241–62.

  1997a. Forging ahead, falling behind and catching-up: a sectoral analysis of Anglo-American productivity differences, 1870–1990. *Research in Economic History* 17: 1–37.

  1997b. Anglo-German productivity differences 1970–1990: a sectoral analysis. *European Review of Economic History* 1: 247–67.

  1997c. *The Productivity Race: British Manufacturing in International Perspective 1850–1990*. Cambridge.

  1998a. How did the United States and Germany overtake Britain? A sectoral analysis of comparative productivity levels, 1870–1990. *Journal of Economic History* 58: 375–407.

  1998b. Human capital and productivity performance: Britain, the United States and Germany, 1870–1990. Unpublished paper, University of Warwick.

  2000. Britain's productivity performance in international perspective 1870–1990. In Barrell *et al.* 2000.

  2003. Human capital and skills. In Floud and Johnson 2003.

Broadberry, S. N. and Crafts, N. F. R. 1992. Britain's productivity gap in the 1930s: some neglected factors. *Journal of Economic History* 52: 531–58.

  1996. British economic policy and industrial performance in the early postwar period. *Business History* 38: 65–91.

  1998. The post-war settlement: not such a good bargain after all. *Business History* 40: 73–9.

  2001. Competition and innovation in 1950s Britain. *Business History* 43: 97–118.

Broadberry, S. N. and Ghosal, S. 2002. From the counting house to the modern office: Anglo-American productivity differences in services, 1870–1990. *Journal of Economic History* 62: 967–98.

Broadberry, S. N. and Howlett, P. 1998. The United Kingdom: 'Victory at all costs'. In Harrison 1998.

forthcoming. Blood, sweat and tears: British mobilisation for World War II. In Chickering and Förster forthcoming.

Broadberry, S. N. and Wagner, K. 1996. Human capital and productivity in manufacturing during the twentieth century: Britain, Germany and the United States. In van Ark and Crafts 1996.

Broadway, F. 1969. *State Intervention in British Industry, 1964–68.*

Brown, G. 2001. The conditions for high and stable growth and employment. *Economic Journal* 111: C30–C44.

Brown, W. 1976. Incomes policy and pay differentials. *Oxford Bulletin of Economics and Statistics* 38: 1.

Brown, W., Deakin, S., Hudson, M., Pratten, C. and Ryan, P. 1998. *The Individualisation of the Employment Contract in Britain.* DTI Research Series.

Brown, W., Deakin, S., Nash, D. and Oxenbridge, S. 2000. The employment contract: from collective procedures to individual rights. *British Journal of Industrial Relations* 38: 611–29.

Bruno, M. and Sachs, J. D. 1985. *Economics of Worldwide Stagflation.* Oxford.

Bryson, A. 2002. Unions and workplace performance: what's going on? Mimeo, Policy Studies Institute, London.

Bryson, A. and Wilkinson, D. 2002. *Collective Bargaining and Workplace Performance: an Investigation using the WERS 1998.* DTI Research Series.

Budd, Alan. 1998. The role and operations of the Bank of England Monetary Policy Committee. *Economic Journal* 108: 1783–94.

Building Societies Association, *Facts and Figures*, various years.

The Building Societies Association Bulletin, various years.

Bullock, A. 1967. *The Life and Times of Ernest Bevin*, II, *Minister of Labour, 1940–1945.*

Burnham, P. 2000. Britain's external economic policy in the 1950s: the historical significance of operation ROBOT. *Twentieth Century British History* 11: 379–408.

Burton, D. 1990. Competition in the UK retail financial services sector: some implications for the spatial distribution and function of bank branches. *Service Industries Journal* 10: 571–88.

Buxton, T., Chapman, P. and Temple, P., eds. 1994. *Britain's Economic Performance.* 1998. *Britain's Economic Performance.* 2nd edn.

Cairncross, A. 1985. *Years of Recovery: British Economic Policy, 1945–1951.*
1986. *The Price of War: British Policy toward German Reparations, 1941–45.* Oxford.
1992. *The British Economy since 1945.*

Cairncross, A. and Eichengreen, B. 1983. *Sterling in Decline.* Oxford.

Cairncross, Alec. 1983. The 1967 devaluation of sterling. In Cairncross and Eichengreen 1983.
1987. Prelude to Radcliffe: monetary policy in the United Kingdom 1948–57. *Rivista di Storia Economica* 4: 1–20.

Cannadine, D. 1997. Apocalypse when? British politicians and British 'decline' in the twentieth century. In Clarke and Trebilcock 1997.

Cantwell, J. A. and Hodson, C. 1991. Global R&D and British companies. In Casson 1991.

Capie, F. and Collins, M. 1992. *Have the Banks Failed Industry?*

Capie, F. and Wood, G. 2002. Price controls in war and peace: a Marshallian conclusion. *Scottish Journal of Political Economy* 49: 39–60.

Capie, Forrest and Webber, Alan. 1985. *A Monetary History of the United Kingdom 1870–1982*, I, *Data, Sources, Methods.*

Carnevali, F. and Scott, P. 1999. The Treasury as venture capitalist: DATAC industrial finance and the Macmillan gap 1945–60. *Financial History Review* 6: 47–65.

Caroli, E. and Van Reenen, J. 2001. Skill-biased organizational change?: evidence from a panel of British and French establishments. *Quarterly Journal of Economics* 116: 1449–92.

Carter, C. F., ed. 1981. *Industrial Policy and Innovation.*

Carter, C. F. and Williams, B. R. 1957. *Industry and Technical Progress.* Oxford.

Casson, M. C., ed. 1991. *Global Research Strategy and International Competitiveness*. Oxford.

Castells, M. 2000. *The Information Age: Economy, Society and Culture*, I, *The Rise of the Network Society*, 2nd edn. Oxford.

Caves, R. *et al.* 1968. *Britain's Economic Prospects*. Washington, DC.

Caves, R. E. and Krause, L. B., eds. 1980. *Britain's Economic Performance*. Washington, DC.

Central Statistical Office (CSO) 1985. *The UK National Accounts: Sources and Methods*, 3rd edn.

  1995. *New Earnings Survey 1995*.

  Annual Abstract of Statistics, various years (see also ONS).

  Economic Trends, various years (see also ONS).

  Regional Trends, various years.

  UK Balance of Payments, various years.

  UK National Accounts, various years (see also ONS).

Central Statistical Office with Howlett, P. 1995. *Fighting With Figures*.

Chada, J. and Dimsdale, N. H. 1999. A long view of real rates. *Oxford Review of Economic Policy* 15: 17–45.

Chalmin, P. 1990. *The Making of a Sugar Giant: Tate and Lyle, 1859–1989*. New York.

Chancellor of the Exchequer. 1969. *Public Expenditure: a New Presentation*. Command 4017.

Chandler, A. D. 1990. *Scale and Scope: the Dynamics of Industrial Competition*. Cambridge, MA.

Channon, D. 1976. Corporate evolution in the service industries. In Hannah 1976.

  1978. *The Service Industries*.

Chapman, K. 1991. *The International Petrochemical Industry: Evolution and Location*. Oxford.

Chester, D. N. 1975. *The Nationalisation of British Industry*.

Chester, D. N., ed. 1951. *Lessons of the British War Economy*. Cambridge.

Chickering, R. and Förster, E., eds. forthcoming. *A World at Total War: Global Conflict and the Politics of Destruction, 1939–1945*. Cambridge.

Church, R. 1994. *The Rise and Decline of the British Motor Industry*.

Churchill, W. S. 1949. *The Second World War*, II, *Their Finest Hour*. 1985 edn.

Cipolla, C., ed. 1973. *The Industrial Revolution*.

Clare Group 1982. Problems of industrial recovery. *Midland Bank Review* Spring: 9–16.

Clark, T. and Dilnot, A. 2002a. Long-term trends in British taxation and spending. Briefing Note 25, IFS; available on-line from www.ifs.org.uk/public/bn25.pdf.

  2002b. Measuring the UK fiscal stance since the Second World War. Briefing Note 26, IFS; available on-line from www.ifs.org.uk/public/bn26.pdf.

Clark, T., Love, S. and Elsby, M. 2001. 25 years of falling investment? Trends in capital spending on public services. Briefing Note 20, IFS; available on-line from www.ifs.org.uk/public/bn20.pdf.

Clarke, M. 1986. *Regulating the City. Competition, Scandal and Reform*. Milton Keynes.

Clarke, P. 1998. *The Keynesian Revolution and its Consequences*. Cheltenham.

Clarke, P. and Trebilcock, C., eds. 1997. *Understanding Decline: Perceptions and Realities of British Economic Performance*. Cambridge.

Clayton, G., Gilbert, J. C. and Sedgwick, R., eds. 1971. *Monetary Theory and Monetary Policy in the 1970s*.

Clegg, H. A. 1976. *Trade Unionism under Collective Bargaining*. Oxford.

Coakley, J. 1988. Bank lending and the control of industry: an empirical study. In Harris *et al.* 1988.

Coakley, J. and Harris, L. 1992. Financial globalisation and deregulation. In Michie 1992.

Coates, D. 1994. *The Question of UK Decline*.

2002. The state as 'lubricator': the impact of New Labour's economic policy. A report on New Labour's first term in office. Mimeo, Wake Forest University, NC.

Cobham, David. 1997. The post-ERM framework for monetary policy in the United Kingdom: bounded credibility. *Economic Journal* 107: 1128–41.

Cockerill, A. 1988. Steel. In P. Johnson, ed., *The Structure of British Industry*, 2nd edn.
    1993. Steel. In P. Johnson, ed., *European Industries: Structure, Conduct and Performance*, Aldershot.

Coleman, D. C. 1980. *Courtaulds: an Economic History*, III, *Crisis and Change, 1940–1965*. Oxford.

Collins, B. and Robbins, K. 1990. *British Culture and Economic Decline*.

Combined Committee on Non-Food Consumption 1945. *The Impact of the War on Civilian Consumption in the United Kingdom, the United States and Canada*.

Conservative Party 1970. *A Better Tomorrow*.

Cooper, M. H. 1966. *Prices and Profits in the Pharmaceutical Industry*. Oxford.

Cosh, A., Hughes, A. and Rowthorn, R. E. 1994. The competitive role of UK manufacturing industry: 1950–2003 – a case analysis. Mimeo, University of Cambridge.

Council of Mortgage Lenders, various years. *Housing Finance, The Quarterly Economics Journal of the Building Societies Association*.

Cowling, K. and Cubbin, J. 1971. Price, quality and advertising competition: the UK car market. *Economica*, 38: 378–94.

Cowling, K., Stoneman, P., Cubbin, J., Cable, J., Hall, G., Domberger, S. and Dutton, P. 1980. *Mergers and Economic Performance*. Cambridge.

Crafts, N. 1992. Productivity growth reconsidered. *Economic Policy* 15 (October): 387–426.
    1993. *Can Deindustrialisation Seriously Damage Your Wealth?*
    1995. The golden age of economic growth in Western Europe, 1950–1973. *Economic History Review* 48: 429–47.
    1996. Deindustrialisation and economic growth. *Economic Journal* 106: 172–83.
    1997a. *Britain's Relative Economic Decline 1870–1995*.
    1997b. Economic growth in East Asia and western Europe since 1950: implications for living standards. *National Institute Economic Review* 162: 75–84.
    1998. *The Conservative Government's Economic Record: an End of Term Report*.
    2000. Economic growth in the twentieth century. *Oxford Review of Economic Policy* 15: 18–34.

Crafts, N., ed. 2002. *Britain's Relative Economic Performance*.

Crafts, N. and O'Mahony, M. 2001. A perspective on UK productivity performance. *Fiscal Studies* 22: 271–306.

Crafts, N. and Toniolo, G., eds. 1996. *Economic Growth in Europe since 1945*. Cambridge.

Crafts, N. F. R. and Mills, T. C. 1996. Europe's golden age: an econometric investigation of changing trend rates of growth. In van Ark and Crafts 1996.

Crafts, N. F. R. and Thomas, M. F. 1986. Comparative advantage in UK manufacturing trade, 1910–1935. *Economic Journal*, 96: 629–45.

Crafts, N. F. R. and Woodward, N. W. C., eds. 1991. *The British Economy since 1945*. Oxford.

Croome, David R. and Johnson, Harry, eds. 1969. *Money in Britain 1959–1969*.

Crosland, C. A. R. 1956. *The Future of Socialism*.

Cullingworth, J. B. 1979. *Environmental Planning, 1939–1969*, III, *New Towns Policy*.

Cunningham, P., ed. 1998. *Science and Technology in the United Kingdom*, 2nd edn.

Daly, A., Hitchens, D. M. W. N. and Wagner, K. 1985. Productivity, machinery and skills in a sample of German and British manufacturing plants. *National Institute Economic Review* 111: 48–61.

Daniels, P. 1982. *Service Industries: Growth and Location*. Cambridge.

Dasgupta, P. and Stoneman, P., eds. 1987. *Economic Policy and Technological Performance*. Cambridge.

David, P. A., Hall, B. H. and Toole, A. A. 2000. Is public R&D a complement or substitute for private R&D?: a review of the econometric evidence. *Research Policy* 29: 497–530.

Davies, G. 1981. *Building Societies and their Branches – A Regional Economic Survey.*

Davies, P. and Freedland, M. 1993. *Labour Legislation and Public Policy.* Oxford.

Dawson, S., Willman, P., Bamford, M. and Clinton A. 1988. *Safety at Work: the Limits of Self-Regulation.* Cambridge.

De Long, B. 1988. Productivity growth, convergence and welfare. *American Economic Review,* 78: 1138–54.

Deakin, S. 1992. Labour law and industrial relations. In Michie 1992.

Deardoff, A. and Stern, R., eds. 1994. *Analytical and Negocial Issues in the Global Trade System.* Ann Arbor.

Denny, K. and Nickell, S. J. 1992. Unions and investment in British industry. *Economic Journal* 102: 874–87.

Dent, H. C. 1970. *1870–1970, Century of Growth in English Education.*

Department of Employment, *Employment Gazette,* various issues.
    Labour Market Trends, various issues.

Department of Employment and Productivity 1971. *British Labour Statistics: Historical Abstract, 1886–1968.*

Department of Health 2002. *Tackling Health Inequalities.*

Diebold, W. 1952. *The End of the ITO.* Princeton, NJ.

Diederen, P., Stoneman, P., Toivanen, O. and Wolters, A. 1999. *Innovation and Research Policies: an International Comparative Analysis.* Cheltenham.

Digby, A. 1989. *British Welfare Policy: Workhouse to Workfare.*

Dilnot, A. and Emmerson, C. 2000. The economic environment. In Halsey and Webb 2000.

Dilnot, A. W., Kay, J. A. and Morris, C. N. 1984. *The Reform of Social Security.* Oxford.

Dintenfass, M. 1982. *The Decline of Industrial Britain, 1870–1990.*

Dobson, A. 1995. *Anglo-American Relations in the Twentieth Century.*

Dormois, J. P. and Dintenfass, M., eds. 1999. *The British Industrial Decline.*

Dornbusch, R. 1976. Expectations and exchange rate dynamics. *Journal of Political Economy* 84: 1161–76.

Dornbusch, R. and Layard, R., eds. 1987. *The Performance of the British Economy.* Oxford.

Dow, J. 1998. *Major Recessions: Britain and the World, 1920–1995.* Oxford.

Dow, J. C. R. 1964. *The Management of the British Economy 1945–60.* Cambridge.

Dow, J. C. R. and Saville, I. D. 1988. *A Critique of Monetary Policy: Theory and British Experience.* Oxford.

Dowrick, S. 1992. Technological catch up and diverging incomes: patterns of economic growth 1960–88. *Economic Journal* 102: 600–10.

Dowrick, S. and Nguyen, D. T. 1989. OECD comparative economic growth, 1950–1985. *American Economic Review* 79: 1010–30.

Drake, L. 1989. *The Building Society Industry in Transition.*

DSS 2000. *The Changing Welfare State: Social Security Spending.*

DTI 2002. *Productivity and Competitiveness Update 2002.*

Dunnett, P. J. S. 1980, *The Decline of the British Motor Industry: the Effects of Government Policy, 1945–1979.*

Durcan, J. W., McCarthy, W. E. J. and Redman, G. P. 1983. *Strikes in Post-War Britain: a Study of Stoppages of Work due to Industrial Disputes, 1946–73.*

Eatwell, J. and Robinson, J. 1973. *An Introduction to Modern Economics.* Maidenhead.

Eatwell, J., Milgate, M. and Newman, P., eds. 1987. *The New Palgrave: a Dictionary of Economics.*

Economist, The 1986. Big Bang Brief.

Edgerton, D. 1991. *England and the Aeroplane.*
    1996a. *Science, Technology and the British Industrial 'Decline', 1870–1970.* Cambridge.
    1996b. The 'white heat' revisited: the British government and technology in the 1960s. *Twentieth Century British History* 7: 53–82.

Edgerton, D. E. H. and Horrocks, S. M. 1994. British industrial research and development before 1945. *Economic History Review* 47: 213–38.

Edwards, P. 1998. Industrial conflict. In M. Poole and M. Warner, eds., *The Handbook of Human Resource Management*.

Edwards, P. and Hyman, R. 1994. Strikes and industrial conflict. In Hyman and Ferner 1994.

Eichengreen, B. 1996. Institutions and economic growth: Europe after World War II. In Crafts and Toniolo 1996.

EIRO (European Industrial Relations Observatory) 2001. *Annual Review 2000*. Dublin.

Elbaum, B. and Lazonick, W., eds. 1986. *The Decline of the British Economy*. Oxford.

Elias, P. 1994. Job-related training, trade union membership and labour mobility. *Oxford Economic Papers* 46: 4.

Elliot, I. 1976. Total factor productivity. In Panic 1976.

Ellison, J. 2000. *Threatening Europe: Britain and the Creation of the European Community, 1955–58*. New York.

Eltis, W. 1996. How low profitability and weak innovativeness undermined UK industrial growth. *Economic Journal* 106 (January): 104–95.

   2002. Forward. In Crafts 2002.

Eltis, W. A. and Sinclair, P. J. N., eds. 1981. *The Money Supply and the Exchange Rate*. Oxford.

Emmerson, C. and Frayne, C. 2001. The government's fiscal rules. Briefing Note 18, IFS; available on-line from www.ifs.org.uk.

English, R. and Kenny, M. eds. 2000. *Rethinking British Decline*.

Ergas, H. 1984. *Economic Evaluation of the Impact of Telecommunications Investment in the Communities*. Berlin.

   1987. The importance of technology policy. In Dasgupta and Stoneman 1987.

Evans, M. 1998. Social security: dismantling the pyramids? In Glennerster and Hills 1998.

Falkingham, J. and Hills, J., eds. 1995. *The Dynamic of Welfare*. Hemel Hempstead.

Federal Statistical Office, various years. *Statistisches Jahrbuch*. Wiesbaden.

Feinstein, C. H. 1972. *National Income, Expenditure and Output of the United Kingdom, 1855–1965*. Cambridge.

   1990. Benefits of backwardness and costs of continuity. In Graham and Seldon 1990.

   1994. Success and failure: British economic growth since 1948. In Floud and McCloskey 1994.

   1999. Structural change in developed countries during the twentieth century. *Oxford Review of Economic Policy* 15: 35–55.

Feinstein, C. H., ed. 1967. *Socialism, Capitalism and Economic Growth: Essays Presented to Maurice Dobb*. Cambridge.

   1983. *The Managed Economy*. Oxford.

Feldstein, M. 1974. Social security, induced retirement and aggregate capital accumulation. *Journal of Political Economy* 82: 905–26.

   1996. The missing piece in policy analysis: social security reform. *American Economic Review* 86: 1–14.

Fernie, S. and Metcalf, D. 1995. Participation, contingent pay, representation and workplace performance: evidence from Great Britain. *British Journal of Industrial Relations* 33: 3.

Fforde, John. 1992. *The Bank of England and Public Policy, 1941–1958*. Cambridge.

Fiegehen, G. C., Lansley, P. S. and Smith, A. D. 1977. *Poverty and Progress in Britain, 1953–73*. Cambridge.

Field, F. and Piachaud, D. 1971. The poverty trap. *New Statesman* 3 December.

Finniston Committee 1980. *Engineering Our Future: Report of the Committee of Inquiry into the Engineering Profession*.

Flaherty, D. 1985. Labor control in the British boot and shoe industry. *Industrial Relations* 24: 339–59.

Flanagan, R. J. 1999. Macroeconomic performance and collective bargaining: an international perspective. *Journal of Economic Literature* 37.

Flanders, A. 1954. Collective bargaining. In Flanders and Clegg 1954.

  1964. *The Fawley Productivity Agreements.*

Flanders, A. and Clegg, H. A., eds. 1954. *The System of Industrial Relations in Great Britain.* Oxford.

Fleming, J. M. 1962. Domestic financial policies under fixed and under floating exchange rates. *IMF Staff Papers* 9: 369–79.

Floud, R. and Johnson, P., eds. 2003. *The Cambridge Economic History of Modern Britain,* II, *Economic Maturity 1860–1939.* Cambridge.

Floud, R. and McCloskey, D., eds. 1994. *The Economic History of Britain since 1700,* III, *1939–1992,* 2nd edn. Cambridge.

Foot, M. D. K. W. 1981. Monetary targets: their nature and record in the major economies. In Griffiths and Wood 1981.

Foreman-Peck, J. 1989. Competition, cooperation and nationalisation in the nineteenth century telegraph system. *Business History* 31: 81–101.

  1991. Trade and the balance of payments. In Crafts and Woodward 1991.

Foreman-Peck, J. and Federico, G., eds. 1999. *European Industrial Policy: the Twentieth Century Experience.* Oxford.

Foreman-Peck, J. and Hannah, L. 1999. Britain: from economic liberalism to socialism – and back? In Foreman-Peck and Federico 1999.

Foreman-Peck, J. and Waterson, M. 1985. The comparative efficiency of public and private enterprises in Britain: electricity generation between the wars. *Economic Journal* 85, supplement: 84–105.

Fothergill, S. and Guy, N. 1990. *Retreat from the Regions: Corporate Change and the Closure of Factories.*

François, J. F. 1990. Producer services, scale and the division of labour. *Oxford Economic Papers* 42: 715–29.

François, J. F. and Reinert, K. A. 1996. The role of services in the structure of production and trade: stylised facts from a cross-country analysis. *Asian Pacific Economic Review* 2: 35–43.

Freeman, C. and Louçã, F. 2001. *As Time Goes By: from the Industrial Revolutions to the Information Revolution.* Oxford.

Freeman, C. and Young, A. 1965. *The R&D Effort in Western Europe, North America and the Soviet Union.* Paris.

Frenkel, M. 1962. The production function in allocation and growth: a synthesis. *American Economic Review* 52: 995–1022.

Friedman, M. 1980. Memorandum of evidence on monetary policy. In House of Commons (1980).

Fuchs, V. 1968. *The Service Economy.* New York.

Fukuyama, F. 1995. Social capital and the global economy, *Foreign Affairs* 74: 89–103.

Furner, M. and Supple, B., eds. 1990. *The State and Economic Knowledge: the American and British Experiences.* Cambridge.

Georghiou, L. 2001. The United Kingdom national system of research, technology and innovation. In Larédo and Mustar 2001.

Geroski, P. 1990. Innovation, technological opportunity and market structure. *Oxford Economic Papers* 42: 586–602.

  1991. Innovation and the sectoral sources of UK productivity growth. *Economic Journal* 101: 1438–51.

Geroski, P., Van Reenen, J. and Walters, C. F. 1997. How persistently do firms innovate? *Research Policy* 26: 33–48.

Giddens, A. 1998. *The Third Way.* Cambridge.

Gilborn, D. and Mirza, H. D. 2000. *Educational Inequality: Mapping Race, Class and Gender.*

Gillespie, B. 1979. British 'safety policy' and pesticides. In Johnston and Gummett 1979.

Glennerster, H. 1980. Public spending and the social services: the end of an era? In Brown and Baldwin 1980.

   2000. *British Social Policy since 1945*, 2nd edn. Oxford.

Glennerster, H. and Hills, J., eds. 1998. *The State of Welfare*, 2nd edn. Oxford.

Goddard, J. B. and Champion, A. G., eds. 1983. *The Urban and Regional Transformation of England.*

Goldin, C. 1998. America's graduation from high school: the evolution and spread of secondary schooling in the twentieth century. *Journal of Economic History* 58: 345–74.

Goodhart, C. 1986. Financial innovation and monetary control. *Oxford Review of Economic Policy* 2: 79–102.

Goodhart, C., Kay, J., Mortimer, K. and Duguid, A. 1988. *Financial Regulation or Over-regulation?*

Goodhart, C. A. E. 1969. The gilt-edged market. In Johnson 1972.

   1975. Problems of monetary management: the UK experience. In Goodhart 1984.

   1982. Structural changes in the banking system and the determination of the stock of money. In Goodhart 1984.

   1984. *Monetary Theory and Practice: the UK Experience.*

   1989. The conduct of monetary policy. *Economic Journal* 99: 293–346.

Goodhart, C. A. E. and Crockett, A. D. 1970. The importance of money. *Bank of England Quarterly Bulletin* 10: 159–98. Reprinted in Johnson 1972.

Goodin, R. C. and Le Grand, J. 1987. *Not Only the Poor: the Middle Classes and the Welfare State.*

Goodman, A. 2001. Inequality and living standards in Great Britain: some facts. Briefing Note 19, IFS.

Goodman, A., Johnson, P. and Webb, S. 1997. *Inequality in the UK.* Oxford.

Goodwin, R. M. 1967. A growth cycle. In Feinstein 1967.

Gordon, I. R. and Molho, I. 1998. A multi-stream analysis of the changing pattern of interregional migration in Great Britain, 1960–1991. *Regional Studies* 32: 309–23.

Gordon, R. J. 1992. Discussion of Crafts. *Economic Policy* 15: 414–21.

   1993. Comment on M. Baily, Competition Regulation and Efficiency in Service Industries. *Brookings Papers in Microeconomics* 2: 131–44.

   2000. Does the new economy measure up to the great inventions of the past? *Journal of Economic Perspectives* 14: 49–74.

Gosden, P. 1983. *The Education System since 1944.* Oxford.

Gosling, A. and Machin, S. 1995. Trade unions and the dispersion of earnings in British establishments 1980–90. *Oxford Bulletin of Economics and Statistics* 57: 167–84.

Gospel, H. F. 1992. *Markets, Firms, and the Management of Labour in Modern Britain.*

   1995. The decline of apprenticeship training in Britain. *Industrial Relations Journal* 25: 32–44.

Gourvish, T. and O'Day, A., eds. 1992. *Britain since 1945.*

Gourvish, T. R. 1986. *British Railways 1948–73: a Business History.* Cambridge.

Gourvish, T. R. and Wilson, R. G. 1994. *The British Brewing Industry, 1830–1980.* Cambridge.

Gowing, M. M. 1972. The organisation of manpower in Britain during the Second World War. *Journal of Contemporary History* 7: 147–67.

Gowland, David. 1978. *Monetary Policy and Credit Control: the UK Experience.*

   1982. *Controlling the Money Supply.*

   1990. *The Regulation of Financial Markets in the 1990s.*

Graham, A. and Seldon, A., eds. 1990. *Government and Economies in the Postwar World.*

Grant, W. and Martinelli, A. 1991. Political turbulence, enterprise crisis and industrial recovery: ICI and Montedison. In Martinelli 1991.

Green, F. 1993. The impact of trade union membership on training in Britain. *Applied Economics* 25.

Green, M. J. 1985. The evolution of market services in the European Community, the USA and Japan. *European Economy* 5.

Greenhalgh, C. 1990. Innovation and trade performance in the United Kingdom. *Economic Journal* 100, supplement: 105–18.

Greenhalgh, C. and Gregory, M. 2000. Labour productivity and product quality: their growth and inter-industry transmission in the UK 1979–90. In Barrell *et al.* 2000.

Greenhalgh, C., Taylor, P. and Wilson, R. 1994. Innovation and export volumes and prices – a disaggregated study. *Oxford Economic Papers* 46: 102–35.

Greenway, D. and Winters, L. A., eds. 1991. *Surveys in International Trade*. Oxford.

Gregg, P. and Wadsworth, J., eds. 1999. *The State of Working Britain*. Manchester.

Griffiths, B. 1973. The development of restrictive practices in the UK monetary system. *Manchester School of Economic and Social Studies* 41: 3–18.

Griffiths, B. and Wood, G. E., eds. 1981. *Monetary Targets*.

Griliches, Z. 1988. Productivity puzzles and R&D; another non-explanation. *Journal of Economic Perspectives* 2: 9–21.

1990. Patent statistics as economic indicators. *Journal of Economic Literature* 28: 1661–707.

1994. Productivity, R&D and the data constraint. *American Economic Review* 84: 1–25.

Grossman, G. M. and Helpman, E. 1991. *Innovation and Growth in the Global Economy*. Cambridge, MA.

Gummett, P. 1991. History, development and organisation of UK science and technology up to 1982. In Nicholson *et al.* 1991.

Hall, M. 1987. *The City Revolution. Causes and Consequences*.

Hall, P. A. and Soskice, D., eds. 2001. *Varieties of Capitalism: the Institutional Foundations of Competitive Advantage*. Oxford.

Hall, Robert. 1989. *The Robert Hall Diaries 1947–1953*, ed. Alec Cairncross.

1991. *The Robert Hall Diaries 1954–1961*, ed. Alec Cairncross.

Halsey, A. H., Heath, A. F. and Ridge, J. M. 1980. *Origins and Destinations*. Oxford.

Halsey, A. H. and Webb, J. 2000. *Twentieth Century British Social Trends*. Oxford.

Hammond, R. J. 1951. *Food, I, The Growth of Policy*.

Hannah, L. 1974. Managerial innovation and the rise of the large-scale company in interwar Britain. *Economic History Review* 27: 252–70.

1979. *Electricity before Nationalisation: a Study of the Development of the Electricity Supply Industry in Britain to 1948*.

1982. *Engineers, Managers and Politicians: the First Fifteen Years of Nationalised Electricity Supply in Britain*.

1990. Economic ideas and government policy on industrial organization in Britain since 1945. In Furner and Supple 1990.

Hannah, L., ed. 1976. *Management Strategy and Business Development*.

Hargreaves, E. L. and Gowing, M. M. 1952. *Civil Industry and Trade*.

Harris, J. 1977. *William Beveridge: a Biography*. Oxford.

1981. Some aspects of social policy in Britain during the Second World War. In Mommsen 1981.

1986. Political ideas and the debate on state welfare, 1940–1945. In Smith 1986.

1992. Enterprise and the welfare state. In O'Day and Gourvish 1992.

Harris, L., Coakley, J., Croasdale, M. and Evans, T., eds. 1988. *New Perspectives on the Financial System*.

Harris, R. I. D. 1988. Market structure and external control in the regional economies of Great Britain. *Scottish Journal of Political Economy* 35, 4: 334–60.

1990. The standard capital grant in Northern Ireland, 1954–1988. *Regional Studies* 24, 4: 343–55.

1991. *Regional Economic Policy in Northern Ireland 1945–1988.* Aldershot.

Harrison, M. 1988. Resource mobilization for World War II: the USA, the UK, USSR and Germany, 1938–1945. *Economic History Review* 41: 171–92.

1990. The volume of Soviet munitions output, 1937–1945: a re-evaluation. *Journal of Economic History* 50: 569–90.

forthcoming. The USSR and Total War: why didn't the Soviet economy collapse in 1942? In Chickering and Förster forthcoming.

Harrison, M., ed. 1998. *The Economics of World War II: Six Great Powers in International Comparison.* Cambridge.

Harrison, R. T. and Hart, M., eds. 1993. *Spatial Policy in a Divided Nation.*

Harrison, T. 2000. *Financial Services Marketing.* Harlow.

Hart, M. and Scott, R. 1994. Measuring the effectiveness of small firm policy: some lessons from Northern Ireland. *Regional Studies* 28, 8: 849–58.

Hartwell, R. M. 1973. The service revolution. In Cipolla 1973.

Hasan, J. 1998. *A History of Water in Modern England and Wales.* Manchester.

Haskel, J. and Heden, Y. 1999. Computers and the demand for skilled labour: industry- and establishment-level panel evidence for the UK. *Economic Journal* 109: 68–79.

Hayek, F. A. 1944. *The Road to Serfdom.*

Haynes, M. and Thompson, S. 2000. Productivity, employment and the 'IT paradox': evidence for financial services. In Barrell *et al.* 2000.

Heald, D. 1980. The economic and financial control of UK nationalised industries. *Economic Journal* 90: 243–65.

Healey, N. M., ed. 1993. *Britain's Economic Miracle: Myth or Reality.*

Heim, C. E. 1987. R&D, defence, and spatial divisions of labour in twentieth-century Britain. *Journal of Economic History* 47: 365–78.

1988. Government research establishments, state capacity and distribution of industry policy in Britain. *Regional Studies* 22: 375–86.

Helpman, E., ed. 1998. *General Purpose Technologies and Economic Growth.* Cambridge, MA.

Henderson, P. D. 1977. Two British errors: their probable size and some possible lessons. *Oxford Economic Papers* 29: 159–205.

Higgins, D. M. 1993. Rings, mules and structural constraints in the Lancashire textile industry, c. 1945 – c. 1965. *Economic History Review* 46: 342–62.

Higgs, R. 1992. Wartime prosperity? A reassessment of the US economy in the 1940s. *Journal of Economic History* 52: 41–60.

Hildreth, A. 1999. What has happened to the union wage differential in Britain in the 1990s? *Oxford Bulletin of Economics and Statistics* 61: 1.

Hills, J. 1993. *The Future of Welfare: a Guide to the Debate.* York.

Hills, J., ed. 1996. *New Inequalities.* Cambridge.

Hirst, P. and Thompson, G. 1999. *Globalization in Question,* 2nd edn. Cambridge.

2000. Globalization in one country? The peculiarities of the British. *Economy and Society* 29: 335–6.

Hirst, P. and Zeitlin, J., eds. 1989. *Reversing Industrial Decline? Industrial Structure and Policy in Britain and Her Competitors.* Oxford.

HM Treasury 1961. *Economic and Financial Objectives of the Nationalised Industries.* Cmnd 1337.

1967. *Nationalised Industries: a Review of Economic and Financial Objectives.* Cmnd 3437.

1978. *The Nationalised Industries.* Cmnd 7131.

2000. *Planning Sustainable Public Spending: Lessons from Previous Policy Experience.*

HMSO 1941. *Analysis of the Sources of War Finance and Estimate of the National Income and Expenditure in 1938 and 1940.* Cmd 621.

various years. *Inland Revenue Statistics.*

Hoekman, B. 1994. Conceptual and political economy issues in liberalising international transactions in services. In Deardoff and Stern 1994.

1995. Regional versus multilateral liberalisation of trade in services. *Journal of Economic Integration* 10: 1–31.

House of Commons 1968. Select Committee on Nationalised Industries. *Ministerial Control of the Nationalised Industries*.

1980. Treasury and Civil Service Committee. *Memoranda on Monetary Policy*.

House of Lords 1984–5. Select Committee. On Overseas Trade. *Report, Oral Evidence, Written Evidence* I, II and III.

Howson, S. 1975. *Domestic Monetary Management in Britain 1919–38*. Cambridge.

1980. *Sterling's Managed Float: the Operations of the Exchange Equalisation Account, 1932–39*.

Howson, S. and Winch, D. 1977. *The Economic Advisory Council 1930–1939*.

Howson, Susan, 1987. The origins of cheaper money, 1945–7. *Economic History Review* 40: 433–52.

1988. 'Socialist' monetary policy: monetary thought in the Labour Party in the 1940s. *History of Political Economy* 20: 543–64.

1989. Cheap money versus cheaper money: a reply to Professor Wood. *Economic History Review* 42: 401–5.

1991. The problem of monetary control in Britain, 1948–51. *Journal of European Economic History* 20: 59–92.

1993. *British Monetary Policy 1945–51*. Oxford.

Hudson, R. and Sadler, D. 1989. *The International Steel Industry: Restructuring, State Policies and Localities*.

Hughes, G. and McCormick, B. 1994. Did migration in the 1980s narrow the north–south divide? *Economica* 61: 509–27.

Hughes, K. 1986. *Exports and Technology*. Cambridge.

Hutton, G. 1953. *We Too Can Prosper*.

Hutton, W. 1995. *The State We're In*.

Hyman, R. and Ferner, A. 1994. *New Frontiers in European Industrial Relations*. Oxford.

Ince, G. 1946. The mobilization of manpower in Great Britain for the Second World War. *Manchester School* 14: 17–52.

International Financial Services 2002. *UK Financial Sector Exports, 2002*; available at www.ifs.org.uk.

International Monetary Fund. *Balance of Payments Yearbook*. Various years. Washington.

2000. *International Financial Statistics*. CD-Rom database. Washington.

Iron and Steel Statistics Bureau Various years. *Iron and Steel Industry Annual Statistics for the United Kingdom*.

James, H. 1996. *International Monetary Co-operation since Bretton Woods*. Washington, DC.

Jenkins, P. 1970. *The Battle of Downing Street*.

Johnson, C. 1982. *MITI and the Japanese Miracle: the Growth of Industrial Policy 1925–1975*. Stanford, CA.

Johnson, H. G., 1952. The new monetary policy and the problem of credit control. *Oxford Bulletin of Economics and Statistics* 14: 117–31.

1958. Towards a general theory of the balance of payments. In H. G. Johnson, *International Trade and Economic Growth*.

Johnson, H. G., ed., 1972. *Readings in British Monetary Economics*. Oxford.

Johnson, P. 1986. Some historical dimensions of the welfare state 'crisis'. *Journal of Social Policy* 15: 443–65.

Johnson, P., ed. 1993. *European Industries: Structure, Conduct and Performance*. Aldershot.

Johnson, P. and Webb, S. 1993. Explaining the growth in UK income inequality. *Economic Journal* 103: 429–43.

Johnston, R. and Gummett, P., eds. 1979. *Directing Technology: Policies for Promotion and Control*.

Jones, C. I. 1995. Time-series tests of endogenous growth models. *Quarterly Journal of Economics* 110: 495–525.

Jones, G. and Morgan, N. J., eds. 1994. *Adding Value: Brands and Marketing in Food and Drink*.

Jones, R. and Marriott, O. 1970. *Anatomy of a Merger: a History of GEC, AEI and English Electric*.

Jones Lang Wootton 1994. *Decentralisation of Offices from Central London*.

Journal of Economic Perspectives, Symposium on Real Business Cycles, summer 1989.

Juergens, U., Malsch, T. and Dohse, K. 1993. *Breaking from Taylorism: Changing Forms of Work in the Automobile Industry*. Cambridge.

Kahn-Freund, O. 1954. Legal framework. In Flanders and Clegg 1954.

Kaldor, M. 1982. *The Baroque Arsenal*.

Kaldor, N. 1970. The new monetarism. *Lloyds Bank Review* 97: 1–18.

    1971. The conflict in national policy objectives. *Economic Journal* 81: 1–18.

    1972. The irrelevance of equilibrium economics. *Economic Journal* 82: 1237–55.

Kaletsky. A. and Jonquieres, G. de. 1987. Why a service economy is no panacea. *Financial Times* 22 May.

Kamien, M. I. and Schwartz, N. L. 1982. *Market Structure and Innovation*. Cambridge.

Kay, J. 2001. Meeting of closed minds. *Financial Times*, 28 November.

    forthcoming. Privatisation in the United Kingdom 1979–1999.

Kealey, T. 1995. *The Economic Laws of Scientific Research*. Basingstoke.

    1998. Why science is endogenous: a debate with Paul David [etc.]. *Research Policy* 26: 897–924.

Keeble, D. 1976. *Industrial Location and Planning in the United Kingdom*.

Kendrick, J. W. 1987. Service sector productivity. *Business Economics* 22: 18–24.

Kennedy, C. 1986. *ICI: the Company that Changed Our Lives*.

Kennedy, C. M. 1952. Monetary policy. In Worswick and Ady 1952.

Keynes, J. M. 1927. J. M. Keynes on banking service. *Journal of the Institute of Bankers* 48: 494–7.

    1940. *How to Pay for the War: a Radical Plan for the Chancellor of the Exchequer*.

Kirby, M. W. 1981. *The Decline of British Economic Power Since 1870*.

Kitson, M. 1995. Seedcorn or chaff? Unemployment and small firm performance. Working Paper 2, ESRC Centre for Business Research.

    1997. The competitive weaknesses of the UK economy. In Arestis *et al.* 1997.

Kitson, M., Martin, R. and Wilkinson, F. 2000. Labour markets, social justice and economic efficiency. *Cambridge Journal of Economics* November 2000.

Kitson, M. and Michie, J. 1996. Britain's industrial performance since 1960: under-investment and relative decline. *Economic Journal* 106: 196–212.

    2000. *The Political Economy of Competitiveness*.

Klug, A. and Smith, G. W. 1999. Suez and sterling, 1956. *Explorations in Economic History* 36: 181–203.

Knack, S. and Keefer, P. 1997. Does social capital have an economic payoff? A cross-country investigation. *Quarterly Journal of Economics* November.

Kochan, T., Katz, H. and McKersie, R. B. 1986. *The Transformation of American Industrial Relations*. New York.

Kohan, C. M. 1952. *Works and Buildings*.

Krueger, A. 1993. How computers have changed the wage structure: evidence from micro-data, 1984–1989. *Quarterly Journal of Economics* 108: 33–61.

Krugman, P. 1989. *Exchange-rate instability*. Cambridge, MA.

Kuznets, S. 1945. *National Product in Wartime*. New York.

Kydland, Finn E. and Prescott, Edward C. 1977. Rules rather than discretion: the inconsistency of optimal plans. *Journal of Political Economy* 85: 473–91.

Labour Party 1976. *Labour Party Annual Conference Report*.

Laidler, D. 1971. The influence of money on economic activity – a survey of some current problems. In Clayton *et al.* 1971.

1976. Inflation in Britain: a monetarist perspective. *American Economic Review* 66: 485–500.

1985. Monetary policy in Britain: success and shortcomings. *Oxford Review of Economic Policy* 1: 35–43.

Laidler, D. and Parkin, J. M. 1970. The demand for money in the United Kingdom 1956–1967: preliminary estimates. *Manchester School of Economic and Social Studies* 38: 187–208. Reprinted in Johnson 1972.

Landau, R., Taylor, T. and Wright, G., eds. 1996. *The Mosaic of Modern Growth*. Stanford, CA.

Landefield, J. S. 1987. International trade in services: its composition, importance and links to merchandise trade. *Business Economics* 22: 25–31.

Landes, D. S. 1972. *The Unbound Prometheus: Technological Change and Industrial Development in Western Europe from 1750 to the Present*. Cambridge.

Larédo, P. and Mustar, P., eds. 2001. *Research and Innovation Policies in the New Global Economy: an International Comparative Analysis*. Cheltenham.

Law, D. and Howes, R. 1972. *Mid-Wales: an Assessment of the Impact of the Development Commission Factory Programme*.

Lawson, N. 1992. *The View from No. 11. Memoirs of a Tory Radical*.

Layard R., Nickell, S. and Jackman, R. 1991. *Unemployment: Macroeconomic Performance and the Labour Market*. Oxford.

Layard, R. and Nickell, S. J. 1986. Unemployment in Britain. *Economica* 53: 121–69.

Lazonick, W. 1986. The cotton industry. In Elbaum and Lazonick 1986.

Le Grand, J. 1982. *The Strategy of Equality*.

Leadbeater, C. 1990. The road to privatisation: political debate too simplistic. *Financial Times* 8 August: 8.

Lee, C. H. 1995. *Scotland and the United Kingdom. The Economy and the Union in the Twentieth Century*. Manchester.

Leibenstein, H. 1966. Allocative efficiency vs 'X' efficiency. *American Economic Review* 56: 392–415.

1976. *Beyond Economic Man*. Cambridge, MA.

Levine, A. L. 1967. *Industrial Retardation in Britain, 1880–1914*. New York.

Levitt, M. S. and Joyce, M. A. S. 1986. Government output in the national accounts. *National Institute Economic Review* 115: 48–51.

Lewchuk, W. 1987. *American Technology and the British Vehicle Industry*. Cambridge.

Lewis, J. 1992. *Women in Britain since 1945*. Oxford.

Liepmann, K. 1960. *Apprenticeship: an Enquiry into its Adequacy in Modern Conditions*.

Llewellyn, D. 1987. When some are more equal than others . . . *Banking World* 5: 32–5.

Llewellyn, D. and Wrigglesworth, J. 1990. Labouring under the Law. *Mortgage Finance* 122: 28–36.

Lloyds Bank various years. *Lloyds Bank Review*.

Lowe, R. 1993. *The Welfare State in Britain since 1945*.

Lucas, R. E. 1988. On the mechanics of economic development. *Journal of Monetary Economics* 22:

Lund, M. and Wright, J. 1999. The financing of small firms in the United Kingdom. *Bank of England Quarterly Bulletin* 39: 195–201.

Lythe, C. and Majmudar, M. 1982. *The Renaissance of the Scottish Economy?*

MacDougall, Donald, 1987. *Don and Mandarin: Memoirs of an Economist*.

Machin, S. 1997. The decline of labour market institutions and the rise in wage inequality in Britain. *European Economic Review* 41: 647–57.

1999. Wage inequality in the 1970s, 1980s and 1990s. In Gregg and Wadsworth 1999.

2001. Does it still pay to be in or to join a union? Working Paper, CEP.

Machin, S. and Stewart, M. 1990. Unions and the financial performance of British private sector establishments. *Journal of Applied Econometrics* 5: 327–50.

1996. Trade unions and financial performance. *Oxford Economic Papers* 48: 213–41.

Machin, S. and Van Reenen, J. 1998. Technology and changes in skill structure: evidence from an international panel of industries. *Quarterly Journal of Economics* 113: 1215–44.

Maclennan, D. and Parr, J. B. 1979. *Regional Policy. Past Experiences and New Directions.* Oxford.

Macleod, I. and Powell, E. 1952. *The Social Services: Needs and Means.*

Macmillan, H. 1971. *Riding the Storm, 1956–59.*

Maddison, A. 1995. *Monitoring the World Economy, 1820–1992.* Paris.

2001. *The World Economy: a Millennial Perspective.* Paris.

Malerba, F. and Orsenigo, L. 1997. Technological regimes and sectoral patterns of innovative activities. *Industrial & Corporate Change* 6: 83–118.

2000. Knowledge, innovative activities and industrial evolution. *Industrial & Corporate Change* 9: 289–314.

Mankiw, N. G. 1995. The growth of nations. *Brookings Papers on Economic Activity* 1: 275–326.

Mansell, K. 1996. New data and the measurement of output for the services sector in the UK. *Review of Income and Wealth* 42: 225–32.

Manser, W. 1971. *Britain in Balance: the Myth of Failure.*

Marquand, J. 1983. The changing distribution of service employment. In Goddard and Champion 1983.

Marris, R. 1985. The paradox of services. *Political Quarterly* 56: 242–52.

Mars, J. 1952. British social income estimates, 1938–1950. *Manchester School* 20: 25–56.

Marsden, D. and Thompson, M. 1990. Flexibility agreements and their significance in the increase in productivity in British manufacturing since 1980. *Work, Employment and Society* 4: 1.

Marshall, A. 1920. *Principles of Economics*, 8th edn.

Marshall, J. N. 1988. *Services and Uneven Development.* Oxford.

Martin, J. F. 2000. *The Development of Modern Agriculture: British Farming since 1931.* Berkeley, CA.

Martin, R. 1988. The political economy of Britain's north–south divide. *Transactions of the Institute of British Geographers* n.s. 13: 389–418.

2002. The limits of a cluster based regional policy. Paper presented to the Cambridge–MIT Conference on The Future of Regional Policy, Cambridge, May 2002.

Martinelli, A., ed. 1991. *International Markets and Global Firms: a Comparative Study of Organized Business in the Chemical Industry.*

Marwick, A. 1974. *War and Social Change in the Twentieth Century.*

Mason, G. 1995. *The New Graduate Supply-Shock: Recruitment and Utilisation of Graduates in British Industry.* National Institute of Economic and Social Research, Report Series 9.

Mason, G. and Finegold, D. 1995. Productivity, machinery and skills in the United States and Western Europe: precision engineering. Discussion Paper 89, National Institute of Economic and Social Research.

1997. Productivity, machinery and skills in the United States and Western Europe. *National Institute Economic Review* 162: 85–98.

Massey, D. 1984. *Spatial Divisions of Labour. Social Structures and the Geography of Production.* Basingstoke.

Matthews, D., Anderson, M. and Edwards, J. R. 1997. The rise of the professional accountant in British management. *Economic History Review* 50:

Matthews, R. C. O., Feinstein, C. H. and Odling-Smee, J. C. 1982. *British Economic Growth, 1856–1973.* Oxford.

Maunder, P. 1988. Food processing. In Johnson 1988.

May, R. 1997. The scientific wealth of nations. *Science* 275: 793–6.

Mayer, C. 1986. Financial innovation: curse or blessing? *Oxford Review of Economic Policy* 2: i–xix.

McCloskey, D. 1991. *If You're So Smart*. Chicago, IL.

McGoldrick, P. J. and Greenland, S. J. 1994. *Retailing of Financial Services*.

McKinsey Global Institute 1992. *Service Sector Productivity*. Washington, DC.

Meade, J. E. and Stone, R. 1941. The construction of tables of national income, expenditure, savings and investment. *Economic Journal* 51: 216–33.

Menezes-Filho, N. A. 1997. Unions and profitability over the 1980s: some evidence on union–firm bargaining in the UK. *Economic Journal* 107: 651–70.

Merrett, A. J., Howe, M. and Newbould, G. D. 1967. *Equity Issues and the London Capital Market*.

Metcalf, D. 1993. Industrial relations and economic performance. *British Journal of Industrial Relations* 31: 255–83.

  1994. Transformation of British industrial relations? Institutions, conduct and outcomes, 1980–1990. In Barrell 1994.

Metcalf, D., Hansen, K. and Charlwood, A. 2001. Unions and the sword of justice: unions and pay systems, pay inequality, pay discrimination and low pay. *National Institute Economic Review* 176: 61–75.

Michie, J., ed. 1992. *The Economic Legacy 1979–1992*.

Michie, J. and Grieve Smith, J., eds. 1997. *Employment and Economic Performance*. Oxford.

Middleton, R. 1996. *Government versus the Market*. Cheltenham.

  2000. *The British Economy since 1945*.

  2001. *Struggling with the Impossible: Sterling, the Balance of Payments and British Economic Policy, 1949–72*.

Midland Bank various years. *Midland Bank Review*.

Milanovic, B. 1989. *Liberalization and Entrepreneurship*. New York.

Miles, D. 1992. Housing and the wider economy in the short and long run. *National Institute Economic Review* 139: 64–77.

  1993. Testing for short-termism in the UK stock market. *Economic Journal* 103: 1379–96.

Mills, G. and Rockoff, H. 1987. Compliance with price controls in the United States and the United Kingdom during World War II. *Journal of Economic History* 47: 197–213.

Millward, N., Bryson, A. and Forth, J. 2000. *All Change at Work?*

Millward, N., Stevens, M., Smart, D. and Hawes, W. R. 1992. *Workplace Industrial Relations in Transition*. Aldershot.

Millward, R. 1990. Productivity in the service sector: historical trends 1856–1985 and comparisons with USA 1950–85. *Oxford Bulletin of Economics and Statistics* 52: 423–36.

  1994. Industrial and commercial performance since 1950. In Floud and McCloskey 1994.

  1999. Industrial performance, the infrastructure and government policy: an international comparison of British performance and policy 1800–1987. In Dormois and Dintenfass 1999.

Millward, R. and Singleton, J., eds. 1995. *The Political Economy of Nationalisation in Britain, 1920–1950*. Cambridge.

Millward, R. and Ward, R. 1987. The costs of public and private gas enterprise in late nineteenth-century Britain. *Oxford Economic Papers* 39: 719–37.

Milner, S., 1995. The coverage of collective pay setting institutions in Britain 1895–1990. *British Journal of Industrial Relations* 33: 69–92.

Milward, A. and Brennan, G. 1996. *Britain's Place in the World: a Historical Inquiry into Import Controls 1945–60*.

Milward, A. S. 1977. *War, Economy, and Society, 1939–1945*.

  1984. *The Economic Effects of the Two World Wars on Britain*, 2nd edn. Basingstoke.

Minford, P. 1991. *The Supply Side Revolution in Britain*.

Ministry of Labour and National Service 1947. *Ministry of Labour and National Service Report for the Years 1939–45*. Cmd 7255.

Mitchell, B. R. 1988. *British Historical Statistics*. Cambridge.

Molyneux, R. and Thompson, D. 1987. Nationalised industry performance: still third rate? *Fiscal Studies* 8: 48–82.

Mommsen, W. J., ed. 1981. *The Emergence of the Welfare State in Britain and Germany, 1850–1950*.

Moore, B. and Rhodes, J. 1973. Evaluating the effects of British regional policy. *Economic Journal* 83: 87–110.

Moore, B., Rhodes, J. and Tyler, P. 1986. *The Effects of Government Regional Economic Policy*.

More, C. 1980. *Skill and the English Working Class, 1870–1914*.

Morgan, K. and Sayer, A. 1988. *Microcircuits of Capital: Sunrise Industry and Uneven Development*. Oxford.

Morison, I. and Shepherdson, I. 1991. *Economics of the City*.

Morris, D., ed. 1985. *The Economic System in the UK*. Oxford.

Morris, P. R. 1990. *A History of the World Semiconductor Industry*.

Moss, M. S. and Hume, J. R. 1981. *The Making of Scotch Whisky: a History of the Scotch Whisky Distilling Industry*. Edinburgh.

Mottershead, P. 1978. Industrial policy. In Blackaby 1978.

Mowery, D. 1986. Industrial research in Britain, 1900–1950. In Elbaum and Lazonick 1986.

Mundell, R. A. 1962. The appropriate use of monetary and fiscal policy for internal and external stability. *IMF Staff Papers* 9: 70–7.

1963. Capital mobility and stabilization policy under fixed and flexible exchange rates. *Canadian Journal of Economics and Political Science* 29: 475–85.

Nabseth, L. and Ray, G. F., eds. 1974. *The Diffusion of Industrial Processes: an International Study*. Cambridge.

Nash, E. F. 1951. Wartime controls of food and agricultural prices. In Chester 1951.

National Statistical Office 2002. *Labour Market Trends*.

Neal, L. and Barbezat, D. 1998. *The Economics of the European Union and the Economies of Europe*. New York.

Nelson, R. R., ed. 1993. *National Innovation Systems: a Comparative Analysis*. New York.

Nichols, T. 1986. *The British Worker Question*.

Nicholson, R., Cunningham, C. M. and Gummett, P., eds. 1991. *Science and Technology in the United Kingdom*.

Nickell, S. 1996. Competition and corporate performance. *Journal of Political Economy* 104: 724–46.

2002. The assessment: the economic record of the Labour Government since 1997. *Oxford Review of Economic Policy* 18: 107–19.

Nickell, S., Wadhwani, S. and Wall, M. 1992. Productivity growth in UK companies 1975–86. *European Economic Review* 36: 1055–85.

Nolan, P. 1989. Walking on water? Performance and industrial relations under Thatcher. *Industrial Relations Journal* 20: 81–92.

1996. Industrial relations and performance since 1945. In Beardwell 1996.

North, D. C. 1981. The second industrial revolution and its consequences. In North, *Structure and Change in Economic History*. New York.

Norton, W. E. 1969. Debt management and monetary policy in the United Kingdom. *Economic Journal* 79: 475–94. Reprinted in Johnson 1972.

O'Day, A. and Gourvish, T., eds. 1992. *Britain since 1945*.

O'Mahony, M. 1992. Productivity levels in British and German manufacturing industry. *National Institute Economic Review* 139: 46–63.

1999. *Britain's Productivity Performance, 1950–1996: an International Perspective*.

2002. *The National Institute Sectorial Productivity Dataset*, www.niesr.ac.uk/research.

O'Mahony, M. and de Boer, W. 2002. Britain's relative productivity performance: updates and extensions. National Institute of Economic and Social Research, London; available from www.niesr.ac.uk.

O'Mahony, M. and Wagner, K. 1994. *Changing Fortunes: An Industry Study of British and German Productivity Growth Over Three Decades*, Report Series No.7, National Institute of Economic and Social Research.

O'Mahony, M., Oulton, N. and Vass, J. 1998. Market services: productivity benchmarks for the UK. *Oxford Bulletin of Economics and Statistics* 60: 529–51.

OECD 1976. *The Footwear Industry: Structure and Governmental Policies*. Paris.

    1981. *The Welfare State in Crisis*. Paris.

    1985. *Social Expenditure 1960–1990*. Paris.

    2000. *Revenue Statistics 1965–1999*. Paris.

    2001. *The Well-being of Nations: the Role of Human and Social Capital*. Paris.

    2002. *Economic Outlook, Statistics and Projections*, no. 72. Paris.

    Economic Outlook, various years. Paris.

Olson, M. 1982. *The Rise and Fall of Nations: Economic Growth, Stagflation and Social Rigidities*. New Haven, CT.

ONS 1998. *United Kingdom National Accounts: Concepts, Sources and Methods*. E. A. Doggett.

    2001a. *UK 2002, The Official Yearbook of Great Britain and Northern Ireland*.

    2001b. *Education Statistics for the UK*.

    Economic Trends, various years.

    Financial Statistics, various years.

    National Income Accounts, 'Blue Books', various years.

    Social Trends, various years.

Oulton, N. 1990. Labour productivity in UK manufacturing in the 1970s and in the 1980s. *National Institute Economic Review* 132: 71–91.

    1995. Supply side reform and the UK economic growth: what happened to the miracle? *National Institute for Economic and Social Research Review* 154: 53–69.

Overy, R. J. 1980. *The Air War 1939–1945*.

    1988. Mobilization for total war in Germany 1939-1941. *English Historical Review* 103: 613–39.

Owen, G. 1992. The British electronics industry from 1960 to the 1990s. Working Paper 324, Centre for Economic Performance, London School of Economics.

    1999. *From Empire to Europe: the Decline and Revival of British Industry Since the Second World War*.

Page, R. M. and Silburn, R. 1999. *British Social Welfare in the Twentieth Century*.

Pain, N., Riley and Weale, M. 2001. The UK economy. *National Institute Economic Review* 178: 48–68.

Paish, F. W. 1965. *Business Finance*.

Panic, M., ed. 1976. *The UK and West German Manufacturing Industry, 1957–72*.

Papp, I. 1975. *Government and Enterprise: an Analysis of the Economics of Governmental Regulation or Control of Industry*.

Parker, D. 1993. Privatisation ten years on. In Healey 1993.

Parker, H. M. D. 1957. *Manpower: a Study of Wartime Policy and Administration*.

Parsons, D. W. 1986. *The Political Economy of British Regional Policy*.

Patel, P. and Pavitt, K. 1989. The technological activities of the UK: a fresh look. In Silberston 1989.

Pathirane, L. and Blades, D. W. 1982. Defining and measuring the public sector: some international comparisons. *Review of Income and Wealth* 28th ser., 3: 261–89.

Pavitt, K. 1981. Technology in British industry: a suitable case for improvement. In Carter 1981.

Pavitt, K., ed. 1980. *Technical Innovation and British Economic Performance*.

Pavitt, K., Robson, M. and Townsend, J. 1987. The size distribution of innovating firms in the UK, 1945–1983. *Journal of Industrial Economics* 35: 297–316.

Peacock, A. and Wiseman, J. 1961. *The Growth of Public Expenditure in the UK*. Princeton.

Peck, M. J. 1968. Science and technology. In Caves *et al.* 1968.

Peden, G. 2000. *The Treasury and British Public Policy 1906–1959*. Oxford.

Peden, G. C. 1985. *British Economic and Social Policy*. Oxford.

Pelling, H. 1984. *The Labour Governments, 1945–51*.

Pember and Boyle, 1950. *British Government Securities in the Twentieth Century*.

Performance and Innovation Unit 2002. Social capital. A discussion paper, Performance and Innovation Unit, The Cabinet Office, London, April.

Petit, P. and Soete, L., eds. 2001. *Technology and the Future of Europe*. Cheltenham.

Pettigrew, A. M. 1985. *The Awakening Giant: Continuity and Change in Imperial Chemical Industries*. Oxford.

Phelps Brown, E. H. 1962. Wage drift. *Economica*.

Piachaud, D. 1987. The growth of poverty. In Walker and Walker 1987.

Pierson, C. 1991. *Beyond the Welfare State?* Cambridge.

Piore, M. J. and Sabel, C. F. 1984. *The Second Industrial Divide: Possibilities for Prosperity*. New York.

Pliatzky, L. 1984. *Getting and Spending. Public Expenditure, Employment and Inflation*, revised edn. Oxford.

Plowden, Edwin. 1989. *An Industrialist in the Treasury: the Post-war Years*.

Political and Economic Planning 1950. *Motor Vehicles: a Report on the Organisation and Structure of the Industry, its Products, and its Market Prospects at Home and Abroad*.

Pollard, S. 1983. *The Development of the British Economy*, 3rd edn.

   1984. *The Wasting of the British Economy*.

Porter, M. E. 1998. *Clusters and Competition: New Agendas for Companies, Governments, and Institutions*, Boston, MA.

Posner, M. 1987. Nationalisation. In Eatwell, Milgate and Newman 1987.

Postan, M. M. 1952. *British War Production*.

Prais, S. J. 1981. *Productivity and Industrial Structure: a Statistical Study of Manufacturing Industry in Britain, Germany and the United States*. Cambridge.

   1988. Qualified manpower in engineering: Britain and other industrially advanced countries. *National Institute Economic Review* 127: 76–83.

   1995. *Productivity, Education and Training: an International Perspective*. Cambridge.

Prais, S. J., Jarvis, V. and Wagner, K. 1989. Productivity and vocational skills in Britain and Germany: hotels. *National Institute Economic Review* 130: 52–74.

Prais, S. J. and Wagner, K. 1988. Productivity and management: the training of foremen in Britain and Germany. *National Institute Economic Review* 123: 34–47.

Pressnell, L. 1986. *External Economic Policy since the War*, I, *The Post-War Financial Settlement*.

Prest, A. and Coppock, D., eds. 1986. *The UK Economy: a Manual of Applied Economics*, 11th edn.

Price, J. 1996. Producer prices for services: development of a new price index. *Economic Trends* 513: 14–18.

Price, L. D. D. 1972. The demand for money in the United Kingdom: a further investigation. *Bank of England Quarterly Bulletin* 12: 43–56.

Propper, C. 2001. Expenditure on healthcare in the UK: a review of the issues. *Fiscal Studies* 22: 151–83.

Pryke, R. 1971. *Public Enterprise in Practice: the British Experience of Nationalisation over Two Decades*.

   1981. *The Nationalised Industries: Policies and Performance since 1968*. Oxford.

   1982. The comparative performance of public and private enterprise. *Fiscal Studies* 3: 68–81.

Pryor, F. L. 2002. *The Future of US Capitalism*. New York.

Puttnam, R. 2000. *Bowling Alone: the Collapse and Revival of American Community*.

Radcliffe Committee on the Working of the Monetary System, 1959. *Report*.

   1960. *Principal Memoranda of Evidence*.

Rahman, M., Palmer, G. and Kenway, P. 2001. *Monitoring Poverty and Social Exclusion 2001*. York.

Ranki, G. 1988. Economy and the Second World War: a few comparative issues. *Journal of European Economic History* 17: 303–47.

Ray, G. F. 1986. Productivity in services. *National Institute of Economic and Social Research Review*: 44–7.

Ray, G. R. 1984. *The Diffusion of Mature Technologies*. Cambridge.

Reddaway, W. B. 1951. Rationing. In Chester 1951.

Regional Studies Association 2001. *Labour's New Regional Policy: an Assessment*.

Reid, Margaret. 1982. *The Secondary Banking Crisis, 1973–75*.

Report of the Committee on Economic and Financial Problems of Provision for Old-age 1954.

Report of the Committee to Review the Functioning of Financial Institutions (Wilson Report) 1980. Cmnd 7937.

Revell, J. 1973. *The British Financial System*.

Rhys, D. G. 1972. *The Motor Industry: an Economic Survey*.

Richardson, J. H. 1938. *Industrial Relations in Great Britain*. Geneva.

Riley, R. and Young, G. 2001. The macroeconomic impact of the New Deal for Young People. Discussion paper 184, August National Institute of Economic and Social Research.

Robinson, E. A. G. 1951. The overall allocation of resources. In Chester 1951.

Robinson, O. and Wallace, J. 1984. Growth and utilisation of part-time labour in GB. *Employment Gazette* September: 391–7.

Robson, M., Townsend, J. and Pavitt, K. 1988. Sectoral patterns of production and use of innovations in the UK: 1945–1983. *Research Policy* 17: 1–14.

Rockoff, H. 1998. The United States: from ploughshares to swords. In Harrison 1998.

Roeber, J. 1975. *Social Change at Work: the ICI Weekly Staff Agreement*.

Rollings, N. 1992. Poor Mr Butskell: a short life, wrecked by schizophrenia. *20th Century British History* 5: 183–205.

Romer, P. 1986. Increasing returns and long-run growth. *Journal of Political Economy* 94: 1002–37.

1994. The origins of endogenous growth. *Journal of Economic Perspectives* 8: 3–22.

Rose, H. 1986. Change in financial intermediation in the UK. *Oxford Review of Economic Policy* 2: 18–40.

Rosevear, S. 1998. Balancing business and the regions: British distribution of industry policy and the Board of Trade, 1945–51. *Business History* 40, 1: 77–99.

Ross, A. M. and Hartman, P. T. 1960. *Changing Patterns of Industrial Conflict*. New York.

Rostas, L. 1948. *Comparative Productivity in British and American Industry*. Cambridge.

Rothschild, V., chair. 1971. *A Framework for Government Research and Development*.

Routh, G. 1965. *Occupation and Pay in Great Britain, 1906–1960*. Cambridge.

1980. *Occupation and Pay in Great Britain 1906–79*.

Rowley, C. K. 1971. *Steel and Public Policy*.

Rowntree, B. S. and Lavers, G. R. 1951. *Poverty and the Welfare State*.

Rowthorn, R. 1999. The political economy of full employment in modern Britain. The Kaleski Memorial Lecture at the Department of Economics, University of Oxford, 19 October 1999.

2001. UK competitiveness, productivity and the knowledge economy. Paper presented at the National Competitiveness Summit, 1 November 2001, Cambridge–MIT Institute, Cambridge.

Rubinstein, W. D. 1993. *Capitalism, Culture and Decline in Britain, 1750–1990*.

Rupp, L. J. 1978. *Mobilizing Women for War*. Princeton, NJ.

Ryan, P. 1996. Factor shares and inequality in the UK. *Oxford Review of Economic Policy* 12: 1.

Rybczynski, T. M. 1988. Financial systems and industrial re-structuring. *National Westminster Bank Quarterly Review*: 3–13.

Salant, W. S. 1980. The collected writings of John Maynard Keynes: activities 1940–43 and 1944–46 – a review article. *Journal of Economic Literature* 18: 1056–62.

Salter, A. J. and Martin, B. R. 2001. The economic benefits of publicly funded basic research: a critical review. *Research Policy* 30: 509–32.

Salter, W. E. G. 1960. *Productivity and Technical Change*. Cambridge.

Salverda, W., Nolan, B. and Lucifora, C., eds. 2000. *Policy Measures for Low-Wage Employment in Europe*. Cheltenham.

Sanderson, M. 1972. *The Universities and British Industry, 1850–1970*.

1988. Education and economic decline, 1890–1980s. *Oxford Review of Economic Policy* 41: 38–50.

Sandy, R. and Elliott, R. F. 1996. Unions and risk. *Economica* 63: 291–309.

Sapir, A. 1991. The structure of services in Europe: a conceptual framework. Discussion Paper 498, Centre for Economic Policy Research.

Sargent, J. 1979. UK performance in services. In Blackaby 1979.

1991. Deregulation, debt and downturn in the UK economy. *National Institute Economic Review* 137: 75–87.

Saul, S. B. 1979. Research and development in British industry from the end of the nineteenth century to the 1960s. In Smout 1979.

Saunders, C. T. 1946. Manpower distribution, 1939–45. *Manchester School* 14: 1–39.

Sayers, R. S. 1956. *Financial Policy, 1939–1945*.

1983. 1941 – the first Keynesian Budget. In Feinstein 1983.

Schenk, C. 1994. *Britain and the Sterling Area: from Devaluation to Convertibility in the 1950s*.

Schenk, W. 1974. Continuous casting of steel. In Nabseth and Ray 1974.

Scherer, F. M. 1980. *Industrial Market Structure and Economic Performance*, 2nd edn. Boston, MA.

Schmookler, J. 1966. *Innovation and Economic Growth*. Cambridge, MA.

Schumpeter, J. A. 1934. *The Theory of Economic Development*. Cambridge, MA.

Scott, M. F. 1989. *A New View of Economic Growth*. Oxford.

Scott, P. 1996a. The worst of both worlds: British regional policy, 1951–64. *Business History* 38, 4: 41–64.

1996b. *The Property Masters: a History of the British Commercial Property Sector*.

1997. British regional policy 1945–51: a lost opportunity. *Twentieth Century British History* 8, 3: 358–82.

2000. The audit of British regional policy: 1934–9. *Regional Studies* 34, 1: 55–65.

Seldon, A. 1957. *Pensions in a Free Society*.

Setterfield, M. 1992. A long run theory of effective demand: modelling macroeconomic systems with hysteresis. PhD thesis, Dalhousie University, Canada.

Shanks, M. 1961. *The Stagnant Society*.

Sharp, M. 1985. *Europe and the New Technologies: Six Case Studies in Innovation and Adjustment*.

2000. The UK experiment: science, technology and industrial policy, 1975–1997. Paper presented at the Triple Helix conference, Rio de Janeiro.

Shaw, C. 1983. The large manufacturing employers of 1907. *Business History* 25: 42–60.

Shaw, G. K. 1992. Policy implications of endogenous growth theory. *Economic Journal* 102, May: 611–21.

Sheldrake, J. and Vickerstaff, S. 1987. *The History of Industrial Training in Britain*. Aldershot.

Sheppard, D. K. 1971. *The Growth and Role of UK Financial Institutions 1880–1962*.

Shonfield, A. 1958. *British Economic Policy since the War*.

1965. *Modern Capitalism: the Changing Balance of Public and Private Power*. Oxford.

Short, J. 1981. *Public Expenditure and Taxation in the UK Regions*.

Silberston, A., ed. 1989. *Technology and Economic Progress*. Basingstoke.

Singh, A. 1975. Takeovers, natural selection and the theory of the firm: evidence from the postwar experience. *Economic Journal* 85: 497–515.

1977. UK industry and the world economy: a case of deindustrialisation. *Cambridge Journal of Economics* 1: 113–36.

Singleton, J. 1986. Lancashire's Last Stand: Declining Employment in the British Cotton Industry, 1950–70. *Economic History Review* 39: 92–107.

1991. *Lancashire on the Scrapheap: the Cotton Industry, 1945–1970*. Oxford.

Skidelsky, R. 2000. *John Maynard Keynes*, III, *Fighting for Britain, 1937–1946*.

Skott, P. and Auerbach, P. 1995. Cumulative causation and the 'new' theories of economic growth. *Journal of Post Keynesian Economics* 17, 3: 381–402.

Small Firms: Report of Committee of Inquiry on Small Firms (Bolton Report) 1971. Cmnd 4811.

Smith, A. D., Hitchens, D. M. W. N. and Davies, S. W. 1982. *International Industrial Productivity: a Comparison of Britain, America and Germany*. Cambridge.

Smith, H. L. 1984. The womanpower problem in Britain during the Second World War. *Historical Journal* 27: 925–45.

Smith, H. L., ed. 1986. *War and Social Change*. Manchester.

Smith, Warren L. and Mikesell, Raymond F. 1957. The effectiveness of monetary policy: recent British experience. *Journal of Political Economy* 65: 18–39.

Smout, T. C., ed. 1979. *The Search for Wealth and Stability*.

Society of Motor Manufacturers and Traders, various years. *The Motor Industry of Great Britain*.

Solow, R. 2001. Information technology and the recent productivity boom in the US. Paper presented to the Cambridge–MIT Institute Summit, Cambridge, MA., November 2001.

Spencer, Peter D. 1981. A model of the demand for British government stocks by non-bank residents 1967–77. *Economic Journal* 91: 938–60.

1986. *Financial Innovation, Efficiency and Disequilibrium: Problems of Monetary Management in the United Kingdom 1971–1981*. Oxford.

SPRU 1996. *The Relationship between Publicly Funded Basic Research and Economic Performance: a SPRU Review*. Brighton.

Steedman, H., Mason, G. and Wagner, K. 1991. Intermediate skills in the workplace: deployment, standards and supply in Britain, France and Germany. *National Institute Economic Review* 136: 60–76.

Steedman, H. and Wagner, K. 1987. A second look at productivity, machinery and skills in Britain and Germany. *National Institute Economic Review* 122: 84–95.

1989. Productivity, machinery and skills: clothing manufacture in Britain and Germany. *National Institute Economic Review* 128: 40–57.

Steiner, V. and Mohr, R. 2000. Industrial change, stability of relative earnings, and substitution of unskilled labour in West Germany. In Salverda *et al.* 2000.

Stelser, I. 1988. Britain's newest import: America's regulatory experience. *Oxford Review of Economic Policy* 4: 68–79.

Stewart, M. 1987. Collective bargaining arrangements, closed shops and relative pay. *Economic Journal* 97: 140–56.

1990. Union wage differentials, product market influences and the division of rents. *Economic Journal* 100: 1122–37.

1991. Union wage differentials in the face of changes in the economic and legal environment. *Economica* 58: 155–72.

1995. Union wage differentials in an era of declining unionisation. *Oxford Bulletin of Economics and Statistics* 57: 143–66.

Stiroh, K. J. 2001. Information technology and the US productivity revival: what do the industry data say? Working Paper 15, Federal Reserve Bank of New York.

Stone, I. and Peck, F. 1996. The foreign-owned manufacturing sector in UK peripheral regions, 1978–1993: restructuring and comparative performance. *Regional Studies* 30, 1: 55–68.

Stone, R. 1951. The use and development of national income and expenditure estimates. In Chester 1951.

Stoneman, P. 1976. *Technological Diffusion and the Computer Revolution: the UK Experience*. Cambridge.

Stoneman, P., ed. 1995. *Handbook of the Economics of Innovation and Technological Change*. Oxford.

Storey, D. 1994. *Understanding the Small Business Sector*.

Sullivan, M. 1999. Democratic socialism and social policy. In Page and Silburn 1999.

Summerfield, P. 1984. *Women Workers in the Second World War: Production and Patriarchy in Conflict*.

1998. *Reconstructing Women's Wartime Lives: Discourse and Subjectivity in Oral Histories*. Manchester.

Summers, R. 1985. Services in the international economy. In Inman 1985.

Supple, B. 1987. *The History of the British Coal Industry, IV, 1913–1946: The Political Economy of Decline*. Oxford.

1994a. British economic decline since 1945. In Floud and McCloskey 1994.

1994b. Fear of failing: economic history and the decline of Britain. *Economic History Review* 47: 441–58.

1997. Introduction: national performance in personal perspective. In Clarke and Trebilcock 1997.

Sutton, J. 1991. *Sunk Costs and Market Structure: Price Competition, Advertising, and the Evolution of Concentration*. Cambridge, MA.

Tanzi, V. and Schuknecht, L. 2000. *Public Spending in the 20th Century*. Cambridge.

Tarling, R. W and Wilkinson, F. 1997. Economic functioning, self sufficiency, and full employments. In Michie and Grieve Smith 1997.

Taylor, B. and Morison, I., eds. 1999. *Driving Strategic Change in Financial Services*. Cambridge.

Taylor, C. T. and Silberston, Z. A. 1973. *The Economic Impact of the Patent System: a Study of the British Experience*. Cambridge.

Taylor, J. and Wren, C. 1997. UK regional policy: an evaluation. *Regional Studies* 31 9: 835–48.

Taylor, R. 2000. *The TUC: from the General Strike to New Unionism*. Basingstoke.

Teeling Smith, G. 1992. The British pharmaceutical industry: 1961–1991. In Teeling Smith 1992.

Teeling Smith, G., ed. 1992. *Innovative Competition in Medicine: a Schumpeterian Analysis of the Pharmaceutical Industry and the NHS*.

Temple, J. 1999. The new growth evidence. *Journal of Economic Literature* 37: 112–56.

Tether, B. S., Smith, I. J. and Thwaites, A. T. 1997. Smaller enterprises and innovation in the UK: the SPRU Innovations Database revisited. *Research Policy* 26: 19–32.

Tew, J. H. B. 1978a. Monetary policy, part I. In Blackaby 1978.

1978b. Policies aimed at improving the balance of payments. In Blackaby 1978.

Thatcher, M. 1993. *The Downing Street Years*.

Thomas, R. 1969. *London's New Towns: a Study of Self-contained and Balanced Communities*. Political and Economic Planning (PEP) Broadsheet No. 510.

Thomas, W. A. 1978. *The Finance of British Industry, 1918–1976*.

Tiratsoo, N. and Tomlinson, J. 1994. Restrictive practices on the shopfloor in Britain, 1945–1960: myth and reality. *Business History* 36: 65–84.

1997. Exporting the 'Gospel of productivity': US technical assistance and British industry 1945–60. *Business History* 71: 41–81.

Titmuss, R. M. 1950. *Problems of Social Policy*.

Tomlinson, J. 1981. The 'economics of politics' and public expenditure. *Economy and Society* 10: 381–402.

1996. Inventing 'decline': the falling behind of the British economy in the postwar years. *Economic History Review* 49: 731–57.

1997. *Democratic Socialism and Economic Policy; the Attlee Years.* Cambridge.

2000. *The Politics of Decline.*

Townsend, P. 1979. *Poverty in the United Kingdom.*

Treasury 2000. *Productivity in the UK: the Evidence and the Government's Approach.*

Trevor, M. 1988. *Toshiba's New Company: Competitiveness through Innovation in Industry.*

Turner, G. 1971. *The Leyland Papers.*

Turner, H. A. 1952. Trade unions, differentials and the levelling of wages. *Manchester School*: 227–82.

Turok, I. and Webster, D. 1998. The new deal: jeopardised by the geography of unemployment? *Local Economy* 12, 4: 309–28.

Twomey, B. 2001. Women in the labour market: results from the Spring Labour Force Survey. *Employment Gazette.* February: 93–106.

Twomey, J. and Taylor, J. 1985. Regional policy and the interregional movement of manufacturing industry in Great Britain. *Scottish Journal of Political Economy* 32, 3: 257–77.

UK 1975. *Royal Commission on the Distribution of Income and Wealth.* Cmnd 6171.

1979. *The Government's Expenditure Plans, 1980–81.*

US Bureau of the Census 2001. *Statistical Abstract of the United States.* Washington, DC.

US Department of Commerce 1965. *Area Redevelopment Policies in Britain and the Countries of the Common Market.* Washington, DC.

US Department of Labor, various years. *Analysis of Work Stoppages.* Washington, DC.

Vaizey, J. 1974. *The History of British Steel.*

Vaizey, J. and Sheehan, J. 1968. *Resources for Education: an Economic Study of Education in the United Kingdom, 1920–1965.*

van Ark, B. 1992. Comparative productivity in British and American manufacturing. *National Institute Economic Review* 142: 63–74.

1996. Sectoral growth accounting and structural change in post-War Europe. In van Ark and Crafts 1996.

van Ark, B. and Crafts, N. F. R., eds. 1996. *Quantitative Aspects of Europe's Postwar Growth.* Cambridge.

Van der Wee, H. 1986. *Prosperity and upheaval: the world economy 1945–1980.* Harmondsworth.

van Stuyvenberg, J. H., ed. 1969. *Margarine: an Economic, Social and Scientific History, 1869–1969.* Liverpool.

Vatter, H. G. 1985. *The US Economy in World War II.* New York.

Vickers, J. and Yarrow, G. 1988. *Privatisation: an Economic Analysis.* Cambridge, MA.

Visser, J. 1989. *European Trade Unions in Figures.* Deventer.

von Tunzelmann, G. N. 2000. Technology generation, technology use and economic growth. *European Review of Economic History* 4: 121–46.

von Tunzelmann, G. N. and Efendioglu, U. D. 2001. Technology, growth and employment in postwar Europe: short-run dynamics and long-run patterns. In Petit and Soete 2001.

Waddington, J. and Hoffman, R. 2001. *Trade Unions in Europe.* Brussels.

Wadhwani, S. 1990. The effects of unions on productivity, growth, investment and employment. *British Journal of Industrial Relations* 28: 371–85.

Wakelin, K. 2001. Productivity growth and R&D expenditure in UK manufacturing firms. *Research Policy* 30: 1079–90.

Walker, A. and Walker, C., eds. 1987. *The Growing Divide: a Social Audit, 1979–1987.*

Walker, W. B. 1980. Britain's industrial performance 1850–1950: a failure to adjust. In Pavitt 1980.

1993. National innovation systems: Britain. In Nelson 1993.

Waller, P. J. 1983. *Town, City and Nation.* Oxford.

Walters, A. A. 1969a. *Money in Boom and Slump.*

1969b. The Radcliffe Report – ten years after: a survey of empirical evidence. In Croome and Johnson 1969.

Weir, R. B. 1994. Managing Decline: Brands and Marketing in Two Mergers, 'The Big Amalgamation' 1925 and Guinness–DCL 1986. In Jones and Morgan 1994.

Wettman, R. W. and Nicol, W. R. 1981. *Deglomeration Policies in the European Community*. Luxembourg.

Whisler, T. R. 1994. The outstanding potential market: the British motor industry and Europe, 1945–75. *Journal of Transport History* 15: 1–19.

— 1995. *At the End of the Road: the Rise and Fall of Austin-Healey, MG, and Triumph Sports Cars*. Greenwich, CT.

White, G. M. 1981. The adoption and transfer of technology and the role of government. In Carter 1981.

Whiteley, P. 1997. *Economic Growth and Social Capital*. Sheffield.

Whiteman, J. C. 1985. North Sea oil. In Morris 1985.

Wicks, M. 1987. *A Future for All: Do We Need a Welfare State?* Harmondsworth.

Wiener, M. 1981. *English Culture and the Decline of the Industrial Spirit*.

Wilensky, H. L. and Lebeaux, C. N. 1958. *Industrial Society and Social Welfare*. New York.

Wilks, S. R. M. 1984. *Industrial Policy and the Motor Industry*. Manchester.

Williams, B. 1967. *Technology, Investment and Growth*.

Williams, G. 1957. *Recruitment to Skilled Trades*.

— 1963. *Apprenticeship in Europe: the Lesson for Britain*.

Williamson, O. 1985. *The Economic Institutions of Capitalism: Firms, Markets, Relational Contracting*. New York.

Wilson, C. 1968. *Unilever, 1945–1965: Challenge and Response in the Post-War Industrial Revolution*.

Wilson, E. 1980. *Only Halfway to Paradise: Women in Postwar Britain, 1945–1968*.

Wilson, K. F. 1983. *British Financial Institutions: Savings and Monetary Policy*.

Wilt, A. F. 2001. *Food for War. Agriculture and Rearmament in Britain Before the Second World War*. Oxford.

Womack, J. P., Jones, D. T. and Roos, D. 1990. *The Machine that Changed the World*. New York.

Wood, A. J. B. 1994. *North–South Trade, Employment, and Inequality*. Oxford.

Worswick, G. D. N. and Ady, P. H., eds. 1952. *The British Economy 1945–1950*. Oxford.

Wray, M. 1957. *The Women's Outerwear Industry*.

Wren, C. 1994. The build-up and duration of subsidy-induced employment: evidence from UK regional policy. *Journal of Regional Science* 34, 3: 387–410.

Wren, C. and Waterson, M. 1991. The direct employment effects of financial assistance to industry. *Oxford Economic Papers* 43: 116–38.

Wrigley, C. 1996. *A History of British Industrial Relations, 1939–1979*. Cheltenham.

Young, S. and Hood, N. 1977. *Chrysler UK: a Corporation in Transition*. New York.

Young, S., Hood, N. and Peters, E. 1994. Multinational enterprises and regional economic development. *Regional Studies* 28, 7: 657–77.

Yoxen, E. 1979. Regulating the exploitation of recombinant biogenetics. In Johnston and Gummett 1979.

Zeitlin, J. and Totterdill, P. 1989. Markets, technology and local intervention: the case of clothing. In Hirst and Zeitlin 1989.

Ziman, J. 1987. *Science in a 'Steady State': the Research System in Transition*.

Zweiniger-Bargielowska, I. 2000. *Austerity in Britain. Rationing, Controls, and Consumption, 1939–1955*. Oxford.

Index